From Slavery to Freedom

A History of African Americans

To Richard and Mary Dunn,
with the cordial best
wishes of

John Hope Franklin

Christmas, 1994

From Slavery to Freedom

A History of African Americans

SEVENTH EDITION

John Hope Franklin

Alfred A. Moss, Jr.

McGraw-Hill, Inc.

New York   St. Louis   San Francisco   Auckland   Bogota   Caracas
Lisbon   London   Madrid   Mexico City   Milan   Montreal
New Delhi   San Juan   Singapore
Sydney   Tokyo   Toronto

From
Slavery
to Freedom

A History of African Americans

Acknowledgments appear on page 635 and on this page by reference.

This book is printed on recycled, acid-free paper containing
10% postconsumer waste.

3 4 5 6 7 8 9 0 DOC DOC 9 0 9 8 7 6 5 4

ISBN 0-07-021907-9

This book was set in Palatino by ComCom, Inc.,
The editors were Peter Labella and Bob Greiner;
the designer was Jo Jones;
the production supervisor was Friederich W. Schulte.
The cover was designed by John Hite.
The photo editor was Fran Antman.
R. R. Donnelley & Sons Company was printer and binder.

Cover Painting

"Family," by Romare Bearden.
Courtesy National Museum of American Art,
Washington, DC/Art Resource, NY.

Back cover photograph of authors: Marvin T. Jones

Library of Congress Cataloging-in-Publication Data

Franklin, John Hope, (date).
   From slavery to freedom: a history of African Americans / John
Hope Franklin, Alfred A. Moss, Jr.—7th ed.
      p.   cm.
   Includes bibliographical references (p.   ) and index.
   ISBN 0-07-021907-9
   1. Afro-Americans—History.   2. Slavery—United States—History.
I. Moss, Alfred A., (date).   II. Title.
E185.F825   1994
973'.0496073—dc20   93-44726

Published September 22, 1947
Second Edition 1956
Third Edition 1967
Fourth Edition 1974
Fifth Edition 1980
Sixth Edition 1988
Seventh Edition 1994

About
the Authors

John Hope Franklin is the James B. Duke Professor Emeritus at Duke University and, for seven years, was Professor of Legal History at Duke University Law School. Born in Oklahoma in 1915, he graduated in 1935 from Fisk University. Harvard University awarded him the master's degree in 1936 and the doctorate in 1941. Professor Franklin has taught at Fisk, St. Augustine's College, North Carolina Central University at Durham, and Howard University. He was Chairman of the Department of History at Brooklyn College and at the University of Chicago, where he remains the John Matthews Manly Distinguished Service Professor Emeritus of History. He was a Fulbright Professor in Australia and Pitt Professor of American History and Institutions at Cambridge University in England.

Dr. Franklin is a former President of the Southern Historical Association, the Organization of American Historians, the American Studies Association, the American Historical Association, and the Society of Phi Beta Kappa. Among Dr. Franklin's awards are the Jefferson Medal of the Council for Advancement and Support of Education, the Clarence Holte Literary Prize, The Jefferson Medal of the American Philosophical Society, and the National Endowment for the Humanities Charles Frankel Award, presented by President Clinton in 1993. He holds one-hundred honorary degrees.

Among his many published works are *The Free Negro in North Carolina, 1790–1860* (1943), *The Militant South 1800–1860* (1956), *Reconstruction after the Civil War* (1961), *The Emancipation Proclamation* (1963), *Racial Equality in America* (1976), *A Southern Odyssey* (1976) *George Washington Williams: A Biography,* (1985), *Race and History* (1989), and *The Color Line: Legacy for the Twenty-First Century* (1993).

Alfred A. Moss, Jr. is Associate Professor of History at the University of Maryland, College Park. After completing his undergraduate work at Lake Forest College, Dr. Moss received his master's degree from the University of Chicago in 1972. He was then awarded his doctorate in 1977, also from the University of Chicago. A graduate of the Episcopal Divinity School, he is also an Episcopal priest. Dr. Moss is the author of *The American Negro Academy: Voice of the Talented Tenth* (1981) and numerous articles; co-author of *Looking at History* (1986); and co-editor of *The Facts of Reconstruction: Essays in Honor of John Hope Franklin* (1991).

■

To Aurelia

Contents

Photographs

Illustrations

Boxes

Maps

Tables

Preface
to the
Seventh Edition

In the nearly half-century since this work first appeared, interest in the subject it covers has quickened considerably. This is evident in the spate of works dealing with various aspects of the subject, in the increase in the number of course offerings in the field at both the secondary and higher-education levels, and in the use of materials related to it in the discussion and formulation of public policy. These developments have in turn had their effect on the several revisions through which this work has gone, and we are ever mindful of the importance of maintaining the integrity and reliability of this work as a contributor to the ongoing discussion of the problems inherent in forging a society characterized by equality, justice, and mutual respect.

In designating the group under discussion as African Americans, we are recognizing the changes that have characterized such designations in previous years. Even during the lifetime of this book, there have been three distinct names by which the group has been called: Negro, black, and African American. (Afro-American and person of color were in use before the end of the nineteenth century.) While African American is increasing in current usage, there is no reason to believe that this is a final designation; for the political and cultural winds that produced it continue to blow, perhaps sweeping before them earlier designations and bringing forth at some later time a designation as yet unknown.

It would be improper as well as awkward to use African American to describe the group before the end of the Civil War. Neither the group nor any others, in law or in practice, conceived of any designation other than black, person of color, or Negro. In recognizing the changes that have come in recent years, we must take care not to impose recent designations on persons of an earlier period. Thus, we have made every attempt to use terms that seem consonant with the period under consideration, recognizing that the search for stylistic felicity invites variation in terminology as long as it is accurate for its own time.

We have made every effort to keep abreast of the wide-ranging and significant scholarship in the field. It has affected our thinking, our approach, even our perspective. At times its effect is quite obvious in the correction of statements of "facts" in earlier editions and in new interpretations gained from new research. Most often its effect is in the way it informs our view of the problem with which we deal and the sense of security it provides in helping us sort out the complexities and meanings of those problems. These effects are at times so subtle as not to be discernable, but this does not diminish their importance. We have also sought to make even more significant some of the features that we introduced in the sixth edition. An example is a marked increase in the number of "box" quotations that provide primary sources that add flavor as well as authority to much of the discussion. Another example is the increased attention given to popular cultures and the role of women. Quite new features in which we, along with the publisher, take particular pride, are the color photographs of early African artifacts and a gallery, in full color, of twentieth-century African-American art. To the many scholars and laypersons who have written on the subject or who have been generous enough to write us and make suggestions, we are grateful for their assistance.

Several scholars, distinguished in the field, have reviewed the Sixth Edition of this work and have given us the benefit of their searching examinations. They are John L. Dabney, San Bernadino Valley College; Joseph Harris, Howard University; Earl Lewis, University of Michigan; Freddie L. Parker, North Carolina Central University; Marshall F. Stevenson, Ohio State University; and Walter B. Weare, University of Wisconsin, Milwaukee. In addition, several friends and colleagues have read portions of the manuscript, made suggestions in the area of their specialty and assisted in other ways to improve the work. Among them are Eric Anderson, Marie Perinbam, Janet Ewald, Robert E. Steele, John Whittington Franklin, Christaud Geary, Genna Rae McNeil, Robyn Muncy, Winthrop R. Wright, George C. Wright, Paul Huebner, Jehu Hunter, Major Clark, Paul Finkelman, and S. O. Y. Keita.

Our families continue to give us their support in every possible way, for which we are most grateful. Margaret Fitzsimmons, beginning in 1964, has served as personal assistant and secretary-editor for five editions of this work. In her various capacities in seeing the book through to completion, she has become indispensable. In expressing our gratitude for all that she has done, we accept all responsibility for errors of fact and judgment.

John Hope Franklin
Alfred A. Moss, Jr.

Preface
to the
Sixth Edition

Forty years ago, one author, with the assistance and encouragement of many others, wrote the first edition of this work. In succeeding years, with the passage of time and the quickening of events, he prepared four succeeding editions, each of which went through numerous printings. Two considerations have led to some major changes in the preparation of the Sixth Edition, which will mark the fortieth anniversary of the book's initial appearance. One has been the growing diversity of interests as well as the increasing complexity of the problems facing Negro Americans, brought on by numerous shifts in strategies initiated by their adversaries as well as by themselves. This has required the constant monitoring and evaluation of virtually everything that occurs. The very magnitude of the task beckons more than one mind and one set of hands. The other is that with the passage of time, the original author has recognized the need for the collaboration of a younger person whose different perspectives and ample energies would assist in giving the new edition the freshness that it requires and deserves.

In this new collaboration we have learned much from each other, and it is our fond hope that our readers will benefit greatly from this joint effort. We have broadened our coverage, expanded our interests, and strengthened our grasp of the basic historical problems with which we have had to deal. We have reexamined every word of the Fifth Edition, reorganized much of the material, rewritten portions, and added a great deal that is entirely new. With the remarkable increase of excellent works in African, Caribbean, and Latin American history, we have not been inclined to repeat or summarize the findings of the scholars in those fields. Rather, we have confined our treatment of those areas to matters of obvious and immediate relevance to the history of Negroes in the United States. Meanwhile, we have brought our treatment of the subject as close to the present as we dared, remembering the wise adage that "current history is not really history, but current events."

As we have reexamined many aspects of the history of black Americans, we have become indebted to many authors for the remarkably rich outpouring of writings on the subject in recent years. Some are mentioned in the text, some in the bibliographical notes, and others remain nameless. We are grateful to them for their contributions to our own knowledge as well as to the field. Several of our colleagues have been especially helpful, among them Marie Perinbam, Eric Anderson, Winthrop R. Wright, Robert Steele, Milton Morris, Janet Ewald, and Evelyn Brooks. In addition, numerous teachers, students, and others who have used earlier editions of this book have been generous in offering corrections, criticisms, and helpful suggestions for its improvement. We also gratefully acknowledge the comments from the following reviewers: Hayward Farrar, Leon F. Litwack, Alan Schaffer, Donald Spivey, and George C. Wright. The libraries, such as the Library of Congress, the Moorland-Spingarn Research Center of Howard University, the Library of the University of Maryland at College Park, North Carolina Central University Library, the Duke University Library, and the Durham County Library, especially its Stanford Warren Branch, have been indispensable. We are deeply grateful to all of these individuals and institutions.

Our families have been generous with their patience and assistance. Serving as personal assistant and secretary-editor, Margaret Fitzsimmons has presided over the preparation of various editions of this work over the past twenty-three years. She has again performed these various functions for this edition, and with greater efficiency, resourcefulness, and wisdom than ever before. We are most grateful to her. Over her protests, we assume responsibility for errors of fact and judgment.

John Hope Franklin
Alfred A. Moss, Jr.

July 4, 1987

Preface
to the
Fifth Edition

It has been more than thirty years since the first edition of this work appeared. These have been momentous years in the history of the world, and Negro Americans, like all others, have been deeply affected by what has transpired. The emergence of the atomic age as well as the space age, either event of sufficient significance to change the course of human history, occurred in this brief period. In like fashion the Black Revolution, with its far-reaching impact on virtually every aspect of life among black Americans, has affected their position in American society as well as the manner in which other Americans view them. The recency of these events, and the consequent lack of adequate perspective, make it difficult to evaluate them with any measure of confidence, and the danger of distortion or exaggeration is very real. I have made every effort to avoid such difficulties. At the same time I have recognized the fact that all events are not of equal importance.

Since the publication of the fourth edition, many works in the general field of Afro-American history have appeared. Some of them have been highly significant and have compelled students of the field to reconsider earlier findings and conclusions. This present edition takes into account these recent developments in historical scholarship, and I am grateful to the many scholars whose works have proved so valuable. I am also grateful to the colleagues, students, and teachers who have been kind enough to offer suggestions or call my attention to errors in previous editions. It would not be possible to revise this work without the continuing assistance of such persons. My research assistants, Michael Lanza and Patrick Thompson, assisted me in more ways than I can acknowledge, and I am grateful to them.

My secretary and administrative assistant, Margaret Fitzsimmons, has not only typed and checked the manuscript but has, as usual, assumed numerous responsibilities beyond the call of duty. She would even be willing to assume some responsibility for textual and other errors, but I can only thank her deeply and assume those myself.

John Hope Franklin

Chicago, Illinois
May 30, 1979

Preface
to the
Fourth Edition

The comments I made in the preface to the third edition regarding the quickened pace of events are even more true for the period since 1966 than before that date. The growing interest in the history of Negro Americans and their greater involvement in the current struggle for equality are part of the far-reaching changes that have occurred in the status of blacks that may be regarded as revolutionary. These developments have made the revision of this work extremely difficult. The study and evaluation of vast quantities of new material, while shedding much light on many aspects of the history of Negro Americans, have also increased the difficulties of revision.

Many readers have been most generous in their observations and criticisms, which I have been most pleased to take into account. My research assistant, Rodney Ross, brought to his task a thorough knowledge of the subject and a high quality of scholarship that greatly eased my own task. My secretary, Margaret Fitzsimmons, not only has typed the manuscript but has greatly assisted with stylistic improvements and in eliminating errors and inconsistencies. To these and to many others I am grateful for their help.

John Hope Franklin

Chicago, Illinois
September 3, 1973

Preface
to the
Third Edition

Almost twenty years ago the first edition of this work appeared. Ten years ago I revised it and brought it up to date. Since that time the very pace at which events have moved has discouraged any effort to prepare a revision that would inevitably be out of date at the time of its publication. It seems fitting, nevertheless, to present a rather extensively revised edition on the occasion of the twentieth anniversary of the first edition.

I feel constrained to add that even the revolutionary developments of the last decade should not obscure the fact that this is essentially a history and not a contemporary tract. Therefore, these developments have been valuable for the historian not only in themselves but also in the new perspectives they provide as one looks at past, even remote, events. These new perspectives are reflected in some of the revisions of the earlier parts of the book.

The revisions have been greatly facilitated by the generous and helpful criticisms and suggestions of my students, colleagues, and friends. Arthur Spingarn and August Meier have assisted me in correcting several serious errors; and Richard Fuke, my research assistant, has been a virtual collaborator in his critical reading of the text and in his valuable updating of much of the material. To these and all the others who have helped in countless ways I am deeply grateful.

John Hope Franklin

Chicago, Illinois
July 4, 1966

Preface
to the
Second Edition

The nine years that have elapsed since this work first appeared have been among the most momentous in the history of the American Negro. The postwar years witnessed vigorous efforts, not always successful, on the part of Negroes and many white Americans to elevate substantially the position of the Negro in American life. The 1954 decision of the Supreme Court in the school desegregation cases was the most dramatic and significant of the frontal attacks on segregation and discrimination, but by no means was it the only one. World attention, moreover, has been focused on the issue of race as never before, and the status of the Negro in the United States has been scrutinized with extreme care by peoples in many other parts of the world. This very scrutiny has had a most salutary effect. The task of the historian in tracing and properly evaluating the numerous developments that have taken place abounds in difficulties, but it nevertheless seems worthwhile at this point to take cognizance of some of the more significant trends.

If this edition is an improvement over the first edition, it is due largely to the able assistance of many persons. The reviewers of the first edition, letters from readers, and my own colleagues and students were not only generous in praise but helpful in pointing out errors and oversights. I am grateful to these careful readers for their thoughtful generosity, and I have taken into consideration their suggestions. The increased interest in the problems of the Negro has stimulated much research and writing in the field; the numerous books and articles on almost every aspect and period of Negro life and history have greatly increased my understanding of the matters with which this book deals. At many points the influence of these works is reflected. I can only hope that I have done violence neither to the diligent work of others nor to the dramatic events that have transpired.

John Hope Franklin

Washington, D.C.
June 15, 1956

Preface
to the
First Edition

In the present work I have undertaken to bring together the essential facts in the history of the American Negro from his ancient African beginnings down to the present time. In doing so it was deemed unnecessary to relate the development of Negro life and history in other parts of the world except where there was a discernible connection with the history of the Negro in the United States. Thus only so much of African history was considered here as evolved in the area from which the vast majority of American Negroes came, and as much more as helped to shape Afro-American institutions in the Old World and the New. On the other hand, it was necessary to consider briefly the Negroes of the Caribbean and of Latin America, because their history belongs to the larger pattern of development of the Negro in the New World. For a similar reason, it was deemed desirable to give some attention to the Negroes of Canada, for they are in a large measure erstwhile citizens or residents of the United States.

I have made a conscious effort to write the history of the Negro in America with due regard for the forces at work which have affected his development. This has involved a continuous recognition of the mainstream of American history and the relationship of the Negro to it. It has been necessary, therefore, to a considerable extent, to retell the story of the evolution of the people of the United States in order to place the Negro in his proper relationship and perspective. To have proceeded otherwise would have been to ignore the indisputable fact that historical forces are all-pervasive and cut through the most rigid barriers of race and caste. It would have been impossible to trace the history of the Negro in America without remaining sensitive to the main currents in the emergence of American civilization.

While I have sought to interpret critically the forces and personalities that have shaped the history of the Negro in the United States, I have attempted to avoid a subjective and unscientific treatment of the subject. This procedure has involved the maintenance of a discreet balance between recognizing the deeds of outstanding persons and depicting the fortunes of the great mass of Negroes. To be sure there were times when dominant personalities forged to the front and assumed roles of responsibility and leadership; these individuals have been recognized. But the history of the Negro in America is essentially the story of the strivings of the nameless millions who have sought adjustment in a new and sometimes hostile world. This work is, therefore, a history of the Negro people, with a proper consideration for anonymous as well as outstanding people.

I have given considerable attention to the task of tracing the interaction of the Negro and the American environment. It can hardly be denied that the course of American history has been vitally affected by his presence. At the same time it must be admitted that the effect of acculturation on the Negro in the United States has been so marked that today he is as truly American as any member of other ethnic groups that make up the American population. That is not to say that the story of the Negro is one solely of achievement or of success. Too frequently the Negro's survival in America has depended on his capacity to adjust—indeed, to accommodate—himself to the dominant culture, and the obstacles have at times been too great to permit him to make significant achievements in the usual sense of the word. The task here has been not to recite his achievements—though naturally some have been so outstanding as to warrant consideration—but to tell the story of the process by which the Negro has sought to cast his lot with an evolving American civilization.

The obligations which I am under for direct and indirect aid received in writing this book are numerous, and it is not possible for me to indicate every instance of assistance which cooperative persons have rendered. Without the research of Carter G. Woodson, Charles H. Wesley, W. E. B. Du Bois, Luther P. Jackson, and many other scholars who have contributed significant writings to the field, it would not have been possible for me to write this book. I am grateful to all these patient, careful scholars for the indispensable services they have performed for all students of American history. I am under special obligation to the Library of Congress, which generously placed its many facilities at my disposal, and to the North Carolina College Library, the Stanford L. Warren Library, the Duke University Library, the New York Public Library, and the American Museum of Natural History for their kind assistance.

I am under obligation to the following publishers for their kind permission to make brief quotations from works published by them: The Columbia University Press: Lorenzo J. Greene, *The Negro in Colonial New England* and

Sterling Spero and Abram L. Harris, *The Black Worker;* Harcourt, Brace and Company: Claude McKay, *Harlem Shadows;* The Macmillan Company: C. Vann Woodward, *Tom Watson, Agrarian Rebel;* The University of Michigan Press: Dwight L. Dumond, *The Antislavery Origins of the Civil War;* The Yale University Press: Bell I. Wiley, *Southern Negroes, 1861–1865;* and Doubleday and Company: R. R. Moton, *Finding a Way Out.*

To Abram L. Harris, C. Vann Woodward, Mrs. Arthur P. Chippey, Howard K. Beale, L. D. Reddick, Rayford W. Logan, Clement Eaton, Mrs. Dorothy Porter, and Arthur S. Link, I am grateful for helpful suggestions and numerous criticisms. Among my colleagues who have assisted me in this effort I am especially grateful to Joseph H. Taylor, Joseph S. Himes, W. Edward Farrison, Albert L. Turner, Charles A. Ray, Albert Manley, and Miss Helen G. Edmonds. President James E. Shepard kindly relieved me of my teaching duties so that I could complete the manuscript, and I am sincerely appreciative of his generosity. The dedication of the work to my wife expresses inadequately my deep gratitude to her for her sacrifices, cooperation, and enthusiastic support of my efforts in historical writing.

John Hope Franklin

Durham, North Carolina
April 4, 1947

African-American Population of the United States, 1860 and 1990

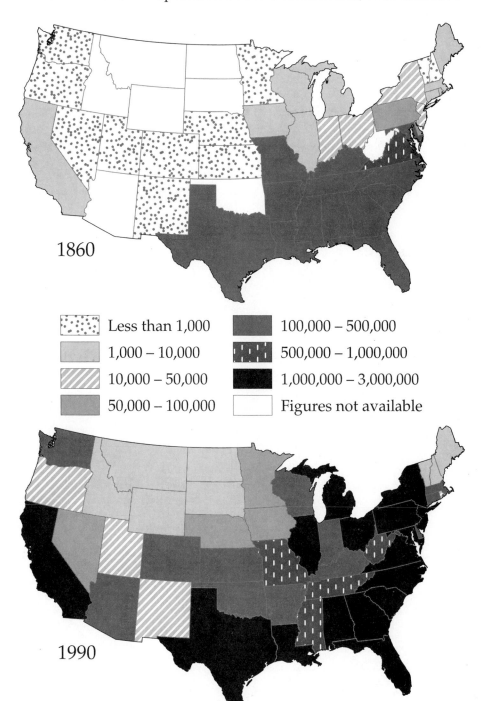

1860

Less than 1,000   100,000 – 500,000

1,000 – 10,000   500,000 – 1,000,000

10,000 – 50,000   1,000,000 – 3,000,000

50,000 – 100,000   Figures not available

1990

CHAPTER 1

Land of Their Ancestors

In the last third of the twentieth century, it became commonplace for African Americans to speak and write sensitively of the land of their ancestors. While some of them could refer to the vast continent of Africa in only the vaguest terms, others could focus quite precisely on the specific areas from which most of their ancestors had come. The emergence of such modern independent states as Ghana, Mali, Chad, Niger, Nigeria, The Gambia, and Upper Volta evoked a deep sense of identification, even though these new countries of the twentieth century have only a slight connection with those nation-states of many centuries ago that bore similar names. The connection is there, nevertheless; and the African who left, say, Whydah, for the New World in 1800 may well have had roots in one of the African states of the Middle Ages. Those states were the land of the ancestors of New World slaves, as indeed they were the land of the forebears of their twentieth-century descendants.

When the Arabs first learned of West Africa, its civilization was already centuries old. Although the land from the Atlantic to the Nile had enjoyed limited contact with other civilized portions of the world, much of the culture that the Arabs found was indigenous to the area. It must be added that the sources of information about the history, as well as the very existence, of these states are increasing but still quite limited. One has to depend primarily on observations of travelers, reports based on information from people two or three times removed from events, and oral tradition.

For centuries some indigenous peoples had no interest in organizing themselves into states, perhaps seeing no need or advantage in erecting political institutions. Others, however, had different attitudes or needs and therefore set out to build governments to meet those needs. Indeed, many well-developed political states had risen and fallen before any lasting contact was established between West Africa and the Near East. These states sprang up in more or less the same general region, from the Mediterranean southward to the Gulf of Guinea and from the Atlantic eastward almost to the Nile. Successively, there arose in the region the states of Ghana, Mali, and Songhay, along with many lesser states.

■ Ghana

The first West African state of which there is any record is Ghana, which lay about 500 miles northwest of its modern namesake. It was also known by its capital, Kumbi Saleh. Although its accurately recorded history does not antedate the seventh century, there is evidence that Ghana's political and cultural history extends back perhaps into the very early Christian era. The earliest observations of Ghana were made when it was a confederacy of settlements extending along the grasslands of the Senegal and the upper Niger. Its boundaries were not well defined, and doubtless they changed with the fortunes of the kingdom. Most of the public offices were hereditary, and the tendency was for the stratified social order to become solidified.

The people of Ghana enjoyed some prosperity as farmers until continuous droughts extended the desert to their lands. As long as they were able to carry on their farming, gardens and date groves dotted the countryside, and there was an abundance of sheep and cattle in the outlying areas. They were also a trading people, and their chief town, Kumbi Saleh, was an important commercial center during the Middle Ages. By the beginning of the tenth century the Muslim influence from the East was present. Kumbi Saleh had a native and an Arab section, and the people were gradually adopting the religion of Islam. The prosperity that came in the wake of Arabian infiltration increased the power of Ghana, and its influence was extended in all directions. In the eleventh century, when the king had become a Muslim, Ghana could boast of a large army and a lucrative trade across the desert. From the Muslim countries came wheat, fruit, and sugar. From across the desert came caravans laden with textiles, brass, pearls, and salt. Ghana exchanged ivory, slaves, and gold from Bambuhu for these commodities. The king, recognizing the value of this commercial intercourse, imposed a tax on imports and exports and appointed a collector to look after his interests.

Under the rulers of the Sisse dynasty, Ghana reached the height of its power. Tribes as far north as Tichit in present Mauritania paid tribute to the king of Ghana, while in the south its influence extended to the gold mines of the Falémé and of the Bambuk. It was the yield from these mines that supplied the coffers of the Sisse with the gold used in trade with Moroccan caravans. In faraway Cairo and Baghdad, Ghana was a subject of discussion among commercial and religious groups.

The reign of Tenkamenin in the eleventh century is an appropriate point at which to observe the kingdom of Ghana. Beginning in 1062 Tenkamenin reigned over a vast empire which, through the taxes and tributes collected by provincial rulers, made him immensely wealthy. Arab writers say that he lived in a fortified castle made beautiful by sculpture, pictures, and windows decorated by royal artists. The grounds also contained temples in which native gods were worshipped, a prison in which political enemies were incarcerated, and the tombs of preceding kings. The king, highly esteemed by his subjects, held court in magnificent splendor.

During Tenkamenin's reign the people of Ghana adhered to a religion based on the belief that every earthly object contained good or evil spirits that had to be satisfied if the people were to prosper. The king, naturally, was at the head of the religion. In 1076, however, a band of Muslims called Almoravids invaded Ghana and brought the area under the influence of their religion and trade. They seized the capital and established the religion of Islam. The strife that ensued was enough to undermine the kingdom of Ghana. By the end of the eleventh century, Ghana entered a period of economic decline brought on by a series of droughts that dried up the important Wagadu and Bagana districts. Under such trying circumstances it fell easy prey to the waves of conquerors who swept in to destroy the kingdom during the twelfth and thirteenth centuries.

■ Mali

As Ghana began to decline, another kingdom in the west arose to supplant it and to exceed the heights that Ghana had reached. Mali, also called Melle, began as an organized kingdom about 1235, but the nucleus of its political organization dates back to the beginning of the seventh century. Until the eleventh century it was relatively insignificant and its mansas, or kings, had no prestige or influence.

The credit for consolidating and strengthening the kingdom of Mali goes to the legendary figure Sundiata Keita. In 1240 he overran the Soso people and leveled the former capital of Ghana. It was a later successor, however, who carried the Malians to new heights. Variously called Gonga-Musa and Mansa-Musa, this remarkable member of the Keita dynasty ruled from 1312 to 1337. With an empire comprising much of what is now francophone Africa, he could devote his attention to encouraging the industry of his people and displaying the wealth of his kingdom. The people of Mali were predominantly agricultural, but a substantial number were engaged in various crafts and

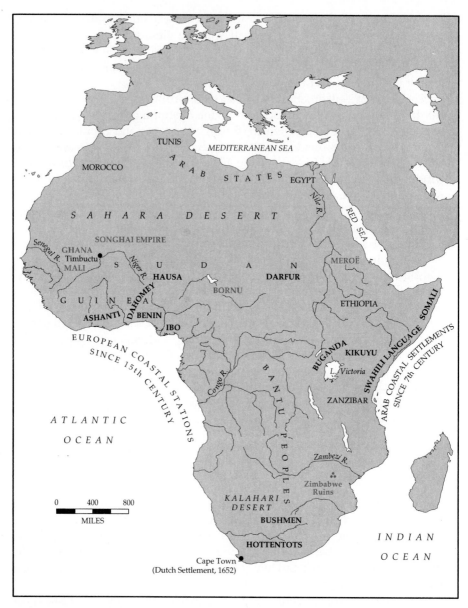

PRECOLONIAL AFRICA. This map shows Africa before European penetration in the nineteenth century. It is difficult to indicate boundaries, for even the most extensive African kingdoms had shifting and indefinite borders. Names in gray designate ancient or medieval centers which no longer exist in modern times.

mining. The fabulously rich mines of Bure were now at their disposal and served to enrich the royal coffers.

The best information that the period affords on the level of attainment of these native kingdoms comes from the accounts of royal pilgrimages to Mecca. The kings, newly converted to the religion, were as ardent and pious as any Arabs of their day. As good Muslims, they looked forward to making the traditional pilgrimage to Mecca. Such a pilgrimage, moreover, was an excellent opportunity to display the wealth of the kingdom and to attract trade. The historic pilgrimage of Mansa-Musa in 1324 exceeded all visits to Mecca by previous royal personages from the West. Cairo's El Omari said that the entourage was composed of thousands of people, a large portion of which constituted a military escort. Gifts were lavished on the populace, and mosques were built where they were needed. As the camels approached Mecca, their burden was considerably lighter than it had been when they departed for the East.

Since any such pilgrimage was a display of wealth and power as well as a holy journey to kiss the black stone of Kaaba, there was no need to proceed directly to and from Mecca. Mansa-Musa first visited various parts of his kingdom to show his subjects and vassals his tremendous wealth and to demonstrate his benevolence. He then proceeded to Tuat, in the land of the Berbers, and after making a deep impression there he crossed the desert, visited Cairo, and finally went to the holy places of Mecca and Medina. He returned by way of Ghadames, in Tripoli, where he received many honors and from which point he was accompanied to his kingdom by El-Momar, a descendant of the founder of the dynasty of the Almohads. A more significant visitor to return with Mansa-Musa was Ibrahim Es Saheli, or Abu Ishak, a distinguished Arabian poet and architect from a Granada family, whom Mansa-Musa engaged to supervise the building of elaborate mosques at Timbuktu, Jenne, Gao, and elsewhere. These structures added further splendor to the already well-developed kingdom of Mali.

When Mansa-Musa died in 1337, Mali could boast of a political state as powerful and as well organized as any of that period. Traveling in the area a few years later, Ibn Batuta, the celebrated Arabian geographer, reported that he was greatly impressed by "the discipline of its officials and provincial governors, the excellent condition of public finance, and the luxury and the rigorous and complicated ceremonial of the royal receptions, and the respect accorded to the decisions of justice and to the authority of the sovereign." In the middle of the fourteenth century Europe was just beginning to feel the effects of its commercial revolution and European states had not yet achieved anything resembling national unity; but Mali under Mansa-Musa and his successor, Suleiman, enjoyed a flourishing economy with good international trade relations and could point with pride to a stable government extending several hundred miles from the Atlantic to Lake Chad. The people adhered to a state religion that had international connections, and learning flourished in the many schools that had been established. It was not until the fifteenth century that the kingdom showed definite signs of decline and disintegration. The powerful blows of the Songhay and the attacks of the Mossi combined to reduce the power of Mali. The decline did not go on indefinitely, however, and Mali continued to exist for many years as a small, semi-independent state.

■ Songhay

The kingdom that was in a position to dispute the power of Mali by the fifteenth century was Songhay. The latter had experienced a long and checkered career as a kingdom. Beginning in the early eighth century at Gao, near the bend of the Niger, it had remained a small, relatively inconsequential state for many years. In fact, it fell under the powerful influence of Mali, and for a time its rulers were vassals of Mansa-Musa and his successors. Undaunted, the Songhay waited for the first opportunity to throw off the yoke of Mali and to assert their own sovereignty. This they had succeeded in doing by 1355, with Sonni Ali (1464–1492) later taking Songhay, as Philip Curtin has said, "from a small riverain state to a great empire."

When Sonni Ali began his rule of the Songhay, most of West Africa was ripe for conquest. Mali was declining, and the lesser states, though ambitious, had neither the leadership nor the resources necessary to achieve dominance. The hour of the Songhay had arrived. Sonni Ali conceived of a plan to conquer the entire Niger region by building a river navy that would seize control of both banks. By 1469 he had conquered the important town of Timbuktu and then proceeded to capture Jenne and other cities. Finally he attacked the kingdom of Mali, and with its conquest the Songhay kingdom was catapulted into a position of primacy in West Africa. Because of his lack of enthusiasm for the religion of Islam, there was considerable opposition to the rise of Sonni Ali, but he was undaunted. Consequently, his years were filled with fighting, but when he died in 1492 the kingdom of Songhay was firmly established as the dominant power of West Africa.

The day of Sonni Ali and his dynasty was over, however, and in 1493 the dynasty was overthrown by a powerful general, Askia Mohammed, who became Songhay's most brilliant ruler. From 1493 to 1529 he devoted his energies to strengthening his empire, making his people prosperous, and encouraging learning. He recruited a professional army of slaves and prisoners of war and left his subjects to engage in farming and commerce. Local rulers, four viceroys, and Askia's brother Omar, as chief lieutenant, maintained peace and administered the empire. In 1494 Omar and the army conquered all of Massina, while in subsequent years most of Mali, the Hausa states, and many other West African kingdoms fell before the power of the Songhay. Finally, the empire of the Songhay was extended from the Atlantic to Bornu and from the Berber country in the north to the Mossi and Benin states in the south. It was easily the largest and most powerful state in the history of West Africa.

To be sure, Askia Mohammed was an orthodox Muslim, but one does not get the impression that his pilgrimage to Mecca in 1497 was either for ostentatious display or merely to pay homage to Allah. This shrewd ruler wanted to improve his empire, and he knew that such a journey would prove profitable from many points of view. His retinue was composed primarily of scholars and officers of state, with a military escort numbering only 1,500 men. He and his followers conversed with doctors, mathematicians, scientists, and scholars, and they doubtless benefited from these contacts. They learned much about how to improve the administration of the government, how to codify the laws of Songhay, how to foster industry and trade, and how to raise the intellectual level of the country. Even Askia Mohammed's investiture as caliph of the Sudan can be interpreted as a move to strengthen his country.

Upon his return from the East, Askia Mohammed and his advisers instituted many of the reforms they had studied. He assigned carefully chosen governors, called *fari,* to rule over subdivisions of the empire. He appointed chiefs, or *noi,* to administer provinces and large cities. He reorganized the army on a more efficient basis. The laws of Mohammed and the Koran were the bases for administering justice. In the area of economic life, banking and credit were improved. A uniform system of weights and measures was established, and scales were inspected. Arabians and the people of Songhay were encouraged to trade with other countries. Traders from Europe and Asia visited the markets of Timbuktu and Gao regularly. With government cooperation all of Songhay became prosperous. Alexander Chamberlain has observed: "In personal character, in administrative ability, in devotion to the welfare of his subjects, in open-mindedness towards foreign influences, . . . King Askia . . . was certainly the equal of the average European monarchs of the time and superior to many of them."

It was in the area of education that Askia made his most significant reforms. He established and encouraged schools everywhere. Gao, Walata, Timbuktu, and Jenne became intellectual centers where the most learned scholars of West Africa were concentrated and where scholars from Asia and Europe came for consultation and study. Scholars like El-Akit and Bagayogo, both jurisconsults, were educated at Timbuktu. By the sixteenth and seventeenth centuries a distinctly Sudanese literature was emerging. At the University of Sankore black and white youths studied grammer, geography, law, literature, and surgery, while in the mosques Askia and his subjects studied the religion of Islam in order to practice and promote it more effectively.

Civil wars, massacres, and unsuccessful military expeditions followed the reign of Askia, who was dethroned by his oldest son. Although there were brief periods of revival, the empire was definitely declining. The Moors viewed the Sudan covetously and began to push down across the desert. With Spanish renegades as their allies, Moroccans overthrew the Songhay state and began their own brief rule in Timbuktu.

■ Other States

Among the other states of West Africa was the empire of Wagadugu, commonly known as the Mossi states. It was founded near the middle of the eleventh century by an adventurer named Ubri. Never a large state, it occupied the area south of the bend of the Niger; but its population was always dense, and its people had a fiercely independent spirit. For a time there were actually five states comprising the loose confederation. Cohesion was greatest in time of emergency, and they managed to repel the attacks of Mali and Songhay and remained more or less independent up until the nineteenth century when France incorporated them into its African empire. The governors of the five states constituted the council of state and served as the chief ministers in the imperial organization. Working with them were eleven ministers overseeing such departments as the army and finance. Beneath them was a hierarchy of officials, which extended to the most insignificant local functionary.

The strength of the Mossi lay in their efficient political and military system. The emperor was absolute. His subordinates operated with carefully worked out and rigidly defined duties. Each morning the emperor received his ministers of state, who reported on the affairs of the realm. In the evening the ruler dealt with matters concerning public order and criminal justice. The procedures of hearings and decisions bore a striking resemblance to the practice of trial by jury. There was no standing army, but the political and social system was so organized as to make possible the calling up for military service of every able-bodied man on the briefest notice. The survival of the Mossi states in an area dominated by powerful empires such as Mali and Songhay is a testimonial to their efficiency and wise leadership.

The Afno, or Hausa, people are said to have had seven original states, the best known of which were Kano, Zaria, and Katsina. The Hausa states occupied roughly the area that today is northern Nigeria. Each kingdom retained its identity, with Kano emerging into the limelight for a while, then yielding to Katsina, and so on. There was commerce with the other African states and across the Sahara. Katsina became a center of learning where law and theology were studied and where the language of the people was refined. It was not until the beginning of the nineteenth century, when Islam made noticeable inroads, that the Hausa states began to yield to outside influences.

To the east and west of Lake Chad resided the people of Kanem and Bornu, respectively. These people were made up of a large number of tribes that had early been attracted to the region by the oases and the lake. Some were Berber, while others were Negroid. As an organized state, Bornu-Kanem dates from about 1220, but instability characterized the government for the next two centuries. The copper mines around the lake brought prosperity to the people, and by the sixteenth century there was a semblance of order under Idris Alooma (1573–1603). In the seventeenth and eighteenth centuries Muslims attempted to subdue these people and convert them, but

Olaudah Equiano (Gustavus Vassa) Describes His Homeland

That part of Africa known by the name of Guinea to which the trade for slaves is carried on extends along the coast above 3,400 miles, from the Senegal to Angola, and includes a variety of kingdoms. Of these the most considerable is the kingdom of Benin, both as to extent and wealth, the richness and cultivation, the power of its king, and the number and warlike disposition of the inhabitants. . . . This kingdom is divided into many provinces or districts, in one of the most remote and fertile of which, called Eboe, I was born in the year 1745, situated in a charming fruitful vale named Essaka. The distance of this province from the capital of Benin and the seacoast must be very considerable, for I had never heard of white men or Europeans, nor of the sea, and our subjection to the king of Benin was little more than nominal; for every transaction of the government . . . was conducted by the chiefs or elders of the place. . . . My father was one of those elders . . . and was styled Embrenche, a term as I remember importing the highest distinction, and signifying in our language a *mark* of grandeur. This mark is conferred on the person entitled to it by cutting the skin across the top of the forehead and drawing it down to the eyebrows, and while it is in this situation applying a warm hand and rubbing it until it shrinks up into a thick *weal* across the lower part of the forehead. . . . My father had long borne it.

We are almost a nation of dancers, musicians and poets. Thus every great event such as a triumphant return from battle or other cause of public rejoicing is celebrated in public dances, which are accompanied with songs and music suited to the occasion. . . . We have many musical instruments, particularly drums of different kinds, a piece of music which resembles a guitar, and another much like a stickado. . . . I was named Olaudah, which in our language signifies vicissitude or fortunate; also, one favoured, and having a loud voice and well spoken. . . .

The Interesting Narrative of the Life of Olaudah Equiano or Gustavus Vassa the African, ed. Paul Edwards (New York, 1966), pp. 1–4.

with only slight success. Complete subjugation by outsiders was not achieved until 1900, when one portion of Bornu became a protectorate of Britain and another came under the influence of France.

The absence of substantial physical barriers in some areas south of the equator made possible the continuous infiltration of migratory tribes, which hampered political stability. The lands of the Bantu, San, Khoikhoi, and Pygmies certainly had some political organizations, and there is considerable anthropological and archaeological evidence to sustain the view that in some areas there existed rather advanced cultures. But it is clear that none of them reached the size or influence of West African states such as Mali and Songhay.

From the mouth of the Niger around to the Cape of Good Hope, there were a number of states that flourished for a time before the sixteenth century. For example, there was the kingdom of the Brama, which lay between Cape Lopez and the mouth of the Congo River and about which practically nothing is known. The so-called Empire of the Congo, founded in the fourteenth century, dominated the area between Setté Cama in the north and Benguella to the south. Inland it reached as far as the upper Zambezi. With its capital at Banya, modern São Salvador, its kings experienced difficulty in maintaining control over the tribes of the Congo Valley, and its boundaries shrank steadily in the seventeenth century because of the chaotic situation resulting from the arrival of Portuguese slavers.

South of the Empire of the Congo was a state near the present city of Mossamedes. Khoikhoi, Damara, and other tribes in the region constituted the population of the kingdom, whose ruler was called the Mataman. In what is modern South Africa there was a large, homogeneous state inhabited by the Bechuana, Basuto, Zulu, and Khoikhoi peoples. On the east coast the Matebelle and Makalaka peoples were incorporated in an ancient state that dated from the tenth century. Its instability was caused by frequent incursions by the Wazimba, a ferocious people living to the west. The remainder of the eastern coast fell early under the influence of the Muslims and became dependencies of various sultanates founded by the Arabs and Persians who gained control of East Africa. In the interior were the kingdoms of the Barotse, the Katanga, and Balubo, extending from the Zambezi to Lake Tanganyika.

The 1591 Moroccan conquest of Songhay had not ended the trans-Saharan trade; the southern terminals had merely shifted eastward to the Hausa states and the Bornu empire. By the early twentieth century, however, when Great Britain, France, and Germany were completing their conquests of West African states, the locus of power in West Africa had long since passed from the savannah kingdoms to forest-belt states located along the Gulf of Guinea to the south. When the Portuguese first sailed down the West African coast in the fifteenth century, they discovered two substantial states: Benin, located to the west of the Niger Delta, and the Kongo kingdom, near the mouth of the Congo River. At Benin, Portuguese sailors bought slaves, beads, and cloth, which they exchanged with Africans further west, along the coast of present-day Ghana, for gold dust. The abundance of certain West African goods so impressed European traders that they named sections of the Guinea coast after these "products"—pepper, ivory, gold, and slaves.

The slave trade, which became the area's dominant form of commerce, played a crucial role as an economic basis for emerging forest-belt kingdoms. The Yoruba people to the west of Benin organized themselves into a series of states, the most powerful of which was Oyo. It was the breakup of this empire in the early nineteenth century that created the unsettling conditions of war and disorder that led in turn to the delivery of large numbers of Yoruba into the transatlantic slave trade. As Oyo declined, Dahomey, a kingdom located within the boundaries of present-day Dahomey, threw off the yoke of its former overlord. Ironically, Dahomey, which owed its seventeenth-century origins to a determination to abstain from the Atlantic slave trade, had by the late eighteenth century become a key West African center for exporting slaves. In the nineteenth century this highly centralized state was transformed from one specializing in the slave trade to one dealing largely in palm oil products. Nonetheless, Europeans used the image of a cruel, barbaric, slaveholding nation as partial justification for the French invasion and conquest in the 1890s.

Another region to share a similar fate was that of the city-states of the Niger River delta. Ibo traders had made the transition from slaves to palm oil only to be thwarted by British commercial attempts to open up Africa to European commerce. Between 1807 and 1901 Britain and the mighty Ashanti nation of present-day Ghana fought ten wars, culminating in a British conquest of that land.

The states described in this chapter are in no way a complete listing of West African political units. Furthermore, there were other African areas that witnessed the development of impressive states. Some like Egypt, Kush, and Carthage flourished during the pre-Christian era. Others came later. Some areas, like Zimbabwe and the savannah lands south of the Congo basin, witnessed different civilizations rising on the sites of their predecessors. Muslim Swahili-speaking city-states located along the Indian Ocean traded with Arabia, India, and Indonesia at a time when European powers were fighting in the Crusades. Ethiopians have a recorded history almost 2,000 years old. Other kingdoms are of more recent origin: the Zulu people, for instance, did not become a powerful nation until the nineteenth century. To a greater or lesser degree, however, all of them had some connection with the inhabiting of the New World with black peoples.

CHAPTER 2

The African Way of Life

It is obviously impossible to make very many generalizations concerning the way of life in a continent as large as Africa, with so many variations in climate, physiography, and population. As in any other area, at any other time, Africa presents variations in degrees of civilization that run the entire gamut from the most simple to remarkably advanced ones. At this point little more can be done than to observe various aspects of the African way of life with a view to understanding more adequately the cultural heritage of these people who have come to claim the concern of Europeans and Americans in recent centuries. If the emphasis here appears to be placed on the way of life in West Africa, it is because there seems to be merit in trying to secure as intimate an understanding as possible of the area in which the bulk of the people lived who later became the black workers of the Americas.

■ Political Institutions

Wherever we observe the peoples of Africa, we find some form of political organization, even among the so-called stateless. They were not all highly organized kingdoms—to be sure, some were simple, isolated family states—but they all seem to indicate the normal capability and desire of establishing governments to solve the problems that every community encounters. The family state prevailed in areas where the territory was divided among a number of distinct families and where there was no inclination or desire to merge resources to organize a stronger state. In such situations the chief of state was extremely powerful because his political strength was supplemented by the strength that was his by virtue of being head of the family. In some instances, several such states, the constituents of which enjoyed a common ancestry, came together to form a more powerful state known as a clan state. If it was possible to surmount the obstacles of tradition and clannishness, several groups could come together and form what came to be known as a village state or tribe seat.

Village states flourished throughout West Africa. The growth and prosperity of some prompted them to merge, voluntarily or by force, to form small kingdoms, the most popular form of government in Africa. These kingdoms, if they met with a favorable set of circumstances—able leadership, adequate resources, and strong military organization—could grow into federations or even empires, such as those of Mali and Songhay. These various degrees of political organization were attained by Africans in their successive stages of development. Despite the fact that the states existed at different times and at different places, it is remarkable that the same essential characteristics seem to have prevailed in all of them.

The power to govern a state usually resided in a given family and was transmitted by it. Two other families, however, performed important functions in establishing a royal personage on the throne, the electing family and the enthroning family. The electing family could exercise a choice within the royal family. In this way Africans recognized the stabilizing effect that a royal family might have on the political fortunes of the people. At the same time, they were practical enough to recognize the fact that the eldest son was not necessarily the ablest or most desirable and felt free to choose their ruler from among any of the male members of the royal family. The new king could exercise no authority until he had been properly invested in office by those so designated by the enthroning family. These practices had the effect of ensuring the people a more satisfactory monarch than automatic descent of authority might give them.

Each African king of any real importance had a group of ministers and advisers. Indeed, in some states custom imposed on the king the obligation of appointing a given number of advisers and delegating real authority to them. Custom generally conferred each ministerial charge on a certain family. These ministers, together with other advisers and members of the nobility, functioned as a kind of parliament, which in some instances exercised substantial authority. It is interesting to observe that a peculiar African custom served to limit the authority of many kings. If the king did not belong to the family of the first person occupying the ground in his kingdom, he had no rights over the land. Any questions involving the land were settled by the descendants of the first occupants, who could conceivably be insignificant subjects of the king or even prisoners of war. It seems that most kings were willing to conform to this ancient custom.

It is possible, however, to overemphasize the importance of the central political organization among Africans. To be sure, the power of the kings, ministers, and subchiefs was considerable, but beneath this semblance of national unity was the individual's strong attachment to local authority and local loyalties. Each locality had its own "king," and in many matters of a purely local nature this royal personage exercised power that was indisputable. It was this concept of the division of authority—a kind of dichotomy of sovereignty—that kept the great kings sensitive to the possibility of conflict within their realms. Few powerful kings of great empires and kingdoms ever achieved so much authority as to destroy completely the feeling of local rulers that they enjoyed a degree of sovereignty themselves. Stability could be achieved only through extensive military organization and a carefully organized central government. That this stability was frequently achieved is a testimonial to the wisdom, strength, and not infrequent ruthlessness of the various kingdoms.

■ Economic Life

It would be erroneous to assume that Africans were either primarily nomadic or simply agricultural. There exists in Africa such a diversity of physical environments that it would be impossible for people to evolve identical ways of life in different parts of the continent. Essentially agricultural, the peoples of Africa displayed a remarkable degree of specialization within this ancient economic pursuit. The African concept of landownership stemmed from the importance of agriculture in the peoples' way of life. The land was considered so important to the entire community that it belonged not to individuals but to the collective community, which was comprised of the first occupants of the soil. One of the most important local dignitaries was the "master of the ground," who was at the same time the grand priest of the local religion and the administrator of the soil. The importance of this official can be clearly seen, it may be recalled, in the fact that not even the political ruler could make any disposition of land without the consent of the master of the ground. Individuals or groups of people could obtain the right to use a given parcel of land, but such permission did not carry with it the right of alienation or any other form of disposition. When the land was not used productively, it reverted to the collective domain.

Whether land was held individually or collectively—and it seems that both practices were in use—the tillers of the soil devoted all their energies to the cultivation of their crops. Soil was cleared by felling trees and burning the underbrush. The ashes were used to fertilize the ground, which was in turn prepared for planting with the use of large spades with short handles. Seeds or sprouts were planted in mounds or embankments that had been carefully prepared. Frequent weeding was necessary, especially in new ground, in order to prevent the young plants from being choked. Millet, wheat, rice, cassava, cotton, fruits, and vegetables were commonly grown. Dotting the countryside were towers from which watchmen drove away birds and grain-eating animals. Harvest time was a particularly busy period during which grain was reaped, threshed, milled, and stored, while other fruits and grains were made into fermented drinks, and cotton was manufactured into thread and cloth.

Domestic animals were a part of almost every farm, but in some areas the rural people devoted most of their attention to the grazing of sheep and cattle and the raising of chickens and other fowl. In northeastern Africa some tribes were known for their great skill in the breeding and care of cattle. In the east many villages ascribed so much importance to the raising of cattle that wealth was measured in terms of heads of cattle. The Bantu and Khoikhoi engaged in farming as well as large-scale cattle raising.

Artisanry was a significant area of economic activity. Even among the so-called backward tribes, there were those who were skilled along various lines. Among many people, there was a remarkable knowledge of basketry, textile weaving, pottery, woodwork, and metallurgy. The Pygmies manufactured bark cloth and fiber baskets. The Khoikhoi devoted much time and attention to making clothing from textiles, skins, and furs. The Ashantis of the Gold Coast wove rugs and carpets and turned and glazed pottery with considerable skill. In many parts of the Sudan there was extensive manufacturing of woodenware, tools, and implements.

The use of iron was developed very early in the economy of Africa. From Ethiopia to the Atlantic, there is much evidence of adroitness in the manufacture and use of iron. Indeed, many careful students of primitive civilizations credit indigenous Africans with the discovery of iron. The anthropologist Franz Boas insisted that Africans were using iron when European peoples were still in the Stone Age. The simple processes that Africans were found to have used and the early date at which they began to make iron suggest that it was the natives of Africa, and not the Hittites, who first discovered its use. Africa exported iron for many years, and blacksmiths and other iron workers were found in many parts of Africa. With simple bellows and a charcoal fire, the native blacksmith smelted his ore and forged implements such as knives, saws, and axes. Africans also worked in silver, gold, copper, and bronze. In Benin, bronze and copper implements and art objects testified to the great skill of the smiths, while many artisans, including those of the Yoruba lands and Mali, devoted their attention to the making of ornamental objects from silver and gold.

The interest of early Africa in the outside world can best be seen in the great attention given to commerce. The tendency of tribes to specialize in some phase of economic activity made it necessary that they maintain commercial contact with other tribes and with other countries in order to secure the things that they did not produce. Some villages, for example, specialized in fishing; others concentrated on metallurgy, while others made weapons, utensils, and so on. In tribes where such specialization was practiced, traders traveled from place to place to barter and to purchase. Upon returning they were laden with goods which they sold to their fellows. Some traders from the west coast went as far north as the Mediterranean and as far east as Egypt, where they exchanged their goods for the wares of traders from other parts of the world. It is to be recalled that the travels of kings and emperors did much to stimulate this international commerce. Africa was, therefore, never a series of isolated, self-sufficient communities, but an area that had far-flung interests based on agriculture, industry, and commerce. The effect of such contacts on the culture was immeasurable. It can only be said here that these routes of commerce were the highways over which civilization as well as goods traveled and that Africa gave much of its own civilization to others and received a good deal in return.

■ Social Organization

As among other peoples, the family was the basis of social organization in early Africa. The foundation of even economic and political life in Africa was the family, with its inestimable influence over individual members. Although the eldest male was usually the head of the family, there was a widespread practice of tracing relationships through the mother instead of the father. In areas where this matrilineal practice was followed, children belonged solely to the family of the mother, whose eldest brother exercised the paternal rights and assumed all responsibility for the children's lives and actions. In tribes that admitted only female relationship, the chief of the family was the brother of the mother on her mother's side. In tribes that were, on the other hand, patrilineal, the chief was the real father. With either group, those forming the family comprised all the living descendants of the same ancestor, female in the matriarchal system and male in the patriarchal system.

In general, a wife was not considered a member of her husband's family. After marriage she continued to be a part of her own family. Since her family continued to manifest a real interest in her welfare, the bride's husband was expected to guarantee good treatment and to pay her family an indemnity, a compensation for taking away a member of the family. This indemnity was not a purchase price, as has frequently been believed. The woman did not legally belong to her husband but to her own family. Naturally, the amount of the indemnity varied both with tribal practice and with the position of the bridegroom. Indeed, in some tribes the tradition was maintained by a mere token payment out of respect for an ancient practice that had once had real significance in intertribal relationships.

Although polygamy existed in virtually every region, it was not universally practiced. The chief of the family would defray the expenses involved in the first marriage of a male member of the family, but if the husband

Salih Bilali Remembers Massina—1844 [as reported in a letter of James Hamilton Couper]

His native town is Kianah, in the district of Temourah and in the Kingdom of Massina. . . . I infer from his conversation, that the town of Kianah . . . is a Foulah or Fellatah colony, established among the older nations of the Soudan, and differing from them in language. . . . The houses consist of two kinds. Those occupied by the richer classes are built of cylindrical bricks, made of clay mixed with rice chaff and dried in the sun. They contain two rooms only; one of which is used as a storeroom, and the other as an eating and sleeping apartment, for the whole family. . . . The poor classes live in small conical huts, made of poles, connected at the tops and covered with straw.

The natives cultivate the soil, and keep large droves of horses, cows, sheep, goats, and some asses. The great grain crop is rice. . . . Besides rice, they cultivate a species of red maize, millet, and Guinea corn. They also grow beans, pumpkins, okra, tomatoes, cucumbers and cotton. . . . The usual food is rice, milk, butter, fish, beef and mutton. The domesticated animals are horses, used for riding, asses and camels for carrying loads; cattle, the bulls of which have lumps on their shoulders, for milk and meat—sheep with very long wool . . . goats and poultry, and dogs for guards. They have no hogs. . . .

His father and mother were persons of considerable property. When about twelve years old, as he was returning from Jenne to Kianah, on horseback, he was seized by a predatory party and carried to Segu, and was transferred from master to master, until he reached the coast, at Anomabu. . . . After leaving Bambara, to use his own expression, the people had no religion, until he came to this country [the Gold Coast].

William B. Hodgson, *Notes on Northern Africa, the Sahara, and the Soudan* (New York, 1844), in Philip D. Curtin, ed., *Africa Remembered* (Madison, 1967), pp. 147–151.

wanted to take a second wife, he would have to meet all the expenses himself. Religion played a part in determining the number of wives a man could have. Local religions did not limit the number. When the Muslims made inroads into the tribes of Africa, they forbade adherents to take more than four wives. Wherever the Christians established a foothold, they insisted on monogamy altogether. Where polygamy was practiced, it does not appear to have produced many evils. As a matter of fact, the division of household duties in a polygamous family had the effect of reducing the duties and responsibilities of each wife, a highly desirable condition from the point of view of the wives if the husband was without servants or slaves.

The clan, the enlarged family, was composed of all families that claimed a common ancestor. The clan would develop in the same community or area, but as it became larger and as some families found more attractive opportunities elsewhere, the clan would separate, and one or more families would go to some other area to live. Unless the separation resulted from a violent quarrel or fight, the departing families regarded themselves as still being attached to the clan. Once the unity was broken by separation, however, the clan tended to disintegrate because cooperation in war, economic activities, and religious life was no longer practicable. Under the strain imposed by separation over the course of time, the traditions and practices of the clan tended to become obscure and unimportant. Consequently, little more than a common name bound members of the same clan together, and new environments and new linguistic influences had the effect of causing clan names to be changed or modified. In such instances, members of the same clan living in different places had no way of recognizing each other.

Early in its development, Africa showed signs of social stratification in its many tribes. At the top was the nobility, "the good men," who could prove that they had descended from free men. Since they could claim the name of a respected clan, they had a right to places and positions of respect in the social order. Next was the great mass of workers, who found it difficult or impossible to raise a genealogical tree that would bear careful scrutiny. Although they might carry a perfectly good clan name, they could not prove their right to it and therefore were not able to qualify for a position in the upper class. At the bottom of the social structure were those who enjoyed no political or social rights. They were slaves, war captives, disgraced or degraded people and those living beyond the pale of the law. It must be added that the social structure had an economic base, and wealth tended to be concentrated in the upper class. Families, moreover, rather than individuals, constituted the several classes. Since families wielded economic power, through their politically important positions or through the domination of certain crafts and other economic pursuits, they had a way of influencing the nature of the social order. Work in itself did not elevate or debase a family, but the particular kind of work did. There was a definite respectability attached to certain types of work, and the gradation toward debasement was equally definite. The working of the soil was the most noble of all pursuits. Following in close order were cattle raising, hunting, fishing, construction, navigation, commerce, gold mining, and the processing of commodities such as soap, oil, and beer. There were variations from tribe to tribe, but everywhere there was the tendency to dignify or to degrade families on the basis of the types of work in which they were engaged.

It must not be assumed that people at the lower levels of the social order enjoyed no privileges or respect. All were regarded as necessary to society and were respected for what they contributed. They were accorded numerous privileges because their acknowledged skills earned for them the right to move from one place to another and entrance into groups that otherwise would have been closed to them. Nor is it to be assumed that there was

Olaudah Equiano (Gustavus Vassa, the African) Is Sold into Slavery—1756

The first object which saluted my eyes when I arrived on the coast was the sea, and a slave ship which was then riding at anchor and waiting for its cargo. . . . When I looked round the ship . . . and saw a large furnace or copper boiling and a multitude of black people of every description chained together, every one of their countenances expressing dejection and sorrow, I no longer doubted my fate; and quite overpowered with horror and anguish, I fell motionless on the deck and fainted. . . . I now saw myself deprived of all chance of returning to my native country [Nigeria] or even the least glimpse of hope of gaining the shore. . . . I was not long suffered to indulge my grief; I was soon put down under the decks, and there I received such a salutation in my nostrils as I had never experienced in my life: so that with the loathsomeness of the stench and crying together, I became so sick and low that I was not able to eat . . . but soon, to my grief, two of the white men offered me eatables, and on my refusing to eat, one of them held me fast . . . and laid me across I think the windlass, and tied my feet while the other flogged me severely. . . . One day, when we had a smooth sea and a moderate wind, two of my wearied countrymen who were chained together . . . preferring death to such a life of misery, somehow made through the nettings and jumped into the sea, immediately another quite dejected fellow . . . also followed; and I believe many more would very soon have done the same if they had not been prevented by the ship's crew. . . .

The Interesting Narrative of the Life of Olaudah Equiano or Gustavus Vassa the African, ed. Paul Edwards (New York, 1966), pp. 25–32.

absolute rigidity in the social structure of tribal Africa. As among other peoples, tact, special knowledge, wealth, or good fortune tended to create a fluidity in African society. By taste, a member of a mining family might choose to farm; although his new occupation did not of itself elevate him from the lower social position of his family, in due time he could gain so much respect and admiration as a farmer that he would be regarded as a legitimate member of the class of noble tillers of the soil. As in almost every society in the world, power and wealth could in many instances be substituted for nobility of origin.

Slavery was an important feature of African social and economic life. The institution was widespread and was perhaps as old as African society itself. Slaves were predominantly people captured in war and could be sold or kept by those who captured them. Slaves were usually regarded as the property of the chief of the tribe or the head of the family. In law, slaves were chattel property, but in practice they often became trusted associates of their owners and enjoyed virtual freedom. Some, however, were sold and exported from the country, while others were sacrificed by kings in the worship of their royal ancestors. The children of slaves could not be sold and thus constituted an integral and inalienable part of the family property. Enjoying such security, it was not uncommon for the children of slaves to be favored with manumission at the hands of their owners.

■ Religion

Certainly up to the period of the many European incursions into Africa the vast majority of the people engaged in religious practices that were indigenous to the continent. These practices were only outward manifestations of certain religious beliefs and, like symbols in other religions, they did not indicate the specific character of the religion. The religion of early Africans can most accurately be described as ancestor worship. Africans believed that the spirits of their ancestors had unlimited power over their lives. In this, as in almost every aspect of African life, the kinship group was important. It was devoutly believed that the spirit that dwelled in a relative was deified upon death and that it continued to live and take an active interest in the family. The spirits of early ancestors had been free to wield an influence for such a long time that they were much more powerful than the spirits of the more recently deceased, hence, the devout worship and the complete deification of early ancestors. Not only were the spirits of deceased members of the family worshipped, but a similar high regard was held for the spirits that dwelt on the family land, in the trees and rocks in the community of the kinship group, and in the sky above the community.

Because of the family character of African religions, the priests of the religions were the patriarchs of the families. They were the oldest living members of the descendants of the initial ancestor and had therefore inherited the earthly prerogatives of their predecessors. Thus, they had dominion over the family grounds, waters, and atmosphere. It was the family patriarch who entered into communication with the souls of his ancestors and the natural forces in his immediate vicinity. He was therefore authorized to conduct ceremonies of worship. The temples of worship could be any structures set aside for that purpose. They contained holy objects, such as the bones of the dead, consecrated pieces of wood, rock, or metal, and statuettes representing objects to be worshipped. Bells or rattles were used to invoke the spirits and the worshippers. The blood of victims—chickens, sheep, goats, or human beings—was offered as a sacrifice to appease the gods. There was never a universal practice of sacrificing human beings in Africa, but in some areas prisoners and captives were sacrificed in worship of the various deities. Libations of palm wine, beer, or some other fermented drink were offered in various forms of worship. Prayers and songs were other expressions of adoration.

It was only natural that in a society such as that found in Africa there would be considerable reliance on the magical power of amulets, talismans, and the like. Anything that helped to explain and answer the imponderables was a welcome addition to tribal practices. Magic was, therefore, practiced on a great scale. By resorting to ill-defined powers, known only to him, the magician invented techniques and created rites designed to secure for individuals the specific ends that they desired. Where religion was a collective attempt to secure satisfaction for the kinship group, magic was an individual attempt to achieve certain satisfactions on the part of a particular person. Even in areas where animistic worship prevailed, belief in magic was widespread. Many had great confidence in the efficacy of magical practices, and it may be that this reliance on the divination of sorcerers was responsible in part for the course that the civilization of Africa took.

The elaborateness of funeral rites all over the continent attests to the regard that Africans had for the idea that the spirits of the dead played an important part in the life of the kinship group. The funeral was the climax of life, and costly and extensive rituals were sacred obligations of the survivors. The dead were generally buried in the ground either beneath the huts in which they had lived or in cemeteries. Burial often took place within a few days after death, but at times the family delayed interment for several weeks or longer. The grave was not completely closed until every member of the family had had an opportunity to present offerings and to participate in some rite incident to interment. Nothing more clearly demonstrates the cohesiveness of the African family than the ceremonies and customs it practiced on the occasion of the death and burial of a member.

In all probability the early influence of the religion of Islam on the African way of life has been greatly exaggerated. This is certainly true for the period before the fourteenth century. Muslims crossed from Arabia over into Egypt in the seventh century. In the following century they swept across North Africa where they met with notable success, but religious conversion was slow below the Sahara in the land of the blacks. It will be recalled that the kingdoms of Ghana, Mali, and Songhay accepted Islam quite reluctantly, while other groups rejected it altogether. Some African kings accepted Islam for what seemed to be economic and political reasons, but their subjects frequently held tenaciously to their tribal religious practices. Muslims were never able, for example, to win over the peoples of Mali, Hausaland, and Yorubaland. The commercial opportunities offered by the Muslims were especially attractive. It must also be added that the followers of the Prophet accepted Africans as social equals and gave them an opportunity to enjoy the advantages of education and of cultural advancement that the religion offered. Even as a slave, the black Muslim was considered a brother. To many black Africans these features were doubtless as important as the purely ritualistic aspects of the new religion. Even so, numberless Africans summarily rejected Islam in preference for the cults and rituals that were historically a part of their way of life.

Christianity became entrenched in North Africa early. It was there when

Islam made its appearance in the seventh century, and these two great faiths engaged in a life-and-death struggle for the control of that area. In West Africa, where the population was especially dense and from which the great bulk of slaves was secured, Christianity was practically unknown until the Portuguese began to establish missions in the area in the sixteenth century. It was a strange religion, this Christianity, which taught equality and brotherhood and at the same time introduced on a large scale the practice of tearing people from their homes and transporting them to a distant land to become slaves. If the Africans south of the Sahara were slow to accept Christianity, it was not only because they were attached to their particular forms of tribal worship but also because they did not have the superhuman capacity to reconcile in their own minds the contradictory character of the new religion.

■ The Arts

In some areas of art Africans attained a high degree of expression. In carvings and sculptures of wood, stone, and ivory, their work displayed an originality both in technique and subject matter that marked them clearly as a people with an abundant capacity for aesthetic expression. There was, of course, a great degree of variation from place to place in the level of expression attained, but hardly any tribe failed to show some inclination toward the use of certain art forms. Benin bronze and brass works of rosettes, doorplates, and metal vases reflect great skill in the use of this difficult medium. Among the Yoruba the delicacy of form seen in the terra-cotta pieces is a testimonial to the rare artistry that these people possessed. The statuettes of people and animals widely used by African tribes in religious rites serve as a reminder that almost everywhere some Africans concerned themselves with artistic activities. From Timbuktu to the Congo there was considerable work in wood, gold, silver, ivory, clay, and the like, and it cannot be denied that many of these pieces bear witness to the fact that African art was not only indigenous but also worthy of the name.

To enhance the beauty and value of the items that they made to be sold or used, Africans decorated them in various ways. Ornamented and glazed pottery, delicately carved spoons and knives, golden jewels of filigree, and elegantly woven mats, cloth, and tapestries are outstanding examples of the application of art in industry. In the construction of houses, royal palaces, and temples, this same proclivity toward ornamentation is apparent. When Muslim architects and scientists came to the region south of the desert, there was a marked improvement in the symmetry and beauty of West African architecture. It must be added, however, that there is abundant evidence to support the view that many basic elements of beauty in African architecture were evident before the incursion of the Muslims.

An important medium of aesthetic expression in Africa is music. Among the principal musical instruments developed in Africa were the xylophone, drum, guitar, zither, harp, and flute. The most frequently used musical form was, of course, the song, with or without instrumental accompaniment. Songs were usually antiphonal and were characterized by highly developed rhythms. Some were quite complex with respect to scale, rhythm, and general organization. There was also great variation in the types of African musical forms, ranging from lullabies and dance songs to work songs and sacred melodies. Likewise, there were many forms of the African dance. Some were for recreational or social purposes, while others served ritualistic or religious functions. Africans regarded both music forms and dance as integral parts of their culture.

The numerous spoken languages found in Africa always constituted a barrier to the development of literary forms. From the Atlantic to Ethiopia, through the heart of the continent, the languages of the Sudanic group are spoken. In the southern half of Africa, Bantu is spoken. There are at least ten Semitic dialects, ranging from the Arabic in North Africa to the Berber dialects heard in the Great Desert. Besides, there are many tribal dialects and languages that have no apparent relationship with the principal language groups. Among these are the languages of Suto, Ruanda, and Banda. Thus, where there is so much heterogeneity in the spoken language, even within a relatively small area, the almost insurmountable difficulties involved in the evolution of adequate means of extensive communication become readily apparent.

In early Africa few of the languages were reduced to writing. The literature was, therefore, predominantly oral, and there was an abundance of it. Handed down principally through the kinship group, the oral literature was composed of supernatural tales, moral tales, proverbs, epic poems, satires, love songs, funeral pieces, and comic tales. Some individuals, griots, made a specialty of collecting these bits of oral literature and purveying them before kings as well as ordinary families. They sang, told stories, and recited poetry. They kept in their memories the history, law, and traditions of their people and were themselves living dictionaries who occasionally performed invaluable services to their communities. The use of Arabic by educated Muslim Africans after the fourteenth century was rather extensive and made possible the reduction of some of the oral literature to permanent form. Examples of this are *Tarikh-es-Soudan*, a history of the Sudan written by Es-Sadi, and *Tarikh-El-Fettach*, written by Kati, a Sudanese. Some African scholars even sought to adapt the Arabic alphabet to the writing of one of the African languages by adding diacritical marks to represent sounds that do not exist in Arabic. This extremely difficult feat made possible the more extensive use of Arabic in developing a written literature among Africans.

Such was the way of life in Africa up until the end of the sixteenth century. It was at this stage of development that Europeans began to make incursions for the purpose of engaging in the trade in humans. It was by no means a simple way of life that the whites found. The basic problems of existence had been solved; political, economic, and social institutions were, on the whole, stable. Whether the states were great empires or modest political entities, they were well organized with limited monarchies and a myriad of public officials. Well-defined concepts of law and order prevailed, and even if there was considerable rivalry and strife among states, there was a remarkable degree of order within the several governments. Citizens seemed to take their responsibilities and loyalties seriously. The peoples of Africa were on the whole well disciplined, and records of rebellions and revolutions are not common. This does not mean that all rulers were benevolent or that all their subjects were completely free from oppression. What it does mean is that a relatively satisfactory balance had been achieved between the people and their government. Usurpers and pretenders did emerge, to be sure, and at times they created considerable chaos, but these situations were perhaps no worse than the strife and chaos that erupted in the states of Europe during the late medieval and the early modern periods.

There was usually enough stability within African states and among them to make possible healthy economic development. The division of labor and the practice of specialization in occupations display a remarkable versatility and variety of talents and tastes. The interest in commerce and the understanding of the economic importance of contact with the European and Asian worlds show a realism similar to that of contemporary states in other parts of the world.

Nothing is more impressive in viewing the social institutions of Africa than the cohesive influence of the family. The immediate family, the clan, and the tribe undergirded every aspect of life. The rule of discipline enforced in the family was responsible in large measure for the stability that has been observed in various aspects of life. The influence and hold that the patriarch had over the members of the family was largely responsible for the stability that was characteristic of the area. The deep loyalty and attachment of the individual to the family approached reverence and indeed was the basis for most of the religious practices, in which ancestor worship played such an important part. The religions of Africa were a product of an environment in which the population lived close to nature. These sacred rites were manifestations of a people who were in a desperate search for answers to the imponderables. Their gods functioned intimately in their daily lives, and the adherents demanded effective, practical demonstrations of their deistical power in terms of better crops and victory over warring enemies. If Africans displayed a measure of religious skepticism in their willingness to accept new tribal gods or even new religions from the outside world, it was because they failed to see why additional gods would give them greater opportunities for success in their undertakings.

These people who of necessity had to devote most of their energies and attention to the important problems of existence did not neglect the aesthetic aspects of life. Evidence can be found everywhere of pronounced proclivities to artistic expression. Whether in painting, sculpture, or carving there is a delicate sensitivity and an appreciation of the beautiful that reflects a basic regard for the finer things of life. Even in the industrial arts and crafts Africans took the time to beautify their products by applying to them the best of their artistic talents and knowledge. Song and dance played an important part in their social life. With stringed and rhythm instruments they made merry with their friends, worshipped their gods, and buried their dead. Nor is their aesthetic proclivity absent from the area of literary achievement. As in every other endeavor, the literary activities of Africans were tied up closely with their everyday life. Their oral literature, made up of tales, proverbs, epics, histories, and laws, served as an educational device, a source of amusement, and a guide for the administration of government and the conduct of religious ceremonies. If their written literature was limited, it was certainly not for a want of literary interests but rather because of the technical obstacles in the way of developing written languages. The extant treatises, largely in Arabic, show that when a written language was mastered, the resulting works were worthy of serious comparison with their contemporaries in other parts of the world. Most important of all, however, is that they were worthy of esteem on their own terms and by their own standards.

■ The Transplantation of African Culture

Students of Africa and America have discussed for many years the question of the extent to which African culture was transplanted and preserved in the New World. Of course, a considerable number of students formerly contended that nothing existed in Africa that approached civilization and that there was, therefore, nothing for Africans to bring with them. As evidence to the contrary began to pile up, that position was no longer tenable. Questions still remained as to whether Africans continued to be African in ways other than color and whether any substantial elements of Africa became part of the general acculturative process taking place in America. Sociologists like E. Franklin Frazier and Robert E. Park have failed to see anything in contemporary African-American life that can be traced to the African background. On the other hand, scholars like Carter G. Woodson, Melville J. Herskovits, Lorenzo Turner, John Blassingame, and Albert Raboteau have insisted that the African cultural heritage can still be seen in many aspects of American life today. In the 1960s and 1970s the debate was revived when many blacks and some whites began to insist that a substantial portion of African culture not only survived the Atlantic crossing but has persisted to the present day. Although the controversy continues unresolved, it nevertheless seems possible to make a tentative statement about this important problem.

African slaves came from a complex social and economic life, and they were not overwhelmed or overawed by their New World experiences. Despite the heterogeneity characteristic of many aspects of African life,

African peoples still had sufficient common experiences to enable them to cooperate in the New World in fashioning new customs and traditions which reflected their African background. To be sure, there were at least two acculturative processes going on side by side in the New World. As Africans of different experiences lived together, there was an interaction of the various African cultures. This produced a somewhat different set of customs and practices, but these were still manifestly rooted deep in the African experience. This was especially true where large numbers of Africans resided in the same place, as in the Sea Islands, where they could preserve certain religious practices and even language patterns. At the same time, there was the interaction of African and Western cultures, which doubtless changed the cultural patterns of both groups. It is to be remembered that European institutions did not exist everywhere with the same degree of fixity, and where European practices were relatively weak the opportunities for African survivals were correspondingly strengthened.

In the cultural conflict that took place in the New World following the introduction of Africans, the acculturative process varied in different places and under different circumstances. In some places it was all but stymied where there was a sufficient consensus of experience among Africans to take the Western culture and reinterpret it almost wholly in terms of their own experiences. In other places, mainly Brazil and some Caribbean islands, successful revolts made possible the transplantation of an African way of life to a considerable degree. Elsewhere, the normal or gradual development of the process can be observed, but always at least some survival of African culture is obvious. When it comes to measuring or evaluating the persistence of African culture in the New World—and especially in the United States—the problem becomes much more difficult. It can be seen in the language in such words as "yam," "goober," "canoe," and "banjo." In literature the persistence of African culture can be seen in the folk tales that have been recorded in recent years by American writers. In religion there are divinations and various cult practices, some of which can be traced to the African background. In work, in play, in social organizations, and in various aesthetic manifestations there are some evidences of African culture.

The survival of varying degrees of African culture in America does not suggest that there has been only a limited adjustment of Africans to the New World situation. On the contrary, it merely points up the fact that they came out of an experience that was sufficiently entrenched to make possible the persistence of some customs and traditions. There is a certain amount of validity in the view that in the conflict of cultures only those practices will survive whose value and superiority give them the strength and tenacity to do so. African survivals in America also suggest a pronounced resiliency in African institutions. There had been sufficient intertribal and interstate intercourse to give Africans the important experience of adopting many of the practices of those with whom they came in contact while at the same time retaining much of their earlier way of life.

CHAPTER 3

The Slave Trade and the New World

■ European and Asian Interests

When the Christians of Western Europe began to turn their attention to the slave trade in the fifteenth and sixteenth centuries, they were not introducing a new practice. Although they displayed much originality in approach and technique, they were engaging in a pursuit that had been a concern for countless centuries. As a matter of fact, slavery was widespread during the earliest known history of Africa as well as of other continents. Doubtless there was cruelty and oppression in African slavery as there was anywhere that the institution developed. At least in some portions of Africa there was no racial basis of slavery. The Egyptians enslaved whatever peoples they captured. At times they were Semitic, at times Mediterranean, and at other times blacks from Nubia. Slavery in the Greek and Roman empires is well known. In both periods the traffic in human beings from western Asia and North Africa brought a continuous stream of slaves to perform personal services and to till the fields for the ruling class. Neither in Greece nor Rome was menial service regarded as degrading. The opportunities for education and cultural advancement were, therefore, opened up to slaves. It was not unusual to find in this class people possessing a degree of intelligence and training not usually associated with slaves.

When the Muslims invaded Africa, they contributed greatly to the development of the institution of slavery by seizing women for their harems and men for military and menial service. By purchase as well as by conquest, the Muslims recruited African slaves and shipped them off to Arabia, Persia, or some other Islamic land. As kings and princes embraced Islam, they cooperated with the Arabians in the exportation of human cargo. Long before the extensive development of the slave trade by Europeans, many of the basic practices of the international slave trade had already been established. It is to be noted, however, that slavery among the Muslims was not an institution utilized primarily for the production of goods from which wealth could be derived. There were no extensive cotton, tobacco, and sugarcane fields in Arabia, Persia, and Egypt. Slaves in these lands were essentially servants, and the extent of the demand for them depended in a large measure on the wealth of the potential masters. Slavery was, therefore, a manifestation of wealth, and the institution showed little of the harshness and severity that it possessed in areas where it was itself the foundation on which wealth was built. Although becoming Muslims did not release slaves from their duties, it did have the effect of elevating their standing and enhancing their dignity among others. While in the face of continued enslavement this was of doubtful value, it could have been viewed by slaves of a later and a more ruthless system as a straw to which to clutch.

It was the forces let loose by the Renaissance and the Commercial Revolution that created the modern institution of slavery and the slave trade. The Renaissance provided a new kind of freedom—the freedom to pursue those ends that would be most beneficial to the soul and the body. It developed into such a passionate search that it resulted in the destruction of long-established practices and beliefs and even in the destruction of the rights of others to pursue the same ends for their own benefit. As W. E. B. Du Bois has pointed out, it was the freedom to destroy freedom, the freedom of some to exploit the rights of others. If, then, people were determined to be free, who was there to tell them that they were not entitled to enslave others?

Coupled with this new concept of freedom was the revitalized economic life of Europe that was brought forth by the Commercial Revolution. The breakdown of feudalism, the rise of towns, the heightened interest in commercial activities, and the new recognition of the strength and power of capital, all of which were essential elements of the Commercial Revolution, brought about a type of competition characterized by ruthless exploitation of any commodities that could be viewed as economic goods. The rise of powerful national states in Western Europe—Spain, France, Portugal, Britain, and, later, Holland—provided the political instrumentalities through which these new forces could be channeled. While the state acted as referee for competitors within its borders, it also served to stimulate competition between its own merchants and traders and those of other countries. The spirit of the Renaissance, with its sanction of ruthless freedom, and the practices of the Commercial Revolution, with its new techniques of exploitation, conspired to bring forth new approaches to the acquisition of wealth and power. Among these was establishment of the institution of modern slavery and the concomitant practice of importing and exporting slaves.

Doubtless, some Africans who were sold to the east and north during the period of Muslim domination found their way into the markets of Western Europe. It was not until the end of the fourteenth century, however, that Europeans themselves began to bring slaves into Europe. Both Spanish and Portuguese sailors were exploring the coast of Africa in the wake of the great wave of expansionism that had swept over Europe. They went to the Canary Islands and to innumerable ports on the mainland as far as the Gulf of Guinea. They took Africans to Europe and made servants of them, feeling justified in doing so because Africans would thereby have the opportunity to cast off their heathenism and embrace the Christian religion. By the middle of the fifteenth century, Europeans were selling in their home markets many African commodities, among them nuts, fruit, olive oil, gold, and slaves. Within a very few years, the slave trade became an accepted and profitable part of European commerce. Largely under the encouragement of Prince Henry, the sailors and merchants of Portugal early saw the economic advantages that the African slave trade afforded. By the time of his death in 1460, 700 or 800 slaves were being transported to Portugal annually.

The last half of the fifteenth century may be considered the years of preparation in the history of the slave trade. Europeans, mainly Spaniards and Portuguese, were establishing orderly trade relations with Africans and were erecting forts and trading posts from which to carry on their business. It was the period in which Europeans were becoming accustomed to having black Africans do their work and were exploring the possibilities of finding new tasks for them. Europeans were attempting to settle among themselves the question of who should and who should not engage in the traffic, and the mad scramble for monopoly even before the close of the century is indicative of the importance with which that traffic was regarded. Finally, this was the period in which Europeans developed a rationalization for their deeds based on Christianity. The Portuguese and the Spaniards led Europeans in invoking the missionary zeal of Christianity to justify their activities on the African coast. If they were chaining Africans together for the purpose of consigning them to a lifetime of enforced servitude, it was a "holy cause" in which they had the blessings of both their king and their church.

There was never any profitable future for African slavery in Europe. Although Europe was undergoing drastic economic change in the fifteenth and sixteenth centuries, its new economic institutions did not utilize Africans on a sufficiently large scale to make the trade excessively profitable. Banking houses, shipyards, mercantile establishments, and the homes of the newly rich could use only a limited number of slaves. To be sure, there were many jobs to be performed, but the large white population that was dispossessed of land by the enclosure movement in England and on the Continent was in search of employment. If there were jobs to be filled, these impecunious Europeans claimed them for themselves. But the new era in economic development ushered in some activities in which Africans could perhaps be used. It was too much to expect that these activities would be confined to Europe as international competition developed. The search for new trade routes, new lands, and new commodities provided the opportunities for the use of African slaves that Europeans had been looking for. It was the New World with its vast natural resources and its undeveloped regions that could make slavery and the slave trade profitable, if indeed it could be profitable anywhere.

■ Africans in the New World

As early as 1920, when Harvard professor Leo Wiener published *Africa and the Discovery of America,* scholars advanced the view that Africans inhabited the New World before Columbus. Wiener and several scholars who followed him (notably Ivan Van Sertima, whose *They Came Before Columbus* was published in 1976) said that numerous evidences of trade and other contacts between Africa and the New World indicate that Africans, not Europeans, were the pioneers of the transatlantic West. Using linguistic as well as archaeological and historical evidence, they vigorously argued their case. Van Sertima declares, for example, that "the case for African contacts with pre-Columbian America . . . is grounded now upon an overwhelming and growing body of reliable witnesses." Although most scholars have not yet accepted these claims, it is not so much because the arguments are not convincing as it is their refusal to deny claims that had become deeply entrenched conventional wisdom for more than four centuries. Consequently the traditional story of the coming of Africans to the New World remains essentially unchanged.

From the very beginning of European exploits in the New World, Africans came as explorers, servants, and slaves. Even if Pedro Alonso Niño of Columbus's crew was not a Negro as has been claimed, there were many blacks who accompanied other European explorers to the New World. As early as 1501, Spain relinquished her earlier ban and permitted Africans to go to Spanish lands in the New World. Thirty Africans, including Nuflo de Olano, were with Balboa when he discovered the Pacific Ocean. Cortés carried blacks with him into Mexico, and one of them planted and harvested the first wheat crop in the New World. Two accompanied Velas in 1520. When Alvarado went to Quito, he took 200 blacks with him. They were with Pizarro on his Peruvian expedition and carried him to the cathedral after he was murdered. The Africans in the expeditions of Almagro and Valdivia saved their Spanish masters from the Indians in 1525.

As Spanish and Portuguese explorers moved into the interior of North America, Africans assisted in the undertakings. They were with Alarcón and Coronado in the conquest of New Mexico. They accompanied Narváez on his expedition of 1527 and were with Cabeza de Vaca in the exploration of the southwestern part of the present United States. One of the outstanding African explorers was Estevanico, who opened up New Mexico and Arizona for the Spaniards. Little Stephen, as Estevanico was known among his fellows, proceeded into the interior and sent back wooden crosses to indicate his progress. When his crosses increased in size until they were as tall as a man, the Spaniards realized that Estevanico had experienced great success. Indians brought news of Little Stephen's approach to the fabulous seven cities about which so much had been heard. Shortly after Stephen entered the city, the Indians killed him, believing him to be an imposter when he said that he was the emissary of two white men. Although Estevanico was murdered, he had prepared the way for the conquest of the Southwest by the Spaniards.

Africans were with the French in their explorations of the New World. In Canadian expeditions, they were with the Jesuit missionaries. When the great conquest of the Mississippi Valley was undertaken by the French in the seventeenth century, Africans constituted a substantial portion of the pioneers who settled in the region. Around 1790, Jean Baptiste Point du Sable, a French-speaking black, erected the first building in a place that came to be known as Chicago. While Africans did not accompany the English on their explorations in the New World, it is not without ironic significance that they were extensively engaged in the task of opening the New World for European development. If blacks helped to raise the curtain on the drama of economic life in the New World, they were to play an even more important part in the exploitation of its resources. Once fastened to a lifetime status of slavery, they became an integral part of the economic life of both the Old World and the New.

When the countries of Europe undertook to develop the New World, they were interested primarily in the exploitation of its natural resources. Labor was obviously necessary, and the cheaper the better. It was only natural that Indians, readily available, would be the first to be used. Europeans displayed excessive inhumanity in the employment of Indian slaves in the mines of Haiti, while working in the fields of the Caribbean almost exterminated them. The great susceptibility of Indians to the diseases carried by Europeans and their simple economic background did not prepare them for the disciplined regimen of the plantation system, which all but eliminated them as workers in the economic system that the Europeans established. Nowhere was Indian slavery profitable. Even if it had been, it would have been insufficient for the robust agricultural life that the European colonies were fostering in the seventeenth century. Other sources of labor supply would have to be tapped if agricultural development in the New World was not to be retarded by an insufficiency of workers. The search for acceptable workers in large quantities became a major preoccupation of the English and Spanish colonists in the seventeenth century.

Although Africans were present in Europe in considerable numbers in the seventeenth century and had been in the New World since at least 1501, European imperialists did not at first regard them as a solution to their labor problems. To be sure, Africans were being employed, but colonists and their Old World sponsors were extremely slow in recognizing them as the best possible labor force for the tasks in the New World. Before they came to see this, they resorted to the poor whites of Europe. In the first half of the seventeenth century, they brought landless, penniless whites over to do the work of clearing the forests and cultivating the fields. When the supply of those who voluntarily indentured themselves for a period of years proved insufficient, the English resorted to more desperate means. Their desperation is clearly seen in the emergence of the wide-spread practice of kidnapping children, women, prisoners, and drunken men. Eric Williams has indicated that the horrors these people experienced on the journey to the New World equaled those experienced by any group before or after. In the English colonies many landlords sought to reduce these servants to the status of slaves. Only gradually did servants achieve a position of respectability in the colonies.

England came to realize that white servants were unsatisfactory. There was the fear that they might become more interested in industry than in agriculture to the detriment of England. Even with all the means used to recruit workers, the supply was still insufficient as the tobacco, rice, and indigo plantations had an almost insatiable appetite for laborers. The terms of service of indentured people were a source of constant irritation for all concerned. Not only did servants chafe under the requirement of remaining until their indenture expired, but many went so far as to sue masters and ship captains for illegal detention. Many of them ran away, and since others of their ilk were migrating into unsettled lands, it became increasingly difficult, as well as expensive, to apprehend them once they had fled. The English began to ask themselves why they should be concerned with white servants when blacks presented so few of the difficulties encountered with whites. Because of their color, Africans could be easily apprehended. Furthermore, they could be purchased outright and a master's labor supply would not be in a state of constant fluctuation. Blacks, from a pagan land and without exposure to the ethical ideals of Christianity, could be handled with more rigid methods of discipline and could be morally and spiritually degraded for the sake of stability on the plantation. In the long run, African slaves were actually cheaper. In a period when economic considerations were so vital, this was especially important. African slavery, then, became a fixed institution, a solution to one of the most difficult New World problems. With the supply of Africans apparently inexhaustible, there would be no more worries about labor. European countries could look back with gratitude to the first of their nationals who explored the coasts of Africa and brought this black gold to Europe. It was the key to the solution of one of America's most pressing problems. At the same time it erected for Europeans one more important economic institution, the slave trade. As perhaps the last major development in the Commercial Revolution, it was in itself a source of great wealth for those who would engage in the traffic of human souls.

■ The Big Business of Slave Trading

When in 1517 Bishop Bartolomeo de Las Casas advocated the encouragement of immigration to the New World by permitting Spaniards to import African slaves, the trading of humans in the New World formally began. Las Casas was so determined to relieve Indians of the onerous burden of slavery that he recommended the enslavement of Africans. (Later, he so deeply regretted having taken this position that he vigorously renounced it.) The ban against the use of Africans was removed, and Charles II issued licenses to several Flemish traders to take Africans to the Spanish colonies. Monopoly of the trade went to the highest bidders. Sometimes it was held by Dutch traders, at other times by Portuguese, French, or English. As West Indian plantations grew in size and importance, the slave trade became a huge, profitable undertaking employing thousands of persons and involving a capital outlay of millions of dollars. By 1540 the annual importation of African slaves into the West Indies was estimated at 10,000.

Although Portugal was the first European country to engage in the African slave trade, it did not become one of the principal countries to realize great profits. At a time when other countries were granting monopolies to powerful, government-supported trading companies, Portugal elected to leave her trade in the hands of merchants, who proved ineffective matches for their competitors from other countries. Not until 1692 did Portugal license the Portuguese Company of Cacheo. By that time several strong companies from other countries had so monopolized the slave trade that Portugal did not have an opportunity to garner more than the proverbial crumbs from the table. Spain had been excluded from Africa by the papal arbitration of 1493 and was forced to content herself with granting the privilege of carrying slaves to her colonies, the much sought after *asiento*, to various companies and individuals from other countries.

The trade in humans that developed into such a big business in the seventeenth and eighteenth centuries was largely in the hands of Dutch, French, and English companies. After Holland extricated itself from the control of Spain in the late sixteenth century, it launched a bold program of competing with other European countries for a share in the wealth of the New World. When they failed to secure Angola and Brazil, the Dutch contented themselves with relatively small territorial possessions and con-centrated their energies on seizing control of the commercial routes to the New World. In 1621 the Dutch West India Company was organized with a monopoly of both the African trade and trade with the Dutch colonies in the New World. The company immediately challenged the claim of Portugal to exclusive trading privileges on the African coast, and by the middle of the century it had gained a substantial foothold there. While England was preoccupied with civil wars at home, Holland was strengthening its position both in Africa and America. Dutch slavers could be seen in the ports of almost all the American colonies in the seventeenth century. They brought the first Africans to several French islands, including Martinique and Guadeloupe. On occasion they even took Africans to the Spanish islands, much against the will of Spain, their former subjector.

Holland's wars with France and England in the late seventeenth century left it considerably weakened and never again did it achieve the dominance in the slave trade that it had formerly held. Many independent Dutch traders sought wealth in Africa, a goal that the company tried to obviate by offering licenses to such people. Because of its aggressiveness in the eighteenth century, Holland encountered new difficulties with other countries. Dutch traders pushed into sections of Africa that were under French influence, while on the Guinea coast Holland's seizure of certain possessions from Portugal caused much concern in England. In the West Indies and in South America, Holland used its holdings as centers for the distribution of slaves throughout the New World. Although the end of the century brought a noticeable decline in Dutch influence both in Africa and the New World, this did not take place until after Dutch traders had reaped a bountiful harvest from the slave trade.

Long before Sir John Hawkins inaugurated the English slave trade, merchants of that country had become interested in trade between Africa and the New World. Before the end of the reign of Henry VIII, traders from Britain were developing relationships along the Guinea coast and along the Brazilian coast. By the middle of the seventeenth century, many individuals and organizations, including the powerful East India Company, showed an interest in the African slave trade. The increased needs of the flourishing English colonies in the New World and the chaotic political conditions at home stimulated concern about as well as investments in the slave trade. The relative stability of the Restoration ushered in a period of renewed activity, which was crowned with eminent success. In 1672 the king chartered the Royal African Company, the reorganized group that had held the monopoly for a decade. For almost half a century this company dominated the English slave trade and indeed became the most important single slave-trading group in the world. It jealously guarded the monopoly that the king had granted, and at the same time it attempted to drive the French and the Dutch out of West Africa. The growing number of independent traders in England bitterly fought the company's exclusive right to enjoy the African trade. Pressures at home resulted in the company's loss of its monopoly in 1698. Though it continued to trade in humans, its margin of profit declined. In 1731 it gave up the slave trade and centered its attention on ivory and gold dust.

Greater success attended England's efforts to control the west coast than the Royal African Company experienced in its efforts at national monopoly. Decisive defeats of the Dutch by the British and the French in the late seventeenth century had the effect of enhancing England's prestige in Africa. The blow sustained by France in the War of the Spanish Succession resulted in England's securing the *asiento*—the exclusive right to take slaves to the

Spanish colonies—for thirty years. With British colonies in the Caribbean and on the mainland paying handsome dividends with their bountiful productivity, England's commerce came to dominate the entire world. With a strengthened navy and almost unlimited resources in capital for investment, England could now undertake to satisfy not only the growing demand of its own colonies for slaves but the demands of other colonies in the New World as well.

During the Seven Years' War England transported more than 10,000 slaves to Cuba and approximately 40,000 to Guadeloupe. By 1788 two-thirds of all slaves brought by England to the New World were sold in foreign colonies. Naturally the planters in the English colonies objected to their competitors in the New World being provided with slaves by British traders. What the planters did not realize, perhaps, was that the slave trade had itself become an important factor in England's economic life. If England's colonies were the foundation of the English economic system, certainly in the eighteenth century the slave trade was an important cornerstone of that system.

Since England came to dominate the slave trade, the machinery for prosecuting the traffic was to a large extent the product of English ingenuity. England certainly had no monopoly on the development of slave-trading practices, but its extensive interests and its great success marked it as the country to be emulated. It is for this reason that these practices are almost invariably associated with England. The techniques of trading in slaves were developed after years of trial and failure. Trading posts, or factories, on the coast were the indispensable bases of operation. Once they had been established, and the more the better, trading could proceed. Ships laden with European goods either brought traders out or furnished those already there with goods to be traded. Cotton textiles of all descriptions, utensils of brass, pewter, and ivory, boxes of beads of many sizes and shapes, guns and gunpowder, spirits—whiskey, brandy, and rum—and a variety of foodstuffs were some of the more important items to be exchanged for slaves. The value of the cargo varied with the size of the ship and the time of trading. A typical cargo would seem to be that of the *King Solomon* which in 1720 had an inventory of £4,250 worth of goods when it left London for Cape Castle on the west coast. At each trading post were stationed a number of factors, slave traders who maintained friendly relations with Africans in order to procure slaves. The posts, often bulging with European goods, were well fortified and guarded by soldiers.

Upon arrival at a post in Africa the trader was ready to establish contacts both with the officials at the post and with local Africans who assisted in securing the desired slaves. The usual procedure was to go to the chief of the tribe, make arrangements with him, and secure "permission" to trade in his domain. The chief, after being properly persuaded with gifts, then appointed various assistants who were at the disposal of the trader. Foremost among these was the caboceer, who assumed the responsibility of gathering up those to be sold—at prices previously agreed upon between the trader and the chief. The trading proceeded apace once the captives were brought before the trader for inspection, the entire process having been promoted by the traders themselves, as Robert Rodney has suggested. It was necessary for the trader to consult with his physician and other advisers concerning purchases. Frequently, the prospective slaves had been so cleanly shaven and soaked in palm oil that it was most difficult to ascertain their age or physical condition. The prices, of course, varied greatly depending on the age and condition of the slave, the period of the trading, and the location of the post. Many transactions were mere barter, but there are accounts that reveal that in the middle of the eighteenth century £20 sterling was a typical price to pay for a healthy young man at Cape Castle or some other important post on the Guinea coast.

It must not be supposed that trading in slaves involved the simple procedure of sailing into a port, loading up with slaves, and sailing away. In addition to the various courtesy visits and negotiations that protocol required and that the traders were inclined to follow in order to keep the local leaders in good humor, it was often difficult to find enough "likely" slaves to fill a ship of considerable size. Frequently, traders had to remain at one place for two or three weeks before enough slaves were rounded up to make the negotiations worthwhile. It was not unusual for a ship to be compelled to call at four or five places in order to purchase as many as 500 slaves. Local inhabitants frequently had to scour the interior and use much coercion to secure enough slaves to meet the demands of the traders.

Another delay came in disposing of the cargo that had been brought from Europe and in provisioning the ship with supplies needed for the voyage to America. Experience taught the traders what to take, but at times they took goods not especially desired at the places where they were able to purchase their slaves. If they could not persuade the permanent post officials to take the goods, they would then have to take them all the way back to England. At the post and from Africans traders obtained supplies for the western voyage across the Atlantic. Indian corn, kidney beans, yams, fruits, coconuts, and plantains were the principal foodstuffs secured. In addition, sundry medicines were stocked so that the physician might administer to the slaves, who were almost certain to become ill en route. The last post at which the slaver could make such transactions was Gorée, on the coast of Senegal.

Africans offered stiff resistance to their capture, sale, and transportation to the unknown New World. Fierce wars broke out between tribes when members of one sought to capture members of another to sell them to traders. Slaves brought to the post for sale were always chained, for the caboceers and slave captains very early learned that without such safeguards the slaves would make their escape. One trader remarked that the "Negroes were so wilful and loth to leave their own country, that they have often leap'd out of the canoes, boat and ship, into the sea, and kept under water till they were drowned" to avoid being taken up by their captors. At the first opportunity, if indeed it ever presented itself, many would leap off the ship into the mouths of hungry sharks to avoid enslavement in the New World.

■ One-Way Passage

The voyage to the Americas, popularly referred to as the "middle passage," was a veritable nightmare. Overcrowding was most common. There are records of ships as small as 90 tons carrying a complement of 390 slaves in addition to crew and provisions. The practice of overcrowding slaves became so common that the British Parliament felt compelled to specify that not more than five slaves could be carried for every 3 tons of the burden of a ship of 200 tons. This regulation, like so many others, was not enforced. More slaves meant greater profits, and few traders could resist the temptation to wedge in a few more. There was hardly standing, lying, or sitting room. Chained together by twos, hands and feet, slaves had no room in which to move about and no freedom to exercise their bodies even in the slightest.

It was doubtless the crowded conditions on the vessels that so greatly increased the incidence of disease and epidemics during the voyage to America. Smallpox was one of the dread diseases of the period, and one experienced observer remarked that few ships that carried slaves escaped without it. Perhaps even more deadly than smallpox was flux, a frequently fatal malady from which whites on board the slave ships were apparently spared. Hunger strikes at times aggravated unfavorable health conditions and induced illnesses where previously there had been none. The filth and stench caused by close quarters and disease brought on more illness, and the mortality rate increased accordingly. Perhaps not more than half the slaves shipped from Africa ever became effective workers in the New World. Many of those that did not die of disease or commit suicide by jumping overboard were permanently disabled by the ravages of some dread disease or by maiming, which often resulted from struggling against the chains. Small wonder that one trader who arrived at Barbados with 372 of his original 700 slaves was moved to remark: "No gold-finders can endure so much noisome slavery as they do who carry Negroes; for those have some respite and satisfaction, but we endure twice the misery; and yet by the mortality our voyages are ruin'd and we pine and fret ourselves to death, to think that we should undergo so much misery, and take so much pains to so little purpose."

It may be reasonably doubted that the situation was as unfavorable as that trader pictured it. To be sure, there were difficulties of many kinds, not the least of which was the great mortality among the whites themselves. Even with the great expenses attached to the trade and the extensive loss sustained in the mortality of slaves in transit, the slave trade was still one of the most important sources of European wealth in the seventeenth and

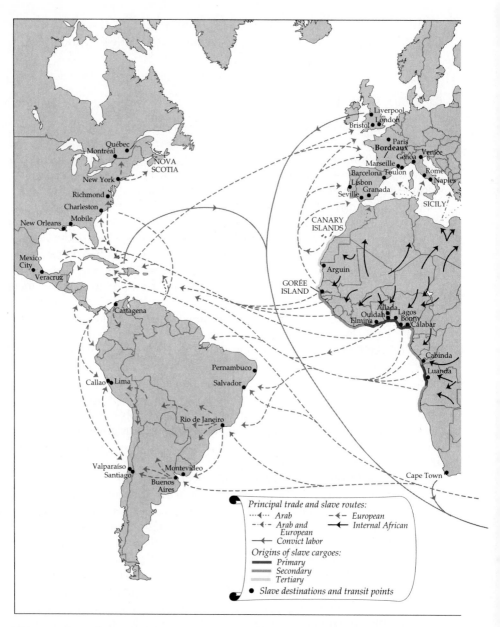

This map shows the general direction of the principal sea routes of Arab, European, and American trade in African slaves up to 1873. The selected destinations include slave debarkation and settlement areas, ports visited by African crewmen, locations of slaves taken on home leave by slaveholders and military officers, and points in England and Canada where slaves were taken following the American War for Independence in 1783.

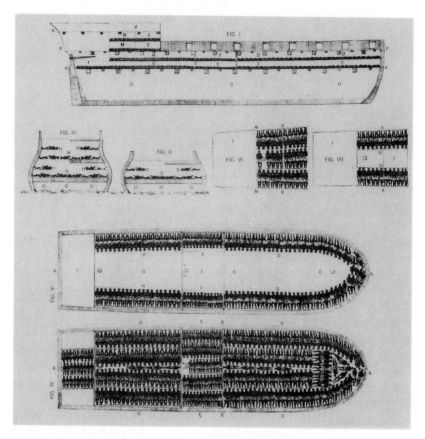

THE PLAN OF THE "BROOKES". A) lower deck; B) lower deck, breadth; C) men's room; D) platforms, men's room; E) boys' room; F) platforms, boys' room; G) women's room; H) platforms, women's rooms; I) gun room; K) quarter-deck; L) cabin; M) half-deck; N) platforms, half-deck; O) hold; P) upper deck. Fig. I) lengthwise cross section; II) breadthwise cross section of men's section; III) breadthwise cross section of women's section; IV) lower deck, with platforms; V) lower deck, without platforms; VI) half-deck, with platforms; VII) half-deck, without platforms. The "Brookes," a 320-ton vessel, was one of the eighteen slave-trading ships examined by a committee before making recommendations to the English Parliament for the regulation of such vessels in 1788. The abolitionists claimed that the "Brookes," built to accommodate 451 persons, carried as many as 609 slaves on one of her voyages. (*From a pamphlet by Thomas Clarkson, London, 1839. Carnegie Institution of Washington.*)

eighteenth centuries. In the late eighteenth century, it was possible for a ship captain to make a commission of £360 on the sale of 307 slaves and for the trader to earn £465 on the same sale. It was not unusual for a ship carrying 250 slaves to net as much as £7,000 on one voyage. Profits of 100 percent were not uncommon for Liverpool merchants. Perhaps those engaged in the trade did undergo much misery, but if they were seeking profits (and who among them had other motives?), it hardly seems accurate for one of them to add that they took "so much pains to so little purpose."

It is not possible to give an accurate figure of the number of slaves imported into the New World from Africa. In eleven years, from 1783 through 1793, Liverpool traders alone were responsible for the importation of 303,737, while in the following eleven years they were certainly responsible for as many more. While the closing years of the eighteenth century represented the peak in the slave trade, the preceding two centuries showed a steady increase leading to the apogee reached in the 1790s.

In 1861 Edward E. Dunbar made estimates of the number of slaves imported into the New World, and these figures were widely accepted during the following century. He estimated that 887,500 were imported in the sixteenth century, 2,750,000 in the seventeenth, 7,000,000 in the eighteenth, and 3,250,000 in the nineteenth. In 1936 R. R. Kuczynski estimated that 14,650,000 Africans had been imported into the New World. In 1969 Philip D. Curtin challenged these estimates. Basing his findings on exhaustive studies of records of slavers, records of slave importations, slave populations in the New World at various times, regional and ethnic origins of slaves imported into the New World, and other pertinent data, Curtin estimated that 241,400 slaves were imported in the sixteenth century, 1,341,100 in the seventeenth, 6,051,700 between 1701 and 1810, and 1,898,400 between 1810 and 1870. His estimate of the total number imported between 1451 and 1870 is 9,566,100. Curtin's figures were in turn challenged by J. E. Inikori, who insisted that the evidence "very strongly suggests a substantial upward revision of the estimates that Curtin made." Declining to give a total figure for the entire slave-trading period, Inikori pointed out that while Curtin's estimate for British exports between 1750 and 1807 was 1,616,100, his own research led him to conclude that the figure was at least 2,365,014. It is obvious that Inikori would place the total estimates much higher than the 9,566,100 estimated by Curtin.

In view of the great numbers that must have been killed while resisting capture, the additional numbers that died during the middle passage, and the millions that were successfully brought to the Americas, the aggregate approaches staggering proportions. The figures, whether Dunbar's, Kuczynski's, Curtin's, or Inikori's, are a testimonial to the fabulous profits realized in such a sordid business, to the ruthlessness with which the traders must have pursued it, and to the tremendous demands made by New World settlers for laborers. Perhaps poet Leopold Sedar Senghor, first president of the republic of Senegal, best summed it up when he declared that the slave trade "ravaged black Africa like a brush fire, wiping out images and values in one vast carnage."

It is more difficult to measure the effect of such an activity on African life than it is to estimate the number of persons removed. The expatriation of millions of Africans in less than four centuries constitutes one of the most far-reaching and drastic social revolutions in the annals of history. It is to be remembered that traders would have none but the best available natives. They demanded the healthiest, the largest, the youngest, the ablest, and the most culturally advanced. The vast majority of the slaving was carried on in the area of West Africa, where civilization had reached its highest point on the continent, with the possible exception of Egypt. The removal of the best of the African population deprived the continent of an invaluable resource. J. E. Inikori insists that the African population and its general well-being would have been much greater by the nineteenth century if the foreign slave trade had not existed. The encouragement that Europeans gave them to fight among themselves with European explosive weapons made it even more difficult for them to recover from the body blow that the slave trade had dealt them. Africa, which culturally was within some measurable distance of Europe at the beginning of the fifteenth century, received the worst possible influence from her Christian neighbors to the north. It was under these adverse circumstances that she entered a recession that in time would suffer the coup de grâce of the imperialistic enslavement thrust upon her in the nineteenth century.

■ Colonial Enterprise in the Caribbean

The slave trade became a tremendously important factor in European economic life primarily because of developments in the New World. The trade in men and women would have remained inconsequential had it been confined to the importation of a few servants into Europe. Its great growth came as the colonies in the New World increased and manifested a pressing need for labor to do the job of clearing the land and tilling the fields. It is, therefore, no mere accident that the seventeenth century, which witnessed the first important advances in the slave trade, also saw the growth of European interest in colonizing and developing the economic life of the New World. The Caribbean was the scene of the first serious effort to develop a lucrative agricultural economy in the New World. It was to the islands in this area that important complements of slaves were sent.

The rivalry among European countries for control of the islands in the seventeenth century presaged the more intense rivalry for hegemony on the mainland that was to develop during the following century. Spain, of course, had prior claim to the islands, thanks to the explorations of its sailors in the fifteenth century and the papal arrangement of 1493. The Spaniards took advantage of this position by channeling their energies and capital into the development of their insular possessions, the most important of which were Cuba, Puerto Rico, Hispaniola, and Jamaica. Although they were to lose some of these and other islands in various conflicts, they nevertheless made the most of them by producing staple crops, especially tobacco and sugar, with slave labor. Early in the sixteenth century large consignments of slaves went to the Spanish islands. In 1518, for example, the king of Spain granted a trader the right to ship 4,000 Africans to the Spanish islands. By 1540 the annual importation had reached approximately 10,000. It must be remembered, moreover, that there was already developing an illicit trade the size of which there was no way of determining.

The breaking of the Spanish monopoly in the Caribbean was closely connected with the slave trade. What the English first sought was an opportunity to share in the Caribbean trade which, during the early years of Elizabeth's reign, already gave promise of being decidedly profitable. When Spain rejected this bid, the English, led in both thought and action by John Hawkins, decided that the monopoly could be broken only by force. Hawkins planned to take slaves to the New World with the hope that the colonists' desire for them would be sufficient to overcome their respect for the royal ban on unlicensed trade. The pattern that he set in selling slaves and other African goods at Hispaniola in 1563 was eagerly followed by other and less discreet English imitators, who were summarily arrested and punished by Spanish officials on the island. Although for the moment Spain had checked the encroachment of Hawkins and others, it was only a matter of time before Spain would have to yield valuable ground in regard both to the commercial and the territorial monopoly it had enjoyed.

In the seventeenth century Spain lost all claim to exclusive control over the islands in the Caribbean. Denmark, Holland, France, and England acquired territory in the area. Dutch buccaneers were entrenched in Curaçao, St. Eustatius, and Tobago by 1640, and the Dutch West India Company, supported enthusiastically by its government, was promoting the slave trade. At about the same time, the French Company of the Islands of America settled Guadeloupe, Martinique, and Marie Galante. In the 1650s St. Lucia and Grenada were acquired by France. The English secured control of St. Christopher in 1623, Barbados in 1625, and Nevis, Antigua, and Montserrat in the 1630s. In 1655 they won one of the great prizes of the Caribbean by driving the Spaniards out of Jamaica. In 1671 the Danes acquired St. Thomas. The Spanish monopoly had indeed been broken, and the West Indies had become not only a pawn in European diplomacy but an important source of revenue for Europeans. African slavery proved to be invaluable in building revenue-producing institutions.

■ The Plantation System

Africans were first used on the tobacco plantations of the Caribbean islands. By 1639, however, European markets had become so glutted with the weed that the price decreased sharply and West Indian planters sustained a great loss. Some of them turned to cotton and indigo, neither of which proved to be as profitable as they had hoped. Some heeded the suggestions of Dutch merchant traders who suggested that they try sugar. It appeared to be a good opportunity, and with capital borrowed from Dutch and English merchants,

West Indian planters began to cultivate sugarcane. The results surpassed their greatest expectations, and they immediately made plans for extension of the cultivation. The problem of labor became acute, and the planters turned more and more to the use of slaves. Thus, in the middle of the seventeenth century, the importation of Africans into the Caribbean islands began in earnest.

In 1640 there were only a few hundred Africans in Barbados. By 1645, after the new sugar plantations had demonstrated their profitableness, there were 6,000, and by the middle of the century the African population had increased to 20,000. Between 4,000 and 5,000 Africans of good quality were delivered to the island in the 1660s, and they found a ready market among the sugar planters. By the end of the century Barbados had a black population of upward of 80,000. A similar growth took place in many of the other Caribbean islands in the seventeenth century. The momentum of importation was so great by the end of the century that in the next 100 years, when the demand for slaves in the islands was declining, importation continued, and in most places it even increased. By 1763, 60,000 African slaves had been imported into Cuba. In the next three decades they came in at a much more rapid rate. Through a system of granting special licenses to importers, Spain was able to bring into Cuba as many as 17,000 Africans in a single year in the 1770s. Between 1763 and 1790, about 41,000 were brought in, while between 1791 and 1825 no less than 320,000 were delivered to Havana alone. Jamaica, Nevis, Montserrat, St. Christopher, St. Vincent, and St. Lucia experienced proportionately similar increases.

The tendency to overpopulate the islands of the Caribbean arose from several important factors. Of course, many slaves who were brought to the islands were to be reexported. Furthermore, there seemed to be no substantial increase in the black population of the islands as a result of births until the emancipation in the 1830s. The death rate was so extraordinarily high that it raises the question of the treatment of slaves. In one year, for example, 2,656 Africans were born in St. Vincent, but in the same year there were 4,205 deaths. On one plantation in Jamaica more than half of the children died in infancy, while miscarriages ran high. Some authorities have attributed the high mortality rate to improper food and the ravages of disease. Doubtless these conditions were present, but the view of many masters that slaves were cheaper to purchase than to breed and the consequent imposition of undue labor on men and women of all conditions and ages apparently caused more deaths than anything else.

There were few evidences of humanitarianism on the plantations of the West Indies. Slavery was essentially an economic institution. Slaves were being extensively used for the sole purpose of producing sugar and other staple crops. Through the use of slaves to produce the rich crops the islands became the favorites of their parent countries. As one writer put it, the islands were "of immense importance to the grandeur and prosperity of England." If the importation of more slaves meant greater prosperity—and it seemed so to the island planters—they were imported with little regard for anything other than economic considerations.

It was absentee landlordism that constituted one of the most important factors in the development of practices that were manifestly destructive of health and life among slaves. Some English landlords pleaded that the climate of the sugar colonies was "so inconvenient for an English constitution that no man will chuse to live there, much less will any man chuse to settle there, without the hopes of at least supporting his family in a more handsome manner, or saving more money than he can do by any business he can expect in England, or in our plantations upon the continent of America." The islands were, therefore, regarded not as a place of residence but merely as a source of wealth. If a planter came out to the Caribbean, he regarded it as a temporary sojourn. Soon he would return to his home country, and with the wealth he had amassed buy an estate and live like a gentleman. Why, then, should he interest himself in schools, churches, and laws that would improve conditions of life for everyone?

Since black slaves were constantly being brought in from Africa, overseers found it necessary to develop a practice of "breaking in" the newcomers. In some areas they were distributed among the seasoned, or veteran, slaves whose duty it was to teach the newly arrived slaves the ways of life in the New World. In other places the newcomers were kept apart and supervised by a special staff of guardians and inspectors who were experienced in breaking in those who might offer resistance to adjusting to their new environment. The mortality rate among newly arrived slaves was exceptionally high, with estimates of deaths running to as much as 30 percent in a seasoning period of three or four years. Old and new diseases, change of climate and food, exposure incurred in running away, suicide, and excessive flogging were among the main causes of the high mortality rate.

In the West Indies slaves were sent to the farms at daybreak, and they labored all day except for a thirty-minute period for breakfast and a two-hour period in the hottest portion of the day, which was frequently the time set aside for doing lighter chores. At harvest time the workday was much longer, sometimes eighteen hours. The driver or overseer did not distinguish between men and women in work requirements or in applying the lash for dereliction of duty. Investigations made by the British Parliament in 1790–1791 brought out the fact that pregnant women were forced to work up to the time of childbirth and that a month was the maximum amount of time allowed for recovery from childbearing. Pregnant women were lashed severely when they were unable to keep pace with the other workers. Women who paused in the fields to care for their babies, whom they carried on their backs, were lashed with cart whips for idling away their time.

Food was on the whole insufficient for slaves. Planters did not often encourage any type of diversified agriculture which would have provided food for the workers. Where this was done at all, slaves were given small plots of land, sometimes far from their houses, that they could cultivate in spare moments. In Barbados, where planters had the reputation of providing for their slaves better than the planters of other islands, slaves were generally ill-fed. On one plantation each adult slave was given a pint of grain and half of a herring (not infrequently rotten) for twenty-four hours. In the famous investigation of 1790–1791 no plantation was found where a slave received more than nine pints of corn and one pound of salt meat per week. Fish of the least desirable grades were imported from the New England colonies, and where this was done the planter acquired a reputation for great benevolence.

On many islands the African population outnumbered the white population. For example, as early as 1673 there were 10,000 blacks in Jamaica and only 8,000 whites. In 1724 there were 32,000 blacks and 14,000 whites. At the end of the century the black population of St. Christopher was over 20,000, "well nigh twenty times that of the white population." It was the preponderance of blacks over whites that promoted the enactment of a slave code of excessive severity. The influence of planters in England made possible the passage, in 1667, of an "Act to regulate the Negroes on the British Plantations." It referred to the Africans in the Caribbean as "of wild, barbarous, and savage nature to be controlled only with strict severity." Slaves were not to leave the plantation without a pass, and they were not allowed to carry any weapons. If a slave struck a Christian, he was to be severely whipped, and for the second offense he was to be branded on the face with a hot iron. If an owner accidentally whipped a slave to death, he or she was not subject to fine or imprisonment. Other European countries had similar laws, but there seemed to have been considerable variation in enforcement. While the well-known French *Code Noir* was relatively humane, it became an agency of great brutality in the hands of some French colonials. When Ogé and his associates were found guilty of conspiring to revolt in the last decade of the eighteenth century, all were cruelly executed. "Their arms, thighs, legs, and backbones were broken with clubs on a scaffold. They were fastened round a wheel in such a manner that their face was turned upward to receive the full glare of the sun." The judge ordered that "Here they are to remain for so long as it shall please God to preserve them alive," after which their heads were to be cut off and exposed on tall poles.

One important ingredient in the seasoning process was the overseer's lash. A typical one was made of plaited cowhide. In the hands of a stern overseer it could draw blood through the breeches of a slave. At times the floggings were so severe as to inflict wounds so large that a finger could be inserted in them. Another favorite type of punishment was to suspend the slave from a tree by ropes and tie iron weights around his or her neck and waist. If these punishments would seem to shorten life and to reduce efficiency, it must be remembered that Africans were being brought in at an increasing rate up until the opening of the nineteenth century and that there was consequently no great inclination to preserve life.

If cruel treatment was designed to prevent uprisings and running away, it was eminently unsuccessful. On almost every island there is a record of some serious revolt against the plantation system, and everywhere there is evidence of constant running away. When the British took Jamaica in the middle of the seventeenth century, most of the slaves promptly escaped to the mountains, where they were frequently joined by other fugitives. These runaways, called Maroons, continuously harassed planters by stealing, trading with slaves, and enticing them to run away. By 1730 these ex-slaves, under Cudgo, their powerful leader, had terrorized whites to such an extent that England was compelled to send out two additional regiments to protect the planters.

Haiti also had its Maroons as early as 1620, and the outlawed colony grew to such proportions that the colonial government recognized it in 1784. It is conceded that they were largely responsible for the Haitian uprisings of 1679, 1691, and 1704. In the middle of the eighteenth century the recalcitrant Negroes of Haiti found a peerless leader in Macandal, a native-born African, who announced that he was the Black Messiah sent to drive the whites from the island. In 1758 he carefully laid his plans for a coup d'état. The water of Le Cap was to be poisoned, and when the whites were in convulsions the Negroes, under the leadership of Macandal and his Maroons, were to seize control. By accident, the plot was discovered, and the fear-stricken planters hunted down Macandal and executed him. At the time of his execution he warned his enemies and comforted his friends by telling them that one day he would return, more terrible than before. Many blacks, and perhaps some whites, were later to believe that Toussaint L'Ouverture was the reincarnation of Macandal.

Even on the small Danish islands there are records of slave resistance. The lack of sufficient food drove many slaves to steal and to refuse to work. In 1726 officials executed seventeen of the leading offenders, but this did not quiet the slaves. The situation worsened, and in 1733 the governor of St. Thomas issued a drastic decree providing for severe punishment of slave offenders by burning, whipping, and hanging. Two months later the Danish islands experienced their worst uprising, which occurred on St. John. Blacks carrying wood entered one of the forts of the Danish West India Company and murdered the guard by stabbing him. Another group of slaves attacked six soldiers and killed five of them. Having captured the garrison, they raised the flag and fired three shots from the cannon, the signal for a general uprising on all the plantations on the island. With flintlocks, pistols, and cane knives the Africans went about the bloody business of murdering all the whites they could find. Only after several days of terror was the uprising brought under control by the captain of the militia.

It was the same everywhere—conspiracies, uprisings, revolts. The seeds of cruelty reaped a bountiful harvest of murder and bloodshed. As the years passed and as slaves learned their duties, they performed them, albeit reluctantly. Time also proved that they could adjust to the climate and food of the New World. Although their terms of service on the islands were by no means satisfactory, they were regarded as seasoned within three or four years and were viewed by mainland planters as much more desirable than the "raw Negroes" fresh from the "wilds" of Africa.

Slaves were being constantly exported from the islands, especially from the British islands. In an effort to capture the slave trade with foreign islands, British traders first brought slaves to some British island and then quietly reexported them to Cuba, Puerto Rico, or some other foreign island. While it is not possible to estimate the number of Africans transported to Cuba from the British islands, it is quite clear that this was Cuba's most important source of slaves. Jamaica alone sent more than 10,000 there in 1756. Of the 90,331 Africans imported into the British West Indies between 1784 and 1787, some 19,964 were reexported; but it is not possible to determine whether they went to French, Spanish, or Portuguese markets, to other British islands, or to the mainland.

As the prosperity of the West Indies declined in the early eighteenth century and as the attention of Europe became focused on the continent of North America, more slaves were doubtless exported from the islands to the mainland. The demand for slaves in the mainland colonies was steadily increasing, and a decided preference for slaves from the islands was manifested. In 1764 several shipments of slaves were made from the West Indies to South Carolina. They came from St. Christopher, Antigua, Barbados, and even Havana. Although the islands could not satisfy the growing demand for slaves on the mainland, they sent some of their surplus yearly, as the records amply testify. Indeed, reexportation itself became a lucrative business in which many persons were engaged. On the islands of St. Christopher, Barbados, and Jamaica some firms carried on a regular business of reexporting slaves to other islands and to the mainland. In the colonies many firms did business directly with traders on the islands.

The cost of producing sugar increased as soil exhaustion manifested itself after a century of intensive cultivation. The price of slaves, moreover, was going up as the demand for them increased on the mainland. White society was so completely without resourceful and imaginative leadership that it was not able to discover areas of economic activity that would compensate for the losses it was sustaining in older activities. Desperate efforts were made both in Europe and in the island colonies to encourage whites to migrate to the Caribbean. Some islands required planters to import propor-tionate numbers of whites for all the slaves they brought, but many planters found it easier to pay the fines. With a surplus of slaves on their hands, the residents of the West Indies were willing to sell many of them to the mainland colonies.

The increasing exportation of slaves from the West Indies is a clear manifestation of social and economic debility. After several centuries of European occupation, religious institutions were still weak, and vice and immorality of all kinds flourished. Education was at an especially low ebb, and ignorance prevailed even among whites. The ineffectiveness of the law showed itself in its inability to prevent running away, insurrections, and widespread miscegenation. In sending many of their slaves to the mainland, the West Indies served notice to the world that they had yielded the long-held economic primacy in the New World to the mainland.

■ Slavery in Mainland Latin America

In 1501 the government in Madrid authorized the introduction of Africans to make up for the deficiency in Indian labor which the Spaniards had been using in the New World, much more than the English ever used. The condition that only such Africans should be taken as had been born under the power of Christian masters was shortly overlooked as the demand for workers increased. They were being brought into Cuba in such large numbers by 1506 that the Spanish government, for fear of a slave uprising, was moved to prohibit their future importation. For a decade the importation of Africans slowed to a trickle, and the extensive use of Indians was resumed. In 1516 Charles II issued licenses to several Flemish traders to take Africans to the Spanish colonies. In the following year the ban against the use of Africans was removed, with the stipulation that one-third of those imported should be women. By the time that Cortés launched his conquest of Mexico, Africans were in all the Spanish island colonies and were being rapidly introduced into the mainland.

In the early years of the Spanish colonies the slave trade was viewed as un-Christian and illegal. To overcome this dual disfavor, it was necessary for traders to secure special permission—the *asiento*—to bring slaves into the Spanish colonies. This made it relatively easy for the crown to subject the traffic in slaves to rigid control. Since the contracts, or permits, were monopolistic, the holders were required to pay a tax to the crown on each slave brought in. The crown reserved the right to revoke the *asiento* if the traders did not make accurate reports on the numbers of slaves imported or if they were either unhealthy or in some other way undesirable as workers. Whether the *asiento* was held by private individuals or companies, by Spaniards, or by foreigners, the crown could use its granting powers as an effective diplomatic and economic weapon to enhance its influence in both hemispheres.

It would be erroneous to assume that slave traders in Spanish America confined their activities to the insular possessions. Almost from the beginning they transported slaves to Mexico, Panama, Colombia, Peru, and Argentina, and from these points the slaves were dispersed in all directions. Only the lines of supply directly from Africa or from the Caribbean entrepôts were officially recognized, but smugglers and interlopers were not averse to bringing Africans from English, French, or Dutch colonies or from other points when it was profitable to do so. By these various routes of commerce more than 60,000 Africans entered Mexico during the first century of conquest. In the following century the number was even greater. While the islands and the adjacent continent possessed a limited capacity to absorb slaves, the Mexican market was a veritable paradise for traders. The Jesuit Father Andrés de Rivas estimated that 3,000 or 4,000 entered the country each year. Gonzalo Aguirre Beltrán, the Mexican historian, asserts that a conservative estimate for the seventeenth century would place the figure at 120,000 slaves. In the eighteenth and early nineteenth centuries importation declined sharply, with no more than 20,000 slaves entering the Viceroyalty of New Spain during that period. When Baron Alexander von Humboldt visited the country in 1793, he said that there were only 10,000 slaves. Certainly 200,000 had entered the country by that time, but the majority had become mixed with the whites and Indians so extensively that perhaps they were no longer recognizable as a distinct element in the population.

During the colonial period Central America was largely a part of the Viceroyalty of New Spain, and no separate figures are available for the importation of slaves into that region. Africans in Central America perhaps were a small but important segment of the population. They were imported into Guatemala as early as 1524, when the Spaniards occupied the land. While the number was never as large as 10,000, they were a considerable source of trouble to the Spanish authorities. Runaways would band together in the woods of Sierra de las Minas and with their bows and arrows harass the countryside for miles around. The entire military force of Guatemala City found it impossible to subdue them. Some slaves became free, developing into substantial citizens. One such freedman became an extensive landowner and herdsman. Although he made a great profit from dairy products that he sold in Guatemala City, the authorities felt that perhaps some hidden treasure was the real source of his wealth. He periodically denied this, and until his death he stood as an example of what an African was able to accomplish in Central America.

Perhaps the largest concentration of blacks in continental Spanish America was to be found in the Viceroyalty of New Granada, comprising the modern states of Panama, Colombia, Venezuela, and Ecuador. The ports along the Caribbean early became entrepôts for Negro slaves and points from which they were distributed to the interior. Panama, Caracas, and Cartagena were among the largest slave markets in the New World. By the time that accurate census figures for the area became available, Negroes were present in considerable numbers. In the Audiencia of Santa Fé—present Panama and Colombia—there were in 1810 approximately 210,000 Negroes and mulattoes, slave and free, in a total population of 1.4 million. In the Captaincy General of Caracas—present Venezuela—Negroes and mulattoes numbered 493,000 in 1810, while the total population was 900,000. About the same time, the Presidency of Quito—present Ecuador—had 50,000 Negroes and mulattoes in a total population of 600,000.

One of the most striking features of the dispersion of Negroes in Spanish America was the presence of large numbers on the Pacific coast in the colonial period. As Fernando Romero pointed out, "the slave trade in the Spanish South American colonies followed well-established lines from north to south and from south to north, the two currents converging on Peru." The Viceroyalty of Peru—roughly present Chile and Peru—was, thus, an area of concentration of Africans. Lima not only received a great share for its own exploitation but also served as a market from which Andean planters and herders could purchase black workers. Some were sent into this remote viceroyalty from Panama and Cartagena, while others were sent directly from Africa around Cape Horn. In 1622 the viceroy reported the presence of 30,000 Negroes in his domain, with 22,000 at Lima. In the middle of the following century one observer declared that there were many blacks, but that it was impossible to ascertain the exact numbers as the owners feared that the government would use the figures as the basis for a new tax.

When the first trustworthy census was taken in 1791, the population of Peru was approximately 1.25 million. Of that number, 40,000 were black and 135,000 were white. The remainder were Indians, *mestizos*—people of Indian and white ancestry—mulattoes, and various combinations of races. Blacks constituted 25 percent of the population of Lima. At about the same time the population of Chile was approximately 500,000, of which 30,000 were Negroes and mulattoes. These figures do not tell the entire story of the African population in the Viceroyalty of Peru. Accurate statistics were always difficult to secure because owners, fearing additional taxation, hid their slaves when census takers came around. The rapid absorption of Africans into the total population, moreover, made it difficult to measure their impact upon the area into which they were sent.

The absence of a considerable population of blacks in modern Uruguay and Argentina does not mean that Spain neglected to furnish these colonies with African slaves. Instead, it is suggestive of the remarkable biological and cultural fusion that occurred. Montevideo and Buenos Aires were major ports of entry for slave traders during colonial days. While there are no figures available for the total African population of the Viceroyalty of La Plata, there can be no doubt that there was a large population of blacks, especially in the area of the estuary of the Rio de la Plata. A contemporary estimated that in 1805 about 2,500 slaves were being imported annually. In 1803 the black population of Montevideo was 1,040 out of a total of 4,726. There is every indication that Buenos Aires also had a substantial black population. As late as 1827 there were seven African societies in the Argentine capital. The disappearance of Africans in the southern part of South America is an eloquent testimony of the complete absorption of a people by the tremendous migration of Europeans that occurred in the last century.

It was only natural that the Portuguese, the first to sense the importance of African slave labor, would undertake to provide their New World empire with Africans. Although they made extensive use of Indian labor throughout the sixteenth century, they introduced Africans into Brazil as early as 1538, when the first shipment from the Guinea coast reached Bahia. It was the introduction of sugar into the colony about 1540 that stimulated the importation of Africans, and after that time the slave trade continued unabated. During the period of Spanish control, 1580–1640, the slave trade to Brazil greatly accelerated. In 1585 there were 14,000 slaves in the colony out of a population of 57,000. Toward the end of the century the Spaniards brought in large numbers of slaves from Guinea, São Thomé, Mozambique, and other parts of Africa. Though there was a tendency for them to be concentrated in Pernambuco, Bahia, and Rio de Janeiro, they fanned out in various directions as sugar and coffee plantations were developed in the fertile interior valleys.

There were five centers of distribution from which slaves were sent into the various parts of Brazil. From Bahia and Sergipe they were taken to plantations and to domestic service on the coast; from Rio de Janeiro and São Paulo they were taken to cane fields and coffee plantations or were kept to work in the capital; from Minas Gerais most slaves were sent to the gold mines, such as those of Goyaz; slaves from the distribution center at Pernambuco supplied the sugar-producing provinces of the northeast, and slaves from Maranhão and Pará were sent to the cotton plantations of the north. In the seventeenth century it was estimated that more than 44,000 Africans were imported annually, while the following century witnessed an annual importation of no less than 55,000 blacks. Estimates of the number of Africans imported into Brazil vary from 5 million to 18 million. Whatever the total figures were, it is clear that between 1538 and 1828 Africans were imported in such large numbers that persons of African descent still constitute a considerable portion of the population.

In 1798 the first reliable estimate of the population listed 406,000 free blacks and 1,582,000 slaves in a total population of 3,250,000. By 1818 the total population had risen to 3,817,000, in which there were 1,930,000 slaves and 585,000 freedmen. Thus, it can be seen that in that twenty-year period Africans were largely responsible for the increase in the total population. In 1830 they constituted 28.6 percent of the population. In 1847, in a total population of 7,360,000, including 800,000 civilized Indians, there were 3,120,000 African slaves, 1,100,000 free persons of color, and 180,000 free native Africans. In 1888, the year of the emancipation of Brazil's slaves, there were 723,419 slaves.

There were three distinct groups of slaves in colonial Brazil. Urban slaves worked as servants in the town homes of planters, in shops, at the docks, and in numerous other capacities. On the whole, their lot was not difficult. Some were specially skilled in arts and crafts and performed invaluable services in helping to improve living conditions in urban areas. Others were kept in homes to render personal service. If there was insufficient work, owners sent their slaves out to find work. These freelancers, *negros de ganho*, often stood on street corners ready to assist shoppers with their packages or went from house to house offering their services to people who did not have servants. Many were able to earn fairly good wages because of their special skills and their ability to read and write. With the opportunity to hire out their own services some slaves not only made money for their masters but also eventually earned enough to purchase their own freedom.

With the discovery of gold in the seventeenth century, large numbers of slaves were employed in the mines. The simultaneous decline in the sugar economy caused many planters either to sell or hire out their slaves to prospectors and mine owners. Black Brazilians began migrating into the interior near Goyaz, Corumba, and the plateau of Matto Grosso. Some were not employed in the mines but demonstrated their aptitudes and abilities in other ways, as iron workers, shoemakers, and even architects and sculptors.

The vast majority of blacks—perhaps five-sixths—were always employed on the great sugar, coffee, cotton, and cacao plantations. These farm workers fared the worst in Brazil. They worked from sunrise to sunset and were supervised for the most part by stewards who, with whips in their hands, threatened, intimidated, and tortured them into performing their work. As in the Spanish colonies, there were laws that sought to protect slaves from cruel masters and overseers, but because such statutes were extremely difficult to enforce, they did not provide much help. The invention of instruments of torture must have taxed the ingenuity of those in command. There was the *tronco,* constructed of wood or iron, by which the slave's ankles were fastened in one place for several days; the *libambo* did the same thing to the arms. *Novenas* and *trezenas* were devices by which a slave was tied, face down, and beaten for nine or thirteen consecutive nights.

There were some mitigating features of Brazil's institution of slavery. Since there was no law against teaching slaves to read and write, many of them became proficient in the use of language. The law required that slaves be baptized within at least one year after their arrival in the country. After this rite was performed, they were expected to attend mass and confession regularly. In addition, the manumission of slaves was actually encouraged in Brazil. Faithful nurses were often set free. There was a general custom that after a slave mother had given birth to ten children she was to be set free. The clergy urged pious communicants to manumit their slaves at death if not sooner. There are perhaps no records of an owner's refusal to emancipate a slave who was able to purchase his or her freedom. Finally, there is the general view that in the colonial period Brazilians felt little, if any, race prejudice. Blacks were given many opportunities for advancement, and free blacks theoretically enjoyed the same rights and privileges before the law that whites did.

While slaves in Brazil and elsewhere were a source of profit, they were also a source of constant trouble. Living in small, crowded huts and subsisting on coarse fare, they frequently became restive and sought to break the chains of slavery. In 1550 the slaves of Santa Marta, Colombia, committed great atrocities and burned the city. Five years later an African calling himself king led a violent insurrection that was subdued only by strenuous exertions of the authorities. One of the most desperate bids for freedom in the New

World occurred in Brazil in the seventeenth century. It was the establishment of the Republic of Palmares, an African state in Alagoas in northeastern Brazil, between 1630 and 1697. Fleeing the towns and plantations between Bahia and Pernambuco, runaway slaves penetrated the heavy forests and settled rustic communities in the Rio Mundahu valley. Despite sieges laid by the Portuguese and by the Dutch, who were attempting to occupy that portion of Brazil in 1644, these Maroons held out until 1697, when the superior forces of the Portuguese soldiers entered the walled city of Palmares. Refusing to surrender, the leader and his principal assistants hurled themselves to certain death from the rocky promontory overlooking the city. Although the other insurrections and Maroon communities established in Spanish and Portuguese America perhaps never equaled Palmares, many of them were greater than any that slaves undertook in British America.

Several factors distinguished slavery in Latin America from that institution in British America. One such factor was the relatively small number of Spaniards and Portuguese in their colonies as compared to the considerable numbers of Britons in the English colonies. It was not at all unusual for slaves to outnumber by a large margin their Spanish and Portuguese owners and officials who frequently had little or no family with them and who were, all too often, infrequent visitors to their New World domains. Such a disproportionate number of blacks facilitated the many more successful insurrections and Maroon communities that arose in Latin American than arose in British America. Perhaps it also had something to do with the strict slave codes which were introduced into Latin America earlier than in British America.

Another factor was the significant role that the Catholic church played in Latin America. Priests often accompanied explorers and were usually present when settlers came. It was they who insisted that slaves be instructed in the Roman Catholic religion and baptized in the church. Owners were not permitted to work their slaves on Sundays and on the approximately thirty feast days during the year. Catholic slaves were married in the church, and the banns were published regularly. There was no law against their learning to read the catechism, and thus the whole world of reading was opened to them. Meanwhile, in the British colonies, where slaves could not enter into any kind of binding agreement, permission of the owner was the only prerequisite for marriage. Although many slaveholders in the British colonies encouraged slaves to be religious and to attend church regularly, the discipline of the Anglican church encouraged but did not require owners to tend the spiritual needs of their slaves. Far from encouraging them to learn to read and write, British colonies generally discouraged such activities, and some of them forbade them altogether. If the church in Latin America had some salutary influence on the treatment of slaves, it did not achieve complete success in eliminating cruelty altogether, as David B. Davis and others have reminded us.

A final factor was that blacks enjoyed a higher level of esteem in the Latin colonies than in the British colonies, which perhaps helps to explain why many more Spaniards and Portuguese than Britons intermarried with blacks. It should be remembered that there were relatively few Spanish and Portuguese women in the New World. Choices were therefore limited. Even so, any stigma attached to intermarrying with blacks was virtually absent, and they did so in the church. Meanwhile, if any British Americans had intimate relationships with blacks, they were generally clandestine and without benefit of clergy.

Still, it does not necessarily follow that slaves fared better in Latin America than in British America. Examples abound of inhuman cruelty in all parts of the New World, and it is well to recall that during the 1830s, long after the United States outlawed the slave trade, Brazil imported 400,000 slaves from Africa. Although converted and baptized as Christians in Latin America, slaves were appraised and sold just like any other merchandise. The point to remember is that it is virtually impossible to speak of slavery other than in terms of its inhumanity, and that few institutions, including the churches, did anything to mitigate its fundamental cruelties and the insensitivity of one person who had complete dominion over another.

CHAPTER 4

Colonial Slavery

■ Virginia and Maryland

The twenty Africans who were put ashore at Jamestown in 1619 by the captain of a Dutch frigate were not slaves in a legal sense. And at the time Virginians seemed not to appreciate the far-reaching significance of the introduction of Africans into the fledgling colony. These newcomers, who happened to be black, were simply more indentured servants. They were listed as servants in the census counts of 1623 and 1624, and as late as 1651 some blacks whose period of service had expired were being assigned land in much the same way that it was being assigned to whites who had completed their indenture. During its first half-century of existence Virginia had many black indentured servants, and the records reveal an increasing number of free blacks.

But as time went on Virginia steadily fell behind in satisfying the labor needs of the colony with Indians and indentured servants. It was then that the colonists began to give serious thought to the "perpetual servitude" of blacks. Virginians began to see what neighboring islands in the Caribbean had already recognized, namely, that blacks could not easily escape without being identified; that they could be disciplined, even punished, with impunity since they were not Christians; and that the supply was apparently inexhaustible. Black labor was precisely what Virginia needed in order to speed up the clearing of the forests and the cultivation of larger and better tobacco crops. All that was required was legislative approval of a practice in which many Virginians were already engaged. Indeed, by 1640, some

Africans in Virginia had become bondservants for life. The distinction between black and white servants was becoming well established. In that year, when three runaway servants, two white and one black, were recaptured, the court ordered the white servants to serve their master one additional year. The black servant, however, was ordered "to serve his said master or his assigns for the time of his natural life here or elsewhere." Thus, within the first generation of Virginia's existence, African servitude was well on the way to becoming African slavery.

The actual statutory recognition of slavery in Virginia came in 1661. The status of blacks already there was not affected if they had completed their indenture and were free. As a matter of fact, the recognition was almost casual and was first indicated in a law directed at white servants: "That in case any English servant shall run away in company with any negroes who are incapable of making satisfaction by addition of time . . . that the English so running away . . . shall serve for the time of the said negroes' absence as they are to for their owne." In the following year, 1662, Virginia took another step toward slavery by indicating in its laws that children born in the colony would be held in bond or free according to the condition of the mother. Some mitigation of slavery was intended by a 1667 law indicating that slaves could be baptized as Christians. In order to protect the institution of slavery, however, this law provided that "the conferring of baptisme doth not alter the condition of the person as to his bondage or freedome." Thus, "diverse masters, freed from this doubt, may more carefully endeavour the propagation of christianity."

At first the black population of Virginia grew quite slowly. In 1625 there were only 23 in the colony, and as late as the middle of the century scarcely 300 could be counted. With the chartering of the Royal African Company in 1672 the shipment of slaves into the colony was accelerated. By the end of the century they were being brought in at the rate of more than 1,000 per year. It was in the eighteenth century that the black population grew at what some Virginians began to view as an alarming rate. In 1708 there were 12,000 blacks and 18,000 whites. By 1756 there were 120,156 blacks and 173,316 whites, with blacks outnumbering whites in many communities.

Although Virginians greatly appreciated the importance of slave labor in the development of the colony, they soon became apprehensive about such large numbers of blacks living among whites. Already whites and blacks were mixing, and a mulatto population was emerging. There were, moreover, persistent rumors of conspiracies of rebellion, and many whites feared for their lives. Those who were apprehensive took the lead in attempting to control the importation of slaves, but commercial interests fought off these attempts with all the resources at their command. For the time being they were successful.

But the fears of insurrection were not groundless. Within two years after the first statutory recognition of slavery, the blacks of Virginia were showing clear signs of dissatisfaction and began to plot rebellion against their masters.

In 1687, while a funeral was taking place, a group of slaves in the northern neck planned an uprising, but the plot was discovered before it could be carried out. Rumors continued, and plots of varying sizes were uncovered. Where there were no plots there was general disobedience and lawlessness. By 1694 Virginia slaves had become so ungovernable that Governor Edmund Andros complained that there was insufficient enforcement of the code which, by that time, had become elaborate enough to cover most of the activities of slaves.

The Virginia slave code, borrowing heavily from practices in the Caribbean and serving as a model for other mainland codes, was comprehensive if it was anything at all. Slaves were not permitted to leave plantations without the written permission of their masters. Slaves wandering about without such permits were to be returned to their masters. Slaves found guilty of murder or rape were to be hanged. For major offenses, such as robbing a house or a store, slaves were to receive sixty lashes and be placed in the pillory, where their ears were to be cut off. For petty offenses, such as insolence and associating with whites or free blacks, they were to be whipped, branded, or maimed. The docility of slaves, about which many masters boasted, was thus achieved through the enactment of a comprehensive code containing provisions for punishment designed to break even the most irascible blacks in the colony. With the sheriffs, the courts, and even slaveless whites on their side, the masters should have experienced no difficulty in maintaining peace among their slaves.

While slavery in Maryland was not recognized by law until 1663, it came into existence shortly after the first settlements were made in 1634. As early as 1638 there was reference to slavery in some of the discussions in the legislature, and in 1641 the governor himself owned a number of slaves. Colonists had no difficulty, therefore, in turning their attention to the problem of the status of blacks and in concluding that legislation was necessary to fix their status as slaves. The law of 1663 was rather drastic. It undertook to reduce to slavery all blacks in the colony even though some were already free, and it sought to impose slave status on all blacks born in the colony regardless of the status of their mothers. It was not until 1681 that the law was brought in line with established practices by declaring that black children of white women and children born of free black women would be free.

The slave population of Maryland was slow to increase, not because of any disinclination on the part of colonists to own slaves but because they were not in ample supply during the colony's early years. This is the principal reason why, during the restoration period, laws were enacted to encourage and facilitate the importation of slaves. In 1671 the legislature declared that the conversion of slaves to Christianity would not affect their status. Masters now felt that they could import African heathens, convert them to Christianity, and thus justify the act of holding them in slavery. By the end of the century the importation of slaves was increasing steadily. In 1708 the governor reported that 600 or 700 had been imported during the preceding ten months. By 1750 there were 40,000 blacks as compared with 100,000 whites.

As in Virginia, blacks in Maryland early showed resentment against their status as slaves. In several instances white masters died at the hands of their slaves, and there was more than one case of a black cook poisoning an owner. In 1742 seven blacks were executed for the murder of their masters. Others were convicted for committing acts of sabotage such as arson, stealing of property, and the brutal treatment of livestock.

The increase in the black population and fear on the part of whites for their own safety led to the enactment of stringent laws covering their conduct and activities. In 1659 came laws relating to the return and treatment of fugitive slaves. Soon there were laws forbidding slaves to deal in stolen goods and liquor, as well as laws providing for the punishment of free blacks and slaves found guilty of murder, arson, larceny, association with whites, insolence, and going about without permission. Punishment ranged from death to branding and whipping. Enforcement was rigorous, but clemency was not rare. There are numerous examples of intervention on behalf of slaves accused by masters who, while approving of the strict enforcement of the law, wanted "on just this occasion" a bit of leniency.

There is a real possibility that the blacks in Maryland were a contributing factor to the religious strife that existed in that colony. From its very beginning in 1634, Maryland had witnessed an intense rivalry between Catholics, favored by the ruling Calverts, and Protestants, who were heartened by the Puritan ascendancy in England. In 1689 there were rumors that the Catholics were plotting against the government of Maryland. Indians were suspected of collusion with the Catholics, and the blacks of some of the southern counties were also watched with suspicious eyes. This doubtless led to the law of 1695 which prevented frequent meetings of blacks. In the eighteenth century when some Maryland colonists hoped for a Jacobite succession in England, those opposed to it continued to keep under surveillance all the Catholics, Indians, and blacks to be certain that they did not conspire to commit some devilish act. No effective rebellion ever materialized, but blacks enjoyed the distinction of being suspected of belonging to an international clique conspiring to overthrow the government of Maryland before handing it over to the French, the Indians, the English Catholics, or all three.

■ The Carolinas and Georgia

It was a foregone conclusion that slaves would be introduced into the Carolinas as soon as it was feasible. After all, four of the proprietors of the colony were members of the Royal African Company and fully appreciated the profits that could come from the slave trade. By 1680, moreover, the

DRIVING NEWLY ARRIVED BLACKS TO THE SLAVE MARKET. Prior to the American Revolution, slavery was sanctioned in all thirteen British North American colonies. As a consequence, slaves of both genders and all ages were appraised and sold just as any other merchandise. *(The Bettmann Archive.)*

examples of Virginia and Maryland led them to believe that Carolina could become prosperous, with plantation slavery as one of the important foundations of the colony's economic life. Perhaps John Locke had these things in mind when, in his *Fundamental Constitutions*, he wrote, "Every freeman of Carolina shall have absolute power and authority over his negro slaves, of what opinion or religion soever." This statement clearly sanctioned slavery and protected it against any possible destruction that might have come through the conversion of slaves to Christianity.

Blacks were present in the Carolina colony virtually from the beginning. This was undoubtedly the result of deliberate encouragement of the impor-

Gallery of African Art

Basket
Rotse peoples, Zambia
Fiber, dye
38.7 cm. (15 1/4 in.)
(Photograph by Jeffrey Ploskonka

Equestrian figure
Inland Delta Region, Mali
Terra cotta
70.5 cm. (27 3/4 in.)
(Photograph by Franko Khoury)

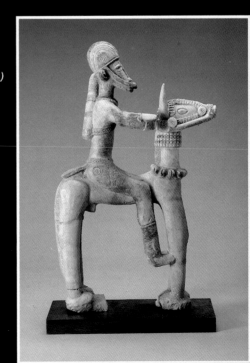

*(All works of art in this insert are courtesy of
the National Museum of African Art, Eliot
Elisofon Archives, Smithsonian Institution.)*

Vessel
Possibly Bamana peoples, Mali
Terra cotta
57.5 cm. (22 5/8 in.)
(Photograph by Delmar Lipp)

Chair
Sourthern Mande or Kru peoples,
Côte d'Ivoire
Wood
32.1 cm. (12 5/8 in.)
(Photograph by Franko Khoury)

Female figure and children
Yoruba peoples, Nigeria
Wood, pigment
38.5 cm. (15 1/4 in.)
(Photograph by Franko Khoury)

Plaque with multiple figures,
Mid-16th-17th century
Edo peoples, Benin Kingdom, Nigeria
Copper alloy
48.6 cm. (19 1/8 in.)

Wrapper
Asante peoples, Ghana
Cotton, silk
159.1 x 101.3 cm. (62 5/8 x 39 7/8 in.)
(Photograph by Franko Khoury)

Pendant
Baule peoples, Côte d'Ivoire
Gold alloy
8 cm. (3 1/2 in.)
(Photograph by Franko Khoury)

tation of slaves by the proprietors. In 1663 they offered to the original settlers twenty acres for every black man slave and ten acres for every black woman slave brought into the colony in the first year. Somewhat smaller incentives were offered for the importation of slaves in subsequent years. Twenty years after the original settlements, the black population in the Carolinas was equal to that of the white. By 1715 blacks outnumbered whites 10,500 to 6,250. In 1724 there were three times as many blacks as whites, and the growth of the black population was to continue for decades to come.

As in the other colonies, the growth of the black population led to the enactment of legislation aimed at controlling the activities of slaves. As early as 1686 the Carolina colony forbade blacks to engage in any kind of trade, and it enjoined them from leaving their masters' plantations without written authorization. In 1722 white justices were authorized to search blacks for guns, swords, "and other offensive weapons" and to capture them unless they could produce a permit less than one month old authorizing them to carry such a weapon. Patrols were given authority to search blacks and to whip those deemed to be dangerous to peace and good order. Punishments for offenses by slaves were summary and severe.

Carolinians had not established their controls too soon, for as early as 1711 there were rumors that blacks were getting out of hand. In 1720 several slaves were burned alive and others were banished because they were implicated in a revolt near Charleston. In subsequent years there were other revolts or rumors of revolts. In 1739 the well-known Stono Rebellion twenty miles west of Charleston threw the countryside into a state of wild excitement. After slaves killed two guards in a warehouse and secured arms, they went on a full-scale drive to destroy slavery in that area. The uprising was put down, but not for several days and not before thirty whites and forty-four blacks had lost their lives. As Peter Wood has said, the black majority in South Carolina would be a continuing cause of apprehension. Later in the century there were other uprisings, and the general state of affairs led to a full-scale revision of the slave code.

Before the Revolution, South Carolina, now divided from North Carolina, had enacted one of the most stringent set of laws governing slaves to be found anywhere in the New World. The selling of liquor to slaves was prohibited. Owners were warned against undue cruelty to slaves which might incite them to revolt. Owners were prohibited from working slaves more than fifteen hours per day between March 25 and September 25 and for more than fourteen hours per day between September 25 and March 25. These last few provisions were a tacit admission that slaves could be driven to revolt. What Carolinians realized all too late was that slaves were not as tractable as they had believed and that the danger of having so large a slave population in their midst was more real than fancied.

If conditions were at all ameliorated among Carolina slaves, it was the result of the efforts of the Society for the Propagation of the Gospel in Foreign Parts. SPG missionaries sought to raise the level of living among both whites and blacks. In some instances they met with considerable success. They suggested that slaves should be given time to study the Scriptures and to learn to read and write. In many cases they taught slaves themselves, and in one notable instance they fostered the establishment of a school for blacks in Charleston in which the teachers were slaves owned by the SPG. While these were significant ameliorations, they were also evidences of acceptance of the basic idea of enslavement, and with the religious sanction that the SPG gave to slavery, planters felt more secure than ever in their belief in the righteousness of the institution.

The presence of Quakers in North Carolina had a salutary effect on the conditions of slaves in the colony. They urged the establishment of regular meetings for slaves, and Quaker slaveholders were urged by their coreligionists to treat their blacks well. Before the end of the colonial period there was some sentiment among the Quakers to discourage members from purchasing slaves, and finally, in 1770, the organization described the slave trade as "an iniquitous practice" and sought its prohibition. Members of the SPG also sought to improve conditions among blacks as well as Indians and, as they had done in South Carolina, blacks encouraged masters to permit their slaves to attend religious services.

It is interesting to note that there was no real slave insurrection in North Carolina during the colonial period. The fact that the slave population was relatively small and that there was little impersonality on North Carolina plantations was doubtless responsible for this peaceful situation. In comparison with neighboring colonies, North Carolina presented a picture of remarkable calm in the period before the War for Independence.

Georgia was the only important New World colony to be established by England in the eighteenth century. It differed in several significant ways from the earlier English colonies: it was to grant no free land titles, to permit the use of no alcoholic beverages, and to allow no slavery. From the time of its establishment in 1733, however, each of these proscriptions was subjected to enormous pressure from the settlers, and one by one the restrictions collapsed. It was in 1750 that the third petition of the colonists brought about the repeal of the hated prohibition against slaves. From that point on the black population grew and slavery flourished. By 1760 there were 6,000 whites and 3,000 blacks. In 1773, when the last estimate was made before the War for Independence, the white population had increased to 18,000, while the black population numbered some 15,000.

Much of Georgia's slave code, adopted in 1755, was taken from the South Carolina code, and it reflected South Carolina's experience rather than Georgia's. For example, the interdiction against more than seven Negroes being out together without a white chaperone indicated South Carolina's general fear of black uprisings. Between Saturday evening and Monday morning, not even those slaves who were authorized to possess firearms were permitted to carry them on their persons. Under no conditions were they to be taught to read and write.

If the slaves of colonial Georgia did not actually engage in rebellion, they nevertheless resisted their enslavement by running away to Florida and by committing acts of sabotage. Strangely enough, Georgia displayed a relative indifference to insurrection by subjecting her slaves to service in the militia. Perhaps the service that Spanish Florida rendered as a place of escape for more discontented blacks made possible the paradoxical practice of using blacks as Georgia militiamen to assist in the return of fugitive slaves to Georgia.

■ The Middle Colonies

Although the Dutch were primarily interested in the slave trade and made great profits from transporting slaves to various colonies, they did not neglect their own New World settlements. There were large plantations in New Netherland, particularly in the valley of the Hudson River, and by 1638 many of them were cultivated largely with slave labor. The institution of slavery, as practiced by the Dutch in the New World, was relatively mild, with slaves receiving fairly humane treatment and many considerations as to their personal rights. The Dutch slave code was not elaborate, and manumission was not an uncommon reward for long or meritorious service. Although the demand for slaves always exceeded the supply, the number imported by the Dutch never reached such proportions as to cause serious apprehension or difficulty during the period of their domination.

The character of the institution of slavery changed when the English took over New Netherland in 1664. In 1665 the colonial assembly recognized the existence of slavery where persons had willingly sold themselves into bondage, and in the statute of 1684 slavery was recognized as a legitimate institution in the province of New York. In subsequent years the black population of New York grew substantially. In 1698 there were only 2,170 blacks in a total population of 18,067, while in 1723 the census listed 6,171 slaves. By 1771 the black population had increased to 19,883 in a total population of 168,007.

The slave code of New York became refined early in the eighteenth century. In 1706 the colony enacted a law stating that baptism of a slave did not provide grounds for a claim to freedom. A further and certainly significant provision was that a slave was at no time a competent witness in a case involving a freeman. In 1715 the legislature enacted a law providing that slaves caught traveling forty miles north of Albany, presumably bound for Canada, were to be executed upon the oath of two credible witnesses. Meanwhile, New York City was enacting ordinances for better control of slaves. In 1710 the city forbade blacks from appearing "in the streets after nightfall without a lantern with a lighted candle in it."

The concentration of an increasing number of slaves in the city of New York brought with it increased dangers to the white population. Blacks defied authority and disobeyed the laws. In 1712 the ungovernable temper of New York blacks flared up into a fully organized insurrection in which twenty-three slaves armed with guns and knives met in an orchard and set fire to a slaveholder's house. During the melee that followed nine whites were killed and six were injured. In the ensuing trial of the accused blacks twenty-one were found guilty and executed.

Almost thirty years later, in 1741, there was a rumor of an even larger insurrection. After a series of fires, the rumor spread that blacks and poor whites were conspiring to destroy law and order in the city and to seize control. After the city offered generous rewards for the apprehension of the conspirators, almost 200 whites and blacks were arrested and prosecuted. At least 100 blacks were convicted, 18 of whom were hanged, 13 burned alive, and 70 banished. Four whites, including 2 women, were hanged. There were no more serious outbursts during the colonial period, and by the time of the Revolution, New York had begun to recognize the moral and economic undesirability of holding human beings in bondage.

South of New York, the colonies of New Jersey, Pennsylvania, and Delaware each in its own way subscribed to the institution of slavery. After the English came to dominate New Jersey, they encouraged slavery in every way. Soon, the black population there was growing steadily: 2,581 in 1726, 3,981 in 1738, and 4,606 in 1745 out of a population of 61,000. In Pennsylvania the growth was not so rapid, largely because of the opposition to slavery by the Quakers. In 1688 Germantown Quakers issued their celebrated protest, and in 1693 George Keith remonstrated with Pennsylvanians for holding persons in perpetual bondage. But in 1685 no less a person than William Penn himself expressed the view that African slaves were more satisfactory workers than white servants, and this had the effect of greatly encouraging slavery in some quarters. In 1721 the black population of Pennsylvania was estimated at between 2,500 and 5,000. Thirty years later there were about 11,000 in the colony. In 1790 there were 10,274 blacks, of whom 3,737 were slaves and 6,537 were free.

In Pennsylvania there was some respect for blacks as human beings, and this attitude led to an early movement for manumission. Even those to whom the institution was acceptable shrank from the wholesale and indiscriminate enslavement of black people simply because it was possible to do so. Pennsylvania was not only relatively free from violence and interracial strife, but the blacks there made strides toward genuine accommodation to their new environment. The lines of communication between blacks and whites were not altogether closed, and the former gained much through these contacts. Schools and churches were a part of the lives of blacks, the institution of marriage was generally respected, and the black family achieved a stability unlike that reached by blacks in most English colonies.

Meanwhile, as early as 1636 slavery existed on the right bank of the Delaware. Since Delaware was a part of Pennsylvania until 1703, the laws of the latter colony applied to Delaware. After that date Delaware was on its own, and the slave population increased at a somewhat more rapid rate

TABLE 1
White and Black Population in the Colonies, 1750
(estimated)

COLONY	WHITE	BLACK
New Hampshire	26,955	550
Massachusetts	183,925	4,075
Rhode Island	29,879	3,347
Connecticut	108,270	3,010
New York	65,682	11,014
New Jersey	66,039	5,354
Pennsylvania	116,794	2,872
Delaware	27,208	1,496
Maryland	97,623	43,450
Virginia	129,581	101,452
North Carolina	53,184	19,800
South Carolina	25,000	39,000
Georgia	4,200	1,000

Source: U.S. Department of Commerce. Historical Statistics of the
United States: Colonial Times to 1970; Part 2. Bureau of the Census.
Washington, D.C. 1975.

than it did in Pennsylvania. As this occurred, Delaware drifted away from the parent colony and became more closely identified with the interests of the neighboring colonies to the south.

Slavery was never really successful in the Middle colonies. Their predominantly commercial economy, supplemented by subsistence agriculture, did not encourage the large-scale employment of slave labor, and many of the slaves that cleared through New York and Pennsylvania ports were later sent into the Southern colonies. Even where there were extensive agricultural enterprises there was no desire for slaves, for the Dutch, Swedes, and Germans cultivated their farms with meticulous care and seemed to prefer to do it themselves. There were those, moreover, who had moral scruples against using slaves. Thus, many in the Middle colonies welcomed the arguments against slavery that became more pronounced during the Revolutionary period.

■ Blacks in Colonial New England

Although New England's primary interest in slavery was in the trade of blacks, some were early introduced into Massachusetts and Connecticut. In 1638 a Salem ship unloaded several Africans in Boston, and in the following year there were blacks in Hartford. Before a decade had passed, blacks were used in the construction of houses and forts in Connecticut. By the middle of the century the refugees who founded Rhode Island were using blacks to help establish that colony. While the status of these early New England blacks was rather uncertain, it gradually became clear in all New England colonies that slavery was a legitimate institution.

Whether slaves landing in New England were to be settled there or shipped to other colonies, they became important to the commercial life of the New England colonies. New England slave traders competed in the trade, although they were at a serious disadvantage compared to the powerful European trading companies. After England secured a monopoly of the slave trade to the New World in 1713, it welcomed New England merchants since there was more than enough for its own traders. In the first half of the eighteenth century New England traders thrived. Boston, Salem, Providence, and New London bustled with activity as outgoing ships were loaded with rum, fish, and dairy products, and as Africans, molasses, and sugar were unloaded from incoming ships. Up until the War for Independence the slave trade was vital to the economic life of New England.

The black population in New England grew slowly. In 1700, when the total population of the entire region was approximately 90,000, there were only 1,000 blacks. In the eighteenth century growth was more rapid. Massachusetts led with 2,000 blacks in 1715 and 5,249 by 1776. Connecticut was second with 1,500 blacks in 1715 and 3,587 by 1756. The largest percentage of blacks was to be found in Rhode Island, where in 1774 there were 3,761 blacks to 54,435 whites. The number in New Hampshire remained negligible all during the colonial period.

New England slavery needed little legal recognition for its growth and development. When the codes emerged late in the seventeenth century, slavery had already become well established. In 1670 Massachusetts enacted a law providing that the children of slaves could be sold into bondage, and ten years later it began to enact measures restricting the movement of blacks. In 1660 Connecticut barred blacks from military service, and thirty years later it restrained them from going beyond the limits of the town without a pass. The restrictions against the education of slaves were not as great as in other regions, and frequently blacks learned to read and write.

Since the number of slaves in New England remained relatively small throughout the colonial period, there was little fear of insurrections. Nevertheless, many slaves indicated their dislike of the institution by running away. Others attacked their masters and even murdered them. Still others plotted to rebel. In 1658 some blacks and Indians in Hartford decided to make a bid for their freedom by destroying several houses of their masters. In the eighteenth century there were a number of conspiracies to rebel in Boston and other towns in Massachusetts. The situation became so serious in Boston in 1723 that the selectmen found it necessary to take precautionary measures by forbidding slaves to be on the streets at night and to be "idling or lurking together."

Phillis Wheatley's "An Address to the Atheist"—1768

Thou who dost not daily feel his hand and rod
Darest thou deny the essence of a God!
If there's no heav'n, ah! whither wilt thou go
Make thy Ilysium in the shades below?
If there's no God from whom did all things spring?
He made the greatest and the minutest Thing.
Angelic ranks no less his power display
Than the least mite scarce visible to Day.

M. A. Richmond, *Bid the Vassal Soar, Interpretive Essays on the Life and Poetry of Phillis Wheatley and George Moses Horton* (Washington, 1974), p. 23.

Despite some restrictions, blacks in New England seemed to have been free to associate with each other and with peaceful Indians. The houses of some free blacks became a rendezvous where they danced, played games, and told stories. Slaves like Lucy Terry of Deerfield, Massachusetts, and Senegambia of Narragansett, Rhode Island, had a seemingly limitless store of tales about Africa and other faraway places that filled many an hour with excitement and pleasure. There was, moreover, ample opportunity for blacks to associate with whites, for hardly a house or church raising, an apple paring, or a corn husking took place without the presence of at least a portion of the slave population. On Guy Fawkes Day, Lorenzo Greene says, "Negroes joined in the boisterous crowds that surged through the streets of Boston, much to the annoyance of pedestrians."

Blacks in New England were in a unique position in colonial America. They were not subjected to the harsh codes or the severe treatment that their fellows received in the colonies of the South. Nevertheless, it is possible to exaggerate the humanitarian aspects of their treatment. Masters in New England held a firm hand on the institution and gave little consideration to the small minority that argued for the freedom of slaves. Although New Englanders took their religion seriously, they did not permit it to interfere with their appreciation of the profits of slavery and the slave trade. At the same time, they did not glut their home market with slaves and increase the number to the point where they would be fearful for their safety. There seemed to be the characteristic Yankee shrewdness in the New Englander's assessment of the importance of slavery to economic and social life.

CHAPTER 5

That All May
Be Free

■ Slavery and the Revolutionary Philosophy

By the middle of the eighteenth century, slavery in the United States was
an integral part of a maturing economic system. There had been protests
against the slave trade, some colonies had imposed almost prohibitive
import duties, and some religious groups, notably the Quakers, had
questioned the right of one person to hold another in bondage. There had
been, however, no frontal attack upon the institution, and even in the
Northern colonies, where there was no extensive use of slaves, the majority
of the articulate colonists paid little attention to slavery. Perhaps it was
the colonists' preoccupation with their economic and political relations
with England that accounted for the widespread indifference with which
they regarded slavery. Colonial problems were so urgent that little time
was left in which colonists could concern themselves with humanitarian
matters. If there could be assurance that blacks would neither conspire to
rebel nor offer aid and comfort to the French or the Indians, there seemed
to be little reason to be concerned over this condition.

This general attitude prevailed up until the end of the French and Indian
War in 1763. This significant year not only marked the beginning of a new
colonial policy for England but also ushered in a new approach, on the part
of the colonists, to the problem of slavery. There was, moreover, a discernible

connection between the two developments. As colonists saw in England's new colonial policy a threat to the economic and political freedom that they had enjoyed for several generations, they also seemed to recognize a marked inconsistency in their position as oppressed colonists *and* slaveholders. John Woolman, a New Jersey Quaker, and Anthony Benezet, a Philadelphia Huguenot, had already begun their anti-slavery activities in the Middle colonies, and others, such as Benjamin Franklin and Benjamin Rush, had joined in the work to free the slaves. But there had been no dramatic denunciation of the institution by any outstanding political leader in the colonies. The resurrection of the hated navigation acts and the imposition of new regulations like the Sugar Act of 1764 brought forth eloquent defenses of the position of the colonists. One act of Parliament had, as James Otis declared, "set people a-thinking in six months, more than they had done in their whole lives before." They began to think of their dual role as oppressed and oppressor. Almost overnight the grave but quiet efforts of Benezet and Woolman bore fruit, as some colonial leaders began to denounce not only England's new imperial policy but slavery and the slave trade as well.

The Whig policy of "benign neglect" lent itself to the flow of ideas across the Atlantic as much as it winked at the clandestine flow of commerce in numerous directions. There is little reason to believe that the colonists were unaware of the revolutionary literature flowing from the pens of such French thinkers as Rousseau. There were enough revolutionary ideas in England, however, to inspire a movement against the proscribing policy of the parent country. Long before 1776 most Americans viewed John Locke's treatises on government as political gospel, and upon numerous occasions after 1763 they used these works to bolster their arguments. Locke's *Constitutions of Carolina* had recognized slavery in that colony, and his treatises on government defended the replacement of James II by William and Mary. If Locke could justify the revolution of 1688, certainly the same line of reasoning could justify the colonial action of the 1760s and 1770s.

It was almost natural for the colonists to link the problem of black slavery to their fight against England. The struggle of blacks to secure their freedom was growing. When James Otis was penning his eloquent protest in the *Rights of the British Colonies,* in which he affirmed the black's inalienable right to freedom, blacks themselves were petitioning the general court of Massachusetts for their freedom on the grounds that it was their natural right. The incident in Boston in March 1770 must have greatly impressed many of the colonists with the incongruity of their position. The presence of British soldiers in Boston excited the indignation of the people, and many wondered what could be done about it. The decision was made by a group, described by defense counsel John Adams at the trial of the British soldiers as "a motley rabble of saucy boys, Negroes and mulattoes, Irish Teagues and outlandish Jack Tars." Led by Crispus Attucks, a runaway slave, and shouting, "The way to get rid of these soldiers is to attack the main guard," they rushed into King Street to protest by action. They were fired upon by several men of Captain Preston's company. Attucks was the first to fall, two others were killed instantly, and two others later died from wounds.

Attucks could hardly be described as a saucy boy. Nor was he deserving of the other harsh things John Adams had to say about those who fell in the Boston Massacre. Attucks was more than forty-seven years old and had made his living during the twenty years after he ran away from his Framingham master by working on ships plying out of Boston harbor. As a seaman he probably felt keenly the restrictions that England's new navigation acts imposed. He had undertaken to make the protest in a form that England would understand. Attucks's martyrdom is significant not as the first life to be offered in the struggle against England. Indeed, there ensued almost five years of peace during which time it appeared as though Samuel Adams and his group would not get their war after all. The significance of Attucks's death seems to lie in the dramatic connection that it pointed out between the colonists' struggle against England and the status of blacks in America. Here was a fugitive slave who, with his bare hands, was willing to resist England to the point of giving his life. It was a remarkable thing, the colonists reasoned, to have their fight for freedom waged by one who was not as free as they.

In the years that followed the Boston Massacre, the colonists, as though pricked by conscience, frequently spoke against slavery and England at the same time. In 1773 the Reverend Isaac Skillman went so far as to assert that in conformity with the laws of nature, slaves should rebel against their masters. In 1774 Abigail Adams wrote her husband: "It always appeared a most iniquitous scheme to me to fight ourselves for what we are daily robbing and plundering from those who have as good a right to freedom as we have." About the same time, Thomas Jefferson wrote "A Summary View of the Rights of British America," in which he said that the abolition of slavery was the great object of desire in the colonies, but that it had become increasingly difficult because Britain had consistently blocked all colonial efforts to put an end to the slave trade.

In their thinking some colonists had thus moved from the position of acceptance of the institution of slavery to the position that it was inconsistent with their fight with England and finally to the view that England was responsible for the continuation of slavery. This view was translated into action in the fall of 1774 when the Continental Congress passed an agreement not to import any slaves after December 1, 1775. Georgia, the only colony not represented, adopted a similar measure in July 1775. These can hardly be regarded as antislavery measures, however. It must be remembered that there was general resentment against England's "Intolerable Acts," passed earlier in the year, and that many of the enactments of the first Continental Congress were retaliatory measures of a temporary nature.

The test of the colonists' regard for slavery came in their reaction to the Declaration of Independence, which was submitted to the Continental Congress by Thomas Jefferson. The formulation of a general political philosophy to justify the drastic step the colonists were taking was generally acceptable, even to the proposition that all people, being created equal, were endowed with "certain unalienable Rights . . . Life, Liberty, and the pursuit of Happiness." Jefferson's specific charges against the king were harsh and uncompromising. Among them were the following:

> He has waged cruel war against human nature itself, violating its most sacred rights of life and liberty in the persons of a distant people who never offended him, captivating and carrying them into slavery in another hemisphere, or to incur miserable death in their transportation thither. This piratical warfare, the opprobrium of *infidel* powers, is the warfare of the Christian king of Great Britain. Determined to keep open a market where MEN should be bought and sold, he has prostituted his negative [veto] for suppressing every legislative attempt to prohibit or to restrain this execrable commerce; and that this assemblage of horrors might want no fact of distinguished die, he is now exciting these very people to rise in arms among us, and to purchase that liberty of which he deprived them, by murdering the people upon whom *he* also obtruded them; thus paying off former crimes committed against the *liberties* of one people, with crimes which he urges them to commit against the *lives* of another.

These charges, described by John Adams as the "vehement philippic against Negro slavery," were unacceptable to the Southern delegation at the Continental Congress and were stricken from the document.

The members of the Continental Congress doubtless realized that Jefferson's bold accusations of the king were at considerable variance with the truth. The slave trade had been carried on not only by British merchants but by colonists as well, and in some colonies no effort had been made even to regulate it. There was, moreover, much favorable disposition to slavery in the Southern colonies, an attitude shared by a larger number than the "few bold and persevering pro-slavery men" described by George Livermore. Those who favored slavery at all realized that if Jefferson's views prevailed in the Declaration of Independence, there would be no justification for the institution once the ties to England were completely cut. It would be better, therefore, to reject the strong language in which the complete responsibility was laid at the door of George III. In thus declining to accuse the king of perpetuating slavery and the slave trade, the colonists contented themselves with engaging in what Rufus Choate later called "glittering generalities" and in connecting all too vaguely the status of blacks with the philosophy of freedom for all people.

The silence of the Declaration of Independence on the matter of slavery and the slave trade was to make it equally difficult for abolitionists and proslavery leaders to look to that document for support. Even if Jefferson did say that all men were created equal, it could not be forgotten that the antislavery passages of the Declaration were ruled out altogether. By endowing all with inalienable rights superior to those of positive law, it was, however, a standing invitation to insurrection that few could accept. The implications of the Declaration, however vague, were so powerful that Southern slave owners found it desirable to deny the self-evident truths that it expounded and were willing to do battle with abolitionists during the period of strain and stress over just what the Declaration meant with regard to society in nineteenth-century America.

■ Blacks Fighting for American Independence

From the beginning of hostilities in 1775, the question of arming blacks, slave and free, consistently plagued the patriots who most of the time had trouble enough without this aggravating situation. The fear of slave insurrections had caused the colonists to exclude blacks from militia service even in Massachusetts in 1656, and in Connecticut in 1660. Despite this exclusion, blacks frequently participated in wars against the French and the Indians, thus developing a tradition of military service that was alive at the time of the War for Independence. As early as the battles of Lexington and Concord in April 1775, blacks took up arms against the British, and their presence at subsequent battles in the spring and summer of that eventful year is an important part of the military history of the struggle.

In May 1775, the Committee on Safety—commonly known as the Hancock and Warren Committee—took up the matter of the use of blacks in the armed forces and came to the significant conclusion that only freemen should be used since the use of slaves would be "inconsistent with the principles that are to be supported." It is doubtful that this policy was adhered to, for evidently slaves, as well as free blacks, fought in the Battle of Bunker Hill. Furthermore, many slaves were manumitted in order to serve in the army. Indeed, one of the outstanding heroes of the battle, Peter Salem, had shortly before the battle been a slave in Framingham, Massachusetts. One story, not thoroughly substantiated, says that Salem won the admiration of his comrades in arms by shooting the British Major Pitcairn. Mounting the redoubt and shouting, "The day is ours," Pitcairn, who displayed more valor than judgment, received the full force of Peter Salem's musket. The death of Pitcairn was a part of the moral victory won by the patriots on June 17, 1775.

Peter Salem was not the only black who succeeded in distinguishing himself at Bunker Hill. Another, Salem Poor, a soldier in a company and regiment made up largely of white men, won the praise of his superiors, who said that in the battle he "behaved like an experienced officer as well as an excellent soldier." In an official commendation presented to the general court of Massachusetts these military leaders said, "We would only beg leave to say, in the person of this said negro centres a brave and gallant soldier. The reward due to so great and distinguished a character, we submit to the Congress." While Peter Salem and Salem Poor stand out for their

AFRICAN-AMERICAN MASON. Prince Hall, fighter in the War for Independence, established Masonry among blacks after he was initiated by a British army lodge in 1775. (*Fisk Archives.*)

extraordinary feats of heroism, other blacks were integrated into the companies of whites and performed services for which they were later commended. Among these were Caesar Brown of Westford, Massachusetts, who was killed in action; Barzillai Lew, a fifer and drummer; Titus Colburn and Alexander Ames of Andover; Prince Hall, later an abolitionist and Masonic leader; and many other Massachusetts blacks: Cuff Hayes, Caesar Dickerson, Cato Tufts, Grant Cooper, and Sampson Talbert. While this is certainly not an exhaustive list, it is indicative of the early use of blacks in the War for Independence.

The black soldier had by no means won the right to fight for the independence of the United States. In the formulation of an overall policy for military service shortly after General Washington took command, it was decided that the services of blacks were not needed. Out of the council of war that Washington held on July 9, 1775, an order was sent to recruiting officers that they were not to enlist "any deserter from the ministerial army, nor any stroller, negro, or vagabond, or person suspected of being an enemy to the liberty of America nor any under eighteen years of age." It was a rather strange expression of gratitude for the services rendered by blacks that Washington and the high command found it desirable to exclude them from enlistment.

The ban on enlistment obviously did not affect blacks already in the service, but within a few months a movement was afoot to rid the army of all blacks. On September 26, 1775, Edward Rutledge of South Carolina moved in the Continental Congress to discharge all blacks in the army. Although he was strongly supported by many Southern delegates, he lost his point. On October 8, however, a council of war composed of Washington, Major Generals Ward, Lee, and Putnam, and several brigadier generals met and considered the use of blacks. It was agreed unanimously to reject all slaves and, by a large majority, to reject blacks altogether. Ten days later a group of civilians, among them Benjamin Franklin and Thomas Lynch, met with Washington and the deputy governors of Rhode Island and Connecticut to discuss plans for recruiting a new army. It was again agreed to reject blacks altogether. On November 12, 1775, General Washington issued an order instructing recruiters not to enlist blacks, boys unable to bear arms, or old men unable to endure the fatigues of campaign.

Thus, the new army under George Washington had settled the question of the black soldier by deciding not to permit any black, slave or free, to enlist. There is no indication that there would have been a change of policy had not the British made a political move that harassed the feeble Continental army almost as much as a significant military maneuver. On November 7, 1775, Lord Dunmore, the governor of Virginia, issued a proclamation that caused immediate concern among the patriots. In part, he said, "I do hereby . . . declare all indentured servants, Negroes, or others (appertaining to rebels) free, that are able and willing to bear arms, they joining his Majesty's troops, as soon as may be, for the more speedily reducing this Colony to a proper dignity." Had Washington known of this proclamation on November 12, he perhaps would not have issued his order prohibiting the enlistment of blacks. As soon as he learned of Dunmore's designs he manifested great concern. During the month of December he was most alarmed at what the consequences of the wholesale enlistment of blacks in the British army might mean in Virginia. In a letter to Richard Henry Lee on the day after Christmas, Washington asserted that if Dunmore was not crushed before spring, he would become the most formidable enemy to the cause of independence. His strength would increase "as a snowball, by rolling; and faster, if some expedient cannot be hit upon to convince the slaves and servants of the impotency of his design."

Washington had to act quickly. On December 31, he partially reversed his policy regarding the enlistment of blacks and in a report to the president of the Continental Congress said that he was permitting the enlistment of free blacks. He said that the free blacks who had served in the army were very much dissatisfied at being discarded. He further reported that it was feared that they would seek service in the British army if they were not permitted to serve with the patriots. On January 16, 1776, the Continental Congress approved a policy permitting free blacks "who had served faithfully in the army at Cambridge" to reenlist but made it clear that no others were to be received.

Virginians were alarmed. The hated Dunmore was openly soliciting support among their slaves. They felt constrained to counteract this bid with pleas and promises to blacks. On November 23, 1775, an article appeared in a Williamsburg paper severely criticizing Dunmore's proclamation and pointing out to blacks that the British motives were entirely selfish. Blacks were urged not to join Dunmore's forces and were promised good treatment if they remained loyal to the Virginia patriots. On December 13, the committee of the Virginia Convention officially answered the Dunmore proclamation. It not only denounced the British for enticing slaves away but also promised pardon to all slaves who returned to duty within ten days.

The alarm of the military high command and of Virginians was fully justified. Edmund Pendleton wrote Richard Henry Lee on November 27, 1775, that slaves were flocking to Dunmore in abundance. In March of the following year, Dunmore reported to the British secretary of state that the enlistment of blacks was proceeding very well, "and would have been in great forwardness, had not a fever crept in amongst them, which carried off a great many fine fellows." During the remainder of the war large numbers of blacks escaped to the British lines, seeking the freedom that had eluded them during their stay in the colonies. Wherever the British armies went they attracted many blacks, and Maryland, Virginia, and South Carolina were especially alarmed over the future of slavery regardless of the outcome of the war. As late as 1781 Richard Henry Lee would write his brother that two neighbors had lost "every slave they had in the world. . . . This has been the general case of all those who were near the enemy."

The presence of British troops in America and the war itself had an unsettling effect on slavery in general. Slaves ran away in large numbers even if they had no intention of reaching the British lines. Thomas Jefferson estimated that in 1778 alone more than 30,000 Virginia slaves ran away. David Ramsay, the South Carolina historian, asserted that between 1775 and 1783 his state lost at least 25,000 blacks. It has been estimated that during the war Georgia lost about 75 percent of its 15,000 slaves. How effective the British were in utilizing this manpower is not at all clear. Here and there, such as at Ft. Cornwallis, there are accounts of blacks serving in the British army. Perhaps their service was more valuable than has been believed, for in 1786 a corps of runaway blacks that had been trained by the British during the siege of Savannah were still calling themselves the "king of England's soldiers" and continued to harass the countryside of Georgia in an eighteenth-century resistance movement.

The British bid for blacks during the war had the effect of liberalizing the policy of the colonists toward them. Not only did Washington order the enlistment of some free blacks, but most of the states, either by specific legislation or merely by a reversal of policy, began to enlist both slaves and free blacks. In 1776 a New York law permitted the substitution of blacks for whites who had been drafted. In the same year Virginia went so far as to permit free mulattoes to serve as drummers, fifers, and pioneers, and in the following year Virginia merely required that all blacks who enlisted should furnish a certificate of freedom secured from a justice of the peace. In 1778 both Rhode Island and Massachusetts permitted slaves to serve as soldiers. In the same year North Carolina, in legislating against fugitive slaves, made it clear that the penalties under the law were not to be applied to liberated slaves in the service of North Carolina or the United States.

Under the more liberal laws of the states, blacks began to enlist in the state and Continental armies in large numbers. In 1778 Massachusetts and Rhode Island felt that enough black soldiers could be raised within their borders to form separate regiments. Indeed, it appeared as though states were now vying with each other in enlisting blacks. New Hampshire offered the same bounty to black soldiers that it was giving to whites, and masters were given bounties as payment for the freedom of their slaves. When the recruiting of white soldiers in Connecticut declined, a vigorous enlistment of blacks began. New York offered freedom to all slaves who would serve in the army for three years, while owners were given a land bounty for their slaves. Before the end of the war most states, as well as the Continental Congress, were enlisting slaves with the understanding that they were to receive their freedom at the end of their service.

Only two states, Georgia and South Carolina, continued to oppose the enlistment of black soldiers. It was a source of considerable embarrassment to Colonel John Laurens, who in 1778 was asked to raise several battalions of blacks in his native South Carolina. In 1779 the Continental Congress recommended that 3,000 blacks be recruited in Georgia and South Carolina. The Congress was to pay the owners not over $1,000 for each slave recruited, and at the end of the war the slave was to be set free and given $50. Georgia and South Carolina were alarmed over the plan and summarily rejected it. Despite several pleas from Laurens, neither state ever permitted such enlistment. By this time, Washington had so completely accepted the idea of blacks as soldiers that he could write of South Carolina and Georgia, "That spirit of freedom which at the commencement of this contest would have gladly sacrificed everything to the attainment of its object, has long since subsided, and every selfish passion has taken its place." Even in these states, however, slaves were running away—to fight with the British and win their own freedom or with the patriots and win the freedom of their country as well as their own.

Of the 300,000 soldiers who served the cause of independence, approximately 5,000 were blacks. Despite the fact that the bulk of the black population was in the South, the majority of black soldiers were from the North. They served in every phase of the war and under every possible condition. Some volunteered, others were drafted, while still others were substituted for white draftees. There were only a few separate black fighting groups. In Massachusetts two black companies were formed, one under Maj. Samuel Lawrence and the other—the Bucks of America—under Middleton, a black commander. Connecticut put a black company in the field under the leadership of Capt. David Humphreys, while the Rhode Island black company was under Col. Jeremiah Olney and later under Col. Christopher Greene. Some of these groups won the admiration and respect of their leaders and of the citizenry. Lawrence's company was described as a group "of whose courage, military discipline, and fidelity" their leader always spoke with respect. On one occasion his men rescued him after he was completely surrounded by the enemy.

The command of an all-black company was, at first, studiously avoided by most of the white officers. There was, therefore, some difficulty in securing a commander for the Connecticut company of blacks. Finally, Captain Humphreys volunteered his services, and under his leadership the group so distinguished itself that thereafter officers were said to have been as desirous of obtaining appointments in that company as they had previously been of avoiding them. In the Battle of Rhode Island, August 29, 1778, the black regiment under Colonel Greene "distinguished itself by deeds of desperate valor." On three occasions they repulsed the Hessian soldiers, who were charging down on them in order to gain a strategic position. In 1781, when Colonel Greene was surprised and killed near Points Bridge, New York, his black soldiers heroically defended him until they were cut to pieces, and the enemy reached him over the dead bodies of his faithful men. One white veteran described them as "brave, hardy troops. They helped to gain our liberty and independence."

The vast majority of black soldiers served in fighting groups made up primarily of white men. The integration of them was so complete that one Hessian officer, Schloezer, declared that "no regiment is to be seen in which there are not Negroes in abundance: and among them are able-bodied, strong, and brave fellows." Not only were they in the regiments of the New England and Middle Atlantic states, but they were also to be found fighting by the side of their white fellows in the Southern states. Hardly a military action between 1775 and 1781 was without some black participants. They were at Lexington, Concord, Ticonderoga, Bunker Hill, Long Island, White Plains, Trenton, Princeton, Bennington, Brandywine, Stillwater, Bemis Heights, Saratoga, Red Bank, Monmouth, Rhode Island, Savannah, Stony Point, Ft. Griswold, Eutaw Springs, and Yorktown.

As in any undertaking that involves large numbers of persons, most of the blacks who served in the War for Independence will forever remain anonymous. There were some, however, who by their outstanding service won recognition from their contemporaries and a conspicuous place in the history of the War for Independence. Two blacks, Prince Whipple and Oliver Cromwell, were with General Washington when he crossed the Delaware

Slaves Want Freedom, Too—1777

To the Honorable Counsel & House of [Representa]tives for the State of Massachusetts Bay in General Court assembled, January 13, 1777.

The petition of A Great Number of Blackes detained in a State of slavery in the Bowels of a free & Christian Country Humbly shuwith that your Petitioners apprehend that they have in Common with all other men a Natural and Unaliable Right to that freedom which the Grat Parent of the Unavers hath Bestowed equalley on all menkind and which they have Never forfuted by any Compact or agreement whatever—but thay wher Unjustly Dragged by the hand of cruel Power from their Derest friends and sum of them Even torn from the Embraces of their tender Parents—from A popolous Pleasant and plentiful contry and in violation of Laws of Nature and off Nations and in defiance of all the tender feelings of humanity Brough hear Either to Be sold Like Beast of Burthen & Like them Condemnd to Slavery for Life—Among A People Profesing the mild Religion of Jesus A people Not Insensible of the Secrets of Rational Being Nor without spirit to Resent the unjust endeavours of others to Reduce them to a state of Bondage and Subjection your honouer Need not be informed that A Life of Slavery Like that of your Petioners Deprived of Every social privilege of Every thing Requiset to Render Life Tolable is far worse than Nonexistance.

Collections, Massachusetts Historical Society, 5th Series, III (Boston, 1877), pp. 436–437.

on Christmas Day 1776. Tack Sisson, by crashing a door open with his head, facilitated the capture of the British general Richard Prescott, at Newport, Rhode Island, July 9, 1777. In the same year, Lemuel Haynes, who was later to become a distinguished minister in white churches, joined in the expedition to Ticonderoga to stop the inroads of Burgoyne's northern army. The victory of Anthony Wayne at Stony Point in 1779 was made possible by the spying of a black soldier by the name of Pompey. At the siege of Savannah in 1779, more than 700 Haitian free blacks were with the French forces that helped save the day. Among the wounded soldiers was Christophe, who was later to play an important role in the liberation of Haiti.

There are many instances of blacks serving in the navy during the War for Independence. Having piloted vessels in coastal waters before the war, their services were finally accepted during the dark days of the war. They were able and ordinary seamen, pilots, boatswain's mates, and gunner's mates. They were among the crews of the coastal galleys that defended Georgia, North Carolina, South Carolina, and Virginia. Luther P. Jackson has called attention to the service of Virginia blacks in the navy of the Revolution. He points out that black sailors fought on the *Patriot, Liberty, Tempest, Dragon, Diligence,* and many other vessels and indicates that some were enlisted for as many as ten or eleven years. In Connecticut and Massachusetts, blacks served in the navy, such as the three black seamen who were on Capt. David Porter's *Aurora* and the four who were on the crew of the privateer *General Putnam.* When he was but fourteen years old, James Forten was a powder boy on Stephen Decatur's *Royal Louis* and participated in the victory over several English vessels. Later, when he was captured and offered a home in England, he refused on the grounds that he felt that he should suffer the prisoner's lot in the cause of independence and to do less would be to betray his country.

Black patriots saw clearly the implications for their own future in their fight against England. They wanted human freedom as well as political independence. Even before Abigail Adams pointed to the inconsistency of fighting for independence while adhering to slavery, blacks spoke out. As early as 1766 they were seeking their freedom in the courts and legislatures. In January 1773 a group of "many slaves" asked the general court of Massachusetts to liberate them "from a State of Slavery." In 1774 a group of blacks expressed their astonishment that the colonists could seek independence from Britain yet give no consideration to the slaves' pleas for freedom. Blacks made literally scores of such representations and, in so doing, contributed significantly to broadening the ideology of the struggle to include at least some human freedom as well as political independence. The fact remained, as Edmund Morgan has observed, that to a large degree "Americans bought their independence with slave labor." It was yet to be seen if human freedom in general was as dear to them as political independence.

■ The Movement to Manumit Slaves

By the end of the War for Independence the ideology of the struggle that had been so clearly defined and so loudly proclaimed at the outset had been dimmed and muffled by the grim and practical realities of the war. Only the perspective of a brief period was needed to realize that the aims of the leaders were more political than social. And yet, some forces had been set in motion that operated to effect a change in the status of blacks. It is no mere coincidence that when the Battle of Lexington was fought the first antislavery society was just beginning to formulate its plans for action. This and similar organizations reflect the social implications of the Revolutionary philosophy. So powerfully did the philosophy act upon the minds of the people that almost every state enlisting slaves to serve in the army either freed them at the outset or promised manumission at the end of service. The records of several states in the 1780s abound in deeds of manumission of black soldiers and their families. While the number is undeterminable, it is not difficult to conclude that hundreds, if not thousands, of slaves secured their freedom at the end of the war.

The freedom that some black soldiers won for themselves did not go uncontested at the end of the war. Some masters sought to repossess slaves who had fought for freedom from Britain, and General Washington found it necessary to authorize several courts of inquiry to establish the validity of such claims. Finally, some states resorted to the enactment of laws such as the one that Virginia passed in 1783 granting freedom to all slaves "who served in the late war." A clear distinction was made, however, between those slaves who served in the army of the American states and those who merely ran away or who escaped to the British lines. Even General Washington expressed alarm at the news that blacks were embarking with the British fleet at various American ports, and he asked a friend in New York to help him retrieve some of his own runaways whom he suspected of being in that vicinity.

Other evidences, besides the manumission of soldier-slaves, that the Revolutionary philosophy was taking effect are seen in the activities of individuals immediately after the war. While no one as prominent as Thomas Jefferson took up the cudgel against slavery, numerous individuals of considerable stature spoke out against the institution. Samuel Hopkins of Rhode Island, Ezra Stiles of Connecticut, and Jeremy Belknap of Massachusetts were outstanding in the group of theologians who expressed antislavery views. In Virginia, St. George Tucker's *Dissertation on Slavery* was studied by the author's students at William and Mary and by Virginia slave owners as well. Other antislavery educators were Jedidiah Morse, the father of American geography, and William Rogers of the College of Philadelphia. Benjamin Franklin and Benjamin Rush continued to speak out against slavery, while the legal profession had outstanding spokesmen in Zepheniah Swift, Noah Webster, and Theodore Dwight.

Manumission and antislavery societies became more widespread after the war. The Quakers, who had organized the first society in 1775, were now joined by many other groups in this and other organizations. In 1785 the New York Society for Promoting the Manumission of Slaves was organized with John Jay as president. In Delaware a similar society was set up in 1788, and by 1792 there were antislavery societies in every state from Massachusetts to Virginia. Some sought to prevent the slave trade, while others were concerned with the deportation of blacks from the state. Most of them envisioned a scheme, however remote, of complete abolition of slavery. Local societies collected information on slavery and published reports on the progress of emancipation. Others published orations and addresses designed to arouse public sentiment against slavery.

The legislation against the slave trade, which began as a measure to combat England's commercial domination before the war, continued after hostilities were over. In 1783 Maryland prohibited the traffic in blacks. In 1786 North Carolina increased substantially the duty on every black imported. A duty of £15, for example, was levied on a black between twelve and thirty years of age imported directly from Africa. This law was repealed in 1790. In 1787 South Carolina prohibited the importation of slaves for several years, an act which was renewed from time to time until 1803, when it was repealed on the grounds that it was unenforceable.

Even before the surrender at Yorktown, the state of Pennsylvania in 1780 had made provisions for the gradual abolition of slavery. The law provided that no black or "Negro" born after that date should be held in bondage after he or she became twenty-eight year old and up to that time was to be treated as an indentured servant or an apprentice. In recalling the struggle against England, Pennsylvanians said that they felt they were called upon to manifest the sincerity of their professions of freedom, and to give substantial proof of gratitude, by extending a portion of their freedom to others, "who, though of a different color, are the work of the same Almighty hand." By 1783 the courts of Massachusetts had abolished slavery by asserting that the constitution of 1780 discountenanced the institution by saying that "all men are born free and equal." In 1784 Connecticut and Rhode Island passed acts that abolished slavery gradually. Manumission acts were passed in New York in 1785 and in New Jersey in 1786, though effective legislation was not achieved in those states until 1799 and 1804, respectively. While the Northern states were thus eradicating the institution, some of the Southern states, such as Virginia and North Carolina, were enacting legislation that facilitated the efforts of slave owners to manumit their human chattel. Perhaps the high-water mark of the postwar anti-slavery movement was reached in 1787 when the Congress added to the Northwest Ordinance the provision that neither slavery nor involuntary servitude should exist in the territory covered by it.

■ The Conservative Reaction

Despite the efforts of antislavery leaders to deal a death blow to slavery after the War for Independence, they were unable to do so. Resistance to abolitionist schemes hardened in the Southern states, where so much capital was invested in slaves and where a new economic importance was already being attached to the institution. In the 1780s, moreover, there was the sobering fear that the social program that grew out of the struggle against Britain would get out of hand and uproot the very foundations of social and economic life in America. As the plain people began to demand liberal and democratic land laws, moratoriums on their debts, and greater guarantees of human rights, they challenged the authority by which the select few ruled the American state. To this "horrid vision of disorder" which the leaders conjured up must be added the loud insistence of antislavery leaders for the destruction of property in human beings and the extension of liberty to all. Where would all this lead? The rebellion of Daniel Shays in Massachusetts suggested the answer: real revolution, pure and simple. The country's leaders had already planned their counterattack in the calling of a convention to meet in Philadelphia in 1787 to stabilize and strengthen the government and to stem the tide of social revolution.

It was only natural that slavery became an important consideration in the Constitutional Convention. In the heated debates over representation in the Congress, the question arose as to how slaves should be counted. Most of the Northern delegates could regard slaves in no light except as property and thus not deserving any representation. Georgia and South Carolina delegates were loud in their demands that blacks be counted equally with whites. Gouverneur Morris declared that the people of Pennsylvania would revolt on being placed on an equal footing with slaves, while Rufus King of Massachusetts flayed slavery in a fiery speech and condemned any proposal that would recognize it in the Constitution. The three-fifths compromise finally written into the Constitution was perhaps satisfactory to no one, but it demonstrates clearly the strength of the proslavery interests at the convention. It was inserted in Article I, Section 2, and reads as follows:

> Representatives and direct Taxes shall be apportioned among the several States which may be included within this Union, according to their respective Numbers, which shall be determined by adding to the whole Number of free Persons, including those bound to Service for a Term of Years, and excluding Indians not taxed, three fifths of all other persons.

It has been seen that several states had already acted to prohibit the slave trade. In 1787 the opponents of the traffic in human beings fervently hoped that the Constitutional Convention would act to stop this evil. To this end the Pennsylvania Abolition Society drafted a memorial imploring the convention to make the slave trade part of its deliberations and gave it to Benjamin Franklin to present. When it became obvious that the convention would consider the problem in any case, he decided not to present the memorial lest the suspicions of Southern members be aroused, thereby doing more harm than good. When the matter came before the convention, an argument ensued that was as fiery as any witnessed by the delegates. Young Charles Pinckney said that South Carolina could never accept a constitution that would prohibit the slave trade. Significantly, he added, "If the States be all left at liberty on this subject, South Carolina may perhaps by degrees do of herself what is wished, as Virginia and Maryland have already done." His cousin, Gen. C. C. Pinckney, was more severe on Virginia and Maryland. He asserted that these states would gain by stopping importations. Virginia's slaves would rise in value, and it would be "unequal to require South Carolina and Georgia to Confederate on such unequal terms." The fear of rupture at this critical moment led the states of the North and Upper South to compromise with the states of the lower South and to extend the slave trade for twenty years. The provision finally adopted in Article I, Section 9, reads:

> The Migration or Importation of such Persons as any of the States now existing shall think proper to admit, shall not be prohibited by the Congress prior to the Year one thousand eight hundred and eight, but a Tax or duty may be imposed on such Importation, not exceeding ten dollars for each Person.

It is significant that there was almost no opposition to the proposal that states give up fugitive slaves to their owners. The public obligation to return fugitive slaves, which had already been provided for in several Indian treaties between 1781 and 1786, was established in the Northwest Territory in 1787 in connection with the prohibition of slavery in that region. When the provision came before the convention for consideration, it was late, August 28, and the delegates were already impatient to return to their homes. Too, the slave owners had already won such sweeping constitutional recognition of slavery that the question of fugitive slaves was an anticlimax to the great debates. When Roger Sherman of Connecticut asserted that he saw "no more propriety in the public seizing and surrendering a slave or servant, than a horse," he found no support even among his New England colleagues. Without serious challenge, therefore, the provision was inserted in Article IV, Section 2:

> No Person held to Service or Labour in one State, under the Laws thereof, escaping into another, shall, in Consequence of any Law or Regulation therein, be discharged from such Service or Labour, but shall be delivered up on Claim of the Party to whom such Service or Labour may be due.

When the delegates to the Constitutional Convention returned to their homes in September 1787, they could look back on three months of political and economic wire pulling that was to check effectively the trend toward social upheaval. Perhaps in no area had there been greater success than in the matter of checking the antislavery movement. Quakers and other groups could view the new document as devoid of guarantees of human liberties, and zealous reformers could regard the Constitution as a victory for reaction; but their objections were silenced by the effective organization for ratification that was in operation even before the convention had adjourned. The fathers of the Constitution were dedicated to the proposition that "government should rest upon the dominion of property." For Southerners this meant slaves, just as surely as it meant commerce and industry for Northerners. In the protection of this property the Constitution had given recognition to the institution of human slavery, and it was to take seventy-five years to undo that which was accomplished in Philadelphia in 1787.

The adoption of the federal Constitution marks the end of an era not only in the political history of the United States but in the history of African Americans as well. With British domination at an end and stable government established, Americans could no longer lay the onus for slavery at the door of the parent country. They proudly accepted the challenge and responsibility of their new political freedom by establishing the machinery and safeguards that ensured the continued enslavement of blacks. Ironically enough, America's freedom was the means of giving slavery itself a longer life than it was to have in the British Empire. New factors on the horizon were about to usher in a new day for slavery as the old day passed away.

CHAPTER 6

Blacks in the New Republic

■ The Black Population in 1790

In the year following the inauguration of George Washington as president of the United States, foreign observers could view with a critical eye the low level of culture and the persistence of slavery in the new republic, but none could deny the happy prospect for permanence that stemmed from a continuously increasing population. There were nearly 4 million inhabitants in the United States, and the most casual observer could see signs of growth everywhere. Among these signs was the black population, which in 1790 numbered slightly more than 750,000. Of course, the vast majority, almost 89 percent, lived in the South Atlantic states where the plantation system was making the greatest demands for black labor. In 1790 Virginia had already taken the lead in black population, which it was to hold during the entire slave period. Virginia's 304,000 blacks were almost three times the number in South Carolina, Virginia's nearest rival. Most of the states in that region, however, presented a picture of an abundant black population. Only two, Georgia and Delaware, which no longer deserved to be classified with Pennsylvania, had less than 100,000 black residents. There were 641,691 slaves in the South Atlantic states and 32,048 free blacks.

Considering their location and economic interests, the Middle Atlantic states of New York, New Jersey, and Pennsylvania had substantial black

TABLE 2 Black Population Census of 1790		
STATE	SLAVES	FREE
Maine		536
New Hampshire	157	630
Vermont		269
Massachusetts		5,369
Rhode Island	958	3,484
Connecticut	2,648	2,771
New York	21,193	4,682
New Jersey	11,423	2,762
Pennsylvania	3,707	6,531
Delaware	8,887	3,899
Maryland	103,036	8,043
Virginia	292,627	12,866
North Carolina	100,783	5,041
South Carolina	107,094	1,801
Georgia	29,264	398
Kentucky	12,430	114
Tennessee	3,417	361
Total	697,624	59,557

Source: Negro Population in the United States 1790–1915. *Arno Press and The New York Times (New York 1968), p. 57.*

populations. Of the 50,000 blacks in the region, approximately one-half lived in New York, while New Jersey followed with 14,000, and Pennsylvania with slightly more than 10,000. The decline of slavery in the region is revealed by the fact that by 1790 there were approximately 14,000 free blacks, comprising about 28 percent of the total black population. This figure is a silent tribute to the unobtrusive but effective work of the antislavery groups that made capital out of the Revolutionary philosophy that was in vogue for a few years following the War for Independence.

By 1790 slavery in New England was dying rapidly. The 3,700 slaves in the region were a mere one-fourth of the total black population of more than 13,000. Indeed, some states, Vermont and Massachusetts, reported no slaves at all. Connecticut, though, was holding on tenaciously to a slave population, and the 2,600 slaves in the state constituted the bulk of the New England slave population. The time was not distant, however, when all the New England states would report that only free blacks lived within their borders.

Although neither Kentucky nor Tennessee had become states in 1790, they were being rapidly settled and were soon to qualify for statehood. Among the inhabitants who were being counted in the quest for the new status were blacks who had been taken there by the Virginians and Carolinians who made their way across the mountains. In 1790 there were more than 12,000 slaves in Kentucky, while Tennessee had 3,400. Together these two prospective states could count only 475 free blacks. The migration of slaves to these new regions set the pattern that became so well established in the nineteenth century.

The black population in 1790 was essentially rural. Some cities and towns, however, could point to a substantial black population. Among these was New York City, which was already known for its heterogeneous population. There were 3,252 blacks, of whom 2,184 were slaves and 1,078 were free. Philadelphia had 1,630 blacks, but only 210 of them were slaves. At the other extreme was Baltimore with 1,578 blacks, of whom only 323 were free. Only one American city could boast that it had no slaves: all of Boston's 761 blacks were free.

There was hardly any indication that the black population would decline in the years following the first decennial census. Indeed, forces were already in operation to fasten slavery on the country with greater permanency and to increase, at least temporarily, slave importations into the country. Ira Berlin has shown that, by the end of the eighteenth century, there were three distinct African-American subcultures—in the North, in the Chesapeake area, and in the deep South—each with its own diverse patterns of black adjustment to, and differentiation from, the dominant white social order. In 1790 the center of black population was twenty miles west-southwest of Petersburg, Dinwiddie County, Virginia. Growth and migration were to cause it to shift with every passing decade. And this phenomenon alone was enough to indicate that the black population was among the most thriving of any of the ethnic groups in America.

■ Slavery and the Industrial Revolution

In the years immediately following the treaty of independence of 1783, the areas where slaves were concentrated experienced a severe depression. Tobacco plantations were plagued by two evils: soil exhaustion and a glutted market. Rice and indigo production brought little profit to the planters of these commodities. The price of slaves was declining, and there was reason to believe that the institution would deteriorate. The planters, however, would not have it so, and they did everything they could to sustain their losses until there was a better day. They did not have long to wait. Already the system of producing cotton textiles was undergoing revolutionary changes in England, and with the invention of spinning and weaving machinery, the manufacturing process was so cheapened that the demand for cotton goods was greatly stimulated. In turn, the demand for cotton fiber to feed the newly developed machinery seemed insatiable, this at a time when the planters of the United States were in desperate need for something that would inject new life into the sluggish plantation system.

For many years the manufacturers of the world had regarded cotton as among the most satisfactory textile materials. Technological difficulties, however, had stood in the way of its being more extensively produced. Now that it could be spun and woven easily, the twofold problem of discovering a variety that could be more easily separated from the seed and of inventing a machine to do this work was all that was left to be solved before cotton could become the world's greatest textile. As early as 1786 planters on the Georgia-Carolina coast began to experiment with growing a long, silky sea-island fiber that was quite superior to the green-seed, short-staple variety that had been cultivated on a small scale for many years. They found it highly satisfactory, and even without machinery to separate the seed from the fiber a greater quantity could be produced because of the ease with which the operation was effected. South Carolinians and Georgians began to plant larger cotton crops and to use slaves not only to cultivate the crops but to separate the fiber from the seeds as well. The areas in which sea-island cotton would grow were limited, however, and until some method was developed by which short-staple cotton, which could flourish in a variety of places, could be seeded there could be no wholesale expansion of cotton culture throughout the South.

Southern planters confidently hoped that in the near future an invention would relieve them of their anxiety. In 1792 Georgia went so far as to appoint a commission to look into the possibility of inventing a cotton gin. In the following year a young Yankee schoolteacher, Eli Whitney, visited the South in search of a position. The talk concerning the difficulties of seeding cotton interested him greatly. He soon grasped the problem and set out to find a solution to it. Within a few days he had made a model which gave promise of being satisfactory. It was only a matter of weeks before the major mechanical difficulties had been mastered, and Whitney and his host, Phineas Miller, began to make plans for the commercial manufacture of cotton gins. Whitney vainly attempted to establish a monopoly over the manufacture of cotton gins, but his failure simply meant that a larger number of these machines would be available at lower prices.

Within a few years after the invention of the cotton gin, the South was on its way to making the economic transition that the new development induced. Since the cultivation of cotton required no large capital, many farmers, even the poorer ones, began to shift from the cultivation of rice, indigo, or tobacco to cotton. Production increased, new lands were cleared, and black labor could now be employed exclusively in the cultivation of the crop instead of in the tedious task of seeding cotton. Exports mounted rapidly, but for many years England and the other manufacturing countries continued to receive, at high prices, all the cotton that the United States could furnish. In the beginning, it seemed that all the Southern farmers would prosper under the stimulation of cotton cultivation. As the years passed, however, and as the more economically resourceful planters began to purchase additional land and slaves, those without capital found themselves at a disadvantage and were forced to yield to those planters who were in a position to carry out large-scale cultivation.

The invention of the cotton gin and the extension of the area of cotton cultivation ushered in a period of economic change in the South that in degree compared favorably with any changes in the history of agriculture. One of the most important manifestations of this change was the increased demand for black slaves. Not only was there now a great opportunity to use the slaves that many had kept against their better judgment, but there was an opportunity to use even more if they could be secured. Thus, in the closing years of the eighteenth century and the opening years of the nineteenth century, the importation of slaves into the United States continued to flourish. In 1803, for example, it was estimated that no less than 20,000 slaves were imported into Georgia and South Carolina. As though they were racing against time, the merchants of New England sought to supply the planters of the South with the precious human cargo, the importation of which was to be outlawed within a few years.

■ Trouble in the Caribbean

While the United States was making an effort to stabilize its political life and the South was desperately attempting to salvage its economic system, there were rumblings not far off that disturbed both the political and the economic equilibrium of the United States. When the French Revolution broke out in 1789, blacks in the French possessions looked toward the prospect of securing for themselves the same elements of freedom for which Frenchmen at home were fighting. On the island of St. Domingue, even the people on the eastern, or Spanish, end of the island sought the equality that the French Revolution promised. When the whites on the island opposed the extension of these rights to blacks, there occurred an uprising in August 1791 which in magnitude and intensity demonstrated the blacks' determination to secure freedom and equality. Blacks so ruthlessly killed their white masters that the National Assembly in France felt compelled to withdraw the rights that it had extended and to send troops to quell the disturbance. The blacks were not awed by the appearance of soldiers from France, and there ensued a bitter struggle that lasted for more than two years. No semblance of order was restored until the French Republic issued a decree granting freedom to all slaves who supported its cause.

The intrepid leader of the black forces in Haiti was Toussaint L'Ouverture. An able and experienced soldier, he cast his lot with the forces of the Republic in 1794. For six years he was the dominant figure on the island, serving in successively higher military positions. By 1800 he was at the height of his power. Napoleon, however, regarded Toussaint as an obstacle to his plan to create a great French empire in the New World. With Louisiana in his hands and with St. Domingue as a key point in the Caribbean area, he could dominate the entire Western Hemisphere, or a substantial portion of it. He therefore dispatched a large army of 25,000 men under General LeClerc to subdue the island. Although the French were successful, by a series of tricks, in capturing Toussaint and taking him to France, they were not successful in subduing the island. Yellow fever and the bitter determination of the followers of Toussaint to be free conspired to defeat the aims of Napoleon.

The effect of these events on the course of American history was extremely important. Of Toussaint, W. E. B. Du Bois said, "He rose to leadership through a bloody terror, which contrived a Negro 'problem' for the Western Hemisphere, intensified and defined the anti-slavery movement, became one of the causes, and probably the prime one, which led Napoleon to sell Louisiana for a song, and finally, through the interworking of all these effects, rendered more certain the final prohibition of the slave-trade by the United States in 1807." Americans were terrified at the news of what was happening in Haiti. For more than a decade beginning in 1791 many Americans were more concerned with events in Haiti than with the life-and-death struggle that was going on between France and England. Despite the fact that Southern states wanted more slaves, they were afraid to import them. In 1792 South Carolina found it inexpedient to allow blacks "from Africa, the West India Islands, or other places beyond the sea" to enter for two years, but many entered illegally. In 1794 North Carolina passed an act "to prevent future importation and bringing of slaves." Virginia and Maryland strengthened their nonimportation laws. Though the Middle Atlantic and New England states did not seem as disturbed over Haiti as their Southern neighbors, there were attempts by Quakers and other humanitarian groups to take advantage of the situation and to strengthen various aspects of antislavery legislation. It would not be too much to say that the revolution in the West Indies did as much as anything else to discourage the importation of slaves into the United States.

As early as 1790 several organizations, including the Yearly Meeting of Friends in New York and the Pennsylvania Abolition Society, presented memorials to Congress requesting immediate legislation against the slave trade. The violent opposition of Southern representatives prevented decisive action. The antislavery organizations continued their activities during the succeeding years. The news from the Caribbean had the effect of hastening action by Congress. In 1794 a bill seeking to prevent slave trade to foreign ports and to prevent the fitting out of foreign vessels for the slave trade in the United States ports was passed by the Senate and the House. This was no victory for the antislavery forces in the United States. Instead, it merely represented the fear of many citizens that the revolution of the Haitian blacks might spread to the United States.

Closely allied with the slave trade was the question of fugitive slaves.

Blacks from the Caribbean had escaped to the United States during the conflict in Haiti and were moving rather freely from place to place. Slaves were escaping from plantations during this troubled period as they had always done. If these trends continued, it was within the realm of possibility that disaffected blacks might attempt some desperate measures to overthrow the institution of slavery. It was deemed wise, therefore, to institute legislation to implement the constitutional provision regarding fugitive slaves. In 1793 the first fugitive slave law was enacted. It empowered the master of an interstate fugitive to seize the slave wherever found, take him or her before any federal or state magistrate in the vicinity, and obtain a certificate warranting the slave's removal to the state from which he or she had fled. This law allowed no trial by jury and required conviction on only the oral testimony of the claimant or on an affidavit certified by a magistrate of the state from which the slave was alleged to have fled. Various groups protested the passage of the act, but to no avail. Although it proved to be exceedingly difficult to enforce, the measure remained part of the federal law and thus, to many, a manifestation of national approval of the institution of slavery.

The purchase of Louisiana was connected with both the trouble in the Caribbean and the institution of slavery in the United States. Louisiana had already become a center of sugarcane cultivation, whether it was in the hands of the French or the Spanish. Both these European groups lived in New Orleans and had spread up the river banks to cultivate the rich lands of the Mississippi delta. Black slaves were introduced into these areas by Creole planters, and by the late eighteenth century some were being brought into Louisiana from the Caribbean. The acquisition of Louisiana by France in 1800 greatly disturbed the United States, since in 1795 the new republic had negotiated a satisfactory arrangement with Spain for navigation of the Mississippi River. Representatives of the United States attempted to secure from France the promise that Western farmers could continue to navigate the river. Instead, the French offered them the whole of Louisiana, which the United States purchased in 1803. Perhaps several reasons caused Napoleon to decide to sell Louisiana. One important reason was his failure to hold Haiti and the consequent dark prospects that existed for his erecting a great empire in the New World with Louisiana and Haiti as important pivotal points. Thus it was the blacks of Haiti who were, to a large degree, responsible for the acquisition of Louisiana by the United States. The purchase of this new land made possible the extension of cotton and sugar culture by planters of the Southern United States and the greater entrenchment of slavery in the region.

■ The Closing of the Slave Trade

Despite the state laws prohibiting it, the African slave trade to the United States continued to flourish during the first decade of the national government. The slave interests were in a curious dilemma. On the one hand they feared the wholesale importation of raw and unruly blacks from Africa or the revolutionary and resourceful blacks from the Caribbean, while on the other hand they were in desperate need of a larger number of slaves to cultivate the cotton that was now in such great demand. The practicality, if not the venality, of merchants and planters compelled them to decide in favor of continued importation, hoping that the safeguards erected by the national and state governments would stem any tide of insurrection that might develop in the United States. In defiance of local laws, New England traders carried on an extensive traffic, while Southern planters were willing to receive slaves from whatever source possible.

Early in the nineteenth century antislavery groups resumed their efforts to secure stringent federal legislation against the slave trade. In January 1800, the free blacks of Philadelphia led the way by requesting Congress to revise the laws on the slave trade and on fugitives. When South Carolina reopened her ports to the trade in 1803, the antislavery forces began to press for action. Resolutions were introduced in the following Congress condemning the slave trade, but no conclusive steps were taken. In 1804 an attempt was made to prevent the importation of slaves into Louisiana, but the resolution presenting this matter received scant attention.

The question of the slave trade was brought dramatically before the country in December 1805, when Senator Stephen R. Bradley of Vermont introduced a bill to prohibit the slave trade after January 1, 1808. After a second reading, consideration of the measure was postponed. In February 1806, Representative Barnabas Bidwell of Massachusetts introduced a similar measure, but nothing was done about it. In his message to Congress on December 2, 1806, President Jefferson called the attention of Congress to the approaching date on which the slave trade could be prohibited. He suggested that measures be taken to "prevent expeditions to Africa that could not be completed before January 1, 1808." On March 2, 1807, the law prohibiting the African slave trade was passed. Persons convicted of violating the act were to be fined and imprisoned. The fines ranged from $800 for knowingly buying illegally imported blacks to $20,000 for equipping a slaver. The disposition of the imported blacks was left to the legislatures of the states. Finally, coastwise trade of slaves was prohibited if it was carried on in vessels of less than forty tons. Every provision of the bill was vehemently debated by representatives of slaveholding and nonslaveholding interests.

Antislavery interests both in England and the United States rejoiced in the year 1807. England had outlawed the slave trade, and in the same year the United States had followed. There was little real reason for rejoicing in the United States, however, for from the beginning, the law went unenforced. Responsibility for the enforcement of the act fell first to the secretary of the treasury, then to the secretary of the navy. At times, even the Department of State was given some duties in connection with its enforcement. In the midst of such shifting of responsibility it is not surprising to find the law poorly enforced. Some Southern states reluctantly passed supplementary acts disposing of illegally imported Africans, while others enacted no such legislation at all. Violations of the law were numerous. New England shipmasters, Middle Atlantic merchants, and Southern planters all disregarded the federal and state legislation when they found it expedient to do so. Those who had an unselfish interest in the closing of the slave trade could say, within a few years after 1808, that hardly anything had happened to the nefarious traffic except that it had been driven underground. The first underground railroad was not that established by abolitionists to transport slaves to freedom but the one used by merchants and others to introduce more blacks into slavery.

■ The Search for Independence

The Industrial Revolution in England, the invention of the cotton gin, the extension of slavery into the new territories, and the persistence of the slave trade into the nineteenth century all had the effect of establishing slavery in the United States on a more permanent basis than ever before. As the nineteenth century opened, there seemed little prospect that slavery would ever cease to exist in the United States. The atmosphere in which blacks lived, whether North or South, was charged with the permanent character of slavery in the United States. Even in the New England states, where laws were putting an end to the institution, blacks could not express much optimism or any great faith in the future, for it was well known that New England merchants were still taking slaves into the South and there was still no great moral indignation against the institution except in isolated areas and groups. Beginning with the Revolutionary period blacks had to seek ways not only of participating in the struggle to secure independence for their country but also to secure for themselves a measure of independence in an atmospehere laden with subordination, subservience, and disrespect for their individuality. This most difficult task involved the effort to forge separate institutions. This phase of black life and history constituted a significant step in the history of adjustment and acculturation in America.

One of the first blacks to make the search for intellectual and spiritual independence was Jupiter Hammon, a slave on Long Island. Growing into manhood during the years when the Wesleyan revival was strong both in England and America, Hammon was greatly influenced by the writings of Charles Wesley and William Cowper. In 1761 he published "An Evening Thought. Salvation by Christ, with Penitential Cries." In 1778 he published a twenty-one stanza poem "To Miss Phillis Wheatley." Other poems and prose pieces appeared in the next two decades. In "An Address to the Negroes of the State of New York," published in 1787, Hammon showed that he felt it his personal duty to bear slavery patiently, but at the same

PHILLIS WHEATLEY. Born in Africa about 1753 and brought to America as a young girl, Wheatley received wide recognition during her lifetime for her essays and poetry, as well as her mastery of Western manners and morals. In 1773 her owners manumitted her and she visited England, where her first book was published. *(The Schomburg Center For Research In Black Culture, The New York Public Library.)*

time he said that it was an evil system and that young blacks should be manumitted. He lived to see his master write a will ordering that certain of his slaves be set free at the age of twenty-eight, and in 1799, the year before his death, Hammon could rejoice that the state of New York had enacted legislation looking to the gradual emancipation of all slaves within the state.

BENJAMIN BANNEKER AND HIS VIRGINIA ALMANACK FOR 1794. Banneker, perhaps the most accomplished black in the early national period, published almanacs, was an astronomer, and served as a member of the commission to define the boundary line and lay out the streets of the District of Columbia. *(The Schomburg Center For Research In Black Culture, The New York Public Library.)*

Perhaps the best-known black of the period was Phillis Wheatley, born in Africa about 1753 and brought to America when still a little girl. In Boston she became the personal maid of Susannah Wheatley and apparently received kindly treatment and an opportunity to cultivate her mind. She rapidly learned to read the Bible and developed an appreciation for history, astronomy, geography, and the Latin classics. In 1770 her first poem, "On the Death of the Reverend George Whitefield," appeared. In 1773 she was manumitted and sent to England for her health. She met the Countess of Huntingdon, to whom one of her first poems was addressed, and rapidly gained popularity. Before leaving England, arrangements were made to have her first book published, *Poems on Various Subjects, Religious and Moral.* Upon her return she composed "His Excellency General Washington," "Liberty and Peace," and numerous other poems before her death in 1784. Phillis Wheatley attempted to write lyric poetry. She was not concerned with the problems of blacks or the country. Even the poem to General Washington is largely impersonal, while her "Liberty and Peace" is only remotely connected with the struggle against England. Her writings are perhaps a good example of the search for independence through the method of escape, which was to become a favorite device of blacks of a later century.

While Gustavus Vassa lived as much in England, Montserrat, and Jamaica as in the United States, the narrative of his life was so frequently printed and read in America that he can be said to represent the growing independence of spirit that blacks were manifesting at the end of the eighteenth century. Vassa was born in Benin in 1745. At the age of eleven he was kidnapped and taken to America. After working on a Virginia plantation he became the servant of a British naval officer. Later, while in the service of a Philadelphia merchant, he saved the money with which he purchased his freedom. Then he went to England, where he made his home between his extensive journeys. He joined in the antislavery movement, and in 1790 he presented to Parliament a petition for suppression of the slave trade. In 1789 he published, in two volumes, *The Interesting Narrative of the Life of Oloudah Equiano, or Gustavus Vassa.* It was immediately successful, and within five years eight editions had been issued. There can be no doubt about Vassa's resentment of slavery, for in his narrative he vigorously condemns Christians for their enslavement of blacks. Only one who had achieved a measure of personal independence could have condemned slavery in the following language:

> O, ye nominal Christians! might not an African ask you—Learned you this from your God, who says unto you, Do unto all men as you would men should do unto you? Is it not enough that we are torn from our country and friends, to toil for your luxury and lust of gain? Must every tender feeling be likewise sacrificed to your avarice? . . . Why are parents to lose their children, brothers their sisters, or husbands their wives? Surely, this is a new refinement in cruelty, which, while it has no advantage to atone for it, thus aggravates distress, and adds fresh horrors even to the wretchedness of slavery.

Perhaps the most accomplished black in the early national period was Benjamin Banneker. Born in 1731 in Maryland, of thrifty and industrious parents, Banneker attended a private school open to whites and blacks near Baltimore and developed a keen interest in science and mathematics. While still a young man he astounded his family and neighbors by constructing a clock from wooden materials. This display of mechanical genius attracted the attention of George Ellicott, a Quaker, who had moved into the neighborhood to establish a flour mill. Banneker frequently visited the Ellicott mills during their construction, and his general knowledge of the mathematical and engineering problems drew him and Ellicott closer together. Soon, Ellicott began to lend Banneker books on mathematics and astronomy. Within a few weeks Banneker had not only mastered the material in the books, but he had even discovered several errors in the calculations of the authors. By 1789 he had become so proficient in astronomy that he could predict a solar eclipse with considerable accuracy.

In 1791 Banneker began issuing his almanacs, a worthy undertaking that lasted until 1802. Among the prominent men attracted by this "black Poor Richard" was James McHenry, later the secretary of war in the cabinet of

---

Benjamin Banneker Writes to Thomas Jefferson—1791

Sir, I have long been convinced that if your love for yourselves, and for those inestimable laws, which preserved to you the rights of human nature, was founded on sincerity, you could not but be solicitous, that every individual, of whatever rank or distinction, might with you equally enjoy the blessings thereof; neither could you rest satisfied short of the most active effusion of your exertions, in order to the promotion from any state of degradation, to which the unjustifiable cruelty and barbarism of men have reduced them. . . .

Benjamin Banneker to Thomas Jefferson, August 19, 1791. Early American Imprints (Microprint), 1639–1800.

President John Adams. Through McHenry, Banneker was able to establish a number of important connections with officials of the national government. McHenry said that Banneker's work "was begun and finished without the least information or assistance from any person, or from any other books." He added that Banneker was "fresh proof that the powers of the mind are disconnected with the color of the skin, or, in other words, a striking contradiction to Mr. [David] Hume's doctrine, that the Negroes are naturally inferior to the whites, and unsusceptible of attainments in arts and sciences."

Banneker sent a manuscript copy of his first almanac to Thomas Jefferson, and in the accompanying letter he made a strong appeal for the exercise of a more liberal attitude toward blacks. He pointed to his own achievements as proof that the "train of absurd and false ideas and opinions which so generally prevails with respect to the Negro should now be eradicated." Jefferson warmly praised the almanac and sent it to Condorcet, the secretary of the Academy of Sciences in Paris, for, as he told Banneker, he considered it "a document to which your whole race had a right for its justifications against the doubts which have been entertained of them."

The most distinguished honor that Banneker received was his appointment to serve with the commission to define the boundary lines and lay out the streets of the District of Columbia. It was perhaps at the suggestion of his friend George Ellicott, himself a member of the commission, that Banneker's name was submitted to President Washington by Jefferson. When he arrived in the federal territory with Major L'Enfant and Ellicott, the Georgetown *Weekly Ledger* described him as "an Ethiopian whose abilities as surveyor and astronomer already prove that Mr. Jefferson's concluding that that race of men were void of mental endowment was without foundation." After his

PAUL CUFFEE AND HIS BRIG, "THE TRAVELLER." Cuffee, a successful businessman, derived his wealth from shipbuilding, a maritime trading fleet, real estate, and landholdings. Seeking to open new opportunities for freedom and economic mobility to his fellow blacks in the United States, he made visits to Africa and provided considerable financial support for African-American colonizationists. *(The Schomburg Center For Research In Black Culture, The New York Public Library.)*

work with the commission, he returned to his home in Maryland, resumed work on his almanacs, and continued his astronomical investigations.

The disastrous wars of 1793 greatly disturbed Banneker, and he devoted considerable attention to devising a means of putting an end to all wars. In his almanac in 1793 he carried a lengthy article by Benjamin Rush, who pointed out that one of the objections to the new government was that it did not have an office in the president's cabinet "for promoting and preserving perpetual peace in our country." Rush proposed the establishment of a secretary of peace, "who shall be perfectly free from all the present absurd and vulgar prejudices of Europe upon the subject of government." There can be no doubt that Banneker published the article by Rush because he subscribed so enthusiastically to the views of Rush on the subject of peace. He often opened the pages of his almanac to those who had constructive suggestions to make for the improvement of mankind. His life was a search for independence through his concern with problems that transcended race and even nation.

A distinguished contemporary of Banneker was James Derham, generally regarded as the first physician of African descent in the United States. Born into slavery in Philadelphia in 1762, Derham's master during his boyhood was a physician who taught him to read and write and to serve as his medical assistant. Later, during the War for Independence, Derham was the property of a British physician from whom he learned a great deal more about the practice of medicine. At the close of the war, he was purchased by a physician in New Orleans under whose tutelage he completed his medical training. He then purchased his freedom and set up his own practice, which soon was large and profitable. Fluent in French, Spanish, and English, Derham's reputation as an able physician spread to many groups. Benjamin Rush regarded Derham as an accomplished and learned practitioner from whom he himself learned much.

Among those who were searching for economic independence and group self-respect during the post-Revolutionary period, Paul Cuffe was one of the most outstanding. Very early in his life he developed an interest in commerce, and at sixteen years of age, in 1775, he secured employment on a whaling vessel. In the following year, during his second voyage, he was captured by the British and detained in New York for three months. During the war he and his brother refused to pay taxes in Massachusetts on the grounds that they were denied the franchise. Shortly thereafter Massachusetts passed a law allowing free blacks liable to taxation all the privileges belonging to other citizens. In 1780 Cuffe began to build ships of his own and to engage in commerce. As profits mounted, he expanded his seagoing activities and built larger vessels. By 1806 he owned one large ship, two brigs, and several smaller vessels, besides considerable property in houses and land. After joining the Society of Friends he became deeply interested, along with many other Quakers, in the welfare of blacks and wanted to engage in some activity that would improve their lot. In 1811 he went to Sierra Leone in his own vessel to investigate the possibilities of taking free blacks back to Africa. The war with England in the following year prevented his carrying out his plans. In 1815, however, he took thirty-eight blacks to Africa at an expense of $3000 or $4000 to himself. He learned, as colonizationists of a later day were to learn, that the expense of taking blacks back to Africa was so great as to be prohibitive.

The individual strivings of Jupiter Hammon, Phillis Wheatley, Gustavus Vassa, Benjamin Banneker, and Paul Cuffe not only represent the effort of blacks to secure a measure of independence for themselves in the post-Revolutionary period but are examples of the movement of Americans toward intellectual and economic self-sufficiency that was so characteristic of the period. Indeed, it can be said that these African Americans were, in a sense, leading the way since they overcame both the degraded position of their race and the psychological and intellectual disadvantage that all Americans of the period suffered. Their search for independence was matched only by the efforts of groups of blacks who found it necessary to forge separate institutions for their people during the same period.

In their efforts to elevate themselves intellectually in the post-Revolutionary period, blacks benefited from the general trend to establish and improve

Philadelphia Blacks Support Cuffe's African Colonization Plan—1815

Whereas Capt. Paul Cuffe, a citizen of the state of Massachusetts, made application to the Congress of the United States, at the session of 1814, for permission to make a voyage to Africa, for the purpose of aiding in the civilization and improvement of the inhabitants of that country and also to promote this desirable object, to take with him a few sober and industrious families, the situation of publick affairs at that period being unfavorable to the design, his proposition failed of success, but now under the blessing of Divine Providence, the causes of obstruction are removed, and he is again preparing to prosecute his voyage, accompanied by two families of this city, who have agreed to visit Africa and settle there.

The African Institution of Philadelphia, established for the promotion of this plan, feel it to be a duty to state, that it cordially unites with Paul Cuffe, in his disinterested and benevolent undertaking, and recommends the families of Anthony Survance and Samuel Wilson to the Friendly Society of Sierra Leone, as persons of good moral character, having satisfactorily settled their outward affairs as far as appears. The Institution likewise solicits on behalf of the adventurers, the friendly notice of all those among whom they may come.

Signed on behalf of the African Institution of Philadelphia

James Forten, Pres't
Russel Parrott, sec'ry

Poulson's American Daily Advertiser, September 20, 1815, from Lamont D. Thomas, *Rise to Be a People: A Biography of Paul Cuffe* (Urbana, Ill., 1986), p. 97.

schools in the new republic. There was also sentiment in favor of educating blacks, which the various abolition and manumission societies expressed before the turn of the century. The New England and Middle Atlantic states were especially active in this area. Whites in Boston were teaching black children both privately and in public institutions. In 1798 a separate school for black children was established by a white teacher in the home of Primus Hall, a prominent African American. Two years later blacks asked the city of Boston for a separate school, but the citizens refused. The blacks established the school anyway, and employed two Harvard men as instructors. The school continued to flourish for many years. Finally, in 1820, the city of Boston opened an elementary school for black children.

One of the best-known schools for blacks during the period was the New York African Free School established in 1787 by the Manumission Society.

When it began it had forty students, and the number never exceeded sixty in its first decade of existence. The opposition to the school was at first keen, but in 1800 constructive interest in the school was evident. New impetus for its continued growth came in 1810 when the state required masters to teach all slave children to read the Scriptures. By 1820 the institution was accommodating more than 500 black children.

New Jersey began educating black children in 1777. By 1801 there had been short-lived schools set up in Burlington, Salem, and Trenton. In addition Quakers and other religious and humanitarian groups were teaching black children privately. As early as 1774 the Quakers of Philadelphia established a school for black children, and after the war, thanks to funds provided by philanthropists like Anthony Benezet, the program was enlarged. In 1787 a school was built, and ten years later there were no less than seven schools for blacks in Philadelphia. This interest in the development of black education continued into the nineteenth century.

The interest in the South was not nearly as great. In 1801 a member of the Abolition Society of Wilmington, Delaware, conducted a school for black children on the first day of each week and taught reading, writing, and arithmetic. In 1816 a school and library were established with a black teacher. A few years later an academy for the instruction of young black women was established. In Maryland plans were made late in the eighteenth century for the opening of an academy, but the school never materialized. In Virginia, however, schools were set up in Richmond, Petersburg, and Norfolk. Quakers like Robert Pleasants offered land and money for the development of schools in Virginia and the Carolinas, but the insurrection of 1800 so frightened Southern planters that further expansion of the education program was discouraged. In the nineteenth century blacks in Southern states had to content themselves, for the most part, with clandestine schools and private teachers.

It was perhaps in the area of religion that African Americans showed the most determined efforts to secure real independence in the post-Revolutionary period. For a time, it seemed that the churches of the embryonic United States would insist upon complete integration of blacks into the religious life of the nation and would spearhead the attack against the institution of slavery. In 1784, for example, the Methodists declared that slavery was "contrary to the golden laws of God" and gave their members twelve months to liberate their slaves. This position proved to be somewhat premature, however, as Virginia and other Southern states forced a suspension of the resolution. In 1789 the Baptists said that slavery was a "violent depredation of the rights of nature and inconsistent with a republican government." Gradually, however, they were forced to recede from this position. After the war many churches accepted blacks, but whites were afraid that too liberal a policy would be disastrous to the effective control of slavery. Black ministers and church officials, it was thought, would exercise too much authority over their slave communicants and would perhaps cause trouble on the plantations.

RICHARD ALLEN. Allen was the leading figure in events that produced the independent black church movement and led to the establishment of the African Methodist Episcopal Church. He served as one of the early bishops of the A.M.E. Church. *(The Schomburg Center For Research In Black Culture, The New York Public Library.)*

American churches were having their own difficulties, and they found little time to devote any attention to the problems of blacks. The Toryism of a great number of the Anglican clergy caused many Americans to insist upon church disestablishment. Every denomination, except Roman Catholicism, moreover, was busy organizing a wing of its church that would be entirely separate from its European sponsor, and even the Catholics of the United States were to be set apart and controlled by a special Prefect Apostolic. These preoccupations tended to crowd the problem of blacks off the church scene and were in part the cause of the establishment of racially separate churches.

During the War for Independence, black Baptist churches began to spring up. George Liele, an industrious and resourceful black leader, founded a Baptist church in Savannah in 1779 before he finally left the country and settled in Jamaica. The work in Georgia was continued by his understudy, Andrew Bryan, who preached to whites as well as blacks. At the end of the war whites sought to close the church by whipping the members and imprisoning Bryan, but his benevolent master supported him, and finally Bryan's church became the nucleus for the organization of black Baptists in Georgia. Virginia blacks organized Baptist churches at Petersburg in 1776, at Richmond in 1780, and at Williamsburg in 1785. In some of these efforts they had the cooperation of white ministers.

It was in Northern communities that blacks went farthest in establishing independent churches. The best example of this trend was the work of Richard Allen and his followers in Philadelphia. This prospective leader demonstrated his industry and determination by saving enough money with which to purchase his freedom from his Delaware master in 1777, the year in which he also was converted. Within a few years he was preaching and winning the favor of Bishop Asbury. In 1786 he moved to Philadelphia, where he began to hold prayer meetings for his own people. His proposal to set up a separate place of worship for blacks was opposed by whites and some blacks. It was only after the officials of St. George's Church, where he frequently preached, proposed to segregate the large number of blacks who came to hear him that it became clear to him and others that blacks should have a separate church. The die was cast when, on one occasion, officials pulled Allen, Absalom Jones, and William White from their knees during prayer. Allen, with the help of Jones, immediately organized the independent Free African Society. Though Jones did not continue to cooperate with him and in 1801 became the first black Episcopal priest, Allen was able to organize and dedicate the Bethel Church in 1794. In 1799 Bishop Asbury ordained him deacon, and later he was elevated to the status of an elder. His church became known as the Bethel African Methodist Episcopal Church.

Branches of the AME church began to spring up in Baltimore, Wilmington, and various Pennsylvania and New Jersey towns, and a number of able persons, such as Daniel Coker, Nicholson Gilliard, and Morris Brown, came to Allen's aid. The church grew in strength until by 1816 it was possible to bind the various congregations together in a formal organization. The conference chose Daniel Coker as its bishop, but he resigned and Allen was elected to fill the position. It adopted a book of discipline similar to that of the Wesleyans and was thus launched on a career that was to make the AME church the leading organization among black Methodists. By 1820 there were 4,000 black Methodists in Philadelphia alone, while in the Baltimore district there were almost 2,000. The organization immediately spread as far west as Pittsburgh and as far south as Charleston. Only the strong opposition to black organizations, brought forth by the Vesey insurrection of 1822 (see Chapter 8), served to check the growth of black Methodism in the Southern states.

The white Methodists of New York had much the same attitude toward their black fellows as did their counterparts in Philadelphia. The result was a withdrawal of blacks from the John Street Methodist Episcopal Zion Church and the establishment of the African Methodist Episcopal Zion Church in 1796. Leading this movement were Peter Williams, James Varick, elected the first bishop in 1822, George Collins, and Christopher Rush. They could find no one in either the Episcopal or the Methodist church who would ordain and consecrate their elders, and finally they had to do it themselves. Overcoming schisms within and opposition without, the church was sufficiently stable by 1822 to elect a bishop and to set up a program of expansion.

The same trend toward independent organizations manifested itself among the Baptists. In 1809 thirteen black members of a white Baptist church in Philadelphia were dismissed to form a church of their own. Under the leadership of Reverend Burrows, a former slave, it became an important institution among the blacks of that community. The black Baptists of Boston, under the leadership of Reverend Thomas Paul, organized their church in 1809. At about the same time, he was assisting in organizing the church in New York that later came to be known as the Abyssinian Baptist Church. In each instance organization was brought about as a result of the separation of blacks from white congregations.

This establishment of separate houses of worship for African Americans, as inconsistent as it may seem with the teachings of the religion that they professed, gave blacks an unusual opportunity to develop leadership. Cut off from participation in the political life of the community and enjoying only very limited educational opportunities, their religious institutions served as a training ground for many types of activities. Although blacks frequently took the initiative in bringing about separation, it appears that such steps were not taken until it was obvious that they were not welcome in white churches. This keen sensitivity to mistreatment and the consequent organization of separate and independent religious organizations of their own were to be the reason for the church occupying such an important place in black life in the nineteenth and twentieth centuries.

Not only were blacks organizing separate churches, but they were also establishing other organizations of a benevolent and fraternal nature. On March 6, 1775, a British army lodge of Freemasons attached to a regiment under General Gage near Boston initiated fifteen blacks, including Prince Hall, a young man who had come to the mainland from Barbados ten years earlier. Hall was a minister and a recognized leader and spokesman of his people. He and his black brothers sought permission from white Americans to establish a chapter of black Masons, but their plea was rejected. In 1784 they applied to the Grand Lodge of England, and a warrant was immediately granted. The organization was not perfected, however, until 1787, with Hall as the master of African Lodge No. 459, located in Boston. In 1792 a black Grand Lodge was organized, with Hall as grand master. Five years later he issued a license to thirteen blacks, who had been initiated in England and Ireland, to set up a lodge in Philadelphia, and another was organized in Providence. Gradually, black Masonry spread over the land as three Grand Lodges came into existence by 1815. Although there was serious objection to black Masons in the beginning, white Masons were visiting the black lodges within a few years and cooperating in a number of ways.

In 1796 the African Society was organized by forty-four blacks in Boston. It declared its objectives to be benevolent and asserted that it would take "no one into the Society who shall commit any injustice or outrage against the laws of their country." It is said that this and similar organizations did much to bind blacks together and give them the experience of leadership and cooperation that was to mean much in a later day. They early sought integration into the political, social, and economic life of the nation. Having been generally rejected, there was no alternative except to forge out of their limited background and training institutions of their own. It is significant, moreover, that in the case of these institutions, just as in the case of individuals, considerable effort was made to share in the general development of the country and to contribute to its growth. The African American search for independence at the turn of the century was essentially, therefore, a struggle to achieve status in the evolving American civilization.

CHAPTER 7

Blacks and Manifest Destiny

■ Frontier Influences

Even before the turn of the century there were unmistakable evidences of profound economic and social changes taking place on the American scene. After 1800 the signs were much more discernible. Already there was talk about industrialization in the United States, and American businesspeople envied developments in England and Europe. Europeans were beginning to resume their migrations to the New World, once more hopeful about the bright future it held for them. The land beyond the areas of settlement was beckoning new settlers and began to exercise an influence on American life that seemed to increase with every passing year. This land beyond, the frontier land, rapidly became an influence in the evolution of the institution of slavery and, therefore, in the history of blacks in America.

In the early nineteenth century the United States could appraise its Western lands as one of its most valuable assets, especially after the purchase of Louisiana in 1803. Although it would be years before this area would be settled, Americans and Europeans were rapidly moving into the area beyond the mountains. Young, adventurous people from the seaboard states and Scotch-Irish and Germans from the Old World pushed back the frontier and became a part of the new states that were added to the American union.

Many of the settlers in the new West were affiliated with religions that emphasized equality and brotherly love, and those who were not ardent believers were without the means considered necessary to build a civilization based on slavery. Thus, a spirit of freedom was dominant on the frontier, but it was destined to be rendered unimportant and ineffective by the economic and social forces at work in the older states. Some residents of the seaboard states became attracted to the new lands because of their inability to adjust to the old environment. Others found it impossible to satisfy their economic needs in the areas already settled, where competition was keen and where the better opportunities were in the hands of a relative few. Still others, many of whom belonged to the upper class, sought new lands on which to grow the cotton for which there was now such a great demand. Frequently this last group had resources, occasionally slaves, with which to dominate the economic and social life of the frontier and to change the character of life there. The frontier, which had formerly been the haven to which social malcontents escaped and to which economic "ne'er do wells" retreated, now became the battleground on which lovers of freedom fought those who sought to entrench the institution of slavery.

It was not possible for the lovers of freedom to win their battle against the slaveholders. The Industrial Revolution and the invention of the cotton gin had already determined the course of events on the American frontier. The ideals of freedom succumbed before the powerful forces demanding slavery, and the attractive lands of the Southern Gulf states made inevitable the establishment of a cotton kingdom based on slavery. At first the frontier settlers fought the whole system of the East, but as the prospects of enrichment for all appeared, even they gradually gave their support to the institution.

Something may be said, moreover, of the manner in which frontier influences may have assisted in the westward march of slavery. The sentiment in favor of freedom and democracy in the West came as much from a new type of settler—German, Scotch-Irish, etc.—as it did from a transformation of the character of the people who moved from the seaboard to the back country. The greater portion of those who moved from the Atlantic coastal states were committed to the institution of slavery and, when possible, demonstrated this commitment by bringing slaves with them. If the spirit of freedom affected them at all, it was in the direction of confirming their right to control the lives of others and to engage in a ruthless exploitation of natural and human resources that was sanctioned by the frontier. The ideal of the West was not so much, as Frederick Jackson Turner, a historian of the frontier, has suggested, the right of everyone to rise to the full measure of his or her own stature. It was the right of everyone to take advantage of every opportunity that presented itself to gain the ends he or she desired and to ignore the basic ethical restraints that would have made some distinction between liberty and license. It was conceivable, therefore, that the frontier, with its attractive land and its spirit of ruthless freedom, may actually have encouraged the westward march of slavery in the early part of the nineteenth century.

■ Black Pioneers in the Westward March

All too frequently, students of history overlook the role of African Americans in the exploration and settlement of the American West. Whenever white Americans undertook the task of winning the West, there were black Americans, slave and free, who were involved in the process. Thus, when Meriwether Lewis and William Clark set out in 1803 under orders from President Jefferson, to explore the Louisiana Territory recently purchased from France, Clark took with him his trusted slave, York. A large and powerful man, York contributed to the success of the expedition by befriending and entertaining the Indians and providing sustenance for the explorers through his considerable skill in hunting and fishing. Upon completion of the expedition Clark emancipated York, and legend has it that York returned to the Western interior where he became a chief in an Indian tribe.

In the immensely profitable fur trade that followed in the wake of the Lewis and Clark expedition, there were black trappers who quite frequently were the most reliable liaison between white entrepreneurs and the Indians. While their reliability and integrity have often suffered at the hands of many recognized historians of the West, their presence and indeed their contributions can hardly be denied. In the 1820s, for example, Edward Rose served as a guide, hunter, and interpreter for the Missouri Fur Company. Despite the fact that Washington Irving was among those who spoke of his bad character and reputation, a contemporary, Col. Henry Leavenworth, wrote in 1823 that Rose had resided among the Indians for several years, "knew their language, and they were much attached to him." Leavenworth and, more recently, Kenneth W. Porter, have spoken of his invaluable services in the fur-trading activities in the West.

In the Minnesota Territory several blacks became prominent as trappers and traders. Among them was Pierre Bonga, a trusted slave of a Canadian fur trapper for the North West Company. Bonga was a skillful interpreter and did much of the negotiating with the Chippewas for his company. His son, George, became even more proficient, having learned English, French, Chippewa, and several other Indian languages. As an assistant and interpreter for Governor Lewis Cass of the Michigan Territory, George Bonga negotiated treaties with the Indians even while working as a voyageur for the American Fur Company. In time he became a free man and a "prominent trader of wealth and consequence." According to William L. Katz, Bonga Township in Cass County, Michigan, is named for his family.

Easily the most intrepid and remarkable of the black explorers of the American West was James P. Beckwourth. Born in 1798 of racially mixed parentage, Beckwourth served an apprenticeship to a St. Louis blacksmith. Desiring more freedom, he fled westward and secured employment with the Rocky Mountain Fur Company. Soon he became an accomplished wilderness fighter, equally skilled in the use of the gun, bowie knife, and tomahawk. In 1824 he was adopted by the Crow Indians, became their beloved "Morning

Star," and married the chief's daughter. He led the Crows in numerous bloody raids and, rising to the position of chief, was known as "Bloody Arm." He had a varied career, serving as a scout in the third Seminole war in Florida and trapping and prospecting for gold in California. In 1850 he discovered the pass in the Sierra Nevada near Reno that still bears his name.

There were others, including John Marsant and John Stewart, who served as missionaries to the Indians. Among other African Americans who participated in the westward march were those who had been emancipated by John Randolph of Virginia and who settled in Ohio; those who migrated from Northampton County, North Carolina, and settled in Indiana; and the celebrated sculptress Edmonia Lewis, part Chippewa, who attended Oberlin College before moving on to Boston, where she studied the art for which she later became famous. There were indeed hundreds of others—some obscure and others well known, at least in their time—who left their mark as black contributors in the winning of the West.

■ The War of 1812

The westward march was not seriously checked by the diplomatic stress and strain of the early nineteenth century or by the war in which it culminated. Indeed, it may be said that the War of 1812 was to some extent a part of the expansionist program of those who were moving westward. There were controversies over the impressment of American sailors by the British and the violation of neutral rights, but there was also the possibility that a war would result in the acquisition of new lands. If the newly acquired lands lay to the north, they could attract Northern settlers who otherwise might go into the emerging cotton kingdom and obstruct the extension of slavery. If, perchance, the expansionists could acquire more lands in the Southwest, it would help to satisfy the appetites of an economic system that was already showing signs of insatiability. In either case, a victorious war would encourage the extension of slavery, and the warhawks and expansionists knew it.

When war finally came in 1812, blacks had an opportunity once more to serve their country. The number who served, however, remained small, perhaps because the areas from which they naturally would have come— New England and the Middle Atlantic states—showed little enthusiasm for the war. There seemed to be no serious objections to blacks' serving in the armed forces of the United States, but there was little inclination to recruit them. New York, however, in 1814, passed an act providing for the raising of two regiments of men of color. Each regiment was to consist of slightly more than 1,000 men, who were to receive the same pay as other soldiers. If slaves enlisted with the permission of their masters, they were to receive their freedom at the end of the war. Doubtless these black soldiers served faithfully, for in 1854 at the New York State Convention of the Soldiers of

1812, a resolution was passed asking Congress to provide the officers, men, and their widows with a liberal annuity "and that such provisions should extend to and include both the Indian and African race . . . who enlisted or served in that war, and who joined with the white man in defending our rights and maintaining our independence."

Scattered through the white units were blacks who served largely in menial capacities. Some, however, fought gallantly, and the records testify to their heroism. One of the outstanding soldiers in the Battle of North Point was William Burleigh, a Philadelphia black. When the city of Washington was taken, Philadelphia and other Eastern cities were alarmed over the possibility of suffering the same fate. The Vigilance Committee of Philadelphia called on three leading black citizens, James Forten, Bishop Richard Allen, and Absalom Jones, and asked that blacks help erect adequate defenses for the city. More than 2,500 blacks met in the statehouse yard, went to Grays Ferry, and worked almost continuously for two days, after which they received the praise of a grateful city. A battalion of blacks was organized in Philadelphia and was on the verge of marching to the front when peace was announced.

A large number of blacks were enrolled in the navy, frequently without reference to race. It is estimated that at least one-tenth of the crews of the fleet on the Upper Lakes were blacks. Capt. Oliver H. Perry was not satisfied with the men, "blacks, soldiers, and boys," that were sent to him. Commodore Chauncey cautioned Perry that he should be proud of whomever he received and added that the fifty blacks on his ship were among the best men he had. Later, after the Battle of Lake Erie, Perry gave unstinted praise to the black members of his crew and declared that "they seemed absolutely insensible to danger." Other naval officers spoke of the gallantry of black seamen. Nathaniel Shaler, the commander of the *Governor Tompkins,* said that the name of John Johnson, a black seaman on his ship, should be registered in the book of fame. As Johnson lay dying after he had been struck by a twenty-four pound shot, he exclaimed, "Fire away my boys; no haul a color down." Another black, John Davis, who was struck in much the same way, begged to be thrown overboard, saying he was only in the way of the others.

It was with Gen. Andrew Jackson that blacks performed their most effective services during the War of 1812. Jackson, needing to augment his forces in the autumn of 1814, called upon the free blacks of Louisiana to answer the appeal from their country. He confessed that the policy of the United States in barring blacks from the service had been a mistake. He promised that all blacks who enlisted would receive the same pay and bounty as white soldiers and that although their officers would be white, their noncommissioned officers would be chosen from among them. Shortly before the Battle of New Orleans, after several units of black soldiers had been recruited and had served in the preliminary campaigns, Jackson told them that in their performance they had surpassed his hopes. He promised that the president would be informed of their conduct and that the "voice of the representatives of the American nation shall applaud your valor, as your general now praises your ardor."

In the Battle of Chalmette Plains, commonly known as the Battle of New Orleans, black soldiers occupied a position of strategic importance. They were very near Jackson's main forces—on the left bank of the Mississippi River, just at the right of the advancing left column of the British. One battalion, under Major Lacoste, was composed of men of color from New Orleans and numbered about 280. The other, under Major Daquin, was composed of blacks from St. Domingue and numbered about 150. These black soldiers erected the cotton-bag defenses for Jackson and contributed substantially to the American victory. As the British, under General Pakenham, attempted to take Jackson's position by assault, frontiersmen, blacks, regular army men, and others opened up a counterattack from behind their breastworks that was disastrous for the British. The war had already ended, but this belated victory for the Americans was significant psychologically as well as from a military viewpoint.

During the war blacks in search of freedom went over to the British. As in the War of Independence the British promised freedom to all fugitive slaves. It is impossible to make any estimate of the number who escaped to the British lines, but it is well known that some were later living in the British West Indies and in Canada. Some of those in the West Indies, however, had been sold into slavery. Many blacks entered the war on the side of America expecting to secure their freedom. Some did, but others were actually sent back to their masters at the end of the struggle. Thus, both sides betrayed, to some extent, the blacks who enlisted in the hope of getting their freedom. The Treaty of Ghent provided for the mutual restoration of properties. This applied to personal property—slaves—as much as to any territories that may have been won during the war. Since the British had been selling fugitive slaves in the West Indies, the Americans sought indemnities for this and other properties that were not restored by the British. It was not until 1828, however, that the British finally acceded to the demands of the United States and granted indemnities of more than $1 million.

■ Emergence of the Cotton Kingdom

The peace that settled over the United States in 1815 made possible the acceleration of the westward movement that was well under way before the war. The men of the South and West, the most enthusiastic supporters of the war, now felt that they had a right to move on to better lands. Many of the Indian dangers had been allayed, and the demand for cotton was increasing now that peace had come to the entire world. The years immediately following the close of the war witnessed an unparalleled movement of the population westward. Into the Gulf region went large numbers of settlers to clear the rich lands and cultivate extensive crops of cotton. Louisiana had become a state in 1812, and the population continued to increase as cotton and sugarcane became profitable crops of slaveholding planters. Mississippi and Alabama became states in 1817 and 1819, respectively. There had been only about 40,000 people in this area in 1810, but by 1820 there were 200,000 inhabitants, and twenty years later the population had almost reached the 1 million mark. The black population had also grown rapidly. In 1820 there were only 75,000 blacks in the Alabama-Mississippi region, while by 1840 almost half a million were in the area. The increase of the white population, coupled with the tremendous growth of the black population, largely slaves, is essentially the story of the emergence of the cotton kingdom.

A considerable number of planters from the seaboard states moved into the cotton kingdom, realizing that only in the new area could slavery have a possibility of becoming profitable. Attempts to grow cotton in Virginia and North Carolina had not been altogether satisfactory. At the beginning of the century the Southeastern states had grown most of the cotton. By 1821, however, the South Central states were producing over one-third of the cotton grown in the United States. By 1834 the coastal states produced 160 million pounds, while Alabama, Mississippi, Louisiana, and the other newly settled areas dominated production with 297.5 million pounds. Small wonder that slaveholders were going into the cotton kingdom. In 1832 the Lynchburg *Virginian* complained that "the constant emigration to the great West of our most substantial citizens, the bone and sinew of the country . . . is the daily subject of complaint among our mercantile men and of which our naked streets and untenanted houses are such emphatic evidence." Four years later a South Carolinian wrote: "The spirit of emigration is still rife in our community. From this cause we have lost many, and we are destined, we fear, to lose more, of our worthiest citizens."

As the income of planters in the new lands grew enormously and as the news of their prosperity found its way back to the seaboard, the wave of migration increased. The demand for slaves grew and, naturally, the prices of slaves went up. This mad scramble for land in the West, for slaves to cultivate the land, and for huge profits with which to expand were the ingredients that made the cotton kingdom one of the most dynamic areas of economic and social activity during the first half of the nineteenth century. The emergence of the cotton kingdom, in which the work was carried on primarily by black slaves, had the effect of committing the Gulf region to a regime of slavery and of unifying the South against any group or section that threatened to destroy those peculiar interests of the South and the cotton kingdom.

The acquisition of Florida in 1819, the settling of Missouri and its entrance into the Union as a slave state in 1821, and the movement culminating in the acquisition of Texas in 1845 were to a large extent a result of the forces that the emergence of the cotton kingdom let loose. In order to safeguard slaveholders against the possibility of losing their slaves through escape to Spanish soil, Florida was considered both desirable and necessary. The controversy over the entrance of Missouri into the Union demonstrated the determination of the South to secure, if possible, a political balance, and an equal determination on the part of the North to maintain political domination. The question of blacks was consequently catapulted into national prominence, and the incident seems to be symbolic of the irrevocable commitment of the South to the institution of slavery. Nothing more clearly demonstrates the insatiable appetite of plantation slavery for new lands than the generation-long struggle for the acquisition of Texas. It was perhaps the high-water mark in the effort of the South to absorb all the lands into which the cotton kingdom could be extended.

Shortly before the beginning of the War of 1812 the people of the West expounded the doctrine that later came to be known as Manifest Destiny. R. M. Johnson of Kentucky, for example, said that he would not die happy until all of Britain's North American possessions were incorporated into the United States. Points of view like this came to be expressed more and more by inhabitants of the slaveholding states, though it is true that many Northerners shared the same ideas. One of the most important motives for expansionism was declared to be the extension of the area of freedom. The area of the United States must be extended so as to make possible the development of a great "empire for liberty" in the New World. It was rather strange, therefore, to hear this doctrine expounded by those who held slaves and who saw little incongruity in their position as slaveholders and their pronouncements in favor of extending freedom and democracy.

It is safe to say that the extension of democracy was probably neither a primary motive of any of the Southern expansionists nor even a secondary motive of many of them. Their preoccupation was with extending the area not of freedom, but of slavery. Many Southerners called for the annexation of new areas as a means of defeating those who were antagonistic to the rights of Southern states. Thus, Manifest Destiny became a platform from which the slaveholder could plead for an extension of the institution of slavery. Southerners, in their thinking, had excluded blacks from their religious and moral conceptions of freedom and had evolved the new notion that the enslavement of blacks was essential to the freedom of whites. It is not too much to say, therefore, that Manifest Destiny, one of America's most dramatic shibboleths in the nineteenth century, contributed substantially to the extension of slavery during the generation immediately preceding the Civil War.

Blacks were not only moving involuntarily into the South Central states, where slavery was deeply entrenched, but they were also moving voluntarily into the North Central states, where presumably slavery would not exist. By 1830 there were more than 16,000 blacks in Ohio, Indiana, Illinois, and Michigan, and although under the Northwest Ordinance slavery was not permitted, there were no fewer than 788 slaves in the region at the time of the fifth census. Some of these migrants were runaway slaves, but others were ex-slaves who were seeking greater opportunities, as were the whites who moved into the North Central states after the War of 1812. An example of a fugitive slave moving into the region was William Trail, who in 1814 ran away from his Maryland master and with the aid of a forged pass went to Indiana. Although he was pursued and captured on two occasions, he finally won his freedom through court action and settled down to become a prosperous landowning farmer in Union County, Indiana. Another example of a free black on the frontier was an individual known as "Free Frank," who was born a slave in Kentucky but subsequently purchased his freedom as well as that of his wife and moved to Illinois. There, in Pike County, he founded the town of New Philadelphia and engaged in a variety of commercial enterprises. An outstanding citizen of Cleveland after 1830 was John Melvin, who moved to that community from Prince County, Virginia, where he was born of a slave father and a free mother. Melvin, through a succession of jobs, amassed sufficient money to purchase a lake vessel and engage in the carrying trade. He helped to organize the First Baptist Church and so vigorously opposed the segregation of blacks that the principle of free seating was adopted. He also assisted in organizing the first school for black children in Cleveland and sponsored the setting up of other such schools in Ohio. Thus, the same search for independence that characterized the efforts of blacks in the seaboard states was to be found in the activities of blacks in the newly settled states in the West.

■ The Domestic Slave Trade

One of the most important single factors augmenting the westward movement was the domestic slave trade. Although many migrants took slaves with them, others, less financially able, did not. Once in the South Central states and having realized some profits from their early ventures, the ambitious farmers began to seek slaves. Perhaps the best sources of supply were the states of the Atlantic seaboard that had found it increasingly difficult to maintain the institution at a profitable level. In the economic reorganization that circumstances forced upon Maryland, Virginia, and the Carolinas, slave trading took its place along with diversified farming as a solution to the difficult problems of economic readjustment. Even before 1800 the domestic slave trade in Maryland and Virginia was well developed. States like South Carolina that forbade importations from Africa permitted their citizens to purchase slaves from other states, thereby stimulating the domestic traffic considerably. Gradually, the interstate trade became profitable, and the consequent rising value of slave property had the effect of destroying much of the antislavery sentiment in Maryland and Virginia after the turn of the century.

With the official closing of the African trade in 1808 the domestic trade became more profitable, and by 1815, about the time of the great movement of the population into the cotton kingdom, it had become a major economic activity in the country. The machinery for handling the traffic developed rapidly, and before the very eyes of Americans there emerged an institution that served as a substitute, or a supplement, for the African trade, which was only slightly less obnoxious in its effects upon the social order. Many business firms that dealt in farm supplies and animals frequently carried a "line" of slaves. Auctioneers who disposed of real estate and personal property sold slaves along with their other commodities. Planters who were abandoning their farms or were undergoing some kind of retrenchment either passed the word around or advertised in the newspapers that they had slaves for sale. Benevolent organizations frequently sold slaves by lottery.

Almost every community in Maryland and Virginia had either traders or their agents scouring the countryside in search of slaves whom they could purchase at the lowest possible price and sell in the cotton kingdom at the highest possible price. Firms like Woolfolk, Saunders, and Overly of Maryland, and Franklin and Armfield of Virginia developed the slave-trading business to a point where it greatly enriched the members of the firm. Although they were generally held in low esteem, they were tolerated because they performed a service that was of great importance both to slaveholders and to those wishing to acquire slaves. Benjamin Lundy called Austin Woolfolk a "monster in human shape." When Woolfolk retaliated by beating Lundy mercilessly, the court fined him only $1, suggesting that the general disapproval of the traders was rather superficial. The newspapers cooperated with the traders in many ways. Not only did they serve them as advertising media, but they often received orders and acted as intermediaries between seller and purchaser.

The slave traders were a ubiquitous lot. They could be seen at general stores, at taverns, at county fairs, and on plantations. Wherever they heard of the possibility of the sale of slaves, they were there. When estates were to be probated or liquidated, they sought out the individuals involved and pressed them for whatever slaves were available. They could convincingly argue that a Virginian no longer needed his slaves, and then with equal firmness they could show a Mississippian that he needed at least ten new hands. Their advertisements are suggestive of twentieth-century methods. In 1834 Franklin and Armfield announced that they would pay cash for 500 blacks and would offer higher prices "than any other purchaser who is now, or may hereafter come into the market." Small wonder that these tycoons were able to move thousands of slaves each year from an area where they were not desired to a section where there was a pressing demand for them.

Baltimore, Washington, Richmond, Norfolk, and Charleston were the principal trading centers in the older states, while Montgomery, Memphis, and New Orleans were the outstanding marts in the newer areas. Although Washington was not the largest slave market, it was the most notorious until 1850 when the slave trade in the District of Columbia was brought to an end. Interstate traders headquartered in the District of Columbia operated in Maryland and Virginia. Alexandria, which was a part of the District of

Columbia until 1846, was, moreover, a good place from which to ship slaves by water or overland. The District of Columbia was aptly called, therefore, "the very seat and center of the slave trade." Foreign visitors to the nation's capital were puzzled at the sight of slave auction blocks, slave jails, and slave pens. Many of them, as well as many Americans, such as John Randolph of Roanoke, roundly condemned the practice of selling human beings in the capital of the world's most democratic nation. Washington was not alone, however, in possessing the various buildings and other symbols of the slave trade. Practically every city in the upper South and lower South had pens, jails, and other necessary accouterments for the effective prosecution of this profitable traffic. Who could deny, anyway, that jails were necessary? Were not some of the slaves unruly, indolent workers or, worse still, under suspicion as conspirators?

Some slaves were sold in the centers of the upper South and shipped to the cotton kingdom via the Atlantic Ocean. As far north as New York and Philadelphia slaves were loaded on cargo ships and sent into the lower South. Chesapeake ports, such as Baltimore, Washington, and Norfolk, were especially important in the slave-trading activity. New Orleans was, of course, the important port of entry and became the most important slave-trading center in the lower South. Other slaves were sent overland, through southwestern Virginia to Tennessee, thence into Alabama, Mississippi, and Louisiana. If they went by land, they frequently walked most of the way. When they reached the Ohio, Tennessee, or Mississippi River, they were placed on flatboats and shipped down the river like any other cargo. In most instances, whether by water or by land, they were taken in chains. More than one traveler was startled at the sight of migrating slaves who were either handcuffed or chained together or both. They were always under the watchful eye of the long-distance traders or their agents, who saw to it that none escaped, lest the profits be therefore proportionally reduced.

There was always a fear that the supply of slaves would become exhausted while the demand was still great. One of the ways in which the slaveholders guarded against this distressing eventuality was the systematic breeding of slaves, one of the most fantastic manipulations of human development in the history of humanity. Despite the denials and apologies of many students of the history of American slavery, there seems to be no doubt that innumerable slaveholders deliberately undertook to increase the number of saleable slaves by advantageously mating them and by encouraging prolificacy in every possible way. As early as 1796 a South Carolina slaveholder declared that the 50 slaves he was offering for sale were purchased for stock and breeding. In 1832 Thomas R. Dew admitted that Virginia was a "Negro raising state" and that it was able to export 6,000 per year because of breeding. Moncure Conway of Fredericksburg, Virginia, boldly asserted that "the chief pecuniary resource in the border states is the breeding of slaves; and I grieve to say that there is too much ground for the charges that general licentiousness among the slaves, for the purpose of a

William Wells Brown Tells about the Domestic Slave Trade—1847

In the course of eight or nine weeks Mr. Walker [slave trader] had his cargo of human flesh made up. There was in this lot a number of old men and women, some of them with gray locks. We left St. Louis in the steamboat Carlton, Captain Swan, bound for New Orleans. . . . I was ordered to have the old men's whiskers shaved off, and the gray hairs plucked out where they were not too numerous, in which case he had a preparation of blacking to color it, and with a blacking-brush we would put it on. This was new business to me, and was performed in a room where the passengers could not see us . . . and after going through the blacking process, they looked ten or fifteen years younger. . . .

The next day [after Natchez] we proceeded to New Orleans. . . . In a short time, the planters came flocking to the pen to purchase slaves. Before the slaves were exhibited for sale, they were dressed and driven out into the yard. Some were set to dancing, some to jumping, some to singing, and some to playing cards. This was done to make them appear cheerful and happy. My business was to see that they were placed in those situations before the arrival of the purchasers, and I have often set them to dancing when their cheeks were wet with tears. As slaves were in good demand at that time, they were all soon disposed of. . . .

William Wells Brown, *Narrative of William Wells Brown, A Fugitive Slave, Written By Himself*, in Gilbert Osofsky, *Puttin' On Ole Massa* (New York, 1969), pp. 191–194.

large increase, is compelled by some masters and encouraged by many." Experiments in slave rearing were carried on, albeit surreptitiously, in much the same way that efforts were made to discover new products that would grow on the exhausted soil. Slave rearing was another evidence of the desperation that gripped the upper South after it lost its economic leadership to the states of the cotton kingdom.

Slave breeding, strangely enough, was one of the most approved methods of increasing agricultural capital. Traders were castigated by the slaveholding gentry as being inhuman, vicious, and extremely venal, but slave-breeding owners were far more common and much more highly esteemed in the community. One respectable Virginia planter boasted that his women were "uncommonly good breeders" and that he never heard of babies coming so fast as they did on his plantation. Of course, the very gratifying thing about it was that "every one of them . . . was worth two hundred dollars . . . the moment it drew breath." Indeed, breeding was so profitable that many slave girls became mothers at thirteen and fourteen years of age. By the time they were twenty, some young women had given birth to as many as five children. Bounties and prizes were offered for great fecundity, and in some instances freedom was granted to mothers who had enriched their masters to the extent of bearing them ten or fifteen children. Arguments denying slave breeding by some recent students of slavery cannot successfully refute these and other contemporary testimonies regarding this practice.

Since the domestic slave trade and slave breeding were essentially economic and not humanitarian activities, it is not surprising to find that in the sale of slaves there was the persistent practice of dividing families. Husbands were separated from their wives, and mothers were separated from their children. This is not to say that there was never any respect manifested for the slave family. Here and there one can find sufficient respect for basic human rights or ample sentimentality to prevent the separation of families, but it was not always good business to keep families together. Since people sold and bought slaves largely for economic reasons, they eschewed the civilities that would have frowned upon separation. Louisiana law forbade separation of a mother from a child under ten years of age, and some other states discouraged the division of families. These laws, if enforced, would have done much to ameliorate the conditions of slavery; but they were almost wholly disregarded.

Few owners were sufficiently insensitive to human decency to admit that they were willing to divide slave families by sale. As a matter of fact, family members were frequently advertised as being for sale together, but they were not always sold together. Slaves often brought higher prices when sold separately. The large number of single slaves on the market bears testimony to the rather ruthless separation of families that went on during the slave period. Frederic Bancroft asserts that "the selling singly of young children privately and publicly was frequent and notorious." It was not unusual to see advertisements in which traders sought young blacks from eight to twelve years of age. Some traders, moreover, announced that they made a specialty of buying and selling young children.

In justification of the practice of separating families it was argued that family ties among slaves were either extremely loose or nonexistent and that slaves were, therefore, indifferent to separation. As Herbert Gutman has shown, this was not the case. Slaves responded to these assaults on familial relations by restructuring their social institutions into new forms, at times based on their African heritage, to establish distinctly African American relationships that often preserved their families in the face of the most adverse conditions. In every coffle of slaves shipped into the cotton kingdom by land or by water, slaves were handcuffed or chained, and hard-boiled traders often admitted that youngsters or oldsters, as the case might be, were unwilling to leave their families. Even more eloquent a denial of the claims of masters that ties of slave families were weak were the advertisements for runaways. All too frequently masters admitted that the fugitives had perhaps gone to a certain place where they were known to have had a wife, husband, or children. The frequency of such advertisements also belies the claim of many that slave families were hardly, if ever, separated.

	1800	1808	1813	1818	1828	1837	1843	1848	1853	1856	1860
TABLE 3 Average Prices of Prime Field Hands (young slave men, able-bodied but unskilled)											
Washington, Richmond, and Norfolk	$ 350	$ 500	$ 400	$ 700		$ 900			$1,250	$1,300	
Charleston, S.C.	500	550	450	850	$ 450	1,200	$ 500	$ 700	900		$1,200
Louisville, Ky.	400		550	800	500	1,200				1,000	1,400
Middle Georgia	450	650	450	1,000	700	1,300	600	900	1,200		1,800
Montgomery, Ala.				800	600	1,200	650	800			1,600
New Orleans, La.	500	600		1,000	700	1,300	800	900	1,250	1,500	1,800

Source: Ulrich Bonnell Phillips. The Slave Economy of the Old South: Selected Essays in Economic and Social History. *Edited by Eugene D. Genovese. Louisiana State University Press (Baton Rouge 1968) p. 142.*

The prices of slaves in the domestic trade reflected all the forces operating to create supply and demand. In the early nineteenth century, the prices of prime field hands were modest, ranging from $350 in Virginia to about $500 in Louisiana. Later, as the demand increased in the lower South, the prices on both the Northern and Southern markets tended to rise. The high point of the number of slaves sold in the domestic market was reached just before the panic of 1837 when Virginia reported that in the previous year no less than 120,000 slaves had been exported into the lower South. After the panic, the slump both in price and in demand became so pronounced that some traders were forced to return to Virginia and Maryland with their slaves and to sustain staggering losses. The forces that operated to increase slave prices in the last decade before the Civil War were largely political and social. In order to convince themselves and the abolitionists that slavery was a moral and economic good and to convince their neighbors of their affluence, planters continued to purchase all the slaves offered on the market. Prices skyrocketed, and by 1860 prime field hands were selling for $1,000 in Virginia and $1,500 in New Orleans.

Closely allied with slave trading was the practice of slave hiring. Owners had various reasons for hiring out their slaves instead of selling them. Some wanted to spread the income from the investment over a long period of time, others wanted to escape whatever stigma there might have been attached to being known as a slave seller, and still others wanted to keep the slaves either for the good of the latter or for the prestige that came from ownership. At any rate, there was almost always an opportunity to make a temporary disposition of slaves because of the constant demand for servants. Some whites hired slaves because the purchase was, for the moment, beyond their means; others merely had a temporary need for the services of a slave and saw no need to purchase one; still others reasoned that it was more economical in the long run to purchase services rather than titles, thereby escaping the responsibility that devolved on the owner during the slave's illness or old age.

Slaves were hired by the day, by the month, or by the year. The employer promised in the agreement to provide food, clothing, shelter, and medical care in addition to the stipulated wage. If the slave became ill or ran away, the wage continued. If the slave died, the wage ceased but the person who had hired the slave was usually compelled to show that he or she was not in any way responsible for the slave's death. Annual contracts ran for fifty-one weeks and did not cover the period from Christmas to New Year's Day. Hiring day was January 1 or some other day early in the new year. Some communities set aside a hiring day and gave all interested persons an opportunity to transact their business with great ease since the owners as well as the hirers would be able to find each other easily. On January 1, 1858, hiring day in Warrenton, Virginia, 500 slaves were advertised as being for hire.

The business of hiring was almost as highly organized as slave trading. There were hiring agents who prepared the papers, collected the money, and performed other similar services. At times these agents were also slave traders. In some instances, however, they were men without the resources necessary to engage in slave trading. Interestingly enough, there was no stigma attached to the business of serving as a hiring agent, and in their advertisements agents frequently proudly listed the names of their "patrons."

Slaves were hired to engage in all kinds of labor, but it was usually customary to state the nature of work in the agreement. They were hired by small farmers who needed a few extra hands at harvest time. They also worked in forests as woodcutters and turpentine hands. Hired slaves could also be found in factories and mines, on railroad construction jobs, and in canal digging. There were, of course, a considerable number in the towns serving as maids, porters, messengers, cooks, and the like. The rates of hire varied considerably depending on the skill of the slave as well as the supply. In 1800 a slave hand brought $100 per year in the lower South. By 1860 the price had increased to $200 or more. Toward the end of the period a young blacksmith in Mississippi was hired for $500, while several hands in Texas brought as much as $600.

Slave trading and hiring were thus essential parts of the economic and social fabric of the South. While practices that may have developed within the system were frowned upon, there was almost universal acceptance of the general principle of buying and selling human beings. To the owners of the upper South it meant the opportunity to dump on the market those individuals who were a serious burden in the period of economic transition. By breeding slaves for the market, moreover, the same owners could go far in the direction of reconstituting themselves economically. To traders it meant commissions and profits that ranged all the way from 5 to 30 percent of the sale price of the slaves, no mean return on a short-term investment. The social stigma of slave trading reduced competition and consequently increased the opportunity for profits. To the planters of the lower South the domestic slave trade provided an opportunity to secure the supply of labor necessary for the development and cultivation of new lands. Without the slaves of the upper South they felt stymied and frustrated. With them their opportunities for amassing wealth and influence were considered almost limitless.

■ Persistence of the African Trade

As the demand for slaves increased in the nineteenth century and as prices went up, merchants and traders experienced a great temptation to engage in the African trade, although it had been officially ended by federal legislation in 1808. The long, unprotected coast, the certain markets, and the prospect of huge profits were too much for American merchants, and they yielded to the temptation. After the War of 1812 it was generally admitted that American capital, American ships, and American sailors were carrying on an extensive slave trade between Africa and the New World. England was greatly distressed because she was committed to a program of eliminating the slave trade. In all her treaties with the new republics of Latin America, England forced them to promise not to engage in the slave trade. But it was embarrassing to England to observe that her recent enemy, with whom she was now on friendly terms, persisted in winking at gross violations of her own laws. There was little that England could do except to bring the pressure of world opinion to bear on the United States, but American citizens were not ashamed of their activities and so did not even heed the words of their own leaders.

In 1839 President Van Buren asked for an amendment of the law against the African slave trade in order to preserve the "integrity and honor of our flag." In June 1841, President Tyler said that there was every reason to believe that the traffic was on the increase. Almost every year witnessed an appeal of the president or some public leader for a more rigid enforcement of the law, but nothing was done. The most flagrant violations did not arouse public opinion to the point of bringing action against those who were profiting from the trade, and in this instance, it was not a sectional profit. New York merchants as well as those of New Orleans were benefiting from the illicit traffic. In 1836 the consul at Havana reported that whole cargoes of slaves fresh from Africa were being shipped daily to Texas in American vessels and that more than 1,000 had been sent within a few months. Two months later it was estimated that 15,000 Africans were annually taken to Texas. Bay Island, in the Gulf of Mexico, was a depot where at times as many as 16,000

Africans were on hand to be shipped to Florida, Texas, Louisiana, and other markets.

By 1854 those engaged in the African slave trade had become so bold as to advocate openly the official reopening of the trade. Between 1854 and 1860 every Southern commercial convention gave consideration to the proposition to reopen the trade. At the Montgomery convention of 1858 a furious debate was carried on over the problem. William L. Yancey, the Alabama "fire eater," argued, with considerable logic, that "if it is right to buy slaves in Virginia and carry them to New Orleans, why is it not right to buy them in Cuba, Brazil, or Africa and carry them there?" The following year, at Vicksburg, the convention voted favorably on a resolution recommending that "all laws, State or Federal, prohibiting the African slave trade, ought to be repealed." Only the states of the upper South, enjoying the profits reaped from the domestic slave trade, were opposed to reopening the African trade.

The federal law of 1808 was so weak and the enforcement of it so lax that a repeal was unnecessary to reopen the trade. When offenders were caught, they were placed under bond, which they promptly forfeited. Sometimes cases involving offenders were never brought before the courts. Thus, for all practical purposes the trade was open in the last decade before the Civil War, much to the distress of the Quakers and similar organizations. As the intersectional strife increased in intensity, importations into Southern ports became "bold, frequent, and notorious." Newly arrived blacks were openly advertised for sale, and most of the cities of the South had depots where they could be purchased if, for some reason, blacks from the upper South were not desired. In doing everything possible to keep the African trade open, Southerners were merely seeking to secure themselves against the possibility that the domestic slave trade would eventually go into a state of decline. There was the possibility, moreover, that if they could increase the supply of slaves, they would be able to secure them at lower prices.

Without slavery and the slave trade the westward movement on the Southern frontier would have been unsuccessful. It was the slaves, brought in either by settlers or traders, who transformed the Southern frontier from a wilderness into flourishing cotton and sugarcane farms and plantations. It was the slaves, moreover, who represented one of the most substantial forms of capital to be found in the cotton kingdom. Frederick Jackson Turner always described the trader as having preceded the farmer. He was, of course, referring to the person who carried on barter with the Indians. In this instance, however, the trader *followed* the farmer. It was the trader who brought the labor supply to the farmer. Although the order is in this case reversed, it would not be too much to say that slave traders with their black workers had a more profound effect on the history of the Southern frontier than Indian traders with their trinkets and fire water.

CHAPTER 8

That Peculiar Institution

■ Scope and Extent

Plantation slavery, as it developed in the cotton kingdom, was something of an anomaly on the American frontier. Although slavery was almost as old as the permanent settlements in America, not until the nineteenth century did it occupy so much of the attention and energy of the settlers as to threaten other forms of labor. The frontier had been a place where one could make or lose a fortune largely by one's own labors. The emergence of the great cotton plantation introduced a kind of exploitation of human and natural resources and fostered a type of discipline in rural areas that created what could at best be called a peculiar situation. Indeed, every aspect of agricultural life in the Southern United States underwent a complete transformation as a result of the new economic and social forces let loose by the Industrial Revolution. And what the Industrial Revolution did to the capitalistic system, new lands and the prospect of wealth from cotton culture did to the system of slavery. Large-scale operations were the order of the day. The farm became a plantation, which in turn became a rural factory with the impersonality of a large-scale economic organization. The face of the Southern frontier had been changed. Cotton and slavery were the great transforming forces.

One of the most rapidly growing elements in the population was the slaves. In 1790 there had been less than 700,000 slaves. By 1830 there were more than 2 million. The South Atlantic states, from Delaware to Florida, were still ahead in numbers, with 1,300,000, while the states of the lower South, none of which had been in the Union in 1790, now had 604,000 slaves. By the last census before the Civil War, the slave population had grown to 3,953,760! The states of the cotton kingdom had taken the lead, with 1,998,000 slaves within their borders. Virginia was still ahead in the number of slaves in a single state, but Alabama and Mississippi were rapidly gaining ground. As a matter of fact, the slave population of all the states of the lower South was increasing rapidly, while that of the upper South was either increasing very slowly or, as in the case of Maryland, was actually declining. The increase in the slave population to virtually 4 million by 1860 is an eloquent testimony to the extent to which slavery had become entrenched in the Southern states.

The impression should not be conveyed that the whites of the South, numbering about 8 million in 1860, generally enjoyed the fruits of slave labor. There was a remarkable concentration of the slave population in the hands of a relative few. In 1860 there were only 384,884 slave owners. Thus, fully three-fourths of the white people of the South had neither slaves nor an immediate economic interest in the maintenance of slavery or the plantation system. And yet, the institution came to dominate the political and economic thinking of the entire South and to shape its social pattern for two principal reasons. The great majority of the staple crops were produced on plantations employing slave labor, thus giving the owners an influence out of proportion to their number. Then, there was the hope on the part of most nonslavehold-ers that they would some day become owners of slaves. Consequently, they took on the habits and patterns of thought of slaveholders before they actually joined that select class.

While slaves were concentrated in areas where the staple crops were produced on a large scale, the bulk of the slave owners were small farmers. It is not too generally known that more than 200,000 owners in 1860 had five slaves or less. Fully 338,000 owners, or 88 percent of all the owners of slaves in 1860, held less than twenty slaves. (One must not be misled by these figures, however, for over one-half of the slaves were employed as field workers on plantations with holdings of more than twenty slaves, and at least 25 percent of the slave community lived on plantations where the number of slaves was in excess of fifty.) It is fairly generally conceded that from thirty to sixty slaves constituted the most profitable agricultural unit. If that is true, there were fewer plantations in the South that had what might be considered a satisfactory working force than has been generally believed. The concentration of 88 percent of all slaveholders in the small slave-owning group is significant for several important reasons. In the first place, it emphasizes the fact that the influence of large owners must have been enormous, since they have been successful in impressing posterity with the erroneous conception that plantations on which there were large numbers of slaves were typical. In the second place, it brings out the fact that the majority of slaveholding was carried on by yeomen rather than gentry. Finally, in a study of the institution of slavery, there is a rather strong indication that some distinction should be made between the possession of one or two slaves and the possession of, say, fifty or more.

But it was the tremendous productivity of the large plantations that placed the large slaveholder in a position of great influence. By 1860 Southern states were producing 5,387,000 bales of cotton annually. Four states, Mississippi, Alabama, Louisiana, and Georgia, produced more than 3,500,000 bales of this crop. It is no mere accident that these same states were also at the top of the list in the number of large slaveholders. Of the states having slaveholders with more than twenty slaves, Mississippi led, just as it did in productivity of cotton, followed by Alabama, Louisiana, and Georgia.

■ The Slave Codes

After the colonies secured their independence and established their own governments, they did not neglect the matter of slavery in the laws that they enacted. Where slavery was growing, as in the lower South in the late eighteenth and early nineteenth centuries, new and more stringent laws were enacted. All over the South, however, there emerged a body of laws generally regarded as the Slave Codes, which covered every aspect of the life of the slave. There were variations from state to state, but the general point of view expressed in most of them was the same: slaves are not people but property; laws should protect the ownership of such property and should also protect whites against any dangers that might arise from the presence of large numbers of slaves. It was also felt that slaves should be maintained in a position of due subordination in order that the optimum of discipline and work could be achieved.

The regulatory statutes were frankly repressive, and whites made no apologies for them. The laws represented merely the reduction to legal phraseology of the philosophy of the South with regard to the institution of slavery. Slaves had no standing in the courts: they could not be a party to a law suit; they could not offer testimony, except against another slave or a free black; and their irresponsibility meant that their oaths were not binding. Thus, they could make no contracts. The ownership of property was generally forbidden them, though some states permitted slaves to have certain types of personal property. A slave could not strike a white person, even in self-defense; but the killing of a slave, however malicious the act, was rarely regarded as murder. The rape of a female slave was regarded as a crime but only because it involved trespassing.

The greater portion of the Slave Codes involved the many restrictions placed on slaves to ensure the maximum protection of the white population and to maintain discipline among slaves. These rules were primarily negative. Slaves could not leave the plantation without authorization, and any white person finding them outside without permission could capture them and turn them over to public officials. They could not possess firearms, and in Mississippi they could not beat drums or blow horns. They could not hire themselves out without permission or in any other way conduct themselves as free people. They could not buy or sell goods. Their relationships with whites and free blacks were to be kept at a minimum. They could not visit the homes of whites or free blacks, and they could not entertain such individuals in their quarters. They were never to assemble unless a white person was present, and they were never to receive, possess, or transmit any incendiary literature calculated to incite insurrections.

Whenever there was an insurrection, or even rumors of one, it was usually the occasion for the enactment of even more stringent laws to control the activities and movements of slaves. For example, after the Vesey insurrection of 1822, South Carolina enacted a law requiring the imprisonment of all black seamen during the stay of their vessel in port. The Nat Turner insurrection of 1831 and the simultaneous drive of abolitionists against slavery brought forth the enactment of many new repressive measures in other parts of the South as well as in Virginia and neighboring states. Long before the end of the slave period the Slave Codes in all the Southern states had become so elaborate that there was hardly need for modification even when new threats arose to shake the foundations of the institution.

Ample machinery was set up to provide for effective enforcement and execution of the Slave Codes. In some states, slaves were tried in regular courts for infractions of the law. In other states, specially constituted slave tribunals had the responsibility of examining evidence and judging the guilt or innocence of slaves. Some states required trials by juries composed of slaveholders, while others merely required the cognizance of one, two, or three justices of the peace. Most petty offenses were punishable by whipping, while more serious ones were punishable by branding, imprisonment, or death. Arson, rape of a white woman, and conspiracy to rebel were capital crimes in all the slaveholding states. There was considerable reluctance to imprison a slave for a long period or to inflict the death penalty for the obvious reason that the slave represented an investment, and to deprive the owner of the slave's labor or life was to deprive the state of just that much wealth. Slaveholders were, therefore, extremely cautious about judging a slave offender hastily because of the danger of losing one of their own slaves through such a process at some later date. This is not to say that slaves enjoyed anything resembling due process of law or justice in any sense in which the term is applied to free persons. Since slaves were always regarded with suspicion and since some crimes were viewed as threats to the social order, they were frequently punished for crimes they did not commit and were helpless before a panic-stricken group of slaveholders who saw in the rumor of an insurrection the slow but certain undermining of their entire system.

One of the devices set up to enforce the Slave Codes and thereby maintain the institution of slavery was the patrol, which has been aptly described as an adaptation of the militia. Counties were usually divided into "beats," or areas of patrol, and free white men were called upon to serve for a stated period of time, one, three, or six months. These patrols were to apprehend slaves out of place and return them to their masters or commit them to jail, to visit slave quarters and search for various kinds of weapons that might be used in an uprising, and to visit assemblies of slaves where disorder might develop or where conspiracy might be planned. This system proved so inconvenient to some citizens that they regularly paid the fines that were imposed for dereliction of duty. A corrupted form of the patrol system was the vigilance committee, which came into existence during the emergencies created by uprisings or rumors of them. At such times, it was not unusual for the committee to disregard all caution and prudence and kill any blacks whom they encountered in their search. Committees like these frequently ended up engaging in nothing except a lynching party.

Despite the elaborateness of the Slave Codes both in the number of statutes and in the machinery of enforcement, there were innumerable infractions that went unpunished altogether. When times were quiet, there was an inclination to disregard the laws and to permit slaves to conduct themselves in a manner that would be regarded as highly offensive during an emergency. There was the desire, moreover, on the part of all masters to take all matters involving their slaves into their own hands and to mete out justice in their own way. The strong individualism that was bred on the frontier plantation and the planter's self-conception as the source of law and justice had the effect of discouraging conformity to statutes even when they were passed in the interest of the plantation system. Slaveholders always had the feeling that they could handle their own slaves, if only something could be done about those on the neighboring plantation. Such a point of view was not conducive to the effective enforcement of the Slave Codes.

■ Plantation Scene

The fact should not be ignored that the primary concern of owners was to get work out of their slaves. And the work of slaves was primarily agricultural. It is estimated that only 400,000 slaves lived in towns and cities in 1850. This left approximately 2.8 million to do the work on farms and plantations. The great bulk of them, 1.8 million, were to be found on cotton plantations, while the remainder were primarily engaged in the cultivation of tobacco, rice, and sugarcane. The cotton farm or plantation was, therefore, the typical locale of the slave. It must be recalled that when a farmer owned a few slaves, as was the case in a vast majority of instances, slaves and owners worked together in the fields and were compelled to engage in a variety of common tasks. On larger plantations, where the organization was so elaborate as to resemble a modern factory, there was extensive supervision by the owner or the overseer or both, and there was considerable division of labor among slaves. A large plantation always had at least two distinct groups of workers, house servants and field hands. The former cared for the house, the yards, and the gardens, cooked the meals, drove the carriages, and performed the other tasks expected of personal servants. The favored ones frequently traveled with their owners and enjoyed other advantages in the way of food, clothing, and education or experience.

Unfortunately, there are few records of the activities of slaves on smaller units. Therefore, a great deal has been made of the existence of a large force of house servants because a considerable number of large slaveholders kept diaries, journals, and other records that have given a clear picture of their activities. In some of these instances there were more house servants than necessary. If a planter could display a considerable number of house servants, he or she could convey the impression, frequently inaccurate, of having great affluence and living in a state bordering on luxury. The house servant group, moreover, tended to perpetuate and even to increase itself. Once a slave had served in a home, the prospect of working in the field was frowned upon and resisted with every available resource. House servants were even anxious to "work" their children into the more desirable situation and to marry them off to the children of other house servants. The result was that the group increased in numbers beyond the point necessary to maintain the average planter's home.

What may be termed the productive work was done in the fields by a force that constituted the principal group of slaves. Where there were not enough slaves to have house servants as well as field hands, agricultural activities seldom suffered. In such instances slaves found it necessary to do the chores around and in the house at times that ordinarily would have been their own time. The cultivation of a crop was a demanding undertaking, and the entire future of both slaves and owners depended on the success with which it was handled. Except on rice plantations, where slaves were given a specific assignment or task each day, the gang system was used. Literally, gangs of slaves were taken to the fields and put to work under the supervision of the owner or the overseer. The leader instructed them about when to begin work, when to eat, and when to quit. Slaves under this system were wholly without responsibility and had little opportunity to develop initiative. Consequently, the claim of some recent writers that owners could have made slavery more bearable to slaves by paying them for their work seems highly unlikely.

It was generally believed that one slave was required for the successful cultivation of three acres of cotton. The planting, cultivation, and picking of cotton required little skill, but a great deal of time. Men, women, and children could be used, though it is to be doubted if the very young and the very old were of any real value to the plantation. Aside from duties in connection with raising the crop, there were other things to do, such as clearing land, burning underbrush, rolling logs, splitting rails, carrying water, mending fences, spreading fertilizer, breaking soil, and the like. Small wonder that

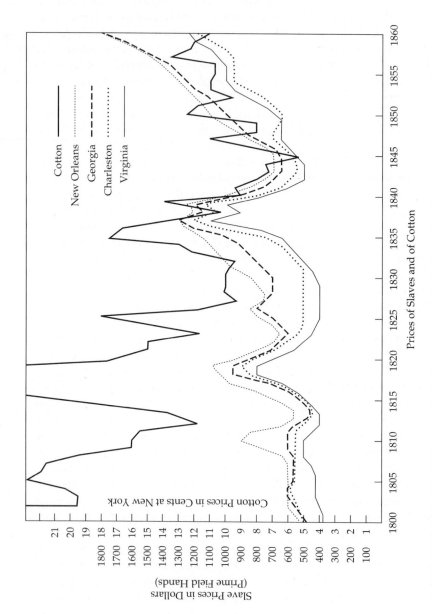

PRICES OF SLAVES AND OF COTTON. As the price of cotton fluctuated on the New York market and the price of slaves fluctuated on the principal slave markets of the South, one can see a clear correlation between the price of cotton and of slaves. (*Ulrich B. Phillips*, American Negro Slavery, *New York, 1966, p. 371.*)

many slaves worked not merely from sunrise to sunset but frequently long after dark. During harvest time the hours were longest since the planter was anxious to harvest the crop before it could be seriously damaged by inclement weather. Under such circumstances slaves were driven almost mercilessly. In 1830, for example, fourteen Mississippi slaves each picked an average of 323 pounds of cotton in one day. It was conceded that if an adult slave picked 150 pounds in one day it was a satisfactory performance. On Louisiana sugarcane plantations it was not unusual for slaves to work eighteen and twenty hours each day during the harvest season.

When there was no watchful supervision, little was accomplished in a slave system. Slaves felt no compulsion to extend themselves in their work unless the planter or overseer forced them. Their benefits would be the same, except on a few plantations where systems of rewards and bounties were developed, whether they worked conscientiously or whether they shirked at every opportunity. There was a great deal of complaining about the idleness and laziness of slaves, but this was inherent in a system of forced labor. On one occasion George Washington said that his slave carpenters were notorious piddlers and not even one of his house servants was worthy of trust. If slaves felt overworked, they frequently feigned illness or simply walked off for a day or so or, perhaps forever. The consistent evasion of work on the part of slaves was one of the reasons why planters always felt in need of more slaves to increase the productivity of their plantations.

In the effort to get work out of slaves the lash was frequently used. There was the general belief, born of a naive or sinister racial justification for the institution of slavery, that Africans were a childlike race and should be punished just as children were punished. Some planters went so far as to specify the size and type of lash to be used and the number of lashes to be given for certain offenses. Almost none disclaimed whipping as an effective form of punishment, and the excessive use of the lash was one of the most flagrant abuses of the institution. Many slaves fled because of brutal beatings by their owner or overseer. Unfortunately, the instances where one can determine the nature and extent of punishment are so few, if they exist at all, that efforts at statistical computation of whippings are pointless if not ridiculous.

The great majority of the plantations were managed by the planters themselves. An overseer was not needed unless there were more than twenty slaves or unless the planter was an absentee landlord. In many instances, moreover, planters worked in the fields and shared the experiences of their slaves. Under such conditions, there was likely to be less brutality on the part of management and more work on the part of the laboring force than under other circumstances. Southern planters were at the center of the economic, social, and political life of their community and naturally had the feeling that they should dominate the lives of their black property completely. If they were inclined to be benevolent and understanding, the slaves were fortunate indeed. If they were inclined to enjoy the exercise of authority and the cruelty that authority frequently fostered, then the slaves probably looked forward to either running away or being sold to a better owner.

It was on plantations where there were overseers that the greatest amount of cruelty and brutality existed. Since overseers came from a nonslaveholding and frequently landless group, they had no interest other than a temporary concern in the institution. Too frequently they hated the system and directed especial contempt toward slaves because they were of the opinion that slavery was responsible for their own unfortunate economic plight. They had the job of managing the entire plantation in the absence of the planter, or if it was too large for the planter to handle alone, the overseer was delegated a considerable portion of the responsibility. In any event, this authority over the slaves was almost unlimited. The owners demanded that the overseers get work out of the slaves and produce a superior crop. With such a mandate overseers were ruthless and excessively cruel in their treatment of slaves. Frequently, fights grew out of attempts of overseers to punish slaves, and in several instances overseers were run off the plantation by irate slaves. Before the planter had the opportunity to reprimand the overseer for his bestiality, he had often done irreparable damage. It must be remembered, moreover, that unless his cruelty bordered on the sensational, many planters were not concerned about it. On some plantations a slave called the driver was selected to assist the owner or overseer in getting work out of the slaves. The other slaves frequently resented this delegation of authority to one among them, and the driver was sometimes viewed as a traitor, especially if he took his duties seriously.

The responsibility of providing the necessities of life for slaves was a major one. The preoccupation with raising the staple crops was so great everywhere that insufficient attention was given to the very important matter of growing food. Charles S. Sydnor has observed that few Mississippi planters raised enough food to supply their needs. Consequently, many plantations were compelled to purchase foodstuffs and other supplies not only for the family of the planter but for the slaves as well. Whether grown on the plantation or brought in from other sections of the country, the fare was not a particularly exciting one, the principal items being meal and meat. On some of the larger plantations there was a central kitchen where the food was prepared, but on the average plantation each slave was responsible for the preparation of his or her own food. Each received a daily or weekly ration of meal and salt pork. For adult persons the weekly ration was about a peck of meal and three to four pounds of meat. This was at times supplemented with sweet potatoes, peas, rice, syrup, and fruit. Some slaves had their own gardens and chickens, but there was always the possibility of incurring the disfavor of the owner or overseer by spending too much time in this pursuit. A further supplement to one's diet could be made by hunting and fishing whenever possible.

It would be too much to suppose that slaves always resisted the temptation to take food from the owner's larder if the opportunity presented itself. The difficulty was that such supplies were locked up, and except for a few house servants, no slaves had access to them. But the house servants, who usually ate the same food as the whites whether they were permitted to do so or not, were perhaps not inclined to take food unless some kind of cabal had been formed for the systematic depletion of the owner's food supply. The break in the monotony of the unattractive fare came on holidays like Christmas when the owner sometimes provided items such as cheese, coffee, and candy as a contribution to the festive spirit.

The filching of perishable items like food was simple when compared with any efforts on the part of slaves to augment their supply of clothing. Some house servants were favored with the castoff garments of their owners, but the average slave wore what was generally described as "Negro clothes." They consisted of jeans, linseys, kerseys, and osnaburgs for the men and calico and homespun fabrics for the women. On some plantations slave women spun and wove the cloth out of which they made their dresses. Shoes, called "Negro brogans," were not provided except for the winter months. No more clothing was furnished than was absolutely necessary. Planters reasoned that slaves perhaps needed ample food in order to work efficiently, but they saw little connection between clothing and work. In a system as harshly materialistic as plantation slavery there was little or no inclination to indulge in any expenditures for slaves that were viewed as unnecessary for increased productivity.

Housing for slaves was especially poor. The small, rude huts were usually inadequate as well as uncomfortable. Windows and floors were almost unheard of. Frederick Olmsted was shocked when he viewed the slave cabins on some of the plantations he visited. They were small and dilapidated with no windows, unchinked walls, and practically no furnishings. One of the better ones had a bed, a chest, a wooden stool, some earthenware, and cooking vessels. Many cabins were wholly without beds, and slaves were compelled to sleep on quilts or blankets with only some straw or shucks between them and the earth. The inadequacy of space was, if possible, even worse than the absence of comforts and conveniences. One Mississippi planter had twenty-four huts, each measuring sixteen by fourteen feet, for his 150 slaves. Ulrich B. Phillips and others have defended the frightfully inadequate housing of slaves on the grounds that, first, the plantation was so close to the frontier that few planters could boast of entirely satisfactory living accommodations and, second, slaves were out of their cabins most of the time and, therefore, did not have a real need for greatly improved housing. In all fairness, these apologists could have added that these unfortunate living conditions go far to explain the crime, delinquency, and aversion to the "civilizing" tendencies of the plantation of which they so loudly accused slaves.

■ Nonagricultural Pursuits

In 1850 there were 400,000 slaves living in urban communities. It may be assumed that a majority were engaged in nonagricultural pursuits and that their number was augmented by plantation slaves whose owners hired them out to townspeople. There is no way of knowing how many such slaves were hired out, but there must have been thousands, especially in the period between the harvest and the new planting. It was in nonagricultural pursuits that slaves displayed the greatest variety of talent and training. Many plantations had slave carpenters, masons, and mechanics, but skilled slaves were to be most frequently found in towns. Indeed, a large number of town slaves possessed some kind of skill. In the Charleston census of 1848, for example, there were more slave carpenters than there were free black and white carpenters. The same was true of slave coopers. In addition, there were slave tailors, shoemakers, cabinetmakers, painters, plasterers, seamstresses, and the like. Many owners realized the wisdom of training their slaves in the trades, for their earning power would be greatly enhanced; and if the slaves were ever offered for sale they would perhaps bring twice as much as field hands of a similar age would bring.

White artisans were violently opposed, for the most part, to the teaching of trades to blacks. One white skilled worker in Mississippi, for example, said that he would starve before he taught a slave his trade. Most of the planters and proslavery leaders advocated training slaves in special skills, not only because it increased their value but because if slave labor were more extensively used, there would be wider and more enthusiastic support of the system. If towns as well as plantations became completely dependent on slave labor, whatever indifference there was to the institution would be transformed into warm advocacy.

Only the most demagogic of the Negrophobes contended that it was not possible to train blacks in artisanry. There were too many examples that belied such a contention. No state and few communities were without highly skilled slaves or slaves employed other than on a plantation. To be sure, the majority of slaves in nonagricultural pursuits found work as domestic servants, porters, or common laborers in towns. But there was a sufficient number of slave artisans to make it clear that they had the capacity to acquire skills. Frequently advertisements for a slave for sale or a runaway slave described him as a "first rate boot and shoe maker," an "experienced weaver and chair spinner," or an "excellent carpenter." In Virginia they were used in mills, iron furnaces, and tobacco factories. The Saluda textile factory in South Carolina at one time employed 98 slave operatives. They were also in the textile mills of Florida, Alabama, Mississippi, and Georgia. In Kentucky they were employed in the saltworks of Clay County and in the iron and lead mines of Caldwell and Crittenden counties. The Southern railroads also employed a considerable number for construction work. It is reported that in 1838 a corporation purchased 140 slaves at a cost of $159,000 to work on the construction of a railroad between Jackson and Brandon, Mississippi. For ten years a slave was the engineer on the West Feliciana Railroad, one of the oldest in the Southern United States. Finally, slaves were frequently employed in river transportation and at docks. Despite Olmsted's observation that Irish workers were employed to unload boats on the Mississippi River because slaves were too valuable, slaves were extensively used in such work. They worked on the docks at New Orleans, Savannah, Charleston, Norfolk, and other Southern ports.

There were even slave inventors. In 1835 and 1836 Henry Blair, designated in the records as a "colored man" of Maryland, received patents for two corn harvesters he had developed. By 1858, however, the attorney general had ruled that since a slave was not a citizen, the government could not enter into an agreement with him by granting him a patent, nor could the slave assign the invention to his owner. Benjamin Montgomery, a slave owned by Jefferson Davis, invented a boat propeller toward the end of the slave period. Davis made an attempt to have it patented, but failed. This perhaps accounts for the passage of a law by the Confederate Congress in 1861 providing that if the owner took an oath that his or her slave had actually invented a device, the patent would be issued to the owner. It was not until after the Civil War that blacks were able to secure patents for their inventions without any difficulty.

■ Social Considerations

It has been assumed too frequently that slavery provided an idyllic existence not only for owners but for slaves as well. The fact is, however, that even for the planter life was not always pleasant. There was little in the way of recreation and other diversions to foster a zest for living either on the plantation or in the Southern towns. Life was so barren generally that it can hardly be described as "the good life" even under the most favorable circumstances. The plantation, with its inherent isolation and consequent social and cultural self-sufficiency, frequently bordering on stagnancy, tended to perpetuate the barrenness. For slaves there was little in the way of enjoyment and satisfaction during the moments or hours they were off the job. It must be remembered that for the most part slaves had no time they could call their own, and not infrequently they worked such long hours that periods of free time necessarily had to be used for rest. Even if there was no work and even if an opportunity for diversion presented itself, slaves could never escape the fact that they were slaves and that their movements as well as their other activities were almost always under the most careful surveillance. If they found it possible to enjoy the periods when they were not on the job, they either possessed a remarkable capacity for accommodation or were totally ignorant of the depth of their degraded position.

Most slave children had the run of the plantation and played with the white children in and out of the "big house," in and out of the cabins, and through the yards without any inhibitions. When blacks reached the useful age, which was very early, much of the playing was over. When they reached the social age, interracial playing was over altogether, and they settled down to the existence that was the inevitable lot of a slave. There was almost nothing of a day-to-day nature for slaves to do in the way of recreation. If the plantation was near a stream it might be possible for them to make it through the woods and spend an hour or so fishing, but not infrequently this was for the specific purpose of supplementing their food supply instead of for recreation. When whites went hunting at night they usually took some slave men, but on a large plantation there were many who never got this opportunity. Races, fairs, militia muster, and election days were occasions for the relaxation of rules on the plantation. Some slaves were favored by being given permission to attend these events. Even if they did not go, there was an opportunity for them to sing, dance, and visit because of the festive spirit that such occasions brought to the plantation.

There were two periods to which slaves could look forward as periods of recreation and relaxation: the summer lay-by and Christmas. At the end of the cultivation period, there was a considerable reduction of duties, which gave slaves an opportunity either to work for themselves or to engage in some kind of recreation. The Christmas season brought a complete suspension of work, except the bare essentials such as cooking and washing, and for one week both town and plantation slaves had a period of merrymaking. On the Atlantic seaboard much of the festivities centered around the John Canoe celebration, a custom practiced in the Caribbean and perhaps in Africa in which slaves engaged in singing, dancing, drinking, and visiting the whites and asking for Christmas presents. Weddings, anniversaries, and the like, whether of whites or blacks, were other opportunities for merrymaking. Some planters even gave dances for their slaves. Doubtless these were exceptions. Few of the 4 million slaves in 1860 led anything except the most barren existence in which their only moments of pleasure were in singing a plaintive melody, strumming a banjo, telling a tale, or playing a game.

As long as proper precautions were taken there was little opposition to some form of religious activity among slaves. Owners had reason to be suspicious if the emphasis was on instruction or if there were slave leaders. Otherwise there was either support of a religious program for slaves or passive indifference. There were some black congregations on the larger plantations and in the towns. Richmond, Charleston, and Lexington, Kentucky, are examples of cities in which churches for slaves were located. One Mississippi planter erected a small Gothic church and paid a clergyman $1,500 to preach to him and his slaves. The number of black preachers was always considerable, and few plantations were without at least one.

When the abolitionists began their crusade against slavery, planters became more cautious regarding religious activities among slaves and undertook to control them more effectively. In most states black preachers were outlawed between 1830 and 1835, and thereafter slave religious services were presided over by a white person. More and more, however, slaves were required to attend the churches of their masters. This ambivalent attitude toward autonomous religious activity reflected whites' fears that it would be difficult, if not impossible, to control and monitor the beliefs and practices of slaves who were devout Christians. Such fears proved accurate, for many of the most pious and influential slaves had a keen understanding of the difference between the gospel of proslavery preachers and the Christian scriptures' message of divine punishment for oppressors and liberation for the faithful. Albert Raboteau has traced some of the numerous ways in which slaves blended their African religious culture with selected aspects of Christianity to produce a sustaining, and at times defiant, religious community—"the invisible institution in the ante-bellum South."

The invitation to slaves to attend white churches, which bordered on compulsion, did not represent a movement in the direction of increased fellowship. Rather, it was the method that whites employed to keep a closer eye on their slaves. It was believed that too many conspiracies had been planned at religious gatherings and that such groups gave abolitionists an opportunity to distribute incendiary ideas and literature. When Bishop Atkinson of North Carolina raised the question "Where are our Negroes," he not only implied that they were in churches other than the Episcopal church but that they were beyond the restraining influence of the conservative element of white society. When slaves attended the churches of planters, they usually sat either in the gallery or in a special section. The earliest examples of racial segregation could be found in churches. In one instance the white congregation constructed a partition several feet high to separate the masters from the slaves.

In the states of the lower South the Baptist and Methodist denominations had the greatest influence on plantation slaves. These were evangelical churches that moved with the population and adjusted their program to the needs of the people. The Methodist camp meetings and the Baptist "protracted" meetings were opportunities not only for religious refreshing but for social intercourse as well. They were the most effective means of releasing the pent-up emotions that the monotonous life of the rural South created. Thus, whites attended in large numbers, and, as Gilbert Seldes has pointed out, they were "times of refreshing." Under such circumstances, whites and Negroes sang together, shouted together, and spent themselves emotionally together. It was the nearest thing to interracial religious fellowship that the South produced.

Once planters were convinced that conversion did not have the effect of emancipating their slaves, they sought to use the church as an agency for maintaining the institution of slavery. Ministers were encouraged to instruct slaves along the lines of obedience and subserviency. Bishops and other high church officials were not above owning slaves and fostering the continuation of slavery. In Louisiana the Episcopal Bishop Polk owned 400 slaves, and although he regularly gave them religious instruction, there is no indication that he attempted to set them free. The Presbyterians and Quakers seemed to have been the most liberal in their attitude toward blacks, but they were not the large slaveholders. The latter were to be found in the Episcopal church

FAMILY WORSHIP ON A SOUTH CAROLINA PLANTATION. This drawing from the *Illustrated London News* for December 5, 1863, was made by an English artist while visiting a plantation near Port Royal, South Carolina. The "state of almost patriarchal simplicity" that characterizes the planter's position reflects the sympathetic attitude that many Englishmen had toward the Confederacy during the Civil War.

on the Atlantic seaboard and in the Baptist and Methodist churches in the cotton kingdom. In the last three decades before the Civil War the church became one of the strongest allies of the proslavery element. Slaves who had found refuge and solace in the religious instructions of the white clergy had reason to believe that they were now trapped by an enemy who had once befriended them.

Despite legal restrictions and despite contentions on the part of Southerners like John Calhoun that Africans could not absorb educative experiences, slaves were receiving education in various parts of the South. It is remarkable how generally the laws against the teaching of slaves were disregarded. Planters became excited over the distribution of abolition literature in the South, but they gave little attention to preventing the training of slaves to read, which would have rendered abolition literature ineffective to a large extent. Indeed, some masters themselves taught their slaves. William Pease of Hardman County, Tennessee, was taught by his owners. There was one strange case in which a planter taught his slaves to spell and read but not to write. One planter in northern Mississippi boasted that all twenty of his slaves could read and that they purchased their own books. The case of Frederick Douglass having been taught by his mistress is perhaps the best-known instance of an owner teaching a slave. In some cases, even when masters were opposed to their slaves receiving instruction, the children of masters would teach slaves to read and write. There are records of hirers and even overseers giving instruction to slaves.

The instruction of one or two slaves, though a violation of the law, was not regarded as serious, and there was hardly any danger of prosecution. But the instruction of slaves in schools was another thing. Even this was undertaken in various parts of the South. Naturally, more care had to be exercised in the selection of students and in the dissemination of information concerning the schools, but there were blacks and whites who were willing to run the risk of legal prosecution and social disapprobation in order to teach slaves. Schools for blacks are known to have existed in Savannah, Georgia; Charleston, South Carolina; Fayetteville, New Bern, and Raleigh, North Carolina; Lexington and Louisville, Kentucky; Fredericksburg and Norfolk, Virginia; and various other cities in Florida, Tennessee, and Louisiana. Francis Cardozo attended school in Charleston until he was twelve years of age. After searching for some time, Frederika Bremer, a European visitor, finally found one of the schools in Charleston and visited it. In 1847 there was a school in Louisville, Kentucky, which slaves were allowed to attend upon presenting permits from their masters.

There is no way of knowing the extent to which blacks attended white schools. In 1840 they were permitted to attend school with white children in Wilmington, Delaware. There is the interesting account, though perhaps fictional, of Julius Melbourn who was sent to a white academy near Raleigh, North Carolina, by his mistress and supposedly remained there until it was discovered that he was not white. Other mulattoes may well have had more success than Melbourn. Nor is there any way of ascertaining with any degree of accuracy the extent of education among slaves. Some Southern whites said that blacks did not have the capacity to learn. Some Northern abolitionists said conditions in the South were so bad that almost no blacks had the opportunity to learn. Amos Dresser believed that 1 out of every 50 slaves in the Southwest could read and write. C. G. Parsons estimated that 5,000 of Georgia's 400,000 slaves were literate. Whatever the number, it represented a clear-cut step in the direction of Americanization and made, at least for some, the process of adjustment to freedom somewhat less difficult.

The slave family experienced great difficulty in maintaining itself on a stable basis in a system where so little opportunity for expression was possible. Too seldom did the owner recognize the slave family as an institution worthy of respect, and frequently the blind forces inherent in the

Harriet Jacobs Remembers Her Life as a Young Slave Girl

But I now entered on my fifteenth year—a sad epoch in the life of a slave girl. My master began to whisper foul words in my ear. Young as I was, I could not remain ignorant of their import. I tried to treat them with indifference or contempt. The master's age, my extreme youth, and the fear that his conduct would be reported to my grandmother, made him bear this treatment for many months. He was a crafty man, and resorted to many means to accomplish his purposes. Sometimes he had stormy, terrific ways, that made his victims tremble; sometimes he assumed a gentleness that he thought must surely subdue. Of the two, I preferred his stormy moods, although they left me trembling. He tried his utmost to corrupt the pure principles my grandmother had instilled. He peopled my young mind with unclean images, such as only a vile monster could think of. I turned from him with disgust and hatred. But he was my master. I was compelled to live under the same roof with him—where I saw a man forty years my senior daily violating the most sacred commandments of nature. He told me I was his property; that I must be subject to his will in all things. My soul revolted against the mean tyranny. But where could I turn for protection? No matter whether the slave girl be as black as ebony or as fair as her mistress. In either case, there is no shadow of law to protect her from insult, from violence, or even from death; all these are inflicted by fiends who bear the shape of men. The mistress, who ought to protect the helpless victim, has no other feelings towards her but those of jealousy and rage.

Harriet A. Jacobs, *Incidents in the Life of a Slave Girl Written By Herself.* (Cambridge, Mass., 1987), pp. 27–28.

system operated to destroy it. Courtship and the normal relationships preliminary to marriage seldom existed. Only when owners manifested some real interest in the religious and moral development of their slaves was there an effort to establish slave families on a stable basis. There are instances where planters insisted on religious ceremonies to unite slave couples, and there is one case of a mistress insisting upon "passing" on all the suitors of her female slaves. One thing that distressed almost all slaveholders was the desire of slaves to marry slaves on other plantations. Such a union, planters knew, would involve one or the other of the slaves being away from his or her own plantation at various times and reduced efficiency as a worker. Slaves were, therefore, encouraged to marry on the plantation if at all possible, and when this was not possible masters sought either to purchase the spouse of their slave or sell their slave to the owner of the spouse.

The permanency of a slave marriage depended on the extent to which the couple had an opportunity to work and live together so that through common experiences they could be drawn closer together. There are numerous examples of the emergence of a stable slave family, especially where there were children to strengthen the bond and where they were not divided through sale. It has been well said by E. Franklin Frazier that the economic interests of the masters were often inimical to the family life of the slaves, but John Blassingame and Herbert Gutman have shown that the slave family was frequently a viable institution.

The bearing of children was often extremely hard for the slave women. Lack of adequate medical care had a particularly negative impact on the health of slave women during pregnancies, childbirths, and the period immediately thereafter, and the high death rate of slave infants in many ways was a reflection of this. Although having learned, by observing the white family unit, certain elements of so-called decency and self-respect, the slave woman was frequently forced into cohabitation and pregnancy by her master. Obviously in such cases the family was established on a very tenuous basis. She may have learned to care for her husband, who had been forced upon her, but the likelihood was not very great. Nor did she have much opportunity to develop any real attachment for her children. Little time off was given for childbearing, and child rearing was of course a haphazard arrangement in which the mother, just like everyone else, was relieved of any responsibility. Nevertheless, the slave mother did what she could to stabilize her family and to keep it together. Division by sale was fiercely resisted. J. W. Loguen's mother, for example, had to be tied to a loom when her children were taken from her to be sold, and Josiah Henson's mother looked on "in an agony of grief" as she saw her children sold one by one.

Sir Charles Lyell said that "one of the most serious evils of slavery is its tendency to blight domestic happiness; and the anxiety of parents for their sons, and constant fear of licentious intercourse with slaves is painfully great." This "evil" not only blighted the happiness of the white family but was one of the powerful forces operating to weaken the slave family altogether. The extensive miscegenation that went on was largely the result of people living and working together at common tasks and the subjection of slave women to the whims and desires of white men. There was some race mixture that resulted from the association of black men and white women, but this was only a small percent of the total. Despite all the laws against the intermingling of the races, the practice continued, and its persistence is another example of the refusal of the members of the dominant group to abide by the laws that they themselves created.

In cities like Charleston, Mobile, and New Orleans there was widespread intermixture. In New Orleans the practice of young white men maintaining young black women in a state of concubinage became so common as almost to gain social acceptability. Some relationships were the result of physical compulsion on the part of the white man, and if resistance was offered it was frequently beaten back in the most vicious manner. Many slave women carried to their graves scars that had been inflicted by their owners or other whites when resistance was offered to their advances. Other slave women did not resist, either because of futility, the prestige that such a relationship could bring, or because of the material advantages that might accrue from it. Children born of such unions were slaves, and the result of such extensive mixing was that by 1850 there were 246,000 mulatto slaves out of a total slave population of 3.2 million. By 1860 there were 411,000 mulatto slaves out of a total slave population of 3.9 million. The number may well have been greater, for census takers counted as mulattoes only those who appeared to be of mixed parentage, but there were many mulattoes who did not appear to be.

The reactions of white fathers to their black progeny were varied. Some had no feeling for them at all and sold them when the opportunity presented itself, just as they would sell any other slave. Not infrequently they were encouraged to do this by their wives, who resented the presence of slave children who had been fathered by their husbands. Other men, however, developed a great fondness for their slave children and emancipated them and provided for them. Frequently, old, repentant men atoned for their youthful waywardness by freeing their mulatto children and giving them land and money. Few, however, bestowed as much as John Stewart of Petersburg, who left to his "natural colored daughter" a house, a lot, and all of his money, which amounted to $19,500.

■ The Slave's Reaction to Bondage

Owners of slaves almost always sought to convey the impression that their human chattel were docile, tractable, and happy. This effort became a part of their defense of the institution, and they went to the extreme in this representation. Frequently, also, the antislavery forces contended that slaves were easily controlled and that was the explanation for their exploitation by their owners. Each group in its own way, therefore, was inclined to overstate the case and to refuse to make a realistic appraisal of a slave's true reaction to his or her status. There is no reason to conclude that the personality of a slave was permanently impaired by engaging in duplicity in the slave-master relationship. It must be remembered that some of the actions of slaves were superficial and were for the purpose of misleading their owners regarding their true feelings. In the process of adjustment innumerable techniques to escape work as well as punishment were developed and in many instances were successful. Any understanding of reactions to slave status must be approached with the realization that the slave at times was possessed of a dual personality and could be one person at one time and quite a different person at another time.

It cannot be denied that as old as the institution of slavery was, human beings had not, by the nineteenth century, brought themselves to the point where they could be subjected to it without protest and resistance. Resistance could be found wherever slavery existed, and slavery in the United States was no exception. Too frequently, misunderstanding, suspicion, and hatred were mutually shared by master and slave. Indeed, they were natural enemies, and on many occasions they conducted themselves as such. There are, of course, numerous examples of kindness and understanding on the part of owners as well as docility—which may be more accurately described as accommodation—and tractability on the part of slaves. But this was an unnatural relationship and was not, by the nature of things, inherent in the system.

The brutality that apparently was indigenous in a system of human exploitation existed in every community where slavery was established. The wastefulness and extravagance of the plantation system made no exception of human resources. Slaves were for economic gain, and if beating them would increase their efficiency—and this was generally believed—then the rod and lash should not be spared. Far from being a civilizing force, moreover, the plantation bred indecency in human relations, and the slave was the immediate victim of the barbarity of a system that commonly exploited the sex of the women and the work of everyone. Finally, the psychological situation that was created by the master-slave relationship stimulated terrorism and brutality because masters felt secure in their position and interpreted their role as calling for that type of conduct. Many masters as well as slaves got the reputation of being "bad," and this did nothing to relieve the tension that seemed to be mounting everywhere as the institution developed.

The laws that were for the purpose of protecting slaves were few and were seldom enforced. It was almost impossible to secure the conviction of a master who mistreated a slave. Knowing that, the owner was inclined to take the law into his or her own hands. Overseers were generally notorious for their brutality, and the accounts of abuse and mistreatment on their part as well as on the part of hirers are numerous. Masters and mistresses were perhaps almost as guilty. In 1827 a Georgia grand jury brought in a true bill of manslaughter against a slave owner for beating his slave to death, but he was acquitted. Several years later Thomas Sorrell of the same state was found guilty of killing one of his slaves with an axe, but the jury recommended him to the mercy of the court. In Kentucky a Mrs. Maxwell had a wide reputation for beating her slaves, both men and women, on the face as well as the body. There is also the shocking account of Mrs. Alpheus Lewis, who burned her slave girl around the neck with hot tongs. Drunken masters had little regard for their slaves, the most sensational example of which is a Kentucky man who dismembered his slave and threw him piece by piece into the fire. One Mississippi master dragged from the bed a slave whom he suspected of theft and inflicted over 1,000 lashes. Repeated descriptions of runaways contained phrases such as "large scar on hip," "no marks except those on his back," "much scarred with the whip," and "will no doubt show the marks of a recent whipping." They suggest a type of brutality that doubtless contributed toward the slave's decision to abscond.

To the demonstrations of brutality as well as to the very institution of slavery itself, slaves reacted in various ways. Thanks to the religion of their masters they could be philosophical about the whole thing and escape through ritual and song. The emphasis on otherworldliness in slave songs certainly suggested grim dissatisfaction with their worldly status. "Dere's a Great Camp Meetin' in de Promised Land," "Look Away in de Heaven, Lord," "Fo' My Soul's Goin' to Heaven Jes' Sho's You Born," and "Heaven, Heaven, Everybody Talkin' 'Bout Heaven Ain't Goin' There" are only a few of the songs that slaves sang in the hope that their burdens would be relieved in the next world. As long as they were in this world they had to make the most of a bad situation by loafing on the job, feigning illness in the fields and on the auction block, and engaging in an elaborate program of sabotage. Slaves were so hard on farming tools that special ones were developed for them. They drove the animals with a cruelty that suggested revenge, and they could be so ruthless in destruction of the fields that the most careful supervision was necessary to ensure survival of the crops until harvest time. Forests, barns, and homes were burned to the extent that members of the patrol were frequently fearful of leaving home lest they be visited with revenge in the form of destruction of their property by fire.

Self-mutilation and suicide were popular forms of resistance to slavery. Slaves cut off their toes and hands and mutilated themselves in other ways so as to render themselves ineffective as workers. One Kentucky slave carpenter, for example, cut off one of his hands and the fingers of the other when he learned that he was to be sold down the river. There were several instances of slaves having shot themselves in the hand or foot, especially upon being recovered from running away. The number of suicides seems relatively high, and certainly the practice was widespread. Slaves fresh from Africa committed suicide in great numbers. In 1807 two boatloads of Africans newly arrived in Charleston starved themselves to death. When his slave woman was found dead by her own hanging in 1829, a Georgia planter was amazed since he saw no reason why she should want to take her own life. When two Louisiana slaves were returned to their master after having been stolen in 1858, they drowned themselves in the bayou. One of the South's wealthiest planters, Charles Manigault, lost a slave by a similar act when the overseer threatened him with punishment. Sometimes slave mothers killed their own children to prevent them from growing up in slavery.

Much more disturbing to the South were the numerous instances of slaves doing violence to the master class. Poisoning was always feared, and perhaps some planters felt a real need for an official taster. As early as 1761 the Charleston *Gazette* remarked that the "Negroes have begun the hellish act of poisoning." Arsenic and other similar compounds were used. Where they were not available, slaves are known to have resorted to mixing ground glass in the gravy for their masters' tables. Numerous slaves were convicted of murdering their masters and overseers, but some escaped. In 1797 a Screven County, Georgia, planter was killed by his newly imported African slave. Another Georgia master was killed by a slave who stabbed him sixteen times.

The slave was later burned alive. The slave of William Pearce of Florida killed his master with an axe when Pearce sought to punish him. Carolina Turner of Kentucky was choked to death by a slave whom she was flogging. Though the citizenry had long complained of the woman's merciless brutality in dealing with her slaves, her killer was summarily hanged for his deed. The times that overseers and masters were killed by slaves in the woods or fields were exceedingly numerous, as the careful reading of almost any Southern newspaper will reveal.

Every Southern community raised its annual crop of runaway slaves. There was both federal and state legislation to aid in their recovery, but many slaves escaped forever. The practice of running away became so widespread that every state sought to strengthen its patrol and other safeguards, but to little avail. Hardly a newspaper went to press without several advertisements listing runaways, and sometimes there were several columns of such advertisements. The following is typical:

> Absconded from the Forest Plantation of the late William Dunbar, on Sunday the 7th instant, a very handsome Mulattress called Harriet, about 13 years old, with straight dark hair and dark eyes. This girl was lately in New Orleans, and is known to have seen there a man whom she claims as her father and who does now or did lately live on the Mississippi, a little above the mouth of the Caffalaya. It is highly probable some plan has been concocted for the girl's escape.

Long before the Underground Railroad was an effective antislavery device (see Chapter 10) slaves were running away: men, women, and children, singly, in pairs, or in groups. At times they went so far as to organize themselves into groups called Maroons and to live in communities, on the order of Palmares in Brazil. The forests, mountains, and swamps of the Southern states were their favorite locations, and they proved to be troublesome to the masters who sought to maintain strict order on their plantations.

Some slaves disguised themselves or armed themselves with free passes in their effort to escape. Others simply walked off, apparently hoping that fate would be kind and assist in their permanent escape. Some were inveterate runaways such as the North Carolina woman who fled from her master's plantation no less than sixteen times. Others were not as daring and gave up after one unsuccessful attempt. While there is no way of even approximating the number of runaways, it is obvious that fleeing from the institution was one of the slaves' most effective means of resistance. It represented the continuous fight that slaves carried on against their masters.

The most sensational and desperate reaction of slaves to their status was the conspiracy to revolt. To those who could summon the nerve to strike for their freedom in a group, it was what might be termed "carrying the fight to the enemy" in the hope that it would end, once and for all, the degradation of human enslavement. To whites it was a mad, sinister act of

Henry Bibb Writes to His Former Master—1844

You may perhaps think hard of us for running away from slavery, but as to myself, I have but one apology to make for it, which is this: I have only to regret that I did not start at an earlier period. I might have been free long before I was. But you had it in your power to have kept me there much longer than you did. I think it is very probable that I should have been a toiling slave on your property to-day, if you had treated me differently.

To be compelled to stand by and see you whip and slash my wife without mercy, when I could afford her no protection, not even by offering myself to suffer the lash in her place, was more than I felt it to be the duty of a slave husband to endure, while the way was open to Canada. My infant child was also frequently flogged by Mrs. Gatewood, for crying, until its skin was bruised literally purple. This kind of treatment was what drove me from home and family, to seek a better home for them. But I am willing to forget the past. I should be pleased to hear from you again, on the reception of this, and should also be very happy to correspond with you often, if it should be agreeable to yourself. I subscribe myself a friend to the oppressed, and Liberty forever.

Narrative of the Life and Adventures of Henry Bibb, an American Slave, in Gilbert Osofsky, ed., *Puttin' on Ole Massa* (New York, 1969), pp. 155–156.

desperate savages, in league with the devil, who could not appreciate the benign influences of the institution and who would dare shed the blood of their benefactors. Inherent in revolts was bloodshed on both sides. Blacks accepted this as the price of liberty, while whites were panic-stricken at the very thought of it. Even rumors of insurrections struck terror in the hearts of slaveholders and called forth the most vigorous efforts to guard against the dreaded eventuality.

Revolts, or conspiracies to revolt, persisted down to 1865. They began with the institution and did not end until slavery was abolished. It can, therefore, be said that they were a part of the institution, a kind of bitterness that whites had to take along with the sweetness of slavery. As the country was turning to Jeffersonian Republicanism at the beginning of the nineteenth century, many people believed that a new day had arrived for the common person. Some blacks, however, felt that they would have to force their new day by breaking away from slavery. In Henrico County, Virginia, they resolved to revolt against the institution under the leadership of Gabriel Prosser and Jack Bowler. For months they planned the desperate move, gathering clubs, swords, and the like for the appointed day. On August 30, 1800, over 1,000 slaves met six miles outside of Richmond and began to march on the city, but a violent storm almost routed the insurgents. Two slaves had already informed the whites, and Governor Monroe, acting promptly, called out more than 600 troops and notified every militia commander in the state. In due time scores of slaves were arrested, and 35 were executed. Gabriel Prosser was captured in late September, and after he refused to talk to anyone he too was executed.

Whites speculated extravagantly over the number of slaves involved in this major uprising. The estimates ran all the way from 2,000 to 50,000. The large numbers, together with the total disregard slaves seemed to have for their own lives, caused the whites to shudder. The "high ground" that slaves took in maintaining silence added to the stark terror of the whole situation. When one was asked what he had to say, he calmly replied:

> I have nothing more to offer than what General Washington would have had to offer, had he been taken by the British officers and put to trial by them. I have ventured my life in endeavouring to obtain the liberty of my country-men, and am a willing sacrifice to their cause; and I beg, as a favour, that I may be immediately led to execution. I know that you have predetermined to shed my blood, why then all this mockery of a trial?

The unrest among slaves, even in Virginia, continued into the following year, and plots were reported in Petersburg and Norfolk and in various places in North Carolina. The latter state became so excited that many slaves were lashed, branded, and cropped, and at least 15 were hanged for alleged implication in conspiracies. In the following years before the war with England there were reports of insurrection up and down the Atlantic seaboard. Conspiracy had crossed the mountains, for in 1810 a plot was uncovered in Lexington, Kentucky. The following year, more than 400 rebellious slaves in Louisiana had to be put down by federal and state troops. At least 75 slaves lost their lives in the encounter and in the trials that ensued. There was another uprising in New Orleans in the following year.

Following the War of 1812 the efforts of slaves to revolt continued. In Virginia in 1815 a white man, George Boxley, decided to attempt to free the slaves. He made elaborate plans, but a slave woman betrayed him and his conspirators. Although Boxley himself escaped, six slaves were hanged and another six were banished. When the revolutions of Latin America and Europe broke out, Americans could not restrain themselves in their praise and support of the fighters for liberty. The South joined in the loud hosannas, while slaves watched the movements for the emancipation of the slaves in Latin America and the Caribbean. Perhaps all these developments had something to do with what was the most elaborate, though not the most effective, conspiracy of the period: the Denmark Vesey insurrection.

Vesey had purchased his freedom in 1800 and for a score of years had made a respectable living as a carpenter in Charleston, South Carolina. He was a sensitive, liberty-loving person and was not satisfied in the enjoyment of his

NAT TURNER EXHORTING HIS FOLLOWERS. The 1831 revolt of Nat Turner and his followers in Virginia resulted in the deaths of his master and numerous other whites. Once the revolt was crushed, dazed whites strengthened slave codes and redoubled vigilance. The artist's depiction reflects whites' fears of the consequences of blacks meeting without the supervision of their masters. *(Culver Pictures.)*

own relatively comfortable existence. He believed in equality for everyone and resolved to do something for his slave brothers and sisters. Over a period of several years he carefully plotted his revolt and chose his assistants. Together they made and collected their weapons: 250 pike heads and bayonets and 300 daggers. Vesey also sought assistance from Haiti. He set the second Sunday in July 1822 for the day of the revolt; and when the word leaked out, he moved it up one month, but his assistants, who were scattered for miles around Charleston, did not all get the word. Meanwhile, the whites were well aware of what was going on and began to round up suspects. At least 139 blacks were arrested, 47 of whom were condemned. Even 4 white men were fined and imprisoned for encouraging them in their work. Estimates of the number of blacks involved in the plot ran as high as 9,000.

The following decade saw the entire South apprehensive over possible uprisings. The revival of the antislavery movement and the publication of such incendiary material as David Walker's *Appeal* put the South's nerves on edge. Several revolts were reported on Louisiana plantations in 1829, and in 1830 a number of citizens of North Carolina asked their legislature for aid because their slaves had become "almost uncountroulable." The panic of the 1820s culminated in 1831 with the insurrection of Nat Turner. This slave from Southampton County, Virginia, was a mystical, rebellious person who had on one occasion run away and then decided to return to his master. Perhaps he had already begun to feel that he had been selected by some divine power to deliver his people from slavery.

Upon the occasion of the solar eclipse in February 1831, Turner decided that the time had come for him to lead his people out of bondage. He selected the Fourth of July as the day, but when he became ill he postponed the revolt until he saw another sign. On August 13, when the sun turned a "peculiar greenish blue," he called the revolt for August 21. He and his followers began by killing Turner's master, Joseph Travis, and his family. In rapid succession other families fell before the blows of the blacks. Within twenty-four hours 60 whites had been killed. The revolt was spreading rapidly when the main group of blacks was met and overpowered by state and federal troops. More than 100 slaves were killed in the encounter, and 13 slaves and 3 free Negroes were immediately hanged. Turner was captured on October 30, and in less than two weeks, on November 11, he was executed.

The South was completely dazed by the Southampton uprising. The situation was grossly exaggerated in many communities. Some reports were that whites had been murdered by the hundreds in Virginia. Small wonder that several states felt it necessary to call special sessions of the legislature to consider the emergency. Most states strengthened their Slave Codes, and citizens literally remained awake nights waiting for slaves to make another break. The uprisings continued. In 1835 several slaves in Monroe County, Georgia, were hanged or whipped to death because of implication in a conspiracy. In the following decade there were several uprisings in Alabama, Louisiana, and Mississippi. In 1853 a serious revolt in New Orleans involving 2,500 slaves was aborted by the informing of a free black. In 1856 the Maroons in Bladen and Robeson counties, North Carolina, "went on the warpath" and terrorized the countryside. Up until and throughout the Civil War, slaves demonstrated their violent antipathy for slavery by continuing to rise against it.

One little-known sidelight of slave revolts is the encouragement and assistance that whites gave to blacks. Two Frenchmen were said to have been involved in Gabriel Prosser's plot. In 1802 a Virginia slave confessed that some white men had promised to help him secure arms and ammunition for an uprising. It will be recalled that four white men were convicted for encouraging Denmark Vesey's uprising. In Mississippi in 1835, twenty-one "bleached and unbleached" conspirators were hanged. In the same year white men in Georgia were involved in a plot, and two whites were hanged in Louisiana for helping to plan an uprising. There were always reports that whites, whose names were most difficult to obtain, were assisting in some way with slave plots. It is not at all strange that some whites sought to encourage the revolts. When consideration is given to the large number of whites in the South who could have traced their economic and social plight directly to slavery, it is surprising to find that there was not a larger number involved in attempts to wipe out the institution of slavery.

■

CHAPTER 9

Quasi-Free Blacks

■ American Anomaly

With the prohibition of slavery in several Northern states and with programs for gradual emancipation in others before the end of the eighteenth century, it was only natural that free blacks would in due time become a substantial element of the population. Slavery, moreover, had been excluded from the Northwest Territory, though it persisted there for several decades after 1787. There had been some free blacks during the entire colonial period, but for the most part they were inconsiderable in number and inconsequential in influence. The Revolution, with its philosophy of egalitarianism, had served to increase the number of free blacks not only in the North but in the South too, where some masters put the philosophy into practice. But in the South the existence of a large group of free blacks proved to be a source of constant embarrassment to slaveholders, for it tended to undermine the very foundation on which slavery was built. The perpetuation of relations between the whites and blacks in the South was predicated upon the indisputable control of the latter by the former. Free blacks, regardless of what their rights were theoretically, could not be an exception. It became necessary, therefore, for Southerners to carry on a campaign of vilification against free blacks in order to "keep them in their place." In the heat of this campaign one antagonist went so far as to describe free blacks as "an incubus upon the land."

Despite Southern opposition to the presence of free blacks, white people themselves were frequently responsible for the increase. Masters, stricken by conscience, impelled by affection, or yielding to the temptation to evade responsibility, manumitted their slaves in large numbers until legislation either discouraged or prevented them from doing so. Many slaves were freed by their masters through deeds of manumission. In some instances the manumitted were children of a master by one of his slaves. Others were manumitted through wills, like the slaves of John Randolph, numbering more than 400, who were set free upon his death in 1833. There were stipulations in some wills that slaves should be set free upon reaching a certain age or upon the death of the testator's heirs. Either individual owners or the state manumitted slaves occasionally for meritorious service. The slave who saved the Georgia capitol from destruction by fire was set free in 1834. Pierre Chastang of Mobile was bought and freed by popular subscription because of his outstanding service in the War of 1812 and in the yellow fever epidemic of 1819.

Enterprising slaves were able to amass sufficient capital to purchase their freedom, especially if their masters were willing to cooperate. There are several examples of masters who set up programs of self-hire for slaves who looked toward purchasing themselves. Some slaves, regardless of their masters' attitude, saved enough money to purchase their freedom. Lunsford Lane of Raleigh, for example, spent his spare time making pipes, raising chickens, and engaging in other tasks in order to realize his ambition of becoming free. A slave could not always trust an owner who promised freedom upon the payment of a certain amount of money, as one of Lane's friends found out after he had given his owner $800 and then had had to run away. Indeed, thousands of slaves secured their freedom by running away.

As the number of free blacks increased by these various methods of obtaining freedom, it also multiplied through the natural excess of births over deaths. Children born of free black mothers were also free, and as the free black family achieved a degree of stability, children became an important factor in adding to their numbers. There was some increase, moreover, from the birth of mulatto children to white mothers. The practice of white women mixing with black men was fairly widespread during the colonial period and had not entirely ceased by 1865.

There were 59,000 free blacks in the United States at the time of the first decennial census in 1790. Slightly more than 27,000 were in the Northern states, and 32,000 in the South. In the next decade they increased by approximately 82 percent, and in the following decade by 71 percent. After 1810 the rate of increase fell sharply, a trend that continued up until 1860. This decline was due largely to laws against manumission and to the opposition of those who viewed their increase with great alarm. Many states required blacks to leave the state upon being manumitted. By 1830 there were 319,000 free blacks in the United States, and thirty years later the number had climbed to 488,000, of whom 44 percent lived in the South Atlantic states and 46 percent in the North. The remainder were to be found in the South Central states and the West. Maryland led all other states with

DEED OF MANUMISSION. Ebenezer Rothwell of Newcastle County, Delaware, promised to set free his twenty-year-old slave, Isaac, when he reached the age of thirty-two. Other popular forms of emancipation were by will and by legislative act. (*Original ms. The Moorland-Spingarn Research Center, Howard University.*)

83,900 free blacks in 1860, a figure only slightly smaller than the slave population. Virginia was next with 58,000, followed closely by Pennsylvania with 56,000, its entire black population.

By 1860 free blacks were concentrated in six areas: the tidewater counties of Virginia and Maryland; the Piedmont region of Virginia and North Carolina; the Southern cities of Baltimore, Washington, Charleston, Mobile, and New Orleans; the Northern cities of Boston, New York, Cincinnati, and Philadelphia; isolated areas in the old Northwest like Cass County, Michigan,

Hammond County, Indiana, and Wilberforce, Ohio; and communities in which blacks had mixed freely with Indians, such as those in Massachusetts, North Carolina, and Florida. Free blacks were inclined to be urban. In 1860 there were 25,600 in Baltimore, 22,000 in Philadelphia, 12,500 in New York, 10,600 in New Orleans, and 3,200 in Charleston. The greater opportunities, both economic and social, doubtless accounted for their tendency to concentrate in cities.

Wherever free blacks settled, they lived somewhat precariously upon the sufferance of the whites. Their legal status was fairly high during the colonial period and was strengthened somewhat during the Revolutionary period. After that time, however, their status deteriorated, until toward the end of the slave period the distinction between slaves and free blacks had diminished to a point where in some instances it was hardly discernible. Free blacks found it especially difficult to maintain their freedom. A white person could claim, however fraudulently, that a black person was a slave, and there was very little he or she could do about it. There was, moreover, the danger of the black person's being kidnapped, as often happened. The chances of being reduced to servitude or slavery by the courts were also great. A large majority of free blacks lived in daily fear of losing what freedom they had. One slip or ignorance of the law would send them back into slavery. Several states, such as Virginia, Tennessee, Georgia, and Mississippi, required registration. Florida, Georgia, and several other states compelled free blacks to have white guardians. All Southern states required them to have passes, and if one was caught without a certificate of freedom, he or she was presumed to be a slave.

The controls that the state and the community exercised over free blacks mounted year by year. One especially annoying regulation limited their movement. In no Southern state could they move about as they wished, and in some Northern communities it was dangerous to try, lest they be thought fugitive slaves. North Carolina prohibited free blacks from going beyond the county adjoining the one in which they resided. As early as 1793 Virginia barred them from entering the state, and by 1835 most of the Southern and several Northern states had restricted or prohibited free black immigration. Penalties for violations of these laws were severe. In Georgia, for example, the offender was fined $100, and failing to pay it—which could be expected—was sold into slavery. There were also laws against free blacks leaving the state for any length of time, such as sixty or ninety days, and returning.

There was a mass of legislation designed to insure the white community against any threats or dangers from free blacks. Virginia, Maryland, and North Carolina were among the states forbidding them to possess or carry arms without a license. This permit was issued annually, and only to those whose conduct was above reproach. By 1835 the right of assembly had been taken away from almost all free blacks in the South. They could not hold church services without the presence of a licensed and respectable white minister. Benevolent societies and similar organizations were not allowed to

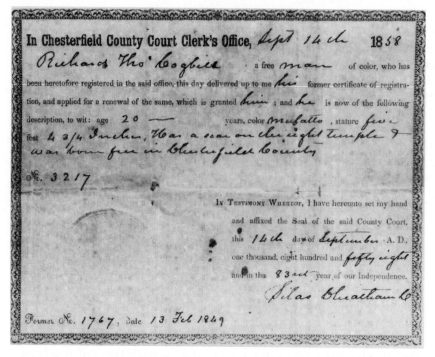

CERTIFICATE OF FREEDOM. Most communities required free blacks to carry such a certificate on their person at all times. Not all of them provided printed forms such as this one, which was issued by the court clerk of Chesterfield County, Virginia. (*Original ms. The Moorland-Spingarn Research Center, Howard University.*)

convene. In Maryland they could not have "lyceums, lodges, fire companies, or literary, dramatic, social, moral, or charitable societies." In many communities contact with slaves was kept at a minimum, and laws against entertaining slaves or visiting them were among those most strenuously enforced.

A number of proscriptions made it especially difficult for free blacks to make a living. In 1805 Maryland prohibited them from selling corn, wheat, or tobacco without a license. In 1829 Georgia made it illegal for them to be employed as typesetters. Two years later North Carolina required all black traders and peddlers to be licensed, while South Carolina forbade the employment of free blacks as clerks. A large number of states made it illegal for them either to purchase or to sell alcoholic beverages. Georgia free blacks could not make purchases on credit without the permission of their guardians. Despite these restrictions every state required free blacks to work, and their means of support had to be visible. As early as 1725 Pennsylvania had set the pattern by ordaining that "if any free negroe, fit to work, shall neglect so to do and loiter and misspend his or her time . . . any two Magistrates . . .

are . . . impowered and required to bind out to service, such negroe, from year to year, as to them may seem meet." Other states passed similar laws during the national period, some going so far as to require free blacks to post bonds as security against becoming public charges. Not only were adult free blacks hired or bound out, but their children were taken and placed in the care of white persons. Illegitimate children whose parents had violated some law or were without means of supporting them were apprenticed out to be taught a trade and to be given moral instruction.

In some states the constitutions written during the Revolutionary period did not exclude free blacks from voting. They voted to a considerable extent in Maryland, North Carolina, New York, and Pennsylvania for several years. All Southern states entering the Union after 1789, except Tennessee, excluded Negroes from the franchise. In a bill signed by President Jefferson in 1802 they were excluded from the franchise in the nation's newly established capital, Washington, D.C. Shortly after the beginning of the nineteenth century, as the campaign to reduce the free black's status got under way, states both in the North and South began to disfranchise them. Maryland's free blacks lost the ballot in 1810. Those in Tennessee were disfranchised in 1834, and in the following year those in North Carolina lost the ballot. Even Pennsylvania confined the privilege to white males in 1838. In its constitution of 1821, New York set up a property qualification of $250 for blacks and a residence requirement of three years for free-black suffrage. Meanwhile, whites had no property requirements for voting and could qualify with only a one year's residency. In states that did not disfranchise blacks, their political influence was taken lightly and there was no extensive voting by blacks anywhere after 1830.

Despite these significant reductions in status, free blacks were expected to bear the burdens that other citizens bore, and in some instances they were expected to do even more. In Pensacola, Florida, they had to pay a tax of $2 for putting on entertainments. In Baltimore in 1859 and in other places as well, they were expected to pay school taxes, but their children were not allowed to attend publicly supported schools. In general they were barred from serving in a state militia except as musicians or servants. Two significant exceptions were the New York law of 1814 raising two black regiments and the Louisiana laws of 1812 authorizing a militia corps of free men of color and, in Natchitoches, a police corps of free blacks.

The right to own and dispose of property was generally conceded to free blacks. When Texas was a republic there was some question as to whether they could own land there, but their right had at least been partially recognized by the time Texas entered the Union in 1845. Only Georgia, in 1818, forbade free blacks to own any real estate or slaves, but the following year the act was repealed, except for Savannah, Augusta, and Darien.

In courts of law the testimony of free blacks was not admissible in cases where whites were parties. Perhaps the clearest example of the disesteem in which free blacks were held was the general policy of permitting slaves, viewed as wholly irresponsible before the law, to testify against them. In practice, however, the courts were fairly lenient toward them. Indeed, from the courts, especially the higher ones, they received the greatest protection. In rejecting the claims of a white person that a black person should be thrown out of court because he had not proved that he was free, the Maryland Court of Appeals said that, in pleading, he did not have to prove his freedom. A justice of the North Carolina Supreme Court went so far as to say that a free black could strike a white man in self-defense: "A free negro, however lowly his condition, is in the 'peace of the State,' and to deprive him of this right would be to put him on the footing of an outlaw."

Slaveholding states had a rather peculiar way of demonstrating their interest in the welfare of free blacks. Since their life was especially difficult, legislators were of the opinion that this class of people should be given the opportunity to choose their masters and reenslave themselves. In 1857 Tennessee enacted a law to facilitate reenslavement. In the following year Texas enacted such a law, and in 1859 and 1860, respectively, Louisiana and Maryland passed similar legislation. Several other states, including North Carolina, seriously considered such statutes, but for various reasons failed to enact them. Perhaps Arkansas went farthest: in 1859 the legislature passed an act to remove free blacks and mulattoes by compelling those who remained in the state at the end of a year to choose masters "who must give bond not to allow such negroes to act as free."

■ Economic and Social Development

It was only natural that free blacks should experience great difficulty in achieving anything resembling economic stability and independence. There was, first of all, the considerable psychological adjustment that had to be made in the transition from enslavement to freedom for all except those who were born free. The success and rapidity of this transition frequently depended upon the responsibility a person had been able to assume while still a slave. Another difficulty, almost insurmountable in some places, was the strong opposition of many white workers to blacks, especially in the artisan class. Whites sought legislation barring them from certain trades; failing in this, they frequently resorted to intimidation and violence in order to eliminate the competition of free blacks. Finally, there was legislation that restricted the movements of free blacks, barred them from certain occupations, and placed them at a disadvantage in other ways. The vast majority were without any special skills and had to content themselves with being agricultural workers or, in urban communities, common laborers. Thanks to the apprenticing system established in some states and to the practice of training many slaves as artisans, a considerable number of free blacks possessed skills that enabled them to achieve a degree of economic independence and affluence before the Civil War.

	TABLE 4		
	Free Black Real Estate Ownership in Fourteen Cities in 1850		
CITIES	VALUE OF REAL ESTATE	NUMBER OF OWNERS	AVERAGE VALUE OF HOLDING
New Orleans	$2,354,640	650	$3,623
Philadelphia	327,000	77	4,248
Cincinnati	317,780	118	2,693
Charleston	200,600	47	4,268
Brooklyn	145,785	98	1,488
Baltimore	137,488	101	1,361
New York	110,010	71	1,549
Washington	108,816	178	611
Louisville	95,650	63	1,518
Pittsburgh	74,200	38	1,953
Buffalo	57,610	41	1,405
St. Louis	49,650	16	3,103
Albany	44,400	32	1,388
Boston	41,900	13	3,223

Source: Leonard P. Curry. The Free Black in Urban America 1800–1850: The Shadow of the Dream. The University of Chicago Press (Chicago, Ill. 1983), p. 267. Reprinted by permission.

Despite the strong opposition of white workers, urban blacks followed their trades if they had any. Even the unskilled found some kind of work to do because they were concentrated in areas that were losing white workers to the West, and in the shortage that prevailed even the labor of the despised black was welcomed. In Charleston, Charles H. Wesley found free blacks engaged in more than 50 occupations, many of them requiring a high degree of skill. They worked in the building trades, made clothing and foods, operated machines, and piloted ships. There were more than 70 occupations in North Carolina in which they were engaged. Among those working in Baltimore in 1860 were several confectioners, druggists, and grocers. Though there were only slightly more than 2,000 free blacks in Boston in 1860, they were scattered among nearly 100 occupations, including paperhanging, engraving, quarrying, photography, and tailoring. They were also in the professions of the ministry, teaching, law, and dentistry. Practically the same can be said for those in New York City and, to a lesser extent, in Cincinnati. In Philadelphia in 1859, they engaged in more than 130 occupations, all of which involved the exercise of skills. Even in the deep South there were free blacks working in occupations and professions that would have disturbed those who were opposed to their progress and surprised those who were convinced of their improvidence. In Atlanta, for example, Roderick Badger was practicing dentistry in 1859. In New Orleans, where in 1845 Norbert Rillieux had invented a vacuum pan for evaporating syrup in the manufacture of sugar, there were teachers, jewelers, architects, and lithographers in 1860. Almost every community had its free black carpenters, barbers, cabinetmakers, and brickmasons; many had shopkeepers, salespeople, and clerks, even where it was in violation of the law.

Aid given by some owners as well as by organizations such as the Society of Friends, the Pennsylvania Society for the Abolition of Slavery, and the North Carolina Manumission Society helped free blacks get a start, and this assistance frequently amounted to enough for them to acquire their first piece of property, usually personal. One benevolent master in Baltimore gave his manumitted slave a house and a lot worth more than $12,000 in 1859. Several gave their freed chattel as much as 100 acres of land. From these benevolences and from their own efforts, free blacks gradually accumulated property. As early as 1800 those in Philadelphia owned nearly 100 houses and lots. By 1837, in New York City, they owned $1.4 million worth of taxable real estate and had $600,000 on deposit in savings banks. In Cincinnati, the property of free blacks was valued at more than $500,000. These evidences of economic stability caused one European observer to describe them as "shrewd and sensible blacks."

Free blacks in the Southern states also accumulated property. In Maryland they paid taxes on more than $1 million of real property in 1860, and 12 owned property valued in excess of $5,000. Luther P. Jackson found that in Virginia in 1860 they owned more than 60,000 acres of farmland and their city real estate was valued at $463,000. In North Carolina they owned $480,000 worth of real property and $564,000 worth of personal property in 1860. In Charleston, 352 blacks paid taxes in 1859 on property valued in excess of $778,000. Tennessee's free blacks owned about $750,000 worth of real and personal property in 1860. The affluence of a large number of free blacks in New Orleans is well known. They owned more than $15 million worth of property in 1860. Small wonder that in the preceding year the *Daily Picayune* was moved to describe them as "a sober, industrious, and moral class, far advanced in education and civilization."

The extent of slaveholding among free blacks has been a matter of only recent concern to the student of history. The majority of black slave owners had some personal interest in their property. Frequently the husband purchased his wife, or vice versa; or the slaves were the children of a free father who had purchased his wife; or they were other relatives or friends who had been rescued from the worst features of the institution by some affluent free black. There were instances, however, in which free blacks had a real economic interest in the institution of slavery and held slaves in order to improve their own economic status. This was true of Cyprian Ricard, who purchased an estate with ninety-one slaves in Louisiana, and of Charles Rogues and Marie Metoyer, who had forty-seven and fifty-eight slaves, respectively. In the Charleston area, as well as around New Orleans, there were several free Negroes who had slaves in such great numbers as to indicate an economic interest in the institution. Free blacks on occasion also employed white people to work for them. Thomas Day, North Carolina's best-known cabinetmaker, employed a white journeyman for several years. Jim Dungey, a wagoner of Nashville, Tennessee, had labor-management problems of his own, for in October 1859 the *Republican Banner* reported that he "got into a fight with a white man in his employ."

Individual cases of affluence among free blacks are numerous. Solomon Humphries of Macon, Georgia, was a leading grocer in the city; before his death he accumulated property worth more than $20,000, including several slaves. Jehu Jones, proprietor of one of Charleston's best hotels, amassed a fortune of more than $40,000 and sent his son to Amherst. James Forten, who had started out as an errand boy on the docks of Philadelphia, became a sailmaker and accumulated a fortune of more than $100,000. Thomy Lafon, the tycoon of New Orleans, was worth $500,000 at his death. He had contributed so much to the development of the city that the state legislature ordered a bust of Lafon to be carved and set up in some public institution in New Orleans. Much closer to the average was James Boon, a North Carolina artisan who, despite his excellence as a carpenter, spent most of his time trying to remain solvent and whose property, what little there was, was in the hands of his creditors more often than in his own.

In the beginning little social distinction was made in America on account of race. As the racial justification for slavery developed, there began to creep into the mores of American society a distinction between blacks and whites. One of its first manifestations was the passage of laws against intermarriage. More and more, however, the real distinction came to be that between whites and those blacks who had some claim to freedom. In the nineteenth century, as the slaveholding class found it necessary to establish safeguards for effective control of free blacks, a veritable wall was erected around the blacks, who found it necessary to develop their own lives and institutions. There existed between them and the rest of the world a minimum of communication, and even this communication steadily decreased.

The free black family evolved as a result of three lines of social relations: marriage within the group; marriage to slaves; and relations, legal or clandestine, with whites and Indians. The free black was not always subjected to the social controls that affected the rest of society. As a result, the relations out of which the free black family sprang were frequently judged immoral and uncivilized according to prevailing social conventions. When free blacks married one another, however, they usually secured licenses and went through a civil or religious ceremony. The marriage of a free black to a slave, which could not be effected without consent of the slave's owner, was more frequently a rather informal union for which no license was secured. Relations with white people were equally informal and consisted of a free black "taking up" with a white person or, as in New

Orleans, a well-to-do white man maintaining a free black woman under a system of *placage*, or concubinage. These relations, together with the manumission of black children by white fathers, accounted for the 159,000 free mulattoes in the United States in 1850.

There was little in the way of organized recreation for free blacks. Their pleasures came from the rather simple experiences of visiting, singing, or attending meetings of organizations to which they belonged. There was considerable drinking, though hardly as much as many whites claimed. Gambling among themselves, with slaves, or with whites, all of which were criminal offenses, was another recreation for them. In urban areas they enjoyed the dances given by various societies and benevolent organizations. Cakewalks and balls were events in Baltimore to which many free blacks looked forward. The best known of the dances were the quadroon balls in New Orleans and a few other Southern cities. These can hardly be called recreation for them, however, since white men were the only males in attendance. Quadroons were either young women whom white men were keeping as concubines or those who were eligible for such relations. Only New York blacks could boast of an "African Theater," which flourished for several years after it was founded in 1821.

Free blacks held their fraternal organizations and benevolent societies in high esteem. The Masons continued to flourish during the generation immediately preceding the Civil War. In Maryland, for example, by 1845 they had grown to the point where it became desirable to form the First Colored Grand Lodge, and two years later another was set up. In 1843, under the leadership of Peter Ogden, a group of them organized the Grand United Order of Odd Fellows, which became one of the major black fraternal organizations. They found it desirable to bind themselves together for social and cultural uplift, economic advancement, and mutual relief. Thus, a large number of benevolent societies sprang into existence, some of which were secret. In Baltimore, there was one as early as 1821, composed of young men, and by 1835 there were thirty-five. The Friendship Benevolent Society for Social Relief, the Star in the East Association, and the Daughters of Jerusalem were some of the more prominent organizations with substantial savings accounts in Baltimore banks. In other cities there were benevolent associations of mechanics, coachmen, caulkers, and other workers, suggesting that blacks were organizing themselves into unions at about the same time as whites. In the deep South such organizations were frowned upon by most whites and were outlawed altogether in many communities. They persisted, however, in some places. As late as 1860 they were being organized in New Orleans, where the Band Society, with the motto Love, Union, Peace, had bylaws requiring its members "to go about once in a while and see one another in love" and to wear the society's regalia on special occasions.

Important to the free black, as to the slave, was the church. Religious services offered opportunities for social intercourse as well as spiritual uplift.

The independent church movement of the North continued to grow. The African Methodist Episcopal Zion church increased its membership and extended its areas of operation. As blacks moved west they founded new congregations of these religious communities. In 1847 the African Methodist Episcopal church began the publication of a weekly magazine, *The Christian Herald,* which was changed to *The Christian Recorder* in 1852. By maintaining national organizations black Methodists were able to make their influence felt through important institutions in American life.

More free blacks belonged to Baptist churches, but because their churches were decentralized, their influence was not as great as that of the Methodists. Where a black Baptist church was associated with other churches, it was usually with white churches in the same area rather than with black churches elsewhere. While this was an important step in Americanization, it left black Baptists without much force among their own people. There were strong Baptist churches in many Northern cities, including Philadelphia, New York, and Boston, and in some towns in the West, such as Cleveland, Cincinnati, Detroit, and Chicago.

The South generally proscribed religious life among blacks between 1820 and 1860. Although the African Methodist Episcopal church had made considerable headway in Charleston, for example, the organization was crushed by the weight of public opinion in 1822. Whites generally believed that black Methodists were implicated in the Denmark Vesey plot. Realizing the futility of trying to carry on against such odds, the Reverend Morris Brown, who later became a bishop, led his flock to the North. Other free black preachers in the South experienced even greater hardships. Although John Chavis was one of North Carolina's most beloved Presbyterian ministers, he was not allowed to preach after 1831. Henry Evans, who organized the first Methodist church in Fayetteville, North Carolina, would doubtless have been evicted from his post had he been alive in 1831. Ralph Freeman, a well-known Baptist minister, was so determined to preach after 1831 that the Pee Dee Baptist Association of North Carolina felt compelled to publish a notice warning him to "refrain from making evening appointments of his own." White Episcopalians and Presbyterians solved the problem of free blacks by admitting them to worship, usually in segregated sections of their churches. As an effective independent institution among free blacks, the church declined before the outbreak of the Civil War.

One unique service that black religious leaders rendered was ministering to whites. Lemuel Haynes, the Revolutionary soldier, had set the example by his long service to white congregations in several Northern towns. Others were Samuel Ringgold Ward, pastor of a white congregation in Cortlandville, New York, and Henry Highland Garnet, who served a white church in Troy, New York. Many Southern black ministers, such as Freeman, Evans, and Chavis, preached to white congregations before the proscriptive laws of the 1820s and 1830s.

In Northern communities the opportunities for blacks to secure an education widened in the nineteenth century. In many places, however, separate schools were maintained. Boston established them for black children in 1820, followed closely by other Massachusetts towns. Antislavery sentiment soon attacked the practice, and by 1855 both Boston and New Bedford permitted black children to attend white public schools. Rhode Island and Connecticut maintained separate schools, but in the last decade before the Civil War, larger funds were given to them. Not until 1824 did the New York Common Council begin to support African Free Schools (see Chapter 6). The city took them over altogether in 1834. Although some communities in the state permitted black children to attend white schools, the legislature made it clear in 1841 that any district could establish separate schools. New Jersey also maintained schools for black children. The citizens of Pennsylvania continued to give both public and private support to schools for blacks as they increased in number, particularly in the western part of the state.

In the West, as more and more blacks migrated, the citizens there were also faced with the problem of education. Ohio excluded them from public schools by law in 1829. Twenty years later the state provided for separate schools, but never appropriated enough funds to set up anything creditable. Citizens of Indiana and Illinois were equally indifferent. Michigan and Wisconsin adopted more democratic policies, but most blacks in the West had to wait until after the Civil War before they could be educated in considerable numbers at public expense.

Free blacks in the South experienced far greater difficulty. Public interest in education was extremely low. Since the responsibility for educating youth was largely a private one, free blacks who would not have benefited directly from public education, did not receive even the indirect benefits of contact with a more educated white populace. There was, moreover, very strong sentiment against educating them. It was believed that they were likely to imbibe seditious and incendiary doctrines through their reading. All the Southern states made it very difficult for them to secure an education by passing laws making it unlawful to instruct free blacks. A surprisingly large number of them nevertheless learned at least the fundamentals. In Baltimore, for example, there were almost 200 adult blacks studying in 1820. Five years later a day and night school was being maintained where many subjects were taught, including Latin and French. The Bethel Charity School, founded by Daniel Coker in 1816 as a part of the enlarged program of the African Methodist Episcopal church, continued to flourish for a number of years. There were several other such schools in Maryland.

Shortly after the settlement of the District of Columbia, several white teachers, including Henry Potter and one Mrs. Haley, taught black children. Later, Maria Billings established a school in Georgetown. In 1807 several free blacks, among them George Bell, Nicholas Franklin, and Moses Liverpool, built the first schoolhouse for blacks in the District of Columbia. It was not until 1824, however, that there was a black teacher, John Adams, in the District. Then schools for blacks began to increase in number, and within a few years

James Thomas, Free Black, Attends School in Tennessee—1830s

A portion of the year (some years) the authorities allowed a school to be kept for teaching the children of Free persons. In that school I learned to read and write. It was surprising to a great many whites to see a colored boy or man with a newspaper. Often they would ask, "Can you read?" It was a question with many people whether it was the proper thing to have a school for the free people for two reasons. First they might write passes for the slaves. Second it might cause the slave to want the same. The law forbid the teaching of the slaves, but many families had servants that were taught by the children and the heads of the family made no objection, rather encouraged it. . . .

School was kept occasionaly. It was regarded a great favor to have it allowed at any time. Each pupil or scollar paid one dollar per month. Often there was no school because there was no teacher. When I was quite young there was a colored man who taught school and was a fine scollar himself. One night he was taken out by what was termed the slicks and whipped pretty near to death. The leader of the gang was a son of the most distinguished Jurist in the state. . . . After that the colored teachers were afraid to try it. Finaly a white man came in and taught. When Mother could spare me from her work I went to school.

From Tennessee Slave to St. Louis Entrepreneur: The Autobiography of James Thomas, ed. by Loren Schweninger (Columbia, Mo., 1984), pp. 31–32.

some of the best were to be found in Washington. Black students came there from Maryland and Virginia to study under teachers of their own race.

Free blacks in Virginia and North Carolina received private instruction from whites and other free blacks, but very little in schools. For almost thirty years John Chavis of Raleigh, North Carolina, maintained a school in which he taught whites during the day and free blacks in the evening, but after 1831 he confined his teaching to white children. The blacks of Fredericksburg, Virginia, sought permission from the state legislature in 1838 to send their children to school out of the state, but their plea was summarily rejected. There is plenty of evidence, however, that many free blacks in Virginia and North Carolina towns were being educated right up until the Civil War. In South Carolina their best opportunity to secure an education was provided in Charleston. As early as 1810 blacks had organized the Minor Society school for orphans, and others also attended. In Florida some free blacks sent their children away to school, while others hired teachers to instruct them, as in St. Augustine and Pensacola. New Orleans had several schools for free blacks. The *Ecole des Orphelins Indigents,* set up in 1840, was generously supported by such wealthy free blacks as Thomy Lafon, Madame Couvent, and Aristide Mary, who bequeathed $5,000 to the school. Some went to France for an education, such as Edward Dede, who studied music in Paris.

From all this educational activity a better trained free black citizenry emerged. There is little doubt that they were eager to secure an education. Of 2,038 in Boston in 1850, almost 1,500 were in school. There were 1,400 at schools in Baltimore and 1,000 in New Orleans. In the states and territories as a whole 32,629 were in school in 1860. In every community they were studying, with an apparent belief that education would solve some of their problems. Where opportunities did not exist, they sought to create them and gave enthusiastic support to their institutions. Just as Lafon and Madame Couvent set examples of philanthropy in New Orleans, so did free blacks in other parts of the country. In several communities they organized Phoenix Societies with the special object of promoting the improvement of "Morals, literature and the mechanic arts." The "Mental Feast," a social occasion, survived thirty years later in the interior towns of Pennsylvania and the West. It was a sign that blacks were part of the great awakening that swept American education in the generation preceding the Civil War.

They also made a start in higher education. In 1826 Edward Jones and John Russwurm graduated from Amherst College and Bowdoin College, respectively, and before the Civil War blacks were attending Oberlin, Franklin, and Rutland colleges, Harvard Medical School, and other institutions of higher learning. The doors of several institutions that were to become predominantly black colleges opened during this period. In 1851 a young white woman from New York, Myrtilla Miner, went to Washington to establish an academy for black females. So much opposition developed that the school was maintained only with difficulty. At the outbreak of the Civil War, it was still a small institution, but the idea had already been conceived for the college in Washington that long bore her name. In 1839 plans were made for an Institute for Colored Youth in Philadelphia. The school was incorporated in 1842 and began to flourish ten years later under the leadership of Charles L. Reason of New York. A bequest for $300,000 by the Reverend Charles Avery led to the establishment in 1849 of a college for blacks in Allegheny City, Pennsylvania, that bore the benefactor's name. With enough funds and an efficient faculty of both races, the institution flourished. Meanwhile, Reason, William G. Allen, and George B. Vashon each taught for a time at Central College, a white institution in McGrawville, New York.

Two denominational institutions founded during the period that have continued to grow are Lincoln University in Pennsylvania and Wilberforce University in Ohio. Lincoln, beginning as Ashmun Institute under Presbyterian sponsorship, was incorporated in 1854 and admitted its first students two years later. In 1855 the Cincinnati Conference of the Methodist Episcopal church decided to raise money to establish a college for black youth which was incorporated the following year as Wilberforce University. Its early students were mainly the mulatto children of Southern planters. After a brief suspension at the beginning of the Civil War, it was reopened under the sponsorship of the African Methodist Episcopal church.

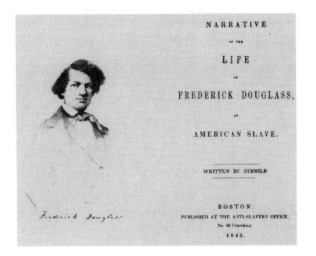

THE NARRATIVE OF FREDERICK DOUGLASS. This is one of many slave narratives written in the antebellum period. Douglass wrote two other autobiographies: *My Bondage and My Freedom* (1855) and *The Life and Times of Frederick Douglass* (1881). (*Courtesy The Schomburg Center for Research in Black Culture, The New York Public Library, Astor, Lenox, and Tilden Foundations.*)

    Blacks became much more articulate in the antebellum years than they had been during the previous century. There were poets, playwrights, historians, newspaper editors, and others who provided a black perspective to the world. In North Carolina, George Moses Horton, who was virtually free, wrote poems that were widely read. In 1829 he published a volume entitled *The Hope of Liberty,* and for the next thirty years wrote for students at the University of North Carolina and for various newspapers. Unfortunately, his interest in poetry diminished as he took to drink; perhaps he realized that for him there was no hope of liberty. Daniel A. Payne, who had a brilliant career as a bishop in the African Methodist Episcopal church, published a small volume in 1850 entitled *Pleasures and Other Miscellaneous Poems.* Though they reveal little imagination, a critic said that "with his love of order and precision he had a sense of versification . . ." Frances Harper, whose *Poems on Miscellaneous Subjects* appeared in 1854, made her most significant contributions after the Civil War. *Our Nig; Or Sketches From the Life of a Free Black,* the first novel by an African American and by an African-American woman appeared in 1859; its author, Harriet E. Wilson, a free black, probably lived in Massachusetts. In the words of its discoverer, Henry Louis Gates, Jr., *Our Nig* "stands as a 'missing link' . . . between the sustained and well developed tradition of black autobiography and the slow emergence of a distinctive black voice in fiction." The cultural life of blacks in New Orleans was best represented by a group of seventeen poets who issued a volume in 1845 entitled *Les Cenelles.* The editor, Armand Lanusse, and several contributors had lived or studied in France, and their work clearly shows the influence of Lamartine and Béranger.

    The largest and perhaps most significant group of black writers consisted of ex-slaves—fugitive or manumitted—who told the stories of their experiences in narratives. Frequently they were inspired and assisted by abolitionists who desired to use their writings as arguments against slavery. Some narratives, however, were the work solely of former slaves who had received the rudiments of an education. Because of the content of these works, most of them have a dramatic quality that the imagination alone, untutored by experience, would have difficulty in achieving. Among former slaves who published their narratives between 1840 and 1860 were William Wells Brown (1842), Lunsford Lane (1842), Moses Grandy (1844), Frederick Douglass (1845), Lewis Clarke (1846), Henry Bibb (1849), J. W. C. Pennington (1850), Solomon Northup (1853), Austin Steward (1857), and J. W. Loguen (1859). Many more narratives were published during and after the Civil War. Despite their subjectivity, they are an important source for the study of slavery in America.

Some of these writers made other contributions. William Wells Brown described his foreign travels vividly in *Three Years in Europe* (1852) and was the first black person to write a play, *The Escape* (1858), and a novel, *Clotel; or the President's Daughter* (1853). J. W. C. Pennington, even before he published his narrative, had written a *Textbook of the Origin and History of the Colored People* (1841). A more capable historian was William C. Nell, whose *Services of Colored Americans in the Wars of 1776 and 1812* first appeared in 1852. Three years later it was issued in a substantially revised edition under the title *The Colored Patriots of the American Revolution with Sketches of Several Distinguished Colored Persons to Which Is Added a Brief Survey of the Condition and Prospects of Colored Americans*. Martin R. Delany, a leading black physician who had studied at Harvard Medical School, published in 1852 *The Condition, Elevation, Emigration and Destiny of the Colored People of the United States*. Seven installments of his novel, *Blake; or the Huts of America*, appeared in *Anglo-African* magazine in 1859. Similar books on the condition of blacks indicated that they were becoming introspective and self-critical, an unmistakable sign of maturity and adjustment. In a class by itself, perhaps, was the work of James McCune Smith of New York. In 1846 this graduate of the medical college at the University of Glasgow published a paper entitled "Influence of Climate on Longevity, with Special Reference to Life Insurance."

Most black newspapers of the period were concerned mainly with the antislavery crusade. Best known were the first one, *Freedom's Journal*, started by Samuel Cornish and John Russwurm in 1827, and the *North Star*, first published by Frederick Douglass in 1847. With its name changed in 1850 to *Frederick Douglass's Paper*, the latter enjoyed wide circulation for several years. Other short-lived periodicals were the *Mystery* (Pittsburgh, 1843), the *Colored Man's Journal* (New York, 1851), the *Mirror of the Times* (San Francisco, 1855), and the *Anglo-African* (New York, 1859).

■ The Struggle in the North and West

For thirty years before the Civil War, blacks were migrating north and west from the South. Not only were slaves running away, but those already free were looking northward in the hope of finding greater opportunities and better treatment. They went to cities in the Northeast in large numbers and also to the old Northwest along with white immigrants from Europe. Between 1850 and 1860, for example, Michigan's black population jumped from 2,500 to 6,700, Iowa's more than tripled, and California's increased from 962 to 4,086. The reaction to this wholesale migration was not pleasant. Northern whites had shown no unusual hostility to blacks who were already in their midst, but they did not welcome the crude, rough type that came from the South. Indeed, they hoped to keep the North and West free not only of slavery but of blacks as well.

Racial animosity grew in both the North and West, and in many instances manifested itself in physical violence. In Philadelphia in 1819, three white women stoned a black woman to death. A few years later, the citizens adopted a policy of driving blacks away from Independence Square on the Fourth of July, since they were considered not to have had any part in establishing the nation. In 1831 the people of New Haven, Connecticut, became alarmed over the proposal of abolitionist Simeon Jocelyn to establish a college for blacks, and they resolved to oppose it with all their resources. When John Randolph's manumitted slaves were taken to Ohio, German settlers opposed their presence so vigorously that Randolph's executor had to find another place for them to settle. More than one interracial fight on the California mining frontier grew out of white resentment at blacks being there.

Sometimes violence reached the proportions of riots. In 1830 a mob drove eight blacks out of Portsmouth, Ohio. For three days in 1829, bands of white ruffians in Cincinnati took the law into their own hands and ran out of the city those blacks who did not have the bonds required by law. More than 1,000 found it advisable to leave. Blacks were also victims of the riot that occurred when the proslavery element of Cincinnati destroyed the office in which James G. Birney had published an antislavery newspaper, the *Philanthropist.* Defenseless blacks were attacked in their homes, and many left the city. The fugitive slave riot in 1841 also involved many blacks who were in no way connected with harboring fugitives.

In New York there were riots in Utica, Palmyra, and New York City in 1834 and 1839. The most serious antiblack outbreaks, however, took place in Pennsylvania. On August 12, 1834, a mob of whites marched into the black section of Philadelphia and committed numerous acts of violence. The following day they wrecked the African Presbyterian Church, burned homes, and mercilessly beat up several blacks. This reign of terror entered its third day before the police put an end to it. Similar uprisings occurred in 1835 and 1842. By the latter year a large number of whites were out of work because of the severe depression, and when blacks were celebrating the abolition of slavery in the West Indies, the unemployed broke up their parade, attacked scores of them, and burned the New African Hall and Presbyterian Church. State troops had to be called to assist the police in quieting the city. In 1839 there had been an outbreak in Pittsburgh during which whites did considerable damage to the black section of the city by burning and tearing down houses.

The South enjoyed playing up Northern hostility toward blacks. When an observer said that in New York and Philadelphia blacks were noted chiefly for their "aversion to labor and proneness to villainy," he was quoted extensively in the Southern press. Southerners recounted with pleasure how a Georgia black returned after attempting to live in Ohio and Canada for two years, learning to dislike each place thoroughly. They also told of the Louisiana blacks who suffered so much in New York City that they begged visiting Southerners to take them back with them. When a North Carolina free black remarked that he had been kicked about and abused so much in Cincinnati that he would like to return to the South, a Greensboro paper not only reported the incident but reprinted the article five years later as though it had just happened.

There can be no doubt that many blacks were sorely mistreated in the North and West. Observers like Fanny Kemble and Frederick L. Olmsted mentioned incidents in their writings. Kemble said of Northern blacks, "They are not slaves indeed, but they are pariahs, debarred from every fellowship save with their own despised race. . . . All hands are extended to thrust them out, all fingers point at their dusky skin, all tongues . . . have learned to turn the very name of their race into an insult and a reproach." Olmsted seems to have believed the Louisiana black who told him that they could associate with whites more easily in the South than in the North and that he preferred to live in the South because he was less likely to be insulted there. Such points of view delighted slaveholders and confirmed their belief that slavery was better than freedom for blacks.

Southerners did not seem to realize, however, that the essential difference between the South and the North and West was that in the latter sections blacks had more of the law on their side and could therefore resist encroachments on their rights. Northern blacks could organize and fight for what they believed to be their rights, and there was a substantial group of white citizens who gave them both moral and material support. In 1830 a convention of blacks with delegates from New York, Pennsylvania, Maryland, Delaware, and Virginia, met in Philadelphia "to devise ways and means for the bettering of our condition." James Forten, John B. Vashon, Samuel Cornish, and other leaders were present. They considered raising funds to establish a college and to encourage blacks to migrate to Canada. Many blacks were opposed to these measures as unsound solutions to their problems, and indeed there were some who opposed the idea of a black convention at all.

For several years, however, these conventions met regularly, and such leading white citizens as Arthur Tappan, John Rankin, and William Lloyd Garrison met with them. In 1847 several delegates, including William C. Nell, met in Troy, New York, and urged that blacks seek admission to white colleges. Nell believed that diligent and outstanding black students would win the respect of enemies and convert them into friends. In 1850 a convention at Columbus, Ohio, resolved to resist all forms of oppression, promote universal education, and encourage blacks to aspire to mechanical, agricultural, and professional pursuits.

In the decade preceding the Civil War, there were more black conventions than ever before. They met in Rochester, Cleveland, New York, Philadelphia, and other cities. One of the most important, held at Rochester in 1853, saw the formation of a National Council of Colored People. A stirring memorial, signed by Frederick Douglass among others, was issued to the American people, asserting that "with the exception of the Jews, under the whole heavens, there is not to be found a people pursued with a more relentless prejudice and persecution, than are the free colored people of the United States." After reciting various ways in which they had been mistreated and humiliated, the memorial declared that no other race could have made more progress "in the midst of such an universal and stringent disparagement. It would humble the proudest, crush the energies of the strongest, and retard the progress of the swiftest. In view of our circumstances, we can, without boasting, thank God, and take courage, having placed ourselves where we may fairly challenge comparison with more highly favored men."

There were also conventions of special groups. In 1848 the Citizens Union of Pennsylvania was organized to fight for first-class citizenship for blacks. In 1850 the American League of Colored Laborers was formed in New York to promote cooperation and to foster the education of young blacks in agriculture, the mechanical arts, and commerce.

■ Colonization

The problem of what to do with blacks who would not "adjust" to American life was an old one. It arose shortly after the arrival of the first Africans in America. Banishment was an early punishment for the crimes of both whites and blacks. As the number of free blacks increased, it was felt that they must be sent out of the country if property in slaves was to be secure. Certainly there could be no complete discipline of slaves as long as free blacks were in their midst. Even Northern communities felt that emancipation and concessions of equality were insufficient because the two races could not always live together in harmony. The prevailing point of view was aptly summed up by J. C. Galloway of North Carolina, who said, "It is impossible for us to be happy, if, after manumission, they are to remain among us."

As early as 1714 a "native American," believed to be a resident of New Jersey, had proposed sending blacks back to Africa. The idea did not die. Just after the War for Independence, Samuel Hopkins and the Reverend Ezra Stiles discussed the possibility of putting this notion into practice. In 1777 a Virginia legislative committee, headed by Thomas Jefferson, set forth a plan of gradual emancipation and deportation. Several organizations for manu-mission, such as the Connecticut Emancipation Society, had as one of their objectives the colonization of free blacks. Perhaps nothing brought coloniza-tion before the country more dramatically than the transporting of thirty-eight blacks to Africa in 1815 by Paul Cuffe, at his own expense. His act suggested what might be done if more people, or even the government, became interested. It suggested, too, that some blacks were indeed interested in leaving the United States.

Within two years after Cuffe's voyage, the American Colonization Society was organized, with Bushrod Washington as president and Henry Clay and John Randolph of Roanoke among its prominent members. Plans were immediately made to establish a colony in Africa, with the aid of federal and state governments, and to educate public opinion to support the project. Agents were sent out to raise funds and to interest free blacks in emigrating to Liberia, whose capital was honored with the name of President Monroe. Soon, thousands of dollars flowed into the society for the purchasing and chartering of ships to transport blacks. By 1832 more than a dozen legislatures had given official approval to the society—even slaveholding states like Maryland, Virginia, and Kentucky. North Carolina, Mississippi, and other states had local colonization societies. At first, only free blacks were transported to Africa. After 1827 some slaves who were manumitted expressly for this purpose were taken to Liberia. By 1830 the society had settled 1,420 blacks in the colony.

The society's first ten years were its best. In 1831 the abolitionists, led by Garrison, who was once a friend of colonization, renounced the scheme. Arthur Tappan, Gerrit Smith, and James G. Birney joined in the attack. Many auxiliary societies, desiring greater autonomy, seceded from the parent organization, which became insolvent in 1834. In Liberia, where the cost of living was high and the colony's affairs were mismanaged, many settlers were unhappy. Dark days thus descended upon the American Colonization Society, but it managed to struggle along for several years before it became moribund in the decade before the Civil War.

Although the American Colonization Society comprised the largest group of individuals interested in deporting blacks, there were other groups and individuals no less interested. Southern newspapers, for example, did what they could to banish free blacks. One Mississippi paper ran an advertisement of how pleasant a place Haiti would be for blacks emigrating from the United States. Indeed, the Haitians were anxious to attract free blacks to their island. A North Carolina newspaper urged free blacks to solve their problems by emigration. It suggested that they go to Canada, Mexico, South America, or the American West. Few whites, however, supported the idea that they should move west after white migration began at the close of the War of 1812.

Despite all the schemes to deport free blacks from the United States, not more than 15,000 migrated. The American Colonization Society was responsible for most of them—approximately 12,000. To places other than Liberia there was less than a trickle. For several reasons all these schemes failed. In the first place, it was not economically feasible to send hundreds of thousands of blacks to Africa or anywhere else. The cost of transporting and maintaining several hundred thousand people would run far into millions if not billions of dollars, and there were not enough supporters of the idea to give it anything like a fair chance of success. In the second place, those who did support it were such a heterogeneous lot that in the long run they could not develop a program agreeable to all. Some advocates of colonization hoped to see an end to slavery and a return of all blacks to their native land. Others supported the schemes because of their conviction that blacks were basically incapable of adjusting to Western civilization and would be better off in their original habitat. Still others saw in colonization an opportunity to carry Christianity and civilization to Africa. Slaveholders hoped, of course, to drain off the free black population, thereby giving great security to the institution of slavery. Motives as varied as these doomed colonization. The attitude of blacks themselves had a great deal to do with its failure.

Shortly after formation of the American Colonization Society a group of free blacks had met in Richmond and mildly approved of the idea of colonization, but they preferred to live elsewhere in the United States, possibly in the Missouri River valley, rather than in Africa. Farther south, free blacks who were weary of fighting a hopeless battle resigned themselves to colonization. The great majority of those who went to Africa were from the slaveholding states. In the North, however, there was almost universal opposition to colonization, particularly in Africa. In Philadelphia 3,000 blacks, led by Richard Allen and James Forten, met in 1817 and registered their objections to colonization, urging the "Humane and Benevolent Inhabitants of Philadelphia" to reject the scheme altogether. They branded it as an "outrage, having no other object in view than the benefit of the slaveholding interests of the country."

Within ten years black opposition had risen to fever pitch. Meetings were held in Baltimore, Boston, New York, Hartford, New Haven, Pittsburgh, and many other cities. New York blacks referred to the supporters of colonization as "men of mistaken views," while those of Lyme, Connecticut, described colonization as "one of the wildest projects ever patronized by enlightened men."

Every convention of blacks opposed colonization, and the leaders spoke and wrote against the scheme. Martin R. Delany was especially hostile to the American Colonization Society, which he described as "anti-Christian in its character and misanthropic in its pretended sympathies." He denounced the leaders as "arrant hypocrites" who were conducting an organization that was obviously "one of the Negro's worst enemies." The main motive of colonization, he claimed, was to eliminate blacks from the United States, and for that purpose a government had been set up in Africa that was "not independent—but a poor *miserable mockery*—a burlesque on a government."

But not all Northern blacks were opposed to colonization. Even Martin Delany thought that blacks would prosper in Central and South America, and on one occasion he described these places as their future home in the New World. He also thought that Canada West (upper Canada) would be a satisfactory home if it were not annexed to the United States. Such an eventuality, he said, would mean that the "fate of the colored man, however free before, is doomed, doomed, forever doomed." Several outstanding ministers supported colonization on the ground that it would extend Christianity to heathen lands. Among them were Daniel A. Payne and Alexander Crummell, who went to Africa in the interest of Christianity and colonization. Lott Cary and Colin Teague went to Liberia in 1821 under the auspices of the Richmond African Baptist Missionary Society and the General Baptist Missionary Convention. While Cary showed no enthusiasm for the policies of the American Colonization Society, he labored among the African settlers until his death in 1828. But colonization itself was doomed: African Americans were as permanent a fixture as there was in America.

Thus blacks went through the terrible ordeal of moving toward freedom. It cannot be said even of the most fortunate that they were entirely free. They suffered indignitites and insults, legal disabilities and economic privations, and violent physical and verbal calumniations. Their reactions, even when sober and considered, were the reactions of a frustrated, stricken people. The mistreatment of free blacks was not sectional. At best the situation in the North was tolerable, but only in a relative sense: it was better than in the South. Small wonder there was so much despair. Small wonder, too, that in the South a few who were free became slaves again. Too few of them saw that in the growing intersectional strife between North and South there was opportunity for the downtrodden and hope for the faint-hearted.

■

CHAPTER 10

Slavery and
Intersectional Strife

■ The North Attacks

The antislavery sentiment generated by the humanitarian philosophy of the eighteenth century never completely died out in America. To be sure, there was a period of quiescence as the South found new opportunities for the profitable employment of slaves and as the North became concerned with its own economic and political problems. But some people continued to oppose slavery as an institution, and long before militant abolitionists appeared on the scene around 1830 the most convincing arguments against slavery had already been developed. Soon after the War of 1812 sectionalism was apparent as the North swung to manufacturing and the South, still wedded to agriculture, came to see clearly that the interests of the two sections were becoming antagonistic. Indeed, the industrial development of the North changed the point of view of that section. As people there were brought closer together, they sought to solve their pressing problems through cooperation. In the South, however, the plantation system tended to preserve frontier independence: there was little communal life, only slight civic responsibility, and little interest in various programs for the improvement of humanity. The contest over Missouri, moreover, crystallized the sectional conflict and emphasized the importance of slavery as a national issue.

Antislavery sentiment in the North increased steadily after 1815 as more ministers, editors, and other leaders of public opinion spoke out against the evils of the institution. Several years passed before almost all these critics were confined to the North. In 1817 Charles Osborn published the *Philanthropist*, an antislavery paper, in Ohio, but two years later he moved to Tennessee and published the *Manumission Intelligencer*. In 1820 Elihu Embree was publishing the *Emancipator* in Jonesboro, Tennessee, while William Swaim was expressing the opposition of Quakers to slavery in his *Patriot*, published at Greensboro, North Carolina. In 1821 the itinerant Benjamin Lundy began editing the *Genius of Universal Emancipation*, in which he set forth a complete program for the emancipation and colonization of blacks. Although he lacked the emotional fervor of later abolitionists, he was not without courage and devotion to the cause of freeing the slaves.

Within ten years after the beginning of Lundy's work, three events indicated that the age of the militant abolitionists had arrived. These were the publication of David Walker's "Appeal," the appearance of William Lloyd Garrison's *Liberator*, and the insurrection of Nat Turner, which many incorrectly thought was inspired by the activities of men like Garrison (see Chapter 8). David Walker was a North Carolina free black who had moved to Boston where he engaged in selling secondhand clothes. His bitter hatred for slavery was not diminished by his leaving the South. If anything, it was increased. In September 1829 his essay appeared: "Walker's Appeal in Four Articles, Together with a Preamble to the Colored Citizens of the World, But in Particular and very Expressly to those of the United States of America." It was one of the most vigorous denunciations of slavery ever printed in the United States. In unmistakable language he called upon blacks to rise up and throw off the yoke of slavery:

> Are we men!! I ask you . . . are we MEN? Did our creator make us to be slaves to dust and ashes like ourselves? Are they not dying worms as well as we? . . . How we could be so *submissive* to a gang of men, whom we cannot tell whether they are as good as ourselves or not, I never conceive. . . . America is more our country than it is the whites—we have enriched it with our *blood and tears*. The greatest riches in all America have arisen from our blood and tears: And they will drive us from our property and homes, which we have earned with our blood.

Walker closed his appeal by quoting the Declaration of Independence to show that blacks were justified in resisting, with force if necessary, the oppression of white masters. A startled country read the words of this black man who called for militant action.

In January 1831 the first issue of Garrison's *Liberator* appeared. Garrison had served his novitiate as Lundy's assistant on the *Genius of Universal Emancipation* and in jail for libelous words against a ship captain who had transported slaves to New Orleans. He was finished with gradualism; he had shifted from supporting colonization to opposing it. In the first issue of his newspaper he also invoked the Declaration of Independence, claiming that the black man was as much entitled to "life, liberty and the pursuit of happiness" as the white man. Immediate and unconditional abolition of slavery was, from his point of view, the only solution. He laid down his challenge to slavery in most dramatic language when he said:

> I *will* be as harsh as truth, and as uncompromising as justice. On this subject, I do not wish to think, to speak, or write, with moderation. . . . I am in earnest—I will not equivocate—I will not excuse—I will not retreat a single inch—AND I WILL BE HEARD.

Thus Garrison became the country's most articulate spokesman for nonviolent militant abolition. For a whole generation he was one of the most important forces working for the freedom of slaves. It was an auspicious beginning for an exciting career. Small wonder that people in the South connected the so-called incendiary writings of Walker and Garrison with the insurrections of Nat Turner and of others; but Garrison always followed a policy of nonviolent, passive resistance.

The militant antislavery movement that had developed by 1831 was in itself a powerful religious crusade—part of the larger humanitarian movement sweeping Europe and the Northern United States. It stemmed from the growing popular concern for the welfare of underprivileged persons, which manifested itself in the antislavery movement, the crusade for better working conditions in England, and the search for a better life in America. It was closely connected, in many respects, with movements for peace, women's rights, temperance, and other reform programs that developed simultaneously. In the West, it was connected with the Great Revival, of which Charles G. Finney was the dominant figure, emphasizing the importance of being useful and thus releasing a powerful impulse toward social reform. The young converts joined Finney's Holy Band, and if the abolition of slavery was a way of serving God, they were anxious to enter into the movement wholeheartedly.

Abolitionists worked out an elaborate argument against the perpetuation of slavery. In the first place, they insisted that it was contrary to the teachings of Christianity, since Jesus taught the doctrine of universal brotherhood and one of the cardinal principles of Christianity was that all men were created in the image of God. James G. Birney's *Letter to the Ministers and Elders* (1834) and Theodore Weld's *The Bible Against Slavery* (1837) carried these religious arguments against slavery to their conclusion. In the second place, abolitionists contended that slavery was contrary to the fundamental principles of the American way of life, which valued freedom as an inalienable right of the individual. Slaves were denied this right: they had no freedom in seeking employment, no religious freedom, no marriage or family rights, no legal protection, and few opportunities to secure an education. They also contended that slavery was economically unsound because the workers could

David Walker Calls for Justice—1829

I ask every man who has a heart, and is blessed with the privilege of believing—Is not God a God of justice to *all* his creatures? Do you say he is? Then if he gives peace and tranquillity to tyrants, and permits them to keep our fathers, our mothers, ourselves and our children in eternal ignorance and wretchedness, to support them and their families, would he be to us a God of *justice*? I ask, O ye *Christians!!!* who hold us and our children in the most abject ignorance and degradation, that ever a people were afflicted with since the world began—I say, if God gives you peace and tranquillity, and suffers you thus to go on afflicting us, and our children, who have never given you the least provocation—would he be to us *a God of justice*? If you will allow that we are MEN, who feel for each other, does not the blood of our fathers and of us their children, cry aloud to the Lord of Sabaoth against you, for the cruelties and murders with which you have, and do continue to afflict us.

Walker's Appeal in Four Articles, Together with a Preamble to the Coloured Citizens of the World, But in Particular, and very Expressly, to those of the United States of America (Boston, 1830), p. 68.

not be expected to be efficient and there was such a waste of physical and human resources in the plantation economy. The culture and civilization of the South suffered, moreover, for the master-slave relationship did not produce a gentility of spirit but brought out instead the baser aspects of the nature of both. Theodore Weld expressed this view succinctly, pointing out that domination of one person by another is essentially uncivilized, when he said, "Arbitrary power is to the mind what alcohol is to the body; it intoxicates." Finally, abolitionists condemned slavery as a menace to the peace and safety of the country. The South was becoming an armed camp where whites lived in constant fear of a widespread uprising of slaves. This fear, it was contended, generated violence and was the cause of bloodshed.

Although antislavery forces had for years believed that colonization was one way of relieving the country of its dreaded "Negro problem," militant abolitionists were on the whole unalterably opposed to colonization. They were suspicious of it because of the support it received from slaveholders, who could not be interested in putting an end to slavery as an institution. Abolitionists felt, as the great majority of blacks did, that colonization was primarily for the purpose of draining off the free black population in order to make slavery even more secure. Garrison said that the American Colonization Society had "inflicted a great injury upon the free and slave population; first by strengthening the prejudices of the people; secondly, by discouraging the education of those who are free; thirdly, by inducing passage of severe legislative enactments; and, finally, by lulling the whole country into a deep sleep." Even more vigorous denunciations appeared in his *Thoughts on Colonization,* published in 1832.

With principles of their own, not necessarily egalitarian, abolitionists were now ready to organize and to wipe out the institution of slavery. In 1831 the New England Anti-Slavery Society was formed. Beginning with a small group of fifteen, Garrison imbued his followers with the idea of immediate emancipation. As their numbers grew, they became more radical and vociferous, the very voice of Garrison. Some, especially in New York and Philadelphia, were from the beginning opposed to Garrison's radical views. Encouraged by the abolition of slavery in the British Empire, this moderate group did much to bring about the organization of the American Anti-Slavery Society in Philadelphia in 1833. Arthur Tappan, a wealthy New York merchant, was the first president. Other important leaders were Theodore Weld, James G. Birney, William Goodell, Joshua Leavitt, Elizur Wright, Samuel May, and Beriah Green, most of whom had been active in local antislavery societies. The organization was dominated by Garrison, however, and when it issued a declaration of sentiments he was successful in getting his views incorporated into the document. A publicity program was drawn up and carried out largely by the New York group. Four periodicals were published: *Human Rights, Anti-Slavery Record, Emancipator,* and *Slave's Friend.* Pamphlets were distributed throughout the North and, when possible, in the South. Through its many agents, local units were organized and money was raised to further the program of emancipation. In 1836 there were seventy lecturers in the field, drawn largely from the ministry, theological seminaries, and colleges.

In the West the antislavery movement had become a crusade by 1830. Most of the leaders who left the South went West. James G. Birney went from Alabama to Kentucky and thence to Ohio. Levi Coffin left North Carolina and carried on his abolition activities in Indiana. Later, these men were joined by others who had found the atmosphere of their home communities peculiarly hostile to antislavery ideas. After Theodore Dwight Weld arrived at Lane Theological Seminary in Cincinnati, the students there were encouraged to discuss the problem of slavery, and the free and open debates won many people, including Southerners, to the cause of abolition. The students put their views into practice by going out into the community to organize groups to assist slaves, and they instructed black youth and participated in the dangerous activities of the Underground Railroad. When the students withdrew from Lane rather than submit to a conservative administration, they went in large numbers to Oberlin College, where a theology department was established with funds provided by such antislavery philanthropists as Arthur and Lewis Tappan of New York. From that time on Oberlin became an important center of antislavery activity. Western Reserve was another college from which students went forth imbued with antislavery ideas. At no other time in American history had colleges played such an important part in a program of social reform.

The zealous Garrison was impatient even with a national organization like the American Anti-Slavery Society, all of whose members were committed to a crusade for the immediate abolition of slavery. They did not press hard enough, they were unwilling to concede equality to women as leaders of the movement, and they hesitated to criticize the churches for not taking an unequivocal stand. In 1839 Garrison and his followers decided to seize control of the national organization. At a convention the following year Garrisonians were elected to the important offices, and women were given positions of responsibility. The New York group, opposed to this bid by Garrison for power, organized under Lewis Tappan the American and Foreign Anti-Slavery Society. It was friendly to churches and sought to use them to end slavery. It believed that political action was necessary to overcome constitutional and legal obstructions to emancipation.

The members of this new society became the nucleus of the Liberty party, which was organized in 1840. In two successive presidential campaigns they nominated James Birney, but at the peak of their strength in 1844 he polled only 60,000 votes. The dismal results proved conclusively that, although millions of people were opposed to slavery, a political party had to offer more than an antislavery platform in order to win support. The Republican party was to demonstrate in the next decade that it had learned this lesson.

By 1840, when the energies of the abolitionists were split into two national bodies, effective work was done by state and local organizations. They maintained agents in the field, published newspapers, and distributed antislavery literature throughout the country. Garrison remained strong to the end in New England. Among his followers he could list John Greenleaf Whittier, the poet of abolition; Wendell Phillips, "abolition's golden trumpet"; and women like Lucretia Mott, Lydia Maria Child, and Maria Weston Chapman. In the border states and the West, however, Birney and Weld were strong, and unlike Garrison they continued to counsel moderation and to insist upon political action.

While "Garrisonism" met with more opposition than other forms of abolition, there was always much sentiment, even in the North, against any kind of antislavery agitation. David M. Reese, for example, called the American Anti-Slavery Society the "purest of all humbugs"; Episcopal Bishop John H. Hopkins of Vermont opposed it because he was convinced that blacks were better off as slaves than as free men. The opposition to abolition frequently became violent. Elijah P. Lovejoy was run out of St. Louis for criticizing the leniency of a judge in the trial of whites accused of burning a black man alive. Later, in Alton, Illinois, he was killed when a mob destroyed for the fourth time the press on which he printed the *Alton Observer*. In Cincinnati a mob destroyed James Birney's press in 1836, and he barely escaped with his life.

Antislavery lecturers often found it difficult to rent halls in which to speak. Even if they succeeded, they could not be certain that their program would go off as planned, for many a meeting was broken up by mobs. Even women who supported the antislavery crusade were in danger of suffering insults and indignities. When Prudence Crandall, a Quaker teacher, admitted a black girl to her school in Canterbury, Connecticut, white patrons boycotted it. After she decided to open a school for black girls, with the aid of abolitionists like Garrison and Lewis Tappan, the citizens broke windows, insulted the teacher, and had her arrested for violating a state law that forbade the teaching of blacks who were not residents of the state.

Abolitionists could expect little help or protection from the federal government. As early as 1828 they submitted a petition to Congress to abolish slavery in the District of Columbia, but nothing was done about it. As petitions against slavery began pouring in, the House of Representatives adopted a rule in 1836 providing that such petitions were to be received and laid on the table. This "gag rule," as abolitionists dubbed it, was vigorously opposed by men like John Quincy Adams of Massachusetts and Joshua Giddings of Ohio, but it was not rescinded until 1845. As long as it stood, abolitionists complained that the sacred right of petitioning the legislature for a redress of grievances was being denied.

It was the countenancing of violence by abolitionists that caused many law-abiding citizens to oppose them and rendered utterly hopeless their schemes to obtain government support. Convinced that slaveholders had the law of the land on their side, abolitionists resorted to the principle of a higher law, which they felt justified their circumventing or breaking the law. Garrison and his followers, although nonviolent, pointed out the inevitability of the violence of the Nat Turner insurrection. In 1839 Jabez Hammond of New York said that only force would end slavery and that military schools for blacks should be set up in Canada and Mexico. When slaves revolted aboard the *Creole* on a voyage from Hampton Roads to New Orleans, Representative Joshua Giddings not only opposed treating the slaves as common criminals but even praised them for seeking freedom. The House of Representatives, shocked by his open defiance of the law, censured Giddings. Forthwith he resigned, went home to Ohio, and was immediately returned to Congress by his antislavery constituency. The redoubtable Giddings later praised other blacks and whites for seeking to abolish slavery, and finally the House became accustomed to his tirades against the institution. By 1850 the philosophy of force was so integral a part of abolitionist doctrine that many viewed it as a movement toward anarchy.

■ Black Abolitionists

Whites were not alone in their opposition to slavery. From the beginning, blacks, who suffered most from the subjugation of their race, gave enthusiastic support to abolition. Indeed, strong abolitionist doctrine had been preached by blacks long before Garrison was born. Before the War for Independence, slaves in Massachusetts brought actions against their masters for the freedom that they regarded as their inalienable right. During and after the Revolutionary War, blacks sought the abolition of slavery by petitioning the state and federal governments to outlaw the slave trade and to embark upon a program of general emancipation. Prince Hall, Benjamin Banneker, Absalom Jones, and Richard Allen issued strong denunciations of slavery before 1800, and organizations like the Free African Society of Philadelphia passed resolutions calling for its abolition. In the nineteenth century blacks organized antislavery societies. By 1830 they had fifty groups, one that was very active in New Haven, and several in Boston, New York, and Philadelphia. One of the strongest was located in New York and named for the famous English antislavery leader Thomas Clarkson.

The year 1829 was especially significant for black abolitionists. Out of Boston came David Walker's *Appeal,* a blast against slavery, and out of Raleigh, North Carolina, came the protest of George Moses Horton in his *Hope of Liberty.* Horton cried out:

> Bid Slavery hide her haggard face,
> And Barbarism fly:
> I scorn to see the sad disgrace
> In which enslaved I lie.

It was in 1829, too, that Robert A. Young published his *Ethiopian Manifesto, issued in defence of the black man's rights, in the scale of universal freedom.* He prophesied, like Walker, that from blacks there would arise a messiah with the strength to liberate his people. Young did not create as much alarm as Walker, although he advocated measures fully as drastic to end slavery.

When the period of militant abolitionism began, black people were ready to join whites in fighting the hated institution. They organized their first national convention in the year before the publication of Garrison's *Liberator* and issued strong denunciations of colonization and slavery that left no doubt in the minds of Americans where they stood. The eagerness of black abolitionists to join the movement for liberation is demonstrated by their reaction to the appearance of the *Liberator.* Of the 450 subscribers in the first year, 400 were blacks, and one enthusiastic, affluent black abolitionist sent Garrison a gift of $50. Such contributions helped to make possible his first trip to England.

Blacks were especially active in organizing the American Anti-Slavery Society. Members whose duty it was to draw up the declaration of sentiments met in Philadelphia at the home of a black man, Lewis Evans. Five leaders served on the first board of managers: Peter Williams, Robert Purvis, George B. Vashon, Abraham Shadd, and James McCrummell. These black "founding fathers" were men of many interests and talents. Purvis, born in Charleston of a well-to-do white father who generously provided for him, had attended Amherst College and was active in many local causes, including the

LEADERS OF THE FREE BLACK COMMUNITY: WILLIAM WELLS BROWN, MARTIN R. DELANEY, HENRY HIGHLAND GARNET, ROBERT PURVIS, SOJOURNER TRUTH (ISABELLA BAUMFREE), AND HARRIET TUBMAN. These brave men and women challenged the mistreatment and humiliation to which their people were subjected. In doing so they refuted the arguments for black inferiority, affirmed the legitimacy of blacks' claims to the rights and privileges of citizenship, and were influential examples to other members of their race. (*The Schomburg Center For Research In Black Culture, The New York Public Library. Sojourner Truth courtesy of Sophia Smith Collection, Smith College.*)

SARAH PARKER REMOND. Abolitionist of Salem, Massachusetts, she lectured against slavery in the United States and Europe. After studying medicine, she married an Italian and settled in Florence, where she practiced medicine until her death at the age of 68. *(Courtesy, Peabody and Essex Museum, Salem, MA.)*

Underground Railroad. Vashon, a graduate of Oberlin College, was a poet, lawyer, and teacher. At most of the annual meetings there were black delegates who spoke out frequently. When the American and Foreign Anti-Slavery Society was organized, blacks were no less active in that body.

Among those who joined in promoting the organization that was committed to political action were Christopher Rush, Samuel Cornish, Charles B. Ray, and James W. C. Pennington.

To local and regional antislavery organizations, which carried the burden of the work, blacks gave their time, energy, and money. The first presiding officer of the Philadelphia Female Anti-Slavery Society was a local dentist, James McCrummell. Frederick Douglass was elected president of the New England Anti-Slavery Society in 1847. Vigilance committees, set up to raise funds to help slaves escaping to freedom, were frequently dominated by blacks. In 1835 David Ruggles became secretary of the New York committee and remained active until his eyesight failed him. In Philadelphia, Robert Purvis had charge of the first vigilance committee, which was headed several years later by William Still.

Blacks were also prominent in the abolition movement as agents and speakers for various societies. Several were full-time employees of local or national bodies. Among the better-known agents were Frederick Douglass, Theodore S. Wright, William Jones, Charles Lenox Remond and his sister Sarah, Frances E. W. Harper, Henry Foster, Lunsford Lane, Henry Highland Garnet, Charles Gardner, Andrew Harris, Abraham Shadd, David Nickens, James Bradley, and William Wells Brown. A notable black abolitionist was Isabella Baumfree, better known by her adopted name Sojourner Truth. From New York she traveled through New England and the West, moving audiences by her quaint speech, a deep, resonant voice, and a hatred for slavery, which she expressed with a unique religious mysticism.

White abolitionists took great pride in introducing black agents to doubting audiences to demonstrate what they could do if given the opportunity. They were among the best speakers. On one occasion, after Douglass had electrified an audience with his remarkable eloquence, Garrison rose to his feet and flung out the question, "Is this a man or a thing?" Henry Highland Garnet spoke with a "terrible pride," and William Wells Brown is reputed to have made a favorable impression wherever he went. Small wonder that many of these speakers were encouraged to carry the message of American abolition to Europe. More than a score of black abolitionists went to England, Scotland, France, and Germany. Among them were Douglass, Brown, Remond, Pennington, Garnet, Nathaniel Paul, Ellen and William Craft, Samuel Ringgold Ward, Sarah Parker Remond, and Alexander Crummell. They were received with enthusiasm almost everywhere and were instrumental in linking up the humanitarian movement in Europe with various reform movements on this side of the Atlantic.

Black abolitionists wrote as well as spoke in favor of emancipation. Most of the black newspapers founded before the Civil War were abolitionist sheets. Perhaps the outstanding journalist was Samuel Cornish, who with John Russwurm had established the first black newspaper, *Freedom's Journal*, in 1827. Two years later, Cornish began his second venture, *Rights of All*, an extremely radical but short-lived paper. In 1836 he published the *Weekly Advocate*, and in the following year, with the help of Charles B. Ray and

Frederick Douglass at Rochester's Independence Day—1852

I am not included within the pale of this glorious anniversary! Your high independence only reveals the immeasurable distance between us. The blessings in which you, this day, rejoice, are not enjoyed in common. The rich inheritance of justice, liberty, prosperity and independence, bequeathed by your fathers, is shared by you, not by me. The sunlight that brought light and healing to you, has brought stripes and death to me. This Fourth July is *yours*, not *mine*. *You* may rejoice, *I* must mourn. To drag a man in fetters into the grand illuminated temple of liberty, and call upon him to join you in joyous anthems, were inhuman mockery and sacrilegious irony. Do you mean, citizens, to mock me, by asking me to speak to-day? If so, there is a parallel to your conduct. And let me warn you that it is dangerous to copy the example of a nation whose crimes, towering up to heaven, were thrown down by the breath of the Almighty, burying that nation in irrevocable ruin! I can to-day take up the plaintive lament of a peeled and woe-smitten people!

"By the rivers of Babylon, there we sat down. Yea! we wept when we remembered Zion. We hanged our harps upon the willows in the midst thereof. For there, they that carried us away captive, required of us a song; and they who wasted us required of us mirth, saying, Sing us one of the songs of Zion. How can we sing the Lord's song in a strange land? If I forget thee, O Jerusalem, let my right hand forget her cunning. If I do not remember thee, let my tongue cleave to the roof of my mouth."

Philip S. Foner, *The Life and Writings of Frederick Douglass*, II (New York, 1950), pp. 181–204.

Phillip A. Bell, he edited the *Colored American*. Other black abolitionist newspapers were the *National Watchman*, edited by William G. Allen and Henry Highland Garnet; the *Mirror of Liberty*, a quarterly issued by David Ruggles; and, of course, the *North Star* of Frederick Douglass.

Douglass was the outstanding black abolitionist. A fugitive slave, he was first introduced to the movement when in 1841 he attended an antislavery convention in Nantucket, Massachusetts. After speaking there he was employed by several societies and rapidly became one of the best-known orators in the United States, lecturing in the North and East, and in England. A narrative of his life was published in 1845. Two years later he started the *North Star*, an incident that led to his break with Garrison, previously one of his chief sponsors. Douglass was active in black conventions, the Underground Railroad, and many other efforts to improve the conditions of his race. He was endowed with the physical attributes of an orator: a magnificient, tall body, a head crowned with a mass of hair, deep-set, flashing eyes, a firm chin, and a rich, melodious voice. Few antislavery leaders did so much to carry the case of the slave to the people of the United States and Europe in the generation before the Civil War.

In their militant bitterness black abolitionists equaled and sometimes surpassed their white brethren. David Walker was by no means alone in demanding violence. In 1844 the Reverend Moses Dickson established in Cincinnati an "order of Twelve of the Knights and Daughters of Tabor" to help overthrow slavery. Two years later he organized the Knights of Liberty in St. Louis. In 1843 Henry Highland Garnet made an address to the Buffalo Convention of Colored Citizens that shocked even many abolitionists: "Brethren, arise, arise! Strike for your lives and liberties. Now is the day and the hour. Let every slave throughout the land do this and the days of slavery are numbered. Rather die freemen than live to be slaves. . . . Awake, Awake, millions of voices are calling you! Let your motto be resistance; no oppressed people have secured their liberty without resistance." Although many blacks viewed his utterances with alarm, by 1854 the black conventions were ready for violence. A resolution adopted at that time declared that "those who, without crime, are outlawed by any Government can owe no allegiance to its enactments [and] . . . we advise all oppressed to adopt the motto, 'Liberty or Death.'" Indeed, black abolitionists had become as ardent in their Garrisonism as any follower of the high priest of abolitionism.

■ The Underground Railroad

Perhaps nothing did more to intensify the strife between North and South, and to emphasize in a most dramatic way the determination of abolitionists to destroy slavery, than the Underground Railroad. Slaves who ran away were irritating and troublesome enough, and the South had been plagued with them from the earliest days of slavery. But when free blacks and whites, fired with an almost fanatical zeal, undertook systematically to wreak havoc on an institution that meant so much to the South, it was almost too much to bear. It was this organized effort to undermine slavery, this manifestation of the workings of a presumably higher law, that put such a strain on intersectional relations and sent antagonists and protagonists of slavery scurrying headlong into the 1850s determined to have their uncompromising way.

The origin of the Underground Railroad goes back to the eighteenth century. Perhaps there were people to help fugitives as early as there were runaway slaves. By the end of the War for Independence, however, organized resistance seemed to be taking shape. At least George Washington thought so when he complained in 1786 of a slave, escaping from Alexandria to Philadelphia, "whom a society of Quakers, formed for such purposes, have attempted to liberate." By the following year Isaac T. Hopper had settled in Philadelphia, and though still in his teens he began to develop a program for the systematic assistance of slaves escaping from the South. Within a few years they were being helped in a number of towns in Pennsylvania and New Jersey. Slowly these antislavery operations spread in various directions.

Henrietta Buckmaster gives 1804 as the year of "incorporation" of the Underground Railroad. It was then that General Thomas Boude, an officer during the Revolution, purchased a slave, Stephen Smith, and brought him home to Columbia, Pennsylvania, followed by Smith's mother, who had escaped to find her son. The Boudes took her in. Within a few weeks the woman who owned Smith's mother arrived and demanded her property. Not only did the Boudes refuse to surrender the slave, but the town supported them. The people of Columbia resolved to champion the cause of fugitives. By 1815 this sentiment was expressed in Ohio. And by 1819 underground methods were used to spirit slaves out of North Carolina. Even before the period of militant abolitionism, the movement that was to be known as the Underground Railroad had grown into a widespread institution.

The name "Underground Railroad" was probably coined shortly after 1831 when steam railroads became popular. There are several versions of how the movement got its name. A plausible one concerns a slave, Tice Davids, who escaped from his Kentucky master in 1831 and got across the Ohio River. Although the master was in hot pursuit, he lost all trace of the slave after crossing the river and was so confounded that he declared the slave must have "gone off on an underground road." That was entirely possible, for by 1831 there were plenty of "underground" roads on the Ohio River, and they had stations, conductors, and means of conveyance. From that time, which coincided exactly with the emergence of Garrison and his militant followers, up until the outbreak of the Civil War, the Underground Railroad operated in flagrant violation of federal fugitive slave laws. It was the most eloquent defiance of slaveholders that abolitionists could make.

In the case of anything so full of adventure and danger as the Underground Railroad, it is difficult to separate fiction from fact. There are stories of breathtaking escapes and exciting experiences that would be quite incredible save for unquestionable verification by reliable sources. After the Railroad had developed an efficient organization, there was a generality of practice that makes possible a brief description of its operation. All, or almost all, of the operations took place at night, for that was the only time when the fugitives and their helpers felt even partially secure. Slaves prepared to make their escape by taking supplies from their masters and, if necessary, by disguising themselves. Those of fair complexion frequently passed as white people and sometimes posed as their own masters. Darker ones posed as servants on their way to meet their owners. There are several cases on record where fugitives were provided at crucial moments with white babies in order to make their claims of being nurses appear more convincing. At times men posed as women and women as men.

In the early days of the Underground Railroad most of the fugitives were men, and they usually traveled on foot. Later, when the traffic was heavy and women and children were fleeing, escorts and vehicles were provided.

The conductors carried their human cargo in covered wagons, closed carriages, and farm wagons specially equipped with closed compartments. Blacks were sometimes put in boxes and shipped as freight by rail or boat. Thus Henry Box Brown was shipped from Richmond to Philadelphia by the Adams Express Company. When traveling by land—and at night—conductors and fugitives were guided by the North Star, by tributaries of the Ohio or other rivers, and by mountain chains. On cloudy nights, when there were no other means of finding directions, they even resorted to feeling the moss on tree trunks and moving north upon discovering it.

Since travel was almost exclusively at night, it was necessary to have stations rather close together, from ten to twenty miles apart, where fugitives could rest, eat, and wait for the next night's journey. During the day they were hidden in barns, in the attics of homes, and in other out-of-the-way places. Meanwhile, the word was passed to succeeding stations, by what was called "the grape vine telegraph," that fugitives were on their way. One ambiguous message mailed by a conductor to the next stationmaster in 1859 gave much more information than a casual glance revealed. It read, "By to-morrow evening's mail, you will receive two volumes of 'The Irrepressible Conflict' bound in black. After perusal, please forward and oblige."

All Underground Railroad lines led north. They began on various plantations in the South and ran vaguely—and dangerously—up rivers and valleys and across mountains to some point on the Ohio or upper Mississippi River in the West, and to points in Pennsylvania and New Jersey in the East. Once the North had been reached, the route was much clearer, though traversed with only slightly less danger, for planters, traders, and sheriffs pursued fugitives relentlessly and resorted to the most desperate means to recover them.

Even if the Underground Railroad did not need papers of incorporation, it needed capital. The fugitives required food and clothing, and frequently there were unexpected expenses such as boarding a train in order to evade a pursuing owner or displaying affluence to convey the impression that one had been free long enough to accumulate wealth. Quakers and similar groups raised funds to carry on the work. The vigilance committees of Philadelphia and New York solicited money. Philanthropists contributed, as did the conductors and other "officials" of the Railroad. Harriet Tubman, one of the greatest of all conductors, would take several months off whenever she was running low in funds and hire herself out as a domestic servant in order to raise money for conveying slaves to freedom.

The Underground Railroad did not seem to suffer for want of operators. Wilbur H. Siebert has catalogued more than 3,200 active workers, and there is every reason to believe that there were many more who will remain forever anonymous. Outstanding among the white workers was Levi Coffin, a Quaker and the so-called president of the Underground Railroad. His strategic location in southern Indiana, as well as his remarkable zeal, made it possible for him to help more than 3,000 slaves escape. Calvin Fairbanks,

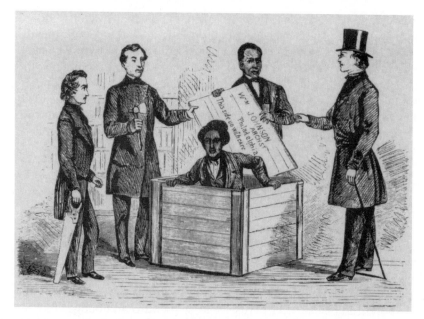

RESURRECTION OF HENRY BOX BROWN. Among the many ways by which slaves escaped to the North was shipment as merchandise. Brown was shipped from Richmond to Philadelphia, a trip requiring twenty-six hours. The white men in the drawing are J. M. McKim, C. D. Cleveland, and Lewis Thompson; the black man is William Still. From William Still, *The Underground Railroad.*

who had learned to hate slavery as a student at Oberlin College, began to travel in the South in 1837 on the dangerous business of freeing slaves. In Kentucky he engaged in a regular business of transporting slaves across the Ohio River. On one occasion, with a teacher from Vermont known as Miss Webster, he helped three slaves escape by posing as her servants. It was said that not one of his fugitives was ever recaptured, though he spent many years in jail because of his work.

In many respects the most daring white conductor on the Underground Railroad was John Fairfield. Son of a Virginia slaveholding family, he would have nothing to do with the institution and decided to live in a free state. Before going north, he helped a slave who was his friend escape to Canada. News of his exploit spread: not only did the whites of his community seek to find and arrest him, but slaves sought his aid to escape. He could not refuse to help, and thus began his career as a conductor on the Underground Railroad. He delivered slaves "on order." Blacks in the North and in Canada would give him money and a description of their friends or relatives and he would deliver them. At times he conveyed as many as fifteen. He posed as a slaveholder, a slave trader, or a peddler of eggs and poultry in Louisiana, Alabama, Mississippi, Tennessee, and Kentucky in order to gain the confidence of slaveholders. He was so convincing in each role that he was seldom suspected of being implicated in a slave's escape. Those that he did not take to Canada he delivered to Levi Coffin, who arranged the rest of their journey. His greatest triumph was in conveying twenty-eight slaves to freedom by organizing them into a funeral procession. He suffered in his work from privation and exposure and one time he was shot, but he persevered in his missions of freedom until his death in 1860, when he is believed to have been killed in an insurrection of slaves in Tennessee. John Brown, dashing from Missouri with twelve slaves and later attacking Harpers Ferry in an attempt at insurrection, has received more notice from historians, but Fairfield was as effective a fighter of slavery as any man who lived before the Civil War.

There were many black officials on the Underground Railroad. Jane Lewis of New Lebanon, Ohio, rowed fugitives regularly across the Ohio River. John Parker, who purchased himself for $2,000, was in league with John Rankin and other white workers on the Railroad. Josiah Henson, born a slave, escaped with his wife and two children to Canada, learned to read and write, and returned south often to assist slaves in their escape. Once he went to Kentucky by a circuitous route through New York, Pennsylvania, and Ohio in order to avoid suspicion. He took 30 refugees out of Kentucky and led them to Toledo within a period of two weeks. Elijah Anderson has been called the general superintendent of the Underground Railroad in northwestern Ohio. From 1850 until his death seven years later in the Kentucky state prison, he worked arduously in behalf of fugitive slaves. By 1855 he had led more than 1,000 to freedom. John Mason, himself a fugitive slave from Kentucky, was one of the most astute conductors. According to William Mitchell, a black missionary in Canada, Mason brought 265 slaves to his home in the course of nineteen months. On one occasion he was captured and sold back into slavery, but again he made good his escape. In all he delivered about 1,300 slaves into free territory.

Easily the most outstanding conductor on the Underground Railroad was Harriet Tubman. Although frail of body and suffering from recurrent spells of dizziness, she not only escaped from slavery herself but also conveyed many others to freedom, including her sister, her two children, and her aged mother and father. She is said to have gone south nineteen times and to have emancipated more than 300 slaves. Unable to read or write, she nevertheless displayed remarkable ingenuity in the management of her runaway caravans. She preferred to start the journey on Saturday night, so that she could be well on her way before the owners had an opportunity the following Monday to advertise the escape of their slaves. She tolerated no cowardice and threatened to kill any slave who wished to turn back. Well known in Philadelphia, New York, and Boston, where she frequently delivered escaped slaves, she preferred to lead them all the way to Canada after the passage of the Fugitive Slave Law in 1850, explaining that she could not trust Uncle Sam with her people any longer.

The very nature of the institution prevents any accurate estimate of the number of slaves who found freedom by the Underground Railroad. Governor Quitman of Mississippi declared that between 1810 and 1850 the South lost 100,000 slaves valued at more than $30 million. This is a much larger figure than the census gives for blacks in the North who were born in slaveholding states, but Wilbur H. Siebert believes that it is fairly accurate. He is certain, for example, that approximately 40,000 passed through Ohio alone.

The Underground Railroad intensified the resentment that the South felt toward outside interference. It was not realized that the Railroad ran inside the South. Not only Northerners participated in its management, but Southern whites and blacks were among its most valuable engineers and conductors, and all the passengers were blacks desperately anxious to get away from the peculiar institution of the South.

■ The South Strikes Back

Despite the fact that there was considerable Southern sentiment against slavery during the colonial and early national periods, the institution always had its defenders. Almost from the beginning no attack on slavery went unanswered. When Samuel Sewall wrote *The Selling of Joseph,* John Saffin answered his attack on slavery with an enthusiastic rebuttal in 1701. Persons of no less stature than George Whitefield, the great evangelist, and his friend James Habersham sprang to the defense of slavery in the middle of the eighteenth century. When there was some doubt regarding the future of slavery under the new national government, most of the Southern congressmen made it clear that they would tolerate no interference with the institution. From the time that Jefferson's *Notes on Virginia* was made public, Southern leaders did not hesitate to use his work to strengthen their contention that blacks were by nature an inferior race and therefore should be enslaved. Some Southerners conceded that slavery was a political evil, but almost none agreed with antislavery antagonists that it was also a great moral evil.

In the early nineteenth century the question of slavery was overshadowed by other problems of a political and economic nature. Foreign relations were strained, and the nation's energies were directed toward trying to stay out of the Napoleonic Wars in Europe. America's preoccupation with becoming more self-sufficient economically caused the North to turn its attention to shipping and, later, manufacturing, while the South made the transition from a tobacco and rice slave economy to one in which cotton was dominant. It would not be accurate, however, to describe sectional attitudes toward slavery during this period as altogether indifferent. As some people continued to attack slavery, its defenders spoke up, gradually developing the classic defense that was to be reiterated with so much feeling in the period ahead.

Even before the great debate over the admission of Missouri, the antislavery movement had assumed something of a sectional character. Emancipation of the slaves in Northern states had proceeded at a time when the institution was becoming more deeply entrenched in the South with the development of the cotton kingdom. Emigration of the majority of antislavery men and women from the slave states, moreover, deprived the South of an opportunity to hear the other side of the argument from its neighbors. Dwight L. Dumond insists that this migration deprived the South of men and women "whose combined intelligence, moral courage, and Christian benevolence would have gone far toward modifying the harsher features of slavery, toward preventing so great a unanimity of opinion in that section in support of slavery as a positive good, and toward keeping alive the spirit of free discussion." Later, as antislavery men and women withdrew from the colonization movement and organized militant antislavery societies, the South found that it could no longer tolerate any enemies of slavery in its midst. The debate over Missouri, the insurrection of Denmark Vesey, and the increased activity of the abolitionists all convinced the residents of the South that they must give more attention to the defense of their institution. When the call went out for defenders, they were sufficient both in number and in zeal. They began to strike back at their Northern traducers, blow for blow.

Southerners were now determined not to apologize for slavery. They stopped thinking of it as having any undesirable aspects. They evolved the idea, and clung to it with ferocious tenacity, that slavery was a positive good. In 1826 Edward Brown brought out *Notes on the Origin and Necessity of Slavery*, which drew heavily from a pamphlet published the previous year by Whitemarsh B. Seabrook. Brown declared that "slavery has ever been the stepping ladder by which countries have passed from barbarism to civilization. . . . It appears . . . to be the only state capable of bringing the love of independence and of ease, inherent in man, to the discipline and shelter necessary to his physical wants." A few months later Thomas Cooper of South Carolina published his first proslavery pamphlet. One by one, Southern educators and ministers joined in the defense of slavery, and the war of words was on.

The proslavery argument was based on a theory of the racial inferiority and biological inequality of blacks. There were four main postulates of the theory. In the first place, it was contended that slave labor was absolutely essential to the economic development and prosperity of the South. Governor Hammond of South Carolina expressed this point of view clearly:

> In all social systems there must be a class to do the menial duties, to perform the drudgery of life. . . . Its requisites are vigor, docility, fidelity. Such a class you must have or you would not have that other class which leads progress, civilization, and refinement. It constitutes the very mud-sill of society and of political government; and you might as well attempt to build a house in the air, as to build either the one or the other, except on this mud-sill.

In the second place, it was asserted that blacks were inferior and destined to occupy a subordinate position. In *Southern Institutes*, George S. Sawyer forcefully stated this point of view:

The social, moral, and political, as well as the physical history of the negro race bears strong testimony against them; it furnishes the most undeniable proof of their mental inferiority. In no age or condition has the real negro shown a capacity to throw off the chains of barbarism and brutality that have long bound down the nations of that race; or to rise above the common cloud of darkness that still broods over them.

Doctors like John H. Van Evrie, Josiah Clark Nott, and many others published works in which they subscribed to an ethnological justification of African slavery.

Another argument of proslavery leaders was that through the ages the church had sanctioned slavery as a means of converting the heathen to Christian civilization. There was, of course, some conflict between the theory that blacks were incapable of improvement and the notion that they could be civilized and Christianized in slavery; but little attention was paid to this apparent contradiction, and each argument was used where it would do the most good. The Reverend James Henley Thornwell, Bishop Stephen Elliott, and Dr. B. M. Palmer were only three among many Southern religious leaders who held fast to this point of view and expressed it in their sermons and writings. With many Northern religious leaders holding opposite points of view, an intersectional clash of denominations was inevitable. Thus fifteen years before the Civil War the Baptists, Methodists, and Presbyterians had each split into two groups.

Finally, the proslavery argument ran, the white race had not degenerated because of slavery but had developed a unique and high degree of culture. George Fitzhugh, Beverly Tucker, and others claimed that a society in which everyone was free was a failure and that the South had solved its problems by acknowledging the fact that culture and civilization could advance only if slaves were available to do the work.

This war of words became so bitter, and the atmosphere in the South so tense, that free inquiry and free speech disappeared. People with points of view at variance with the accepted proslavery creed were run out of the South. Colleges became hotbeds of secession, and every agency in the community was employed to defend slavery. Even men of letters, like William Gilmore Simms, wrote proslavery essays, poems, and songs. In words the South struck back with a vengeance.

The South loved action too well, however, to let the conflict remain on an academic level. It was a practical matter too: the vociferous antislavery preachers must be silenced if they were not to do irreparable damage to Southern institutions. In October 1831, the Georgia legislature offered $4,000 for the arrest of Garrison. There was a price on the head of Arthur Tappan, $12,000 in Macon and $20,000 in New Orleans. The vigilance committee of South Carolina offered $1,500 for the arrest of any person distributing the *Liberator* or Walker's *Appeal*. Most of the leading participants in the abolition movement and the activities of the Underground Railroad could boast that they were officially wanted in the South.

Pushing their program of resistance a step further, Southern leaders were resolved to keep the writings of abolitionists out of their communities, by force if necessary. They worked up such popular resentment to the circulation of abolitionist literature in the South that citizens took the matter into their own hands. In July 1835 a group broke into the Charleston post office, seized antislavery newspapers, and made a bonfire out of them in the public square. Many other cities followed this example. When it appeared that the federal government would not punish them for their actions, Southern postmasters of their own accord began to take abolitionist literature out of the mails.

People living in the South, whether natives or from the North, found it desirable to speak with extreme caution on the question of slavery. One white man was lashed in Petersburg, Virginia, and ordered to leave the town for expressing the view that "black men have, in the abstract, a right to their freedom." A Georgian who subscribed to the *Liberator* was dragged from his home by a mob, tarred and feathered, set afire, ducked in the river, and then tied to a post and whipped. Amos Dresser, a former student at Lane Seminary, went into Tennessee to sell Bibles. When it could not be proved in court that he was spreading abolitionist doctrine, a mob lashed him one midnight in a public square, with the hearty approval of several thousand onlookers. Whites who associated with blacks on any basis that suggested equality were severely dealt with. Several, for example, were murdered in Georgia and South Carolina for the "crime" of mixing with blacks in public.

Proslavery leaders even carried the fight into enemy territory. They not only went North in pursuit of their runaway slaves, but they sought to spread proslavery doctrine and to spy on abolitionists. A Kentucky slaveholder, dressed in the garb of a Quaker, went to Indiana to get information on the Underground Railroad. Because he knew so little about Quaker speech and customs, he was soon discovered. Another went so far as to pose as an antislavery lecturer. Visiting several communities in Indiana and Ohio, he discovered that fugitives were hiding out and notified their masters, who promptly came and claimed their property. He was in a community, however, that was hostile to slavery, and the citizens insisted that the slaves be given a hearing. In court it was decided that the masters' claims were invalid, and the slaves were set free.

In the decade before the Civil War intersectional strife reached a new peak. There was division and dissension among abolitionists with regard to policy, but there was more unity than ever among proslavery leaders. In both sections the war of words had failed to bring satisfactory results. In the North the practical abolitionists resolved to destroy slavery by perfecting the Underground Railroad and delivering slaves into free territory. In the South the practical proslavery leaders resolved to keep the institution of slavery inviolate by destroying every vestige of thought that was at variance with it. If conformity involved burning books or newspapers, spying on the enemy in order to be able to counterattack successfully, or even killing blacks or whites, then in a situation where so much was at stake it simply had to be done.

■ Stress and Strain in the 1850s

Perhaps no decade in the history of the United States has been so filled with tense and crucial moments as the ten years leading to the Civil War, and closely connected with most of these crises was the problem of slavery. The period was ushered in by the controversy over slavery in the newly acquired territory in the Southwest. With the discovery of gold in California in 1848 and with the rapid peopling of many areas in the Mexican cession, a policy had to be decided upon. Some leaders held that the new territory should be divided into slave and free sections as in the Missouri Compromise. The abolitionists, of course, and many others in the North, wanted a total exclusion of slavery from the territories, a point of view expressed in the Wilmot Proviso. Still others were of the opinion that the question should be decided by the people who lived in the new territories, an approach to the problem which was popularized by Stephen A. Douglas. Finally, there were those who insisted that slavery could not be legally excluded anywhere, a view vigorously advanced by John C. Calhoun. The question of fugitive slaves, moreover, was very much alive. Southern owners had never had too much luck in recovering them. In 1842, in the case of *Prigg v. Pennsylvania*, the Supreme Court ruled that state officials were not required to assist in the return of fugitives, and the decision did much to render ineffective all efforts to recover slaves.

In 1850 these questions were thoroughly aired in Congress, and a desperate effort was made to work out a solution that would diminish intersectional strife. After considerable debate by Clay, Calhoun, Douglas, Seward, and Chase, an agreement was reached which provided that (1) California should enter the Union as a free state; (2) the other territories would be organized without mention of slavery; (3) Texas should cede certain lands to New Mexico and be compensated; (4) slaveholders would be better protected by a stringent fugitive slave law; and (5) there should be no slave trade in the District of Columbia. The Compromise of 1850 was by no means satisfactory to all, and Georgia, Mississippi, Alabama, and South Carolina seriously considered secession. Southerners said they would remain in the Union only as long as there was strict adherence to the compromise, especially in enforcing the fugitive slave act.

It soon became clear that neither section was seriously reconciled to the Compromise of 1850 as a final settlement of the slavery question. Militant abolitionists were still determined to assist runaways, and new federal legislation could not deter them. In 1851 they went so far as to rescue a slave, Shadrach, from a United States marshal in Boston who was preparing to return him to his owner. It was the zeal of the slaveholders that especially irritated the abolitionists. With the new law against fugitives, slaveholders put on intensive hunts, determined to drive back into slavery even those fugitives who had lived free for years. For example, they seized Jerry McHenry, who had lived in Syracuse for several years and was regarded as a substantial citizen; but members of the Liberty party convening there were led by Gerrit Smith and William Seward to rescue McHenry and send him on his way. These are merely two examples of what came to be open defiance of the law on the part of militant abolitionists. Their attitude convinced the South that the North was not willing to abide by the Compromise of 1850.

The appearance of *Uncle Tom's Cabin* in 1852 increased the strain on intersectional relations. This novel by Harriet Beecher Stowe sold more than 300,000 copies in the first year of publication and was soon dramatized in theaters throughout the North. Its story of abject cruelty on the part of masters and overseers, its description of the privation and suffering of slaves, and its complete condemnation of Southern civilization won countless thousands over to abolition and left Southern leaders busy denying the truth of the novel. The damage had been done, however, and when Southerners counted their losses from this one blow, they found them to be staggering indeed.

The sectional truce brought about by the Compromise of 1850 was at an end, but if it needed a legislative act to destroy it, the Kansas-Nebraska Act of 1854 was precisely the thing. Introduced into the Senate by Stephen A. Douglas of Illinois, the act provided that Kansas and Nebraska should be organized as territories and that the question of slavery should be decided by territorial legislatures. Whatever the motives of Douglas may have been, the passage of the act precipitated a desperate struggle between North and South for the control of Kansas. The Missouri Compromise had been in effect repealed, and those forces that mustered the greatest strength in Kansas could win it. In the ensuing years abolitionist and proslavery factions fought and bled for Kansas, and the land became a preliminary battleground of the Civil War. No longer was there much semblance of intersectional peace. Although the climate of Kansas would have prevented any extensive development of plantation slavery there, the principle was important to both sides, and they conducted themselves accordingly.

The Kansas-Nebraska Act persuaded many antislavery leaders that political action was necessary to combat the relentless drive of proslavery forces to extend slavery. Northern Whigs, Free Soilers, and Democrats who had fought the passage of the act came together, and out of their discussions arose the Republican party. This new political organization, unalterably antislavery in its point of view, profited by the mistake of earlier antislavery parties and evolved a program broad enough to attract voters who were indifferent to slavery. Southerners, meanwhile, sought to counteract this new party by demanding further extension of slavery and the reopening of the African slave trade.

The significance of these trends had hardly become apparent when the

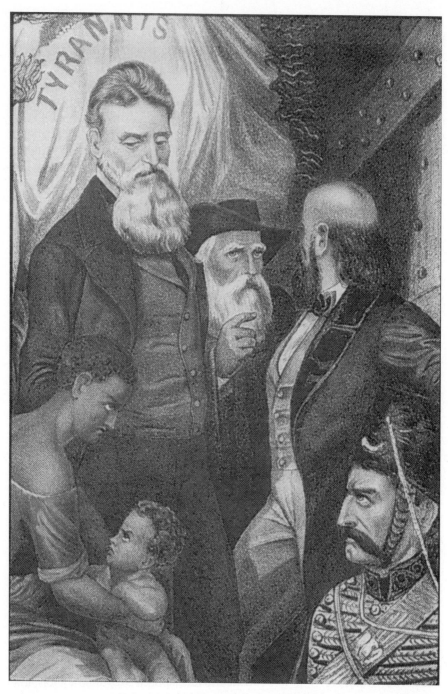

JOHN BROWN MEETING THE SLAVE MOTHER. Brown was hanged in 1859, following his unsuccessful attempt to launch an assault on slavery by seizing the federal arsenal at Harper's Ferry. On his way to the place of execution, he greeted a slave mother and her child. *(John Hope Franklin Collection.)*

Supreme Court in 1857 handed down a decision in the case of *Scott v. Sanford* that had the effect of widening the breach between North and South. Dred Scott was a Missouri slave whose master had first taken him to live in free Illinois and subsequently to a fort in the northern part of the Louisiana purchase, where slavery had been excluded by the Missouri Compromise. Upon his return to Missouri, Scott sued for his freedom on the ground that residence on free soil had liberated him. The majority of the Court held that Scott was not a citizen and therefore could not bring suit in the courts. Chief Justice Roger B. Taney, speaking for the Court, added that since the Missouri Compromise was unconstitutional, masters could take their slaves anywhere in the territories and retain title to them. The decision was a clear-cut victory for the South, and the North viewed it with genuine alarm. With the highest court in the land openly preaching the proslavery doctrine, there was little hope that anything short of a most drastic political or social revolution would bring an end to slavery. All abolitionists were not as optimistic as Frederick Douglass, but they hoped with him that "The Supreme Court . . . [was] not the only power in this world. We, the abolitionists and colored people, should meet this decision, unlooked for and monstrous as it appears, in a cheerful spirit. This very attempt to blot out forever the hopes of an enslaved people may be one necessary link in the chain of events preparatory to the complete overthrow of the whole slave system."

Indeed, only two more links were needed to bring on the bitter war that gave freedom to the slaves: one was the raid of John Brown, and the other was a Republican victory at the polls in 1860. Brown had worked in the cause of freedom for many years. He had done his part to aid the antislavery forces in Kansas, and he had worked on the Underground Railroad out of Missouri. By 1859 he was anxious to strike a more significant blow for the freedom of slaves. He traveled through the North raising money and talking with white and black abolitionists. Finally, he laid his plans to attack slaveholders and liberate their slaves. On Sunday night, October 16, with a small band of less than fifty men he seized the federal arsenal at Harpers Ferry, Virginia, in the hope of securing sufficient ammunition to carry out a large-scale operation against the Virginia slaveholders. Immediately the countryside was alerted, and both federal and state governments dispatched troops which overwhelmed Brown and his men. Among those with Brown were several blacks, including Lewis Sheridan Leary, Dangerfield Newby, John Anthony Copeland, Shields Green, and Osborn Perry Anderson. Leary and Newby were killed; Copeland and Green were hanged; and Anderson escaped.

The effect of this raid on the South was electrifying. It made slaveholders think that abolitionists would stop at nothing to wipe out slavery. No one felt secure because there were rumors of other insurrections to come and widespread complaints that slaves were insolent because they knew their day of liberation was near. The whole South was put on a semi-war footing, with troops drilling regularly as far south as Georgia and with increasing demands for arms and ammunition by the militia commanders of most states.

On December 2, 1859, John Brown was hanged, but not before he had dazzled the country by his words and his conduct after the trial. He told a reporter from the *New York Herald*, "I pity the poor in bondage that have none to help them; that is why I am here; not to gratify any personal animosity, revenge or vindictive spirit. It is my sympathy with the oppressed and wronged, that are as good as you and as precious in the sight of God. . . . You may dispose of me easily, but this question is still to be settled—the negro question—the end of that is not yet." Upon hearing his sentence he calmly said, "Now, if it is deemed necessary that I should forfeit my life for the furtherance of the ends of justice, and mingle my blood further with the blood of my children and with the blood of millions in this slave country whose rights are disregarded by wicked, cruel, and unjust enactments, I say, let it be done."

Some people said that Brown was a madman, but few who saw him and listened to him thought so. Governor Wise of Virginia said, "They are themselves mistaken who take him to be a madman. . . . He is a man of clear head, of courage, of fortitude and simple ingenuousness." He terrified the South and captivated the North by his deed. Many had died fighting for freedom, but none had done it so heroically or at such a propitious moment. The crusade against slavery now had a martyr, and nothing wins followers to a cause like a martyr. Literally thousands of people who had been indifferent were now persuaded that slavery must be abolished. There can be no doubt that many voted for the Republican ticket in 1860 because of this conviction.

When it became clear that the Republican candidate would stand on an antislavery platform, the South began once more to utter threats of secession. But with the nomination of Abraham Lincoln, instead of a pronounced abolitionist like Seward of New York or Chase of Ohio, it was the abolitionists who were worried. They were not sure how far Lincoln would go to put an end to slavery. And yet, as Dwight Dumond has pointed out, his words and deeds for twenty years had clearly been antislavery. He had said many times that slavery was hostile to the poor man. During his one term in Congress he had done what he could to keep the territories free, so that poor people could feel secure there. He had said that blacks should be protected in their right to the enjoyment of the fruits of their own labor, and he had vigorously denounced the Dred Scott decision. Nevertheless, Garrison, Phillips, Sumner, and other abolitionists were skeptical of him because he was not one of them.

Lincoln's election, which many Democrats conceded after they split into factions at the Charleston and Baltimore conventions, marked the elevation to power of a party whose philosophy was, from the Southern point of view, revolutionary and destructive. There was no place in the Union for states unalterably committed to the maintenance and extension of slavery. The November election returns, which gave victory to the Republicans, were the signal for calling conventions in the South to take the step that fire-eaters and proslavery leaders had already decided upon.

It was in an atmosphere of slavery that the weapons for waging the Civil War were sharpened. It was the question of slavery that sundered the sections and forced them to settle the question by a bloody war. The humanitarian reform movement would have proceeded apace had there been no slaves, for temperance, women's rights, and the like would have received generous support in communities where there was a tendency to assume civic responsibility. It was the question of slavery, however, that intensified the reform crusade and brought the country to the impasse of 1860. Without slavery the question of the extent of federal authority in the territories would have remained academic and could have been debated openly and peaceably. Without slavery the South would have remained a land where freedom of thought could command respect and where all institutions would not feel compelled to pursue a course of action prescribed by the planting aristocracy. Just as the antislavery movement had its roots deep in the liberal philosophy of the Revolutionary period, so intersectional strife and the Civil War itself had their roots in the question of the future of black people in the United States.

CHAPTER 11

Civil War

■ Uncertain Federal Policy

When President-Elect Lincoln arrived in Washington late in February 1861, the nation he was to administer during the next four years was rapidly falling apart. Seven states in the lower South had already seceded, and there was talk of the same momentous step being taken in each of the other slave states. Even before his inauguration Lincoln perceived that his most important and difficult task was stemming the tide of national disintegration. In his carefully worded inaugural address he condemned the Southern citizens—not the states—who were in insurrection, and thus he may have won friends in the doubtful border states. But his words were hardly encouraging to abolitionists, who felt that the time for words was over. Action was needed, in their opinion, to bring an end to an institution against which the Republican party had taken a stand during the election campaign. But Lincoln had to move cautiously lest he offend the eight slave states that still remained in the Union. No amount of caution, however, could maintain peace indefinitely without surrendering the authority of the federal government in the South. When the time came to defend Fort Sumter, Lincoln acted promptly, but the defense of the fort cost him four more slave states and plunged the country into civil war.

Even if there had not been the problem of keeping the remaining slave states—Delaware, Maryland, Kentucky, and Missouri—in the Union, there were still many people in the North who would have recoiled from a war against slavery. Lincoln not only had to mollify the border slave states but also had to avoid any policy offensive to thousands throughout the North who had grown weary of the abolition movement. He could hope in the meantime to soften the attacks that abolitionists were bound to make on him by giving ground to them on less dangerous matters.

When blacks rushed to offer their services to the Union, they were rejected. In almost every town of any size there were large numbers of blacks who sought to serve in the Union army. Failing to be enlisted, they bided their time and did whatever they could to assist. In New York they formed a military club and drilled regularly until the police stopped them. Several Philadelphia blacks offered to go south and organize slave revolts, but this was unthinkable. In the nation's capital they made repeated requests of the War Department to be received into the army. At a meeting in Boston they passed a resolution urging the government to enlist them: "Our feelings urge us to say to our countrymen that we are ready to stand by and defend our Government as the equals of its white defenders; to do so with 'our lives, our fortunes, and our sacred honor,' for the sake of freedom, and as good citizens; and we ask you to modify your laws, that we may enlist,—that full scope may be given to the patriotic feelings burning in the colored man's breast."

Abolitionists began to wonder if they had supported the wrong candidate in Lincoln. They were filled with even greater despair when they observed the vacillating policy adopted by the government with reference to slaves who escaped to federal lines. Indeed, there was no policy; each commander used his own discretion. In the spring of 1861, blacks sought refuge within federal lines near Fortress Monroe in Virginia. When General Butler learned that slaves had been employed in erecting Confederate defenses, he immediately declared that they were "contraband of war" and should not be returned to their owners. Instead, they were put to work for the Union forces. For several months it was not at all clear that the authorities in Washington would endorse his action, and several replies from the War Department to his requests for a clarification of policy were evasive.

In June 1861 several military officers spoke out in favor of returning all fugitives. In the West, General Halleck adopted this policy. But the lack of any uniform policy was clearly indicated by two developments in July 1861. On July 9 the House of Representatives passed a resolution declaring it was not the duty of federal troops to capture or return fugitive slaves. One week later, General Winfield Scott wrote Brigadier General McDowell, in the name of President Lincoln, asking him to allow owners of fugitive slaves in Virginia to cross the Potomac and recover runaways who had taken refuge behind Union lines. Small wonder that there was so much dissatisfaction among abolitionists with regard to federal policy. Phillips, Sumner, and Garrison openly attacked the government and demanded a more forthright stand on fugitives and emancipation. It was not until the passage of the Confiscation Act of August 6, 1861, that anything resembling uniform treatment was applied to fugitives by the federal government. The act provided that any property used with the owner's consent and with his or her knowledge in aiding or abetting insurrection against the United States was the lawful subject of prize and capture wherever found. When the property consisted of slaves, they were to be forever free.

As Union armies pushed into the South, blacks poured over Union lines by the thousands. Yet federal policy regarding their relief and employment was hardly more clear-cut than it had been when the legality of receiving them at all was doubtful. Again each commanding officer seemed to use his own discretion. In western Tennessee, General Grant found it necessary to appoint John Eaton to take charge of all fugitives in his area in November 1862. A special camp was set up for blacks at Grand Junction, Tennessee, where Eaton supervised the hiring out of these ex-slaves, leased abandoned plantations to whites who hired them, and saw to it that they were paid for their work. In Louisiana, General Benjamin Butler leased blacks to loyal planters who paid them $10 a month. It was most difficult to secure the cooperation of soldiers and officers, who did not want to appear to be serving with blacks. The transition period for them was extremely difficult, and because of the confused and changing federal policy, they endured at times both hunger and exposure. While they did not suffer cruel punishment, there were many instances of unfair treatment, a most perplexing problem to the officers whose principal responsibility was to take the war to the enemy.

In December 1862 Rufus Saxton, head of the Department of the South, sought to reduce the confusion involving the employment and relief of fugitives by issuing an order for a general plan to be followed everywhere. Abandoned lands were to be used for the benefit of ex-slaves. Black families were allotted two acres for each working hand. They were to plant corn and potatoes for their own use, with tools to be furnished by the government, and the plowing was to be done by those assigned to that task. All blacks were required to raise a certain amount of cotton for government use. In many areas superintendents of "Negro affairs" were appointed, whose duties were to take a census of the black population, see that blacks were employed and had the necessaries of life, take charge of land set aside by the government for their use, and protect those who had hired themselves out to white employers. Some superintendents, like the Reverend Horace James of the North Carolina area, performed their duties conscientiously, but others did not show much interest in the problems of blacks.

Relief was almost always difficult because of the small amount of land available for the use of blacks. In his report in 1864 the Reverend Mr. James said, "We control indeed a broad area of navigable waters, and command the approaches from the sea, but have scarcely room enough on land to spread our tents upon." The government was selling much of the land held for nonpayment of taxes to private parties. Eastern capitalists and philanthropists bought most of the available land in South Carolina, and frequently, though not always, these new owners had little interest in the plight of blacks.

Another difficulty arose out of the fact that the Treasury Department contested the right of the War Department to administer the affairs of black people. Although the secretary of war desired the Treasury to control all confiscated property, except that used by the military, officers in the field were of the opinion that they could best handle everything. While the controversy raged during 1863 and 1864, blacks suffered for want of any coordinated supervision. In his message to the Confederate Congress in the fall of 1863, President Davis excoriated Northern conduct of black affairs. After describing the starvation and suffering among blacks in contraband camps, he said that "there is little hazard in predicting that in all localities where the enemy have gained a temporary foothold, the negroes, who under our care increased sixfold in number . . . will have been reduced by mortality during the war to not more than one-half their previous number." While his criticism was by no means objective, there was indeed much suffering and death among blacks. In 1864 a Union official admitted that mortality in black camps was "frightful" and that "most competent judges place it at not less than twenty-five percent in the last two years."

The federal policy for relief of former slaves developed so slowly that private citizens, both black and white, undertook to supplement it. As early as February 1862 meetings were held in Boston, New York, and other Northern cities for the express purpose of rendering more effective aid to Southern blacks. On February 22 the National Freedmen's Relief Association was organized in New York, and soon thereafter came the Contraband Relief Association in Cincinnati, which later changed its name to the Western Freedmen's Aid Commission. The Friends Association for the Relief of Colored Freedmen was established in Philadelphia, and a group of Chicago citizens formed the Northwestern Freedmen's Aid Commission. In 1865 all were united in the American Freedmen's Aid Commission. Religious organizations, such as the United States Christian Commission and the American Missionary Association, joined in providing relief for blacks. Collections were taken up, clothing and food solicited, and agents sent south to minister to the needs of ex-slaves.

A significant contribution of private agencies toward the adjustment of former slaves to their new status was in education. Although the federal government had no policy in this matter, it was not averse to cooperating with philanthropic organizations. Their work in educating blacks began in 1861 when Lewis Tappan, treasurer of the American Missionary Association, wrote General Butler to offer the services of his organization. Butler welcomed such aid, and the Reverend L. C. Lockwood was sent to develop a program. On September 15, 1861, he opened a Sunday School for blacks in the home of former President Tyler, and two days later he began the first day school, with Mary S. Peake as the teacher. Within a few months the American Missionary Association had established schools for blacks at Hampton, Norfolk, Portsmouth, and Newport News, Virginia, and on several plantations. By 1864 more than 3,000 blacks were in school with 52 teachers, of whom at least 5 were black. They were paid by the associations, but the government furnished subsistence.

Several schools were established in Washington for refugees, and the freedmen's relief associations of Boston and Philadelphia supplied teachers. In North Carolina, the chaplains of Northern regiments took an early interest in the education of blacks, and later the American Missionary Association and relief organizations extended their programs into this area. The first day schools were set up in July 1863. One year later there were schools at Beaufort, Washington, Plymouth, Morehead, and other places, with 3,000 students and 66 teachers. Evening schools were also established for adults. General Butler took great interest in this work and sponsored the erection of a large building at Hampton to accommodate 800 students.

The New England Freedmen's Aid Society started education for blacks in South Carolina in 1862 when 31 men and women arrived as teachers. Schools were established on larger plantations and in towns, and by June 1863 it was estimated that 5,000 blacks were in school. Gradually education for blacks was extended to most areas occupied by Union troops. In 1863 General Banks established a system of public education under the Department of the Gulf, and a Board of Education for Freedmen supervised the schools. By the end of the next year ninety-five schools had been set up under the department, with 162 teachers, of whom 130 were Southerners including several blacks. There were 9,571 students in day schools, and another 2,000 in evening schools.

The enthusiasm of Northerners for the education of blacks was tremendous. In the last year of the war at least 1,000 young Northern men and women were teaching and caring for ex-slaves. They brought with them slates, pencils, spelling books, readers, blackboards, and chalk. While they met strong opposition from a majority of Southern whites, there were some who not only favored but contributed to the success of schools for blacks. All through the South were to be found native whites teaching blacks before the close of the war.

Some blacks established schools for their own people. In Natchez, for example, three schools were started during the war by black women. In Savannah, blacks could boast not only of two large schools that they had founded, but also of a black board of education to determine their policies. Most schools for blacks had poor facilities, inadequate supplies, and insufficient teachers, but African Americans attended them in larger and larger numbers. The people responsible for establishing these schools—Northerners and Southerners, whites and blacks—made a most significant contribution to the adjustment of a people emerging from slavery.

The opposition of the government early in the war to using black soldiers evoked unfavorable criticism from abolitionists. There was considerable agitation for arming blacks. Garrison and Phillips believed that it was cruel to deprive blacks of the opportunity to fight for the freedom of their brothers. White Northerners who were not abolitionists objected to fighting for the freedom of blacks when blacks themselves were not fighting. There were many, however, including some soldiers, who did not want blacks to wear the uniform of the Union, feeling that it should be reserved for those whose citizenship was unquestioned. Lincoln feared that the border states would take exception to a policy of arming blacks and that it would seriously alienate support in the North. He therefore gave no serious consideration to arming them until the spring of 1862, and then it was forced on him.

As a result of considerable pressure from officers in the field, the acting secretary of war authorized Gen. Thomas W. Sherman in October 1861 to "employ fugitive slaves in such services as they may be fitted for . . . with such organization as you may deem most beneficial to the service; this, however, not being a general arming of them for military service." While Sherman did not take advantage of this authorization to arm some slaves, his successor, David Hunter, sent out a call in May 1862 for blacks to serve in the army. Within a few months enough had responded for the First South Carolina Volunteer Regiment to be activated, but almost immediately Hunter was forced to disband the group, and the men were sent home unpaid and dissatisfied. In the autumn of 1862, however, Lincoln permitted the enlistment of some blacks. General B. F. Butler mustered a whole regiment of free blacks in Louisiana, and Hunter's South Carolina regiment was reorganized by General Saxton. In December, Gen. Augustus Chetlain assumed control of blacks volunteering in Tennessee, and thereafter the program was definitely considered a successful venture.

Machinery for recruiting black soldiers in the South was set up in the spring of 1863 by Adj. Gen. Lorenzo Thomas, who was sent to the Mississippi Valley to put it into operation. A special bureau was established in his office for the "conduct of all matters referring to the organization of Negro troops." Recruiting agents were selected and stations established in Maryland, Tennessee, Missouri, and at other strategic points. All able-bodied black men were eligible for military employment. Where loyal masters consented to the enlistment of their slaves, the masters were to receive $300 for each one. If sufficient recruits were not obtained in an area within thirty days, slaves were taken without consent of loyal owners. Although two years had elapsed before the federal government adopted a clear-cut policy regarding black soldiers, it demonstrated that when the circumstances were favorable, it could pursue a policy vigorous enough to satisfy even the most zealous abolitionists.

These months of vacillation on the treatment of runaway slaves, the relief of blacks, and their military service had a disquieting effect on their status during the Civil War. If the federal government would not take a stand to uphold them, they could expect little from private citizens. White reformers joined with such black leaders as Douglass, Langston, Remond, and Brown in fighting for recognition, but they achieved small results. Newspapers in the North opposed to the Lincoln administration complained that the government had plunged the country into a costly war to help undeserving

Susie King Taylor Wishes to See the Yankees—1862

. . . I had been reading so much about the "Yankees" I was very anxious to see them. The whites would tell their colored people not to go to the Yankees, for they would harness them to carts and make them pull the carts around, in place of horses. I asked grandmother, one day, if this was true. She replied, "Certainly not!" that the white people did not want slaves to go over to the Yankees, and told them these things to frighten them. . . . I wanted to see these wonderful "Yankees" so much, as I heard my parents say the Yankee was going to set all the slaves free. Oh, how those people prayed for freedom! I remember, one night, my grandmother went out into the suburbs of the city to a church meeting, and they were fervently singing this old hymn,

> Yes, we all shall be free,
> Yes, we all shall be free,
> Yes, we all shall be free,
> When the lord shall appear.

when the police came in and arrested all who were there, saying they were planning freedom, and sang "the lord," in place of "Yankee," to blind any one who might be listening.

Susie King Taylor, *Reminiscences of My Life in Camp* (Boston, 1902), pp. 7–8.

blacks. The Philadelphia *Age* said that abolitionists had brought on the war to fulfill their "ebony ideals," ignoring the interests of millions of free white men. The editors of these papers strove to create unfavorable public opinion, and not infrequently they succeeded. They headlined any allegations of the rape of white women by black men and insisted that abolitionists were encouraging miscegenation. This sensational and irresponsible journalism had the desired effect: hostility toward blacks actually increased in many Northern communities during the war.

Such hostility was most clearly shown by white workers of the North. They feared that emancipation of the slaves would cause a general exodus of former slaves to the North and that the ensuing competition for work would depress wages and create unemployment. White laborers in many places sought to raise their wages by striking, but the willingness of employers to use black strikebreakers convinced them that competition with black workers had already materialized. The result was that fights and riots occurred where blacks sought work. In New York in 1862, a group of black women and children who worked in a tobacco factory were mobbed. The use of black workers on the Camden and Amboy Railroad in New Jersey caused considerable agitation and threats of reprisals by unemployed whites. Longshoremen in Chicago, Detroit, Cleveland, Buffalo, New York, and Boston fought black workers whenever they were brought on the job.

The New York draft riots of 1863 were closely connected with the competition between whites and blacks for work. Shortly before the riots began, 3,000 longshoremen went on strike for higher wages. Blacks, with police protection, took their places. When the government began drafting unemployed whites, they looked upon it as adding insult to injury: they had been displaced on their jobs by blacks and were now being sent off to fight in a war to set more of them free. Consequently, they resisted conscription to the point of violence. During the riots in July, many homes and business places of blacks were burned, and freedmen's associations, organized to help in the relief of Southern blacks, found it necessary to aid blacks in New York. Perhaps it is not too much to suggest that there was a discernible correlation between the uncertainty of federal policy and the hostile attitude of many white citizens in the North toward their darker fellows.

■ Moving toward Freedom

From the very beginning of the war there had been speculation as to whether or when the slaves would be emancipated. Most Northern Democrats were opposed and said unequivocally that slavery was the best status for blacks. Abolitionists supported the Republicans in 1860 principally because their platform was antislavery, and they demanded that the party fulfill its pledge by setting the slaves free. Lincoln had to move cautiously, however, for constitutional, political, and military reasons. His views on emancipation were well known. As early as 1849 he had introduced a bill in Congress for the gradual emancipation of slaves in the District of Columbia, and in the ensuing decade he stated his position on several occasions. For the abolitionists, gradual emancipation was bad enough, but not even to take definite steps in that direction was unforgivable.

The whole matter caused Lincoln grave concern. As he evolved his plan of emancipation, he was viewed all the more unfavorably because he felt it necessary to restrain enthusiastic officers who emancipated slaves without his authorization. In 1861 Gen. John C. Frémont proclaimed military emancipation in Missouri, but Lincoln had to modify his action in keeping with the Confiscation Act. In 1862 Gen. David Hunter proclaimed that slaves in Georgia, Florida, and South Carolina were to be forever free. When Lincoln learned of this order ten days after it was announced, he immediately issued a proclamation nullifying it and reminding slaveholders that they could still adopt his plan of compensated emancipation.

President Lincoln was going ahead with this plan for solving the problem of blacks in America. He hoped to achieve emancipation by compensating owners for their human property, and then he looked forward to colonizing them in some other part of the world. In the fall of 1861 he attempted an experiment with compensated emancipation in Delaware. He urged his friends there to propose it to the Delaware legislature. He went so far as to write a draft of the bill, which provided for gradual emancipation, and then he composed another, which provided that the federal government would share the expenses of compensating masters for their slaves. Although these bills were much discussed, there was too much opposition to introduce them.

More definite steps in the direction of emancipation were taken in the spring of 1862. In a special message to Congress, President Lincoln recommended that a resolution be passed announcing that the United States would cooperate with any state adopting a plan of gradual emancipation together with satisfactory compensation of the owners. He urged the congressional delegations from Delaware, Maryland, West Virginia, Kentucky, and Missouri to support his policy. They opposed it, however, because their constituents were unwilling to give up their slaves. A joint resolution introduced by Roscoe Conkling nevertheless passed both houses and was approved by the president on April 10, 1862. The abolitionists were furious; they felt that Southern slaveholders should not be paid to surrender property they did not rightfully possess. Wendell Phillips, speaking in Cincinnati before a crowd hostile to his views, criticized the administration, declaring that the right hand of Southern aristocracy was slavery and the left hand the ignorant white man. All over the North abolitionists denounced Lincoln's plan of compensated emancipation.

Another of Lincoln's recommendations, which became law in April 1862, provided for the emancipation of slaves in the District of Columbia. There would be compensation, of course, but not exceeding $300 for each slave. A significant feature was the provision of $100,000 to support the voluntary emigration of freedmen to Haiti and Liberia. Colonization seemed almost as important to Lincoln as emancipation. In August 1862 he called a group of prominent free blacks to the White House and urged them to support colonization. He told them, "Your race suffer greatly, many of them, by living among us, while ours suffer from your presence. In a word we suffer on each side. If this is admitted, it affords a reason why we should be separated." Perhaps some of them pledged their support, for in his second annual message he was able to say that many free blacks had asked to be colonized. Largely at Lincoln's suggestion, the State Department made inquiries of South American governments and of some insular and African governments concerning the possibility of colonizing black Americans. Only two replies were entirely satisfactory to Lincoln; they suggested that colonies of former slaves be established in Panama and on the Ile à Vache, in the Caribbean. Up until the end of the war Lincoln held out hope for colonizing at least some of the slaves who were being set free.

From June 1862 the policy of the government toward emancipation took shape rapidly. On June 19 the president signed a bill abolishing slavery in the territories. On July 17 a measure became law setting free all slaves coming from disloyal masters into Union-held territory. Lincoln again called together congressmen from the border slave states and told them that since slavery would be destroyed if the war lasted long enough, they should accept his plan of compensated emancipation. His plea fell on deaf ears. Having gone as far as he had, however, Lincoln considered emancipating by proclamation all slaves in rebellious states, an idea that he discussed with his secretaries of state and navy, Seward and Welles.

For two days, July 21 and 22, the cabinet debated the draft of an emancipation proclamation that Lincoln read to them. Rebels were to be warned of the penalties of the Confiscation Act and reminded of the possibility of emancipating their slaves and receiving compensation. All slaves were to be set free on January 1, 1863. Only two cabinet members, Seward and Chase, agreed even in part with Lincoln's proposed proclamation, and Seward strongly advised him not to issue it until the military situation was more favorable. Apparently there was some hope, based on rumor, that the president would issue the proclamation in August. When it was not forthcoming, advocates of emancipation were sorely disappointed. Horace Greeley, writing in the *New York Tribune,* urged Lincoln to proclaim emancipation. Antislavery delegations called upon him. Interestingly enough, the president told one delegation that he could not free slaves under the Constitution because it could not be enforced in the rebel states. Any proclamation would be about as effective, from Lincoln's point of view, "as the Pope's bull against the comet."

It was the Union victory at Antietam on September 17, 1862, that caused Lincoln to act. Five days later he issued a preliminary proclamation. In this document he revived the possibility of compensated emancipation and said that he would continue to encourage the voluntary colonization of blacks "upon this continent or elsewhere." The time had come, however, when more direct action was needed. So he proclaimed that on January 1, 1863, "all persons held as slaves within any State, or designated part of the State, the people whereof shall be in rebellion against the United States, shall be then, thenceforward, and forever free."

The general reaction in the North was unfavorable. Many whites felt that the war was no longer to save the Union but to free the slaves, and some soldiers resigned rather than participate in such a struggle. The Peace Democrats accused the administration of wasting the lives of white citizens in a costly abolitionist war. Abolitionists hesitated to condemn the proclamation since it was better than nothing, but to them it seemed at best very poor compensation for all the struggles and sacrifices they had made for more than a generation. Furthermore, what if the war should end and there were no rebellious states on the first of January 1863? The prospect sent cold shivers through every ardent abolitionist. The real reaction was seen at the November elections. Although the Republicans maintained a majority in

Congress, the Democrats won in many Northern communities and gained substantially in both the House and Senate.

The preliminary proclamation, despite this critical reaction, captured the imagination of workers in many parts of the world, who viewed it as a great humanitarian document, and whenever slaves learned of it they laid down their tools and took on the mantle of their newly found freedom. By the end of December 1862, the suspense attending the final proclamation was so great that even before it was read it had assumed the significance of one of the great documents of all times. On December 31 watch meetings were held by blacks and whites in many parts of the country at which prayers of thanksgiving were offered for the deliverance of the slave. At Tremont Temple in Boston, Frederick Douglass, William Wells Brown, William Lloyd Garrison, Harriet Beecher Stowe, Charles B. Ray, and other fighters for freedom heard on January 1 the words that emancipated more than three-fourths of the slaves. President Lincoln set free all slaves except those in states or parts of states not in rebellion against the United States at that time. These exceptions, in addition to the four loyal slave states, were thirteen parishes of Louisiana, including the city of New Orleans; the forty-eight counties of Virginia, which had become West Virginia; and seven counties in eastern Virginia, including the cities of Norfolk and Portsmouth.

Lincoln left no doubt of his justification for the Emancipation Proclamation. Twice he mentioned the *military* necessity of pursuing this course. He described it as a "fit and necessary war measure" for suppressing the rebellion which he could take by virtue of the power vested in him as commander in chief of the army and navy. In the last paragraph of the proclamation he said that it was "sincerely believed to be an act of justice, warranted by the Constitution upon military necessity." He counseled slaves, however, to abstain from all violence except in self-defense and to work faithfully for reasonable wages.

If the Emancipation Proclamation was essentially a war measure, it had the desired effect of creating confusion in the South and depriving the Confederacy of much of its valuable labor force. If it was a diplomatic document, it succeeded in rallying to the Northern cause thousands of English and European laborers who were anxious to see workers gain their freedom throughout the world. If it was a humanitarian document, it gave hope to millions of blacks that a better day lay ahead, and it renewed the faith of thousands of crusaders who had fought long to win freedom in America.

During the war years slaves had moved significantly toward freedom. Many of them were among the first, however, to realize that it had not been achieved. Even after the proclamation was issued there were more than 800,000 slaves in the border states untouched by it, to say nothing of the hundreds of thousands if not millions in the Confederacy who were not even to hear about the proclamation until months later. Political and economic freedom, moreover, blacks had neither in the South nor in the North. Their leaders were concerned about these matters. The National Convention of Colored Men, which met at Syracuse in October 1864, discussed the questions of employment, enfranchisement, and the extension of freedom. If blacks had no answers to these questions, it was because of the complexity and magnitude of the problems involved in adjusting more than 4 million people to a new climate of freedom.

■ Confederate Policy

One of the greatest anxieties of the South at the beginning of the war was the conduct of slaves. The reaction of slaves to their status involved not only the security of the white civilian population but also the maintenance of a stable economic system without which there was no hope of prosecuting the war successfully. The owners took no chances. It was all right to talk about the love of slaves for their masters during times of peace, but in war idle talk and wishful thinking were not the stuff of victories. There was widespread sentiment for much closer control of slaves. Patrol laws all over the Confederacy were strengthened. Instead of biweekly patrols, Florida in 1861 required them to make their rounds once a week, and even more often "when informed by a creditable citizen of evidence of insubordination or threatened outbreak, or insurrection of slaves." In 1862 Georgia canceled exemptions from patrol duty, and Louisiana imposed a fine of $10 or twenty-four hours' imprisonment for failure to perform it.

The fears of white Southerners appeared to be fully justified. Ordinary emergencies might not excite the slaves, but gradually they became aware that in this war their freedom was at stake. To be sure, there were slaves who remained on the plantation, worked faithfully for their masters, and protected their mistresses, but as Bell I. Wiley has pointed out, "these acts of loyalty, in the light of contemporary evidence, must be considered as exceptional." The most widespread form of disloyalty was desertion. It could hardly be called running away in the sense that it was before the war. Between 1861 and 1865 black men and women simply walked off plantations, and when Union forces came close, they went to their lines and got food and clothing. In Arkansas, according to Thomas Staples, "whenever federal forces appeared, most of the able-bodied adult Negores left their owners and sought refuge within the Union lines." Almost the entire slave population of the Shirley plantation in Virginia deserted to the Union lines. In August 1862 a Confederate general estimated that slaves worth at least $1 million were escaping to the federals in North Carolina.

Confederate and state officials sought to halt the wholesale exodus of slaves by having planters engage in what was called "running the Negroes." When an area was threatened with invasion by federal troops, the planters would remove their slaves to safety, usually in the interior. More than 2,000 were transferred from Washington and Tyrell counties to the interior of

ROBERT SMALLS. Smalls, a slave pilot in Charleston, became a Civil War hero when he sailed with his family out of the harbor aboard a Confederate steamer, *The Planter,* of which he had taken control, and delivered it to the Union squadron that was block-ing the harbor. After the Civil War, Smalls served five terms in the United States House of Representatives as a member from South Carolina. *(Schomburg Center For Re-search in Black Culture, New York Public Library.)*

North Carolina in the autumn of 1862. It was an interesting sight to see planters moving with "black capital," sometimes on foot, sometimes by wagon or cart, but always in haste. Not all blacks were amenable to the idea of "refugeeing," at least not with their masters, and at times they openly resisted them and went off in the opposite direction—toward Union troops.

Slaves were often insolent toward whites, especially when their lands were being invaded by Union armies. In 1862 a Mississippi citizen wrote the governor that "there is greatly needed in this county a company of mounted rangers . . . to keep the Negroes in awe, who are getting quite impudent. Our proximity to the enemy has had a perceptible influence on them." The situation became so disturbing in Georgia that a bill was introduced in the legislature "to punish slaves and free persons of color for abusive and insulting language to white persons." The Richmond *Enquirer* reported that a coachman, upon learning that he was free, "went straightly to his master's chamber, dressed himself in his best clothes, put on his best watch and chain, took his stick, and returning to the parlor where his master was, insolently informed him that he might for the future drive his own coach." A North Carolina citizen summed up the prevailing white point of view in 1864: "Our Negroes are beginning to show that they understand the state of affairs, and insolence and insubordination are quite common."

As the war entered its more desperate stages, many slaves refused to work or to submit to punishment. A South Carolina planter complained in 1862 that "we have had hard work to get along this season, the Negroes are unwilling to do any work, no matter what it is." Another exasperated planter said, *"I wish every negro would leave the place* as they will do only what pleases them, go out in the morning when it suits them, come in when they please, etc." Some Louisiana slaves demanded wages for their labor. In Texas, a slave cursed his master "all to pieces" when the latter attempted to punish him. Relations became so strained in some areas that masters and mistresses stopped trying to punish their slaves, lest they resort to desperate reprisals.

Other acts of slave disloyalty were giving information and guidance to federal troops, seizing the master's property upon arrival of these troops and helping to destroy it, and inflicting bodily harm upon white civilians. Most white Southerners lived in constant fear of slave uprisings during the war, especially after the Emancipation Proclamation. Rumors of uprisings became common, and slaveholders were so terrified at the prospect of bloody insurrections that they frequently appealed to Union troops for protection.

One of the main objections of white Southerners to conscription was that it would drain off the white male population and encourage blacks to revolt. In 1864 the Richmond *Whig* said, "Take away all, or nearly all the vigorous whites, and leave the negro to the feeble control of women, children, and old men, and the danger is that famine will be superadded to insurrection." In several Alabama and Georgia towns slaves were hanged for plotting insurrection; many were committed to jail for implication in these plots. The number of actual insurrections was relatively small because slaves were able to secure their freedom without committing violence. The practice in the South, moreover, was to act summarily in the case of people suspected of insurrection in order to discourage any large-scale revolt.

Since Southern agriculture had been based on staple crops, there was great difficulty in making the transition to a wartime economy that would provide the food necessary for the fighting forces. In most places cotton acreage was forcibly reduced by law, and there was a wholesale conversion of land to corn, wheat, and other cereal grains. The laboring force was the greatest problem. The supervision of slaves, who knew little about grain production and were not interested in it, fell into the hands of white women, disabled white men, and faithful slaves.

Slaves were employed not only on farms but in factories as well. The ironworks of Virginia and Alabama used them throughout the struggle. In 1862 the famous Tredegar Works advertised for 1,000 slaves. At the ironworks they cut the wood for charcoal, hauled iron to shipping points, and engaged in various types of skilled labor. In 1864 there were 4,301 blacks and 2,518 whites in the iron mines of the Confederate states east of the Mississippi. Slaves were also to be found mining coal and working in salt factories. Historian James Brewer has shown how indispensable they were in Virginia's war effort. Relying on the skills of slaves could be a dangerous business, however. Robert Smalls, a slave pilot in Charleston, sailed with his family out of the harbor aboard a Confederate steamer, *The Planter*, of which he had taken control, and delivered it to the Union squadron that was blocking the harbor.

Confederate and state governments relied on slave and free black labor to do much of the hard work involved in prosecuting the war. Slave laborers were secured by contracts with their masters, by hiring them for short periods, and by impressment. By the fall of 1862 the labor shortage was so acute in the South that most states had authorized the impressment of slaves. In 1863 a desperate Confederate government passed a general impressment law, and one year later voted to impress 20,000 slaves. Up until the close of the war President Davis constantly urged that more slaves be impressed. The results were not at all gratifying. In the first place, the owners of slaves did not like the principle of impressment, by which their property could be seized at a price set by the government. Consequently, they simply refused to cooperate in many instances. Slaves did not like impressment, because to work for military authorities involved vastly more strenuous work than what they were accustomed to doing for their own masters, if they chose to work at all. With master *and* slave opposed to impressment, there was little chance for its success.

Even without it Confederate and state governments were able to secure the services of thousands of slaves who performed many important tasks. Most of the cooks in the Confederate army were slaves, and the government recognized their value to the morale and physical fitness of the soldiers by designating four cooks for each company and providing that each one should receive $15 a month as well as clothing. There were also slave teamsters, mechanics, hospital attendants, ambulance drivers, and common laborers. Much of the work in the construction of fortifications was done by slaves. As Union armies invaded the South, tearing up railroads and wrecking bridges, gangs of slave and free black workers repaired them. They were also extensively employed in the manufacture of powder and arms. Of 400 workers at the naval arsenal in Selma, Alabama, 310 were black in 1865.

Affluent Confederates took their body servants to war with them. These workers kept the quarters clean, washed clothes, groomed uniforms, polished swords, buckles, and spurs, ran errands, secured rations, cut hair, and groomed the animals. Some even took part in fighting. In November 1861 it was reported that one servant "fought manfully" and killed four Union soldiers. As the fighting grew desperate, and rations shorter, most servants were sent home. The Confederate soldiers had come to realize that outside medieval romances there was no place for body servants on the field of battle.

It was one thing to have blacks performing all types of work, even with the army, and quite another to put weapons in their hands. Some white Southerners had wanted to arm blacks from the beginning, and local authorities had permitted free blacks to enroll for military service. In 1861 the Tennessee legislature authorized the governor to enlist all free blacks between fifteen and fifty years of age in the state militia. Memphis went so far as to open a recruiting office for them. Public opinion, however, was generally against arming blacks. There was, of course, the fear that they would turn on their masters. To accept them for military service, moreover, would be an acknowledgment of their equality with whites. When a company of sixty free blacks presented themselves for service at Richmond in 1861, they were thanked and sent home. A company of free blacks in New Orleans was allowed to parade but not to go into battle.

Despite the stern opposition of Southern leaders to enlisting blacks, agitation in favor of it continued throughout the war. After reverses in the autumn of 1863 the debate increased, and the Alabama legislature recommended arming a large number of slaves. In 1864 Gen. Patrick Cleburne proposed to officers in the Tennessee army that they organize a large force of slaves and promise them freedom at the end of the war. This proposal, coming from a high army official, provoked considerable discussion, and President Davis, fearing that it did the Confederate cause no good, ordered that no such force of slaves be organized. Discussion continued, however, and at a meeting of the governors of North and South Carolina, Georgia, Alabama, and Mississippi in October 1864, a resolution was adopted suggesting the use of slaves as soldiers. Davis was still opposed to the proposition. In his message to the Confederate Congress the following month he said as much but added: "Should the alternative ever be presented of subjugation or of the employment of the slave as a soldier, there seems no reason to doubt what should then be our decision."

The Confederate Congress in the winter of 1864–1865 openly debated arming the slaves. A representative from Mississippi deplored any suggestion that slaves should be armed and cried out, "God forbid that this Trojan horse should be introduced among us." The outspoken editor of the Charleston *Mercury* declared that South Carolina would no longer be interested in prosecuting the war if slaves were armed.

A bill was introduced in the Confederate Senate in 1865 providing for the enlistment of 200,000 blacks and their emancipation if they remained loyal through the war. Advocates of the measure sought the approval of Gen. Robert E. Lee. The South's most respected soldier said that the measure was not only expedient but also necessary, that blacks would make efficient soldiers, and that those who served should be freed at the end of the war. On March 13, 1865, a bill was signed by President Davis which authorized him to call on each state for its quota of additional troops, irrespective of color, on the condition that the slaves recruited from any state should not exceed 25 percent of the able-bodied male slave population between eighteen and forty-five. Recruiting officers were immediately appointed to enroll blacks for the Confederate army.

The enlistment of blacks was very slow in the West. A Mississippian wrote his governor that they were fleeing to avoid conscription. Enlistment went better on the Eastern seaboard, where officers resorted to dances and parades to work up enthusiasm among blacks for the Confederate cause. It was too late, however, for the Confederacy had already been destroyed by the onslaught of Union forces and by its own internal strife and disorganization. There are unconfirmed reports that some black troops saw action on the side of the Confederacy, but if they did, their number was very small. Had the Confederacy reached a decision to use black troops two years earlier, a considerable force might have been enlisted. But in view of so much slave disloyalty, there is little reason to believe that they would have fought effectively for the Confederate cause.

■ Blacks Fighting for the Union

When blacks were finally permitted to enlist in the Union army, they did so with alacrity and enthusiasm. In the North leading blacks like Frederick Douglass served as recruiting agents. Rallies were held at which speakers urged blacks to enlist, and in Boston, New York, and Philadelphia blacks went to recruiting stations in large numbers. In the South, too, there were many who enlisted, but not all saw the necessity of fighting when they were winning their freedom without it. Enlistment of blacks was, however, a notable success: more than 186,000 had enrolled in the Union army by the end of the war. From the seceded states came 93,000, and from the border slave states, 40,000. The remainder, approximately 53,000, were from free states. It is possible that the total figure was larger, for some contemporaries insisted that many mulattoes served in white regiments without being designated as blacks.

Black troops were organized into regiments of light and heavy artillery, cavalry, infantry, and engineers. To distinguish them from white soldiers, they were called United States Colored Troops, and for the most part they were led by white officers with some black noncommissioned officers. At first it was difficult to secure white officers for black outfits, because regular army men were generally opposed to having blacks in the service. Joseph T. Wilson says that West Pointers were especially averse to the idea of commanding black troops and ostracized their fellows who undertook the task. There were those, however, who enthusiastically assumed the responsibility and made such a reputation for themselves and their men that it was not difficult to secure white officers for black outfits toward the close of the war. Among those who were outstanding as leaders were Col. Thomas Wentworth Higginson of the First South Carolina Volunteers, Col. Robert Gould Shaw of the Fifty-fourth Massachusetts Regiment, and Gen. N. P. Banks, who for a time had the First and Third Louisiana Native Guards under his command.

Some blacks held commissions in the Union army. Two regiments of General Butler's *Corps d'Afrique* were entirely staffed by black officers, including Maj. F. E. Dumas and Capt. P. B. S. Pinchback. An independent battery at Lawrence, Kansas, was led by Capt. H. Ford Douglass and 1st Lt. W. D. Matthews. The 104th Regiment had two black officers, Maj. Martin R. Delany and Capt. O. S. B. Wall. Among the black surgeons who received commissions were Alexander T. Augusta of the 7th Regiment and John V. DeGrasse of the 35th. Charles B. Purvis, Alpheus Tucker, John Rapier, William Ellis, Anderson Abbott, and William Powell were hospital surgeons in Washington. Among the black chaplains with commissions were Henry M. Turner, William Hunter, James Underdue, Williams Waring, Samuel Harrison, William Jackson, and John R. Bowles.

At the beginning there was discrimination in the pay of white and black soldiers. The Enlistment Act of July 17, 1862, provided that whites with the rank of private should receive $13 a month and $3.50 for clothing, but blacks of the same rank were to receive only $7 and $3, respectively. Black soldiers and their white officers objected vigorously to this discrimination. The Fifty-fourth Massachusetts Regiment served a year without pay rather than accept discriminatory wages and went into battle in Florida in 1864 singing "Three cheers for Massachusetts and seven dollars a month." In the Third South Carolina Regiment, Sgt. William Walker was shot, by order of court martial, for "leading the company to stack arms before their captain's tent, on the avowed ground that they were released from duty by the refusal of the government to fulfill its share of the contract." After many protests the War Department, beginning in 1864, granted equal pay for black soldiers.

Blacks performed all kinds of services in the Union army. Organized into raiding parties, they were sent through Confederate lines to destroy fortifications and supplies. Since they knew the Southern countryside better than most white soldiers and could pass themselves off as slaves, they were extensively used as spies and scouts. White officers relied upon information secured by black spies. Harriet Tubman was a spy for Union troops at many points on the eastern seaboard.

Black soldiers built fortifications along the coasts and up the rivers. They were engaged so much in menial tasks, instead of fighting, that their officers made numerous complaints. One said that he would rather carry his rifle in the ranks of fighting men than be overseer to black laborers. In 1864 Adj. Gen. Lorenzo Thomas took notice of the situation and issued an order that there should be no excessive impositions upon black troops and "that they will be only required to take their fair share of fatigue duty with white troops. This is necessary to prepare them for the higher duties of conflicts with the enemies."

The "higher duties of conflicts" had already begun, for blacks saw action against Confederate forces as early as the fall of 1862. Hardly a battle was fought up to the end of the war in which some black troops did not meet the enemy. They saw action, according to George Washington Williams, in more than 250 skirmishes. In the Battle of Port Hudson, eight black infantry regiments fought.

Naturally the Confederacy was outraged by the Northern use of black troops. The question immediately arose as to whether they should be treated as soldiers of the enemy or slaves in insurrection. The vast majority of white Southerners viewed black soldiers as rebellious slaves and insisted that they should be treated as such. In 1862 President Davis ordered that all slaves captured in arms were to be delivered to the state from which they came, to be dealt with according to state laws. Union officials insisted that captured blacks should be treated as prisoners of war, but the Confederates did not accept that point of view until 1864.

Some captured blacks, perhaps not many, were sold into slavery. Others were killed. The Confederate secretary of war countenanced the killing of some black prisoners in order to make an example of them. In 1864 a Confederate officer, Col. W. P. Shingler, told his subordinates not to report the capture of any more blacks. The worst case was the Fort Pillow affair. On April 12, 1864, the fort fell to Confederate forces under the command of Gen. Nathan B. Forrest. Blacks who were there were not permitted to surrender; they were shot, and some were burned alive. Yet many black troops were captured and held as prisoners of war by the South. In 1863 General Butler reported that 3,000 black troops were prisoners of the Confederates. Late in 1864 nearly 1,000 black prisoners worked on Confederate fortifications at Mobile.

Blacks saw action in every theater of operation during the Civil War. They were at Milliken's Bend in Louisiana, at Olustee in Florida, at Vicksburg in Mississippi, and at the siege of Savannah. They fought in Arkansas, Kentucky, Tennessee, and North Carolina. They played a part in the reduction of Petersburg and were at Appomattox Court House, April 9, 1865. Congress awarded a medal to Decatur Dorsey for gallantry while acting as color-sergeant of the Thirty-ninth United States Colored Troops at Petersburg on July 30, 1864. James Gardner, of the Thirty-sixth, received a medal for rushing in advance of his brigade to shoot a Confederate officer leading his men into action. Four men of the Fifty-fourth Massachusetts Infantry earned the Gilmore Medal for gallantry in the assault on Fort Wagner, in which their commanding officer, Col. Robert Gould Shaw, lost his life. Maj. Gen. Gilmore issued the following order to commend black soldiers under his command for a daring exploit:

> On March 7, 1865, a party of Colored soldiers and scouts, thirty in number . . . left Jacksonville, Florida, and penetrated into the interior through Marion County. They rescued ninety-one Negroes from slavery, captured four white prisoners, two wagons, and twenty-four horses and mules; destroyed a sugarmill and a distillery . . . and burned the bridge over the Oclawaha River. When returning they were attacked by a band of over fifty cavalry, whom they defeated and drove off with a loss of more than thirty to the rebels. . . . This expedition, planned and executed by Colored men under the command of a Colored noncommissioned officer, reflects credit upon the brave participants and their leader.

ROBERT GOULD SHAW AND THE MEN OF THE FIFTY-FOURTH MASSACHUSETTS INFANTRY. This monumental frieze by Augustus Saint-Gaudens on the Boston Commons commemorates the heroic service during the Civil War of the all-black army unit and its commanding officer. It has come to symbolize the contributions of all the blacks who fought for the freedom of their people and to ensure the preservation of the Union. *(Courtesy Barbara W. Moore.)*

Testimonies similar to this were given by Maj. Gen. E. R. S. Canby, Godfry Weitzel, James G. Blunt, S. A. Hurlbut, Alfred H. Terry, and W. F. Smith, as well as by men of other ranks. The most significant thing about their words of praise is that they bear witness to the fact that black soldiers did what they could to save the Union and secure their freedom.

More than 38,000 black soldiers lost their lives in the Civil War. It has been estimated that their rate of mortality was nearly 40 percent greater than that among white troops. In the Fifth United States Colored Heavy Artillery, for example, 829 men died, the largest number of deaths in any outfit in the Union army. The Sixty-fifth Colored Infantry lost more than 600 men from disease alone. The high mortality rate among blacks is to be explained by several unfavorable conditions. Among them were excessive fatigue details, poor equipment, bad medical care, the recklessness and haste with which they were sent into battle, and the "no quarter" policy (namely, the refusal to regard them as soldiers fighting under the accepted rules of war) with which Confederates fought them. It is impossible to estimate the number of blacks who died at the hands of their enemy, but it must have run into many thousands. There can be no doubt, therefore, that blacks contributed heavily to the victory of Union forces in the second great war for freedom.

■ Victory!

The surrender of the Confederate army in 1865 meant victory not only for the powerful military forces of the North but also for an indestructible Union. Once and for all the question of whether states had a right to secede from the Union was settled. The question of the exact relation of a state to the federal government could arise again, but all states were bound henceforth to recognize the superior sovereignty of the federal government.

The surrender of the Confederacy was also a personal victory for President Lincoln and his policies. It was he who evolved the theory that the states had not seceded but that rebellious citizens had gotten out of hand. Now he could use this theory, magnanimous as it was, to hasten binding up the nation's wounds. Almost as long as any man in public life, Lincoln had spoken out against slavery. Now he could view with satisfaction its abolition, which began with his war proclamations and ended with the adoption of the Thirteenth Amendment late in 1865.

The end of the war marked a victory for the abolitionists. At no time in the nation's history had a pressure group done so much to shape public opinion and then to move opinion to action. For a generation they had labored tirelessly, suffering abuse and even bodily harm. With them, however, it was a moral crusade and they were blind to personal indignities and insensible to suffering. More effectively than ever before in our history they had roused the nation's conscience to its sins and misdeeds. Up until the present day, Americans still feel the effects of the morality in human relations which was the creed of abolitionists.

For blacks, Lee's surrender was a victory. At last they had achieved what human beings everywhere have always wanted—freedom. The end of the war brought to a close a period of enslavement that had lasted for almost 250 years. The desire for freedom had been kept alive through the centuries by those blacks who demonstrated by their conduct that freedom and the right to it transcended racial lines. The victory was won in part by their struggles through the centuries as well as by their service in the final battles.

Paradoxically, the end of the war was also a victory for the South. To be sure, it had suffered military reverses and lost much. But it had been delivered from the domination of an institution that had stifled its economic development and rendered completely ineffective its intellectual life. Opportunities for extensive development in new areas of economic activity had hardly existed in the South, and because it was sensitive to criticism of slavery, the region had expelled both freedom of speech and the talents that flourish only in freedom. It was a great day for the South when at last it could be realistic in economic life and its churches, schools, and writers could face the truth and express it as they saw it. At least, no system of slavery any longer demanded that they do otherwise.

The end of the war was, moreover, the beginning of a new era in the history of the United States. The economic revolution ushered in by the

COMPANY E, 4TH UNITED STATES COLORED INFANTRY. Over 186,000 blacks fought under the Union flag during the Civil War. Company E was one of the detachments assigned to guard the nation's capital. *(Library of Congress.)*

tremendous forces let loose in war was to transform every phase of American life and to create new problems and injustices for reformers to solve. In the new era the Republicans would have to find a new faith for their party, and the abolitionists new social ills to eradicate. Blacks would have to perfect their freedom in a society that was changing so rapidly that adjustment would be difficult even for the best educated of them. For all Americans, perhaps the greatest problem that arose out of the Civil War and its economic aftermath was to find a way to retain freedom, the desire for which had become almost an obsession, and yet at the same time to enjoy security, which was becoming more precarious in the new economic order. As black people and white people set out to find the perfect balance between freedom and security in post-Civil War America, democracy faced a new test.

CHAPTER 12

The Effort to Attain Peace

■ Reconstruction and the Nation

In few periods of our history has the whole fabric of American life been altered so drastically as during the Civil War and the period immediately following it. To be sure, there were the social and economic changes arising from the emancipation of 4 million slaves in the South, but these changes were so completely interwoven with other consequences of the war as to make them wholly inseparable. Although the South, for example, did not experience great industrial development during the war, the North did; and the forces let loose were so powerful that they affected the entire course of Reconstruction. The political changes that began with the secession of the Southern states affected the whole nation, but the economic transformation brought on by numerous changes in production and distribution demanded the attention of every practical-minded person in the United States.

It must be remembered, as Howard K. Beale has pointed out, that there is no way of understanding Reconstruction unless an attempt is made to study it in its setting. It is not a history of "Negro rule," as many historians have dubbed the period of Radical Reconstruction, nor is it merely Southern history, however much students in the past have approached it from a regional point of view. It is an integral part of the national history, and one may find an explanation for strange events in Alabama not only in the activities of people in that state but in the movements and transactions of

220

citizens in Boston, New York, or Philadelphia as well. From 1865 to the end of the century, the United States was picking up the threads of its social, political, and economic life, which were so abruptly cut in 1861, and attempting to weave them into a new pattern. South Carolina's political life after 1865 was affected by more than the presence of blacks in the state legislature or in other positions of public trust. It was affected, as well, by the dynamic changes of economic reconstruction. Reconstruction in 1865 was indeed nationwide.

White Southerners who traveled in the North after the Civil War were amazed at the changes that a few years had wrought in the economic life of the section. The pressing military needs, the extensive inflation of Union currency, and the stimulating effect of protective tariff legislation had all conspired to industrialize the North. Steel factories were producing much more than what was needed for the prosecution of war; railroads were rapidly connecting the North and West in one large community. Hundreds of technological developments made possible the production of commodities, the conception of which would have strained the imagination two decades earlier. New forms of economic organization emerged whose possibilities for expansion throughout the nation and the world were almost unlimited and whose leaders were filled with a desperate anxiety to create monopolies and reap huge profits. Northerners were as anxious to sell to ex-Confederates as they were to Northerners. The most discerning white Southerners must have seen that the new order of things was the result of the triumph of industrialism over the agrarian way of life. The new and old bustling cities were symbols of the triumph, while the wasted and abandoned lands of the South signified the defeat of the old agrarianism. White Southerners could also see that if their section was not careful, its economic and psychological defeat would be as complete as its military downfall.

The political situation was much disturbed in the period after the Civil War, and the problem of the reorganization of the seceded states was only part of the unsettled state of political affairs. During the war the president had wielded many powers that would not be tolerated in peace, and even before the war's end Congress signified by its choleric temper that it was anxious to restore the balance of the three branches of government. From the point of view of many men in Congress, the pendulum had to swing back, and not even a Lincoln should obstruct the delicate operations of constitutional government. The unexpected accession to the presidency of Andrew Johnson merely complicated matters and made Congress more determined than ever to have a full share in governing the country. The fear of Republicans that they would lose political control, the pressure of new industrialists for favorable legislation, and conflicting philosophies of Reconstruction are all considerations that cannot be overlooked in studying the politics of the period.

The political chaos that followed in the wake of war carried with it the inherent element of corruption. There was an extravagance in wartime spending that encouraged corruption, and the beneficiaries of graft and bribery had no intention of retiring at the end of the war. Indeed, many wartime profiteers kept within the bounds of respectability, but in the postwar period adhering to the restraints of respectability was no longer desirable. As the more able men went into industry and other economic activities, incompetent people, the easy prey of cunning industrialists and unscrupulous politicians, took over the management of political affairs. Sound economic and political reconstruction became all the more difficult, and the United States became a prime example of corruption during the postwar years.

The problem of American political immaturity after the Civil War cannot be dismissed merely by observing that there were 4 million blacks who were without any experience in public affairs. To these must be added the millions of Europeans who poured into the country and muddied the political waters considerably. Many of them had not participated in any kind of government, and most of them had no understanding of the workings of representative government. The vast majority, moreover, spoke "strange" languages and were poorly educated. These factors, in addition to their low standard of living, made adjustment in the New World even more difficult. They were, of course, exposed to venal and corrupt politicians and frequently became unwitting accessories to the crimes of corrupt governments. Towns were attracting millions of people from the country. Although they were for the most part American citizens, they were so ignorant of the ways of urban life that they fell victims of scheming city politicians. All these elements added to the political chaos of Reconstruction and made it more difficult.

The immediate problems of Reconstruction were numerous. One of the most important was the rebuilding of the war-torn South and the restoration of its economic life on the basis of free labor. At the end of the war there was no civil authority in the Carolinas, Georgia, Florida, Alabama, Mississippi, and Texas. Many despondent Southerners abandoned their farms or left the South altogether. Others, willing to start over again, did not know where to begin. Much of the countryside had been devastated by Union armies. Public buildings and private homes had been burned. The lands had deteriorated under poor cultivation or none at all, and titles to lands and crops in many areas were in dispute. Everywhere there was suffering from starvation and disease. Many former slaves, homeless and without jobs, wandered from place to place, much to the disgust and fear of whites. The ideological aberrations of whites were disturbing: they had difficulty in thinking of a black as a free person, and this problem of reconciling themselves to this new status loomed larger and larger before their vision, blinding them to an objective consideration of other pressing problems.

The needs of the South were great, both in number and variety. There was the important problem of finding a way to restore the seceded states to their places in the Union. It was not as simple as welcoming a prodigal back into the family. Precautions had to be taken to make sure that state governments did not fall into the hands of irreconcilable ex-Confederates who might undo the accomplishments of the war. Involved in this problem were the questions of how much punishment the leaders of the Confederate states should suffer and whether their states had indeed seceded at all. Tedious as the problem was, it appeared that it might soon be solved, and that the United States would once more be truly united.

Inseparably connected with the problems of rebuilding the South and bringing it back into the Union was the question of ex-slaves. There was no dispute over the fact that they were in dire need, but there was serious debate over who could best serve their needs. There was no question of their status as free individuals but conflict arose over the possible distinctions between them and white people. Even more serious was the problem of whether their status should be settled and their condition improved before the Southern states were permitted to return to the Union.

A barrier to the solution of these pressing postwar troubles was the legacy of hate inherited from a generation of bitter intersectional strife. Perhaps this animosity was the most grievous wound to heal, for it lay deep in the hearts of whites, North and South, and none knew how to attend it. There was no hope of solving any problem until a new spirit of conciliation and good will could be created. In this intangible and elusive area lay the key to intersectional peace.

Thus Reconstruction was essentially a national, not merely a sectional or racial, problem. The major obstacles in the way of a satisfactory settlement grew out of developments that were for the most part national. With the perspective of more than 100 years it becomes increasingly clear today that few crises in the history of the United States have so urgently demanded national action. Almost as obvious is the fact that the problem of Reconstruction was essentially the problem of how to move the nation toward greater economic and political democracy.

■ Conflicting Policies

Lincoln early saw the need for a policy of dealing with the states of the South as they capitulated to the Union army and of handling the large number of blacks who came under the control of the United States before the end of the war. Since he had insisted that the war was a rebellion of Southern citizens rather than a revolt of the states, he could deal with citizens of the Confederacy on the assumption that they had misled their state governments. It was the function of the president, he believed, to undertake whatever measures were necessary to reorganize the states in the South. As states collapsed, Lincoln appointed military governors who had complete power until civil authority could be established. In December 1863 he outlined to Congress his comprehensive plan for Reconstruction and issued a proclamation containing its essential features.

Acting on the assumption that Reconstruction was an executive problem, President Lincoln extended general amnesty to the people of the South, except for certain high Confederate civil and military officials, and called on them to swear allegiance to the United States. When as many as one-tenth of the people of a state as had cast votes in the election of 1860 complied with the proclamation, a government could be established that would be recognized by the president. Although his proclamation was generally well received and the Southern states proceeded to reconstruct themselves under its provisions, some members of Congress were of the opinion that the president was too lenient and that Reconstruction was a matter to be handled by Congress. They enacted their own measure, the Wade-Davis Bill, which disfranchised a larger number of ex-Confederates, delayed action until a majority of whites had qualified as loyal voters, and required greater assurances of loyalty from reconstructed governments. The president refused to sign the bill but granted that it provided one way for a state to reorganize if it chose to do so.

As far as the former slaves were concerned, Lincoln realized that there must be a satisfactory settlement of their status if peace was to be secured in the South. All during the war Lincoln had entertained the hope that a substantial number of blacks would choose to emigrate from the United States, and he had tried to secure congressional cooperation in encouraging them to do so. It must have become obvious to him that the problem could not be solved in this way, and he was faced with having to reach some solution based on the continued presence of blacks in the United States and in the South. He permitted the establishment of a number of departments of "Negro affairs," which assumed responsibility for administering to the needs of blacks in the early years of the war. Gradually, the work of these departments was taken over by the Freedmen's Bureau.

Concerning the recognition of black citizenship, Lincoln was of the opinion that with education blacks would qualify for it, at least on a restricted basis. In 1864 he wrote to Governor Georg M. Hahn of Louisiana asking "whether some of the colored people may not be let in [to the elective franchise] as, for instance, the very intelligent, and especially those who have fought gallantly in our ranks." Doubtless he was disappointed when the new legislature met in the fall of 1864 and failed to extend the franchise to any Louisiana blacks, despite the fact that many of them were individuals of considerable intellectual and economic achievement.

There was some evidence of a conflict between the president and Congress over the policy of reconstructing the South before the death of Lincoln in April 1865. Shortly after Andrew Johnson took office as president, he made it clear that he would follow essentially the plan of Reconstruction outlined by Lincoln. There were some signs that he might go beyond it. When Charles Sumner, the ardent protagonist of black rights, conferred with Johnson shortly after he became president, Johnson assured him that they were agreed on black suffrage. In his proclamation of May 1865, he called for complete abolition of slavery, repudiation of Confederate war debts, nullification of the ordinances of secession, and disqualification of the people Lincoln had disfranchised as well as all Southerners worth $20,000 or more. He appointed provisional governors in the Southern states, and legislatures, based on white suffrage, were called to modify their constitutions in harmony with that of the United States.

Through 1865 and 1866 Southern whites gradually assumed the responsibility of governing their people. The greatest concern of Southerners was the problem of controlling blacks. There were all sorts of ugly rumors of a general uprising in which blacks would take vengeance on whites and dispossess them of their property. Most Southern whites, although willing to concede the end of slavery even to the point of voting for adoption of the Thirteenth Amendment, were convinced that laws should be speedily enacted to curb blacks and to ensure their role as a laboring force in the South. These laws, called Black Codes, bore a remarkable resemblance to the antebellum Slave Codes (see Chapter 8) and can hardly be described as measures that respected the rights of blacks as free individuals. Several of them undertook to limit the areas in which blacks could purchase or rent property. Vagrancy laws imposed heavy penalties that were designed to force all blacks to work whether they wanted to or not. The control of blacks by white employers was about as great as that which slaveholders had exercised. Blacks who quit their jobs could be arrested and imprisoned for breach of contract. They were not allowed to testify in court except in cases involving members of their race. Numerous fines were imposed for seditious speeches, insulting gestures or acts, absence from work, violating curfew, and the possession of firearms. There was, of course, no enfranchisement of blacks and no indication that in the future they could look forward to full citizenship and participation in a democracy.

As it became clear to Northern protagonists of blacks that the Reconstruction policy of President Johnson sanctioned white home rule in the South in ways strikingly similar to those existing before the Civil War, they became furious. Friends of blacks refused to tolerate a policy that would nullify the gains made during the war. Abolitionists, roused again to their crusade, demanded that blacks be enfranchised and a harsher policy adopted toward the South. Practical Republicans, fearful of the political consequences of a South dominated by Democrats, became convinced that black suffrage in the South would aid in the continued growth of the Republican party. Industrialists with an eye on markets and cheap labor in the South, were fearful that the old agrarian system would be resurrected by the Democrats. These groups began to pool their interests in order to modify substantially the Johnson policy of Reconstruction.

When Congress met in December 1865, it was determined to take charge of Reconstruction. If there had been any doubt as to the direction in which the South was moving, it was dispelled by the character of the representatives sent to Congress. One had been vice president of the Confederacy, and there were four Confederate generals, five Confederate colonels, six Confederate cabinet officers, and fifty-eight members of the Confederate Congress. Although none could take the oath of office, their election indicated that the South stood solidly behind its defeated leaders. Thaddeus Stevens, a wily Republican leader and vigorous supporter of a stern policy toward the South, was exasperated. He proposed that Congress assume control of Reconstruction, asserting that the president's policy had been essentially provisional. Congress adopted a Stevens resolution creating the Joint Committee on Reconstruction to inquire into the condition of the Southern states and to make recommendations for a new policy.

In two bills, one to strengthen the Freedmen's Bureau and extend its life and the other to guarantee civil rights to blacks, Congress sought to exercise its influence in behalf of blacks. President Johnson vetoed the Freedmen's Bureau bill on the grounds that it was unconstitutional and proposed to do more for blacks than had ever been done for whites. The attempt to override the veto failed. He likewise vetoed the civil rights bill and declared that blacks were not yet ready for the privileges and equalities of citizens. Johnson's veto of these two bills, his condemnation of the proposed Fourteenth Amendment, and his attack on Stevens, Sumner, and other Northern leaders, put Congress in an angry mood. Consequently, on April 9, 1866, it passed the civil rights bill over his veto.

The fight between the president and Congress was now out in the open. Both believed that they could muster enough strength to have their way. Johnson was so confident that he decided to carry the fight to the people and call on them to return men to Congress in the fall of 1866 who would support his program. His conduct during the well-known "swing around the circle" was so unbecoming and his utterances so indiscreet that the entire country was outraged. He was soundly repudiated at the polls when the nation elected to Congress an overwhelming majority to oppose him and his Reconstruction program.

The rejection of the Fourteenth Amendment by the Southern states, their enactment of Black Codes, the widespread disorder in the South, and President Johnson's growing obstinacy persuaded many people that the South had to be dealt with harshly. Consequently, the Joint Committee presented to Congress a measure that ultimately was the basis of the principal Reconstruction Act of 1867. Through this measure the ex-Confederate states except Tennessee, where Reconstruction was moving satisfactorily, were divided into five military districts in which martial law was to prevail. On the basis of universal male suffrage a convention in each state was to draw up a new constitution acceptable to Congress. No state was to be admitted until it ratified the Fourteenth Amendment. Former rebels who could not take the ironclad oath were of course disfranchised. President Johnson vetoed the bill, contending that it was unconstitutional, that it was unfair to the states that had been reorganized, and that blacks, not having asked to vote, did not even understand what the franchise was. Congress overrode the veto and proceeded to enact other measures in the new program of Reconstruction.

The victory of Congress over the president was complete. It had enfranchised blacks in the District of Columbia, put the Freedmen's Bureau on a firm footing, carried forward its program of reconstructing the South through stern and severe treatment, and laid plans for subordination of the presidency by removal of its incumbent. The victory of Congress not only marked the beginning of a harsh policy toward the South but also signified the triumph of a coalition of interests—crusaders, politicians, and industrialists—all of whom hoped to gain something substantial through congressional reconstruction. It produced new conflicts, more bitter than preceding ones, and created so much confusion and chaos in almost every aspect of life that many of the problems would persist for more than a century.

■ Relief and Rehabilitation

In the closing months of the war and afterward, the South suffered acutely. The abandoned lands, the want of food and clothing, the thousands of displaced persons, and the absence of organized civil authority to cope with the emergency merely suggest the nature of the disorder and suffering. A most interesting and poignant feature of the time was ex-slaves searching for husbands, wives, or children who years earlier had been separated by sale or other transactions. As Herbert Gutman stated so pointedly, nothing better illustrated the remarkable stability and resiliency of the black family than their efforts to reunite and, in many instances, their taking steps to make their marriages and children legitimate after years and decades of living together as slaves with no marriage contract. Blacks were distressed, moreover, not only because they lacked the necessaries of life but also because they genuinely feared, especially after the death of President Lincoln, that they would gradually slip back into a condition hardly better than that of slaves. Leon Litwack indicated in *Been in the Storm So Long* that ex-slaves were constantly facing the question of what it meant to be free; indeed, how free was free? In those early days following the close of the war, they found it increasingly difficult to live out their notions of freedom as they had dreamed of it during slavery. In the summer and fall of 1865 they held several conventions, all looking toward an improvement in their condition. A black convention in Nashville protested seating the Tennessee delegation to Congress because the legislature had not passed just laws for African Americans. It also demanded that Congress recognize black citizenship. A group of 120, meeting in Raleigh, North Carolina, declared that they wanted fair wages, education for their children, and repeal of the discriminatory laws passed by the state legislature. Mississippi blacks protested reactionary policies in their state and asked Congress to extend the franchise to them. It was the same thing in Charleston and

North Carolina Blacks Seek Relief—1865

We are fully conscious that we cannot long expect the presence of Government agents, or of the troops to secure us against evil treatment from unreasonable, prejudiced, and unjust men. We have no desire to look abroad for protection and sympathy. We know we must find both at home, among the people of our own State, and merit them by our industry, sobriety and respectful demeanor, or suffer long and grievous evils. . . .

We most earnestly desire to have the disabilities under which we have formerly lived removed; to have all the oppressive laws which make unjust discriminations on account of race or color wiped from the statutes of the State. We invoke your protection for the sanctity of our family relations. Is this asking too much? . . . .

Though associated with many memories of suffering as well as of enjoyment, we have always loved our homes, and dreaded, as the worst of evils, a forcible separation from them. Now that Freedom and a new career are before us, we love this land and people more than ever before. Here we have toiled and suffered; our parents, wives and children are buried here, and in this land we will remain, unless forcibly driven away. . . .

"Address from the Convention of the Colored People of North Carolina," New York, *Daily Tribune*, October 7, 1865.

Mobile: blacks were demanding suffrage, the abolition of Black Codes, and measures for the relief of suffering.

While the pleas of blacks were largely ignored in the South, there were Northerners of both races who worked to relieve their distress. Private organizations had taken up this work during the war, and considerable pressure was applied to Congress as early as 1863 to assume responsibility for the welfare of needy whites and blacks in the South. Military commanders did whatever they could or wanted to do with regard to relief.

The need, however, was for a comprehensive and unified service for freedmen. It was not until March 1865 that the Bureau of Refugees, Freedmen, and Abandoned Lands, better known as the Freedmen's Bureau, was established. With officials in each of the Southern states, the bureau aided white refugees and former slaves by furnishing supplies and medical services, establishing schools, supervising contracts between ex-slaves and their employers, and managing confiscated or abandoned lands, leasing and selling some of them to former slaves.

The atmosphere in which the Freedmen's Bureau worked was one of hostility. Many white Northerners looked upon it as an expensive agency, the existence of which could not be justified in time of peace. In the South opposition to the bureau was vehement. There was serious objection to

CHARLOTTE FORTEN, TEACHER AMONG FLORMER SLAVES. Born in Philadelphia and educated in Salem, Massachusetts, Charlotte Forten began her teaching career in St. Helena's Island, South Carolina, in 1862. *(Moorland Springarn Research Center, Howard University.)*

federal interference with the relations between worker and employer. It was believed, moreover, that the bureau had a political program for enfranchising blacks and establishing a strong Republican party in the South.

There can be no doubt that the Freedmen's Bureau relieved much suffering among blacks and whites. Between 1865 and 1869, for example, the bureau issued 21 million rations, approximately 5 million going to whites and 15 million to blacks. By 1867 there were forty-six hospitals under the bureau staffed by physicians, surgeons, and nurses. The medical department spent over $2 million to improve the health of ex-slaves and treated more than 450,000 cases of illness. The death rate among former slaves was reduced, and sanitary conditions were improved.

The bureau undertook to resettle many people who had been displaced during the war. Because of the urgent need for labor to cultivate the land, free transportation was furnished ex-slaves to leave congested areas and to become self-supporting. By 1870 more than 30,000 had been moved. Although abandoned and confiscated lands were generally restored to their owners under the amnesty proclamations of Lincoln and Johnson, the bureau distributed some land to former slaves. Colonies of infirm, destitute, and vagrant blacks were set up in several states. Small parcels of land were first allotted and then leased to them for management and cultivation.

The bureau sought to protect blacks in their freedom to choose their own employer and to work at a fair wage. Both parties were required to live up to their contract. Agents of the bureau consulted with planters and ex-slaves, urging the former to be fair in their dealings and instructing the latter in the necessity of working to provide for their families and to achieve independence and security. Thousands of blacks returned to work under conditions more satisfactory than those that had existed before the bureau supervised their relations with employers. Gen. Oliver Otis Howard, the bureau's commissioner, reported that "in a single state not less than fifty thousand [labor] contracts were drawn." Even when they did not know all the stipulations of the contracts, many former slaves suspected that their employers would not live up to them. The "fust dif'culty," a South Carolina freedman said, was that "we gits no meat," although he assumed from the contract that they would.

When it was felt that the interest of blacks could not be safely entrusted to local courts, the bureau organized "freedmen's" courts and boards of arbitration. They had civil and criminal jurisdiction over minor cases where one or both parties were ex-slaves. Frequently an expression of the bureau's interest was sufficient to secure justice for former slaves in the regular courts. In Maryland, for example, the case of a white physician who assaulted a black without provocation was taken by the bureau agent to the state supreme court, which admitted the testimony of blacks and convicted the physician.

The bureau achieved its greatest successes in education. It set up or supervised all kinds of schools: day, night, Sunday, and industrial schools, as well as colleges. It cooperated closely with philanthropic and religious organizations in the North in the establishment of many institutions. Among the schools founded in this period that received aid from the bureau were Howard University, Hampton Institute, St. Augustine's College, Atlanta University, Fisk University, Storer College, and Biddle Memorial Institute (now Johnson C. Smith University). The American Missionary Association and the Baptists, Methodists, Presbyterians, and Episcopalians were all active in establishing schools. Education was promoted so vigorously that by 1867 schools had been set up in "the remotest counties of each of the confederate states."

Teachers came down from the North in large numbers. Besides Edmund Ware at Atlanta, Samuel C. Armstrong at Hampton, and Erastus M. Cravath at Fisk, there were hundreds whose services were not as widely known. In 1869 there were 9,503 teachers in schools for former slaves in the South. Although some of the white teachers were Southerners, a majority of whites came from the North. In *Reading, 'Riting, and Reconstruction,* Robert Morris reminds us that many white teachers discriminated against their black colleagues. Noticing the obvious differences in how the white veteran antislavery leader, the Reverend Sela G. Wright, treated white and black teachers under his supervision, a black resident of Natchez, Mississippi, referred to him as a "copperhead preacher." The number of black teachers nevertheless was growing, and gradually they took over supervision of some schools.

By 1870, when the educational work of the bureau stopped, there were 247,333 pupils in 4,329 schools. Reports from all quarters "showed a marked increase in attendance, and advance in scholarship, and a record of punctuality and regularity which compared favorably with the schools in the north." The bureau had spent more than $5 million in schooling ex-slaves. The shortcomings in the education of blacks arose not from a want of zeal on the part of teachers but from ignorance of the needs of blacks and from the necessary preoccupation of students with the problem of survival in a hostile world.

Despite Southern hostility to the bureau and the inefficiency of many officials, it performed a vastly important task. As a relief agency it deserves to be ranked with the great efforts of recent depressions and wars. It demonstrated that the government could administer an extensive program of relief and rehabilitation and suggested a way in which the nation could grapple with its pressing social problems. To be sure, there was corruption and inefficiency, but not enough to prevent the bureau from achieving notable success in ministering to human welfare.

Another agency that offered both spiritual and material relief during Reconstruction was the black church. The end of the war led to the expansion of independent churches among blacks. There were no longer Southern laws to silence black preachers and proscribe separate organizations. Blacks began to withdraw from white churches once they had secured their freedom, and consequently the black church grew rapidly after the war. In 1865 black members of the white Primitive Baptist churches of the South established a separate organization called the Colored Primitive Baptists in America. In 1869 the General Assembly of the Cumberland Presbyterian church organized its black members in the Colored Cumberland Presbyterian church. One of the most important separate churches emerged in the Colored Methodist Episcopal church. By 1870, when blacks had organized five conferences, the first general conference was held, and white bishops came to consecrate W. H. Miles and R. H. Vanderhorst as the first black bishops, to be followed three years later by L. H. Holsey, J. A. Beebe, and Isaac Lane.

Older black churches entered a new stage of growth. The African Methodist Episcopal church, which had only 20,000 members in 1856, boasted 75,000 ten years later. In 1876 its membership exceeded 200,000, and its influence and material possessions had increased proportionally. The Baptists likewise enjoyed phenomenal growth. Local churches sprang up overnight under the ministry of unlettered but inspired preachers. In 1866 the black Baptists of North Carolina organized the first state convention. Within a few years every Southern state had a large black Baptist organization. Total membership increased from 150,000 in 1850 to 500,000 in 1870. As the first social institution fully controlled by blacks in America, these churches gave them an opportunity to develop leadership, and it is no coincidence that many outstanding Reconstruction leaders were ministers. Bishop H. M. Turner of Georgia, the Reverend R. H. Cain of South Carolina, and Bishop J. W. Hood of North Carolina were a few of the political leaders who gained much of their experience in the black church.

■ Economic Adjustment

It was one thing to provide temporary relief for former slaves and another to guide them along the road to economic stability and independence. The release from bondage of 4 million persons had serious implications for the economic structure of the South at a time when it could least afford to be disturbed. To be sure, many ex-slaves would not work, at first, because they were exhilarated by their new liberty, and still others scorned low wages and lacked confidence in their employers. But many were active, and all were potential competitors in the labor market. To white workers the situation was extremely disturbing. White planters, however, in an effort to reestablish themselves, were anxious to secure labor at the lowest possible price, and if in their own minds they conceded the right of blacks to be free, they were seldom able to realize that blacks also had a right to refuse work. Many prospective employers therefore sought to force blacks to work. The Black Codes were in many instances formulated with this specific end in view.

The Black Codes represented the effort of the South to solve problems created by the presence of former slaves, as the Freedmen's Bureau represented the efforts of the federal government to achieve the same end. Establishment of the Freedmen's Bureau and of Radical Reconstruction governments did not mean that the Black Codes had failed, but rather that political power over the South had been transferred to Washington. In the final analysis, neither the Black Codes nor Radical Reconstruction solved the economic problems of ex-slaves. What solution there was, however unsatisfactory, came by negotiations between the white employer and the black worker, in some instances under the supervision of the Freedmen's Bureau. Because the federal government failed to give blacks much land, they slowly returned to the farms and resumed work under circumstances scarcely more favorable than those prevailing before the war. Black agricultural workers found themselves at the mercy of white planters. Labor contracts drawn up to bind both parties were frequently disregarded, employers failing to pay stipulated wages and workers failing to perform tasks outlined in their contracts.

Once blacks were back on the farm as workers, they were paid either in

Dr. Norton Discusses
Ex-Confederates—1866

Washington, February 3, 1866

Dr. Daniel Norton (colored) sworn and examined.
By Mr. [Jacob M.] Howard, [Senator from Michigan]

Question. Where do you reside?
Answer.   I reside in Yorktown, Virginia.

Question. How old are you?
Answer.   About 26 years old.

Question. Are you a regularly licensed physician?
Answer.   I am.

Question. Where were you educated?
Answer.   In the State of New York. I studied privately under Dr. Warren. . . .

Question. Are you a native of Virginia?
Answer.   Yes, sir. I was born in Williamsburg, Virginia.

Question. What is the feeling among the rebels in the neighborhood of Yorktown
           towards the government of the United States?
Answer.   They do not manifest a very cordial feeling toward the government of
           the United States. There are some, of course who do, but the majority
           do not seem to manifest a good spirit or feeling. . . .

Question. How do the colored people feel toward the government of the United
           States?
Answer.   They feel determined to be law-abiding citizens. There is no other
           feeling among them.

Question. Are you a delegate sent to the city of Washington by some association?
Answer.   I am. I was sent by three counties; I represent, perhaps, something like
           fifteen or twenty thousand people. The great trouble, in my opinion, is
           that the colored people are not more disposed to return to their former
           homes on account of the treatment which those who have gone back
           have received.

Question. State generally whether or not the treatment which those colored people
           receive at the hands of their old white masters is kind or unkind.
Answer.   It is not what I would consider kind or good treatment. . . .

Question. In case of the removal of the military force from among you, and also
           of the Freedmen's Bureau, what would the whites do with you?
Answer.   I do not think that the colored people would be safe. They would be in
           danger of being hunted and killed. The spirit of the whites against the
           blacks is much worse than it was before the war. . . .

Report of the Joint Committee on Reconstruction (Washington, 1866), pp. 51–52.

monthly wages or a share of the crop. Plantation wages ranged from $9 to $15 a month for men and from $5 to $10 for women, in addition to food, shelter, and fuel. Where the sharecropping system prevailed, former slaves were allowed from one-quarter to one-half of the cotton and corn; they were also provided with a house, fuel, and in some cases food. There was every opportunity for the contracting parties not to live up to their word; good faith was the only effective way to keep agreements. It need not be added that where hatred and bitterness prevailed, as in so many parts of the South, relations between employer and worker often militated against efficient production.

There can be no question that the majority of blacks worked, despite Southern doubts of their efficiency as free laborers. Many of them resented the suggestion that they would not work. The editor of a black newspaper declared in 1865 that black people need not be reminded to avoid idleness and vagrancy. After all, he concluded, "the necessity of working is perfectly understood by men who have worked all their lives." The same could be said of women. They had no other choice but to cast their lot with their former masters and assist them in restoring economic stability to the rural South. By 1870 the cotton kingdom had retrieved much of its losses, and by 1875 the white South had come to realize that cheap labor could be the basis for a profitable agricultural system. The cotton crop of 1870 had not reached the level of production achieved just before the war, but by 1880 the South was producing more cotton than ever. While the sugar crop recovered more slowly, its continued improvement was marked. Thus black farm workers contributed greatly to the economic recovery of the South. As free workers, however, they gained but little. The wages paid them in 1867 were lower than those that had been paid to hired slaves. In the sharecropping system the cost of maintenance was so great that at the end of the year ex-slaves were indebted to their employers for most of what they had made and sometimes more than they had made. The white South generally recovered much more rapidly than the former slaves.

Many former slaves had received the impression that abandoned and confiscated lands were to be distributed to them in lots of forty acres by January 1866. This impression stemmed from the Confederate apprehension during the war that the Union government planned to seize their land and convey it to ex-slaves, and from the bill creating the Freedmen's Bureau, which gave tacit encouragement to such a plan. Although nothing came of it, the federal government sought to encourage the dispersion of populations from congested centers by opening public lands, under the Southern Homestead Act of 1866, in Alabama, Mississippi, Louisiana, Arkansas, and Florida to all settlers regardless of race. Eighty acres were available for the head of each family. Within a year ex-slaves secured homesteads in Florida covering 160,960 acres, and in Arkansas they occupied 116 out of 243 homesteads. By 1874 blacks in Georgia owned more than 350,000 acres of land. "Forty acres and a mule" as a gift of the government had not been realized, but wherever possible blacks were acquiring land in their effort to achieve economic security.

Neither white nor black Southerners were fully aware of the revolutionary implications of the industrial changes taking place. While the South was preoccupied with the restoration of an agricultural regime, the rest of the country responded to the quickened pace of living ushered in by industrialization. Most blacks remained in rural areas, but a considerable number joined their fellows in the urban centers of both the North and South. They migrated to the cities not because they knew of their industrial development but because of a repugnance for plantation life, which they still associated with slavery. The war was hardly over before the sharp cleavage between white and black workers became apparent. White artisans and factory hands were keenly aware of the same threat to their security that had embittered the landless whites of the South before the war. African-American blacksmiths, bricklayers, pilots, cabinet makers, painters, and other skilled workers met stern opposition from white artisans wherever they sought employment. In many instances the opposition led to violence, in the North as well as in the South.

The use of black labor had the curious effect of making it more difficult for black workers to achieve security and respectability in the world of labor. Manufacturers and entrepreneurs did not hesitate to employ blacks in order to undermine white labor unions. In 1867, for example, black ship caulkers were brought from Portsmouth, Virginia, to Boston to defeat white workers' efforts to secure an eight-hour day. Operators of iron and cotton mills and railroad builders all looked south for cheap labor, even if it meant the displacement of workers with a much higher standard of living. The deliberate degradation of black labor by white employers in all sections of the country made it impossible for black and white workers to join hands or to present a solid front to management.

On the whole blacks were not welcomed into labor organizations in the postwar period. Some local unions admitted them, like the carpenters and joiners in Boston in 1866, but most locals would not. The locals, moreover, prevented national unions from adopting a nondiscriminatory policy on the grounds that local autonomy must be preserved. When the National Labor Union was organized in Baltimore in 1866, blacks were invited to cooperate in the general movement, but it was made clear that if they were to be regarded as trustworthy, they must adhere to the true principles of labor reform. It looked as though blacks were to be effectively barred from the white labor movement, and as a result a group of black workers met in December 1869 to organize the National Negro Labor Union. During the next few years this organization sought affiliation with white labor, but without much success. Local black organizations advanced the cause of the black worker. But white workers did everything possible to retard the growth of a black labor movement, and black leaders too frequently sought to use their organizations for political purposes. Until after 1880 black workers remained, involuntarily, outside the organized labor movement. Meanwhile, as victims of ruthless and unscrupulous employers, they acquired the reputation of being strikebreakers who worked for lower wages than whites. This reputation was to follow them for several generations after the Civil War.

Since Reconstruction was a period in which efforts were made by citizens everywhere to achieve economic independence through various forms of business enterprise, blacks did likewise. Lack of capital was an obstacle to their success in business. In 1865 blacks in Baltimore organized the Chesapeake and Marine Railway and Dry Dock Company, capitalized at $40,000 with the stock divided into 8,000 shares. At the end of five years the company purchased a shipyard and was apparently prospering, but profits began to decline in 1877, and in 1883 the company went out of existence. In Savannah, blacks invested $50,000 in a business venture that proved worthless. They also failed in an effort to run a land and lumber enterprise in which they had invested $40,000. There were other groups and individuals who sought to make a living by opening shops, but many of them failed, for they had no knowledge of how to operate a business, and those who knew how were caught in the depression following the panic of 1873.

One effort to assist former slaves in their economic adjustment was the encouragement given them to save their money. There had been several experiments with savings banks for blacks during the war. After the allotment system was developed, many soldiers saved regularly in banks established for that purpose. Outstanding were the Free Labor Bank set up by General Banks at New Orleans, and another established by General Butler at Norfolk. Toward the end of the war, blacks were given an opportunity to save at the Freedmen's Savings and Trust Company, which was chartered by the federal government in 1865. The business of the organization, with William Booth as president, was confined to the black race, and two-thirds of the deposits were to be invested in securities of the United States.

On April 4, 1865, the headquarters of the Freedmen's Bank, as it was called, was opened in New York. Within the next few months branches were started in Washington, New Orleans, Nashville, Vicksburg, Louisville, and Memphis. By 1872 there were thirty-four branches, with only the New York and Philadelphia offices in the North; by 1874 the deposits in all branches totaled $3,299,201.

But unmistakable evidences of failure were apparent: there was inaccurate bookkeeping, and some of the cashiers were incompetent. There had been almost no black employees at the beginning, but gradually they were hired. Some, but not all, proved able to perform their tasks. Political influence was used to secure loans. At a time when his business was tottering, Jay Cooke borrowed $500,000 at only 5 percent interest, and Henry Cooke together with other financiers unloaded bad loans on the bank. After the big financial houses failed in 1873, there was a run on the bank, and many speculating officials resigned, leaving blacks to take the blame. In March

1874 Frederick Douglass was made president, but the bank was already a failure, although neither he nor the public was aware of the fact. When he realized the truth, he resorted to desperate means to save the bank, using his own money and appealing to the Senate Finance Committee for more. The bank was placed in liquidation by Congress so that it could be reorganized, but it was too late. Confidence in the bank had been completely shattered, and on June 28, 1874, it closed. Thousands of black depositors suffered losses they could ill afford. Black leaders, some of whom were blameless, were castigated by their fellows, while the Cookes and others, who benefited most, escaped without public censure.

Perhaps the greatest failure of Reconstruction was economic. At the end of the period both white and black workers in the South were suffering from want and privation. In the North, where their lot was substantially better, they had not yet learned to cope with the powerful industrialists who were using political agencies as their most reliable allies and bribing officials with greater regularity than they paid their employees. While the white leaders of the South were preoccupied with opposing black suffrage and civil rights, Northern financiers and industrialists took advantage of the opportunity to impose their economic control on the South, and much of it endured for generations. The inability of blacks to solve their problems was not altogether to their discredit. It was merely a symptom of the complexity of the new industrial America, which baffled even the most astute of its citizens.

■ Political Currents

The Reconstruction Act of 1867 imposed on the white South a regime more difficult to bear than defeat. Vast numbers of white Southerners were to be disfranchised; blacks and their allies, loyal whites and those from the North who apparently had come to stay, were to enjoy the ballot. Constitutional conventions were called for the express purpose of eradicating the last vestiges of the old order. From the white Southerners' point of view all power was to be placed in the hands of those least qualified to control their destiny. Two years of white home rule were discredited because it was said that white Southerners had tried to turn the clock back to the years before the war. White Southerners thought the clock was now being turned back to the days of barbarism.

The constitutional conventions called in pursuance of the Reconstruction Act all contained black members. Only in South Carolina did they make up a majority of delegates, and in Louisiana they were equal to the whites, each having forty-nine delegates. In some states the ratio of blacks to whites was small, as in Texas where only nine out of ninety members of the convention were black. In most states blacks constituted only a respectable minority of the delegates. In six states native white Southerners were in the majority. Some black members had been slaves, but others had always been free, and among them were emigrants from the North. Some blacks were of considerable intellectual stature. In Florida it was generally conceded that Jonathan Gibbs was "the most cultured member of the convention." For the most part, the black members of the conventions were men of moderation. A generous appraisal of the personnel of a black delegation was made by the Charleston *Daily News:* "Beyond all question, the best men in the convention are the colored members. Considering the influences under which they were called together, and their imperfect acquaintance with parliamentary law, they have displayed, for the most part, remarkable moderation and dignity. . . . They have assembled neither to pull wires like some, nor to make money like others; but to legislate for the welfare of the race to which they belong." Typical of the magnanimity of the black members are the words of Beverly Nash before the constitutional convention of South Carolina:

> I believe, my friends and fellow-citizens, we are not prepared for this suffrage. But we can learn. Give a man tools and let him commence to use them, and in time he will learn a trade. So it is with voting. We may not understand it at the start, but in time we shall learn to do our duty. . . . We recognize the Southern white man as the true friend of the black man. . . . In these public affairs we must unite with our white fellow-citizens. They tell us that they have been disfranchised, yet we tell the North that we shall never let the halls of Congress be silent until we remove that disability.

The state constitutions drawn up in 1867 and 1868 were the most progressive the South had ever known. Most of them abolished property qualifications for voting and holding office; some of them abolished imprisonment for debt. All of them abolished slavery, and several sought to eliminate race distinctions in the possession or inheritance of property. Although the planters of Louisiana thought their constitution was the "work of the lowest and most corrupt body of men ever assembled in the South," the laws codified on the basis of this constitution, together with laws adopted later in three codes, remain even today the basic law of the state. In every state the ballot was extended to all male residents, except for certain classes of Confederates, and it is significant that some blacks, like Nash of South Carolina and Pinchback of Louisiana, were vigorously opposed to any disqualification of Confederates.

The conservative elements of the South almost unanimously denounced the new constitutions and fought to defeat their ratification. When they gained power at the end of Reconstruction, however, they seemed anxious to rewrite only those clauses of the constitutions that had enfranchised blacks. Florida finally adopted a new constitution in 1885, Mississippi in 1890, South Carolina in 1895, Louisiana in 1898, and Virginia in 1902. Like those written soon after the overthrow of Reconstruction, they were remarkably similar to the documents that had been so roundly condemned. Victors in the campaigns for white supremacy were wise enough to retain the public school systems, the modernized machinery of local government, and other measures

FIRST AFRICAN-AMERICAN GOVERNOR.
P. B. S. Pinchback, the elected lieutenant governor
of Louisiana, served as governor for forty-one days
when H. C. Warmoth was removed from office.
(Culver Pictures.)

in the Reconstruction constitutions that pointed toward a more progressive
South.

During Reconstruction, blacks held public offices in Southern states. They
sat in the legislatures and assisted in enacting laws that won both the praise
and the condemnation of bitter partisans. It was in South Carolina that they
wielded the greatest influence. In the first legislature there were eighty-seven
blacks and forty whites. From the outset, however, the whites controlled the
state senate, and in 1874 the lower house as well. At all times there was a
white governor. It can be said, therefore, that at no time were blacks in control
of South Carolina. There were two black lieutenant governors, Alonzo J.
Ransier in 1870 and Richard H. Gleaves in 1872. Samuel J. Lee was speaker
of the house in 1872, and Robert B. Elliott occupied that position in 1874.
Francis L. Cardozo, an accomplished black who had been educated at the
University of Glasgow and in London, was secretary of state from 1868 to
1872 and treasurer from 1872 to 1876. He was regarded by friends and
enemies, says A. A. Taylor, as one of the best-educated men in South
Carolina, regardless of color.

The blacks of Mississippi were not as largely represented in their new
government. In the first Reconstruction legislature there were forty black
members, some of whom had been slaves. In 1873 they held three significant
positions: A. K. Davis was lieutenant governor; James Hill, secretary of state;
and T. W. Cardozo, superintendent of education. On the whole, blacks took
little part in legislation, but a few were chairmen of important legislative
committees. In 1872 John R. Lynch was Speaker of the House, and at the end
of the session a white Democrat praised him "for his dignity, impartiality,
and courtesy as a presiding officer."

Between 1868 and 1896 Louisiana had 133 black legislators, of whom 38
were senators and 95 were representatives. At no time did they approach
control of public affairs. John W. Menard was elected to Congress but was
denied a seat. Three blacks, Oscar J. Dunn, P. B. S. Pinchback, and C. C.

SOUTH CAROLINA'S SUPREME COURT JUSTICE. Jonathan Jasper Wright, the first African American elected to the Pennsylvania bar (1866). He went to South Carolina, was elected to the state supreme court in 1870 and served until 1876. (*Courtesy of the South Carolina Library, University of South Carolina.*)

Antoine, served as lieutenant governor, and Pinchback was acting governor for forty-three days in the winter of 1873 when Henry C. Warmoth was removed from office. Although blacks were not in control, they sought to improve political conditions. Oscar J. Dunn, for example, led the fight against corruption and extravagance.

Blacks were not significant in the leadership of Alabama during Reconstruction. They were in both houses of the legislature, but not in sufficient numbers to secure positions of power. They helped to adopt the Fourteenth and Fifteenth Amendments, however, and put a state system of schools into operation.

Although blacks were elected to the first Reconstruction legislature of Georgia, they had difficulty in securing and retaining their seats. In September 1868 the legislature declared that all black members were ineligible, and not until almost a year later, when the state supreme court declared them eligible, were they able to regain their seats. The black members introduced many bills on education, the jury system, city government reform, and women's suffrage. Two able black legislators, Jefferson Long and H. M. Turner, sought better wages for black workers but got little support from their colleagues, who in many instances supported the industrialists seeking to exploit all forms of natural and human resources.

In Florida and North Carolina black members of the Reconstruction government were primarily interested in relief, education, and suffrage. In

MISSISSIPPI'S SPEAKER OF THE HOUSE. Elected to the State legislature in 1869, John Roy Lynch became speaker in 1872 before going on to serve three terms in the United States House of Representatives. (*Culver Pictures.*)

Jonathan Gibbs, superintendent of public instruction from 1872 to 1874, they had an able leader, a champion of equal rights. H. S. Harmon led the fight for a satisfactory school law. With other black legislators he supported a homestead law and such measures as would provide greater economic security for the mass of citizens. North Carolina blacks helped to inaugurate a system of public schools. An outstanding worker in the field of education was the Reverend J. W. Hood, who had helped write the constitution of 1868 and served as assistant superintendent of education.

Very few blacks held office in the new government of Virginia. Twenty-seven sat in the first legislature, and others served in minor posts. They were never powerful enough to determine any policy of the government except, as A. A. Taylor says, on a few occasions where they held the balance between militant white factions. So far as the exercise of influence is concerned, the same thing can be said of blacks in Tennessee, Arkansas, and Texas.

An important way in which blacks participated in politics was by election to Congress. Between 1869 and 1901, two served in the Senate and twenty in the House of Representatives. The two senators were Hiram R. Revels and Blanche K. Bruce, both representing Mississippi. Revels was a North Carolina free black who had migrated to Indiana, Ohio, and Illinois, receiving his education at a seminary in Ohio and at Knox College in Illinois. By the time of the Civil War he had been ordained a minister in the African Methodist Episcopal church and had taught school in several places. During the war he recruited blacks for the Union army, founded a school for freedmen in St. Louis, and joined the army as chaplain of a black regiment in Mississippi. After the war he settled in Natchez and became prominent in state politics. In 1870 he was elected to the United States Senate to fill the seat previously occupied by Jefferson Davis. He favored the removal of all disqualifications on ex-Confederates and worked diligently in the interest of his state. He admitted that during his year in the Senate he received fair treatment even in the matter of patronage.

In 1874 Blanche K. Bruce was elected to the Senate, the only black to be elected to a full term until the election in 1966 of Edward Brooke, a Republican from Massachusetts. Bruce had been born a slave in Virginia. When the war came, he escaped from St. Louis to Hannibal, Missouri, and established a school for blacks. After the war he studied in the North for several years. In 1869 he went to Mississippi, entered politics, and worked up through a succession of offices from tax collector to sheriff and then superintendent of schools. In the Senate he usually voted with his party and introduced a number of bills to improve the conditions of blacks. When P. B. S. Pinchback was denied a seat in the Senate, to which he had been elected from Louisiana, Bruce spoke for him in vain. He succeeded in having some pension bills passed, but his chief work was with the Manufactures, Education, and Labor Committee and the Pensions Committee. As chairman of the select committee on the Freedmen's Bank, he conducted a thorough investigation of the causes for its failure. His wide range of interests as a lawmaker is seen in the introduction of bills on the Geneva award for Alabama claims, another for aid to education and railroad construction, and one for reimbursement of depositors in the Freedmen's Bank.

Of the twenty blacks who served in the House of Representatives, South Carolina sent the largest number, eight, and North Carolina followed with four, three of whom served after Reconstruction. Alabama sent three, and Georgia, Mississippi, Florida, Louisiana, and Virginia, one each. It was in the Forty-first Congress, in 1869, that blacks, three of them, first made their appearance in the federal legislature. In the next Congress there were five. The peak was reached in the Forty-third and Forty-fourth Congresses when seven black men sat in the House of Representatives. In length of service, J. H. Rainey and Robert Smalls, both of South Carolina, led with five terms for each. John R. Lynch of Mississippi and J. T. Walls of Florida both served three terms, and six others served two terms each.

Most of the blacks in Congress had had some experience in public service before going to Washington, as delegates to constitutional conventions, as

AN EARLY MIXED JURY IN THE UNITED STATES. This group of men was impanelled to serve on a jury to try Jefferson Davis, the president of the Confederacy. Although he had been held in prison since his capture, he was released without trial shortly after the impanelling had been made. *(Courtesy The Moorland-Springarn Research Center, Howard University.)*

state senators and representatives, or as state or local officials. While they were chiefly concerned with civil rights and education, their efforts were not by any means confined to problems of blacks. Many fought for local improvements such as new public buildings and appropriations for rivers and harbors. Several, like Walls of Florida and Lynch of Mississippi, promoted protective tariffs for home products. Walls was also interested in the recognition of Cuba. Hyman of North Carolina advanced a program for relief of the Indians, and Nash of Louisiana uttered a plea for intersectional peace.

Concerning the work of black members of Congress, the white historian James Ford Rhodes wrote: "They left no mark on the legislation of their time; none of them, in comparison with their white associates, attained the least distinction." It must be remembered, however, that if few measures introduced by blacks were enacted into law, there were other ways in which as members of Congress they served effectively. Many bills that they introduced were deemed unworthy of serious consideration, but this was also true of a majority of the bills presented to Congress. Others died a natural death on the tortuous road from one house to the other and to the president's desk. None of the black members enjoyed the prestige of chairing important committees, and they had great difficulty in winning the respect even of colleagues in their own party. At a time when Congress could count among its members men affiliated with the most scandalous and corrupt deals in the history of the country, it was not without significance that a former

**FIRST AFRICAN AMERICAN IN THE UNITED STATES
SENATE.** Hiram R. Revels was elected in 1870 to fill the
seat previously occupied by confederate President Jefferson
Davis. *(Bettmann Archive.)*

congressman and ex-Confederate general, Roger A. Pryor, was moved to say
in 1873: "We have not yet heard that a Negro congressman was in any way
implicated in the Credit Mobilier scandal." To James G. Blaine, who knew
most of the black congressmen, "the colored men who took seats in both
Senate and House did not appear ignorant or helpless. They were as a rule
studious, earnest, ambitious men, whose public conduct . . . would be
honorable to any race."

More important than the men, white or black, who held office during
Reconstruction were the forces operating to influence their actions. Although
blacks were members of Congress, lieutenant governors, sheriffs, prosecuting
attorneys, and recorders of deeds, at no time was there black rule anywhere
in the South. Indeed, it can be said with some reason that there was no
carpetbag rule as the term is commonly understood. The South, as well as
the North, was subject to the most dynamic political and economic currents
that had ever stirred American life. Economic revolution, not Reconstruction,

BLANCHE KELSO BRUCE—MISSISSIPPI TEACHER, PLANTER, AND POLITICIAN.
Bruce was the first African American to win a full term in the United States Senate.
(Moorland Spingarn Research Center, Howard University.)

determined the pattern of public action after 1865. Tariff legislation was more important than civil rights; railroad subsidies were more important than the suffrage. The industrialists of the North, who had come to control the Republican party, wanted a satisfactory settlement of the Southern problem in order to hasten the exploitation of Southern resources and to capture Southern markets. When the Radical Reconstruction program served their purposes, they cooperated, as in the period when they sought favorable consideration from the Southern legislatures; but when the program failed to bring peace and order, thereby postponing prosperity, they helped to restore home rule to the South.

It is significant that Northern industrialists were active in the South throughout Reconstruction. As Horace Mann Bond points out, William D. Kelly and other Northern capitalists were so anxious to exploit the rich resources and cheap labor of Alabama that they used their influence to bring about a hasty, if not satisfactory, reconstruction of the state. Iron and railroad interests were powerful in Alabama, and many Northern capitalists worked behind the scenes, manipulating the actors on the Reconstruction stage. In

1867, for example, the legislature granted $12,000 a mile to companies building railroads and later increased this sum to $16,000. Between 1867 and 1871 the Louisville and Nashville Railroad and the Alabama and Chattanooga Railroad received $17 million in endorsements and loans. These subsidies became part of the Reconstruction debt.

It has been estimated that of $305 million owed by eleven Southern states in 1871, at least $100 million of the debt consisted of contingent and prospective liabilities incurred by the issue of railroad bonds. Southerners and Northerners, Republicans and Democrats, had cooperated in lending the credit of these states to railroad investments. A survey of the Reconstruction debt shows clearly that Southern legislatures were not as extravagant in the purchase of whiskey and cigars for their members as in yielding to the pressure of Northern money interests for favorable and costly legislation. In addition, the expenses of carrying out legitimate programs for improved roads, public education, and other social services accounted for much of the Reconstruction debt.

The graft and corruption of the period were neither new nor peculiar to the South. Public office has been used for personal gain too frequently to ascribe the practice to any particular group, section, or period. The Southern land agents who stole public funds during Van Buren's day would qualify as excellent thieves today. The North descended to a new level of public immorality after the Civil War. Bribery and thievery were rampant in the South during Reconstruction, but doubtless they stemmed from the same forces that made the Tweed Ring in New York and numerous scandals in the Grant administration disgraces to the whole nation. Similar forces have created similar situations in the America of later days.

From a national point of view Reconstruction was a period in which the country moved steadily toward a more powerful position in the world economy, thereby making possible the exercise of tremendous influence on world affairs in succeeding years. The Fourteenth Amendment gave Americans their first clear-cut definition of citizenship and strengthened their position as individuals in a complex social order. It also gave corporations an opportunity to flourish under the broad interpretation that the Supreme Court soon put upon the amendment. In the Fifteenth Amendment, a wider exercise of the franchise was guaranteed along with the removal of race as a disability. In the South, Reconstruction laid the foundations for more democratic living by sweeping away all qualifications for voting and holding office and by establishing a system of universal free public education. In failing to provide adequate economic security for former slaves, Reconstruction left them no alternative but to submit to their old masters, a submission that made easier the efforts of Southern whites to overthrow Reconstruction and restore a system based on white supremacy.

CHAPTER 13

Losing the Peace

■ The Struggle for Domination

The war was hardly over before the victors found out that it was easy to sit in Washington and proclaim peace by presidential decree or legislative enactment but very difficult to establish peace in a country so recently torn apart by civil conflict. Despite the fact that General Grant thought that the South would accept the verdict of the battlefield, there were others who believed that the South was irreconcilable. Carl Schurz returned from a tour of the region with the verdict that the South had submitted only because it saw no alternative. He was alarmed at having found "no expression of hearty attachment to the great republic." To his horror, treason was not odious in the South. The tragic dispersion of the Confederate troops at the end of the war contrasted miserably with the presence of Northern invaders—not only white soldiers but also black troops, in fact, far fewer than the former Confederates claimed—stationed at strategic points to maintain the peace. This was evidence of the North's conviction that the South was barbarous and that the spirit of slavery had "debased the Southern mind, destroyed liberty and law, and vitiated all white elements upon which a restored union might be erected." Each section was thoroughly convinced that the other was wicked and, under the circumstances, not to be trusted to do the right thing.

The Republicans, having the upper hand even in the early years of Reconstruction, were determined to strengthen their position and perpetuate their power. They had effective propaganda for these purposes. They could remind the country that it was the South which had treasonably fought to destroy the Union, that old slaveholders were only waiting for an opportunity to reenslave blacks, and that the Republican party had saved the nation from complete ruin at the hands of Democrats, North and South. The vulnerable position of the Democrats was summed up by Schurz: "There is no heavier burden for a political party to bear, than to have appeared unpatriotic in war." To be sure, the Democrats claimed they were dedicated to peace and union, but it was a modest claim compared to the extravagant and righteous pretensions of the Republicans. Many Republicans, whatever their altruistic motives, were moved to adopt the cause of blacks almost solely by considerations of political expediency and strategy. It would have been unnatural for them not to have strengthened their party by enfranchising African Americans and enlisting them as loyal voters. It would have been equally unnatural for the Democrats, especially the Southern wing, to have abided this clever political maneuver.

The struggle of these two parties to dominate national politics shaped the history of Reconstruction and led to the final defeat of both in attaining peace. Democrats generally opposed all Republican measures regardless of their merits. Republicans, convinced of the perfidy if not downright treason of the Democrats, sought to create a coalition that was too self-centered to be either altruistic or effective. To each party must be ascribed some share of the guilt for their utter failure to establish peace between the sections and the races.

With Union troops in the South and an increasing number of federal officials, most of whom were loyal Republicans, the latter sought to build up a strong Southern wing of their party. Many Freedmen's Bureau officials were interested not only in the welfare of the freedman but in the growth of the Republican party as well. Moreover, missionary groups and teachers from the North, who saw in the Republican party an instrument by which the South could be saved from barbarism, supported it enthusiastically. It would be incorrect, however, to conclude that these groups were primarily political in their motives or activities. But the special agency that recruited Republicans, primarily among blacks, was the Union League.

The Union League of America was organized in the North during the war. It did an effective job in rallying support for the war wherever there was much opposition. Later it branched out into the South to protect the fruits of Northern victory. As a protective and benevolent society, it welcomed black members and catechized them on political activity. As the Freedmen's Bureau and other Northern agencies grew in the South, the Union League became powerful, attracting a large number of blacks. With the establishment of Radical Reconstruction, the league became the spearhead for Southern Republicanism. Since blacks were the most numerous enfranchised group in many areas, the league depended on them for the bulk of Republican strength.

By the fall of 1867 there were chapters of the league all over the South.

South Carolina alone had eighty-eight, and it was said that almost every black in the state was enrolled. Ritual, secrecy, night meetings, and an avowed devotion to freedom and equal rights made the league especially attractive to blacks. At elections they looked to their chapters for guidance on voting. If they had any doubt about the straight Republican ticket, the league had only to remind them that this was the party of Abraham Lincoln and of deliverance. A vote for Democrats, they said, was a vote for the return of slavery. During most of Reconstruction, the Union League and such smaller organizations as the Lincoln Brotherhood and the Red Strings delivered the black vote to the Republican party in national as well as state and local elections.

As long as Lincoln and Johnson permitted some Southern whites to participate in Reconstruction, the whites believed that they could handle blacks and resurrect the Democratic party. Even when the presence of black troops outraged them, they could protest vigorously to the president, as Wade Hampton did in 1866, and expect quick relief. These white Southerners were determined to guide their own destiny and control blacks. When Radical Reconstruction made this impossible, in 1867 they struck with fury and rage.

The violence, which culminated in the Ku Klux Klan movement, did not arise solely, however, from the establishment of Radical Reconstruction and the consequent elimination of many Southern white men from public life. As early as 1866, when Southern whites had almost complete charge of Reconstruction, a kind of guerrilla warfare was carried on against both blacks and whites who represented the Washington government in the South. The head of the Freedmen's Bureau in Georgia, for example, complained that bands of men calling themselves Regulators, Jayhawkers, and the Black Horse Cavalry were committing the "most fiendish and diabolical outrages on the freedmen" with the sympathy not only of the populace but of the reconstructed governments too. There were scores of these coercive organizations all over the South. They were formed as white protective societies, and while Southern leaders enacted the new Black Codes, they were engaged in "keeping the Negro in his place" and sniping at Northerners who had come south.

Secret societies grew and spread when it became apparent to Southerners that their control was to be broken by Radical Reconstruction. For ten years after 1867 there flourished the Knights of the White Camelia, the Constitutional Union Guards, the Pale Faces, the White Brotherhood, the Council of Safety, the '76 Association, and the Knights of the Ku Klux Klan. Among the numerous local organizations were the White League of Louisiana, the White Line of Mississippi, and the Rifle Clubs of South Carolina. White Southerners expected to do by extralegal or blatantly illegal means what had not been allowed by law: to exercise absolute control over blacks, drive them and their fellows from power, and establish "white supremacy." Radical Reconstruction was to be ended at all costs, and the tactics of terrorist groups were the first step of Southern white leaders toward achieving this goal.

The Camelias and the Klan were the most powerful of the secret orders. Armed with guns, swords, or other weapons, their members patrolled some parts of the South day and night. Scattered Union troops proved wholly ineffectual in coping with them, for the members were sworn to secrecy, disguised themselves and their deeds in many ways, and had the respect and support of the white community. They used intimidation, force, ostracism in business and society, bribery at the polls, arson, and even murder to accomplish their deeds. Depriving blacks of political equality became, to them, a holy crusade in which a noble end justified any means. Blacks were run out of communities if they disobeyed orders to desist from voting, and the more resolute and therefore insubordinate blacks were whipped, maimed, and hanged. In 1871 several black officials in South Carolina were given fifteen days to resign, and they were warned that if they failed to do so, "then retributive justice will as surely be used as night follows day." A similar situation prevailed in Kentucky where the major purpose of violence against blacks was to eliminate their participation in politics. In 1874 a committee of the Colored Convention assembled in Atlanta informed the state legislature that they could not point "to any locality in Georgia where we can in truth say that our lives and our liberties are perfectly secure."

Local efforts to suppress the outlaw organizations were on the whole unsuccessful. In 1868 Alabama, for example, passed a law imposing heavy fines and long jail sentences on anyone caught away from home wearing a mask or committing such acts as destroying property and molesting people, but this law was generally disregarded. Congress undertook to suppress the Klan and similar groups in a series of laws passed in 1870 and 1871. It was a punishable crime for any person to prevent another from voting by bribery, force, or intimidation, and the president was authorized to use land and naval forces to prevent such crimes. In 1871 a second law was passed to strengthen the first. After an extensive investigation, members of Congress were convinced that the Klan was still active, and in April 1871 a law designed to put an end to the movement was enacted. The president was authorized to suspend the writ of habeas corpus in order to suppress "armed combinations." Acts of conspiracy were declared tantamount to rebellion and were to be punished accordingly. As a result, hundreds of arrests were made, and many were found guilty of conspiracy. In South Carolina alone, nearly 100 were sentenced and fined in one year.

The struggle between organized Southern whites on the one hand and the Union League, Freedmen's Bureau, federal troops, and blacks on the other was essentially a struggle for political control of the South. From the Northern point of view it was a question of whether the gains of the war were to be nullified by the rebels who had brought the nation to the brink of disaster in 1861. From the Southern point of view it was a question of home rule—a right that they would defend to the end—and of who should rule at home, which they felt was largely academic since blacks were not qualified. As surely as the struggle between 1861 and 1865 was civil war, so was the conflict from 1865 to 1877, with as much bitterness and hatred but less bloodshed. The peace was being lost because of the vigorous efforts of both parties and sections to recruit their strength from the ruins of war. Peace could not prevail in such a warlike environment.

■ The Overthrow of Reconstruction

Reconstruction did not end abruptly as the result of congressional or presidential action. Rather it came to a gradual end as restraints were relaxed and stringent legislation repealed. Just as Reconstruction had begun long before the war was over, so it drew to a close long before the final withdrawal of troops from Southern soil. As early as 1865 many white Southerners had resumed their places at home as respected citizens of their communities, and they entered affairs on taking the oath of allegiance. Even during Radical Reconstruction they continued to return to the fold and to aid in restoring home rule. In 1869 the ex-Confederates of Tennessee were enfranchised. Within a few months large numbers of white Southerners in other states reclaimed their citizenship through individual acts of amnesty. In 1871 the "ironclad" oath, which Congress had imposed at the beginning of Radical Reconstruction to disqualify many ex-Confederates, was repealed. In the following year a general amnesty restored the franchise to all but about 600 ex-Confederate officials. It then became possible for the South to take up where it left off in 1861 and to govern itself.

The effect of pardoning white Southerners was seen early in the revival of the Democratic party. In 1870 the border states began to go Democratic; North Carolina and Virginia came under the control of Conservatives, who outnumbered the Republican combination of blacks, scalawags, and carpet-baggers. In the following year Georgia Democrats returned to power. In other states controlled by Republicans, Democrats won partial control, especially in the so-called white counties. In 1874 and 1875 they resumed the rule of Texas, Arkansas, and Alabama. All that Republicans could claim in the South by 1876 were South Carolina, Florida, and Louisiana. The cause of the Democrats had gained so much momentum that the overthrow of Republicanism was regarded by many as a crusade.

It looked as though the Civil War would break out anew as the Democrats resorted to every possible device to overthrow the Radicals. In 1875 Mississippi was on the verge of war. The black militia maintained by Governor Adelbert Ames was especially offensive to the resurgent Democrats, and when the governor ordered 100 copies of *Infantry Tactics*, presumably for the blacks, the whites thought it time for a "protective" white militia to step forward. Both sides imported arms, paraded, and actually skirmished. Although Ames promised to disband the black militia, disorder and killings continued until the election, when the Democrats carried the state by more than 30,000. Within two months the Republican party was dissolved. In

John R. Lynch Foresees End of Republican Rule—1874

I was well aware of the fact . . . that it was the result of the state and congressional elections at the North in 1874 that had convinced the Southern Democrats that Republican ascendancy in the national government would soon be a thing of the past—that the Democrats would be successful in the presidential and congressional elections of 1876 and that that party would no doubt remain in power for at least a quarter of a century. It was this, and not the unsuccessful effort to pass a Federal Elections Bill that produced the marked change that was noticeable on every hand. Every indication seemed to point to a confirmation of the impression that Democratic national success was practically an assured fact.

There had been a disastrous financial panic in 1873 which was no doubt largely responsible for the political upheaval in 1874, but that was lost sight of in accounting for that result. In fact, they made no effort to explain it or account for it except in their own way. The Democrats had carried the country, the reasons for which they construed to suit themselves. The construction they placed upon it was that it was a national condemnation and repudiation of the congressional plan of reconstruction and they intended to govern themselves accordingly.

John Roy Lynch, *Reminiscences of an Active Life* (Chicago, 1970), pp. 164–165.

Louisiana, the Conservatives organized "White Leagues" and apparently planned to overthrow the Radical government by violence as early as 1874. The Radicals tried to seize the arms of the White Leagues, an attempt that resulted in a riot in New Orleans, killing 40 and wounding more than a 100 people. Intermittent warfare continued through the election of 1876, and there was no peace until President Hayes withdrew the federal troops the following year. In South Carolina, the "Red Shirts" dominated campaign meetings and openly carried arms as a measure of "protection" against Radical "tyranny." Workingmen's Democratic Associations were organized, and whites were urged to employ only Democrats. Many sections of the state were in constant turmoil, particularly Edgefield County, where Ben Tillman was rapidly becoming a public figure.

The town of Hamburg, South Carolina, was the scene of one of the bloodiest race clashes. When the black militia paraded on July 4, 1876, several blacks were arrested on a charge of blocking traffic. And when their trial was postponed, a large number of armed white men, estimated at several hundred, came into town to see that justice was meted out to the black offenders. An ex-Confederate general ordered the blacks to apologize and to surrender their arms, which they refused to do; heavier arms and more

munitions were then imported by the whites. Gunfire followed. The blacks tried to escape, but too late, and several were killed in the attempt, besides five who were killed after being captured. It was not until Wade Hampton succeeded Daniel H. Chamberlain as governor in 1877 that South Carolina had even a semblance of peace.

The overthrow of the Radicals was accomplished not only by Southerners returning to political action and restoring Conservative governments but also by other circumstances favorable to white Southerners. Intimidation of blacks was effective. Even where there were no riots, whites kept blacks from the polls by terrorism and thus ensured Democratic victory. After the official dissolution of the Ku Klux Klan in 1869, other methods of intimidation were employed to render blacks politically inconsequential. Indeed, intimidation was most effective after 1870, although the Ku Klux Klan disclaimed all responsibility because of its increasing violence. The crops of blacks were destroyed, their barns and houses burned, and they were whipped and lynched for voting Republican. Organized whites became bolder as they patrolled polling places to guarantee "fair, peaceful, and Democratic" elections. Blacks more and more remained at home, and political power changed from Republican to Democratic hands.

Disclosures of corruption in Republican governments served to hasten the overthrow of Radical Reconstruction. The case for Democrats was strengthened considerably as they pointed to misgovernment through bribery, embezzlement, misappropriation of funds, and other corrupt practices. The federal government was unable to rush to the defense of Southern Republican governments because it was having difficulty in purging itself of corruption. It did not matter that white Southerners had also been corrupt before the war or that the provisional governments under Johnson were extravagant and corrupt. The Democrats were not in power in 1874 and consequently had all the advantages that the "outs" usually enjoy in such cases. Corruption discredited Radical Reconstruction, and with the loss of conscientious but disillusioned supporters, complete white home rule could be restored in the South.

The North had grown weary of the crusade for blacks. Perhaps Stevens, Sumner, Butler, and old antislavery leaders could have gone on with it, but younger people, with less zeal for blacks, took their places. They were loyal party men, practical politicians who cared more about industrial interests in the North and South than Radical governments in the South. The assumption of Republican leadership by men like Rutherford B. Hayes, James G. Blaine, Roscoe Conkling, and John A. Logan was a signal for the party to turn to more profitable and practical pursuits.

Not even the Supreme Court postponed the overthrow of Radical Reconstruction. As a matter of fact, its decisions had the effect of hastening the end. In 1875, several indictments under the Enforcement Act of 1870 charged defendants with preventing blacks from exercising their right to vote in elections. In *United States v. Reese* the Court declared that the Fifteenth

Amendment did not confer the right of suffrage upon anyone. "It prevents the States or the United States . . . from giving preference . . . to one citizen of the United States over another on account of race, color, or previous condition of servitude," the Court declared. In *United States v. Cruikshank* the Court held that the Enforcement Act of 1870 covered more offenses than were punishable under the terms of the Fifteenth Amendment and was, therefore, unconstitutional. Neither blacks nor Republicans could expect much support from a court that brushed aside the very laws with which they hoped to implement the franchise amendment. As far as the Court was concerned, the South was free to settle its problems as best it could.

The campaign of 1876 was the great test for both parties. The Democrats were committed to a program to end Reconstruction in the South; the Republicans had not openly promised to do so, but there was at least one wing of the party that was willing to withdraw troops and leave the South to its own devices. In the three states that had not been "redeemed," South Carolina, Louisiana, and Florida, the election campaign approached civil war. The result was, in the case of the first two, a hotly disputed election with both sides claiming victory and establishing dual governments. The presidency of the United States hung on the decision regarding their disputed votes. To break the impasse, the Republicans promised not only to withdraw troops but also to assist the South in its long-cherished ambition to obtain federal subsidies for internal improvements and better representation in affairs in Washington. Thus when Hayes became president, the South was soon assuaged in its grief by his prompt withdrawal of troops. At last the South could rule itself without Northern interference or black influence.

With troops out of the South and in a spirit of great conciliation, Congress removed other restrictions. In 1878 the use of armed forces in elections was forbidden. In 1894 appropriations for special federal marshals and supervisors of elections were cut off. In 1898 the last disabilities laid on disloyal and rebellious Southerners were removed in a final amnesty. Before the dawn of a new century there was complete recognition in law of what the South had itself accomplished in fact even before the election of 1876.

■ The Movement for Disfranchisement

After the Democrats returned to power in the South, they confronted the problem of finding ways either to nullify the political strength of blacks or to disfranchise them altogether. Complete disfranchisement by state legislation was viewed with some misgivings as long as the Fourteenth and Fifteenth Amendments remained a part of the fundamental law. Until it was feasible, the Democrats contented themselves with other methods—some extralegal, others incorporated in state codes—of preventing black participation in politics. Intimidation continued on an extensive scale. Earlier it had been justified in order to wrest political control from unworthy Republicans, both white and black, but once control was secured, it appeared irresponsible to the more sensitive white Southerners to depend upon night riders and Red Shirts to maintain them in power. For many white Southerners, however, violence was still the surest means of keeping blacks politically impotent, and in countless communities they were not allowed, under penalties of severe reprisals, to show their faces in town on election day.

Other devices, hardly more legal than violence and intimidation, had a more respectable appearance. Polling places were frequently set up far from black communities, and the more diligent blacks failed to reach them upon finding roads blocked and ferries conveniently out of repair at election time. Polling places were sometimes changed without notifying black voters; or, if they were notified, election officials thought nothing of making a last-minute decision not to change the place after all. Election laws were so imperfect that in many communities uniform ballots were not required, and officials winked at Democrats who made up several extra ballots to cast with the one given them. The practice of stuffing ballot boxes was widespread. Criminal manipulation of the counting gave point to the assertion of an enthusiastic Democrat that "the white and black Republicans may outvote us, but we can outcount them."

For what black votes were cast and counted, the white factions vied with each other. Dances and parties, with plenty of barbecue and whiskey, were held for black voters on election eve as a reminder that they should vote for their benefactors. Some planters brought their black workers to the polls and "voted them like a senseless herd of cattle." At times black candidates were nominated by whites in order to divide the vote of the race, while the whites all voted for one of their own race. A few candidates sought black votes by advocating measures favorable to them. In 1882, when he was running for the Georgia legislature, Tom Watson won many black votes by demanding free black schools and condemning the convict lease system, which was especially burdensome to blacks.

Where possible the legislatures, now controlled by zealous white-supremacy Democrats, helped to disfranchise blacks. Areas with a heavy concentration of blacks were divided by a system of gerrymandering that rendered the black vote ineffective. Poll tax requirements, elaborate and confusing election schemes, complicated balloting processes, and highly centralized election codes were all statutory techniques by which blacks were disfranchised. Some states went the limit in establishing "legal" barriers to black suffrage. Virginia, for example, reapportioned, or gerrymandered, its voting districts five times within seventeen years in order to nullify black ballots. Petty larceny, of which countless blacks were convicted, was added to the long list of suffrage disqualifications, and the poll tax was made a prerequisite for voting. The elaborate election code of 1894 required that registration and poll tax certificates be shown at the polls, that the names of candidates be printed on the ballot not by party but by office (an extremely confusing arrangement for semiliterate and illiterate voters), and that if others were waiting to vote, an elector must not remain in a booth more than two and a half minutes. Such requirements virtually disfranchised Virginia's illiterate voters, whether white or black.

South Carolina was most adroit in making voting difficult. The law of 1882 required that special ballots and boxes be placed at every polling place for each office on the ballot and that voters put their ballots in the correct boxes. No one was allowed to speak to a voter, and if he failed to find the correct box his vote was thrown out. South Carolina and Virginia were not alone in devising ingenious schemes to render the black vote ineffective. All the Southern states used some device or other. The result appeared so satisfactory on the whole that by 1889 Henry W. Grady could say, "The Negro as a political force has dropped out of serious consideration."

Strangely enough, however, the elimination of blacks from the political picture created circumstances that brought them back into the picture. By the 1880s the menace of black Republicanism had disappeared, and with it the great cohesive force among Southern whites. Almost immediately sharp class lines appeared, and irregularity in party voting cropped out. Now that white Southern farmers did not fear "Negro rule," they were more concerned with their own plight and held the dominant white groups responsible for their impending ruin. The coalition of classes that had united only to oppose another race began to disintegrate, as the poor whites came to distrust the Bourbons for substantial economic and political reasons.

An agricultural depression, caused largely by the overexpansion and increased production of cotton, settled down on the South after 1870. The panic of 1873 was especially disastrous because thousands of small farmers lost their land. In their distress they turned upon the money powers that foreclosed their mortgages, the railroads that charged excessive freight rates but received subsidies from state and federal taxes, the corporations that sought higher tariffs and charged higher prices for farm machinery, and the government that steadily raised taxes. In the South, moreover, a significant change had taken place in the leadership of the Democratic party. It no longer followed solely the plantation aristocrats, with whom the small farmers felt that they had something in common; industrialists and merchants, whom the small farmers disliked intensely, had come forward and were assuming important roles in party politics. In some states they were the dominant figures. The radical farmers, who wanted regulation of railroads, state aid for agriculture, and higher taxes on corporations, did not take to these new leaders and consequently wavered in their party regularity. The threat of a black balance of power did not frighten hungry white farmers, whose unconcern about race alarmed loyal Democrats. Small wonder that Henry W. Grady deplored the defections he saw everywhere among whites.

Radical agrarian organizations had flourished all over the United States after the Civil War. The National Grange, or Patrons of Husbandry, was attracting thousands of farmers by 1870, but it was kept within bounds in the South during Reconstruction because of the dangers of "Negro-Radical" rule. Prostrated by depression, however, Southern farmers organized and adopted a radical program. By 1889 the Southern Farmers' Alliance had branches in every Southern state. Although they did not admit black members, they believed that blacks should at least be lined up in a parallel organization. In 1886, therefore, the Colored Farmers' National Alliance and Cooperative Union came into existence. It grew rapidly and by 1891 claimed more than a million members in twelve state organizations. There were local chapters wherever black farmers were sufficiently numerous. After a national organization was perfected in 1888, there was for a time close cooperation between the white and black groups. But when the Colored Farmers' Alliance proposed to call a general strike of black cotton pickers, Leonidas L. Polk, president of the National Farmers' Alliance, opposed it with the argument that blacks were attempting to better their condition at the expense of whites. He insisted that farmers should leave their cotton in the field rather than pay 50 cents per 100 pounds to have it picked.

As the program of radical agrarianism evolved during the last two decades of the century, however, black and white farmers in the South drifted closer together and white solidarity became more difficult to maintain. Radical leaders like Tom Watson of Georgia told poor whites and blacks that they were being deliberately kept apart and fleeced. He called on them to stand together and work for the common good. Along with other leaders, he was at the time opposed to black disfranchisement and looked forward to a coalition of black and white farmers to drive the Bourbons from power. Then it would be possible to adopt progressive laws especially beneficial to the poor man. C. Vann Woodward says that under the tutelage of radical agrarian leaders the white masses of the South were learning to regard blacks as political allies bound to them by economic ties and a common destiny. "Never before or since have the two races in the South come so close together as they did during the Populist struggles."

The Populist, or People's, party was the political agency of these resurgent farmers. In 1892 the Populists sought to win the black vote in most of the Southern states and in many instances resorted to desperate means to secure the franchise for blacks in communities where by custom and practice they had been barred from voting for more than a decade. The Democrats, alarmed to desperation, made overtures to the Populists, but to no avail. They then turned to the blacks. In some communities blacks were forced to vote for Democrats by the very people who had dared them to attempt such an exercise of the "white man's prerogative" only a few years before. Blacks were hauled to towns in wagons and made to vote repeatedly. In Augusta, Georgia, they were even imported from South Carolina to vote for Democrats.

Many blacks, however, stood by the Populists, who advocated political if not social equality. One of the most zealous advocates of Tom Watson in Georgia was a young Negro preacher, H. S. Doyle, who made sixty-three speeches for Watson in the face of numerous threats. Democrats resorted to violence. A black Populist in Dalton, Georgia, was murdered in his home, and it is estimated that fifteen were killed in Georgia during the state elections of 1892. Riots also broke out in Virginia and North Carolina. If black rule meant chaos and disorder to the Democrats, the mere threat of it was enough for them to resort to violence themselves.

In some states there was a successful fusion between the newly organized Populists and the remnants of old Republican organizations. In 1894 such a combination seized control of the North Carolina legislature. The Democratic election machinery was immediately dismantled, and voting was made easier so that more blacks could vote and make their influence felt once more. Black officeholding soon became common in the eastern black belt of the state. The action of the fusion legislature of 1895 led to the election of 300 black magistrates. Many counties had black deputy sheriffs. Wilmington had 14 black police officers, and New Bern had both black policemen and aldermen. One prominent black, James H. Young, was made chief fertilizer inspector and a director of the state asylum for the blind; another, John C. Dancy, was appointed collector for the port of Wilmington.

White Conservatives who witnessed the political resurgence of blacks in North Carolina, Georgia, and other Southern states deeply resented the blacks' exercise of power when they were unable to control them. As blacks returned to prominence, either as electors or as an election issue, sentiment against their participation in politics grew. The Democrats, failing to control the black vote, moaned dismally about the return of black Republicanism. Even when they controlled them, they said that they made for corruption in politics. Although the Populists could on occasion have had the black vote, apparently they preferred not to have it because of the dangers involved. The election laws, as they stood, might actually be turned against poor, ignorant whites if the Democrats became vindictive and sought to disfranchise the Populists as well as their black allies. It was much better, therefore, to have clear-cut constitutional disfranchisement of blacks and to leave white groups to fight elections out among themselves. Where the Populists were unable to control the black vote, as in Georgia in 1894, they believed that the Democrats had never completely disfranchised blacks because their votes were needed if the Democrats were to stay in power. This belief led the defeated and disappointed Tom Watson to support a constitutional amendment excluding blacks from the franchise—a complete reversal of his position in denouncing South Carolina for adopting such an amendment in 1895.

With the collapse of the agrarian revolt in 1896, the movement for complete disfranchisement of blacks helped to reunite the white South. The poor, ignorant white farmers reverted to their old habits of thinking and acting, comforted in their poverty by Conservative assurances that "Negro rule" must be avoided at any cost. They might look back to the time in the 1890s when they were on the verge of joining their darker brothers and sisters to fight for a common cause. The poor whites could say with one of their leaders that the "Negro question" was an everlasting, overshadowing problem that served to hamper the progress of poor whites and prevent them from becoming realistic in social, economic, and political matters.

■ The Triumph of White Supremacy

When it became evident that white factions would compete with one another for the black vote and thus frequently give blacks the balance of power, it was time for complete disfranchisement of blacks, the Fifteenth Amendment notwithstanding. On this, most Southern whites were agreed. They differed only over the method of disfranchising blacks. The view prevailed that none but people of property and intelligence were entitled to suffrage. As one writer put it, white Southerners believed that "no person should enjoy the suffrage unless he gives sufficient evidence of his permanent interest in and attachment to the community." And yet there were many who opposed such stringent disfranchisement because it would disqualify numerous whites. Not surprisingly, poor whites were especially apprehensive. Some of them had been disfranchised by earlier measures, and when competition grew keen between rival white groups, the Conservatives actually barred Radical whites from the polls and at the same time permitted their own black supporters to vote. More poor whites were bound to be disfranchised by any new measures. The sponsors of a stricter suffrage had to be certain that they did not contravene the Fifteenth Amendment. Despite the fact that the Supreme Court had refused to apply it in the Reese and Cruikshank cases, there was no guarantee that the Court would view so favorably any state action obviously designed to disfranchise a group because of its race.

These were the problems that had to be solved by state constitutional conventions when they undertook to write into their fundamental law a guarantee of white supremacy. It was in Mississippi, where a majority of the population was black, that the problem was first faced and solved. As early as 1886 sentiment was strong for constitutional revision; a convention met in 1890 for the primary purpose of disfranchising blacks. A suffrage amendment was written that imposed a poll tax of $2 and excluded voters convicted of bribery, burglary, theft, arson, perjury, murder, or bigamy. It also barred all who could not read any section of the state constitution, or understand it when read, or give a reasonable interpretation of it. Isaiah T. Montgomery, the only black delegate to the convention, said that the poll tax and education requirements would disfranchise 123,000 blacks and only 11,000 whites. He, nevertheless, supported the proposed amendments. Before the convention, black delegates from forty counties had met and protested their impending disfranchisement to President Harrison. Doubtless they would have fought ratification, but the Conservatives would run no risk of having their handiwork rejected; after the convention approved the constitution, it was promulgated and declared to be in effect.

South Carolina followed Mississippi by disfranchising blacks in 1895. Ben

Tillman had worked toward this goal after he was elected governor in 1890, but he was unable to obtain sufficient support for a constitutional convention until 1894. Tillman was then in the United States Senate, but he returned to the convention to serve as chairman of the Committee on Rights of Suffrage and thus to be certain that blacks were effectively disfranchised. The clause, when adopted, called for two years' residence, a poll tax of $1, the ability to read and write any section of the constitution or to understand it when read aloud, or the owning of property worth $300, and the disqualification of convicts.

Black delegates bitterly denounced this sweeping disfranchisement. In answer to Tillman's charge that blacks had done nothing to demonstrate their capacity in government, Thomas E. Miller replied that they were largely responsible for "the laws relative to finance, the building of penal and charitable institutions, and, greatest of all, the establishment of the public school system." He declared that numerous reform laws "touching every department of state, county, municipal and town governments . . . stand as living witnesses [on the statute books of South Carolina] of the Negro's fitness to vote and legislate on the rights of mankind." James Wigg of Beaufort County said,

> The Negro . . . has a right to demand that in accordance with his wealth, his intelligence and his services to the state he be accorded an equal and exact share in its government. . . . You charge that the Negro is too ignorant to be trusted with the suffrage. I answer that you have not, nor dare you, make a purely educational test of the right to vote. You say that he is a figurehead, an encumbrance to the state, that he pays little or no taxes. I answer you, you have not, nor dare you make a purely property test of the right to vote. . . . We submit our cause to the judgment of an enlightened public opinion and to the arbitrament of a Christian civilization.

Only two whites joined the six blacks in voting against the constitution of 1895.

The story was essentially the same in Louisiana in 1898 when a new device, the "grandfather clause," was written into the constitution. This called for an addition to the permanent registration list of the names of all male persons whose fathers and grandfathers were qualified to vote on January 1, 1867. At that time, of course, no blacks were qualified to vote in Louisiana. If any blacks were to vote, they would have to comply with educational and property requirements. Booker Washington attempted to prick the conscience of Louisiana Democrats by writing them that he hoped the law would be so clear that "no one clothed with state authority will be tempted to perjure and degrade himself by putting one interpretation upon it for the white man and another for the black man." Blacks led by T. B. Stamps and D. W. Boatner appeared before the suffrage committee and admitted that a qualified suffrage might remedy demoralized conditions, but they pleaded for an honest test, honestly administered.

By 1898 the pattern for constitutional disfranchisement of blacks had been completely drawn. In subsequent years other states followed the lead of Mississippi, South Carolina, and Louisiana. By 1910 blacks had been effectively disfranchised by constitutional provisions in North Carolina, Alabama, Virginia, Georgia, and Oklahoma. The tension arising from campaigns for white suffrage sometimes flared up into violent race wars. In Wilmington, North Carolina, three white men were wounded and eleven blacks killed and twenty-five wounded in a riot in 1898. In Atlanta, there were four days of rioting after an election in 1906 in which disfranchisement was the main issue. Robbery, murder, and brutality were not uncommon during this period.

For the cause of white supremacy the effect was most salutary. In 1896 there were 130,344 blacks registered in Louisiana, constituting a majority in twenty-six parishes. In 1900, two years after the adoption of the new constitution, only 5,320 blacks were on the registration books, and in no parish did they make up a majority of voters. Of 181,471 black males of voting age in Alabama in 1900, only 3,000 registered after the new constitutional provisions went into effect. On the floor of the Virginia convention Carter Glass had said that the delegates were elected "to discriminate to the very extremity of permissible action under the limitations of the Federal Constitution, with a view to the elimination of every Negro voter who can be gotten rid of, legally, without materially impairing the numerical strength of the white electorate." This was accomplished not only in Virginia, but in every state where whites resorted to such means.

The South universally hailed the disfranchisement of blacks as a constructive act of statesmanship. African Americans were viewed as aliens whose ignorance, poverty, and racial inferiority were incompatible with logical and orderly processes of government. Southern whites said that blacks had done nothing to warrant suffrage. But as blacks made progress in many walks of life, it became increasingly difficult to allege that they were naturally shiftless and incapable of advancement. The framers of the new suffrage laws, however, were committed to the complete and permanent disfranchisement of blacks regardless of their progress. The Southern white view was summed up by J. K. Vardaman of Mississippi: "I am just as opposed to Booker Washington as a voter, with all his Anglo-Saxon re-enforcements, as I am to the coconut-headed, chocolate-colored, typical little coon, Andy Dotson, who blacks my shoes every morning. Neither is fit to perform the supreme function of citizenship." Southerners would have to depend on administration of the suffrage laws to keep blacks disfranchised, for there were many who would gradually meet even the most stringent constitutional qualifications. White supremacy would require an abiding belief in racial inequality, reinforced perhaps by hatred born of bitter memories.

Once blacks were disfranchised, everything else necessary for white supremacy could be done. With the emergence of white Democratic primaries, from which all blacks were excluded by the rules of the party, whites

TABLE 5
Population by Race (White and Black) in the Former
Confederate States of America As Shown in 1880

STATE	WHITE (In Thousands)	BLACK (In Thousands)
Alabama	662	600
Arkansas	592	211
Florida	143	127
Georgia	817	725
Louisiana	455	484
Mississippi	479	650
North Carolina	867	531
South Carolina	391	604
Tennessee	1,139	403
Texas	1,197	393
Virginia	881	632

Source: U.S. Bureau of the Census, *Historical Statistics of the United States, Colonial Times to 1970, Bicentennial Edition* [Part 2]. Washington, D.C., 1975, pp. 24–37.

planned their strategy in caucuses, and the party itself became the government in the South. Whites solemnly resolved to keep the races completely separate, for there could be no normal relationships between them. Laws for racial segregation had made a brief appearance during Reconstruction, only to disappear by 1868. When the Conservatives resumed power, they revived the segregation of the races. Beginning in Tennessee in 1870, white Southerners enacted laws against intermarriage of the races in every Southern state. Five years later, Tennessee adopted the first "Jim Crow" law, and the rest of the South rapidly fell in line. Blacks and whites were separated on trains, in depots, and on wharves. After the Supreme Court in 1883 outlawed the Civil Rights Acts of 1875, blacks were banned from white hotels, barber shops, restaurants, and theaters. By 1885 most Southern states had laws requiring separate schools. With the adoption of new constitutions the states firmly established the color line by the most stringent segregation of the races, and in 1896 the Supreme Court upheld segregation in its "separate but equal" doctrine set forth in *Plessy v. Ferguson*.

It was a dear price that the whites of the South paid for this color line. Since all other issues were subordinated to the issue of "the Negro," it became impossible to have free and open discussion of problems affecting all the people. There could be no two-party system, for the temptation to call upon blacks to decide between opposing factions would be too great. Interest in politics waned to a point where only professionals, who skillfully deflected the interest from issues to races, were concerned with public life. The expense of maintaining a double system of schools and of other public institutions was high, but not too high for advocates of white supremacy, who kept the races apart in order to maintain things as they were.

Peace had not yet come to the South. The new century opened tragically with 214 lynchings in the first two years. Clashes between the races occurred almost daily, and the atmosphere of tension in which people of both races lived was conducive to little more than a struggle for mere survival, with a feeble groping in the direction of progress. The law, the courts, the schools, and almost every institution in the South favored whites. This was white supremacy.

CHAPTER 14

Philanthropy and Self-Help

■ Northern Philanthropy and African-American Education

The end of Reconstruction brought little improvement in the economic and social status of African Americans. Meanwhile, their political gains rapidly disappeared before the vigorous, all-out efforts of Southern whites to wipe them out altogether. They could be certain of an improved status only in the field of education, for many of the schools that had been founded in the days immediately following the war were still flourishing (see Chapter 12). Despite the opposition of many white Southerners to black schools, there seemed to be a greater willingness to tolerate the growing educational institutions than any of the other agencies that blacks established in order to improve themselves. The pursuit of education, therefore, came to be one of the great preoccupations of African Americans, and enlightenment was viewed by many as the greatest single opportunity to escape the increasing proscriptions and indignities that whites heaped upon blacks. Small wonder that black children were sent to school even when it was a great inconvenience to their parents. Black fathers and mothers made untold sacrifices to secure for their children the learning that they had been denied.

Coincident with the growth of African-American schools in the South was the emergence of a new stimulus for educational institutions in the form of philanthropy. As the Freedmen's Bureau withdrew, the only outside assistance that the impoverished black schools had was help from denominational boards. The American Missionary Association continued its work, administering the interesting experiment for the coeducation of the races at Berea College in Kentucky, as well as financing and operating academies and colleges throughout the South. The Freedmen's Aid Society of the Methodist Episcopal church had broadened its scope by 1878 to include not only secondary schools and colleges but also two medical colleges and three theological schools. Baptists were working effectively through their Home Mission Society, while Presbyterians, Episcopalians, and Catholics increased their activities. Each of the major black denominations maintained secondary schools and colleges, and blacks themselves seemed to be increasingly interested in their schools.

To many the church organizations appeared, undoubtedly incorrectly, to be interested merely in strengthening their denominations instead of improving the status of blacks. Consequently, the appearance of large educational foundations, established for the most part by the new group of wealthy Americans, stimulated a broadening of the concept of education for African Americans in the South. These newly rich Americans by no means confined their interests to blacks, for the period between 1860 and 1900 witnessed the founding of 260 institutions of higher learning, many of which were primarily white institutions. Vanderbilt (1873), Johns Hopkins (1876), Leland Stanford (1885), and the University of Chicago (1892), all financed by wealthy philanthropists, are cases in point. It was an age of philanthropy, and African-American education benefited substantially. Between the end of the Civil War and the beginning of World War I several large educational foundations were established which worked directly to advance Southern African-American education: the Peabody Education Fund, the John F. Slater Fund, the General Education Board, the Anna T. Jeanes Fund, the Julius Rosenwald Fund, and the Phelps-Stokes Fund.

George Peabody, who had amassed a fortune as a merchant and financier in England and America, not only founded the institute at Baltimore and the museums at Harvard and Yale that bear his name but also established an education fund in 1867 "for the promotion and encouragement of intellectual, moral, or industrial education among the young people of the more destitute portions of the Southern and Southwestern States." In two separate grants he gave almost $2.5 million to be administered by a board of trustees that was empowered to use the interest and 40 percent of the principal. The grants were to be used to promote common school education immediately and assist in the establishment of a permanent system of public education in the South. Between 1867 and 1914 the fund provided more than $3.5 million for the advancement of education in the South.

In 1882 John F. Slater, a textile industrialist from Norwich, Connecticut, founded the fund that bears his name. Stimulated by the success of the Peabody Education Fund, Slater gave $1 million "for uplifting the lately emancipated population of the Southern states and their posterity, by conferring on them the blessings of Christian education." The board of trustees, headed by former President Rutherford B. Hayes, undertook immediately to assist twelve schools that were training African-American teachers. Between 1882 and 1911 the fund assisted both private and church schools in their teacher-training programs and made donations to public schools where the need and the work justified it. In 1911 the fund began its support of country training schools, and within a decade more than 100 such institutions had been assisted. The program of expenditures for the Peabody and Slater funds was administered largely by J. L. M. Curry, who was also the adviser to the Southern Education Board, made up of most of the influential Northern philanthropists.

In 1902 John D. Rockefeller, who had been giving largely to Baptist schools and who had financed the establishment of the University of Chicago, pledged $1 million to an agency created to promote education without distinction of race, sex, or creed. In the following year the General Education Board was incorporated and set about to support various programs for the diffusion of knowledge over a wide range. Among its major objectives were the general improvement of higher education in the United States, the support of education in the South, and the assistance of private and public institutions for the education of African Americans. Between 1902 and 1909 Rockefeller gave $53 million to the board and empowered its trustees to dispose of the principal whenever they saw fit. The board seemed especially interested in providing means for the preparation of teachers for African-American schools throughout the South and consequently gave generously to institutions that were undertaking the task.

In 1905 Anna T. Jeanes, the Quaker daughter of a wealthy Philadelphia merchant, gave $200,000 to the General Education Board to help improve black rural schools in the South. The money was set aside for that purpose and named the Anna T. Jeanes Fund for the Assistance of Negro Rural Schools in the South. Two years later Miss Jeanes gave $1 million for the enlargement of the program. Under the guidance of James H. Dillard, the fund sought the appointment of teachers to do industrial work in rural schools and special teachers to do extension work. County agents, whose function was to improve rural homes and schools and create public sentiment for better African-American schools, were also appointed. The fund paid the salaries of these special teachers, and county officials gradually assumed part of the responsibility. The work of the fund attracted additional contributions from several other philanthropic agencies.

In 1910, in accordance with the will of Caroline Phelps-Stokes, a fund bearing her name was established. From the beginning, the fund manifested a special though not an exclusive interest in African-American education. It gave considerable attention to the improvement of existing institutions of proved experience and ensured stability and made specialized studies of educational institutions and problems, the results of which would help plan future educational programs.

As early as 1910 Julius Rosenwald became interested in the improvement of conditions among blacks. In the following year he visited Tuskegee Institute and accepted a place on its board of trustees in 1912. His interest in rural African-American schools and his active assistance dated from this time. Beginning as a small donor of amounts of $5,000, he soon became a major contributor to the improvement of educational facilities for Southern blacks (see Chapter 20).

One of the major differences between church philanthropy and the large educational foundations—aside from the much larger amounts of money available for the direct funding of education—was one of motive. While church philanthropy either served some recognized social need or supported agencies for the promotion of its own interests, the educational foundations usually were interested in stimulating the public to recognize certain existent needs as yet unfelt by society. These new agencies hoped to establish the principle of self-help for the individual as well as for the state. Perhaps the interests of Northern businesspeople in the South were correlated with their efforts to improve Southern citizenry, both black and white. In 1882 Dexter Hawkins, a New York lawyer, argued that the development of education in the South would enable that section to bear a larger proportion of national taxes. In 1888 the Reverend A. D. Mayo asserted that Northern capital could be attracted and Southern resources properly developed only if the working masses were educated in skill and dependability. As Northern industrialists moved into the South and invested heavily in railroads, textile mills, and steel mills, they became increasingly aware of the need for a trained working force to operate the machines and perform the other tasks required in an industrialized economy. Thus, they were at least interested in the improvement of the common schools, and some even contributed to the improvement of higher education. Critics have accused Northern philanthropists of seeking the education of blacks as well as whites in order to play one off against the other in the competition for jobs. Regardless of the validity of this charge, the fact remains that both blacks and whites benefited substantially from their generosity.

There was the motive, moreover, that stemmed from the successful businessperson's sense of noblesse oblige. The contributions of large foundations as well as those of individuals like Robert C. Ogden, H. H. Rogers, Collis P. Huntington, Andrew Carnegie, and William Baldwin were motivated, at least in part, by their feeling that they should assume responsibility for bestowing what the economic system failed to provide directly for social need. Thus, the industrialists of the United States had a feeling of duty toward those who were not reaping benefits from the economic order.

The philanthropists contributed substantially toward bringing about a new day for education in the South. By conditional grants in aid to those instititutions that had proved their worth, philanthropists did much to stimulate self-help on the part of the individual, the institution, and the states of the South. Public education was greatly improved as the boards supplemented teachers' salaries, bought equipment, and built schools. There was general approval of Northern philanthropy when the white citizens of the South discovered that their benefactors showed little or no interest in establishing racial equality or upsetting white supremacy.

Although philanthropists effected a greater support of public education in the South, they did little to encourage the equitable distribution of public funds for the education of all Southern children. Perhaps the whites of the South took the position that if the philanthropists were going to educate blacks, the taxpayers' money could be used to educate whites. Too, they were strongly of the opinion that since blacks paid little in the way of taxes, they were not entitled to receive very much support for their educational institutions. Thus, in 1898 Florida's per capita cost of education was $5.92 for whites and $2.27 for blacks. Two years later the citizens of Adams County, Mississippi, were spending $22.25 for the education of each white child and only $2 for the education of each black child. African Americans, of course, denied that they were not supporting their own institutions through taxation. At the Sixth Atlanta Conference for the Study of Negro Problems in 1901 it was reported that between 1870 and 1899 blacks paid a total of $25 million in direct school taxes, while the indirect taxes that they paid amounted to more than $45 million. It was also reported that they had paid more than $15 million in tuition and fees to private institutions. With a strong assertion that they had done much to help themselves in the generation following Reconstruction, the report concluded, "It is a conservative statement to say ... that American Negroes have in a generation paid directly forty millions of dollars in hard earned cash for educating their children."

The schools had also done much to sustain themselves. The Jubilee Singers of Fisk University set an example for other institutions. The treasurer of the college, George L. White, conceived the idea that through the singing of a group of young African Americans, the hearts and hence the pockets of the Northern citizens could be reached. Therefore, with money borrowed from the teachers and the citizens of Nashville, White took a group of students in 1875 to Oberlin, Ohio, where the National Council of Congregational Churches was meeting. The council was captivated by the way in which the young blacks sang the spirituals and work songs of their people, and the fame of the group spread rapidly. In the East they sang in many halls under the sponsorship of Henry Ward Beecher of Brooklyn. Numerous engagements followed, and the money flowed in. Later they went to England, Germany, and other European countries and appeared before several royal audiences. Within seven years they had raised $150,000, a part of which was used in the construction of Jubilee Hall. Student quartets, speakers, and other groups went out from other schools. In some communities money was raised at fairs and demonstrations. In many ways, the schools were learning that they could contribute to their own continuation and growth through the resources of their students.

The results of the efforts to ensure the education of African Americans were gratifying. In 1900 there were 28,560 black teachers. At the same time

JUBILEE HALL, FISK UNIVERSITY. Funds for construction of this building were raised primarily by students who traveled through the North and Europe. It is an example of self-help in the period following emancipation. *(Courtesy Alumni Office, Fisk University.)*

there were more than 1.5 million black children in school. Thirty-four institutions for African Americans were giving collegiate training, and a larger number of African Americans were entering the universities and colleges of the North. Virginia, Arkansas, Georgia, and Delaware each had a state college for blacks; other institutions, begun by private groups or individuals, were later to be taken over by the states. By 1900 more than 2,000 African Americans had graduated from institutions of higher learning, while more than 700 were in college at that time. The great educational awakening that pervaded the United States in the closing years of the nineteenth century and the opening years of the twentieth century was certainly as clearly manifested among blacks as it was among other ethnic groups in the population.

For African Americans, however, the problem of education was complicated in a way that it was not for any other group. There was the feeling on the part of most white people that the success or failure of African Americans to adjust depended on the type of education to which they were exposed. There were those who felt that the amount of education that blacks could or should receive was limited, perhaps to the rudiments. Others were of the opinion that African Americans should not be regarded as a group for which a special amount or kind of education should be provided. Still others contended that African Americans, at their present stage of development, could best serve themselves and their country with a type of education that could most rapidly help them find an indispensable place in the American social order. Into the controversy stepped Booker T. Washington, who for more than thirty years so completely dominated the scene as to stamp upon the period his own name and personality.

■ The Age of Booker T. Washington

Writing in 1903 W. E. B. Du Bois said, "Easily the most striking thing in the history of the American Negro since 1876 is the ascendancy of Mr. Booker T. Washington." The ascendancy of this man is one of the most dramatic and significant episodes in the history of American education and of race relations. In 1872 Washington, a lad about sixteen years old, arrived at Hampton Institute, a school molded from the ideas of practical education of its founder, Samuel Chapman Armstrong. Armstrong taught his students that labor was a "spiritual force, that physical work not only increased wage-earning capacity but promoted fidelity, accuracy, honesty, persistence, and intelligence." He emphasized the value of acquiring land and homes, vocations and skills. Washington drank deeply of Armstrong's teachings and in time became the most eloquent exponent of Armstrong's ideals. By the time that Washington graduated he was convinced that in order for African Americans to achieve success they must do some useful service that the world wanted. It was his great preoccupation from that point on to find the ways in which his people could be most useful.

When Washington went to Tuskegee in 1881, he found none of the equipment with which to develop an educational institution, and he found a white community hostile to the idea of a school for blacks. He, therefore, set about the twofold task of securing the necessary resources with which to conduct a school and of conciliating the whites. It was an ideal situation in which to relate education to life. Students cooperated in doing all the necessary work at Tuskegee, constructing the buildings, producing and cooking the food, and performing innumerable other tasks. The community was given assurances in many ways that the students were there to serve and not to antagonize. Washington believed that Southern whites had to be convinced that the education of blacks was in the true interest of the South. The students provided many of the services and much of the produce that the white community needed, and hostility to the new school began to diminish. Washington counseled his people to respect the law and to cooperate with white authorities in maintaining peace. In this way he won the good will of the ruling class.

As Washington saw the salutary effects that his program was having on the white South as well as on his black students, he became more and more convinced that this was the pattern for strengthening the position of African Americans throughout the area. He became the apostle of a form of industrial education that would not antagonize the white South and would at the same time carve out a place of service for blacks in their communities. Certainly a program of training African Americans to become farmers, mechanics, and domestic servants would be more acceptable to Mississippi's J. K. Vardaman than the program of classical education advocated by many Northern educators. Earlier Vardaman had said, "What the North is sending South is not money but dynamite; this education is ruining our Negroes. They're

FOUNDERS LIBRARY, HOWARD UNIVERSITY. Built in 1937 at a cost of approximately $1 million, this structure might be regarded as a symbol of the ideal of twentieth-century American education. *(Scurlock Studios.)*

demanding equality." Washington was not demanding that, and it pleased Southern whites to hear him say at the Atlanta Exposition in 1895, "In all things that are purely social we can be as separate as the five fingers, yet one as the hand in all things essential to mutual progress." To his own people he uttered this admonition: "To those of my race who depend upon bettering their condition in a foreign land or who underestimate the importance of cultivating friendly relations with the Southern white man . . . I would say 'Cast down your bucket where you are'—cast it down in making friends in every manly way of the people of all races by whom we are surrounded. Cast it down in agriculture, in mechanics, in commerce, in domestic service, and in the professions."

Washington never tired of urging blacks to develop habits and skills that would win places for them in their Southern communities. Intelligent management of farms, ownership of land, habits of thrift, patience, and perseverance, and the cultivation of high morals and good manners were encouraged. He said that African Americans must learn that all races have got on their feet largely by laying an economic foundation and, in general, by beginning in a proper cultivation and ownership of the soil. He was greatly distressed by the mass movement of blacks from the country to the city and did what he could to persuade them to return. He did not deprecate the study of such subjects as science, mathematics, and history, but he indicated on many occasions that he regarded them as impractical. He said that he believed that "for years to come the education of the people of my race should be so directed that the greatest proportion of the mental strength of the masses will be brought to bear upon the everyday practical things of life, upon something that is needed to be done, and something which they will be permitted to do in the community in which they reside."

The Washington doctrine of industrial education, or, more properly, vocational education, for the great mass of blacks was hailed by whites in the North and in the South. Some Northern whites, weary of racial and sectional conflicts, saw in it a formula for peace in the South with the establishment of a satisfactory economic and social equilibrium between the races. Others, skeptical of the capacity of African Americans to become completely assimilated in a highly complex civilization, viewed it as leading blacks to their "proper place" in American life. Still other Northerners, with an eye on markets and a cheap labor supply in the South, thought it would perhaps make possible the greater economic development of the South. For all these reasons, some historians of the period have described the educational foundations and the white South's support of Washington and his philosophy as promoting "education for the new slavery."

White Southerners liked Washington's relative disinterest in political and civil rights for blacks. They liked the way in which he placed confidence in the Southern whites regarding their good treatment of blacks who proved themselves to be useful, law-abiding citizens. They agreed with his advocacy of a type of education that they believed would consign African Americans to an inferior economic and social status in Southern life. Finally, they admired the tact and diplomacy with which he conciliated all groups, North and South, although they were not always pleased that he spoke for the white South as well as the black South. Only twice did he threaten his position among whites in the South. Speaking on one occasion in Chicago he lashed out at race prejudice and asserted that it was eating away the vitals of the South. On another occasion he visited the White House and had lunch with President Theodore Roosevelt, an incident that was regarded by most Southerners as a serious breach of racial etiquette (see Chapter 15). After fourteen years of intimate association with Washington, J. L. M. Curry, a leading white Southern educator, could say that he had never once known the principal of Tuskegee to say or to do an unwise thing. Curry surely did not know that Washington was quietly financing some of the earliest court cases against segregation. Indeed, as Louis R. Harlan has made clear, "by

Booker T. Washington on Racial Harmony and Black Progress—1884

Any movement for the elevation of the Southern Negro, in order to be successful, must have to a certain extent the cooperation of the Southern whites. They control government and own the property—whatever benefits the black man benefits the white man. . . .

Brains, property, and character for the Negro will settle the question of civil rights. The best course to pursue in regard to the civil rights bill in the South is to let it alone; let it alone and it will settle itself. . . . Let there be in a community a Negro who by virtue of his superior knowledge . . . can raise fifty bushels of corn to the acre while his white neighbor only raises thirty; and the white man will come to the black man to learn. . . .

Now, in regard to what I have said about the relations of the two races, there should be no unmanly cowering or stooping to satisfy unreasonable whims of the Southern white man, but it is charity and wisdom to keep in mind the two hundred years' schooling in prejudice against the Negro which the exslaveholders are called upon to conquer. . . . Just here the great mission of industrial education coupled with the mental comes in. It 'kills two birds with one stone,' viz: secures the cooperation of the whites, and does the best possible thing for the black man. . . . Educate the black man, mentally and industrially, and there will be no doubt of his prosperity; for a race who has lived at all, and paid, for the last twenty years, twenty-five and thirty per cent interest on the dollar advanced for food, with almost no education, can certainly take care of itself when educated mentally and industrially.

Booker T. Washington, "A Speech before the National Educational Association," Madison, Wisconsin, July 16, 1884, in Louis R. Harlan, *The Booker T. Washington Papers*, Volume 2 (Urbana, 1972), pp. 255–262.

private action [he] fought lynching, disfranchisement, peonage, educational discrimination, and segregation."

Because of their intense interest in the immediate goals of Washington, few whites saw that this leader looked forward to the complete acceptance and integration of blacks into American life. On one occasion he said, "I would set no limits to the attainments of the Negro in arts, in letters or statesmanship, but I believe the surest way to reach those ends is by laying the foundation in the little things of life that lie immediately about one's door. I plead for industrial education and development for the Negro not because I want to cramp him, but because I want to free him. I want to see him enter the all-powerful business and commercial world." He always advocated the entrance of African Americans into the professions and other fields, and, it will be recalled, he urged them to make friends with their white neighbors in every "manly" way. Washington believed that African Americans, starting with so little, would have to work up gradually before they could attain a position of power and respectability in the South. Whites, on the other hand, looking at Washington's program of expediency, frequently regarded it as the ultimate solution to the "Negro problem" and believed that the latter's place would be permanently fixed by the Washington formula.

As Washington's prestige grew to the point where he was regarded as not only the outstanding exponent of industrial education but also the spokesperson for millions of African Americans, opposition among his own people increased. Of course, some of it was envy, but a relatively small group of blacks took serious exception both to the point of view of the Washington philosophy and to the techniques he employed in implementing it. Foremost among the opponents was W. E. B. Du Bois, a young African American who was trained at Fisk, Harvard (where he received the degree of Doctor of Philosophy), and Berlin. Although born in Massachusetts, Du Bois was teaching at Atlanta University, and the series of studies he was making of the conditions of African Americans in the South had furnished him with considerable firsthand information concerning the group for which he spoke. In books, essays, and addresses Du Bois opposed what he viewed as the narrow educational program of Washington, which was too predominantly economic in its objectives. His *Souls of Black Folk* (1903) contained several searchingly critical essays on Washington. He accused Washington of preaching a "gospel of Work and Money to such an extent as apparently almost completely to overshadow the higher aims of life." In an essay entitled "The Talented Tenth" Du Bois said, "If we make money the object of man-training, we shall develop money-makers but not necessarily men; if we make technical skill the object of education, we may possess artisans but not, in nature, men. Men we shall have only as we make manhood the object of the work of the schools—intelligence, broad sympathy, knowledge of the world that was and is, and of the relation of men to it—this is the curriculum of that Higher Education which must underlie true life." He especially denounced the manner in which Washington deprecated institutions of higher learning, and he insisted that neither the black common schools nor Tuskegee could remain open one day were it not for the teachers trained in black colleges or trained by their graduates.

Du Bois did not approve of the manner in which Washington ignored or winked at the white South's virtual destruction of the political and civil status of African Americans. He believed that the extension of the olive branch to white Southerners had resulted in the disfranchisement of blacks and the legal creation of a distinct status of civil inferiority. Du Bois contended that it was not possible, under modern competitive methods, for black artisans, businesspeople, and property owners to defend their rights and exist without the suffrage. Furthermore, he maintained that the counsel of silent submission to civic inferiority would surely sap the strength of any race in the long run. He called Washington's Atlanta Exposition speech the "Atlanta Compromise," describing it as "the most notable thing in Mr. Washington's career" and conceding that it made him the most distinguished Southerner since Jefferson Davis. It also made him the leader of his people, not by their own choice, but by the manner in which he was acclaimed by whites in the North and in the South. He became "a compromiser between the South, the North, and the Negro" and was consulted whenever any matters arose affecting blacks anywhere in the United States. As the most eloquent spokesman for a growing number of blacks, Du Bois was alarmed by the ultimate effect of Washington's leadership.

While there was much to be said for the position that Washington took (and Du Bois admitted the importance of many of Washington's teachings), his doctrine contained some weaknesses that are perhaps more obvious today than they were then. He accepted uncritically the dominant philosophy of American business when he insisted that everyone had their future in their own hands, "that success came to him who was worthy of it, and that the greater the obstacles, the greater the victory over them." It was a doctrine of triumphant capitalism, which was strengthened by his contacts with Ogden, Huntington, and other wealthy American businesspeople. The Negro Business League, which Washington organized in 1900 to foster business and industry, was based on the philosophy that if one could make a better article and sell it cheaper, one could command the markets of the world, and that if one produced something someone else wanted, the purchaser would not ask who the seller is. Add to this a generous amount of tact, good manners, resolute will, and a tireless capacity for hard work, and success in business would be the reward. As Sterling Spero and Abram Harris have pointed out, this philosophy was an adaptation of the theories of free competition and political individualism that had been taught by the school of classical political economy and was becoming more fictitious than ever by 1900. The spread of "vertical and horizontal combinations capitalized in hundreds of millions was discrediting the idea that a man of small capital could raise himself to affluence and power through hard work and thrift." Washington showed little understanding of these realities as he developed a program for the economic salvation of African Americans.

The particular type of industrial education that Washington emphasized, with much attention given to the development of a class of artisans, was outmoded even at the time he enunciated it. He did not seem to grasp fully the effect of the Industrial Revolution upon the tasks that had been performed by the hands of workers for centuries. To be sure, brickmasons, carpenters, blacksmiths, and the like would still be needed, but their tasks were being reduced to a minimum in the industrial age; many of the occupations that Washington was urging African Americans to enter were disappearing almost altogether. As training grounds for industrial workers, the curriculums and the institutions urged by Washington were not at all

BOOKER T. WASHINGTON. This bust of the distinguished African American educator was done by Richmond Barthé, one of America's leading sculptors. It is in the New York University Hall of Fame, to which Washington was elected in 1945, thus becoming the first African American to be so honored. *(Courtesy The Hall of Fame for Great Americans at New York University.)*

satisfactory. Neither Washington nor the industrial schools for blacks took cognizance of the problems peculiar to the wage earner in modern industry. In speaking of organized labor, Washington went so far as to say that blacks did not like an "organization which seems to be founded on a sort of impersonal enmity to the man by whom he is employed." He therefore utterly failed to see the relation of the laboring class to the Industrial Revolution and counseled an approach to the labor problem that had the effect of perpetuating the master-slave tradition.

In counseling blacks to remain in rural areas, Washington failed to see not only that the advent of expensive farm machinery put the impoverished African-American farmer at a serious disadvantage but also that the industrial urban community was infinitely more attractive to blacks as well as whites. There were, on the surface at least, innumerable economic opportunities in the city. Furthermore, the city offered incomparable advantages for cultural and intellectual growth. If Washington wished for his people educational and economic opportunities that would facilitate their assimilation and acceptance, the urban centers seemed to be, by far, the oases in the desert of despair. Indeed, it would seem that nothing represented more vividly blacks' reflection of a typical American reaction than their inclination to move from the country to the city in the late nineteenth and early twentieth centuries.

Despite the fact that there were blacks who vigorously opposed Washington's leadership and that there were some valid exceptions to his program for the salvation of his people, he was unquestionably the central figure—the dominant personality—in the history of African Americans until his death in 1915. The vast majority of blacks acclaimed him as their leader, and few whites ventured into the matter of race relations without his counsel. During his lifetime lynchings decreased only slightly, blacks were effectively disfranchised, and black workers were systematically excluded from the major labor organizations, but Washington's influence, sometimes for better and sometimes for worse, was so great that there is considerable justification in calling the period the Age of Booker T. Washington.

■ Struggles in the Economic Sphere

While Northern philanthropists contributed increasingly to the education of African Americans, and while the controversy raged over the most practicable and effective type of education for them, the vast majority faced the difficult task of making a living and were becoming more and more convinced that they would have to work out their own salvation in terms of the means at their immediate disposal. Since more than 75 percent of the African Americans in the United States were still in the former Confederate states in 1880 and were primarily engaged in agricultural work, it appeared that most of them would be compelled to make some sort of economic adjustment on the farms. They were without capital with which to purchase land, and they continued to engage in the various forms of tenancy and sharecropping that had evolved during Reconstruction. Indeed, large numbers were mere farm laborers with no greater stake in agricultural production than their own labor, for which they were paid scant wages. In 1902 farm workers in South Carolina were receiving $10.79 per month, while those in New York were receiving $26.13. Some were paid by the week or month, while others were paid at the end of the season, a method designed to hold workers on the farm until the crop was harvested.

It was difficult for African Americans to purchase desirable farmland even if they had the capital. With the destruction of the institution of slavery, whites looked upon land as their only important capital investment, and they were reluctant to sell land to blacks, whom they did not want to enjoy the power that came from the ownership of land in the South. The number of black farm owners remained small in the entire period before World War I. In the South, where blacks constituted approximately 50 percent of the population in 1900, they owned 158,479 farms, while whites in the South owned 1,078,635 farms. Before 1890 almost nothing had been done to educate African Americans in the use of modern agricultural methods, and, as a result, productivity was low and there was general ignorance of the problems of marketing crops and purchasing supplies. Booker T. Washington sought to improve this situation in 1892 when he issued the first call for a conference of farmers at Tuskegee. In this and succeeding years African Americans from

WILLIAM EDWARD BURG-
HARDT Du BOIS. This photograph of the eminent editor,
author, and leader of his people
was made by Carl Van Vechten,
who was interested in African
American life and culture for
more than thirty years. Van
Vechten noted that the background of the photograph is a
"Hindu design, a variation, indeed, of the swastika. It is well
known in the Orient. The significance in this case is that Dr. Du
Bois is interested in colored peoples everywhere." *(Courtesy The
Moorland-Spingarn Research Center, Howard University.)*

the surrounding countryside listened to discussions on "the evils of the
mortgage system, the one-room cabin, buying on credit, the importance of
owning a home and of putting money in the bank, how to build school-
houses and prolong the school term, and to improve moral and religious
conditions." Small tracts and circulars containing some essentials of farm
improvement were distributed to the farmers, and from time to time the
institute mailed them others. After 1907, thanks to the contributions of
philanthropists and the cooperation of Southern boards of education, farm
demonstration agents helped to improve conditions.

Despite the efforts of African-American farmers to adjust to the rural
economy, the farm ceased to be attractive to many. The return of ex-Confederates to power, intermittent agricultural depressions, unfair and sometimes cruel treatment by landlords and merchants, and rumors of rich
opportunities in the cities and in other parts of the country stimulated an
exodus of blacks from the rural South that began as early as 1879. Thousands
of them left Mississippi, Louisiana, Alabama, and Georgia and went to the
North and West. There was a minor stampede to Kansas, with Henry Adams
of Louisiana and "Pap" Singleton of Tennessee assuming the leadership.
Adams claimed to have organized 98,000 African Americans to go west.

THE BLACK EXODUS—THE OLD STYLE AND THE NEW. In the exodus of 1879 thousands of Negroes left the farms and towns of the South in search of a better life. Their departure greatly contrasted with the manner in which blacks left the region in the period before 1865. *(From* Harper's Weekly, *May 1, 1880.)*

Perhaps he at least collected the names of that many who expressed a willingness to go. Singleton distributed a circular entitled "The Advantage of Living in a Free State" and actually caused several thousand to leave. Charles Banks and Isaiah Montgomery in Mississippi, Edward P. McCabe in Kansas and Oklahoma, Allen Allensworth in California, and Oklahomans David Turner, Thomas Haynes, and James E. Thompson were leaders in efforts to establish and promote economically viable and politically independent all-black towns and agricultural settlements as the solution to the black dilemma. Most of these ventures were abject failures.

Some blacks seriously considered the possibility of going to Africa and sought help from the American Colonization Society. Southern whites became visibly alarmed over the movement of blacks and the prospects of ever-increasing numbers leaving. Various methods were used to keep blacks on Southern plantations—the enforcement of vagrancy and labor contract laws, the enactment of legislation imposing penalties for enticing laborers away, and the establishment of systems of peonage by which blacks were hired out by the county in order to pay the fine for a crime or to pay a debt. More tactful whites sought to persuade blacks to remain by promising them good treatment and high wages.

African-American leaders were in wide disagreement among themselves over whether their people should leave the South. Frederick Douglass opposed the exodus on the grounds that the government should protect citizens wherever they lived and that emigration was no permanent remedy for their plight. He feared that blacks would become nomads and lose what strength a sedentary existence would give them in the South, where they were concentrated. Richard T. Greener, Harvard's first African-American graduate and a former professor at the University of South Carolina, insisted that blacks should migrate in order to put an end to the bad treatment they received at the hands of Southern whites. He declared that the exodus would not only carry blacks to better economic and educational opportunities but would also benefit those who remained in the South. Perhaps none of these arguments had any telling effect. Forces rather than words decided the fate of African Americans. Most of them had neither the resources nor the initiative to go to new areas. Those who did go were lured just as other rural Americans of the period. They simply could not resist the temptation to move into the industrial communities of the North and a few cities in the South and cast their lot with the new way of life.

In the last two decades of the nineteenth century the South began to feel the impact of the economic revolution that had already enveloped the North. The iron industry was growing in Tennessee and Alabama, cloth was being manufactured in the Carolinas, and the business of transporting manufactured goods to Northern and Southern consumers was becoming a major economic activity. The new opportunities were numerous, and blacks as well as whites attempted to take advantage of them. For the most part blacks in Southern towns experienced great difficulty in securing some of the benefits of the new economic growth. In 1891 only 196 industrial employers of the South were using 7,395 African Americans. Ten years later the number had increased substantially, and some were employed in cottonseed-oil mills, sawmills, and furniture factories, and in foundries, machine shops, boiler works, and the like. By 1910 African-American factory workers had increased to more than 350,000, generally holding the least attractive jobs. Southern urban blacks even found it difficult to render their customary personal services to city dwellers. Barbers met with foreign-born competition, while cooks and caterers were displaced by palatial hotels which frequently did not hire blacks. Everywhere there was sentiment against hiring blacks in jobs that had even the least semblance of respectability. Blacks living in cities in the South discovered that urban life could be almost as frustrating as rural life.

African Americans themselves had made some contribution toward the growing industrialization of America. Jan E. Matzeliger, who had been an apprenticed cobbler in Philadelphia and in Lynn, Massachusetts, invented the shoe lasting machine. It was purchased by the United Shoe Machinery Company of Boston and effectively reduced the cost of manufacturing shoes by more than 50 percent. In 1884 John P. Parker invented a "screw for tobacco presses." He established the Ripley Foundry and Machine Company and made presses for many businesses. Elijah McCoy patented fifty different inventions relating principally to automatic lubricators for machines. It was the claim for the genuineness of one of his products that led to the expression, "the real McCoy." Granville T. Woods, who began inventing in 1885, made significant contributions in the fields of electricity, steam boilers, and automatic air brakes. Several of his inventions were assigned to the General Electric Company, the Westinghouse Air Brake Company, and the American Bell Telephone Company.

The urban African-American laborer, both in the North and in the South, had to face the problem of obtaining membership in the labor unions that came more and more to dominate the industrial picture. Prejudice against the black worker and the refusal of numbers of whites to work with blacks served to exclude many from membership. Other factors, however, also contributed to blocking entrance of blacks into the industrial scene through organized labor. Most of them lacked the skills prerequisite to membership in many of the craft unions. There were those, moreover, who insisted that blacks were temperamentally unfit for skilled mechanical work. In 1893 the *Manufacturers Record* of Baltimore reported that in a study made of employers' reactions to black factory workers it was found that blacks were unfit for manufacturing. Although these points of view were not based on conclusive proof, they persuaded some manufacturers that hiring black workers was unsound.

Among the large post-Civil War labor organizations, only the Knights of Labor, which placed little emphasis on skills, showed any enthusiasm for securing African-American members. In 1885 the national convention proposed that an African-American organizer be appointed for each of the Southern states, and although the resolution was approved, no further action was taken on the matter. In the following year the secretary-treasurer rejoiced that African Americans were flocking to the Knights of Labor and manifesting a desire to be organized and educated. Some locals had black and white members, while others had separate organizations. Approximately 60,000 African Americans had become members of the Knights of Labor by 1886. This organization was losing ground, however, because of the infiltration of radical foreign elements and its alleged involvement in the Haymarket Square riots in Chicago in 1886.

Meanwhile, the American Federation of Labor (AFL), a confederation of autonomous craft unions, was growing in influence. At first the American Federation of Labor took a positive stand against discrimination against African Americans. In 1890 the convention declared that it looked "with disfavor upon trade unions having provisions which exclude from membership persons on account of race and color," a resolution that was readopted in 1893. The leaders, however, began to realize that this unequivocal stand

MADAM C J WALKER and daughter on a sight — seeing tour

WOMAN OF WEALTH AND INFLUENCE. Madam C. J. Walker and daughter on a sightseeing tour. *(Courtesy Walker Collection of A'Lelia Bundles.)*

on the race question was preventing the expansion of the organization, for some independent craft unions that would not accept African-American memberships refused to join.

In order to attract powerful organizations like the National Machinists Union, the American Federation of Labor allowed unions to enter if they did not openly exclude African Americans in their constitutions. The exclusion then was merely transferred from the constitution to the ritual, and members were pledged to present for membership only white workers. Many all-white labor unions joined the American Federation of Labor, and the membership grew rapidly. In order not to exclude African Americans altogether, the federation began to charter locals composed solely of African Americans, but this was seldom done if such a move was not acceptable to the white workers of the same community. In the effective exclusion of blacks from the strong labor organizations, either by constitution or by ritual, white unions made it impossible for them to participate to any considerable degree in the great industrial activity that was taking place. Some efforts were made to organize independent African-American unions, such as the National Association of Afro-American Steam and Gas Engineers and Skilled Workers of Pittsburgh, but none of them was able to make any headway against the monopoly that white labor unions had established in the various industries.

It was only natural that African Americans observing the success of various individuals during the age of heroic business enterprise, should enter the fields of business and industry. Frustrated in their efforts to participate in the development of the businesses of whites, they embarked on a program of "Negro business enterprise" in which they undertook to be their own producers and employers. African-American leaders, taking their cue from the almost hopeless plight of millions of blacks in the South, urged their followers to escape poverty and achieve economic independence by entering business and manufacturing themselves. Speaking before the Fourth Atlanta University Conference in 1898, John Hope, a professor at the university, said that the plight of African Americans was not due altogether to ignorance and incompetence but at least in part to competition between the races for employment in new fields. He therefore called upon blacks to escape the wage-earning class and become their own employers. The conference adopted resolutions declaring that "Negroes ought to enter into business life in increasing numbers" and that "the mass of Negroes must learn to patronize business enterprises conducted by their own race, even at some slight disadvantage. We must cooperate or we are lost." The conference also called for the dissemination of information concerning the need for African-American businesses and the organization of local, state, and national Negro Business Men's Leagues.

By 1900 Booker T. Washington had concluded that African-American business must be immediately stimulated and upgraded. He called a group of African-American businessmen together in Boston and organized the National Negro Business League. More than 400 delegates came from thirty-four states and elected Washington as their first president. Washington, believing that taxpaying African Americans of intelligence and high character almost invariably were treated with respect by whites, urged that shiftless, idle, and useless African Americans be transformed into valuable, law-abiding citizens. He also urged that a larger number of blacks enter various business fields. In *The Negro in Business* he stated that he was gratified by the large number of new business enterprises that had sprung up during the first year of the league's existence. Many local organizations were formed, and by 1907 the national organization had 320 branches.

At the end of the century African Americans were engaged in innumerable types and sizes of business. They operated grocery stores, general merchandise stores, and drugstores; they were restaurant keepers, caterers, confectioners, bakers, tailors, builders, and contractors. Some operated shirt factories, cotton mills, rubber goods shops, lumber mills, and carpet factories. There were many cooperative businesses, such as the Bay Shore Hotel Company of Hampton, Virginia; the Capital Trust Company of Jacksonville, Florida; the South View Cemetery Association of Atlanta, Georgia; and the Southern Stove Hollow-Ware and Foundry Company of Chattanooga,

A LEADER IN BUSINESS AND SELF-HELP. As president of Richmond's Consolidated Bank and Trust Company and the Richmond Council of Negro Women, Maggie L. Walker (standing at right) was a leader in supporting a training school for girls, a tuberculosis sanitorium, a community center, and a nursing home. In Richmond, a street, theater, and school have been named for her. *(Courtesy of Richmond National Battlefield Park, U.S. Department of the Interior.)*

Tennessee. The success of some black businesspeople, while failing to approach the success of whites during the same period, was nevertheless significant. One of the new, flourishing businesses was Madam C. J. Walker's establishment for making hair and skin preparations, the first of a large number of such businesses to spring up in the next fifty years. In 1898 there were two real estate agents in New York City worth more than $150,000 each, and one in Cleveland had property valued at $100,000. A fish dealer in Concord, North Carolina, was worth $25,000, while several builders, contractors, and merchants were worth more than $10,000. Large industries, department stores, and trusts were making it daily more difficult for the small capitalist with slender resources, whether black or white, to survive, and it is not surprising that each year witnessed the failure of many such enterprises.

In the field of banking, African Americans made a special effort to establish themselves firmly, a difficult task after the failure of the Freedman's Bank in 1874. In 1888 the Reverend W. W. Browne organized in Richmond the first bank to be administered solely by blacks, the Savings Bank of the Grand Fountain United Order of True Reformers. Later in the same year the Capital Savings Bank of Washington was organized. In 1889 the Mutual Bank and Trust Company of Chattanooga was founded, followed by the establishment of the Alabama Penny Savings Bank of Birmingham. By 1914 approximately fifty-five black banks had been organized. Most of them were closely connected with fraternal insurance organizations or churches or both. Most of the banks were short-lived, however, because African-American depositors and borrowers did not engage in trade, industry, and commerce in a sufficient volume to support the financial institutions satisfactorily. Perhaps the real significance of the organization of these banks lies in the fact that they represent an effort on the part of African Americans to adopt the business ideals and social values of the rest of America and, thus, to assimilate themselves more completely.

■ Social and Cultural Growth

It was more important for African Americans to maintain a separate existence socially and culturally than it was for them to do so economically. Whites in the South and, to a considerable extent, in the North kept a discreet distance from the everyday lives of blacks, and as the problems of migration and existence in a complex industrial society multiplied their difficulties, blacks had to work out their own formulas for survival. An important agency for maintaining group cohesion and rendering self-help was the church. Although church membership was increasing, organized religious bodies were going through a period that was as critical for blacks as for whites. The conservative element, devoting its attention to denouncing the sins of young people and concerned largely with otherworldliness, was in control. Its leadership, however, was being effectively challenged by a rising progressive element, which refused to accept the crude notions of Biblical interpretation and the "grotesque vision of the hereafter" portrayed by the conservatives. Educated African Americans began to reject the church as the agency of salvation and turned their attention more and more to the immediate problems at hand. They did not hesitate to register their impatience with their leaders. They demanded a change in management that would give them more influence in the church and insisted upon changes in forms of worship that were more in keeping with their improved intellectual level. Frequently progressives withdrew from Baptist and Methodist denominations and joined Congregational, Presbyterian, Episcopalian, and Catholic churches, some of which seemed to have a more flexible attitude toward the reforms upon which the progressives insisted.

Among Baptists there was not only a conflict between progressives and conservatives but also a struggle between whites and blacks. In many localities whites undertook to control black Baptist associations and conventions, much to the distress of the African-American leaders. When they were refused the privilege of participating in management of the American Baptist Home Mission Society, the strife began. A serious breach developed when the American Baptist Publication Society, under pressure from Southern churches, refused to accept contributions of African-Americans to Sunday School literature. In 1886 they organized the National Baptist Convention in an attempt to reduce the influence of white national bodies among blacks. Soon the National Baptist Publishing House, under R. H. Boyd, began to circulate its own Sunday School literature. Some blacks continued to use the materials of the white organizations, while others used the materials issued by Boyd's house. The resulting strife and confusion lasted well into the twentieth century.

Despite the disagreement within the church, religious bodies continued, and even increased, their responsibility in ministering to the needs of their people. Even the conservatives yielded to the demands of more enlightened members that the church serve as an agency for improvement of the social and moral conditions among African Americans. As before the Civil War, the church promoted education, largely by encouraging its members to become Bible readers. It also encouraged the formation of literary societies among its young people. The greatest evidence of its socialization, however, was its increasing function as a welfare agency. Innumerable services were rendered to the community by the new institutional churches. Some worked in slums and jails, several established missions in the slums of both the North and South, while others established or supported homes for the aged and for orphans. In Atlanta, H. H. Proctor's Congregational church organized a day nursery, kindergarten, gymnasium, school of music, employment bureau, and Bible school. W. N. DeBerry of Springfield, Massachusetts, led his Congregational members in the establishment of a home for working girls in Amherst, a welfare league for women, handicraft clubs for boys and girls, an evening school of domestic training, and a free employment bureau. Churches in New York, Detroit, Chicago, St. Louis, and other cities engaged in similar activities. This progressive development served not only to contribute to the improvement of conditions in urban communities but also to attract better-trained young men to the ministry of African-American churches.

Another manifestation of the struggle of African Americans to become socially self-sufficient was the remarkable growth of fraternal orders and benefit associations. Masons and Odd Fellows maintained large black memberships; in addition, organizations like the Knights of Pythias and the Knights of Tabor competed for membership among black men. Organizations for black women included the Order of the Eastern Star and Sisters of Calanthe. Other secret orders—the International Order of Good Samaritans, the Ancient Sons of Israel, the Grand United Order of True Reformers, and the Independent Order of St. Luke—offered insurance against sickness and death, aided widows and orphans of deceased members, and gave opportunities for social intercourse. Some were strong only in certain localities; others had memberships that extended over several states and owned the buildings housing their main offices as well as other property which they rented to black businesses.

A variation of fraternal organizations, without the feature of secret rituals, was the beneficial and insurance societies which became numerous during the period. These organizations usually collected weekly dues ranging from 25 cents to 50 cents from their members. The Young Mutual Society of Augusta, Georgia, organized in 1886, and the Beneficial Association of Petersburg, Virginia, organized in 1893, are examples of local benefit societies. Larger in scope and membership was the Workers Mutual Aid Association of Virginia. By 1898, four years after its founding, it had a membership of more than 4,000. Although these societies imposed relatively exorbitant dues on their members, they served as important training grounds where African Americans could secure business experience, and they helped to develop habits of self-help that seemed to be more imperative as the new century opened.

A logical outcome of the mutual benefit societies was black insurance companies, which were more economic than social in their functions. In Washington, D.C., S. W. Rutherford severed his connections with the True Reformers and organized a society that finally became the National Benefit Life Insurance Company, which remained the largest African-American organization of its kind for more than a generation. In Durham, North Carolina, John Merrick, who had been an extension worker for the True Reformers, was able to interest several influential citizens in organizing an insurance company. He, together with A. M. Moore, James E. Shepard, W. G. Pearson, and others, in 1898 became charter members of the organization that later became known as the North Carolina Mutual Life Insurance Company. Its period of substantial growth dates from 1899, when C. C. Spaulding was added to the board and the company was reorganized. In Atlanta, Georgia, A. F. Herndon secured control of the Atlanta Mutual Aid Association and reorganized it into the powerful Atlanta Life Insurance Company. These and similar businesses grew as some white companies became more and more reluctant to insure African Americans when they were learning the value of purchasing various types of insurance.

While little surplus capital among African Americans could be channeled into philanthropic and charitable undertakings, a surprising amount of effort was devoted to helping the unfortunate and underprivileged. Orphanages, homes for the aged, hospitals, and sanitariums were established in many communities; some of them were maintained solely by African Americans. The Tennessee Orphanage and Industrial School at Nashville, the Carrie Steele Orphanage at Atlanta, Georgia, and the Pickford Tuberculosis Sanitarium of Southern Pines, North Carolina, for example, were supported exclusively or principally by funds raised among African Americans. Many organizations were founded primarily for charitable purposes. Among them was the Louisiana Association for the Benefit of Colored Orphans, to which

Thomy Lafon, a wealthy black real estate broker of New Orleans, contributed generously. In 1895 the National Association of Colored Women was established. Living up to its motto, "Lifting As We Climb," the organization through its local clubs set up girls' homes, hospitals, and other social agencies. The Colored Women's League of Washington, organized in 1892, established a kindergarten and did considerable rescue work, while the Farmers' Improvement Society of Texas instituted in 1891 a program of benevolent activities that reached out to thirty-six towns in the state. Both the Young Men's Christian Association and the Young Women's Christian Association were extending their activities to African Americans during this period.

Although there were no conventions quite comparable to those of the period before the Civil War, the "Negro problem" was the subject of a number of conferences held toward the end of the century. It will be remembered that Booker T. Washington had two such projects in the annual Farmers' Conference that met at Tuskegee and the National Negro Business League. There was also the Lake Mohonk Conference on the Negro Question in 1890, at which prominent white citizens discussed the educational, religious, and economic problems affecting blacks. No African Americans attended this conference. The Hampton Conference, conducted in part by African Americans, dealt with problems peculiar to African Americans, while the Capon Springs Conference undertook a similar task.

With the founding of the Afro-American League of the United States in 1890, black self-help efforts reached an important critical juncture. Under the leadership of T. Thomas Fortune more than 100 African Americans from many parts of the country met in Chicago and pledged themselves to fight any and all forms of segregation and discrimination. Seven years later, Alexander Crummell, W. E. B. Du Bois, John W. Cromwell, Kelly Miller, and other African-American intellectuals established the American Negro Academy, a national organization whose members included some of the best educated and most prominent of the black elite. Their great hope was that these "trained and scholarly men" would take the lead in shaping and directing "the opinions and habits of the crude masses," while at the same time defending African Americans from the assaults of those who despised them. For thirty-one years, through annual meetings, special conferences, the publication of occasional papers, the collection of printed materials on blacks, and lobbying for the creation of research centers devoted to the study of Africa and the African-American community, the academy promoted the exchange of ideas among black intellectuals and helped perpetuate the black protest tradition in an age of accommodation and proscription.

Another of these efforts was the Conference on Negro Problems, which was held annually at Atlanta University between 1896 and 1914 under the general direction of W. E. B. Du Bois. Not only did African Americans come together to discuss their problems, but each year a study of some phase of African-American life was made. Guy B. Johnson regarded these efforts as "the first real sociological research in the South." Du Bois indicated that the 2,172 pages of the published reports formed a "current encyclopedia on the American Negro problems." Among the more valuable publications of the conference were *Some Efforts of Negroes for Social Betterment* (1898), *the Negro in Business* (1899), *The College-bred Negro* (1900), and *The Negro Common School* (1901). Several of the reports were enlarged and brought up-to-date at later conferences.

Thus, in many ways African Americans were attempting to take their fate into their own hands and solve their problems as best they could. The techniques used were those commonly known to Americans of all races. They were the use of agencies already in existence, such as the school and the church, and the establishment of new agencies, such as mutual aid societies and business leagues. Small wonder that the editor of the Atlanta University publications could say in 1898:

> Compared with modern civilized groups the organization of action among American Negroes is extremely simple. . . . And yet there are among them 23,000 churches, with unusually wide activities, and spending annually at least $10,000,000. There are thousands of secret societies with their insurance and social features, large numbers of beneficial societies . . . there is the slowly expanding seed of cooperative business efforts. . . . Finally there are the slowly evolving organs by which the group seeks to stop and minimize the anti-social deeds and accidents of its members. This is a picture of all human striving— unusually simple, . . . but strikingly human and worth further study and attention.

One result of the social and cultural strivings was the emergence of a substantial number of blacks who gave evidence of intellectual growth and a satisfactory assimilation into American life. This growth was notably reflected in the literary activity of the period. In history and biography there was a tendency, so generally characteristic of the writing of the time, to portray heroic deeds and dramatic successes. In *The Colored Cadet at West Point* (1889) Henry Ossian Flipper told of his experiences in becoming the first African American to receive a commission from the United States Military Academy. In 1881 Frederick Douglass brought his colorful career up-to-date in *The Life and Times of Frederick Douglass,* which was enlarged in 1892. The outstanding piece of autobiographical writing was Booker T. Washington's *Up from Slavery* (1900), which was to become one of the classics in American biography. It is the type of success story that many white Americans were telling. Other African-American leaders, such as Bishop Daniel A. Payne and John M. Langston, wrote their autobiographies during the period. Two of the better biographical studies were Sarah Bradford's work on the life of Harriet Tubman, *Harriet, the Moses of Her People* (1886), and Charles W. Chesnutt's *Frederick Douglass* (1899).

In 1872 William Still issued his *Underground Rail Road,* which, while hardly qualifying as a historical narrative, reflected the new interest of

IDA B. WELLS, CRUSADER FOR JUS-
TICE. She was run out of Memphis,
Tennessee, where she edited a paper,
for condemning violence, especially
lynching. She continued her crusade in
Chicago, where she also criticized the
Columbian Exposition in 1892 for not
including African Americans in its exhib-
its. *(Schomburg Center for Research in
Black Culture, New York Public Library.)*

African Americans in their past. Numerous church histories, written principally by ministers and church officials, were more important as source
materials than as authoritative studies. Joseph T. Wilson wrote several
histories during the period, including *Emancipation; Its Course and Progress
from 1481 B.C. to A.D. 1875* (1882) and *The Black Phalanx* (1888), a history of
blacks in the Civil War. Similar historians were John Wallace, who wrote
Carpetbag Rule in Florida (1888), and E. A. Johnson, author of *A School History
of the Negro Race in America* (1891). A much abler historian was George
Washington Williams, a Pennsylvanian who had served as a soldier in the
Civil War and had been educated in Massachusetts. In 1882 G. P. Putnam's
Sons published in two volumes his *History of the Negro Race in America from
1619 to 1880,* the result of years of painstaking and laborious research. It was
the first historical study by an African American to be taken seriously by
American scholars, and one newspaper hailed him as the "Negro Bancroft."
Five years later Harper and Brothers brought out his *History of the Negro
Troops in the Rebellion.* Booker T. Washington's *Story of the Negro* in two
volumes (1909) made no improvement on the earlier work of Williams. In
1896 the first scientific historical monograph written by an African American
appeared. It was W. E. B. Du Bois's *The Suppression of the African Slave Trade,
1638–1870,* which became the first work in the Harvard Historical Studies.
It was a landmark in the intellectual growth of African Americans and is
still regarded favorably by serious students of history.

In economics, sociology, and political science, the writings of African

FRANCES ELLEN WAT-
KINS HARPER. While
still a young woman,
Harper, a poet, novelist,
lecturer, and essayist, became active in the anti-
slavery movement. Be-
fore and after the Civil
War, she used her tal-
ents for racial justice,
women's rights, and
temperance, remaining
an active figure in social
reform until her death
in 1911. *(Schomburg
Center For Research In
Black Culture, New York
Public Library.)*

Americans were generally neither as numerous nor as satisfactory as in the field of history. There were of course the Atlanta University studies written primarily by Du Bois, to which reference has already been made. While serving as an assistant instructor at the University of Pennsylvania, Du Bois gathered material on the black community of Philadelphia which appeared as *The Philadelphia Negro* in 1900. In 1892 Ida B. Wells began her long crusade with the publication of *A Red Record, Tabulated Statistics and Alleged Causes of Lynching in the United States.* That same year, in a volume of essays titled *A Voice From the South: By a Black Woman of the South,* Anna Julia Cooper wrote with great insight about the challenges and opportunities that faced African-American women as they tried to make their way in a white capitalist society that oppressed blacks and a patriarchal society that oppressed women. Booker T. Washington wrote numerous books in the fields of education, race relations, economics, and sociology. Some of the titles are *The Future of the American Negro* (1899), *The Education of the Negro* (1900), *Tuskegee and Its People* (1905), and *The Negro in Business* (1907). They were largely restatements of his position regarding the place of blacks in American life. T. Thomas Fortune made several contributions to economics and political science, including *Black and White: Land, Labor and Politics in the South* (1884) and *The Negro in Politics* (1885). The former is in support of organized labor among blacks, while the latter is a vigorous attack upon Frederick Douglass's assertion that for African Americans "The Republican Party is the ship, all else is the ocean."

In the field of fiction some antislavery leaders were still writing short stories and sketches of life in the South. In 1880 William Wells Brown published his last book, *My Southern Home.* The writer who made the greatest impression during the period, however, was Charles W. Chesnutt, whose novels and short stories were widely read and generously praised. Between 1899 and 1905 four books written by him were favorably received because of their vivid portrayal of character and their quality as lively narratives. They were *The Conjure Woman* (1899), *The House Behind the Cedars* (1900), *The Marrow of Tradition* (1901), and *The Colonel's Dream* (1905). Of *The Conjure Woman* Vernon Loggins has said that such a sincere work of art was "positive evidence that Negro literature was coming of age." The NAACP's bestowal of the Spingarn Medal on Chesnutt toward the end of his career was only the most notable expression of the African-American community's appreciation of his work.

While Paul Laurence Dunbar wrote several novels during his short life, including *The Uncalled* (1898) and *The Love of Landry* (1900), he is best known for his poems, which led William Dean Howells to describe him as the first African-American "to feel the Negro life aesthetically and express it lyrically." Frederick Douglass considered Dunbar to be "the most promising black man of his time," and writer Ralph Ellison has described him as the first African American to introduce into American literature the "something else which makes for our [African-American] strength, which makes for our endurance and promise." Few poets in America had been able to capture so completely the spirit of some aspect of American life and to distill it into such delightful verse. His *Oak and Ivy* (1893), *Majors and Minors* (1896), and *Lyrics of Lowly Life* (1896) have caused many critics to refer to him as the "poet laureate of the Negro race." His poems went through many editions, and before he died in 1906 he had become one of America's famous men of letters. It was the enthusiastic acclaim of Dunbar that overshadowed the works of James Madison Bell, Albery A. Whitman, and Frances E. W. Harper, who otherwise might have been regarded much more highly as poets of a race coming of age.

Although African-American editors did not have the same battles to fight as Frederick Douglass and Samuel Cornish had, they were no less preoccupied with the problem of fighting for the greater integration of African-American citizens in American life. Even in the postwar years, the *New National Era*, owned by Douglass, was a failure, while its successor, *The Commoner*, edited by George W. Williams in Washington in 1875, lasted only a few weeks. Magazines like *The Southern Workman*, published at Hampton after 1872, and the *AME Review*, which was begun in 1884, were concerned primarily with educational, literary, and religious matters; but the newspapers were fighting economic and political battles. In 1900 there were 3 African-American daily newspapers—at Norfolk, Virginia, Kansas City, Kansas, and Washington, D.C.—all of which were short-lived. At the same time there were approximately 150 weekly newspapers that were widely

Anna J. Cooper on the Challenges and Opportunities for "Colored Women" Facing the Twentieth Century

The colored woman of to-day occupies, one may say, a unique position in this country. . . . She is confronted by both a woman question and a race problem, and is as yet an unknown or an unacknowledged factor in both. While the women of the white race can with calm assurance enter upon the work they feel by nature appointed to do, while their men give loyal support and appreciative countenance to their efforts . . . the colored woman too often finds herself hampered and shamed by a less liberal sentiment and a more conservative attitude on the part of those for whose opinions she cares most. That is not universally true I am glad to admit. There are to be found both intensely conservative white men and exceedingly liberal colored men. But as far as my experience goes the average man of our race is less frequently ready to admit the actual need among the sturdier forces of the world for woman's help or influence. . . .

But to be a woman of the Negro race in America, and to be able to grasp the deep significance of the possibilities of the crisis, is to have a heritage, it seems to me, unique in the ages. In the first place, the race is young and full of the elasticity and hopefulness of youth. It does not look on the masterly triumphs of nineteenth century civilization with that blasé world-weary look which characterizes the old washed out and worn out races which have already, so to speak, seen their best days.

Said a European writer recently: "Except the Slavonic, the Negro is the only original and distinctive genius which has yet to come to growth—and the feeling is to cherish and develop it."

Anna J. Cooper, "The Status of Women in America," in A Voice from the South. Xenia, Ohio, 1892.

read among African Americans. Georgia and Texas had no less than 23 each, while North Carolina had ten. The others were scattered in twenty-six states. Some were widely read and provoked considerable discussion. In Boston, in 1901, for example, George Forbes and Monroe Trotter began publication of the *Guardian*, which fought the program of Booker T. Washington and demanded full and immediate equality for African Americans. While Washington controlled some of them, the majority of the newspapers were uncompromising, and their titles suggest the temperament and spirit of the editors. Among them were the *San Antonio X-Ray*, the *Austin Searchlight*, the *Baltimore Crusader*, the *Columbus New Light*, and the *Albany Iconoclast*.

The end of the century found African Americans in a stronger position in that they had educational institutions in which to develop and social agencies by which they could improve their status. The help that they received from philanthropists did much to make their lot easier, but their experiences in the economic and social world of whites convinced them more and more that the brunt of the burden of black development would have to be borne by African Americans themselves. They assumed this responsibility without hesitation and in typically American fashion sought a larger share of the blessings of liberty. But as blacks developed their own institutions and, to a considerable extent, their own cultural life, it became clearer that the American melting pot, so far as African Americans were concerned, was not boiling; it was hardly simmering.

CHAPTER 15

The Color Line

■ The New American Imperialism

One of the most far-reaching consequences of Reconstruction and the economic revolution that accompanied it was the recurrence of a strong American nationalism, which had only temporarily given way to sectional strife. Once again Americans looked upon themselves as the guardians of civilization in the New World and consequently desired to extend to other peoples the blessings they enjoyed. Once more a united people, Americans felt compelled to wield the kind of influence in the New World that had earlier characterized their policy. A bigger and better navy was viewed as necessary in order to protect the New World against the encroachments of the Old, and missionaries extended their activities to the islands of the Caribbean, Latin America, and even the Pacific world.

Such a point of view had its logical culmination in the disintegration of national isolation and the pursuit of an imperialism similar to that of several European countries. The United States observed with interest the increased imperialistic activities of France and England and of the newcomers to the field, Belgium, Italy, and Germany. David Livingstone, Cecil Rhodes, and Henry M. Stanley dramatized the importance of Africa to an industrialized world, while Leopold of Belgium, Wilhelm of Germany, and Victoria of England became the political agents in whose names the Dark Continent was divided. In the winter of 1884–1885 an international conference was held in Berlin to discuss the question of Africa. The great basin of the Congo was given to Leopold of Belgium, and the conference paved the way for the acquisition of East Africa, Southwest Africa, Togoland, and Kamerun by Germany, a vast expanse of land from the Cape to Cairo by England, and a considerable portion of West Africa by France. By the end of the century Africa was effectively divided among the great powers of Europe, and they were looking for more fields to conquer. But at least one African American, George Washington Williams—historian, politician, and Ohio legislator—was bitterly critical of King Leopold's policies in the Congo.

The United States had not been wholly inactive in the field of imperialism during the post-Civil War period. As industrial production increased, American manufacturers began to search for new markets as well as for new sources of raw materials. The great industrialists, their pockets bulging with surplus capital, began to search for areas in which to invest their profits. Consequently, exports increased enormously and foreign investments sky-rocketed. As immigrants continued to come to the United States in larger numbers, the land in the West rapidly filled up, and as at other periods in its history, the United States felt the need for *Lebensraum*. A newly confident America was turning its eyes outward. Sectional strife was over, the economic revolution had surmounted its greatest obstacles, and the people were tired of the relatively unexciting question of the perfection of a national economy. The United States was ready to assume a role in world affairs.

In some respects the territorial growth of the United States from the acquisition of Louisiana in 1803 may be regarded as an imperialistic development, but the lands west of the Alleghenies were contiguous to the United States and, except for American Indians, were populated by people similar in cultural heritage to the majority of early American settlers. Long before the end of the nineteenth century, however, the United States had become initiated into the fraternity of imperialistic powers by the purchase of Alaska from Russia in 1867. Although at first some serious opposition was raised to the acquisition of Russia's "icebox," the objections soon melted before the intense fire of a new manifest destiny.

Already the Hawaiian Islands were attracting the attention of many American traders. As more of them visited the islands, they saw their value as a site for a naval base, a coaling station, and a cable landing. In 1875 sugar and other Hawaiian products were given free entry into the United States. In 1884 the United States leased Pearl Harbor on the island of Oahu as a naval station. With this added military protection, American investors poured capital into the islands, so that by 1890 American plantations there were worth more than $25 million. Despite the fact that the Hawaiian people had racial and cultural heritages vastly different from those of any American group, sentiment for annexation of the islands to the United States grew steadily. In 1898, after some maneuvering on the islands and on the mainland, Congress annexed them by joint resolution. Likewise, arrange-ments were made to secure Tutuila when the Samoan Islands were divided among Britain, Germany, and the United States.

Meanwhile, the United States was acquiring jurisdiction over many other small islands in the Pacific, including Wake, Midway, Palmyra, and How-land. Before the end of the century the United States was well on its way toward acquiring an empire composed primarily of darker peoples—Poly-nesian, Japanese, Chinese, and others. In so doing, the leading power in the Western Hemisphere was conforming to the prevailing pattern of imperial-ism that had swept the world: the injection of the spirit of industrialism into a program to dominate the less-developed areas of the world. Invariably, these peoples were dark, and frequently they were of African descent.

It was in the Americas, of course, that the United States pursued its new imperialistic policy most vigorously, and even where territory was not at stake, financial and political influence wrought wonders. Thus, as America focused on South America and the Caribbean world, it brought into its orbit millions of people of African or mixed descent. It was in the Caribbean where the influence of the United States was most dramatically and effectively wielded.

By the end of the Civil War, Spain could claim only two islands, Cuba and Puerto Rico, of a vast New World empire that had once extended from the upper Mississippi River to Cape Horn. Spain's steady decline as a major imperial power had not left the country chastened or any the wiser in dealing with dependent peoples. On Spain's two islands a policy was pursued that was no more enlightened than the one followed in the seventeenth century. Spain had remained unaffected by the new trends in imperialism, and England's gestures of conceding self-government, even to some of the more backward areas, apparently did not impress Spain at all. Repression and rigid control of every aspect of life in Cuba had inspired numerous revolts against Spain, and they were becoming more frequent and more intense by the middle of the nineteenth century.

Toward the end of the century, Cubans became more determined to have their independence. This determination happily coincided with the increas-ing interest in the island on the part of citizens of the United States who had already made sizable investments in Cuba. By 1890 Americans had invested more than $50 million in plantations and sugar refineries. When, therefore, the Cubans revolted in 1895, the United States became alarmed over the damage that was done to American fields and factories on the island. Their material interest was broadened into a humanitarian interest in the following year when Spain sent Gen. Valeriano Weyler to put down the insurrection. With more determination than wisdom Weyler ordered much of the rural population to be placed in concentration camps since it was extremely difficult to separate the loyalists from the insurgents. The starvation and disease that followed took such a toll of Cuban lives that the American press dubbed the Spanish leader "Butcher" Weyler. In the province of Havana alone, for example, more than 50,000 people died.

It was inconceivable to Americans that such brutality could exist so close to the center of freedom in the Western world. An outraged America, for the moment, forgot the heated presidential campaign of 1896, as well as the campaign to disfranchise blacks in the South. The so-called yellow journals fanned the flames of indignation in America to the point where Congress finally recognized the belligerency of the Cubans. Only the firmness of President Cleveland prevented the country from going further. With some encouragement from the United States, Cubans were more determined than ever to have their independence. Under the leadership of Antonio Maceo, a mulatto general, and Quintin Bandera, known as "The Black Thunderbolt," the insurgents carried on a campaign of systematic devastation that won greater support among the Americans. In January 1898 the American battleship *Maine* was ordered to Havana to protect American life and property and to impress on the Spaniards that the government of the United States was willing to take energetic action. On February 15, 1898, an explosion sank the *Maine* in Havana harbor with a loss of more than 250 officers and enlisted men. The incident set off a train of events that culminated in war between the United States and Spain two months later. It was America's first international conflict in more than fifty years, and it was more than anything else a clear-cut demonstration of America's growing interest in affairs outside her own territorial limits.

From the beginning, African Americans were involved in the war against Spain. Indeed, there were at least thirty blacks on the *Maine* when it exploded. Twenty-two were killed, four were injured, and four others escaped injury. African Americans had already been inspired by the soldiers of Maceo and Bandera and regarded "Weylerism as the synonym of barbarous warfare." The majority of African Americans were anxious to vindicate the honor of the United States and help bring independence and freedom to Cubans, whom they regarded as blacks and mulattoes. When, therefore, the president called for 200,000 volunteers to supplement the inadequate regular army, blacks were as enthusiastic about enlisting as any group in America. Some African Americans, however, were vocal anti-imperialists who argued that the United States' acquisition of colonies only boded ill for current and potential nonwhite members of the American community. These dissenters, most of whom identified with the Cuban rebels (especially those who were blacks), stressed repeatedly that Spain, though cruel and undemocratic, had not imposed a racial caste system on Cuba. They refused to be a part of a war in which African Americans, themselves victims of discriminatory laws and racist practices, were used to subject nonwhite colonials to that same system.

Among the regular army that numbered only 28,000 troops in 1898, there were four African-American outfits, all of which had been used in actions against the Indians in the West. The Ninth Cavalry was in the Department of the Platte, and the Tenth Cavalry was stationed at Assiniboine, Montana. The Twenty-fourth Infantry was at Fort Douglas, near Salt Lake City, Utah, and the Twenty-fifth Infantry was in Missoula, Montana. These organizations had been activated shortly after the close of the Civil War and had performed numerous duties in the Indian wars and in border service. The Ninth

Cavalry, for example, had served at Fort Lancaster, Texas, at Santa Fe, New Mexico, at Fort Riley, Kansas, and at Fort McKinney, Wyoming. These troops were often referred to as the "Buffalo Soldiers," a name given them by the Kiowa, Cheyenne, and Apache tribes they encountered. When they, along with other black and white regulars, were called to service in the Spanish-American War, they were ill-prepared both in equipment and training for action in a tropical theater.

Besides the four black outfits in the regular army and the four outfits that were recruited under a special act of the Congress, numerous other African-American groups served in the war against Spain. Several states permitted African Americans to organize outfits and enter the service, among them the Third Alabama Infantry of Volunteers, the Third North Carolina Infantry, the Sixth Virginia Infantry, the Ninth Ohio Infantry, the Twenty-third Kansas Infantry, the Eighth Illinois Infantry, two companies of the Indiana Infantry, and several smaller groups. Company L of the Sixth Massachusetts Infantry was the only black company that was mustered in as an integral part of a white regiment. It had African-American officers and, having been created during the War for Independence as the "Bucks of America," boasted that it was the oldest African-American military organization in America.

The question of African-American officers plagued military leaders from the beginning. Even when Congress authorized the four new black outfits, the War Department insisted on white staff and line officers above the rank of second lieutenant. The majority of the white soldiers in the regular army regarded blacks as unfit for leadership and pointed to the fact that although there were four black outfits in the regular army there was only one African-American commissioned officer, West Pointer Charles Young. The president finally commissioned about 100 African-American second lieutenants in the volunteer service, while the majority of the black military organizations in the service of the states were officered by African-American men. The Third North Carolina Infantry had all African-American officers. The commanding officer was Col. James H. Young, a prominent leader in the state; his immediate aides were Lt. Col. C. S. Taylor and Maj. Andrew Walker. The Eighth Illinois was commanded by Col. John R. Marshall; Charles Young was made a brevet major and placed in command of the Ninth Ohio. The Massachusetts company also had African-American officers. The Sixth Virginia was staffed with white officers, but some changes were made when several black soldiers resigned because they had enlisted with the understanding that they were to have African-American officers.

Six noncommissioned officers were commissioned as second lieutenants in the field because they had "rendered particularly gallant and meritorious services in the face of enemy action." Among the other special commissions issued were those to two paymasters with the rank of major. Recipients were John R. Lynch, former congressman from Mississippi and former fourth auditor of the treasury, and Richard R. Wright, president of the Agricultural and Mechanical College of Georgia. Two African-American ministers were commissioned as chaplains, the Reverend C. T. Walker of Georgia and the Reverend Richard Carroll of South Carolina. Dr. Arthur M. Brown was appointed assistant surgeon with the Tenth Cavalry, and from August 2 to October 8, 1898, he was the commanding officer of his outfit.

The treatment of black troops throughout the war reflected how entrapped African Americans were in a Jim Crow society, no matter how vital or brave their service. Wherever they were stationed, black regiments excited hostility from whites who were opposed to armed blacks wearing the uniform of their country. Blacks were subject to racial insults and to exclusion from places of public accommodation which were open to their white counterparts. African-American soldiers vigorously protested these and other insults to their officers and, through letters to newspapers, to the American public. The fact that they were armed, in uniform, and traveling in large numbers led some of them, on occasion, to challenge Jim Crow practices or to use violence to punish their detractors. Most exercised restraint, however, enduring insults and mistreatment in the belief that by demonstrating an indifference to racism, as well as by showing their patriotism, they would strengthen their race's claims to equal treatment. But their additional, and ultimately less successful, war against racism took its toll in disillusionment and bitterness.

In the swift and decisive action that brought victory to the United States, the only African Americans who saw considerable service were in the four regular outfits. In June 1898 these groups sailed out of various Southern ports for Cuba. The Twenty-fifth Infantry, for example, sailed on June 7 from Tampa, Florida, on a government transport. During the week that the men were delayed at Tampa they were not allowed to go ashore to bathe and exercise unless an officer escorted the entire company. Upon embarkation, the Twenty-fifth was assigned to the bottom deck where there was no light, except that which came through the small portholes, and very little air. Blacks and whites were not permitted to mingle with each other on board ship. When they disembarked at Daiquiri in Guantanamo Bay on June 22, the campaign for the reduction of the Spanish forces in Cuba began.

The African-American contingents saw action with the forces principally at El Caney, Las Guasimas, and San Juan Hill. On June 24 two battalions of the First Volunteer Cavalry (Theodore Roosevelt's Rough Riders) moved up the Santiago Road toward Las Guasimas, where they met the enemy. At a crucial moment in the fighting, several blacks from the Ninth and Tenth Cavalries came up, knocked down the enemy's improvised fort, cut the barbed wire, and made an opening for the Rough Riders, who then routed the Spaniards. One African-American corporal who manned a Hotchkiss gun during the action was killed at his post. At El Caney, on June 30, the Twenty-fifth was ordered up to reinforce the Rough Riders. In this decisive action many of the African-American troops were under fire for the better part of the day, with strict orders not to return the enemy fire. In three days of fighting most of the black regulars in Cuba saw action and won the praise of practically all of their officers.

It has been claimed by many that the Ninth and Tenth Cavalries saved the Rough Riders from complete annihilation at Las Guasimas. One Southern white officer, said, "If it had not been for the Negro cavalry the Rough Riders would have been exterminated. I am not a Negro lover. My father fought with Mosby's Rangers, and I was born in the South, but the Negroes saved that fight, and the day will come when General Shafter will give them credit for the bravery." Another said, "I am a Southerner by birth, and I never thought much of the colored man. But, somehow, now I feel very differently toward them. . . . I never saw such fighting as those Tenth Cavalry men did. They didn't seem to know what fear was, and their battle hymn was 'There'll be a hot time in the old town tonight.'" Even among those who did not claim that the African Americans saved the Rough Riders, the praise was generous. Lt. Thomas Roberts said, "I have naught but the highest praise for the swarthy warriors on the field of carnage. Led by brave men, they will go into the thickest of the fight, even to the wicked mouths of deadly cannon, unflinchingly." The *New York Mail and Express* said:

> All honor to the black troops of the gallant Tenth: No more striking example of bravery and coolness has been shown since the destruction of the *Maine* than by the colored veterans of the Tenth Cavalry during the attack upon Caney on Saturday. By the side of the Rough Riders they followed their leader up the terrible hill from whose crest the desperate Spaniards poured down a deadly fire of shell and musketry. They never faltered. . . . Firing as they marched, their aim was splendid, their coolness was superb, and their courage aroused the admiration of their comrades. . . . The war has not shown greater heroism.

The reaction of Theodore Roosevelt to the performance of the African-American troops was varied, depending upon the occasion. When he made his farewell address to the rather incongruous group of Indians, ranchers, cowboys, college athletes, and African-Americans who served under him, Roosevelt had words of unqualified praise for the black soldiers. "The Spaniards called them 'Smoked Yankees,'" he said, "but we found them to be an excellent breed of Yankees. I am sure that I speak the sentiments of officers and men in the assemblage when I say that between you and the other cavalry regiments there exists a tie which we trust will never be broken." When campaigning for the office of governor of New York in October 1898, Roosevelt said, "As I heard one of the Rough Riders say after the charge at San Juan: 'Well, the Ninth and Tenth men are all right. They can drink out of our canteens.'" Roosevelt expressed the highest praise for the African Americans who charged up San Juan with his Rough Riders and concluded, "I don't think that any Rough Rider will ever forget the tie that binds us to the Ninth and Tenth Cavalry." Writing in *Scribner's Magazine* in April of the following year, however, Roosevelt said that the blacks behaved well, but "They are, of course, peculiarly dependent on their white officers. . . . None of the white regulars of Rough Riders showed the slightest sign of weakening; but under the strain the colored infantrymen . . . began to get a little uneasy and to drift to the rear." Roosevelt said that he could not allow this and drew his revolver in order to halt the retreating blacks. He said that he would shoot any man who went to the rear under any pretense whatever.

The explanation for this retreat was not given by Roosevelt but was supplied by Sgt. Preston Holliday of the Tenth Cavalry writing in the *New York Age,* May 11, 1899. Holliday said that the African Americans who were going to the rear had been ordered to do so by Lieutenant Fleming to bring up rations and entrenching tools and to carry the wounded men to safer places. Fleming at the time made the explanation to Colonel Roosevelt, and some of the Rough Riders told Roosevelt that he would not have to shoot the blacks. The reply of the black men was, "We will stay with you, Colonel." On the following day, Roosevelt admitted that he had misunderstood the actions of the African-American soldiers and expressed regret at having spoken harshly to them. African-American soldiers and civilians were, therefore, keenly hurt when Roosevelt wrote unfavorably of them less than a year later. They could be consoled, however, by the remarks of Maj. Gen. Nelson A. Miles, the ranking officer of the United States Army, who said at a peace jubilee in October 1898: "The white race was accompanied by the gallantry of the black as they swept over intrenched lines and later volunteered to succor the sick, nurse the dying and bury the dead in the hospitals and the Cuban camps." Major General Miles probably had in mind the manner in which almost 100 men of the Twenty-fourth Infantry answered the call for volunteer nurses when the yellow fever epidemic broke out.

African-American soldiers served as occupation troops at the close of the war. Some African-American troops, including the Third North Carolina, served in the Pacific. The Twenty-third Kansas Infantry did garrison duty in Cuba, and the Eighth Illinois, which did not arrive in Cuba until August 1898, did garrison duty in the province of Santiago. When an editorial appeared in the *Washington Post* discrediting black troops with black officers, Maj. Charles Douglass, writing in the *Colored American* on August 17, 1898, pointed out that the Eighth Illinois had been selected to replace a disorderly white regiment. He said in conclusion, "The generals at the front know the value of Negro troops, whether the quill-drivers in the rear do or not." During this tour of duty Col. John R. Marshall served for a while as governor of San Luis, while Maj. R. R. Jackson acted as mayor of El Paso, Cuba.

Citizens of the United States did not view with complete favor the arming of African Americans to fight in the war and to serve as troops of occupation. As troops passed through the South en route to ports of embarkation, they were frequently treated with contempt by white Southerners. At the end of the war, when the Third North Carolina Volunteers were moved from Macon, Georgia, the *Atlanta Journal* carried an editorial entitled "A Happy Riddance." Among other things, the editor said that the army and the country were to be congratulated on mustering out the North Carolina blacks, for "a tougher and more turbulent set of Negroes were probably never gotten together before. . . . While stationed in Macon several of its members were killed either by their own comrades in drunken brawls or by citizens in self-defense." Charles F. Meserve, the white president of Shaw University, visited the North Carolinians at their camp and had nothing but praise for them. He described Col. James H. Young as possessing in "a marked degree a quality of leadership as important as it is rare" and said that the men were well disciplined on and off the post.

■ America's Empire of Darker Peoples

At the end of the Spanish-American War the United States could regard itself as one of the great powers of the world. The victory over Spain was so quick and decisive that it was only natural for many to expect that the United States would supplant Spain as a leading imperial power. The Treaty of Paris between the two powers left little doubt as to the direction in which the United States was moving. It provided that Spain was to relinquish all claim to sovereignty over Cuba. In lieu of a war indemnity Spain ceded to the United States the island of Puerto Rico and the other Spanish insular possessions in the West Indies. Upon payment of $20 million by the United States, Spain was to relinquish the Philippines to the victor. Although it was not immediately clear just what disposition the United States would make of Cuba, it was quite evident that the island would remain under the political and economic domination of the United States for an indefinite period. Puerto Rico was, from the outset, to become a part of America's growing empire, one that was constituted almost wholly of undeveloped peoples. The Philippines gave to the United States the foothold that it needed in the Orient if it was to compete with Britain, France, and Russia.

Whether it was American or European imperialism, the areas brought under control abounded in resources that would supply the needs of highly industrialized economic systems and in human beings that were potential consumers of commodities provided by the advanced countries. The areas were uniformly populated by so-called backward peoples, and in most cases they were darker peoples. In Africa they were, of course, black; in Asia they were yellow. In the American empire they were black, white, and yellow, or a mixture. In Cuba there were more than 600,000 blacks and persons having African blood. In Puerto Rico there were more than 300,000 such persons. Even in Hawaii and the Philippines there were some blacks, with the majority of the population in both cases composed primarily of darker peoples. When the United States acquired the Canal Zone in 1903, many blacks lived in the vicinity, and many more were brought in from the Caribbean islands to work on the Panama Canal.

It was ironic that African-American soldiers, themselves subject to Jim Crow restrictions and viewed as inferiors by most white Americans, should have played a part in bringing extensive numbers of other nonwhites under United States domination. For Howard University professor Kelly Miller and journalist John W. Cromwell—both imperialists and prominent members of the African-American community—America's victory over Spain provided opportunities for blacks to help uplift members of the "weaker races." Miller urged that Howard be employed by the federal government to educate and Americanize Cuban, Philippine, and Puerto Rican youth. He also called upon enterprising African Americans to exploit the economic opportunities in these places, "where the field is not preempted, as in America, and where race proscription is not so discouraging." Although Cromwell expressed similar sentiments, he did concede to the inhabitants of Spain's former colonies one advanced trait, a history of "fraternity between the races." The most negative black reaction to America's new imperialist policies came in the Philippines, where from 1899 to 1902 United States military forces were engaged in crushing the independence movement led by Emilio Aguinaldo. There, as Willard Gatewood has shown, "an unusually large number of Negro troops deserted" to join the Filipino Insurrectos, "whose struggle they interpreted as the struggle of all colored people."

One of the most salient features of the American imperial problem was that the United States, unlike the other imperial powers, had a color problem at home and therefore had to pursue a policy with regard to race that would not upset the racial equilibrium within the United States. In Puerto Rico, for example, approximately one-third of the population was distinctly of African descent, and many so-called white Puerto Ricans had sufficient black blood in their veins to qualify as African Americans in the United States. In 1900, when the first organic act of Puerto Rico was passed by Congress, the Southern members of that body—and some Northern members, too—were concerned not only with the fact that Puerto Ricans should be carefully supervised in the operation of their government but also that the blacks of the island should not enjoy political liberties that would inspire the African Americans to fight for greater political opportunities. The governor and all of the important officials were to be appointed by the president of the United States, and Americans were to outnumber Puerto Ricans on the important Executive Council. The second organic act of 1917 remodeled the local government to resemble one of the states of the United States. Two legislative houses were established, members were to be elected by universal male suffrage, and all Puerto Ricans were to enjoy American citizenship. The power of appointing all the major officials of the island, however, was reserved for the president of the United States.

The major efforts of the United States in Puerto Rico were directed toward the improvement of health, education, and public works and toward the Americanization of Puerto Ricans. In all these areas there were notable advancements, but the low economic level of the people, stemming largely from the concentration of wealth in the hands of a few, prevented greater improvement and caused hundreds of thousands to migrate to the mainland. Since American investors on the island reaped considerable profits, especially in the cultivation of sugar, there was an inclination on the part of the cursory observer to view the period of American control as very successful. The high mortality rate, the abject poverty of the masses, and the cultural and social debility of the people seemed to indicate the need for a new imperial outlook that would foster greater improvement for the inhabitants of the island. The effort of Puerto Ricans to break up the large plantations in order to redistribute the land and the unfavorable reaction of American investors suggested that any improvements would be slow indeed in coming.

A significant expansion of America's black empire came with the purchase of the Danish West Indies in 1917, culminating a half-century of effort to acquire the islands. In August 1916 a treaty for the purchase of the islands for $25 million was negotiated, and in January of the following year the ratifications of the two countries were exchanged. American marines landed shortly after the purchase, and a military government was established which lasted until 1931, when President Hoover signed an order creating a civil government for the Virgin Islands.

Although the islands were acquired largely because of their military and strategic value in the Caribbean, the United States felt some responsibility for the improvement of conditions there. With whites comprising less than 10 percent of the population of approximately 25,000, the problem of the islands was viewed by the United States as essentially a black problem. In 1924, because of unrest in the islands, President Coolidge appointed a federal commission of five black Americans to investigate conditions. In its report the commission criticized particularly the tax laws and the judicial system. It recommended the passage of a new organic act "so as to authorize the adoption of a new code of laws based upon American ideals and calculated to insure an administration and enforcement of the laws in keeping with American practices." In 1937 President Roosevelt appointed William Hastie, a distinguished African-American attorney, as the federal judge of the islands. In 1946 President Truman appointed Hastie governor of the islands. The inhabitants regarded these appointments as an indication of a new and enlightened interest on the part of the government and the people of the United States. Later, governors would be appointed from among Virgin Islanders themselves.

America's empire of darker peoples was substantially enlarged through the manner in which the United States wielded influence over independent nations of darker peoples. In Santo Domingo, for example, the control that the United States exercised in the twentieth century was so extensive as to constitute almost complete domination. After its separation from Haiti in 1844, this country, composed largely of blacks and mulattoes, demonstrated a remarkable similarity to other Latin American nations in its inability to establish stable political and economic conditions. It, therefore, succumbed to American "dollar diplomacy," which brought one Latin American nation after another within the sphere of influence of the United States. In 1907 an American citizen was named the general receiver of customs with authority to deposit $100,000 each month toward the interest and sinking fund that was held in trust for all national creditors. In May 1916 the United States landed marines in Santo Domingo to preserve order, and within a few months civil government had disappeared altogether. Despite the vigorous protests of the Dominican minister in Washington, the marines remained there until 1924. By that time peace and order had been restored, and the commercial relationship between the United States and the black republic had become so intimate as to guarantee the domination of its economic life for an indefinite period.

Haiti's experience with the United States was similar to that of the Dominican Republic. Within a year after the beginning of World War I the United States and Haiti negotiated and ratified a treaty that permitted the United States to have control over Haiti's finances and police for a period of ten years. This gave the United States a pretext to dominate every phase of life in the second oldest republic in the New World. In 1917 the United States placed the country under complete military rule and forced extension of the treaty of 1915 for another ten years. The nature of the intervention was clearly demonstrated by a telegram that an American sent to the secretary of the navy: "Next Thursday . . . unless otherwise directed, I will permit Congress to elect a president." Almost from the beginning the Haitians resented American occupation of their country, and it was necessary for the marines to shoot more than 2,000 inhabitants in order to restore peace and order.

The widespread sympathy that Haitians elicited is clearly demonstrated by the fact that in 1922 a group of distinguished Americans, including Felix Frankfurter, Zechariah Chafee, Jr., and Moorfield Storey, issued a booklet entitled *The Seizure of Haiti by the United States, A Report of the Military Occupation of the Republic of Haiti and the History of the Treaty Forced upon Her.* The authors declared that the United States should immediately abrogate the treaty of 1915, "unconditionally and without qualifications" and that a new treaty should be negotiated that would be mutually satisfactory to both countries and "by methods that obtain between free and independent sovereign states." In 1924 Dantes Bellegarde, the Haitian delegate to the League of Nations, brought the matter to the attention of the League. Although the League refused to place the matter on its agenda, it was a victory for Haiti that Bellegarde was permitted to place the question before the League at all. The agitation continued, and in 1934, after nineteen years of occupation, American troops evacuated Haiti. Haiti had already become, for all practical purposes, a part of America's empire of darker peoples.

From the outset Liberia was of course regarded by realists as a protectorate of the United States. Early in the twentieth century, however, a closer economic relationship between the two countries began to develop. In 1909, at the request of Liberia, the United States government sent three commissioners there to report on boundary disputes between that country and Great Britain and France and to study conditions there with a view to making recommendations. In the following year the United States expressed a willingness to help Liberia by taking charge of its finances, its military organization, and any boundary questions that might arise. During World War I American interest in Liberia increased. In 1921 the United States arranged a loan of $5 million to Liberia, but Congress would not approve the transaction. In 1927 the Liberian government entered into a contract with the Firestone Rubber Company of Akron, Ohio, for a loan of $5 million on the condition that Liberia would give to the company 2,000 acres of land for experimental purposes, that the company would be given the opportunity to lease up to 1 million acres of rubber land, and that the company would construct a harbor at Monrovia out of its own funds and with its own engineers. These expenditures were later to be paid by the Liberian government. With the government of the United States committed to a policy of protection and with a powerful American industrial organization actively participating in the economic life of the country, the United States could well boast that, like the powers of Europe, it had substantial interests in the Dark Continent.

African Americans themselves played an important part in extending the empire of the United States. From the end of Reconstruction up until the beginning of World War I, American ministers to Haiti were largely blacks, and they manifested a keen interest in the extension of American influence. John M. Langston, for example, went to Haiti as the official representative of the government of the United States in 1877 and interested himself in the political and economic conditions of the island. He was quite disturbed about the unsettled political scene and made many suggestions to his government on the ways in which trade relations could be improved. Both J. E. W. Thompson, who went out in 1885, and Frederick Douglass, who became the American minister in 1889, were very much concerned over the treatment of American vessels in Haitian ports. William F. Powell, who was the minister in 1897, vigorously fought discriminating taxes against foreign merchants, while Henry W. Furness, a later minister, concerned himself primarily with seeking advantages for American merchants in the matters of tariffs and customs duties.

From 1871 up until the present time most of the American ministers to Liberia have been blacks. Beginning in 1871 J. Milton Turner helped to establish closer commercial relations between Liberia and the United States. Several others, including John Henry Smyth, E. E. Smith, and Ernest W. Lyon, praised the resources of the country and sought to encourage Americans to help develop the commercial and economic life of Liberia. Lyon, for example, is credited with having had a great deal to do with the organization of the New York Liberia Steamship Line in 1905. In the 1970s John Reinhardt and W. Beverly Carter continued the tradition of African-American ambassadors to Liberia.

Credit has always been given to the United States for having had an imperial policy that was more enlightened than that of any of the European powers. The efforts to improve the health, education, and general well-being of the backward peoples of the American empire were viewed to be genuine even when they were not very successful. But the great influence of industrialists and financiers led to a foreign policy characterized by dollar diplomacy in areas enjoying a semblance of independence and to a policy of neglect or maladministration in dependent areas. There was too great an inclination, moreover, to exercise military authority over nations whose territorial integrity and sovereignty the United States was supposed to respect. In many instances it was argued that the landing of marines in Haiti, Santo Domingo, and other nations was for purposes of security, but it was doubtless indicative of the anxiety of a nation having so recently entered the family of great powers to demonstrate its strength. Perhaps it was also a manifestation of jealousy, born of fear, of the powers of Europe, whose experience in the field served to excite the suspicions of the United States. The specter of color in America's empire hung over the United States like the sword of Damocles and was a constant reminder that its imperial policy should take cognizance of that fact. For an America that would like to boast of having the most enlightened policy in the world, the problem of color at home served to check the liberalism of that policy in the empire of darker peoples.

■ Urban Problems

The new century was one of hope for almost everyone in America. During the previous generation the country had emerged as a highly industrialized nation with a productive capacity far beyond its own needs. Toward the end of the period America acquired an empire that placed it in fair competition with the great powers of the world. It was confidently believed that the new era would bring prosperity and plenty to everyone. The most unfavorable sign on the horizon was the natural tendency of business combinations to increase to unmanageable proportions and to exploit people. There was, moreover, an increase in social and political problems in the city as urban populations grew to unprecedented numbers. Few people worried very much about these national ills, for they were considered to be inherent pains of growth. Even so, several steps had been taken to ease these pains. The Interstate Commerce Act had been passed in 1887 to curb the railroads, the Sherman Antitrust Act had been passed in 1898 to check the growth of monopolies, and the industrialists themselves were vying with each other in pouring money into educational and charitable enterprises. Americans thus faced the new century with resolution and optimism.

There were slight signs of hope even for African Americans. Despite the fact that they were disfranchised in the Southern states and were experiencing difficulties in the economic world, their hopes for the future soared with those of other Americans. One major reason for the new hope was the succession of Theodore Roosevelt to the presidency in 1901. African Americans had been shocked by Roosevelt's article partially discrediting the service of black soldiers in the Spanish-American War. He was not long in office, however, before he satisfied the majority of African Americans, at least temporarily, that he favored the equality of all. When he had been president only a month, he invited Booker T. Washington to the White House and dined with him during the course of the interview. Southerners were outraged. The Richmond *Dispatch* exclaimed: "That was a deliberate act . . . and may be taken as outlining his policy toward the Negro as a factor in Washington society. . . . With our long-matured views on the subject of social intercourse between blacks and whites, the least we can say now is that we deplore the President's taste, and we distrust his wisdom." Blacks all over the country were delighted at this signal recognition of their leader. The Washington *Bee* asserted, "The Southern Democrats hoped and expected to blarney the President so as to continue unrestrained in their wicked reign of terror and proscription against the coloured race. They are shocked, boiled, smitten, and exasperated. In one fell swoop Mr. Roosevelt has smashed to smithereens their fondest idol. They are fuming with dire imprecations against him, and all because he took a meal of victuals with a coloured gentleman who had been entertained by the nobility of England, and the best people of America."

The debate over the incident continued for many months, with the president taking no cognizance of the matter at all. Less than two years later he appointed an outstanding African-American citizen, William D. Crum, to the collectorship of the port of Charleston, South Carolina. Once more, Southern citizens attacked the president. In this instance the appointment of Crum set no precedent. African Americans had served in similar capacities in Wilmington, North Carolina, and Savannah, Georgia. Whites, however, had looked forward to the elimination of blacks from officeholding in the South, but the ascendancy of Booker T. Washington caused them to fear that he was dictating White House Southern policy. African Americans promptly forgot that within nineteen months in 1899 and 1900 McKinley had appointed twice as many blacks to federal positions as any previous president. Roosevelt further pleased them by declaring that unless some valid reason other than color could be urged against Crum, the appointment would stand. In a letter to a Charleston citizen he said that he would not close the door of hope to any American citizen. This avowed position of the president prompted one black editor to say that Roosevelt's words were "full of hope for the Negro and deadly miasma for the Southern whites." When Crum was confirmed, the editor of the *Colored American* said that the African American "had witnessed his greatest political triumph in twenty years. . . . In this crusade against the confirmation of Crum, the South has greatly weakened the growing regard which the North has here of late entertained for it."

A third incident that heartened African Americans and led them to believe that they would flourish under Roosevelt's "Square Deal" was the resignation of the postmistress at Indianola, Mississippi. This African-American woman, Minnie M. Cox, had been in office since Harrison's administration, but because of pressure from the white citizens of the town she resigned. The Post Office Department, however, refused to accept her resignation, and when she would not serve, the post office was closed. Several months passed before the office was reopened with a white postmaster in charge. Meanwhile, African Americans warmly praised Roosevelt and referred to him as "our President—the first since Lincoln set us free."

Not until Roosevelt was far into what he called his second term did African Americans begin to understand that his friendship was neither systematic nor sustained. Before that time, however, they had come to realize that the new century had brought with it all the difficulties they had experienced in the previous one and had added some new ones of its own. In the search for better economic opportunities, blacks, like their white neighbors, continued to move into urban areas of both the North and South. Compelled by the objections that rural poor whites registered to their presence, they divorced themselves from the soil as life became almost intolerable under dishonest merchants and cruel, unscrupulous landlords. They were being run out of many parts of Arkansas, for example, and even before Oklahoma became a state the white citizens of Lawton demanded that the blacks leave within twenty-four hours.

Coincident with the rise of the city in American life was the rise of the African-American community within the city, a kind of *imperium in imperio* so far as the social aspects of their existence were concerned. In 1900 there were seventy-two cities with more than 5,000 blacks. Washington had more than 86,000, Baltimore 79,000, and New Orleans 77,000; Philadelphia, New York, and Memphis each had more than 50,000. The African-American populations of these cities, as well as of Louisville and Atlanta, were growing rapidly. Blacks outnumbered whites in Charleston, Savannah, Montgomery, Jacksonville, Shreveport, Vicksburg, Baton Rouge, and several other Southern cities. More than half of the black population of Missouri lived in towns and cities, while one-third of the black population of Kentucky lived in urban areas. If cities afforded larger opportunities, African Americans hoped to benefit from them.

Employment opportunities were fewer than the number of people coming to urban areas, and African Americans found great difficulty in securing anything except the more onerous and less attractive jobs. They continued to exist around the "ragged edge of industry" with organized labor evincing a pronounced feeling of hostility (see Chapter 14). Only the Cigarmakers' International Union and the United Mine Workers of America seemed to welcome African Americans into membership, although some other unions did have black members. African-American women easily found employment as household servants, and the more certain employment of women had the effect of attracting a larger number of women than men to the cities. Many white industrialists claimed that blacks were inefficient, while others refused to hire them because of objections raised by white employees.

Although the prospects of securing satisfactory employment were not great, African Americans continued to migrate to the cities, thereby multiplying the difficulties of those already there.

The problem of housing, common to all migrating to the city, was aggravated for African Americans by the determination of white citizens to segregate them in one section of the city. The exploitation by white landlords of the newly arrived blacks was made easier since the latter had little choice in selecting places of residence. Municipalities gave sanction to this practice by enacting segregation ordinances. The first group of such laws was passed by Louisville, Baltimore, Richmond, and Atlanta in 1912 and 1913. Blocks containing a majority of white people were to be designated as white blocks, and blocks containing a majority of African Americans were to be designated as black blocks. No blacks could move into white blocks, and vice versa. The extreme congestion that resulted from the restriction upon the choice of residence and the occupancy of small, unsanitary homes by large families led naturally to poor health and a high mortality rate.

All of the ills usually associated with maladjustment in urban life arose in the unfavorable conditions among blacks in American cities, North and South. Juvenile delinquency became rampant as slum areas grew steadily worse and as too few corrective measures were taken by either public agencies or private individuals. The parks and playgrounds movement that was developing throughout the country early in the century did little for blacks, and when they attempted to avail themselves of the opportunity to use public recreational facilities, violence and bloodshed frequently resulted. Family disorganization and disintegration were a logical consequence of the innumerable difficulties that African Americans faced, and although the church was assuming a greater responsibility for helping black communities, problems increased far more rapidly than it could solve them. The century, which had opened on such a note of optimism, very early revealed overtones of despair that equaled, if they did not surpass, any which African Americans had experienced. Perhaps the systematic movement to disfranchise and to degrade African Americans was the trend, and the Washington-Roosevelt dinner and the Crum appointment merely aberrations. The Progressive movement of the early years of the new century seemed to be "for whites only."

Even as urban problems became more aggravated as the years passed, African Americans found themselves attempting to cope with many other problems that plagued the country at the opening of the century. Exploitation of the people by unscrupulous businesses was general; the struggle for survival in a complex urban society was no respecter of races. African Americans experienced the difficulties common to all, together with the peculiar obstacles placed before them because of their color. The opening of the century witnessed, moreover, a vigorous assault on privilege and exploitation by a group of writers dubbed by Theodore Roosevelt as the "muckrakers." They attacked slum conditions, huge business combinations, corruption in city government, dishonesty in the United States Senate, the malodorous operations of the railroads, and numerous other wretched conditions. An aroused public opinion was determined to eradicate these social ills and proceeded to press for legislation to effect these ends. One muckraker, Ray Stannard Baker, studied the problem of the African American in American life, but his book, *Following the Color Line,* was hardly in the muckraking tradition. Baker, while not defending lynching, sought to explain it in terms of the distrust of Southern whites of their own judicial processes. While muckrakers usually advocated legislation to correct social ills, Baker counseled that time, patience, and education were the only solutions to the "Negro problem." African Americans could look neither to the White House nor to the muckrakers for substantial assistance. They had to grope toward a new solution to their old problems. Before this approach could be made, however, there had to be a more dramatic and violent manifestation of the problem, in order to impress both blacks and whites with the urgency of the situation.

■ The Pattern of Violence

Violent manifestations of hostility toward African Americans in the North and in the South were not new. They had persisted almost from the beginning of blacks' presence in the New World (see especially Chapters 9 and 13). In the last sixteen years of the nineteenth century there had been more than 2,500 lynchings, the great majority of which were of African Americans, with Mississippi, Alabama, Georgia, and Louisiana leading the nation. In the year of the Spanish-American War there had been the violence and bloodshed of the Wilmington, North Carolina, riot. Some considered this the dying gasp of a reign of terror. Few regarded these manifestations of violence as an inherent part of the industrial imperialism to which America was committed, although, to be sure, an integral part of that imperialistic ideology was the subjection of blacks to caste control and wage slavery. Whatever the motives, all were soon to realize that for African Americans the new century meant more violence and more bloodshed, a kind of organized brigandage of life and property against which all America revolted whenever it was practiced by lawless immigrants from Europe.

In the very first year of the new century more than 100 African Americans were lynched, and before the outbreak of World War I the number for the century had soared to more than 1,100. The South was far ahead of the rest of the country, but several Northern states, notably those in the Midwest, adhered to this ancient barbaric ritual of total disregard for the law. Although the impression was widely held that most of the blacks lynched had been accused of raping white women, the records do not sustain this impression. In the first fourteen years of the twentieth century only 315 lynch victims were accused of rape or attempted rape, while more than 500 were accused of homicide and the others were accused of robbery, insulting white people, and numerous other "offenses." Regardless of the alleged crime of the victim, lynching in the twentieth century continued to be an important if illegal part of the system of punishment in the United States.

It was the epidemic of race riots that swept the country early in the century that aroused the greatest anxiety and discomfort among the African-American population. Although lynchings were decreasing slightly, riots were perceptibly increasing, and their dramatic nature had the effect of emphasizing the insecurity of blacks throughout the country. In August 1904 the state of Georgia was rocked by occurrences in the small town of Statesboro. Two African Americans were accused of the brutal murder of a white farmer, his wife, and three children. After two weeks of "safe keeping" in Savannah, the blacks were brought back to Statesboro for trial. They were convicted and sentenced to be hanged. Meanwhile, the white citizens had worked themselves into a frenzy of race hatred. There was constant talk of the way in which blacks were becoming insolent. When the sentences were passed on the defendants, a mob that had formed surged upstairs and forced itself into the courtroom after overpowering a company of Savannah militia whose rifles were not loaded "in tender consideration for the feelings of the mob." The African Americans were dragged out and burned alive. This was the signal for wholesale terrorism against African Americans. One black was severely whipped for riding a bicycle on the sidewalk, while another was lashed "on general principles." The black mother of a three-day-old infant was beaten and kicked, and her husband was killed. Houses were wrecked, and countless terrified blacks left the country. Although there was talk of punishing the leaders of the mob, nothing was ever done.

As events in Statesboro made clear, African Americans of both genders and all ages were victims of racial violence. When Marie Thompson, a black woman in Lebanon Junction, Kentucky, killed a white man during an argument, her claim of self-defense—"a statement that would have undoubtedly saved her if she was a white woman"—produced a lynch mob that took her unopposed from the jail and attempted to "lynch her from a tree in the jail yard." The Louisville *Courier-Journal* reported that Thompson fought her murderers to the end:

> The woman was struggling and fighting like a tiger all the time, but the mob was too much for her, and a minute later she was swinging in the air, with her feet several inches from the ground. All of a sudden she twisted around and grabbed a man by the collar, jerked a knife from his hands and cut the rope that was choking the life out of her.

Once on the ground, Thompson attempted to force her way through the lynch mob but was "shot down in a hail of gunfire." This lynching in Kentucky and numerous others in communities throughout the nation confirms George C. Wright's judgment that "whites . . . did not hesitate to take the law into their own hands, to turn to the rope or the rifle to keep blacks in their place, and to stamp out any acts that suggested militancy on the part of Afro-Americans."

The South's most sensational riot occurred in Atlanta in September 1906. For months the city had been lashed into a fury of race hatred by loose talk and by the movement to disfranchise African Americans (see Chapter 13). An irresponsible press published articles that intensified the feeling against blacks. One editor called for the revival of the Ku Klux Klan, while another went so far as to offer a reward for a "lynching bee" in Atlanta. On Saturday, September 22, newspapers told of four successive assaults on white women by blacks. The country people, in town for the day, joined with the urban element in creating an outraged, panic-stricken mob. Whites began to attack every black person they saw.

The following day was quiet, but the rioting broke out again on Monday in Brownsville, a suburb of Atlanta. African Americans there had heard that their fellows in Atlanta were being slaughtered en masse. Some sought asylum in two black institutions in the neighborhood, Clark University and Gammon Theological Seminary. Others, who were determined to defend themselves to the end, collected arms. When officers of the law came out, they began rounding up blacks and arresting them for being armed. One officer shot into a crowd of blacks. The fire was returned, killing one officer and wounding another. The whites then threw discretion aside and set out upon a general destruction of black property and lives. Four African Americans, all of whom were substantial citizens, were killed, and many were injured. J. W. E. Bowen, the president of Gammon, was beaten over the head with a rifle butt by a police official. Houses of blacks were looted and burned. For several days the city was paralyzed: factories were closed and all transportation stopped. Numerous blacks sold their property and left. The whites confessed their shame and condemned the rioters. A group of responsible black and white citizens came together and organized the Atlanta Civic League to work for the improvement of social conditions and to prevent other riots. Nothing was done to the rioters. Despairing African Americans loudly protested, but no one listened. Even Roosevelt's "door of hope" was apparently being shut in their faces.

President Roosevelt's handling of the riot in Brownsville, Texas, convinced many African Americans that he had no genuine interest in their plight. In August 1906 three companies of the Twenty-fifth Regiment, composed of African Americans, were involved in a riot in Brownsville, Texas; one citizen was killed, another wounded, and the chief of police injured. Whites reported that blacks had "shot up the town," and race passion was stirred to a fever pitch. Only the firm stand of the commander at Fort Brown prevented the riot from reaching a more desperate level. In November, on the basis of the report of an inspector who had said that blacks had murdered and maimed the citizens of Brownsville, President Roosevelt dismissed the entire battalion without honor and disqualified its members for service in either the military or the civil service of the United States. African Americans, who had always taken pride in the service of their soldiers, were outraged. Many whites protested, among them John Milholland, who through the Constitution League carried on a relentless fight for the soldiers. Even Senator Tillman, doubtless in order to embarrass the president, called it an "executive lynching."

When Congress met in December, Sen. Joseph B. Foraker of Ohio insisted that a full and fair trial should have preceded such drastic punishment. On January 22 the Senate authorized a general investigation of the whole matter, the president having revoked the civil disability of the discharged soldiers a week earlier. After several months of study the majority of the Senate committee upheld the president's handling of the affair. A stinging minority report by Senator Foraker denounced the findings of the majority. The Ohio senator did not give up the fight. In 1909 he succeeded in forcing through an act of Congress establishing a court of inquiry to pass on the cases of the discharged soldiers. It provided that all of the discharged soldiers who were found to be qualified for reenlistment were to be deemed eligible and that if they reenlisted they were to be considered as having enlisted immediately after their discharge more than two years earlier. Any such soldier was to receive the "pay, allowances, and other rights and benefits that he would have been entitled to receive according to his rank from said date of discharge as if he had been honorably discharged . . . and had reenlisted immediately." While some regarded the establishment of the court of inquiry as the "most pointed and signal defeat of Roosevelt's administration," most African Americans looked upon the Brownsville incident as one more piece of evidence of the helplessness of a minority in a hostile land. Not until 1972, some sixty-six years after the incident, did Congress rescind the dishonorable discharge and restore the black members of the regiment, most of whom were dead, to good standing in the army.

The South was not the only area of America that was hostile to African Americans in the early years of the new century. Crowds of white hoodlums frequently attacked blacks in large Northern cities. On several occasions whites dragged blacks off the streetcars of Philadelphia, with cries of "Lynch him! Kill him!" As the migration of African Americans to the North increased, hostility toward them grew. Some towns tolerated them; others did not. Syracuse, Ohio, forbade any blacks to settle there, and several towns in Indiana did not permit any African-American residents within their limits.

Rioting in the North was as vicious and almost as prevalent as it was in the South. Springfield, Ohio, had two riots within a few years. The one in 1904 conformed perfectly to the pattern of violence that had characterized rioting in other parts of the country. In an altercation an African American shot and killed a white officer. A mob gathered and broke into the jail where the black was being held. The citizens murdered the black in the doorway of the jail, hung him on a telegraph pole, and riddled his body with bullets. They then proceeded to wreak destruction on the black section of the town.

Colored Methodist Bishops Appeal to White America—1908

To enumerate the civil, social, moral, judicial and political injustices that today exasperate and annoy the members of our race, would be a hard task . . . whereever this race turns . . . it is restricted within certain narrow limits by the "Color Line." It is "thus far" in the North, and "thus far" in the South. . . .

We appeal to the friends of humanity to use their influence to rid this glorious country of mob violence which is sending so many to an untimely grave.

We appeal to all who believe in fair play to assist us in banishing from our land the peonage and convict labor system, which are degrading and destroying the very vestige of manhood and relegating many to the most galling serfdom.

We appeal to the liberty loving men in authority to lend us their assistance by influence, by legislation for the removal of the 'Jim Crow' car laws. . . .

We appeal to the Judges of the Supreme Court to annul laws in violation of the Federal Constitution, to members of the several Southern States where disfranchisement laws have been enacted, and to the Congress of the United States to repeal the enactments which have robbed us of the rights guaranteed to us by the Federal Constitution [rights] which were gained upon the field of conquest by blood shed by black men as well as white men.

The Christian Index, March 19, 1908, in Herbert Aptheker, ed., A *Documentary History of the Negro People in the United States, 1661–1910* (New York, 1951), pp. 896–897.

When they had finished, eight buildings had been burned, many blacks had been beaten, and others had fled, never to return. Two years later, in Greensburg, Indiana, a portion of the act was repeated. A retarded black was convicted for criminally assaulting his employer, a white widow. The mob that gathered did not succeed in taking the black from the authorities, but it was not daunted. Many homes of African Americans were damaged, several innocent persons were beaten, and some were driven out of town.

The Northern riot that shook the entire country was the one that occurred in Springfield, Illinois, in August 1908. The wife of a streetcar conductor claimed that she had been dragged from her bed and raped by someone whom she identified as an African American, George Richardson, who had been working in the neighborhood. Richardson was arrested and jailed. Before a special grand jury the woman admitted that she had been severely beaten by a white man whose identity she refused to disclose and that Richardson had had no connection with the incident. By this time, however, feeling was running high against Richardson. As a precautionary measure the officials took him and another black, held in connection with the murder of a white man, to a nearby town where they boarded the train for

Bloomington. When the mob that was gathering learned that the blacks had been removed, they were furious. They wrecked the restaurant of an operator whose car had been used to transport the blacks and began to surge through the town.

The town officials saw that the mob was becoming unruly, and several unsuccessful efforts were made to disperse it. Finally the governor called out the militia. The mob, oblivious to the appeals of high state officials, raided secondhand stores, secured guns, axes, and other weapons, and began to destroy African-American businesses and to drive blacks from their homes. They set fire to a building in which a black owned a barber shop. The barber was lynched in the yard behind his shop, and the mob, after dragging his body through the streets, was preparing to burn it when the militia from Decatur dispersed the crowd by firing into it. On the following night an eighty-four-year-old African American, who had been married to a white woman for more than thirty years, was lynched within a block of the statehouse. Before order was restored more than 5,000 militia men were patrolling the streets. In the final count, two blacks had been lynched, four white men had been killed, and more than seventy persons had been injured. More than 100 arrests were made, and approximately fifty indictments were returned. The alleged leaders of the mob went unpunished.

The news of the riot was almost more than African Americans could bear. It seemed to them a perverse manner in which to approach the centennial of the birth of Lincoln. African Americans were actually lynched within half a mile of the only home Lincoln ever owned and within two miles of his final resting place. Their cup was filled, and they hardly had the voice to cry out against this most recent outrage. These realities certainly made a mockery of Booker T. Washington's well-publicized philosophy of uplift and accommodation, clearly negating his oft-repeated belief that no intelligent, virtuous, and economically independent black "shall very long be denied the proper respect and consideration." It was time for drastic action. Somehow, some solution had to be found to the problem of color, which Du Bois had already called the greatest problem of the twentieth century.

■ New Solutions for Old Problems

The sordid picture of African-American life in America in the twentieth century had moved a group of young African Americans as early as 1905 to organize for determined and aggressive action in order to secure full citizenship. They reasoned that the day of temporizing was over; a war was on, and they decided to fight to the finish. This group, under the leadership of W. E. B. Du Bois, met at Niagara Falls, Canada, in June 1905 and drew up a platform for aggressive action. Among other things, they demanded freedom of speech and criticism, manhood suffrage, the abolition of all distinctions based on race, the recognition of the basic principles of human fellowship, and respect for the working person. Despite the open attack that was made on them for their radicalism, they incorporated themselves as the Niagara Movement and met at Harpers Ferry in the following year.

The resolutions that were drawn up at Harpers Ferry were written by Du Bois in what he admitted was a "tumult of emotion." Kelly Miller described this manifesto as "scarcely distinguishable from a wild and frantic shriek." It was indeed the wailings of a despondent but courageous group calling out for consideration on the basis of the common humanity of all people. In part, it said:

> In the past year the work of the Negro hater has flourished in the land. Step by step the defenders of the rights of American citizens have retreated. The work of stealing the black man's ballot has progressed and the fifty and more representatives of stolen votes still sit in the nation's capital. . . . Never before in the modern age has a great and civilized folk threatened to adopt so cowardly a creed in the treatment of its fellow-citizens, born and bred on its soil. Stripped of verbose subterfuge and in its naked nastiness, the new American creed says: fear to let black men even try to rise lest they become the equals of the white. And this in the land that professes to follow Jesus Christ. The blasphemy of such a course is only matched by its cowardice.

The Niagara Movement met in Boston in 1907, and at the session in Faneuil Hall did much to revive the old spirit of abolitionism. Organizations such as the New England Suffrage League and the Equal Rights League of Georgia supported the work of the Niagara Movement. In the following year the meeting was held at Oberlin, Ohio. The organization had now met at Oberlin, a hotbed of Western abolitionism; at Boston, the center of Eastern abolitionism; at Harpers Ferry, the scene of John Brown's martyrdom; and at Niagara Falls, an important terminus on the Underground Railroad. But there were to be no more meetings, for soon the Niagara Movement was absorbed by a new and more resourceful organization.

The Springfield riots shocked the sensibilities of many whites. Among them was William English Walling, a distinguished writer, who went to the scene and gathered data for an article. In "Race War in the North," a piece which appeared in the *Independent,* Walling described the Springfield atrocities and declared, "Either the spirit of the abolitionists, of Lincoln and of Lovejoy, must be revived and we must come to treat the Negro on a plane of absolute political and social equality or Vardaman and Tillman will soon have transferred the Race War to the North. . . . Yet who realizes the seriousness of the situation and what large and powerful body of citizens is ready to come to their aid?" Mary White Ovington, a New York social worker already interested in the problems of blacks, read the article and took the matter up with Walling and Henry Moskowitz. They decided to call a conference for Lincoln's birthday in 1909 to accept Walling's challenge. Oswald Garrison Villard, the grandson of William Lloyd Garrison, wrote the call, in which he said, "We call upon all believers in democracy to join in a

National conference for the discussion of present evils, the voicing of protests, and the renewal of the struggle for civil and political liberty." Abolitionism had become reincarnate in the progeny of its greatest exponent.

The young radicals of the Niagara Movement were invited to the conference, and most of them accepted. Among those who did not was Monroe Trotter, who was suspicious of the motives of white people. It was a distinguished gathering of educators, professors, publicists, bishops, judges, and social workers. Among those who participated were Jane Addams, William Dean Howells, Ida B. Wells, John Dewey, John Milholland, Du Bois, and Villard. Plans were made to establish a permanent organization, which came to be known as the National Association for the Advancement of Colored People (NAACP). A program of action was also agreed upon. The organization pledged itself to work for the abolition of all forced segregation, equal education for black and white children, the complete enfranchisement of African Americans, and the enforcement of the Fourteenth and Fifteenth Amendments. A formal organization was perfected in May 1910, with Moorfield Storey of Boston as president and William E. Walling as chairman of the executive committee. W. E. B. Du Bois, as the director of publicity and research, was the only African-American officer. The presence of Du Bois on the staff branded the organization as radical from the beginning. Many feared that it would be a capricious, irresponsible organization that would draw its main inspiration from the dreamings of the Niagara Movement. It was denounced by most white philanthropists, and even some blacks thought it unwise.

In the first year of its existence the NAACP launched a program to widen the industrial opportunities for African Americans, to seek greater police protection for them in the South, and to carry on a crusade against lynching and lawlessness. Important instrumentalities in carrying out its program were the publication *Crisis* and the Legal Redress Committee. It was the primary task of Du Bois to get the magazine going. In November 1910 the first issue appeared. One thousand copies were rapidly sold, and the circulation figures increased until they reached 100,000 per month by 1918. The magazine waged a vigorous campaign against lynching and mob law. Its phenomenal success in circulation was equaled by the effectiveness with which it dealt with the pressing problems of blacks.

Arthur B. Spingarn, who with his brother Joel had become a member of the biracial board of directors, was chairman of the legal committee. White and black attorneys worked closely with him, and within fifteen years they had won three important decisions before the United States Supreme Court. In 1915, in the case of *Guinn v. United States*, the Supreme Court declared the grandfather clauses in the Maryland and Oklahoma constitutions to be repugnant to the Fifteenth Amendment and therefore null and void. In 1917, in the case of *Buchanan v. Warley*, the Court declared unconstitutional the Louisville ordinance requiring Negroes to live in certain sections of the city. In 1923, in the case of *Moore v. Dempsey*, the Court ordered a new trial in the

Arkansas courts for an African American who had been convicted of murder. The representatives of the NAACP had argued that the Arkansas peon had not received a fair trial because, among other things, African Americans were excluded from the jury. The Court accepted this view. Resorting to the courts thus became an effective weapon in the fight for full citizenship.

As the work of the NAACP became better organized, it was extended by the establishment of branches. Shortly after the initial organization the first branch was established in Chicago. Within two years, nine others had been formed. Each year up until the outbreak of the First World War the number doubled, and by 1921 there were more than 400 branches scattered all over the United States, gathering information for the association and carrying out, on the local front, the aims of the parent organization. It was not long before the NAACP extended its activities across national boundaries. Du Bois was sent to the International Congress of Races in London, partly to represent the association at that important gathering and partly to follow Booker T. Washington, who had made a tour of Europe in 1910. In his speeches before the congress Du Bois made it clear that contrary to Washington's claims African Americans in the United States were suffering under grave legal and civil disabilities. He won new friends for the NAACP among the delegates from many lands. These contacts were to strengthen the program of the association at home during and after the war.

Although the NAACP included in its program a plan for widening the economic opportunities of African Americans, it did not find time to do much in this area. The need for organized effort in the economic sphere was no less pressing, however, and an organization emerged that devoted its attention to this matter. At the time that the Niagara Movement was getting under way in 1905, two organizations were established in New York City, and these became the nucleus for a national agency. They were the Committee for Improving Industrial Conditions of Negroes in New York and the National League for the Protection of Colored Women. Among the distinguished whites supporting the latter organization were Mrs. W. H. Baldwin, W. J. Schiefflin, and A. S. Frissell. Meanwhile, George Edmund Haynes, a young black graduate student at Columbia University, was making an extensive study of social and economic conditions among the African Americans of New York City. He made a report of his findings to a joint meeting of the two organizations. Interest was so great in his findings, later published as *The Negro at Work in New York City*, that a committee was formed to act as a coordinating agency in the effort to round out a larger program of community life for the blacks of New York.

Plans were laid before the committee for improving social and economic conditions among African Americans. Haynes, who maintained a keen interest in the project, went to Fisk University to develop a department of sociology and to establish a training center for social workers. The experience and data he secured were placed at the disposal of the committee, and as the program evolved, a formal organization was perfected. In 1911 the three organizations merged to form the National League on Urban Conditions among Negroes (commonly known as the National Urban League), with Haynes and Eugene Kinckle Jones as executive officers. E. R. A. Seligman of Columbia University was the first chairman of the league, and it received support from Julius Rosenwald, Mrs. Baldwin, and others. Among the sponsors were Booker T. Washington, Kelly Miller, Roger N. Baldwin, Robert R. Moton, and L. Hollingsworth Wood.

The league undertook to open up new opportunities for African Americans in industry and to assist newly arrived blacks in their adjustment to urban centers. Branches were opened in many of the large cities, and programs were started for meeting migrants, directing them to jobs and lodgings, and offering information on how to live in the city. It did an effective job in bringing employer and employee together and in easing the difficulties of mutual adjustment. The league also developed a program for the training of young men and women for social work. It established fellowships to support them while studying at the School of Philanthropy in New York, and "part fellowships" to make possible in-service training at the national office in preparation for carrying on work in the field. Its program of training made possible the education of many of America's most distinguished black social-work leaders in the next generation.

Among the other organizations that assisted in the adjustment of African Americans to city life were the Young Men's Christian Association (YMCA) and the Young Women's Christian Association (YWCA). The first black YMCA had been organized as early as 1853 in Washington, but not until after the Civil War was it connected with the white movement. In 1888 William A. Hunton was placed on the national staff as its first salaried black officer, and in 1898 Jesse E. Moorland joined him to give special attention to the problems of African Americans in urban areas. Early in the new century several city association branches were organized. Buildings that could be used as headquarters and recreational centers were constructed. In 1907 George Foster Peabody gave a building for black men and boys in his native city of Columbus, Georgia. In 1910 Julius Rosenwald, in his initial contribution to the YMCA movement among African Americans, gave $25,000 toward the erection of the Wabash Avenue building in Chicago. In the succeeding years his gifts for thirteen buildings amounted to $325,000. In the absence of an effective public program of wholesome recreation and guidance, the YMCA, even with its segregated facilities, which in the long run would prove counterproductive, provided some services to the communities where it existed.

By 1906 there were small YWCAs for African Americans in Washington, Philadelphia, New York, and Baltimore. Gradually, with an awakened social consciousness, city and student work developed. Not until the outbreak of World War I did a strong movement develop for the work among African-American women. Several substantial buildings were erected in strategic centers, and with the cooperation of philanthropists like Rosenwald and

Rockefeller, the YWCA acquired physical plants in which it could carry out a program of social improvement and education for young black women that did much to assist them with their problems in urban communities.

There were scattered efforts to solve local problems, such as the Flanner Settlement House in Indianapolis and the neighborhood associations in New York. Efforts were also made to improve housing, such as the Octavia Hill Association in Philadelphia and the Model Homes Company in Cincinnati. They were indeed new solutions for old problems. But the problems of African Americans in the United States at the opening of the twentieth century were so broad in scope and so deep in implication that only a large-scale, comprehensive attack on them could hope to make more than a dent in solving them. The programs of the National Association for the Advancement of Colored People and the National Urban League were broadly conceived to meet this challenge, but there was no guarantee that these agencies had the right formula. In the difficult task of social reform and regeneration, science and reason together could scarcely keep the door of hope open if passion and prejudice were pressing with all their might to close it.

CHAPTER 16

In Pursuit of Democracy

■ World War I

The discerning observer at the International Races Congress in London in 1911 could see the unmistakable signs of war clouds gathering in Europe. Despite the multiplication of peace agencies in the Old World as well as the New, the armed competition between two rival coalitions in Europe for markets, cheap materials, and cheap labor was well under way several years before the actual outbreak of the war. What observers could not see, however, was that civilized countries would be willing to pay a price as dear as a world conflagration for a "place in the sun." Germany and its satellites were more determined than ever to wield a controlling influence in Europe, Africa, and Asia, while Russia, France, and Great Britain were equally determined to see to it that such ambitions were effectively curbed. Confusion and antagonism were everywhere, as the game of intrigue became more complicated and as all semblances of international law broke down.

When war came in 1914 the American people were wholly unprepared even to stand on the sidelines and watch the world plunge itself into the madness and insanity of war. Americans had been peculiarly preoccupied with their own domestic problems, and Woodrow Wilson's promise of a "New Freedom" had focused attention on the economic and social maladjustments that were the legacies of the great industrial upheaval of the previous generation. African Americans certainly were not concerned with

Europe's problems. They already had more than enough difficulties to claim their attention. Having been skeptical of the Democratic party since the days of Reconstruction, they kept their eyes fastened on Washington to see what the first Southern-born president since the Civil War would do.

In 1912 African Americans were sorely distressed by the political picture. They had become suspicious of Theodore Roosevelt because of his handling of the Brownsville incident (see Chapter 15), and they did not have any confidence in President Taft. Many of them were willing, however, to follow Roosevelt in the formation of a new party if they could receive assurances that the new party would stand unequivocally for full citizenship for all. Officials of the NAACP went so far as to draft a statement, which they wanted placed in the Progressive Republican platform, calling for the repeal of discriminatory laws and for complete enfranchisement. When Roosevelt permitted the Southern white delegates to have their way in ignoring the statement and in barring some black delegates from the convention, African Americans realized that the Bull Moose movement offered them very little. As skeptical of the Democratic party as they were, some of them turned to it. They were considerably heartened by Wilson's assertion that he wished to see "justice done to the colored people in every matter; and not mere grudging justice, but justice executed with liberality and cordial good feeling." Many African Americans were won over to the Wilson camp by the candidate's clear-cut expressions of good will. One of these was: "I want to assure them that should I become President of the United States they may count upon me for absolute fair dealing, for everything by which I could assist in advancing the interests of their race in the United States." Black support of Wilson was by no means decisive, but it was far greater than many Republicans would have believed possible.

In the early years of the Wilson administration, therefore, African Americans were watching Washington, rather than Paris and Berlin. What they saw dismayed them greatly. They had little immediate interest in tariff and banking reforms, and since they were excluded from so many labor unions, they benefited little from the labor exemption provisions of the Clayton Antitrust Act. Washington had not forgotten them, however. The first Congress of Wilson's administration received the greatest flood of bills proposing discriminatory legislation against blacks that had ever been introduced into Congress. At least twenty bills advocated the segregation of the races on public carriers in the District of Columbia, the exclusion of blacks from commissions in the army and navy, separate accommodations for black and white federal employees, and the exclusion of all immigrants of African descent. There were similar proposals in the next Congress. Although most of the legislation failed to pass, Wilson, by executive order, segregated African-American federal employees so far as eating and rest room facilities were concerned and phased out most of them from civil service.

When President Wilson issued his proclamation of neutrality in 1914, African Americans, like most Americans, thought little of the possibility of

America's entry into the war. Blacks continued to concern themselves with their own peculiar problems. Some went to the White House with Monroe Trotter to protest the segregation of African-American federal employees but were dismissed because Wilson regarded Trotter's language as "insulting." Others began to fight residential segregation ordinances that were springing up all over the country. When the president ordered the occupation of Haiti by the marines in 1915, African Americans loudly protested the violation of that country's sovereignty and territorial integrity; and the killing of several hundred Haitians in order to restore peace and order was particularly repulsive to them. In the same year the most notable motion picture yet produced, *The Birth of a Nation,* was released. Based on the violently antiblack writings of Thomas Dixon, it told a most sordid and obviously distorted story of black emancipation, enfranchisement, and debauchery of white womanhood. And it did more than any other single thing to nurture and promote the myth of black domination and debauchery during Reconstruction. Lynchings and other forms of violence increased, to add to the concern of African Americans. In 1916 Jesse Washington was publicly burned in Waco, Texas, before a cheering mob of thousands of men, women, and children. In South Carolina a well-to-do black farmer, Anthony Crawford, was mobbed and killed for "impudence" in refusing to agree to a price for his cottonseed. In Mexico twenty-two blacks from the Tenth Cavalry were killed while on a mission pursuing a deserter.

In the midst of this great distress, late in 1915, Booker T. Washington died. Now there was no leader among blacks whom the majority of the citizens of the United States respected. At the same time, though, there was no one left with the prestige of Washington who would counsel patience and moderation. This was the time, some of the more aggressive leaders believed, to consolidate and achieve a unity in thought and action that had been hitherto impossible. To this end a conference was called in 1916 at Joel Spingarn's home in Amenia, New York, to discuss the plight of African Americans. This conference brought together perhaps the most distinguished African Americans to assemble in recent years. It drew up no impassioned manifesto, and its resolutions showed no bitterness. But all participants agreed to work quietly and earnestly for enfranchisement, the abolition of lynching, and the enforcement of laws protecting civil rights. It was a happy prelude to America's entry into the war. With a calm but firm unanimity among African-American leaders, the black citizens of the United States could pursue more intelligently and relentlessly the democracy that the allies were seeking to extend to all the world.

■ The Enlistment of African Americans

Of the 750,000 men in the regular army and the National Guard at the beginning of the war, approximately 20,000 were black. There were 10,000 in the black units of the regular army, the Ninth and Tenth Cavalries and the Twenty-fourth and Twenty-fifth Infantries. Another 10,000 were in various units of the National Guard: the Eighth Illinois, the Fifteenth New York, the separate battalions of the District of Columbia and of Ohio, and the separate companies of Maryland, Connecticut, Massachusetts, and Tennessee. As early as March 25, 1917, two weeks before the United States formally declared war, blacks from the District of Columbia National Guard had been called out to protect the capital. Between July and September, other black units were called into active service.

African Americans were among those who thronged the recruiting stations in April 1917 seeking to volunteer their services, but for the most part they were not accepted. The passage of the Selective Service Act on May 18, however, provided for the enlistment of all able-bodied Americans between the ages of twenty-one and thirty-one. On July 5, registration day, more than 700,000 blacks registered. Before the end of the Selective Service enlistments, 2,290,525 blacks had registered, 367,000 of whom were called into the service. Approximately 31 percent of all blacks who registered were accepted, while 26 percent of whites who registered were accepted. This was due not to the superior physical and mental qualifications of African Americans, but to the inclination of some draft boards to discriminate against blacks in the matter of exemptions. One board in Georgia, for example, was discharged because of its flagrant discrimination against blacks in exemptions. There were numerous complaints against other boards. There were no outstanding examples of draft-dodging blacks, and even those who were opposed to the war on the grounds that it was an imperialistic conflict answered the call of their draft boards.

African Americans were especially eager to participate in the struggle not only as enlisted men but as officers. They were greatly disheartened by the retirement of the highest-ranking black officer, Col. Charles Young, because of alleged high blood pressure. To prove his physical fitness, Colonel Young rode on horseback from Ohio to the nation's capital, but the retirement board remained adamant. In an effort to secure the commissioning of African-American officers, blacks met stern resistance in many high places in Washington. Congress was creating training camps for white officers but was making no provisions for the training of black officers. A committee of representative citizens, headed by Joel Spingarn, went to Washington and conferred with military authorities, but it was a fruitless venture. Almost immediately college students at Howard, Fisk, Atlanta, Tuskegee, and other black institutions began a program of agitation for the training of African-American officers. When Spingarn took the matter up with Gen. Leonard Wood, the latter said that if 200 trained blacks of college grade could be secured, he would see to it that a training camp was established for them. Early in May 1917 a Central Committee of Negro College Men was set up at Howard University, and within ten days it had collected the names of 1,500 African-American college men who wanted to become officers in the

United States Army. The committee interviewed numerous members of Congress and presented them with a statement justifying the establishment of an officers' reserve training camp for blacks. More than 300 senators and representatives approved the proposal, and the movement to establish the camp began in earnest. Mass meetings were held, the African-American press vigorously supported the training of African Americans as officers, and students raised funds to carry on the fight.

Some blacks denounced the idea of a separate camp, contending that such an establishment would defeat the struggle for full citizenship. The NAACP, however, supported the proposal. When the government finally authorized the camp, Spingarn, a leader in the association as well as in the fight for the camp, said: "The army officials want the camp to fail. The last thing they want is to help colored men to become commissioned officers. The camp is intended to fight segregation, not to encourage it. Colored men in a camp by themselves would all get a fair chance for promotion. Opposition on the part of Negroes is helping the South, which does not want the Negroes to have any kind of military training." On October 15, 1917, at Fort Des Moines, Iowa, 639 African Americans were commissioned—106 captains, 329 first lieutenants, and 204 second lieutenants. Later, at nonsegregated camps and in the field, other blacks received commissions in the army. At colleges and high schools throughout the country, blacks prepared to become officer candidates and to serve the army in a variety of ways in the Students' Army Training Corps and the Reserve Officers Training Corps.

Because of the mounting race friction that attended the migration of African Americans to the North, the continued lynching of black men and women, and the German propaganda that was circulated in the United States, it was deemed wise to bring into the government an African American who could advise on matters affecting blacks and who enjoyed the confidence of his people. Consequently, Newton D. Baker, the secretary of war, announced on October 5, 1917, the appointment of Emmett J. Scott, who for eighteen years had been the secretary to Booker T. Washington, as a special assistant to the secretary of war. Scott was to serve as "confidential advisor in matters affecting the interests of the ten million Negroes of the United States and the part they are to play in connection with the present war." Baker was widely commended by whites and blacks for making the appointment. The *Mobile News Item* said, "The appointment is a wise move and a wise selection. While the government is coordinating all the interests of the country in the movement to win the war . . . it should not overlook the colored people." Kelly Miller of Howard University said, "I regard the appointment of Mr. Scott . . . as the most significant appointment that has yet come to the colored race."

Scott's functions were primarily to urge the equal and impartial application of Selective Service regulations and to formulate plans to promote healthy morale among black soldiers and civilians. He was called upon to express an opinion regarding almost every phase of African-American life and was required to answer thousands of inquiries from blacks on every conceivable subject. He investigated scores of cases in which unfair treatment was charged, and he looked into many cases relating to voluntary and compulsory allotments, war risk insurance, and government allowances and compensation. He also worked with the Committee on Public Information in releasing news concerning black soldiers as well as various activities on the home front.

While African Americans were barred altogether from the marines and permitted to serve in the navy only in the most menial capacities, they served in almost every branch of the army except the pilot section of the aviation corps. After a long struggle they were permitted to join units of coast and field artillery. They were in the cavalry, infantry, engineer corps, signal corps, medical corps, hospital and ambulance corps, veterinary corps, sanitary and ammunition trains, stevedore regiments, labor battalions, and depot brigades. Blacks also served as regimental adjutants, judge advocates, chaplains, intelligence officers, chemists, clerks, surveyors, draftsmen, auto repairmen, motor truck operators, and mechanics.

The problem of training African-American soldiers while in the United States was one that plagued the War Department from the beginning. Although the army was committed to the activation of an all-black division, the Ninety-second, no arrangements were made to train the men at the same camp. Thus the men of the all-black division were trained at seven widely separated camps, all the way from Camp Grant in Rockford, Illinois, to Camp Upton in Yaphank, New York. It was the only instance in which a division was never actually brought together until it reached the fighting front. Another black division, the Ninety-third, was never brought up to its full strength, and after training in different places the units that were organized were sent overseas at different times to join various fighting units of the French army. White Southerners objected strenuously to the army's sending Northern African Americans into the South for training. The objections became so persistent that it was necessary for officials in Washington to call a conference in August 1917 to discuss the matter. It was agreed that "while the South might object to having colored men from Northern states sent into the various camps and cantonments of the South, it could not well refuse an acceptance of the principles of having such colored selectmen as might be called in such states trained in the cantonments of the states in which they lived." This arrangement worked such a hardship upon the administration of the army's program that long before the war was over, blacks were being sent to the camp, North or South, that best served the interests of the prosecution of the war.

There was much discrimination in the army and in the civilian agencies that served the army, and it required a great deal of tact and prompt action to prevent more serious outbreaks than there were. The Federal Council of Churches created a Committee on the Welfare of Negro Troops of which Bishop W. P. Thirkield, Robert R. Moton, James H. Dillard, and John R.

Hawkins were prominent members. The two field secretaries of the committee were Charles H. Williams of Hampton and G. Lake Imes of Tuskegee. They investigated conditions at home and abroad and found many outstanding examples of discrimination and segregation among the service agencies. At Camp Greene, near Charlotte, North Carolina, they found that there were five YMCA buildings, but none for the 10,000 African Americans stationed there. A sign over one of the buildings read "This building is for white men only," and the secretary placed outside the building a table for black soldiers to use in writing letters. At Camp Lee, near Petersburg, Virginia, white soldiers patrolled the grounds around a white prayer meeting to see to it that no blacks attempted to enter.

Complaints flooded the War Department that blacks were continuously insulted by white officers. They referred to African Americans as "coons," "niggers," and "darkies" and frequently forced them to work under unhealthy and difficult conditions. Many black soldiers contended that white officers made it extremely hard for them to advance and that they indiscriminately assigned them to labor battalions even when they were qualified for other posts requiring higher skills and intelligence. The friction between black soldiers and the military police grew in intensity as the war progressed, and although the War Department issued orders calling for fair and impartial treatment of black soldiers, there was little discernible improvement.

The hostility that white civilians displayed toward black soldiers made it difficult for African Americans to remain enthusiastic about serving their country. In many places in the North they were denied service in restaurants and admission to theaters. When African Americans insisted on attending the theater at Fort Riley, Kansas, Gen. C. C. Ballou, commander of the Ninety-second Division, issued an order commanding his men not to go where their presence was resented. He reminded them that "white men had made the Division, and they can break it just as easily if it becomes a trouble maker." A howl of resentment was immediately raised in the black press, and African Americans were not consoled by the fact that Gen. Ballou was pressing legal charges against the theater operators that discriminated against his men.

Friction in the South caused the greatest concern. In August 1917, for example, the men of the Twenty-fourth Infantry became involved in a riot with white civilians in Houston, Texas. After much goading and many insults by the white citizens, the black soldiers were disarmed when it was feared that they would use their weapons in defending themselves. Refusing to be outdone, the soldiers seized arms and killed seventeen whites. With only a slight pretense of a trial, thirteen African-American soldiers were hanged for murder and mutiny, forty-one were imprisoned for life, and forty others were held pending further investigation. Nothing since the Brownsville incident had done so much to wound the pride of African Americans or to shake their faith in their government. Houston native Emmett J. Scott's assertion that the incident "did not dampen the ardor of the colored men who went to the front for the Stars and Stripes" seems hardly accurate. Many men of the Twenty-fourth swore vengeance on the officials whom they accused of unjust treatment. A black newspaper in Baltimore exclaimed, "The Negroes of the entire country will regard the thirteen Negro soldiers of the Twenty-fourth Infantry executed as martyrs," while the *New York Age* declared, "Strict justice has been done, but full justice has not been done. . . . And so sure as there is a God in heaven, at some time and in some way full justice will be done."

At Spartanburg, South Carolina, where the Fifteenth New York Infantry was in training, white citizens felt that something was needed to put the jaunty New York blacks in their place. In October 1917, when Noble Sissle, the talented drum major of the infantry band, went into a hotel to purchase a newspaper, the proprietor cursed him and asked him why he did not remove his hat. Before Sissle could answer, the white man knocked his hat from his head. As the young soldier stooped to pick up his hat he was struck several times and kicked out of the place. Upon discovering what had happened, black militiamen, joined by their incensed white comrades from New York, started to "rush the hotel." But Lt. James R. Europe, the bandmaster, who happened to be passing, called the men to attention and ordered them to disperse. The following evening the soldiers planned to "shoot up" the town of Spartanburg, but the commanding officer, Col. William Hayward, overtook them as they were leaving and ordered them back to camp.

Emmett J. Scott rushed to the scene to investigate the incident and to plead with the men to do nothing to bring dishonor on the regiment or the race. The War Department had three possible courses: it could keep the regiment at Camp Wadsworth and face a violent eruption; it could remove the regiment to another camp, thereby conveying the impression that whenever any community exerted sufficient pressure it could force the War Department to remove undesirable soldiers from its midst; or it could order the regiment overseas. The last alternative was decided upon. As the 15th New York Regiment, now the 369th of the United States Army, made its way to Europe to become the first contingent of African-American combat troops to reach the theater of war, it could well reason that there could be a more successful pursuit of democracy in Europe than at home. Many could not have resisted the temptation to conclude that the penalty for insisting upon full equality in the United States was a sentence to face, for a full season, the onslaught of German armies.

■ Service Overseas

The first African Americans to arrive in Europe after the United States entered the war, and indeed among the first Americans to reach the war zone, were laborers and stevedores sent to assist in the tremendous task of providing the Allies with materials of war. The first black stevedore battalion arrived in France in June 1917. From that date to the end of the war, they came in larger numbers. They were classified as stevedore regiments, engineer service battalions, labor battalions, butchery companies, and pioneer infantry battalions. Before the end of the war there were more than 50,000 in 115 different outfits, more than one-third of the entire American force. At Brest, St. Nazaire, Bordeaux, Le Havre, and Marseilles, black stevedores worked in mud and rain, sometimes in twenty-four-hour shifts, unloading supplies from the United States. At one port a crew of black stevedores amazed the French by unloading 1,200 tons of flour in nine and one-half hours, after it had been estimated that such an undertaking would require several days. In September 1918 at American base ports in France, 767,648 tons were handled largely by blacks, an average of more than 25,000 tons per day. An American war correspondent was moved to remark, "One who sees the Negro stevedores work notes with what rapidity and cheerfulness they work and what a very important cog they are in the war machinery."

The African-American combat troops originally intended for the 93rd Division were among the first to be sent overseas; they were placed in various divisions of the French army. After many hardships at sea, including breakdown, fire, and collision, the 369th United States Infantry arrived in France early in 1918, and some of the men went immediately to a French divisional training school. There they learned to throw grenades, use bayonets, and handle French weapons. In April 1918, almost exactly one year after the formal entry of the United States into the war, they moved up to the fighting front. By May they were in the thick of the fight, in Champagne, holding for a time a complete sector constituting 20 percent of all the territory held by American troops. After some relief they were placed in the path of the expected German offensive at Minaucourt, where they bore the brunt of the German attacks in the middle of July. From that time until the end of hostilities the men of the 369th were almost continuously in action against the Germans. The feats they could boast of at the end of the war were many. Theirs was the first unit of the Allied armies to reach the Rhine. The regiment never lost a man through capture, and it never gave up a trench or a foot of ground. It saw the first and longest service of any American regiment as part of a foreign army, having been in the trenches for 191 days. It won the unique distinction of being called the "Hell Fighters" by the Germans. The entire regiment won the Croix de Guerre for its action at Maison-en-Champagne, and 171 individual officers and enlisted men were cited for the Croix de Guerre and the Legion of Honor for exceptional gallantry in action.

The 8th Illinois Infantry, renamed the 370th United States Infantry, reached France in June 1918. It was equipped with French arms and sent to the front. After service in the St. Mihiel sector, it was withdrawn and sent to the Argonne Forest, where it remained for the better part of July and August. In September, under the 59th Division of the French army, it took over a full regimental sector in the area of Mont des Tombes and Les Tueries. From that time until the end of the war, the 370th, in concert with several units of the French army, pursued the enemy out of France into Belgium. Twenty-one men received the Distinguished Service Cross, one received the Distinguished Service Medal, while sixty-eight received various grades of the Croix de Guerre. They were the first American troops to enter the French fortress of Laon when it was wrested from the Germans after four years of war. The 370th fought the last battle of the war, capturing a German wagon train of fifty wagons and crews a half-hour after the Armistice went into effect.

The 371st Infantry Regiment, which had been organized in August 1917 at Camp Jackson, South Carolina, arrived in France late in April 1918. It was then reorganized on the French plan and attached to the 157th French Division, the famous "Red Hand," under General Goybet. It remained in the front lines for more than three months, holding first the Avocourt and later the Verrières subsectors, northwest of Verdun. In the great September offensive it took several important places near Monthois and captured a number of prisoners, many machine guns and other weapons, a munitions depot, several railroad cars, and many other supplies. For its action its regimental colors were decorated by the French government. Three officers won the French Legion of Honor, while thirty-four officers and eighty-nine enlisted men won the Croix de Guerre. Fourteen officers and twelve enlisted men won the Distinguished Service Cross.

One of the enlisted men in the 371st, Corporal Freddie Stowers of Sandy Spring, South Carolina, was recommended by his commanding officer for the Congressional Medal of Honor, the nation's highest military award. Stowers had led his company in a victorious charge against a German-held hill, an assault that left over 50 percent of his company dead. Because the recommendation was "misplaced," Stowers, the only black member of America's World War I military forces to be recommended for the Medal of Honor, would wait seventy-three years to receive it. In April 1991 President George Bush, following historian Leroy Ramsey's criticism of the United States military for failure to award the Medal of Honor to any of the 1.5 million blacks who had served in World War I and World War II, presented the decoration posthumously to Stowers' elderly sisters.

The 372nd United States Infantry was something of a catch-all outfit, composed of African-American National Guardsmen from the District of Columbia, Ohio, Massachusetts, and Maryland, and about 250 men who had entered the army through the Selective Service. After a period of training in the United States the regiment reached France in April 1918 and was, along with the 371st, brigaded with the French Red Hand Division. Late in May it took over the job of holding the Argonne west sector and was in the front-line trenches on May 31. During the summer it was subjected to heavy shelling in the Verdun sector, and in September it went in pursuit of the retreating enemy. For its gallantry in the final campaign, Vice Admiral Moreau decorated the colors of the regiment with the Croix de Guerre and palm just before the men sailed for America. Many individual honors were also won, especially by the men of the First Battalion of the District of Columbia National Guard.

Because of the rather irregular procedure of training the units in separate camps, the Ninety-second Division was late in becoming welded into an efficient fighting unit. There were eight weeks of intensive training after its arrival in France in June 1918. By August 7, it was ready to move up to the front by stages and take over its first sector. Late in the month it took over the St. Die sector, relieving several regiments of the American and French forces. At the time, the enemy was on the offensive, and almost immediately the only all-black division received its baptism of war in the form of shrapnel and gas. The division was eager to attack the enemy, and early in September the opportunity came. The encounter resulted in the capture of several Germans by the black troops and the capture of two blacks by the Germans.

When it became clear to the Germans that the division consisted almost entirely of African Americans, they launched a propaganda campaign to accomplish with words what they had not been able to accomplish with arms. They had sought to demoralize other African-American troops, but apparently the Germans reserved their most powerful propaganda offensive for the Ninety-second Division. On September 12 they scattered over the lines a circular that sought to persuade the blacks to lay down their arms. They told them that they should not be deluded into thinking that they were fighting for humanity and democracy. "What is Democracy? Personal freedom, all citizens enjoying the same rights socially and before the law. Do you enjoy the same rights as the white people do in America, the land of Freedom and Democracy, or are you rather not treated over there as second-class citizens? Can you go into a restaurant where white people dine? Can you get a seat in the theater where white people sit? . . . Is lynching and the most horrible crimes connected therewith a lawful proceeding in a democratic country?" The circular asserted that Germans liked blacks and treated them as gentlemen in Germany. "Why, then, fight the Germans only for the benefit of the Wall Street robbers and to protect the millions they have loaned to the British, French, and Italians?" The African Americans were invited to come over to the German lines, where they would find friends who would help them in the cause of liberty and democracy. None deserted, and all seemed to have continued to fight against the enemy even more energetically.

In September and October the 92nd did its share of the fighting by holding two sectors during the heavy fighting of that period. There were numerous casualties from gas and enemy artillery fire. The official reports state that it became difficult in some regiments to send out small patrols, for every officer and enlisted man desired to participate. Company commanders solved disputes over priority among the volunteers for night patrols and raiding parties by promising places days in advance. The awards and citations that the men of the 92nd received were numerous. The entire first battalion of the 369th Infantry was cited for bravery in its participation in the drive toward Metz and was awarded the Croix de Guerre, while the colors of the regiment were decorated by order of the French high command. In the division forty-three enlisted men and fourteen African American officers were cited for bravery in action and awarded the Distinguished Service Cross. Both the French and American governments cited numerous individual soldiers of the division for their heroism and awarded them appropriate decorations.

The feats of gallantry of African Americans in the service were similar to those performed by other American soldiers. Two examples will suffice. On November 10, 1918, a shell struck the house in which the switchboard was being operated at Point-à-Mousson. Sgt. Rufus B. Atwood rendered valuable assistance in reconstructing the switchboard and connecting new lines under heavy shell fire. The official order reported,

> After repairs were made from the first explosion, there were two to follow which completely wrecked the switchboard room and tore out all the lines which were newly fixed. Sergeant Atwood was left alone, and he established a new switchboard and the same connections they had at first. The coolness with which he went about his work and the initiative he took in handling the situation justifies his being mentioned in orders.

One of the most sensational feats in the war was that performed by two privates, Henry Johnson of Albany, New York, and Needham Roberts of Trenton, New Jersey, both members of the 369th Infantry. While the men were on guard at a small outpost in May 1918, a strong raiding party of Germans numbering almost twenty made a surprise attack, wounding the two blacks. When the Germans were within fighting distance, Johnson opened fire, and Roberts, lying on the ground, threw grenades. The Germans continued to advance, and as the two black men were about to be captured, Johnson drew his bolo knife from his belt and attacked the Germans in a hand-to-hand encounter. He succeeded in freeing Roberts from the Germans who were dragging him away and slashed several so mercilessly that they died of their wounds. The killing of at least four of the enemy and the wounding of perhaps twice as many more have caused this encounter to become known as "The Battle of Henry Johnson." Both men received the Croix de Guerre for their gallantry.

The casualties of African-American soldiers seem to indicate the general disregard for personal safety that characterized the American army and which contributed substantially to the victory of November 11, 1918. In the 92nd Division, for example, 208 enlisted men were killed in action, while 40 others died of wounds received in battle. There were 551 who were wounded in action and 672 who were gassed. In some of the black regiments attached to the French army the proportion of casualties was even higher. In the 371st

Regiment, 113 men were killed in action, 25 died of wounds, and 859 were wounded.

That the price African Americans paid for victory was highly regarded by the Allies is clearly seen in the praise accorded them by ranking military officials. General Goybet, the commanding officer of the 157th French Division said, "Never will the 157th Division forget the indomitable dash, the heroic rush of the American regiments (Negro) up the observatory ridge and into the plains of Monthois. . . . These crack regiments overcame every obstacle with a most complete contempt for danger. Through their steady devotion, the 'Red Hand Division' for nine whole days of severe struggle was constantly leading the way for the victorious advance of the Fourth Army." In January 1919 General Pershing, commander of the American Expeditionary Forces, said, "I want you officers and soldiers of the 92nd Division to know that the 92nd Division stands second to none in the record you have made since your arrival in France. I am proud of the part you have played in the great conflict which ended on the 11th of November."

Some effort was made to maintain high morale among African Americans during their tour of duty in France. Most of the combat units had their own bands. One of the best known was the 369th Regiment Band under the direction of James R. Europe, assisted by Noble Sissle. Another was the 350th Field Artillery Band under J. T. Bynum. It was said that these musical organizations "filled France with jazz" and won for their members the admiration of their hosts. There were no African-American theatrical entertainers overseas. A unit, headed by the Reverend H. H. Proctor, speaker, J. E. Blanton, song leader, and Helen Hagan, pianist, traveled through France and staged programs for the soldiers. White entertainment groups almost always bypassed black soldiers.

Welfare work was carried out largely by the YMCA and the YWCA, although the Knights of Columbus and the Federal Council of Churches devoted some attention to the soldiers. Of the 7,850 "Y" workers who went overseas, 87 were black, 19 of whom were women. Only 3 of the women, however, were in France during the actual fighting. At the base ports, it was the task of the "Y" huts to provide classes for illiterates, maintain libraries, operate canteens, provide letter-writing facilities, and perform innumerable other services for the comfort of the men. Among the African Americans engaged in this work were Matthew Bullock, J. C. Croom, John Hope, W. J. Faulkner, Max Yergan, Addie Hunton, and Kathryn Johnson. Of the 60 African-American chaplains in the United States Army, approximately 20 ministered to the spiritual needs of black soldiers overseas. Although the African-American nurses in the United States offered their services in large numbers, the government did not see fit to accept and send them overseas until the fighting had ended. During periods of rest and recuperation, as well as after hostilities were over, some blacks attended several French universities, including those in Paris, Bordeaux, Toulouse, and Marseilles.

An important aspect of the welfare of African-American soldiers was the

"SINGING BUFFALOES." Members of the 367th Infantry Regiment on parade after their return from the battle front in France. *(Scott's Official History of the Negro in the Great War.)*

manner in which they were treated by the French. For the most part they moved about freely in France and associated pleasantly with French men and women, much to the chagrin of many white American soldiers. Some whites took it upon themselves to warn the French against African Americans. American whites told the French that blacks could not be treated with common civility, that they were rapists, and that Americans were compelled to lynch and burn blacks in order to keep them in their place. In August 1918 a document was circulated among the French, *Secret Information Concerning Black Troops*. It was necessary, the document asserted, to maintain complete separation of blacks and whites, lest blacks assault and rape white women. It would be unfortunate if French officers associated socially with black officers or had any contact with them outside the requirements of military service. Neither the civilians nor the soldiers of France seemed to take seriously the counsel that was offered to them by white Americans, for they continued to welcome African Americans into their homes and sought to make their black defenders as comfortable as possible.

Toward the end of the war, reports came to the United States that African-American soldiers were attacking and criminally assaulting French women in large numbers. The fear was expressed openly that African Americans in France had developed habits and practices that would be detrimental to interracial stability upon their return to the United States. The

WOMEN'S WAR WORK. Red Cross nurses on duty at the base hospital at Camp Grant, Illinois. *(Scott's Official History of the Negro in the Great War.)*

matter was of such concern that in December 1918 Robert R. Moton, Booker T. Washington's successor at Tuskegee, was asked to go to France to investigate the rumors and to examine the conditions affecting African-American soldiers. The secretary of war and the president placed every facility at Moton's disposal and made it possible for him to travel freely among the black troops. The commanding general of the 92nd Division asserted that the crime of rape was very prevalent among his men and that there had been at least twenty-six cases within recent months. Upon examination of the records, which the general furnished, Moton found that in the division of more than 1,200 men only seven cases involved the crime. Only 2 men had been found guilty, and one of the two convictions had been turned down at general headquarters. In other places it became clear that charges against African Americans were few and that convictions were fewer still. Moton also found that, contrary to persistent rumors, the Ninety-second Division had not been a failure, and that only a very small detachment of a single battalion of one regiment had failed. General Pershing assured him that it was probable that any officers under similar adverse circumstances would have failed.

Moton made many speeches to groups of African-American soldiers. In his autobiography he reports that he told them:

> You have been tremendously tested. . . . Your record has sent a thrill of joy and satisfaction to the hearts of millions of black and white Americans, rich and poor, high and low. . . . You will go back to America heroes, as you really are. You will go back as you have carried yourselves over here—in a straightforward, manly, and modest way. If I were you, I would find a job as soon as possible and get to work. . . . I hope no one will do anything in peace to spoil the magnificent record you have made in war.[1]

African-American soldiers who heard Moton reported that he told them not to expect in the United States the kind of freedom they had enjoyed in France and that they must remain content with the same position they had always occupied at home. African-American soldiers and civilians were outraged and spoke of Moton in the harshest manner. Regardless of what he actually said, it became clear that he did little to allay the fears of blacks or to prepare them for their return to the United States.

Many African Americans both in the United States and in other parts of the world desired to bring the plight of darker peoples before the peace conference that met in Versailles at the end of the war. Some Americans opposed the treaty because they feared that the membership of darker countries would make the permanent peace organization a "colored league of nations." Others feared that some agencies of the League of Nations might attempt to exercise influence in the domestic affairs of the United States. The only consideration that the darker peoples received was the disposition that was made of the African colonies of the defeated countries. The mandates system gave England, France, Belgium, and the Union of South Africa the administration of the former German colonies under the supervision of the League of Nations. By 1979 all mandated areas had become

---

[1]R. R. Moton, *Finding a Way Out* (Garden City, New York: Doubleday and Co., 1920), p. 263.

independent with the exception of Southwest Africa (Namibia), which had been under the supervision of South Africa. Its rich natural resources and excellent harbor were assets that South Africa did not wish to give up. But the latter was experiencing difficulty in withstanding the pressure from a number of sources, including the United Nations Security Council, the Southwest Africa People's Organization, and opponents of South Africa's system of apartheid.

Hoping to place the cause of darker peoples before the world in a dramatic way, W. E. B. Du Bois called a Pan-African Congress to meet in Paris simultaneously with the peace conference. Du Bois had been asked by the NAACP to go to France in December 1918 to investigate the treatment of African-American soldiers and to collect information concerning their participation in the war. Through Blaise Diagne, a Senegalese member of the Chamber of Deputies who was highly respected in French circles, Du Bois secured Clemenceau's permission to hold the congress in the Grand Hotel in Paris in February 1919. There were fifty-seven delegates, including sixteen African Americans, twenty West Indians, and twelve Africans. Although the results of the meeting were limited, it called the attention of the world to the fact that darker people in various parts of the world had a material interest in the deliberations at Paris and that they were seeking for themselves the democratic treatment for which they had fought. It also served to stimulate interest in the several congresses that were held in subsequent years.

■ On the Home Front

African Americans who remained at home during the struggle were no less enthusiastic in their support of the war than those who faced the Germans on the Western front. It has been estimated, for example, that in the five loan campaigns blacks purchased more than $250 million worth of bonds and stamps. Mary B. Talbert, president of the National Association of Colored Women, reported that African-American women alone purchased more than $5 million worth of bonds in the Third Liberty Loan. When a black cook in Memphis was approached by her employer regarding the purchase of a $100 bond, she replied that she didn't want such a small bond. "I want a thousand dollar bond, and I'll pay cash for it." A black farmer in Georgia, with two sons in the army, bought a $1,000 bond, thereby putting fresh spirit into the local campaign. Black insurance companies purchased large quantities of bonds in each drive. The North Carolina Mutual Life Insurance Company, for example, purchased $300,000 worth of bonds in less than two years. Similar support was given to the fund-raising campaigns of the "Y" organizations and the American Red Cross.

The United States found itself especially dependent on African Americans in the program to produce and conserve food because of the large number of black farmers and cooks. Some work was done among blacks through the educational department of the Food Administration under the direction of A. U. Craig of Washington's Dunbar High School. Herbert Hoover, director of the Food Administration, sought to enlarge the work among blacks, and to that end he appointed Ernest Atwell of Tuskegee as field worker for Alabama and later for the other Southern states. In September 1918 Atwell went to Washington where he served as director of the activities of African Americans from the headquarters of the Food Administration and circulated an open letter to the African Americans of the United States asking for their cooperation in general food conservation. Black directors were appointed in eighteen states, and organizations were perfected to carry forward the program of food conservation.

One of the most important social and economic phenomena on the home front was the migration of hundreds of thousands of African-American men and women out of the South during the war. The fundamental cause of the exodus was economic, though there were certainly some important social considerations. The severe labor depression in the South in 1914 and 1915 sent wages down to 75 cents per day and less. The damage of the boll weevil to cotton crops in 1915 and 1916 discouraged many who were dependent on cotton for their subsistence. Floods in the summer of 1915 left thousands of blacks destitute and homeless and ready to accept almost anything in preference to the uncertainty of life in the South. Meanwhile, the wheels of Northern industry were turning more rapidly than ever, and the demand for laborers was increasing. The sharp decline in foreign immigration from more than 1 million in 1914 to slightly more than 300,000 in the following year created a labor shortage that sent agents scurrying to the South to entice blacks as well as whites to move North to work in industry. Injustice in the Southern courts, the lack of privileges, disfranchisement, segregation, and lynching served as important stimuli for blacks to move out of the South. The North was regarded as the "land of promise," and the African-American press did much to persuade Southern blacks to abandon the existence that held nothing better for them than second-class citizenship. The *Chicago Defender* exclaimed, "To die from the bite of frost is far more glorious than at the hands of a mob." In 1917 the *Christian Recorder* wrote, "If a million Negroes move north and west in the next twelve-month, it will be one of the greatest things for the Negro since the Emancipation Proclamation."

In 1916 the movement spread like wildfire among African Americans. By the summer of that year the migration had reached flood tide in the states of the deep South. The Pennsylvania Railroad brought 12,000 to work in its yards and on its tracks; all but 2,000 came from Florida and Georgia. Even black professionals moved north to continue to serve their clientele. The South was alarmed. Officials of Jacksonville, Florida, passed an ordinance requiring migration agents to pay a license fee of $1,000. White citizens of many Southern towns threatened blacks, while the white press urged them to remain in the South. Homes were without servants, farms were without laborers, churches were empty, and houses were deserted. It was estimated that by the end of 1918 more than 1 million African Americans had left the South. This estimate seems too generous, for the Bureau of the Census reported that the states of the North and West showed a net gain of 330,000 African Americans for the decade ending in 1920.

Although numerous unfortunate incidents resulted from the wholesale movement of African Americans into the North and West, the migration, coming when it did, gave them an opportunity for industrial employment that they had never enjoyed before, and it relieved the labor shortage during the crucial years of the war. The Department of Labor, taking cognizance of the importance of black labor early in the war, created a Division of Negro Economics under the direction of George Edmund Haynes. The division was to advise the secretary of labor and the heads of bureaus of plans and policies for improving conditions of black workers and for securing their full cooperation with white workers and employers for maximum production. Several state and local advisory committees were set up to carry out the work of cooperation and to reduce friction between white and black workers. State conferences were held in twelve states, with the cooperation of the governors, employment agencies, employers, and workers. When the year's report of the Negro Worker's Advisory Committee of North Carolina was released, Governor Bickett said, "If every man, white and black, in the United States could read and digest this report, it would go a great way toward solving all our race questions."

The National Urban League was also active in helping with the adjustment of African Americans who had recently moved to the industrial centers of the North. In 1916 it held a National Conference on Migration in New York and issued recommendations and advice to employers and migrants. It established branches in cities like Chicago, Detroit, Cleveland, St. Louis, Philadelphia, and Pittsburgh and assisted in the adjustment and distribution of black labor. The league also sought to solve some of the delicate problems arising out of black migration, such as housing, recreation facilities, and the relation of blacks to organized labor.

African Americans were suspicious of organized labor because of its history of systematic exclusion of black workers. They therefore organized several labor groups of their own, such as the Associated Colored Employees of America. In 1917 the American Federation of Labor (AFL) expressed the view that the workers of all races should unite and present a common front to industry. It was hoped that African Americans could be brought into the labor movement in order to prevent them from breaking strikes. In 1918 the Council of the American Federation of Labor invited several prominent African Americans to discuss the matter. Among them were Robert R. Moton of Tuskegee, Emmett J. Scott of the War Department, Eugene Kinckle Jones of the National Urban League, and Fred Moore of the *New York Age*. Little came of the deliberations except an expression of the willingness of both sides to cooperate further. During the war few unions of organized labor accepted blacks into full membership.

SILENT PROTEST PARADE ON FIFTH AVENUE IN NEW YORK.
Staged by the NAACP on July 28, 1917, in protest to the East St. Louis
riots and other violence to blacks. Other banners carried in the parade
read, "Mother, do lynchers go to heaven?"; "Mr. President, why not
make America safe for Democracy?"; and "Pray for the Lady Macbeths
of East St. Louis." (*Underwood Collection/The Bettmann Archive.*)

African Americans found employment in most of the industries of the
North during the war. They were engaged in the manufacture of ammunition
and of iron and steel products. They were in the meat-packing industries,
and worked in large numbers in automobile and truck production and in
the manufacture of electrical products. There were 26,648 blacks in 46 of the
55 occupations incident to shipbuilding under the United States Shipping
Board. A black, Charles Knight, at the Bethlehem Steel Corporation plant at
Sparrow's Point, Maryland, broke the world's record for driving rivets in
building steel ships. A black pile-driving crew building shipways at Hog
Island, near Philadelphia, broke the world's record for driving piles. More
than 75,000 blacks worked in the coal mines of Alabama, Illinois, Pennsylvania, Ohio, and West Virginia. Approximately 150,000 blacks assisted in
the operation of the railroads, while another 150,000 served to keep up other
vital means of communication. In 152 typical industrial plants there were
21,547 black women performing 75 specific tasks.

High government officials very properly concerned themselves with the
problems of African-American morale during the war, for there were many
indications that while there was a vigorous pursuit of democracy in Europe,
there was widespread destruction of it at home. At least thirty-eight African
Americans lost their lives at the hands of lynching parties in 1917, while in

TABLE 6
African-American Population, by States, in 1920

State	African-American Population (In Thousands)
Alabama	901
Alaska	(a)
Arizona	8
Arkansas	472
California	39
Colorado	11
Connecticut	21
Delaware	30
Dist. of Columbia	110
Florida	329
Georgia	1,206
Hawaii	(a)
Idaho	1
Illinois	182
Indiana	81
Iowa	19
Kansas	58
Kentucky	236
Louisiana	700
Maine	1
Maryland	244
Massachusetts	45
Michigan	60
Minnesota	9
Mississippi	935
Missouri	178
Montana	2
Nebraska	13
Nevada	(a)
New Hampshire	1
New Jersey	117
New Mexico	6
New York	198
North Carolina	763
North Dakota	(a)
Ohio	186

TABLE 6
African-American Population, by States, in 1920
(*Continued*)

State	African-American Population (In Thousands)
Oklahoma	149
Oregon	2
Pennsylvania	285
Rhode Island	10
South Carolina	865
South Dakota	1
Tennessee	452
Texas	742
Utah	1
Vermont	1
Virginia	690
Washington	7
West Virginia	86
Wisconsin	5
Wyoming	1

(a) Indicates less than 500 persons.
Source: U.S. Bureau of the Census, *Historical Statistics of the United States, Colonial Times to 1970, Bicentennial Edition* [Part 2]. Washington, D.C., pp. 24–37.

the following year the number rose to fifty-eight. Race clashes in the North and South did not diminish. In Tennessee more than 3,000 spectators responded to the invitation of a newspaper to come out and witness the burning of a "live Negro." In East St. Louis, Illinois, at least forty blacks lost their lives in a riot that grew out of the employment of blacks in a factory holding government contracts. African Americans were stabbed, clubbed, and hanged, and one two-year-old African American was shot and thrown in the doorway of a burning building. The Germans made the most of these unfortunate incidents in their effort to spread antiwar sentiment among blacks. They kept a careful record of lynchings and the attacks of whites on blacks and urged African Americans to desert the struggle from which they were gaining nothing. While the propaganda had no noticeable effect on the morale of blacks, the president of the United States finally saw fit to issue a strong public statement against lynching and mob violence.

The African-American press, for the most part, supported the war enthusiastically. In June 1918 Emmett J. Scott held a conference of thirty-one leading black newspapermen, who, while pledging their support of the war, drew up a bill of particulars in which they denounced mob violence, called for the use of black Red Cross nurses, requested the return of Col. Charles Young to active service, and asked for the appointment of a black war correspondent. Most of their requests were granted, though somewhat belatedly. Ralph Tyler of Columbus, Ohio, was designated by the Committee on Public Information as a war correspondent and went to Europe to send back dispatches about the exploits of African-American soldiers. African-American newspapers carried his stories, which were generally glowing accounts of the gallantry and heroism of the black outfits. The *Messenger*, a newspaper published in New York by A. Philip Randolph and Chandler Owen, was one of the few black journals that refused to go along in an all-out support of the war. For the article "Pro-Germanism among Negroes" the editors were sentenced to jail for two and one-half years and their second-class mailing privileges were rescinded. The war effort received unexpected support, however, from the *Crisis*, whose editor, W. E. B. Du Bois, wrote an editorial in July 1918 entitled "Close Ranks." In part he said, "Let us not hesitate. Let us, while this war lasts, forget our special grievances and close our ranks shoulder to shoulder with our white citizens and the allied nations that are fighting for democracy."

The talk of democracy during the war had raised vague hopes even among the most militant African Americans. Both at home and abroad they had supported the war that was to make the world safe for democracy. Perhaps it was too much that there could be the full realization of democracy within the foreseeable future. It was not too much, most African Americans reasoned, to hope that the war's end would usher in a new period of opportunity both in the area of economic life and in the sphere of civil rights. Doubtless they realized that the pursuit of democracy was a continuing process that had to be carried on long after the last gun was fired. They hardly realized, however, that many of the forces that operated to prevent the establishment of an enduring peace for the entire world, as well as the peculiar local forces that had flourished in the very warp and woof of American civilization, would serve to make democracy seem for them as elusive and as ephemeral as the lengthening shadows of evening.

CHAPTER 17

Democracy Escapes

■ The Reaction

Although some African-American soldiers who served in France were hesitant about making the return trip to the United States lest they lose what democracy and freedom they had found in faraway places, the great majority seemed anxious to return. Some doubtless believed that conditions would be better than before the war, while others were indifferent to the future, thinking only of the pleasures of being home again. They were not required to wait very long before finding out what changes had taken placed in the United States, for shortly after the Armistice was signed American military authorities began to make preparations for the return and demobilization of American troops. Some African-American troops were detained to assist in the tasks of cleaning up camp sites and clearing away debris left from the battles, but the greater part of them were en route to the United States within four months after the end of the war. By April 1919 many troops were already in the United States, and some of them were being demobilized.

Since most of the African-American troops disembarked in the New York area, their first reception in the United States was enthusiastic. New York City seemed never to tire of the apparently endless parades of troops, both black and white, that proceeded almost immediately from their ships to the triumphal march up Fifth Avenue. When New York's own black regiment, the 369th, returned on February 17, 1919, approximately 1 million people witnessed their parade from lower New York up Fifth Avenue to Harlem. A similar reception was given various units of the 92nd Division, the last of whose troops landed at Hoboken on March 12, 1919. Other cities, however, vied with New York in welcoming their black troops. Buffalo turned out en masse to receive its darker brothers, while huge crowds filled the streets of St. Louis to cheer the blacks who had fought in Europe. When the 370th, the "Old Eighth Illinois," reached Chicago, much of the business of the city was suspended to welcome the veterans. The soldiers paraded through the Loop as well as through the thickly populated black South Side, and in many places the crowds were so dense that the troops could not march in regular formation. If the parades were not so large and the enthusiasm not so great in the South, it could easily be attributed to the fact that no black units came from single communities, as well as to the fact that Southern whites did not enjoy seeing African Americans armed with powerful weapons. Few stopped to give much consideration to such a matter, however. It was a time of jubilation, and African Americans were determined to enjoy it while it lasted.

The period of jubilation was short-lived, however, for the business of settling down to postwar living became more urgent with every passing day. Indeed, all America was anxious to forget the war and return to a peacetime existence. Industry wanted to begin the task of filling the huge backlog of orders for goods that had not been produced during the war. Labor was ready to press for demands that it could not afford to make during the war. Politicians could hardly wait to get the peace treaties out of the way in order to wage a campaign in 1920 that they hoped would be free of the issues of the war. Militant black leaders were anxious, too. They did not want to return to a prewar normalcy but to move forward to a new basis for democratic living in the United States. In May 1919 the editor of the *Crisis* undertook to speak for returning black soldiers when he said:

> We return from the slavery of uniform which the world's madness demanded us to don to the freedom of civil garb. We stand again to look America squarely in the face and call a spade a spade. We sing: This country of ours, despite all its better souls have done and dreamed, is yet a shameful land.
> It *lynches*. . . . It *disfranchises* its own citizens. . . . It encourages *ignorance*. . . . It steals from us. . . . It insults us. . . .
> We *return*. We *return from fighting*. We *return fighting*.
> Make way for Democracy! We saved it in France, and by the Great Jehovah, we will save it in the U.S.A., or know the reason why.

The editor had not spoken too early, for if he and other blacks were determined to secure a larger share of democracy for themselves, there were many whites who were as determined to see that there should be no wholesale distribution of the blessings of liberty. Whites had steeled themselves against the day when black soldiers would return and make demands for first-class citizenship, and they were ready to put the machinery they had perfected into operation. The Ku Klux Klan had been revived in the Southern states as early as 1915. Its growth was slow until the end of the war, at which time it came forth with a broad program for "uniting native-born white Christians for concerted action in the preservation of American institutions and the supremacy of the white race." Within a year it grew from an impotent organization of a few thousand members to a militant union of more than 100,000 white-hooded knights. It declared itself against "Negroes," Japanese and other Orientals, Roman Catholics, Jews, and all foreign-born individuals. It capitalized on the isolationist reaction that followed the war and spread into areas where previously there had been few bold manifestations of race hatred. It assumed the responsibility for punishing people whom it considered dangerous to the growth of its ideas and spearheaded a drive for violence and intimidation toward African Americans. Within ten months, shortly after the close of the war, the Klan made more than 200 public appearances in twenty-seven states. Cells of the organization flourished in several New England states, as well as in New York, Indiana, Illinois, Michigan, and other Northern and Midwestern states. In many communities candidates for public office feared defeat if they were not on good terms with the Klan, preferably as members. Its assumption of a semiofficial role, in taking the law into its own hands and in luring public servants into its membership, stimulated the lawlessness and violence that characterized the postwar period in the United States.

At a public meeting one Klansman exclaimed, "We would not rob the colored population of their rights, but we demand that they respect the rights of the white race in whose country they are permitted to reside." Actually, there were few rights of African Americans that the Klan felt obliged to respect, and this militant organization acted in a manner confirming its contention that the United States was a "white man's country." In Texas the Klan became the instrument of a new enslavement, forcing blacks to work and pick cotton at wages they would not have accepted if the decision had been left to them. Throughout the South and Southwest African Americans lived in constant fear of the hooded bands of night riders who burned crosses to terrify those whom they considered undesirables. In the West the Klan was also active, especially against the Japanese population. Wherever it established itself it was blamed, correctly or incorrectly, for the atrocities committed in the vicinity. There were floggings, brandings with acid, episodes of tarring and feathering, hangings, and burnings. The victims were largely, though not entirely, African Americans. It was a new day, indeed—a new day of violence and terror.

White citizens, in and out of the Klan, poured out wrath upon the black population shortly after the war that could hardly be viewed as fit punishment even for traitors. More than seventy blacks were lynched during the first year of the postwar period. Ten black soldiers, several still in their uniforms, were lynched. Mississippi and Georgia mobs each murdered three returned soldiers, in Arkansas two were lynched, while Florida and Alabama each took the life of a black soldier by mob violence. Fourteen Negroes were burned publicly, eleven of whom were burned alive. In utter despair an African-American editor in Charleston, South Carolina, cried out, "There is

Reverend Francis J. Grimke Welcomes Returning Black Soldiers—1919

Young gentlemen, I am glad to welcome you home again after months of absence in a foreign land in obedience to the call of your country—glad that you returned to us without any serious casualties. . . .

We, who remained at home, followed you while you were away, with the deepest interest; and, our hearts burned with indignation when tidings came to us, as it did from time to time, of the manner in which you were treated by those over you, from whom you had every reason, in view of the circumstances that took you abroad, and what it was costing you, to expect decent, humane treatment, instead of the treatment that was accorded you. The physical hardships, incident to a soldier's life in times of war, are trying enough, are hard enough to bear. . . . To add to these the insults, the studied insults that were heaped upon you, and for no reason except that you were colored, is so shocking that were it not for positive evidence, it would be almost unbelievable. . . .

Again, most gladly do I welcome you back home; and most earnestly do we express the hope that every man of you will play a man's part in the longer and more arduous struggle that is before us in battling for our rights at home. If it was worth going abroad to make the world safe for democracy, it is equally worth laboring no less earnestly to make it safe at home. We shall be greatly disappointed if you do not do this—if you fail to do your part.

Francis J. Grimke, *The Works of Francis J. Grimke*, Carter G. Woodson, ed., Volume I, *Addresses Mainly Personal and Racial* (Washington, 1942), pp. 589–591.

scarcely a day that passes that newspapers don't tell about a Negro soldier lynched in his uniform. Why do they lynch Negroes, anyhow? With a white judge, a white jury, white public sentiment, white officers of the law, it is just as impossible for a Negro accused of crime, or even suspected of crime, to escape the white man's vengeance or his justice as it would be for a fawn to escape that wanders accidentally into a den of hungry lions. So why not give him the semblance of a trial?"

It was the summer of 1919, called by James Weldon Johnson the "Red Summer," that ushered in the greatest period of interracial strife the nation had ever witnessed. From June to the end of the year there were approximately twenty-five race riots. Some were large, others were small, and all were indicative of a thoroughly malodorous situation in race relations. Even after the war the migration of African Americans to urban centers continued and, in some areas, increased. Jobs were not so plentiful as during the war years, and competition strained the relations of whites and blacks. Meanwhile, the high rents in the segregated residential areas continued. Unrest and disappointment seized a considerable portion of the African-American population, and when it became clear that many whites were seeking to deprive them of some of the gains they had made during the war, blacks bristled into action and showed a willingness to defend themselves that they had not shown before. The riots were not confined to any section of the country. They were Northern and Southern, Eastern and Western—wherever whites and blacks undertook the task of living together. Egged on by native fascist organizations like the Ku Klux Klan, the lawless element of the population undertook to terrorize blacks into submission.

In July 1919 Longview, Texas, witnessed the nightmare of a race riot. Several white men were shot when they went into the black section of the town in search of a black schoolteacher who was accused of sending a release to the *Chicago Defender* concerning the lynching of an African American during the previous month. Whites in the town were alarmed over this show of strength among blacks, and they poured into the black section determined to teach them a lesson. Many homes were burned, a black school principal was flogged on the streets, and several leading citizens were run out of town. It was several days before the town returned to normal. In the following week a riot of more violent proportions broke out in the nation's capital. Newspaper reports of blacks assaulting white women whipped the irresponsible elements of the population into a frenzy, although it early became clear that the reports had no basis in fact. Mobs, consisting primarily of white sailors, soldiers, and marines, ran amok through the streets of Washington for three days, killing several African Americans and injuring scores of others. On the third day blacks retaliated when hoodlums sought to invade and burn their section of the city. The casualty list mounted, but before order was restored the number of whites killed and wounded had increased considerably as a result of the belated but stern action that blacks took.

The most serious racial outbreak occurred in Chicago late in July of the so-called Red Summer. Chicago had become to Southern blacks "the top of the world," and thousands had migrated there during and after the war in search of employment and freedom. Within less than a decade the black population of the city had more then doubled, and the census of 1920 showed approximately 109,000 living there. There was, of course, some friction in industry, but because of the abundance of jobs it had remained at a minimum. The most serious friction came in housing and recreation. Blacks were spreading into white neighborhoods, whereupon the whites sought to prevent the infiltration by bombing the homes of blacks. Groups of young whites took it upon themselves to frighten the blacks into submission and to prevent their continued movement into white sections of the city. In June two blacks were murdered, an act that ushered in a month of terror.

The riot that began on July 27 had its immediate origin in an altercation at a Lake Michigan beach. A young African American swimming offshore had drifted into water that was customarily used by whites. White swimmers commanded him to return to his part of the beach, and some threw stones at him. When the young man went down and drowned, blacks declared that he had been murdered. Although his recovered body showed no marks of having been stoned, it was too late to save the city from a riot that was already in progress. Distorted rumors circulated among blacks and whites concerning the incident and the subsequent events at the beach. Mobs sprang up in various parts of the city, and during the entire night there was sporadic fighting. In the next afternoon white bystanders meddled with blacks as they went home from work. Some were pulled off streetcars and whipped. Many people of both races were injured in these clashes, and at least five were killed. On the South Side a group of young blacks stabbed an old Italian peddler to death, and a white laundry operator was also stabbed to death. During that day and the next the riot spread, with mobs of both races doing what they could to terrorize the opposite group. For thirteen days Chicago was without law and order, despite the fact that the militia was called out on the fourth day of the riot. When the authorities counted the casualties, the tally sheet gave the appearance of the results of a miniature war. Thirty-eight people had been killed, including 15 whites and 23 blacks; of the 537 injured, 178 were white and 342 were black. There is no record of the racial identity of the remaining 17. More than 1,000 families, mostly black, were homeless as a result of the burnings and general destruction of property. It was the nation's worst race war and shocked even the most indifferent observers into the realization that interracial conflicts in the United States had reached a serious stage.

During the next two months riots occurred in, among other places, Knoxville, Tennessee; Omaha, Nebraska; and Elaine, Arkansas. The Knoxville riot began when a white woman stumbled and fatally injured herself while running from a black man who was later accused of attempting to assault her. When he was arrested, a mob formed and an attempt was made to take him from the jail. During the general riot that followed, scores of people were injured, some fatally, and more than $50,000 worth of property was destroyed. The troops that were called out went into the black section and "shot it up" when a false rumor was circulated that some blacks had killed two white men. Black people were stopped on the streets and searched. A black newspaper declared, "The indignities which colored women suffered at the hands of these soldiers would make the devil blush for shame."

In Omaha a mob almost completely destroyed the county courthouse by fire in order to secure a black man who was in jail on a charge of attacking a white girl. The group succeeded in seizing him, whereupon he was dragged through the streets, shot more than 1,000 times, and mutilated beyond recognition. He was finally hanged downtown at one of the busiest intersections. Meanwhile, much damage was done to property, and several blacks were severely beaten. Blacks in Elaine, Arkansas, met to make plans to force their landlords to make a fair settlement with them. The meeting was broken up by a deputy sheriff and a posse, and in the melee the deputy was killed. A reign of terror began in which scores of blacks were shot and several killed. In the trials, which lasted less than an hour, twelve black farmers were sentenced to death and sixty-seven others were given long prison terms. The decisions were later nullified by the Supreme Court, which found that the African Americans had not been given a fair trial.

Although rioting continued for the next few years, few outbreaks equaled in proportion those of 1919. Two years later, in June 1921, the blacks and whites of Tulsa, Oklahoma, engaged in fighting, which some residents preferred to call a "race war," in which nine whites and twenty-one blacks were known to have been killed and several hundred injured. On hearing that a black had been accused of assaulting a young white woman, blacks took arms to the jail to protect the accused person, who, it was rumored, would be lynched. Altercations between whites and blacks at the jail spread to other parts of the city, and general rioting, looting, and house burning began. Four companies of the National Guard were called out, but by the time order was restored more than $1 million worth of property had been destroyed or damaged. In 1925 Detroit joined the ranks by seeking to prevent an African-American physician, O. H. Sweet, from living in a home he had purchased in a white neighborhood. When a mob gathered around his home and threw stones, a white man was killed by gunfire coming from the house. Sweet, his brother, and his friends in the house were brought to trial. The National Association for the Advancement of Colored People came to their defense, employing Clarence Darrow and Arthur Garfield Hays as defense attorneys. All were finally acquitted, but irreparable damage had been done not only to the Sweet family but also to race relations in Detroit.

In the postwar racial strife the willingness of African Americans to fight and to die in their own defense injected a new factor into America's most perplexing social problem. It was no longer a case of one race intimidating another into submission. Now it was war in the full sense of the word, and blacks were as determined to win it as they had been in Europe. The increasing urbanization of blacks, with its accompanying stimulation of self-respect and racial cohesiveness, had much to do with the resistance that they offered to their would-be oppressors. They had, moreover, imbibed freely of the democratic doctrine that had been expounded so generally during the war. Even if they could not win in the one-sided struggle, they sought to make a good showing. One of the outstanding poets of the period, Claude McKay, expressed the feelings of a great many African Americans when he wrote:

> If we must die, let it not be like hogs
> Hunted and penned in an inglorious spot,
> While round us bark the mad and hungry dogs,
> Making their mock at our accursed lot.
> If we must die, O let us nobly die,

W. E. B. Du Bois on "The Souls of White Folk"—1920

High in the tower, where I sit above the loud complaining of the human sea, I know many souls that toss and whirl and pass, but none there are that intrigue me more than the Souls of White Folk.

Of them I am singularly clairvoyant. I see in and through them. I view them from unusual points of vantage. Not as a foreigner do I come, for I am native, not foreign, bone of their thought and flesh of their language. Mine is not the knowledge of the traveler or the colonial composite of dear memories, words, and wonder. Nor yet is my knowledge that which servants have of masters, or mass of class, or capitalist of artisan. Rather, I see the working of their entrails. I know their thoughts and they know that I know. This knowledge makes them now embarrassed, now furious! They deny my right to live and be and call me misbirth! My word is to them mere bitterness and my soul, pessimism. And yet as they preach and strut and shout and threaten, crouching as they clutch at rags of facts and fancies to hide their nakedness, they go twisting, flying by my tired eyes and I see them ever stripped—ugly, human.

The discovery of personal whiteness among the world's peoples is a very modern thing—a nineteenth- and twentieth-century matter, indeed. The ancient world would have laughed at such a distinction. The Middle Ages regarded skin color with mild curiosity; and even up into the eighteenth century we were hammering our national manikins into one, great, Universal Man, with fine frenzy which ignored color and race even more than birth. Today we have changed all that, and the world in a sudden, emotional conversion has discovered that it is white and by that token, wonderful!

W. E. B. Du Bois, *Darkwater, Voices from Within the Veil* (New York, 1920), pp. 29–30.

So that our precious blood may not be shed
In vain; then even the monsters we defy
Shall be constrained to honor us though dead!
O kinsmen! we must meet the common foe!
Though far outnumbered let us show brave,
And for their thousand blows deal one deathblow!
What though before us lies the open grave?
Like men we'll face the murderous, cowardly pack,
Pressed to the wall, dying but fighting back!

Many whites freely intimated that it was foreign influences, especially the association on the basis of equality with the French during the war and the propaganda of Bolshevists after the war, that caused blacks to fight back. Blacks, however, ridiculed this view and contended that they were fighting only for what they thought was right. In October 1919 the *Pittsburgh Courier* declared, "As long as the Negro submits to lynchings, burnings, and oppressions—and says nothing he is a loyal American citizen. But when he decides that lynchings and burnings shall cease even at the cost of some bloodshed in America, then he is a Bolshevist." The militant *Crusader* regarded such accusations as a compliment. In a scathing denunciation of mob violence and rioting in America its editor asserted, "If to fight for one's rights is to be Bolshevists, then we are Bolshevists and let them make the most of it!"

In radical and conservative organizations, African Americans loudly protested against practices that they termed injustices and oppressions. They freely admitted that democracy had escaped, despite the fact that they had pursued it with an earnestness and vigor of which few other races could boast. Disillusionment and despair settled over them, and they could express little but dejection in their utterances, which were largely directed rather indiscriminately toward the white population. After describing the burning alive of a young black boy in Vicksburg, Mississippi, *Challenge Magazine* of Chicago exclaimed, "The 'German Hun' is beaten but the world is made no safer for Democracy. Humanity has been defended but lifted no higher. . . . I hate every Hun, and the worst I know are the ones that thrive under the free institutions of America." It would take more than utterances to gain a respected place for African Americans in American life. Indeed, it became increasingly clear that it would take more than the feverish fighting back that they courageously performed in times of crisis. Intelligent planning and action were needed, but the difficulty lay in taking any kind of bold and decisive steps in a climate so completely charged with emotion and tension. Small wonder that the programs for salvation were of such varied approaches and such diverse goals.

■ The Voice of Protest Rises

In the years immediately following World War I no meeting of a national organization of African Americans neglected to register its protest against the failure of the United States to grant them first-class citizenship. In July 1919 the National Association for the Advancement of Colored People meeting in Cleveland adopted resolutions expressing its great concern over the status of blacks. In September of the same year the National Equal Rights League, meeting in Washington, followed the lead of the NAACP. During the next month the National Race Congress also met in Washington and passed resolutions of protest. At about the same time the National Baptist Convention declared itself in favor of a more complete integration of African Americans into American life. It was the NAACP, however, that took the leadership in setting up a program of assault against bigotry and injustice in America. In May 1919 it had held a national conference on lynching at which the chief speaker was Charles Evans Hughes. The organization decided to carry on a relentless crusade against lynching and to raise funds to publicize its program and to defend persecuted African Americans. Largely through the efforts of Mary Talbert and others, the NAACP raised more than $45,000 by 1924.

Late in 1919 the association took the first steps toward securing the passage of a federal law against lynching. After carefully working to secure the support of senators and representatives, James Weldon Johnson, the secretary of the association, succeeded in 1921 in getting Rep. L. C. Dyer of Missouri to introduce in the House a bill "to assure to persons within the jurisdiction of every state the equal protection of the laws, and to punish the crime of lynching." Representatives from the Southern states immediately began organizing to defeat the proposed bill. They spoke on the floor of Congress in favor of mob rule and defied the federal government to interfere with the police power of the states. It was not possible for them to prevent a vote in the House of Representatives, and the bill passed, 230 to 119. The task in the Senate was infinitely more difficult, and the NAACP doubled its efforts to achieve the herculean task of securing passage of the bill there. A memorial signed by twenty-four governors, thirty-nine mayors, twenty-nine college presidents and professors, and a large number of editors, jurists, and lawyers was sent to the Senate urging its passage. The association published full-page advertisements in such newspapers as the *New York Times* and the *Atlanta Constitution* calling attention to the necessity for such a bill. When the bill reached the floor of the Senate the Southern senators, led by Underwood of Alabama and Harrison of Mississippi, succeeded in organizing a filibuster that ultimately prevented a vote on the measure. The Republicans, showing a decided lack of interest, voted to abandon it. Numerous similar bills were later introduced, including the Costigan-Wagner bill of 1935 and the Wagner-Gavagan bill of 1940, but all of them met a similar fate.

The NAACP undertook to make a thorough investigation of crimes committed against African Americans and to inform the public concerning them. In 1919 it published *Thirty Years of Lynching in the United States, 1889–1918*, which was a revelation with regard to the causes of lynchings and the circumstances under which the crimes occurred. A young light-skinned investigator, Walter White, was hired to go to the scenes of crimes and to secure as much data as possible concerning the tragedies. These reports were published by the association and distributed widely. In 1929 White brought out a work entitled *Rope and Faggot, A Biography of Judge Lynch*, based on his findings over a period of ten years. The association held meetings to protest lynching. In 1921, for example, more than 200 such meetings were held in various parts of the United States. The columns of its official organ, the *Crisis,* were filled with reports of crimes against African Americans, as well as appeals for support of the program of the organization.

The NAACP undertook to secure in the courts the rights that blacks could not otherwise obtain. Encouraged by its success in the cases involving grandfather clauses, residential segregation, and the Arkansas peons, it sought to break down the practice of Southern states of excluding blacks from Democratic primaries. It succeeded, in the case of *Nixon v. Herndon,* in having the Supreme Court of the United States declare null and void a Texas statute that excluded blacks from Democratic primaries in the state. When the Texas legislature enacted a law giving the party's executive committee the authority to fix the qualifications for party membership, the association, in *Nixon v. Condon,* succeeded in having the law nullified by arguing that the statute had set up a party committee and made it a state agency with certain powers and duties. It suffered a setback, however, in 1935 when, in *Grovey v. Townsend,* the Court refused to interfere with the exclusion of African Americans from Democratic primaries when such an exclusion had been effected by a resolution of the state convention of the party. It recovered its lost ground in 1944, in *Smith v. Allwright,* when the Supreme Court decided that the exclusion of African Americans from the Democratic primary was a clear violation of the Fifteenth Amendment. Thus the association, as well as many blacks, came to regard the Court as the most reliable safeguard of the rights of all citizens.

Another interracial organization that interested itself in race problems was the Commission on Interracial Cooperation. Organized in 1919, it set out "to quench, if possible, the fires of racial antagonism which were flaming at that time with such deadly menace in all sections of the country." The commission worked primarily in the South and, through Will W. Alexander and other prominent white Southerners, set up a program of education in race relations on state and community levels. Several ten-day schools for whites and for blacks were held to train leaders in promoting interracial work. Local interracial committees were organized, and upon the creation of sufficient interest state committees were set up. While the commission did not attack segregation, it spoke out against discrimination. Through its monthly publication, the *Southern Frontier,* and through other mediums it pressed for equal participation in government welfare programs, equal justice under the law, the abolition of lynching, and the ballot for all citizens. From its offices in Atlanta it carried on a program of research and education on Southern problems, devoting considerable attention to agriculture, health, and education.

Despite their vigorous efforts, the National Association for the Advancement of Colored People and the Commission on Interracial Cooperation failed to reach more than a small minority of blacks and whites, and although they succeeded in achieving ends that were beneficial to all African Americans, they failed to capture the imagination and secure the following of the masses. African Americans on the lower social and economic levels were inclined to regard such organizations as agencies of upper-class blacks and liberal whites who failed to join hands with them in their efforts to rise. It

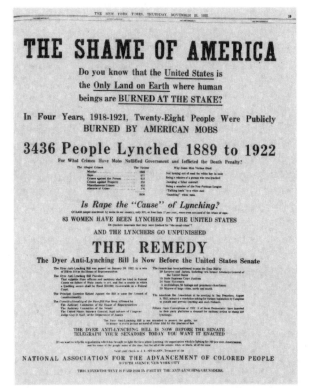

THIS FULL-PAGE ADVER-
TISEMENT appeared on
November 23, 1922, in
The New York Times, At-
lanta Constitution, and
several other leading newspapers. It was part of the
NAACP's campaign to se-
cure passage of the Dyer
antilynching bill.

was this feeling, regardless of its justification, that made possible the rise of
Marcus Garvey and his Universal Negro Improvement Association (UNIA).
Garvey had begun this organization in his native Jamaica in 1914. Two years
later he came to the United States to organize a New York chapter of the
UNIA. At the end of the war the association grew rapidly, and according to
its leader there were more than thirty branches by the middle of 1919.

The basis for Garvey's wide popularity was his appeal to race pride at a
time when African Americans generally had so little of which to be proud.
The strain and stress of living in hostile urban communities created a state
of mind upon which Garvey capitalized. He called upon African Americans,
especially those of the darker hue, to follow him. Garvey exalted everything
black; he insisted that black stood for strength and beauty, not inferiority.
He asserted that Africans had a noble past, and he declared that American
blacks should be proud of their ancestry. In his newspaper, the *Negro World,*
he told blacks that racial prejudice was so much a part of the civilization of
whites that it was futile to appeal to their sense of justice and their
high-sounding democratic principles. With an eye on the growing sentiment
favoring self-determination of dependent peoples, Garvey said that the only

hope for African Americans was to flee America and return to Africa and build up a country of their own. On one occasion Garvey cried out: "Wake up Ethiopia! Wake up Africa! Let us work toward the one glorious end of a free, redeemed and mighty nation. Let Africa be a bright star among the constellations of nations."

As a man of action Garvey began to put his program into operation. He appealed to the League of Nations for permission to settle a colony in Africa and opened negotiations with Liberia. Failing to secure entry into Africa by peaceful means, he organized the Universal African Legion to drive the white usurpers out. Other auxiliary organizations consisted of the Universal Black Cross Nurses, the Universal African Motor Corps, the Black Eagle Flying Corps, and the Black Star Steamship Line. In 1921 Garvey announced the formal organization of the Empire of Africa and appointed himself provisional president. He ruled with the assistance of one potentate and one supreme deputy potentate. Among the nobility he created were knights of the Nile, knights of the distinguished service order of Ethiopia, and dukes of the Niger and of Uganda. In New York and other large cities members of the Universal Negro Improvement Association, now citizens of a new empire, paraded in elaborate uniforms and held conferences and conventions.

The effect of the Garvey doctrines on the unlettered and inexperienced urban element, recently removed from the farm, was magnetic. Thousands hailed him as the true leader of the black race. Although Garvey's claim that he had 4 million followers in 1920 and 6 million three years later is doubtless exaggerated, even his severest critics admitted that there were perhaps a half-million members of the UNIA. Most African-American leaders denounced him bitterly as an insincere, selfish imposter, but he countered that they were opportunists, liars, thieves, and traitors. Du Bois was especially critical of Garvey and called the UNIA "bombastic and impracticable." Du Bois later admitted that Garvey's schemes made difficult the effective development of the Pan-African congresses. When the third congress met in 1923 signs of decline were clearly discernible, and the fourth one in 1927 was nothing more than an "empty gesture to keep the idea alive." Garvey was especially contemptuous of Du Bois and other leaders of the NAACP. On one occasion he wrote, "The N.A.A.C.P. wants us all to become white by amalgamation, but they are not honest enough to come out with the truth. To be a Negro is no disgrace, but an honor, and we of the U.N.I.A. do not want to become white. . . . We are proud and honorable. We love our race and respect and adore our mothers."

Garvey's conduct of his steamship line finally put an end to his meteoric rise. According to his wife he had collected $10 million between 1919 and 1921. More than $1 million had been spent in purchasing and equipping ships for the Black Star Line. In 1923 Garvey went on trial before a federal judge on a charge of using the mails to defraud in raising money for his steamship line. He was found guilty, and two years later entered the Atlanta penitentiary to serve a five-year term. Perhaps Arthur Brisbane's assertion that to hold him was equivalent to "jailing a rainbow" was an overstatement, but he continued to conduct the movement from his cell in Atlanta. In one letter to his followers he said:

> My months of forcible removal from among you, being imprisoned as a punishment for advocating the cause of our real emancipation, have not left me hopeless or despondent; but to the contrary, I see a great ray of light and the bursting of a mighty political cloud which will bring you complete freedom. . . .
>
> We have gradually won our way back into the confidence of the God of Africa, and He shall speak with a voice of thunder, that shall shake the pillars of a corrupt and unjust world, and once more restore Ethiopia to her ancient glory. . . .
>
> Hold fast to the Faith. Desert not the ranks, but as brave soldiers march on to victory. I am happy, and shall remain so, as long as you keep the flag flying.

Garvey remained in prison until President Coolidge pardoned him in 1927 and ordered his deportation as an undesirable alien. Although he made efforts to revive his movement in Jamaica and later in London, where he died in 1940, "Negro Zionism" was doomed to failure. Regardless of how dissatisfied African Americans were with conditions in the United States, they were unwilling in the 1920s, as their forebears had been a century earlier, to undertake the uncertain task of redeeming Africa. The widespread interest in Garvey's program was more a protest against the anti-black reaction of the postwar period than an approbation of the fantastic schemes of the black leader. Its significance lies in the fact that it was the first mass movement among African Americans and that it indicated the extent to which they entertained doubts concerning the hope for first-class citizenship in the only homeland they knew.

While most blacks were content to remain in the United States and strive to improve conditions through the regular channels open to all citizens or through special agencies like the NAACP, others looked toward a rapid transformation of life into a veritable heaven. Among these were the followers of George Baker, more commonly called Father Divine. Beginning in 1919 with a small group in Sayville, New York, this remarkable man built up a following within the next two decades that amused some observers and perplexed others. Although his followers deserted their churches and began to call him God, it was as much a social as a religious movement. By 1930 he was holding open house and feeding thousands in places that came to be known as heavens. When people wondered where he secured the money for the elaborate feasts, he merely answered in an almost unintelligible torrent of words, "I have harnessed your consciousness as Franklin did electricity and it is for you to use your emotions as Edison handled the electricity

Marcus Garvey Dreams of a Better World for Blacks—1923

I read of the conditions in America. I read "Up from Slavery" by Booker T. Washington, and then my doom—if I may so call it—of being a race leader dawned upon me in London after I had traveled through almost half of Europe.

I asked, "Where is the black man's Government?" "Where is his King and his kingdom?" "Where is his President, his country, and his ambassador, his army, his navy, his men of big affairs?" I could not find them, and then I declared, "I will help to make them."

. . . I was determined that the black man would not continue to be kicked about by all the other races and nations of the world, as I saw it in the West Indies, South and Central America and Europe, and as I read of it in America. My young and ambitious mind led me into flights of great imagination. I saw before me then, even as I do now, a new world of black men, not peons, serfs, dogs and slaves, but a nation of sturdy men making their impress upon civilization and causing a new light to dawn upon the human race. I could not remain in London any more. My brain was afire. There was a world of thought to conquer. I had to start ere it became too late and the work be not done. Immediately I boarded a ship at Southampton for Jamaica, where I arrived on July 15, 1914. The Universal Negro Improvement Association and African Communities (Imperial) League was founded and organized five days after my arrival, with the program of uniting all the negro peoples of the world into one great body to establish a country and Government absolutely their own.

Marcus Garvey, *Current History*, XVIII (September 1923), pp. 951–957.

uncovered by Franklin." His following grew enormously in the 1930s, and heavens or peace missions were founded in many Eastern cities as well as in some Midwestern communities. The movement became interracial as early as 1926, and within a few years had attracted a considerable number of white followers, some of whom were wealthy. That such a movement flourished during the period is a testimonial of the extent of the social ills from which the body politic suffered and was one more indication of the tremendous frustration that characterized many blacks and some whites as well.

CHAPTER 18

The Harlem Renaissance and the Politics of African-American Culture

■ Socioeconomic Problems and African-American Literature

During the postwar period a distinctly new literary movement emerged in the United States. In the early part of the century there had been the shocking revelations of the muckrakers and the tendency toward greater realism in the works of Howells and others. The war had, however, produced such an intense air of patriotism that more energy was expended on praising the American way of life than on criticizing it. It looked as though there would be no further criticism of American life, as everyone appeared content to return to normalcy, to forget whatever was wrong with America, and to concentrate on enjoying the blessings of the existing system. There was, moreover, the spread of bolshevism, which alarmed Americans so that they became intolerant of cynics who insisted on finding fault with things as they were. There were, nevertheless, a few writers who emerged from the calm surrounding America's enjoyment of peace and prosperity and called attention to the failings and inadequacies of capitalistic democracy in America. In 1920 Sinclair Lewis in *Main Street* emphasized the superficiality and false values of American urban life. Two years later he delivered a shocking indictment of the American businessman in *Babbitt*. In 1925 Theodore Dreiser showed the deleterious effects of the false values of the commercial civilization in *An American Tragedy*.

American writers interested themselves in numerous social and economic problems. Labor problems received considerable attention, as did housing, crime, social planning, and disarmament. Novelists, dramatists, publicists, and other writers also turned to the American race problem. Perhaps no other subject lent itself to such a variety of treatments, and writers made the most of it. In 1919 Robert Kerlin collected the points of view of African-American newspapers in *Voice of the Negro*. Shortly thereafter Moorfield Storey pricked the conscience of America regarding blacks in his *Problems of Today*; and in 1924 Frank Tannenbaum described the plight of Southern blacks in *Darker Phases of the South*. Among the white dramatists who experimented with African-American materials, Eugene O'Neill was outstanding with *The Emperor Jones* (1920) and *All God's Chillun Got Wings* (1924). In 1926 Paul Green's *In Abraham's Bosom*, produced with a predominantly African-American cast, won him the Pulitzer Prize. Carl Van Vechten, Victor F. Calverton, Joel Spingarn, and others were lending their pens to the encouragement of African Americans and the use of their own materials. In her own inimitable way, Zora Neale Hurston would label as "Negrotarians" those whites who were, in one way or another, fascinated with life in Harlem and similar black communities and who wrote about it for whatever reasons. With such a profusion of writing about blacks, America became somewhat more conscious of the race problem and was willing to listen to what African Americans had to say about it.

There can be no doubt that the emergence of African-American writers in the postwar period stemmed in part from the fact that they were inclined to exploit the opportunity to write about themselves. It was more than that, however. The movement that has been variously called the Harlem Renaissance, the Black Renaissance, and the New Negro Movement was essentially a part of the growing interest of American literary circles in the immediate and pressing social and economic problems facing the country. This increasing interest coincided with two developments in African-American life that fostered the growth of the New Negro Movement. The migration that had begun during the war had thrown the destiny of blacks into their own hands more than ever before. They developed a responsibility and a self-confidence that they had not previously known. During the war they learned from no less a person than their president the promise of freedom, and on the battlefield black men served their country. They began to see the discrepancies between the promise of freedom and the reality of their experiences. They became defiant, bitter, and impatient. It was not the timorous, docile black of the past who said, "The next time white folks pick on colored folks, something's going to drop—dead white folks."

In the riots and clashes that followed the war, blacks fought back with surprising audacity. By this time, moreover, they had achieved a level of articulation that made it possible for them to transform their feelings into a variety of literary forms. Despite their intense feelings of hate and hurt, they possessed enough restraint and objectivity to use their materials artistically.

They were sufficiently in touch with the main currents of American literary thought, moreover, to adapt the accepted forms of expression to their own materials and therefore gain a wider acceptance. These two factors, the keener realization of injustice and the improvement of the capacity for expression, produced the crop of black writers who constituted the Harlem Renaissance. Although few of the black writers would concede it, there could be no denying that Marcus Garvey was one of the great energizers of the New Negro Movement. By raising the consciousness of millions of black Americans, by outraging many of their articulate leaders such as W. E. B. Du Bois and James Weldon Johnson, and by creating so much excitement in Harlem for black and white alike, Garvey stimulated a variety of forms of expression. Caught up in the controversies of which Garvey was the center, or brooding over the conditions in American life to which he pointed, many blacks began to write about them, as though reacting to Garvey's harangues, even if they seldom agreed with him.

Those who contributed to the literature of the Harlem Renaissance were deeply aware of belonging to a group that not only was a minority but also was set apart in numerous ways, many of which were degrading. If black writers accepted this separateness, it was not so much because they wanted to be what others wanted them to be, that is, a distinct and even exotic group in the eyes of the more patronizing whites. Rather, it was because their experiences had given them some appreciation of their own distinct and unique cultural heritage and traditions. The plantation, the slave quarters, the proscriptions even in freedom, the lynchings and the riots, and the segregation and discrimination had created a body of common experiences that in turn helped to promote the idea of a distinct and authentic cultural community. This community had its own spokespersons who, in the years following the First World War, protested all the social and economic wrongs. They stood for full equality, but they celebrated the strength of their own integrity as a people. While they had a vision of social and economic freedom, they cherished the very unhappy experiences that had drawn them closer together. They also had a vision, as Nathan Huggins has suggested, "of themselves as actors and creators of a people's birth (or rebirth)."

The writers of the Harlem Renaissance, bitter and cynical as some of them were, were more intent on confronting American racists than on embracing the doctrines of the Socialists and Communists. The editor of the *Messenger* ventured the opinion that the New Negro was the "product of the same world-wide forces that have brought into being the great liberal and radical movements that are now seizing the reins of political, social, and economic power in all the civilized countries of the world." Such forces may have produced the New Negro, but the more articulate of the group did not seek to subvert American constitutional government. Indeed, the writers of the Harlem Renaissance were not so much revolting against the system as they were protesting the unjust operation of the system. In this approach they proved to be as characteristically American as any writers of the period. Like their white contemporaries, black writers were merely becoming more aware of America's pressing social problems, especially those dealing with race, and like the others, they were willing to use their art, not only to contribute to the great body of American culture but also to improve the culture and civilization of which they were a part.

All the black writers of this period cannot be described as crusaders, for not all of them assumed this role. Some were not immediately concerned with the injustices heaped on Negroes. Some created poems, novels, and songs merely for the sake of art, while others took up their pens to escape the sordid aspects of their existence. If there is an element of race in the works of these writers, it is because their material flows out of their individual and group experiences, which reflect the emergence of a distinct cultural community. This is not to say that such writings were not effective as protest literature, but rather that not all the authors were conscious crusaders for a better world. As a matter of fact, it was this detachment, this objectivity, that made it possible for many of the writers of the Harlem Renaissance to achieve a nobility of expression and a poignancy of feeling in their writings that placed them among the great masters of twentieth-century American literature.

■ Harlem, the Seat and Center

The city of New York had long been the center of the intellectual and cultural life of black America. It was only natural that the Negro Renaissance should have developed in the capital of the American black world. The riot of 1900 had stirred the African-American population to a great degree of self-assertion, which culminated in the organization of the Citizens Protective League. Under the editorship of T. Thomas Fortune the militant *New York Age* fought for equality of opportunity for blacks and equal protection under the law. Within a few years James Weldon Johnson had moved from Florida to New York, and shortly after the organization of the National Association for the Advancement of Colored People, W. E. B. Du Bois left Atlanta and took up residence there. Du Bois continued his creative writing, bringing out two novels, *The Quest of the Silver Fleece* (1900) and *The Dark Princess* (1928), and two volumes of poems and essays, *Darkwater* (1920) and *The Gift of Black Folk* (1924). Militant blacks from the West Indies migrated to the great city in large numbers and were ready to join in any movement for the improvement of conditions among blacks. During World War I, with the migration of large numbers of African Americans from Southern states and with greater opportunities for work, the black community of Harlem became a prosperous and important part of the metropolitan community.

It was in New York that African Americans made their most eloquent demands for equality during and after World War I. There were no serious race clashes, such as those in East St. Louis and Chicago, but there was the

CLAUDE McKAY, NOVELIST, ESSAYIST, POET. Many regarded him as the first significant writer of the Harlem Renaissance. A native of Jamaica, some of his best work was about his homeland, but he quickly displayed a talent for capturing the spirit of Harlem and other places in his adopted home. *(Schomburg Center for Research in Black Culture.)*

impressive silent protest parade in 1917, the vigorous denunciations of injustice in the columns of the *Crisis*, and the radical utterances of the *Messenger*. There was, moreover, some flirtation on the part of African Americans with Communists and Socialists, though it was short-lived. New York was already the center of American literary and artistic activity. Talented authors, playwrights, painters, and sculptors came to the big city to sell their wares and to increase their output. Publishers and other purveyors of arts and letters remained sensitive to any production that had the promise of benefiting all parties concerned. It was only natural, therefore, that any substantial growth of African-American literature would take place in a climate congenial to its development.

A few blacks, such as Du Bois, had written artistic works of protest for many years. "The Litany of Atlanta," which Du Bois composed on the occasion of the Atlanta riot in 1906, was in the spirit of the New Negro; but there were too few such works at that time to describe their appearance as part of a movement. As a prelude to the emergence of an abundant crop of African-American writers, James Weldon Johnson published *Fifty Years and Other Poems* in 1917. The title poem, written on the anniversary of the signing of the Emancipation Proclamation, made it clear that African Americans were determined to remain in America and to enjoy the full fruits of their labors. Johnson thus became the advance herald of the Harlem Renaissance and remained an integral part of that movement. In 1922 he published *The Book of American Negro Poetry*, which contains the works of outstanding contemporary black poets. His preface to the work, a survey of African-American

CIVIL LEADER, PUBLIC SERVANT, AND WRITER. James
Weldon Johnson was perhaps the best known writer of the
Harlem Renaissance. *(Courtesy, Beinecke Rare Book and Manu-
script Library, Yale University.)*

poetry from George Moses Horton to Claude McKay, did much to emphasize
the value of such efforts to the cultural life of America. He participated
further in the movement by editing, in collaboration with J. Rosamond
Johnson, his brother, two books of American Negro spirituals in 1925 and
1926. In 1927 there appeared his *God's Trombones,* Negro sermons in verse,
and in 1930 his *Saint Peter Relates an Incident of the Resurrection Day,* a burning
indictment of the discrimination against Negro Gold Star mothers. In 1927
his *Autobiography of an Ex-Coloured Man,* originally published in 1912, was
reissued. In two works, *Black Manhattan* (1930) and *Along This Way* (1933),
an autobiography, he chronicled the Harlem Renaissance, of which he was
a leading participant. As a precursor of, participant in, and historian of the
movement, James Weldon Johnson, whom Nathan Huggins called the
compeer of the New Negro, had as much to do with the rise of the Harlem
Renaissance as any one person.

James Weldon Johnson's Harlem— The 1920s

This was the era in which was achieved the Harlem of story and song; the era in which Harlem's fame for exotic flavor and colorful sensuousness was spread to all parts of the world; when Harlem was made known as the scene of laughter, singing, dancing, and primitive passions, as the center of the new Negro literature and art; the era in which it gained its place in the list of famous sections of great cities. This universal reputation was the work of writers. The picturesque Harlem was real, but it was the writers who discovered its artistic values and, in giving literary expression to them, actually created the Harlem that caught the world's imagination. Very early, Langston Hughes discovered these values and gave them their first expression in poetry. The prose about this Harlem is voluminous. The writers who came to parties and went sightseeing in Harlem found stimulating material for their pens. Then other writers flocked there; many came from far, and depicted it in many ways and in many languages. They still come; the Harlem of story and song still fascinates them.

James Weldon Johnson, *Along This Way: The Autobiography of James Weldon Johnson* (New York, 1933), p. 380.

Claude McKay is regarded by most critics, including James Weldon Johnson, as having been the first significant writer of the Harlem Renaissance. When McKay came from his native Jamaica in 1912 at twenty-one years of age, he had already won distinction as a poet. In 1911 his *Songs of Jamaica* had been published. After attending Tuskegee Institute and Kansas State University in Manhattan, McKay went to New York and witnessed the evolution of Harlem into an integral part of the great metropolis. He published poems in several magazines, but it was the appearance of *Harlem Shadows* (1922) that placed him in the front ranks of postwar American writers. In "The Lynching," "If We Must Die" (see Chapter 16), and "To the White Fiends" there is expressed in eloquent verse a proud defiance and bitter contempt that became two of the salient characteristics of the Harlem Renaissance. As though he had expended all of his poetic talents, McKay next turned his attention to prose. In 1928 he brought out a novel of African-American life in New York, *Home to Harlem*. In the following year there appeared another novel, *Banjo*, the scene of which is laid in Marseilles. Later he was to publish his autobiography, *A Long Way from Home* (1937), and a panorama of African-American life in New York, *Harlem: Negro Metropolis* (1940). Even after McKay turned his attention to other matters the movement that he stimulated grew to enormous proportions.

Jean Toomer was one of the most talented of the African-American writers. He had studied in France, where he developed the art of introspective contemplation. He moved freely among European and American literary circles and drank deeply of a variety of experiences. In 1923 he published *Cane*, which ranked with McKay's *Harlem Shadows* in its significance for the literary movement. This only contribution of Toomer to the Harlem Renaissance was a series of realistic stories about black life, together with a number of extraordinarily moving lyrics. Both the poetry and prose of *Cane* reflect an enormous capacity for self-revelation, which Toomer had developed in France. His writings are unrestrained, yet objective, passionate, but proud. They are full of love and pride of race, and they reveal the inner yearnings as well as the joys and hurts of the New Negro. Shortly after the appearance of *Cane*, Toomer retired from active participation in the literary awakening and disappeared into the larger community of American life.

A new high was reached in the Harlem Renaissance with the appearance of Countee Cullen's first volume of poems, *Color*, in 1925. Though only twenty-two years old, this New York-born son of a Methodist minister and later son-in-law of Du Bois, gave numerous evidences of being a true lyric poet. He doubtless felt as keenly about the race problem as McKay, but his protests are couched in some of the most delicate, gentle lyrics of the postwar poetry. He was at his best when writing verse dealing with aspects of the race problem, but the beauty and effectiveness of his lines do not depend on the use of racial experiences. Typical of the quality of his writings are these two lines, perhaps the best known of all of Cullen's work:

> Yet do I marvel at this curious thing:
> To make a poet black, and bid him sing!

The lyric quality, rich imagination, and intellectual content of his works make him one of the major poets of twentieth-century America. In 1927 he brought out two books, *The Ballad of the Brown Girl* and *Copper Sun,* as well as an anthology, *Caroling Dusk.* Two years later his *Black Christ* appeared, while in 1932 he published *One Way to Heaven.*

During the Harlem Renaissance, New York attracted from Missouri via Mexico, Africa, and Europe its most cosmopolitan as well as its most prolific writer, Langston Hughes. Few writers in America had such rich and varied experiences, and few were so indiscriminate in selecting materials for their writings. While Hughes was a true rebel poet, writing in the best traditions of the New Negro, he did not cry or moan. Frequently he laughed, revealing a freedom from the restrictions of race that equaled his freedom from the restrictions of form. He could compose deeply moving verses full of pride of race, such as "The Negro Speaks of Rivers," or he could write of the most humble walks of life, as in "Brass Spittoons," with a freedom and nobility of expression that raised them many levels higher. In 1926 his *Weary Blues* appeared, followed in the next year by *Fine Clothes to the Jew.* He demonstrated his versatility by bringing out a novel, *Not Without Laughter,* in 1930,

POET LAUREATE OF THE HARLEM RENAISSANCE. Langston Hughes, shown here at his typewriter, also wrote novels,
essays, and plays. *(Springer/Bettmann Film Archive.)*

and a volume of short stories, *The Ways of White Folks,* in 1934. At a later
time he experimented with pieces for the theater, and in 1940 his autobiography, *The Big Sea,* appeared. Numerous smaller works of his were published,
and as he moved about the country ever broadening the scope of his art and
continuously experimenting with new forms of expression, there appeared
to be some justification for regarding him as "Shakespeare in Harlem."
Hughes, as Arnold Rampersad has noted, "liberal and generous in his spirit,
and well aware of the demands of the modern world" on his people, wrote
both to address and give voice to the African-American masses, fashioning
"out of his imagination . . . an aesthetic to suit, above all, their needs, not to
amuse their masters."

   The period produced numerous other poets, who published their works
either in slender volumes or in the columns of Charles S. Johnson's
Opportunity, published by the Urban League, Du Bois's *Crisis,* or other New
York periodicals. They were overshadowed, however, by the novelists, some
of whom ranked with the major poets of the period. One of those who

YOUNG BLACK WRITERS AND SCHOLARS ATTEND FASHIONABLE WEDDING.
When Countee Cullen married Yolande, the daughter of W. E. B. Du Bois, on April
10, 1928, among the groomsmen were Langston Hughes and Arna Bontemps (top row,
center), Alpheus Hunton (standing, second from right), Robert C. Weaver (extreme
left, standing), Cullen (fourth from left, second row); Dr. and Mrs. Du Bois are seated
at the right. (*Courtesy Schomburg Center for Research in Black Culture.*)

employed the medium of fiction quite successfully was Jessie Redmond
Fauset. She brought to her work an ample education from Cornell University
and the University of Pennsylvania and used her spare moments to translate
the works of some of the black poets of the French West Indies and to write
verse of her own. It was her novel *There Is Confusion* (1924) that won for her
a place among the more select in the new literary movement. In employing
characters from well-to-do African-American families, Fauset created a new
setting in the treatment of African Americans in literary works. While the
problem of race is present in her works, it does not obscure the problems
that confront anyone of similar economic and social position. It seems that
her characters merely emphasize the growing Americanization of blacks and
the fact that in a given situation they react as other people do. In 1929 Fauset's
second novel, *Plum Bun,* appeared and was followed in 1931 by *The
Chinaberry Tree* and in 1933 by *Comedy: American Style.* While there is a pride
of race running through most of her works, they do much to carry
African-American fiction above the complex problem of race and place it in
the company of general American literature.

In 1924 Walter White published *Fire in the Flint,* a swiftly moving, tragic

JESSIE FAUSET, POET, ESSAYIST, EDITOR, NOVELIST, TRANSLATOR, EDUCATOR. She ranged widely in her search for a proper and powerful means of communicating. *(Courtesy, Moorland Spingarn Research Center, Howard University)*

story of Negro life in the South. Two years later, in *Flight,* he sought to picture the emotional struggles of a young woman light enough to pass as white. In 1929 White deserted the field of fiction and wrote *Rope and Faggot: A Biography of Judge Lynch,* an authoritative and searching analysis of lynching, which was based on his own investigations. In *Quicksand* (1928) and *Passing* (1929), Nella Larsen sought to explore the innumerable social problems of young African-American women in their efforts to struggle upward both in American and in Europe. Among the other works of fiction during the period were Wallace Thurman's *The Blacker the Berry* (1929) and *Infants of the Spring* (1932), Eric Walrond's *Tropic Death* (1926), Rudolph Fisher's *The Walls of Jericho* (1928) and *The Conjure Woman Dies* (1932), and George S. Schuyler's *Black No More* (1931).

A considerable amount of nonfiction prose was an integral part of the new literary movement. *Crisis* and *Opportunity* kept their columns open to young African-American authors and offered prizes to stimulate writing. Other periodicals in the New York area, such as *Survey Graphic, Current History,* the *Modern Quarterly,* the *Nation,* the *New Masses,* and the *American Mercury,* also encouraged writers by publishing their works. In addition to the writings of Du Bois, James W. Johnson, and Schuyler, essays were published by Abram L. Harris, E. Franklin Frazier, Arthur A. Schomburg, Benjamin Brawley, J. A. Rogers, and Alain Locke. In 1925 the Renaissance received its most significant recognition with the appearance of a special

Harlem number of *Survey Graphic,* edited by Alain Locke. Later in the same year the articles were collected and enlarged in a volume, *The New Negro.* Indeed, the literary phase of the Harlem Renaissance had come of age.

There were other mediums through which African Americans expressed themselves during this period, not the least of which was the stage. After 1910 blacks disappeared almost altogether from the stages of downtown theaters in New York. In the ensuing years there grew up in Harlem a real African-American theater in which black actors performed before predominantly African-American audiences. It was no longer necessary for blacks to attempt only those roles that were acceptable to white audiences. The Lafayette Players presented almost every type of play, including such stalwarts as *Madame X, The Servant in the House, On Trial,* and *Within the Law.* Similar works were produced at the Lincoln Theater. A large group of able and popular players emerged, including Abbie Mitchell, Laura Bowman, Edna Thomas, Charles Gilpin, Frank Wilson, Clarence Muse, and Jack Carter. In 1917 a group of black actors under the sponsorship of Emily Hapgood presented three one-act plays by Ridgely Torrence at the Garden Theater in Madison Square Garden. The presentation of the plays, *The Rider of Dreams, Granny Maumee,* and *Simon the Cyrenian,* marked the first time that African-American actors had commanded the serious attention of the critics and the general press. Because the United States entered the war on the day following the opening of the plays, blacks in the theater were forced to wait until a later period before they could claim a substantial place in American public entertainment.

In 1919 there was a revival of interest in African Americans in the theater with the appearance of Charles Gilpin as the Reverend William Custis in John Drinkwater's *Abraham Lincoln.* In the following year Gilpin won acclaim for himself and for Eugene O'Neill in the creation of the title role in *The Emperor Jones.* For his outstanding performance he received an award from the Drama League of New York as well as the Spingarn Medal. Some critics predicted for him a career similar to that of Ira Aldridge, who had captivated European audiences with his Shakespearean roles in the previous century. In 1924 Paul Robeson played the leading role in O'Neill's *All God's Chillun Got Wings.* It was the first time in American history that a black man had taken a principal role opposite a white woman, and the anticipated riot did not materialize. In 1926 Paul Green of the University of North Carolina brought to New York *In Abraham's Bosom,* in which Jules Bledsoe played the leading role, ably assisted by Rose McClendon, Abbie Mitchell, and Frank Wilson. The play was a distinct success and demonstrated both the adaptability of African-American life to the theater and the ability of African-American actors in the theater. In the following year *Porgy,* a folk play of black life in Charleston by Dorothy and DuBose Heyward, was produced by the Theater Guild. Once more Rose McClendon, Frank Wilson, and the others in the cast captivated New York audiences by the seriousness with which they plied their art. These plays about black life by white authors reached a

EUBIE BLAKE AND NO-BLE SISSLE. Among the most talented of their time, they wrote the lyrics and composed the music for several Broadway hits. (*The Bettmann Achive.*)

high-water mark with the production in 1930 of Marc Connelly's *The Green Pastures*, a fable of a black person's conception of the Old Testament, with Richard B. Harrison as the Lord. With its long run in New York and on the road, the play should have convinced America that there was a place for African Americans on the legitimate stage.

The Harlem Renaissance produced more than writers of serious poetry and prose and skilled dramatic actors. It was only natural for New York to expect that in the field of lighter entertainment performances by African Americans would reach a new high. Ever since Bert Williams and George Walker reached New York in 1896 and introduced their highly successful vaudeville team, blacks had furnished a considerable portion of New York's entertainment. Aside from making the cakewalk fashionable, they appeared in numerous revues and became world-famous for their rollicking, carefree wisecracking. There were also Bob Cole and J. Rosamond Johnson, whose *Shoofly Regiment* and *Red Moon* were successes in the field of musical comedy before World War I. By 1920, when Bert Williams was making his final appearances, New York was as ready for New Negro musical shows as it was for New Negro poetry.

In the summer of 1921 *Shuffle Along* opened in New York, the most brilliant African-American revue New York had ever witnessed. Its popular songs, including "I'm Just Wild about Harry," "Love Will Find a Way," and "Shuffle Along," were worthy of the talented singers and beautiful chorus that sang and danced the tunes. The settings and costumes were in the best traditions of the musical extravaganza. The show was written and produced by blacks—F. E. Miller, Aubrey Lyle, Eubie Blake, and Noble Sissle. It was indeed record-breaking and epoch-making. Its New York run lasted more than a year, and it was on the road for more than two years. The production was the highest type of musical comedy entertainment that African Americans had yet produced, and it was easily the most popular show in New York in 1921 and 1922. There was another fairly popular African-American show, *Put and Take,* by Irving Miller, but because of the extraordinary success of *Shuffle Along,* it did not receive the recognition that it deserved.

During the remainder of the 1920s, New York witnessed a succession of top-flight African-American musical revues. In 1923 there was Irving Miller's *'Liza.* In the same year there was *Runnin' Wild,* by Miller and Lyle, as well as *Chocolate Dandies* by Blake and Sissle, a show that introduced Josephine Baker to theatergoers. In 1924 *Dixie to Broadway,* starring Florence Mills, opened. Since African-American revues had previously starred two black-face comedians, the domination of the show by Florence Mills was a break with long-established traditions. The production of *Blackbirds* in 1926 was a signal triumph for this talented black woman, who captivated audiences in America and in Europe with her pantomiming, singing, and dancing. Her untimely death in 1927 removed the brightest star on the musical comedy horizon. Ethel Waters in *Africana* and other shows, Adelaide Hall and Ada Ward in *Blackbirds of 1928,* and Bill Robinson in a succession of hits sought to maintain the high standards set by Florence Mills and others in earlier productions.

Some observers were already calling this "the Jazz Age," a tribute to the numerous African-American musicians whose compositions and performances made jazz so popular among Americans of all classes and races by the early twentieth century. One of the earliest contributors was the composer-pianist Scott Joplin who, before his death in 1917, was known as "the king of ragtime." Perhaps no one gave more substance and depth to the meaning of the term "the Jazz Age" than Ferdinand "Jelly Roll" Morton, composer, pianist, and raconteur. By World War I, Morton had composed a number of works, including "The New Orleans Blues" and "The Jelly Roll Blues," that won for him, in Eileen Southern's view, recognition as the first true jazz composer. Meanwhile, Morton's contemporary, virtuoso cornetist Joseph "King" Oliver, moved his operation from New Orleans to Chicago, setting the stage for that city to become a major center of jazz. There would be others also—such as the young second cornetist in Oliver's band, Louis Armstrong, and clarinetist Johnny Dodds—who would excite scores of thousands with their new synthesis of blues and ragtime and would inspire generations of musicians to come.

There was also what some called serious music. Harry T. Burleigh, R. Nathaniel Dett, Carl Diton, and J. Rosamond Johnson were writing and editing Negro spirituals as well as other musical scores. Paul Robeson, Lawrence Brown, and Taylor Gordon were giving programs made up exclusively of African-American songs, while Jules Bledsoe, Abbie Mitchell, and others included Negro spirituals in their repertoire. Roland Hayes was acclaimed both in Europe and in America for his rare gifts in interpreting songs as well as Negro spirituals. Meanwhile, the father of the blues, W. C. Handy, moved from Memphis to New York, where his influence and popularity increased enormously. The spirit of the New Negro was as alive in the serious and popular music of the period as in the other mediums.

The origins of the African-American academic tradition in art can be traced back to Edward Mitchell Bannister. Born in 1828 and largely self-taught, by the late 1850s Bannister was a highly respected portrait painter. After the Civil War, wealthy whites and blacks were frequent purchasers of his canvases. Bannister served on the original board of the Rhode Island School of Design and when in 1876 a landscape he submitted won a first prize at the Centennial Exposition in Philadelphia, he became the first African American to receive a national art award.

During the late nineteenth and early twentieth centuries, however, no African-American artist measured up to the stature of Henry Ossawa Tanner, who was one of the world's outstanding painters at the turn of the century. His works won medals at the Paris Exposition of 1900, the Pan-American Exposition of 1901, and the St. Louis Exposition of 1904. Today, many of his paintings hang in the better art galleries of Europe and America. In the period after World War I Aaron Douglas began to receive recognition for his black-and-white drawings and his illustrations. His growing reputation brought him significant commissions, one of which was to do the murals for the Fisk University Library in 1929. As the illustrator of many works by James Weldon Johnson and others, and as a significant muralist who depicted the history of black Americans, Douglas was the leading graphic artist of the Harlem Renaissance. Archibald J. Motley, Jr., who spent most of his life in Chicago, painted vibrant scenes of African-American life in that city and portraits of his family and friends that are powerful reflections of the mood, the spirit, and the concerns of the New Negro. Laura Wheeler Waring painted scenes from the life of upper-class African Americans, examples of which are *The Coed* and *The Musician,* while Edward A. Harleston contented himself with subjects from what may be called the black proletariat, examples of which are his *Old Servant* and *Negro Soldier.* Among the white painters who gave attention to black subjects were Miguel Covarrubias, whose caricatures of prominent African Americans are well known, and Winold Reiss, who provided the illustrations for Alain Locke's *The New Negro.* In the field of sculpture Meta Warrick Fuller, who had won considerable recognition before World War I, continued to do significant work in the decade following the war.

The African-American community's negative reaction in 1915 to D. W. Griffith's racist motion picture, "The Birth of A Nation," was a stimulus for the birth of the black film movement. And the atmosphere and mood of the Harlem Renaissance sustained and expanded it. Beginning in 1916, black film companies began to appear. While all were short-lived, they produced a steady stream of films with all-black casts. These films, Donald Bogle tells us, were shown "at segregated theaters in the South, at big-city ghetto movie houses in the North, and on occasion at black churches, schools, and social gatherings—almost anyplace where it was possible to reach a black audience." The most significant of the black companies were the Lincoln Motion Picture Company established by brothers George and Noble Johnson in 1916 and Oscar Micheaux's film and book company begun in 1918. Before Lincoln's demise in 1923 the Johnsons produced at least six films and pioneered in establishing patterns for advertising, booking, and promotion that would be imitated by other black independent filmmakers. Micheaux, a man of great drive, energy, and shrewd business acumen, was the most important and prolific producer of black films during the 1920s. He and other African Americans in this field were never able to overcome the restrictions imposed by limited capital, inability to purchase state-of-the-art equipment, and the vast advertising budgets and powerful distribution systems of the white filmmakers with whom they competed in the African-American community. The existence of black independent filmmakers during this period was made possible largely by the great hunger of the African-American masses for films that featured members of their race and addressed issues that affected their lives.

It was only natural that leaders of the Harlem Renaissance in New York would tend to move in the same social circles. There was a community of spirit and point of view that found its expression not only in the cooperative ventures of a professional nature but also in the intimate social relationships that developed. Perhaps these Harlemites felt that form and substance could be given to their efforts through the interchange of ideas in moments of informality. In *When Harlem Was in Vogue,* David Lewis has described the Harlem of the mid-1920s as "overcrowded, vulgar, and wicked." These qualities helped give it the exotic flavor that made it attractive to so many whites. There was Small's Paradise, the Savoy, and the Cotton Club to which whites flocked, providing them with opportunities to meet the crowd that Zora Neale Hurston dubbed "the Niggerati." It was indeed *Nigger Heaven,* as Carl Van Vechten called his Harlem novel that offended not a few black contemporaries and that grew out of his own infatuation with life north of New York's Central Park. There were many literary parties in Harlem and downtown New York at which most of these leaders could be found. In Harlem the regular hostess was A'Lelia Walker, the heiress of Madam C. J. Walker, although Jessie Fauset, the James Weldon Johnsons, Wallace Thurman, and others also entertained the literary set with regularity. Downtown, when he was not uptown, the most regular host was Carl Van Vechten. It was not at all unusual to discover Clarence Darrow, or a distinguished publisher, or a British lord moving freely among the guests. The fellowship of intellectual colleagues was a cohesive force in the efforts of the group, while the interracial aspect of the gatherings doubtless had the effect of giving them a sense of belonging to the larger community.

■ The Circle Widens

Although New York was the center of the Harlem Renaissance, it could not claim a complete monopoly on African-American literary activity in the decades following World War I. In Boston William Stanley Braithwaite, who had won recognition early in the century with his *Lyrics of Life* (1904) and *The House of Falling Leaves* (1908), continued to issue his yearly anthologies of magazine verse and to write verse of his own. Although none of his poetry is racial, he interested himself in the new movement and did what he could to encourage younger poets. In Washington, Georgia Douglas Johnson emerged as the first outstanding African-American woman poet since Frances Harper. In 1918 her *The Heart of a Woman* was published, followed in 1922 by *Bronze. An Autumn Love Cycle* was published in 1928. Johnson's poems are unsophisticated and emotional. Some may be classified as protest pieces. All of them are characterized by a sincerity that gives them their greatest appeal. Another important poet from Washington was Angelina W. Grimké. While teaching at Dunbar High School, she wrote a number of poems, among them "A Winter Twilight" and "When the Green Lies over the Earth."

Toward the end of the literary movement two young Washington poets emerged and won immediate recognition as writers of talent. Waring Cuney won the *Opportunity* poetry contest of 1926 with his "No Images" and followed this up with the composition of several poems of protest that were recorded by Josh White in an album entitled *Southern Exposure*. Although his first volume of poems, *Southern Road*, was not issued until 1932, Sterling Brown had been writing verse for several years. His "Long Gone," "Slim in Hell," and "Break of Day" reveal a remarkable capacity for effectively using African-American materials. In Washington while professor of philosophy at Howard University, Alain Locke was also active in the new literary movement. He did much to steer its course and to interpret it to the world at large. In many respects he may be regarded as the liaison officer of the Negro Renaissance.

The circle widened to include blacks who were removed from New York and the forces that produced a profusion of writers in that city. Anne Spencer lived and worked in Lynchburg, Virginia, but found time to write verse that reflects both maturity and detachment. Her "Before the Feast of Shushan," "At the Carnival," and "Dunbar" won for her a secure place in the new movement. In Louisville, Kentucky, Joseph Seamon Cotter, Jr., had already

INTERPRETER OF THE HARLEM RENAISSANCE. Alain L. Locke, Professor of Philosophy at Howard University, edited *The New Negro*, which revealed the many facets of African-American life after World War I. *(Courtesy, Moorland Spingarn Research Center, Howard University.)*

begun to follow in the footsteps of his poet-father by publishing in 1918 a slender volume of verse, *The Band of Gideon*. His death at twenty-four cut off what promised to be a rich and influential life. Frank Horne, a New Yorker who worked in Chicago and Fort Valley, Georgia, won the *Crisis* contest in 1925 with his "Letters Found near a Suicide." Other well-known poems of his are "Nigger: A Chant for Children" and "On Seeing Two Brown Boys in a Catholic Church." In California, Arna Bontemps, who later was to join the New York group, began writing verse, and in 1926 he won *Opportunity's* Alexander Pushkin Award for Poetry with "Golgotha Is a Mountain." In the following year he received the same award for "Nocturne at Bethesda."

Gradually the scope of the Harlem Renaissance came to be the whole of the United States. African Americans everywhere became more articulate. There were poetry circles in Houston and Detroit, little theaters in Chicago and Los Angeles, and interested students of painting in Cleveland and

THE HARLEM RENAIS-SANCE'S INTELLECTUAL. Arriving on the scene late, when many writers were well established, Zora Neale Hurston was both brilliant and prolific. *(Courtesy, Beinecke Rare Book and Manuscript Library, Yale University.)*

Nashville. Long before the beginning of the Depression the groups in Harlem could claim no monopoly, but they could claim some credit for the widespread interest in the new efforts at self-expression in various parts of the country. Du Bois lectured in almost every community where there was a substantial number of African Americans, and frequently he spoke on subjects somewhat removed from the crusading activities of the NAACP. African-American book dealers and publishers effectively distributed the works of the writers of the movement. Richard B. Harrison gave dramatic readings in the South and Midwest long before he became famous in *The Green Pastures.* It was no more possible for the Harlem Renaissance to remain confined to upper Manhattan than it was for other elements in American social and cultural life to remain isolated in one area of the United States. The literary and cultural aspects of the New Negro Movement had indeed become national before the end of the 1920s.

Many students of the period regard the Harlem Renaissance as having ended with the production of *The Green Pastures* in 1930. To be sure, there was less activity among the Harlem writers at that time, and their works were not as sensational. The group that had been concentrated in New York scattered to all parts of the world. Claude McKay spent much of his time in France, Langston Hughes resumed his worldwide travels, and James Weldon Johnson accepted a professorship in creative literature at Fisk University in Nashville. The Depression settled over the country, and it was naturally more difficult for those in the arts and letters to ply their trade. Many writers, singers, and artists found it impossible to stay off relief, and thanks to the broad scope of federal relief projects they could continue to write and to sing and receive a check from the government for their efforts.

Out of the Federal Writers' Project, for which Sterling Brown was the Negro Adviser, came many evidences that the Harlem Renaissance had not ended. Even the older writers continued their efforts. Langston Hughes continued to write, as did Jessie Fauset, Countee Cullen, Claude McKay, and others. There were, moreover, several who, having begun toward the end of the 1920s, seemed to flourish in the darkest days of the Depression. One of them, Zora Neale Hurston, effectively bridged the gap between what may be described as the first and second stages of the Harlem Renaissance. This young anthropologist, a student of Franz Boas at Columbia, began to write short stories in the late 1920s and collected a mass of folklore in the United States and the Caribbean area on which many of her later works were to be based. In rapid succession she wrote novels, collected short stories, issued scholarly pieces on folklore, and wrote authoritatively on Haiti and Jamaica. Between 1931 and 1943 she published *Moses, Man of the Mountain; Jonah's Gourd Vine; Mules and Men; Their Eyes Were Watching God; Tell My Horse;* and *Dust Tracks on a Road.* Certainly in view of Zora Neale Hurston's work, it could hardly be said that the Harlem Renaissance was over.

In one sense the Harlem Renaissance would not end in the foreseeable future for, through their creativity, black writers and artists would continue to claim the attention of an ever-increasing number of readers, listeners, and observers in many parts of the world. The 1920s and 1930s, however, were quite special since they marked the emergence of the African-American artist who could say something significant, in so many different ways, about life in this country. The African-American participant in the Harlem Renaissance inherited a legacy of expression from those of an earlier period and in using it transformed it into a powerful, relevant statement that would greatly influence succeeding generations.

Gallery of Twentieth-Century African-American Artists

Henry Ossawa Tanner
"The Banjo Lesson"
1893
Oil on canvas
(Hampton University Museum)

Archibald Motley
"Saturday Night"
1935
Oil on canvas, 32 x 40 in.
(The Howard University Gallery of Art)

(Left)
William H. Johnson
"Swing Low Sweet Chariot"
ca. 1944
Oil on paperboard, 28 5/8 x 26 1/2 in.
*(National Museum of American Art,
Washington, D.C./Art Resource, NY)*

(Opposite top)
Lois Mailou Jones
"Jardin du Luxembourg"
1948
Oil on canvas, 23 3/4 x 28 3/4 in.
*(National Museum of American Art,
Washington, D.C./Art Resource, NY)*

(Opposite bottom)
Jacob Lawrence
"The Library"
1960
Tempera on fiberboard
*(National Museum of American Art,
Washington, D.C./Art Resource, NY)*

Aaron Douglas
"Inspiration"
1966
Tempera on canvas
(John Hope Franklin)

Richard Hunt
"Orpheus"
1979
Welded bronze, 14 ft. high
(Gwenda Jay Gallery)

Elizabeth Catlett
"Glory"
1981
Bronze
(Elizabeth Catlett)

CHAPTER 19

The New Deal

■ Depression

In the decade following World War I the number of African-American potential wage earners expanded considerably. As migration to the industrial centers continued, some found employment in factories and in personal service, while others joined the ranks of the unemployed. Blacks were found in increasing numbers in the automobile and allied industries, in glass factories, in paper and bag companies, and in tobacco factories. They also made gains in the clothing and food industries, while thousands were able to earn a living in transportation and communication. The textile industry in the South grew tremendously, but only a small number of blacks found employment there. Almost everywhere white labor tended to exclude black workers from unions. A large number of affiliated unions of the American Federation of Labor barred or segregated blacks, while the various railway brotherhoods excluded them altogether, even though on one large railroad of the South alone, slightly more than 80 percent of the firemen were blacks before World War I. Within ten years after the end of the war only 10 percent of the firemen were blacks. In 1927 the Atlanta joint terminals entered into an agreement that white firemen were to be given preference over black firemen. In some instances white workers were violent in their attempts to drive blacks out of the transportation field, as in 1932 when white employees of the Illinois Central Railroad engaged in a fight with black workers that resulted in the death of ten black trainmen.

Despite the continued employment of African Americans in some industrial centers, hostility to them at the end of the war was sufficient to cause a group to organize the Friends of Negro Freedom in 1920. This organization, composed primarily of New York radicals, hoped to unionize black migrants, protect black tenants, advance black cooperation, and organize forums through which to educate the masses. Through the branches that it intended to set up throughout the country, the Friends of Negro Freedom hoped to fight racial discrimination in employment by use of the boycott. During the three years of its existence, however, only a few locals were established, and their work proved largely ineffective. A similar organization, the National Association for the Promotion of Labor Unionism among Negroes, was organized about the same time under the direction of Chandler Owen and A. Philip Randolph, publishers of the *Messenger*. An advisory board was composed of white labor radicals and intellectuals, including Morris Hillquit, Joseph D. Cannon, and Charles W. Ervin. After its futile effort to organize black laundry workers, the association ceased to function. The American Negro Labor Congress, meeting for the first time in Chicago in October 1925, sought to unify the efforts of all organizations of African-American workers and farmers, as well as similar interracial organizations. It desired to abolish discrimination against, and exploitation of, African Americans and workers generally and looked toward bringing blacks into trade unions and the general labor movement with white workers. The congress hoped to form local councils through which it would work to secure the total integration of black workers. The local councils were never formed, and the objectives of the organization never realized. Like its predecessors, it succumbed under the weight of disunity among blacks and indifference and hostility among whites.

The most significant step toward the unionization of African Americans was the organization of the Brotherhood of Sleeping Car Porters and Maids by A. Philip Randolph in 1925. When an effort was made to secure from the Pullman Company better working conditions and higher wages, the employer would have nothing to do with the brotherhood. It attacked the brotherhood as a dangerous radical organization and condemned Randolph as a professional agitator. Considerable opposition to the brotherhood arose from both white and black groups, but its endorsement by the American Federation of Labor, the NAACP, and the National Urban League bolstered its fight considerably. Partial recognition came in 1926 and 1929 in wage agreements; full recognition of the brotherhood as the bargaining agency for the porters and maids employed by the Pullman Company came only in 1937, when more than 8,000 employees benefited by a wage increase of $1,152,000.

Although the number of black business enterprises increased after World War I, the proportion of African Americans among all retail dealers tended to decrease. In the black community, however, African Americans who were engaged in business remained important because of their social and political influence, as well as for the economic strength that they wielded. Black undertakers, barbers, beauticians, insurance companies, and mercantile houses constituted the more important enterprises, but a variety of small business institutions performed personal services that increased the number of blacks in the white-collar group. The success of these businesses depended peculiarly upon the income of the skilled and unskilled African-American laborer who worked primarily for whites and who traded with blacks. When adverse circumstances in the economy caused a curtailment of employment or a reduction in wages, black businesses were affected immediately. The African-American community in this period was, therefore, hardly more independent of general trends than African Americans had been a century earlier.

The flight of thousands of African Americans from Southern farms during and after the war did not seem to improve the conditions of those who remained. To the general poverty and land exploitation that prevailed were added the ravages of the boll weevil. In many areas the destruction was so extensive that farms were temporarily or permanently abandoned, and black and white farm laborers were thrown out of work. The suffering of tenants can hardly be overestimated. Early in the 1920s the Depression had already begun for them. Meanwhile, the number of African-American farm owners was gradually declining. Soil erosion, the boll weevil, and the southwestern shift in cotton cultivation played havoc on black and white farmers alike. The growing importance of foreign tobacco, cotton, and sugarcane on the international market created conditions of competition beyond the control of American farmers, and the tariff legislation of the Republicans did little to relieve the situation. It was an unfavorable sign of the times that the agrarian population of the United States, which included the majority of African Americans, was without the necessary purchasing power to enjoy the opulence of the 1920s.

As the stock market soared to unprecedented heights, as urban land values increased continuously, and as people spoke confidently of a new era of abundance and prosperity, little attention was given to the fact that prosperity was unevenly distributed. Only those who were immediately concerned, together with a few "gloomy experts," complained that people working in agriculture, shipbuilding, coal mining, and the textile and shoe industries were not enjoying the prosperity of the so-called new economic era. When the first signs of recession appeared in the middle of the 1920s, thousands of African Americans lost their jobs, but they were counted as casualties of a technological age in which several million people were expected to be unemployed. When the crash came in October of 1929, many blacks were already suffering from economic depression. As businesses closed, banks failed, and mines shut down, a larger number of black workers became unemployed. In cities they lost their jobs rapidly, while in rural areas they were driven to starvation wages. In household jobs and personal service occupations, where so many were to be found, there was immediate curtailment. Because of blacks' small or nonexistent reserve of capital, it was not long before there was dire want and untold suffering.

Within a few years after the beginning of the Great Depression millions of American citizens were regarded as incapable of self-support in any occupation. By 1934, for example, 17 percent of whites and 38 percent of blacks were placed in this category. Everywhere the relief rolls soared. In October 1933, between 25 and 40 percent of the African Americans in several large urban centers were on relief, a figure three or four times the number of whites on relief at the time. Approximately one-fourth of the 1.5 million black domestic workers were on relief in 1935. In some Southern cities the size of black relief rolls was appalling. In Atlanta in 1935, 65 percent of African-American employables were in need of public assistance, while in Norfolk no less than 80 percent of the group were on relief. Small wonder that there was utter distress and pessimism among African Americans generally. Added to the denials of freedom and democracy was the specter of starvation.

Even in starvation there was discrimination, for in few places was relief administered on a nonracial basis. Some religious and charitable organizations, in the North as well as the South, excluded African Americans from the soup kitchens they operated to relieve the suffering. In many of the communities where relief work was offered, blacks were discriminated against, while in the early programs of public assistance there was in some places as much as a $6 differential in the monthly aid given to white and black families. This was final proof for African Americans that democracy had escaped. More and more, they began to feel that if it was to be retrieved at all, it could come only through political influence. It was an awakened consciousness, brought on by suffering and discrimination, that drove African Americans to this conclusion.

■ Political Regeneration

Although there was little opportunity to participate in the affairs of government, African Americans remained an issue in American politics from the Civil War up until the end of World War I. What patronage they enjoyed under Republican presidents during the late nineteenth and early twentieth centuries had diminished perceptibly under Wilson, and an almost impenetrable pall of gloom settled over their political prospects before the end of the first administration of the exponent of the New Freedom. The period of the war brought new economic opportunities to the blacks of the United States, and there came in its wake a new hope for the greater exercise of political power. This hope stemmed from practical situations much more than it did from any national policies or promises of wartime leaders. The migration of large numbers to Northern urban centers and the ambitious and restless nature of many of the newcomers combined to produce a new power which some were quick to realize. In consequence of the concentration of African Americans in Northern cities there developed a political resurgence that placed them once more in the thick of American politics and gave them the kind of strength that they had not exercised since Reconstruction.

It was only natural that the resurgence would manifest itself first in the centers where the African-American population had grown most rapidly. In Chicago political leaders realized the growing power of the black vote when, in 1915, Oscar DePriest was elected alderman from the densely populated South Side. In New York blacks had gained enough strength by 1917 to send Edward A. Johnson, the historian and teacher, to the state assembly. In each succeeding year African Americans became more aware of their political potentialities and took advantage of their opportunities. The breaking away from tradition, which had characterized the literary movement in the 1920s, was likewise found in politics. There seemed to be an interest not so much in patronage as in overall programs for improvement in the condition of African Americans. Whereas earlier many blacks had been satisfied with President Taft's appointment of William H. Lewis of Boston as assistant attorney general of the United States and with President Wilson's appointment of Robert H. Terrell of Washington as judge of the municipal court of the District of Columbia, now few regarded such appointments as more than tokenism. In 1924 when the Democratic candidate for president, John W. Davis, promised that if elected he would make no distinctions on the basis of race or creed, and when the Progressive candidate, Robert LaFollette, made a similar statement, African Americans began to desert the Republican party.

The real disaffection with the party of Lincoln began in 1928 when Republicans attempted to resurrect a strong party in the South with white leadership. Prominent African-American Republican leaders, such as Benjamin Davis of Georgia, Perry Howard of Mississippi, and William McDonald of Texas, lost influence in their states as the Republican high command began to recognize white leaders in those states and to seat white delegates at the national convention instead of black delegates who presented themselves. Leaders like Robert Church of Memphis were so incensed about the lily-white Republican movement in the South that they refused to serve on the national advisory committee. The Baltimore *Afro-American*, Norfolk *Journal and Guide*, and Boston *Guardian*, all black newspapers, supported Alfred E. Smith rather than Herbert Hoover.

The Hoover upset—he carried Florida, Kentucky, North Carolina, Tennessee, Texas, Virginia, and West Virginia—demonstrated the Republicans' capability of amassing strength among white Southerners, especially when the Democratic candidate, Alfred E. Smith, was a Roman Catholic, an advocate of the repeal of prohibition, and a reputed friend of African Americans. It also showed the extent to which the Republican party was willing to alienate the black vote in an effort to build up a following that could crack the Southern Democratic stronghold. By 1928 African Americans were beginning to learn to vote for candidates who were not Republicans. At a time when more and more independent thought was motivating the actions of blacks, Republicans could ill afford to jeopardize their leadership of a group that was gaining political strength. After the election, to add insult to injury, the new president is reported to have said that he was very much interested in building up a Republican party in the South "such as could commend itself to the citizens of those states." He meant white citizens, of course.

The election of Oscar DePriest to the House of Representatives in 1928 compensated for the disappointment of blacks who opposed Herbert Hoover, and it also gave them new hope concerning their political future. DePriest had moved to Chicago from his Alabama home in 1899, and almost immediately he developed an interest in politics and worked his way up from a ward committeeman to become the first African-American alderman. As early as 1923 he was mentioned as a possible candidate for Congress, and with the cooperation of William H. Thompson his influence steadily increased. With the death of Martin B. Madden, who had been renominated by the Republicans in 1928, DePriest's big opportunity came. He announced his candidacy, and with the help of powerful Republican interests he was able to overcome the opposition of his enemies and to win the seat from the First Illinois Congressional District by a plurality of 3,800. George White's prediction of 1901 that African Americans would return to Congress had come true. And for the first time in the nation's history a Northern black sat in the nation's lawmaking body.

DePriest's position was peculiar. He represented not only his own district but all the blacks of the United States. During his three terms in office he was in great demand as a speaker and was pointed out by African Americans everywhere as the realization of their fondest dreams. One black newspaper said that his presence in Washington gave the race "new hope, new courage, and new inspiration." The white South was alarmed that a black had achieved so high a distinction in American political life. When Mrs. DePriest attended a tea at the White House for the wives and families of members of Congress, Southerners were outraged, and several Southern legislatures passed resolutions "condemning certain social policies of the administration in entertaining Negroes in the White House on a parity with white ladies." In Birmingham, where DePriest was scheduled to speak, the Ku Klux Klan burned him in effigy. Through all the insults heaped upon him, DePriest maintained an imperturbable calm and continued to try to secure greater recognition for African Americans in the national government. Much of his energy was doubtless dissipated by the peculiar demands of his role, but his presence in Washington symbolized the regeneration of blacks in politics and prepared the way for his successors both in Congress and in other high places.

More and more African Americans were using their votes to register protests. They studied the voting records of members of Congress and watched the utterances and policies of presidents in order to ferret out those whom they considered their enemies. As early as 1923 they began to fight those senators who were responsible for the defeat of the Dyer antilynching bill. In 1930 they vigorously opposed the confirmation of John J. Parker to

the United States Supreme Court because he was reported to have said that the "participation of the Negro in politics is a source of evil and danger to both races." When his name was finally rejected by the Senate, African Americans began to turn their guns on those senators who had voted for his confirmation. Thus, they helped to defeat Henry J. Allen of Kansas and Roscoe McCulloch of Ohio. Despite the fact that blacks had helped elect Samuel Shortridge of California to the Senate in 1926, they turned against him in 1932 and helped to bring about his defeat. Many blacks who had supported President Hoover now began to regard him as their enemy. They did not like the manner in which he supported the lily-white Republican movement in the South, and they openly censured him for his appointment of Judge Parker to the Supreme Court. They noticed, also, a decline in the patronage that was given to African-American Republicans. Like many other Americans, moreover, some blacks placed the responsibility for the Depression on the shoulders of the president and roundly condemned the relief policy that he fostered. Some African-American leaders grumbled that it would take a long time for the funds of the Reconstruction Finance Corporation to trickle down through the giant but defunct industrial firms to the African Americans who were at the bottom. They were ready, therefore, to try something else at the end of Hoover's first term in office.

It was not easy for blacks to desert the Republican party in 1932, and many of them remained true to the tradition and voted for the party of Lincoln. They continued to feel that the "best people" voted Republican. Few African Americans outside New York were acquainted with Franklin D. Roosevelt, and he had aroused little enthusiasm as a public figure. They were fearful, moreover, that a Democratic victory would lead to the ascendancy of Southern politicians in Washington, with the consequent degradation of blacks, as had happened during Wilson's administration. Finally, rumors of Roosevelt's ill health terrified some African Americans as they thought of the possibility of the succession of John Nance Garner of Texas to the presidency. Only in New York City had black Democratic organizations been able to draw large numbers into their folds. Theirs was a difficult task, and African Americans showed great reluctance to break with the past and vote Democratic. In Chicago, for example, only 23 percent of the black vote was for Democrats in the election of 1932. Among those who deserted the Republican party few were willing to "throw their votes away" by voting the Communist ticket, although a black, James W. Ford, was the vice-presidential candidate in 1932, 1936, and 1940.

There were some African Americans, a smaller number than many whites feared, who were indeed attracted to the Communists. The "so-called better class of Negroes" might join the NAACP, as long-time black Communist, Hosea Hudson, observed, but working-class African Americans were not comfortable with that organization. A few highly placed blacks and those like Hudson trickled into the Communist party, but the numbers remained small. Party members such as Hudson tended to exaggerate the importance of the party in the 1930s and 1940s, claiming that it formed the basis for the civil rights movement of the following decades. Nell Painter discounts this claim, reminding us of the work of other groups such as the Southern Conference for Human Welfare, the Interracial Commission, the Southern Regional Council, and the NAACP, which "also helped to change the South" in Hudson's time.

Individual Communists, nevertheless, as well as Communist-affiliated organizations, played their roles with dramatic success in the Depression and New Deal years. Among them was a young crusading Birmingham coal miner, Angelo Herndon. After years of privation, discrimination, and disillusionment, he joined the Communist party and sought to persuade others to do likewise. In 1932 he was arrested, tried, convicted, and sentenced to eighteen years in prison on a charge of inciting to insurrection. After a five-year court battle, the International Labor Defense (ILD) secured his freedom. Meanwhile, nine young blacks, the youngest of whom was thirteen, were arrested and jailed in Scottsboro, Alabama, and sentenced to death on charges of raping two white women on a freight train. After a fight with NAACP lawyers, ILD lawyers and the Communist party made an international issue of the case. The Supreme Court ordered a new trial when it was proved that at the original trial the defendants did not have adequate counsel. In the new trial the Scottsboro boys were sentenced to terms up to ninety-nine years, but by 1950 the last of them had been released.

In the 1930s the Communists made an effort to join with so-called middle-class black organizations in an all-out United Front Against Fascism. They worked primarily through the National Negro Congress, organized in 1936 to coalesce the efforts of many black groups fighting for equality. As the Communists moved to the right for tactical reasons, their general posture was not significantly different from the views expressed by the president of the congress, A. Philip Randolph. Consequently, they were unable to attract any considerable following among black Americans.

President Roosevelt was not long in office before he gained a large following among African Americans. The dramatic manner in which he tackled the problems before him captured the imagination of blacks just as it did that of most Americans, and his fireside chats gave many a feeling of belonging that they had never experienced before. African Americans early regarded the relief and recovery programs that he advocated as especially beneficial to them, although later there were many black critics of the New Deal's administration of relief. The president frequently received African-American visitors, and it was widely known that Robert L. Vann of Pittsburgh, Julian Rainey of Boston, William T. Thompkins of Kansas City, and F. B. Ransom of Indianapolis were high in the Democratic councils. Roosevelt visited and sent messages to African-American organizations and institutions, thus adding to his popularity with black groups. His physical handicap and the strength he brought to bear in overcoming this enormous difficulty were a source of inspiration to them.

Eleanor Roosevelt was especially friendly to African Americans. She was known to be on intimate terms with Mary McLeod Bethune, and she invited the National Council of Negro Women, of which Mrs. Bethune was president, to have tea at the White House. She visited black schools and federal projects and spoke to numerous groups. When she was photographed while being escorted by two ROTC cadets of Howard University, African Americans circulated the picture widely as an example of the broad egalitarianism of the occupants of the White House, while Southern whites circulated it to show the depth to which the occupants of the White House had descended. These and many more indications of serious interest in the problems of blacks caused thousands of them to change their party allegiance in the years following Roosevelt's election in 1932.

The extent of the shift of African-American allegiance was demonstrated in 1934 when Arthur W. Mitchell, who only four years earlier had been registered as a Republican, was elected to Congress on the Democratic ticket to replace Oscar DePriest. Mitchell was the first black Democrat ever to sit in Congress, and it was a source of considerable embarrassment to his Southern colleagues to have him as a member of their majority. All over the country African Americans were not only changing from the party of Lincoln to the party of Roosevelt, but they were becoming increasingly active in politics. Black newspapers and various black groups showed a spirited interest in the campaign of 1936, and while the majority of them supported Roosevelt, Alf Landon and the Republicans were not without their African-American enthusiasts. For example, twelve of the fourteen bishops of the AME Church supported Landon. In *Farewell to the Party of Lincoln*, Nancy Weiss has pointed out that, while blacks favored many New Deal policies, this shift to the Democratic party was part of a larger process of a change in attitude toward politics on the part of blacks. This involved not only a swing away from the Republican party but increased participation by new black voters who entered the political arena and simultaneously acquired a party identification. By 1940 some opposition to Roosevelt had developed, and there was a substantial decline in the black support that he received. African Americans accused the administration of discriminating in some of the relief agencies and of excluding them from preliminary defense preparations. Some African Americans, moreover, discovered a ring of sincerity in Wendell Willkie's promises and were inclined to desert what they were pleased to call "The Dirty Deal."

In the years that followed, the black vote came to be more evenly divided, with the groups in the great urban centers of the North still showing an inclination toward the politics of the New Deal but wielding sufficient influence in pivotal states such as Illinois, Ohio, Pennsylvania, and new York to cause much anxiety in both Republican and Democratic circles. Labor matters, foreign policy, and other issues influenced urban black voters just as they did white voters. African Americans, sensing their strength and importance as voters, felt that they could now demand a high price for their

THE PRESIDENTS EXCHANGE VISITS. When President Roosevelt went
to Africa in 1943, he took the opportunity to visit President Edwin Barclay, inspect American troops stationed in Liberia, and cement the
friendship between that country and the United States. In May 1943,
President Edwin Barclay and President-Elect William V. Tubman returned the visit and consulted with State Department officials. The
close relationship that developed during the war was described by some
writers as the "Washington-Monrovia Axis." *(Photo by Army Air Forces
from Wide World Photos.)*

support. In addition to demanding that a candidate reflect their views on
public questions that interested all Americans, they could also demand that
a candidate's views on questions of race be acceptable.

The strength of African Americans during the period of political regeneration was manifested not only in the consideration that both major parties
gave them in national elections but also in their successes in state and local
elections. An increasing number of blacks secured seats in state legislatures
in the 1930s and 1940s. After 1932 black legislators in California, Illinois,
Indiana, Kansas, Kentucky, New Jersey, New York, Ohio, Pennsylvania, and
West Virginia became commonplace, and both the Republican and Democratic parties were represented. The reapportionment of seats in state
legislatures, ordered by the Supreme Court in 1962, increased the opportunities for African Americans to win elections. The greater concentration of
blacks in urban centers and their increased political consciousness were
additional factors. In 1946 some 30 blacks secured seats in the legislatures
of ten states. Twenty years later 104 blacks—4 Republicans and 100 Democrats—sat in the legislatures of twenty-four states, including 10 in the two
houses of the Georgia legislature.

After 1930, when two African Americans were elected to municipal
judgeships in New York City, other municipalities elected or appointed
blacks to judicial positions. In 1947 there were black judges in Cleveland,

Chicago, Los Angeles, Washington, and several other cities, while the number had increased to seven in New York City. By the late 1960s the number of black judges in New York had more than doubled, while the number had significantly increased in the other cities mentioned above. And more than a dozen new cities boasted black judges. In many American cities African Americans helped to manage the affairs of government as members of boards of education and city councils, as members of the prosecuting attorneys' staffs, as police officers, and as tax commissioners and corporation counsels. The fruits of political activity were enjoyed in a very real way by the faithful servants of the parties, and there was an increasing recognition of the contributions that qualified blacks could make to the improvement of the life of the whole community.

■ Roosevelt's "Black Cabinet"

One of the most important factors in the achievement of political respectability on the part of blacks was the New Deal policy of securing the assistance of African-American specialists and advisers in various governmental departments. Seeking the advice of blacks was not a Roosevelt innovation. Other presidents had sought the pulse of the black population through one or more leaders of the black community. Booker T. Washington was merely an outstanding example of a long-established practice. For example, in 1889, upon learning that historian-lawyer George Washington Williams would be making a visit to the Congo, President Benjamin Harrison asked Williams to submit a report which could be used in determining what this nation's policy should be toward the Congo. In most instances, of course, the African-American advisers were faithful members of the president's party who gave counsel in the matter of patronage. Roosevelt's group of black advisers differed from the others in several important respects. In the first place, the number of "black cabineteers" was fairly large, in contrast to the small number on whom previous presidents had relied for advice. It is not possible to set an arbitrary number because it was changing constantly and because it is difficult to be sure whether certain appointees were actually members of the select circle that could be regarded as a "cabinet." Nor can it be said that these black leaders had access to the president. Time and again, they sought to speak with the president personally, only to be rebuffed, told that he was too busy, or forced to see one of his many subordinates instead. Roosevelt's black advisers nevertheless differed from their counterparts in previous administrations in that they were placed in positions of sufficient importance that both the government and the African-American population generally regarded the appointment as significant. They were not people whose relationship with the government was nebulous and unofficial. They were oath-bound servants of the citizens of the United States, although they could not be described as policy makers.

Members of Roosevelt's black cabinet were not politicians, for the most part. To be sure, there were black political advisers to the president, but few of them were in positions of trust in the government. It was later said that they were mere salesmen for the New Deal, but it could not be said that they were brought in because of faithful political service during campaigns. And finally, they were highly intelligent and highly trained people who were called in to perform specific functions. To that extent their appointments were in line with the tendency of the New Deal administration to commandeer the services of the best-trained people in the country to assist in developing programs of relief, recovery, and reform. They were called by some, therefore, the black brain trust, for among them were doctors of juridical science, doctors of philosophy, and college presidents. Some African Americans complained that it was most unfortunate that they were confined to problems affecting their race, and one severe critic said that they could be described as "Porkbarrelensis Africanus" because of that fact. Few could deny, however, that they were well qualified to perform many functions, and indeed on occasion many of them worked in areas that only indirectly touched on racial issues.

It was Harold L. Ickes, a former president of the Chicago branch of the NAACP, who, as secretary of the interior, began to hire racial advisers in the early days of the New Deal. The first was Clark Foreman, a white liberal from Atlanta. He used African Americans as his own advisers on the legal staff of the Department of the Interior and in other agencies such as the National Park Service. Later, some of them transferred to other departments, thereby enlarging the area in which blacks exercised some influence in the national government. Eleanor Roosevelt is credited with having enlarged the size of the black cabinet, while Will W. Alexander, who was for a time the head of the Farm Security Administration (FSA), was also instrumental in having African Americans appointed to positions that were regarded as having black cabinet rank.

Among the African Americans who occupied high places in New Deal councils was Robert L. Vann, the editor of the *Pittsburgh Courier*, who served as a special assistant to the attorney general. William H. Hastie, the dean of Howard University Law School, entered government service as assistant solicitor in the Department of the Interior. He went on to serve as the judge of the Virgin Islands and later as civilian aide to the secretary of war. In 1946 he was appointed governor of the Virgin Islands. Robert C. Weaver was the first black to be the racial adviser in the Department of the Interior. Subsequently he served in several agencies, including the Federal Housing Authority, Office of Emergency Management, and War Manpower Commission. In 1966 he became the first African-American member of the president's cabinet when the Housing and Home Finance Agency, which he headed, became a department in the executive branch of the federal government. Eugene Kinckle Jones, executive secretary of the National Urban League, went to Washington in the early days of the New Deal and for a period was

MARY McLEOD BETHUNE IN THE FEDERAL SERVICE. Bethune, founder of Bethune-Cookman College and the National Council of Negro Women, served the New Deal as Director of Negro Affairs of the National Youth Administration. Here she confers with Eleanor Roosevelt and Aubrey Williams, Director of the NYA. *(UPI/Bettmann Newsphotos.)*

adviser on "Negro affairs" in the Department of Commerce. Lawrence A. Oxley, veteran social worker, was chief of the division of Negro labor in the Department of Labor. Mary McLeod Bethune, founder-president of Bethune-Cookman College, was active for several years as the director of the division of Negro affairs of the National Youth Administration. Edgar Brown, president of the United Government Employees, was adviser on Negro affairs in the Civilian Conservation Corps. Frank S. Horne, poet and teacher, served in several capacities, primarily with federal housing programs. William J. Trent was racial adviser in the Department of the Interior before going to the Federal Works Agency as the racial relations officer.

The list of African Americans in such positions with the federal government could be expanded. Some of them remained only a few months, while others found government service so much to their liking that they stayed on during the Truman administration. With the onset of the war emergency the number was substantially increased. Crystal Bird Fauset, a former member of the Pennsylvania legislature, went to Washington as the racial relations adviser in the Office of Civilian Defense. Ted Poston, veteran New York newspaperman, served as racial adviser in the Office of War Information. Col. Campbell Johnson became an executive assistant to Gen. Lewis B.

Hershey, head of the National Selective Service. Others served with the War Production Board, War Manpower Commission, Office of Price Administration, and Social Security Board. Numerous consultants served only temporarily: Abram L. Harris with the National Recovery Administration (NRA), William H. Dean with the National Resources Planning Board, Ralph Bunche with the Library of Congress and later with the Department of State, Rayford W. Logan with the Coordinator of Inter-American Affairs, and Ira DeA. Reid with the Social Security Board's Bureau of Employment.

The task of "top Negroes" in the federal government was a difficult and delicate one: to press for economic and political equality for their race in America. This task was all the more peculiar because they were seeking to bring about an integration that was antithetical to their own roles. Almost all of them were unalterably opposed to racial separatism. When the suggestion was made that there should perhaps be a "Negro bureau" to deal with all matters affecting the race, several African-American cabineteers combined their energies to oppose it on the grounds that it would tend to make blacks wards of the government, thus extending and perpetuating segregation. These leaders also sought to increase opportunities for the employment of African Americans in government and in industry. They attempted to secure employment for blacks on the basis of ability and training rather than color. They worked closely with the black press and with other agencies of influence, through members of Congress, and through powerful white citizens in public and private stations. The aggressive temper of the African-American population, the war emergency, and the inclination of many New Dealers to increase equal opportunities served to make possible the achievement of a measure of success by black New Dealers.

If these officials smarted under the roles assigned to them as advisers on "Negro affairs," they could look with satisfaction at the increasing number of blacks who were serving their government in many capacities. Thanks to new Civil Service regulations it was no longer necessary to indicate one's race on applications or to attach a photograph to the forms, but after personal interviews, hiring officials sometimes avoided hiring African Americans by availing themselves of the Civil Service Commission's "rule of three," by which they could select a white who ranked second or third over a black who ranked first. Even so, African-American employees on the federal payroll increased from about 50,000 in 1933 to approximately 200,000 before the end of 1946. It is only fair to add, however, that the majority of the newly employed blacks were in the low, unskilled, and semiskilled brackets, and that there was only a sprinkling of economists, statisticians, chemists, physicists, and other specialists. In some portions of the government the segregation of whites and blacks was abolished, while most government cafeterias were opened to blacks. While the black cabineteers were not responsible for all of the improvements in the condition of African-American federal employees, they could view with pride all of the changes and could claim as their handiwork a considerable number of them.

■ Government Agencies and Relief for Blacks

As the Roosevelt administration established numerous agencies to aid the total population in recovering from the severe depression, African Americans, to be sure, benefited from the amelioration of conditions. However, because of the long custom of discriminating against blacks, it was inevitable that in these agencies there were variations between black and white relief grants, numbers of workers, salaries, and the like. The National Industrial Recovery Act, which sought to stimulate industry, established codes of fair competition that provided for a minimum wage scale of $12 to $15 per week, a forty-hour week, and the abolition of child labor under the age of sixteen. Few African Americans represented their group at code hearings, and cost-of-living differentials were set up that discriminated against the groups in which most black workers were found. In the steel, laundry, tobacco, and other codes African Americans frequently received lower minimum wages than whites. The compliance boards that were to enforce the codes were frequently made up of employers who were themselves violating the codes. African Americans seldom complained, for fear of losing their jobs. When wages were raised in compliance with the codes, employers frequently dismissed black workers and paid higher wages to whites. Few African Americans lamented the fact that the Supreme Court in 1935 declared the NIRA unconstitutional.

A larger number of blacks were affected by the various New Deal measures to provide relief to farmers and agricultural workers. In the crop reduction program of the Agricultural Adjustment Administration (AAA) farmers received cash benefits for plowing under their cotton, wheat, and tobacco crops and for slaughtering their hogs. While the farmers' cash benefits rose to billions of dollars under the AAA, many of the grants intended for African-American farmers were dissipated and misappropriated. Many landlords took advantage of illiterate sharecroppers and tenants and kept the checks intended for them. It was this dishonesty, which hurt both white and black farm workers, that led to the organization of the unfortunate victims into such groups as the Southern Tenant Farmers Union. Planters vigorously opposed such unions and appealed to race prejudice in an effort to break up cooperation between black and white farmers. Even after administrative rules were changed to provide for payments to be made directly to the tenants, many blacks suffered; for then white landlords merely removed them from the land and received the benefits themselves. Aside from the benefits that some African-American farmers received in the form of cash payments, they obtained valuable experience in voting in AAA referenda on such important questions as establishing marketing quotas. They demonstrated conclusively that blacks and whites could vote together on important economic questions, even though blacks were still effectively disfranchised in regular elections in most Southern states.

From the Tennessee Valley Authority, Rural Electrification Administra-

THE DESTRUCTION OF NEGRO SLUMS. These substandard homes were replaced by 480 units of public housing, called Yamacrow Village, which were completed in March 1941, Savannah, Georgia. (*Courtesy U.S. Department of Housing and Urban Development.*)

tion, Federal Land Bank, and local production credit associations, African Americans received benefits, though infrequently in proportion to their number or their needs. They were substantially aided by the program of the Farm Security Administration (FSA) which in 1937 took over the work of the Resettlement Administration. Unfortunately, the FSA had an appropriation only one-fifth of the amount appropriated for the AAA, but it undertook to establish communities of small farmers who rented land from the FSA and to make loans to those who desired to purchase their own farms. An extensive educational program was carried out in which, among other things, new methods of production and marketing were introduced. Under the program African Americans received a large share of the benefits, and thousands, for the first time in their lives, were able to purchase land. The FSA, largely because of the capable leadership of Will W. Alexander, insisted that there be no discrimination between white and black farmers. Because of its racial policies and because of its program of settling farmers in communities, it was almost always under fire. The attacks grew so vehement that in 1942 the enemies of the FSA managed to cut appropriations so drastically that the greater part of its program was ended.

The National Youth Administration (NYA) and the Civilian Conservation Corps (CCC) undertook to provide relief for the youth of America. Under Aubrey Williams, a white Mississippian, the NYA set up a liberal program for the benefit of African-American youth. Not only was Mrs. Bethune invited to Washington to head the division of Negro affairs, but black state and local supervisors were appointed in the districts where large numbers of African Americans lived. In the out-of-school programs, 13 percent of the enrollees were blacks, and they learned a variety of trades that were to be beneficial in the war emergency. In the student work program, more than 64,000, or 10 percent, were black. Young African Americans, all the way from grade school to graduate school, found it possible to continue their education by means of the benefits obtained from the NYA. The CCC maintained a policy of strict segregation, but during its lifetime from 1933 to 1942, approximately 200,000 African-American boys and young men worked in camps established by the agency. In addition to the work of conservation, reforestation, and prevention of soil erosion, the agency set up an educational program under the supervision of black advisers. A measurable amount of illiteracy was eliminated, and juvenile delinquency was doubtless curtailed. Although many critics raised serious doubts as to the wisdom of the program, it can hardly be argued that the CCC did not relieve the suffering of many young men during the depths of the Depression.

The New Deal housing program aided blacks not only in their efforts to keep their homes and to acquire better living accommodations but also in the matter of providing employment on projects under construction. Some African Americans secured loans from the Home Owners Loan Corporation in order to make payments on their homes during the Depression. A limited number were able to borrow money to build homes with loans guaranteed by the Federal Housing Authority. In many communities, however, some banks were not inclined to lend money to African Americans because they regarded them as poor risks and because of the uncertain future value of houses occupied by blacks. The most widely beneficial federal housing program for African Americans was the encouragement that local housing authorities received to construct low-cost housing projects with subsidies from the United States Housing Authority, later the Federal Public Housing Authority. In some Northern communities the projects were occupied jointly by blacks and whites, while in each Southern community the principle of segregation was maintained. Approximately one-third of the units constructed were occupied by African-American families. These modern units, with electric or gas appliances and facilities for recreation, gave thousands of these families an opportunity to live in a kind of environment that previously was wholly unknown to them.

Under the Public Works Administration and similar agencies, a considerable number of black hospitals and other public buildings were constructed. Through an arrangement with local and state governments, these federal agencies subsidized the construction of buildings at black colleges, playgrounds, community centers, and the like. Despite the provisions of the contracts that called for the employment of a proportionate number of African-American workers in the construction of these buildings, the stipulations were frequently disregarded. In some cities, where as many as a score of buildings were constructed with public funds, no African Americans were employed. In other cities, however, there was some employment of black workers. In very few instances did African Americans secure the amount of employment to which they were entitled under the provisions of the contracts.

During the darkest days of the Depression, it was not possible, for either the government or private business, to employ a sufficient number of people to relieve satisfactorily the plight of the unemployed. The Federal Emergency Relief Administration and later the Works Progress Administration (renamed the Work Projects Administration WPA) provided both for relief in kind— food, clothing, and commodity surpluses—and in employment. There was a greater inclination toward fairness to African Americans in providing material relief than in providing employment. Under the WPA there was such a variation in policy from place to place as to make impossible any general statement with regard to the treatment of blacks. In some communities blacks secured employment on professional and clerical levels. Thus, African-American actors, writers, and artists in cities like New York and Chicago carried on their activities under the WPA. In some other localities, however, it was almost impossible even for unskilled blacks to secure any benefits from the relief agencies. The wage differentials in some communities were great, and administrators made no apologies for them. Even so, more than a million blacks owed their living to the WPA in 1939, and this and similar relief agencies became so important that they were surpassed only by agriculture and domestic service as sources of income.

When the Social Security Board was established in 1935, provisions were made for old age assistance and unemployment benefits in a large number of occupational categories. Since agricultural and domestic workers were excluded, however, a tremendous proportion of the black population failed

AFRICAN AMERICANS SEEK RELIEF. In 1937 Margaret Bourke-White took this picture of a line of unemployed African Americans seeking food supplies. *(Margaret Bourke-White, Life Magazine © 1937 Time, Inc.)*

to qualify for the benefits provided by the act. Even in the program of old age assistance, there was a tendency to grant lower sums, especially in the South, to aged blacks than to aged whites.

Although there was outright discrimination against African Americans in the local administration of most of the New Deal measures in the South, some substantial progress was made toward breaking down the traditional pattern of discrimination. Many white Southern leaders found the New Deal distasteful because it concentrated too much power in Washington. Furthermore, it relieved the suffering of a considerable number of whites and blacks on whose poverty many Southern white politicians had climbed to power, and occasionally it undertook to force equality in the administration of its benefits. They could ill afford to break with the Roosevelt administration, however, because it gave them national power through their control of congressional committees and their voice in party politics. They had to pay lip service, for the most part, to the liberal measures of the New Deal and to compromise on many issues. The entrance of highly trained blacks into the government in Washington and federal agencies in the South gave white Southerners a new experience in their relationships with blacks. The consequences of this new experience could not be measured until years after the New Deal had ended.

Unemployed, poverty-stricken African Americans could not always wait for the New Deal to provide them with the necessities of life. At times they found it desirable to use what force they could command to secure employment and relief. In 1929 Albon Holsey of the National Negro Business League organized the Colored Merchants Association, which undertook to establish stores in New York and to purchase merchandise cooperatively. African Americans were urged to buy from these merchants because their patronage would provide jobs for their racial community. The stores survived less than two years of the severe depression, however. Shortly thereafter the Jobs-for-Negroes movement began in earnest in St. Louis, where the Urban League led a boycott against a white-owned chain store whose trade was almost exclusively black but whose payroll showed that it employed no blacks. The movement spread to Pittsburgh, Chicago, Cleveland, and other Midwestern cities, and many African Americans found employment because of the pressure brought on white employers in black sections. The most intensive campaign was carried on in New York City, where African Americans organized the Citizens' League for Fair Play in 1933. Under the leadership of the Reverend John H. Johnson the committee attempted to persuade white merchants to use black clerks. When their first efforts failed, they resorted to picketing the stores and appealing to blacks with the motto, "Don't Buy Where You Can't Work." On street corners blacks harangued their listeners concerning the injustice of whites refusing to hire black workers. Intense feelings developed, and the movement almost got out of hand when some people took advantage of the situation to advance their own interests. The campaign resulted in hundreds of African Americans obtaining employment in stores in Harlem and with public utilities such as the telephone, electric, and bus companies.

In 1935 the intense feeling against the white merchants and landlords in Harlem led to a riot of considerable proportions. An African-American youth was caught stealing a small knife from the counter of one of the stores on 125th Street. He succeeded in escaping, but there were rumors that he had been beaten to death. Black crowds gathered and loudly accused the police of brutality and the white merchants of discrimination in employment. The mob began to smash store windows and to raid the shelves. During most of the night of March 19 the rioting went on. Three blacks were killed, 200 store windows were smashed, and more than $2 million worth of damage was done. The city was both outraged and ashamed. Mayor La Guardia appointed an interracial Committee on Conditions in Harlem. A staff of investigators, headed by E. Franklin Frazier, studied the causes of the riot and concluded that the lawlessness was provoked by "resentments against racial discrimination and poverty in the midst of plenty." There was insufficient relief of a private and public nature to stem the tide of social unrest that prevailed in Harlem and other black communities. Picketing and other measures continued. Blacks were encouraged greatly by the decision of the Supreme Court in 1937 declaring that the picketing of firms that refused to employ African Americans was a legal technique of securing relief.

■ Black Labor and the Unions

The Great Depression worked a real hardship on the labor movement in the United States, and African-American workers, who even during the days of prosperity found the going very difficult, now met almost insurmountable barriers against their employment. Section 7a of the National Industrial Recovery Act provided that employees should have the right to organize and bargain collectively through representatives of their own choosing without "interference, restraint, or coercion of employers of labor." The National Labor Board (NLB) was set up to enforce these provisions of the statute. While the average white employee found it especially difficult to press for higher wages and keep his or her job, black workers found it almost impossible. Indeed, the discriminatory policies of the major labor unions were still in effect, and, therefore, the majority of black workers were outside whatever protection Section 7a offered. In 1935 the Wagner Act gave permanency and strength to the National Labor Relations Board (NLRB) that had replaced the NLB the previous year. It established clear-cut rules for collective bargaining and set up twenty-two regional boards to conduct elections in industry to determine what group of employees was entitled to bargain with the employer. It was also given wide powers in handling labor disputes and in settling strikes. It was indeed labor's "bill of rights," and if black workers could succeed in breaking the barriers that excluded them from unions, they could enter a new period of security and prosperity in the enjoyment of these rights.

In 1938 the Congress passed the Fair Labor Standards Act, better known as the wages and hours bill. It was another step in the direction of the emancipation of the worker. It established a minimum wage of 25 cents per hour, which was to be increased to 40 cents by 1945, and a maximum week of forty hours, any excess of which was to be paid on the basis of time and a half. While perhaps better than 1 million African Americans were affected by the act, several millions were not, since it excluded agricultural and domestic workers, just as the Social Security Act did. Here again, the law meant little if blacks were unable to secure employment in the industries covered by it.

In an effort to keep whites employed during the Depression, labor unions maintained their exclusion policies on a stricter basis than ever. The bulk of African Americans that found employment fell into the unskilled and semiskilled categories where there was little or no union organization. They were thus without the protection that the NLRB granted to workers. There were few unions like the United Mine Workers, which brought together in one union all the workers in a given industry and which, since its organiza-

A. Philip Randolph Demands a
New Deal—1937

. . . it is more and more becoming correctly understood that the task of realizing full citizenship for the Negro people is largely in the hands of the Negro people themselves. Assuring full citizenship rights to [the] Afro-American is the duty and responsibility of the State, but securing them is the task of the Negro; it is the task of Labor and the progressive and liberal forces of the nation. Freedom is never given; it is won. And the Negro people must win their freedom. They must achieve justice. This involves struggle, continuous struggle.

True liberation can be acquired and maintained only when the Negro people possess power; and power is the product and flower of organization—organization of the masses, the masses in the mills and mines, on the farms, in the factories, in churches, in fraternal organizations, in homes, colleges, women's clubs, student groups, trade unions, tenants' leagues, in cooperative guilds, political organizations and civil rights associations.

A. Philip Randolph, "The Crisis of the Negro and the Constitution," in *Official Proceedings, Second National Negro Congress, 1937,* in August Meier and others, *Black Protest Thought in the Twentieth Century* (New York, 1965), pp. 202–203.

---

tion in 1890, had encouraged the organization and participation of African-American workers. By 1934 even a considerable number of white workers had come to the conclusion that the labor movement in the United States could have great success only by organizing the mass-production industries which employed hundreds of thousands, indeed millions, of men and women. William Green, the president of the American Federation of Labor, had said that he would organize 25 million workers, but he had failed miserably. Meanwhile, the industrial bloc in the American Federation of Labor was demanding that mass-production industries be organized, and on an industrywide basis rather than on the basis of crafts.

In 1935 the industrial bloc, led by John L. Lewis of the United Mine Workers, became more insistent, and when the American Federation of Labor remained adamant, Lewis called a meeting for November 9, 1935, out of which grew the Committee for Industrial Organization (CIO). Even after the organization of the CIO, Lewis attempted to force the American Federation of Labor to foster the organization of mass-production industries on a craft basis, but the older organization spurned all offers by Lewis, even to the point of rejecting $500,000 which he offered to finance such a campaign. The break with the American Federation of Labor became clean, and the CIO began to make plans to conduct such a campaign itself. With the resources of its own member unions, among which were the United Mine Workers, the Amalgamated Clothing Workers, and the International Ladies' Garment Workers (ILGW), the CIO undertook to organize the mass-production industries. From the beginning the CIO made it clear that it sought to organize workers regardless of race. When the Steel Workers Organizing Committee (SWOC) set out in 1936 to organize the workers in the steel industry, the United Mine Workers transferred many of its African-American organizers to the SWOC. In some places blacks joined enthusiastically, but in others they were skeptical, having learned through bitter experience to distrust all labor unions. The National Urban League and other black organizations urged African-American steel workers to join the CIO affiliate. Finally, the vast majority of black workers joined the SWOC, and when the great steel companies capitulated in 1937 and agreed to bargain with the organization under the NLRB, thousands of black workers benefited from the pay raises for which the contract called.

In the meat-packing industry, where many African Americans were already employed, 5,000 enrolled in the Chicago locals of the Amalgamated Meat Cutters and Butcher Workmen after adoption of the blanket code under the NRA. There was similar affiliation in Kansas City and St. Louis. When the union showed signs of weakness, especially after the demise of the NRA, many blacks dropped out. In 1936 the CIO, with its United Packing House Workers' Industrial Union, sought to organize the industry, but its efforts gave new life to the older union. Although there was considerable success on the part of the CIO union, to which many blacks belonged, competition was keen and both unions still maintained organizations in the meat-packing industry.

In the clothing industry the International Ladies' Garment Workers Union and the Amalgamated Clothing Workers had long had a liberal policy toward the organization of black workers. Although relatively few blacks were employed in the clothing industry, by far the great majority of them belonged to these two unions, with the ILGWU having the larger number. When the CIO was organized, the program of equality among workers was extended, and they became exemplary unions in equality of treatment of their members. In the textile industry, on the other hand, African Americans had little opportunity to work either in Northern or Southern mills. The CIO affiliate, the Textile Workers Union, undertook to organize the workers, but it made little headway except in the North. In the unions of Virginia and North Carolina, there were separate white and black locals, perhaps the only CIO unions where such an arrangement existed. In making this compromise with its policy the CIO attempted to face realistically the extremely difficult task of organizing an industry whose white workers historically had viewed these jobs as belonging exclusively to them.

In 1940 African Americans constituted more than 30 percent of all the longshoremen in the United States because whites viewed work on the docks as undesirable. Since its beginning in 1892, the International Longshoremen's Association (ILA), an affiliate of the American Federation of Labor which dominated the Atlantic and Gulf ports, had opposed racial discrimination.

Several of its vice presidents were black, but in some ports there were separate black and white locals. In 1937 the International Longshoremen's and Warehousemen's Union (IL&WU) was organized on the West Coast and affiliated with the CIO. In the beginning it did not seem to welcome African-American workers, but after the strike of 1934 Harry Bridges, the leader, made it clear that black labor would receive equal treatment in the IL&WU. Special antidiscrimination committees were organized to see that no worker was discharged or intimidated on account of race or color. Various efforts were made by the IL&WU to organize the workers of the Atlantic and Gulf ports, but because of the fairly satisfactory policy of the ILA, little headway was made. Some observers believed that the vigorous nondiscrimination policy of the West Coast union had a salutary effect on the policy of the ILA.

It was during World War I that African Americans forced open the doors of the automobile industry. Even so, there were only 20,720 black automobile workers as late as 1940, constituting 3.8 percent of the total work force. After that time, however, both the number and proportion of blacks in the industry increased substantially. Except at Ford's River Rouge factory, the great majority of African Americans in the automobile industry were employed in unskilled jobs. The unionization of automobile workers was largely the work of the CIO, and since blacks were not in special crafts in the industry, they were fortunate that a union adhering to the industrial principle organized the workers. The United Automobile Workers of the CIO succeeded in forcing all the major automobile manufacturers to recognize it as the legal collective bargaining agent for the workers, with the Ford plant finally capitulating after a bitter fight in 1941. Although some white members opposed the union's fight for equal opportunities for blacks in the automobile industry, the union continued its struggle. The new opportunities that the war provided for the employment of African Americans in the automobile industry created innumerable social as well as economic problems, especially in the Detroit area, which the shedding of blood did not altogether solve.

Substantial progress was made in the organization of African Americans in other industries. In the tobacco industry, the building trades, and the aircraft industry, for example, blacks were included in the organization. The CIO was, for the most part, consistently opposed to discrimination on the basis of race; and while it did not always have great success in its efforts to organize, as with the tobacco workers, for example, its use of black organizers and its election of black officers had wide appeal among blacks. The stand of the CIO Committee to Abolish Racial Discrimination and the liberal program of the Political Action Committee gave new hope to many African Americans. They were no longer suspicious of labor organizations per se and were inclined to join in the program of strikes with as much enthusiasm as other workers. A feeling of security and belonging arose among black workers that was one of the most significant developments in their struggle for greater integration into American life.

CHAPTER 20

The American Dilemma

■ Trends in Education

In the twentieth century African Americans manifested the same intense interest in education as they had in the period immediately following emancipation. More and more the public assumed the responsibility that earlier had been borne by philanthropy and self-help, but the triumph of white supremacy meant that blacks would not share in educational opportunities on any basis that even remotely approached equality. The school enrollment of African Americans increased steadily. In 1880 there were 714,884 blacks in school in Alabama, Arkansas, Florida, Georgia, Louisiana, Mississippi, North and South Carolina, Tennessee, and Texas. By 1910 the number had increased to 1,426,102, and by 1930 there were 1,893,068 in school. In the same states the enrollment of white children increased even more rapidly, with the consequent diversion of educational funds to schools for whites, thereby depriving blacks of adequate facilities and well-trained teachers. In 1899 the Supreme Court had set the stage for flagrant discrimination against blacks in education. In *Cumming v. School Board of Richmond County, Ga.*, Justice John Marshall Harlan, speaking for a unanimous court, refused to grant any relief to blacks whose high school had been closed by county officials while two high schools for whites remained open. For the first half of the twentieth century the bulk of African-American children in school at all attended impoverished, small, short-term schools with pronounced inadequacies in every phase of the educational program.

The movement of large numbers of African Americans from rural areas to urban centers resulted in some substantial improvement in educational opportunities. In urban areas there was much more taxable wealth, the income from which was sometimes made available for educational purposes. The concentration of the population in urban centers, moreover, had the effect of reducing the per capita cost of education even when many inadequacies remained. Finally, in cities there was a greater opportunity to impose various forms of taxes, thereby increasing the opportunities for the diversion of some of the income to schools for blacks. This is not to say that blacks received an equitable share of the school funds in any of the Southern states. By 1900 every state in the South had enacted laws that provided for separate schools for blacks and whites, and through the years the courts made it clear that even though the law did not specify that the schools for both races should be equal, the law assumed that they would be equal. The compliance in the South with the provision of equality in educational facilities was nowhere more than slight; and in most instances there was a studied disregard for the principle of equality.

Nothing was more persistent in the first half of the twentieth century than the disparity between the money spent for the education of white children and that spent for the education of black children. In fact, in many instances the differential increased as time went on. In 1900 for every $2 spent for the education of blacks in the South, $3 was spent on whites; but in 1930 $7 was spent for whites to every $2 spent for blacks. In 1935–1936 the current expenditures per white pupil in ten Southern states averaged $37.87, while such expenditures per black pupil averaged $13.09. In the new educational services, such as transportation, visual aids, laboratory equipment, modern buildings, and the like, the differentials were even greater. In North Carolina, for example, where greater attention was consistently given to the education of African Americans than in most other Southern states, more money was spent in 1929–1930 for school trucks for white children than was spent for new schools for black children.

The work of the Julius Rosenwald Fund in assisting in the construction of school buildings for Negroes in the South helped to provide better facilities. Between 1913 and 1932 the fund aided in the construction of more than five thousand African-American school buildings in fifteen Southern states. Approximately 64 percent of the expenditure of $28 million came from the tax funds; 15 percent was contributed by the Rosenwald Fund; 4 percent came from interested white persons; while 17 percent was made up of a "flood of small contributions of Negroes themselves—striking evidence of the desire of members of this race for schooling for their children." Even so, the value of African-American school sites, buildings, and equipment per pupil enrolled was less than one-fifth as great as the per pupil value of property in white schools.

Only in teachers' salaries was there a noticeable decline in the differentials between black and white education by 1945. In most instances where equalization was achieved, it came only after a court battle that was vigorously contested by school authorities. Several counties of Virginia, Maryland, and South Carolina equalized the salaries of white and black teachers after court action was either instituted or threatened. In 1940 Judge John J. Parker of the United States Circuit Court of Appeals ruled in a case arising in Norfolk, Virginia, that a double salary standard based on race was an unconstitutional discrimination. Although this had the effect of forcing equalization in the county in which the case arose, there was no wholesale equalization in the South as a result of the Parker decision. In 1944 North Carolina completed its program of gradually reducing the differential and proudly announced that it had brought about equalization without court action.

While the Great Depression hurt education all over the country, it worked a special hardship on Southern black schools. Construction of new school buildings stopped almost entirely, the teaching staffs were curtailed to the point where effective teaching was practically impossible, and miserably low salaries were further reduced. Southern states curtailed expenditures for black schools in the same or greater proportion that they were curtailed in white schools. While no Southern community could afford to cut its educational expenditures without seriously impairing the effectiveness of its program, the slightest cut in African-American education often had the effect of taking away the barest essentials in the educational program, including the teacher.

As the black population moved north in the twentieth century, especially during and after World War I, black children were forced, or at least urged, to attend schools that were predominantly black. This was not too difficult, since in most communities blacks lived in restricted areas. Few states followed the lead of New York, which, in 1900, prohibited separate schools. Most of the Northern states were inclined to provide separate schools for blacks, especially where white patrons brought pressure to bear upon school officials. In several Northern states, such as New Jersey, Ohio, Illinois, and Indiana, there were separate schools as well as some integrated schools. In Kansas and Arizona, racially separate education was mandatory only on the elementary level; but in both these states several communities had separate schools on the secondary level. In large cities, such as Gary and Indianapolis, Indiana, where separate high schools were established, the schools constructed for the use of African Americans were modern and adequate in almost every detail. Some suggested that meticulous care was taken in the construction of schools for blacks in such communities in order that they would not feel that they were being deprived of equal education in attending exclusively black institutions. The tendency toward segregation increased as white students engaged in strikes and violence in the effort to prevent African-American students from attending schools open to all, and as white parents kept children away from school in the effort to force the authorities to set aside separate facilities for blacks.

It is not possible to measure the effects that separate and unequal education had on both white and black populations in the areas where it was maintained. Separate schools were doubtless one of the strongest supports of the concept of white supremacy in the South. Separate schools, moreover, contributed to the perpetuation of a leadership that was devoted not only to the idea of separate education but also to the maintenance of economic and political inequalities between the white and black populations. Even under such handicaps, there was a notable decline in illiteracy among blacks. In 1870 at least 81 percent of all African Americans above ten years old were illiterate. Sixty years later only 16 percent were illiterate. In 1946 Ambrose Caliver of the United States Office of Education undertook to establish a program that would wipe out the last remnants of illiteracy among blacks. The decline of illiteracy was a clear indication that African Americans were gradually coming into possession of those skills and that in due time they would not suffer the personal handicaps that had so often made them the dupes of those who sought to control them.

Predominantly black colleges increased from one in 1854 to more than 100 by the middle of the next century. They were of three general types: church-related colleges, privately endowed colleges, and public colleges. While the period of their most rapid growth was the thirty years following the Civil War, the twentieth century witnessed some increase. States and cities established colleges for the education of blacks and also took over church-supported institutions. An example of the latter procedure was the assumption by North Carolina in 1923 of the support of the National Religious Training School of Durham, which had been founded in 1910 by James E. Shepard. The name of the institution was changed to the North Carolina College for Negroes (again changed to the North Carolina College at Durham in 1947 and North Carolina Central University in 1970).

The enrollment of African Americans in institutions of higher learning increased steadily in the years following World War I. By 1933 more than 38,000 blacks were receiving collegiate instruction, and 97 percent of these students were in colleges in Southern states. Despite the Depression, which forced the curtailment of expenditures, the physical plants of black colleges were improved and teachers continued to increase their training. The problems of black colleges had not been solved, however, and several gave evidence of long-term planning by consolidating their resources. In 1929 Morehouse College, Spelman College, and Atlanta University combined to form the Atlanta University System under John Hope. A few years later two institutions in New Orleans, Straight College and New Orleans University, gave up their separate identities and became Dillard University, receiving considerable support from the Rosenwald Fund and the General Education Board. Operating expenses had become such a problem at private institutions by 1943 that thirty-three of them pooled their solicitation resources and organized the United Negro College Fund. White philanthropists, such as John D. Rockefeller, Jr., Walter Hoving, and Thomas A. Morgan, assisted in the multimillion-dollar annual campaigns.

Three significant trends in the higher education of African Americans became noticeable in the second half of the twentieth century. One was the dramatic increase in the enrollment of blacks in predominantly white colleges and universities. Before World War II, it was most unusual to see more than a dozen or so African Americans in such institutions, and these were invariably located in the North. From the 1960s the numbers increased steadily, and by 1970 there were some 378,000 African Americans in higher institutions that were not predominantly black. By 1977 there were 1.1 million blacks in colleges and universities, accounting for 9.3 percent of the nation-wide enrollment that year. Within a few years, however, there was a noticeable decline in the number of African Americans attending institutions of higher education. By 1984 the number had dropped to 993,574; of these, 267,000 were in historically black institutions, which continued to provide more than half of all the bachelors degrees received by African Americans.

The number of black administrators in higher education increased markedly. In 1945 many black colleges, such as Fisk, Tougaloo, Virginia Union, St. Augustine's, and Talladega, had white presidents. Twenty years later there were no white presidents in black colleges. Meanwhile, black presidents, vice presidents, deans, and other administrative officials increased in predominantly white colleges. In 1970 Clifton Wharton became the first African-American president of a major white institution when he assumed his duties at Michigan State University. Eight years later he became chancellor of the largest institution of higher education in the nation, the ninety-campus State University of New York. In 1976 Mary Frances Berry became chancellor of the University of Colorado before going to Washington the following year to become assistant secretary for education in the Department of Health, Education, and Welfare. Marguerite Ross Barnett joined this select group in 1986 when she became Chancellor of the University of Missouri–St. Louis before going on to become president of the University of Houston.

The number of African-American professors at white colleges and universities steadily increased, partly because of the growing demand for teachers of black studies and partly because of the demand for a black presence among the teaching personnel at institutions where the number of black students was increasing. Another contributing factor was the requirement in the 1970s by the Department of Health, Education, and Welfare that institutions have affirmative action programs in connection with their hiring practices. By the early 1970s many colleges and universities were actively recruiting African-American professors in their effort to conform to the demands of black students and the federal government. The picture of hundreds of black professors at predominantly white universities in 1973 was a marked contrast to the assistant instructorship that W. E. B. Du Bois had held at the University of Pennsylvania in 1899 and the nonteaching position that William Hinton had held at Harvard Medical School from 1905 to 1949 when he was appointed to a professorship on the eve of his retirement. Even so, black professors were recruited for black studies more often than not, and the number of black professors with tenure remained relatively small.

Graduate and professional training of blacks increased as a larger number of them sought such opportunities. Early in the twentieth century graduate training was available only at a few Northern universities and at some privately supported black institutions. After World War I Howard University, Fisk University, and Atlanta University increased their emphasis on graduate education, but it was not possible for these institutions to serve African Americans in all the areas of training that they were demanding, and not many students could afford to study in Northern universities even if they gained admission. The feeling increased, moreover, that the public should provide graduate and professional training for blacks as well as for whites. Several Southern states took cognizance of this, and by 1935 they had appropriated money for out-of-state graduate training of African Americans. Blacks were willing to resort to court action to force states to discharge their obligations to African-American citizens. As early as 1933 Thomas Hocutt of North Carolina sought admission to the school of pharmacy at the University of North Carolina by bringing court action against the university. The applicant lost his suit on a technicality when he failed to establish his eligibility for admission. In 1935 Donald Murray was successful in gaining admission to the law school of the University of Maryland. The Maryland court of appeals made it clear that it regarded out-of-state tuition scholarships as unequal and, therefore, a violation of the law.

The most significant step toward providing graduate and professional training for African Americans grew out of the decision of the Supreme Court in the case of *Missouri ex rel. Gaines v. Canada, Registrar of the University, et al.* In 1936 Lloyd Gaines applied for admission to the law school of the University of Missouri. When rejected he took his case to the courts, and when the state courts denied him relief he appealed to the federal courts. In the decision of the Supreme Court in 1938 Chief Justice Hughes said that it was the duty of the state to provide education for all its citizens and that the provision must be made *within the state*. To provide legal education for white residents within the state and to fail to do so for blacks "is a denial of the equality of legal right to the enjoyment of the privilege which the State has set up, and the provision for the payment of tuition fees in another State does not remove the discrimination."

The decision caused immediate consternation in states having separate systems of education, but they begrudgingly sought to provide opportunities for graduate and professional training at colleges already in operation. Missouri established a law school; Virginia increased its provisions for out-of-state aid; South Carolina established a "chair of law" at the State Agricultural and Mechanical Institute at Orangeburg. Only Maryland and West Virginia moved in the direction of making it possible for blacks to attend institutions that had heretofore been used exclusively by white residents.

In succeeding years the fight for graduate education continued. The issue was clearly defined in a decision of a Texas state court that an African American who applied for admission to the University of Texas Law School either must be admitted or a law school had to be established for him that was substantially equal to the one in existence. The problem had plagued the Conference of Southern Governors, as well as the Conference of Deans of Southern Graduate Schools. In 1945 the latter organization made a thorough study of the needs of African Americans for graduate instruction, and its interest in the politics of education led it to observe that blacks were on the whole strong in their demands for equal educational opportunities within the states where they resided. The idea of regional graduate and professional schools for African Americans was receiving much more support from whites than from blacks by 1946.

In 1946 the struggle assumed critical proportions when Ada Sipuel sought admission to the law school of the University of Oklahoma. When the United States Supreme Court ordered the state to provide facilities for her, the university regents arranged for the establishment of a separate law school. She declined to attend this institution, which had been set up within two weeks, began the litigation all over again, and finally gained admission to the university law school in 1949. Meanwhile, another Oklahoma black, G. W. McLaurin, demanded and gained admission to the graduate school of the state university. When university officials segregated him in the classroom, library, and cafeteria, McLaurin sued again, and on June 5, 1950, the Supreme Court ordered an end to these segregation practices. On the same day the Court ordered the law school of the University of Texas to open its doors to Heman Sweatt, a black applicant, despite the fact that the state maintained a separate law school for African Americans. It was not possible, Chief Justice Vinson declared, for the black law school to provide the student with an education equal to that of the university law school, which had a strong faculty, experienced administrators, influential alumni, standing in the community, tradition, and prestige.

To white Southerners this was a frightening departure from the separate but equal doctrine that had been laid down in *Plessy v. Ferguson* in 1896. For most Southern states, it also was convincing proof that the Court would, in time, open all public institutions of higher education to African Americans. Arkansas had already voluntarily admitted its first black in 1947. In 1951 the University of Louisville absorbed the Municipal College for Negroes and employed one black professor. Within a few years, either voluntarily or by court order, several Southern state universities had admitted African Americans.

Both friends and foes of segregation in education conceded that the bitter fight would be waged on the level of the elementary and secondary schools, and the fight was not long in coming. Segregationists hoped that they would be able to prevent or forestall indefinitely the admission of blacks to white elementary and secondary schools by moving toward the equalization of black schools. Thus, as the Supreme Court moved away from the doctrine of separate but equal in a succession of cases, Southern states spent funds, almost desperately, on black schools. Within a few years some of the most modern schools to be found anywhere in the United States had been constructed for African-American children in Southern communities. Southern leaders pledged themselves to equalize white and black schools as rapidly as possible.

The determination of the South to provide better public schools for African Americans brought its resources to one of its major problems in a tardy and inadequate fashion. Not only were the black schools so inadequate that it would take years to achieve even a semblance of equality, but by 1951 the NAACP had decided to attack the very principle of segregation as unconstitutional and a clear contravention of the "basic ethical concepts of our Judaeo-Christian tradition." To test the validity of segregated schools the NAACP, in 1952, took to the Supreme Court five cases arising in South Carolina, Virginia, Kansas, Delaware, and the District of Columbia. Many organizations entered briefs in behalf of the blacks' position, and the attorney general of the United States asked that the separate but equal doctrine be struck down. "Racial discrimination," he declared, "furnishes grist for the Communist propaganda mills, and it raises doubt even among friendly nations as to the intensity of our devotion to the democratic faith."

Perhaps no public question in the United States in the twentieth century aroused more interest at home and abroad than the debate about the constitutionality of segregated public schools. It was presented on the platform and in the press as well as before the Supreme Court of the United States. The decision of the Court in *Brown v. Board of Education* on May 17, 1954, was unequivocal in outlawing segregated public schools. Speaking for a unanimous Court, Chief Justice Earl Warren said:

> Separate educational facilities are inherently unequal. Therefore, we hold that the plaintiffs and others similarly situated for whom the actions have been brought are, by reason of the segregation complained of, deprived of the equal protection of the laws guaranteed by the Fourteenth Amendment.

The chief justice then conceded that formulation of the decrees presented problems of "considerable complexity" because of the great variety of local conditions and because of the wide applicability of the decision. He therefore invited the parties to the suits, the attorney general of the United States, and the attorneys general of the states requiring or permitting segregation in public education to offer suggestions during the next term of court regarding the manner in which relief should be granted.

Reaction to the decision was mixed. There was the anticipated defiance in such states as South Carolina, Georgia, and Mississippi, whose governors had threatened to abolish public schools rather than permit white and black children to attend the same schools. Fiery crosses were burned in some Texas and Florida towns, and scattered groups of whites organized to resist the decision. If the *Knoxville Journal* surprised some, it spoke for many when it said, "No citizen, fitted by character and intelligence to sit as a justice of the Supreme Court, and sworn to uphold the Constitution of the United States, could have decided this question other than the way it was decided." A group of leading African-American educators praised the decision in a statement entitled "It Was The Right and Moral Thing To Do," and several groups of white churchwomen in the South declared that they accepted the decision "with humility."

A year later, May 31, 1955, the Supreme Court remanded the cases to the courts of origin "because of their proximity to local conditions." The Court made it clear, however, that although the lower courts should be guided by equitable principles including practical flexibility, adjustment, and reconciliation of public and private needs, the vitality of the constitutional principles set forth in its 1954 decision could not "be allowed to yield simply because of disagreement with them." It then instructed the courts to require the defendants to make "a prompt and reasonable start toward full compliance" with the ruling of May 17, 1954.

Indefinite delay now seemed impossible, and adverse Southern reaction to the Court's decision was pronounced. An editorial in a Richmond newspaper referred to the Supreme Court justices as an "inept fraternity of politicians and professors" and declared that the Court "repudiated the Constitution, spit upon the Tenth Amendment, and rewrote the fundamental law of this land to suit their own gauzy concepts of sociology." The legislature of one state, by unanimous vote, passed a resolution declaring it impossible to educate the children of both races in the same school. But the president of the Southern Regional Council called the decree "wise, moderate, and workable," while a South Carolina newspaper, in an editorial entitled "We Can't Win," said, "Segregation is going—it's all but gone. South Carolina and the rest of the South can't reverse the trend." Even if the South could not win, it was not ready to admit defeat (see Chapter 22).

Among the other means of education in which blacks manifested an interest in the twentieth century were the public libraries. The South lagged behind the rest of the nation in extending the use of its resources and facilities to blacks. Between 1900 and 1910 a number of public libraries in the South began to extend their services to African Americans, either through restricted privileges at the main library or through the establishment of black branches. In 1903 the Cossitt Library of Memphis agreed to furnish a librarian and the books if Lemoyne College would provide a room for African-American readers. In the same year the Charlotte, North Carolina, Carnegie Public Library fostered the establishment of a separate library for African Americans with its own board of management. The extension of public service to blacks in the South was indeed slow. As late as 1935, for example, only eighty-three of the 565 public libraries in thirteen Southern states were reported to be giving service to African Americans. The Hampton Library School furnished the major portion of the trained black librarians during its years of existence between 1925 and 1939. Later, schools of library service were established at Atlanta University and North Carolina College.

Surprisingly enough, out of the confused pattern of education for African Americans in the United States there emerged a body of highly trained men and women who were scholars by any criterion. Most of them had received their graduate and professional training at Northern and European universities, but many were products of separate colleges and schools. While W. E. B. Du Bois may be regarded as the pioneer African-American scholar in the period following the Civil War, there were numerous others with whom he had to share honors. Indeed the numbers increased dramatically by midcentury and in the years that followed. Some black scholars wrote widely in the field of sociology and came to be regarded as authorities, among them George E. Haynes, Charles S. Johnson, and E. Franklin Frazier. Scholars in the field of economics included Abram L. Harris, Sadie T. Alexander, and Robert C. Weaver. Carter G. Woodson, Charles H. Wesley, Rayford Logan, A. A. Taylor, Merze Tate, Dorothy Porter, Benjamin Quarles, Ralph Bunche, and Kenneth Clark were among the most distinguished in the other social sciences. In the humanities some leading figures were Alain Locke, J. Saunders Redding, Sterling Brown, and Ulysses Lee. A growing number of scholars in the various scientific fields included George W. Carver, Elmer S. Imes, Ernest E. Just, Julian Lewis, William A. Hinton, Percy Julian, Charles Drew, and Daniel Hale Williams. In the next generation the list would be too long to provide, but one, David Blackwell, was elected to the National Academy of Science.

African-American scholars became increasingly articulate and contributed articles to learned journals and published numerous books. While some of their works were accepted in many white journals, they saw fit, in several fields, to establish journals of their own. In 1916 the Association for the Study of Negro Life and History (renamed the Association for the Study of Afro-American Life and History in 1976) began publishing the *Journal of Negro History* with Carter G. Woodson as editor, and it remained a major historical journal in succeeding years. The Bureau of Educational Research at Howard University began publishing the *Journal of Negro Education*, edited by Charles H. Thompson, in 1931. Its yearbook issue became one of the most important sources of information on the historical, sociological, and educational aspects of African-American life. At Atlanta University in 1940, W. E. B. Du Bois started a magazine entitled *Phylon, A Journal of Race and Culture*, which served as a broad medium of articulation for black scholars. White scholars also contributed generously to all these publications. Some colleges sponsored periodicals for African-American scholars, such as Johnson C.

Smith University's *Quarterly Review of Higher Education among Negroes* and Wilberforce University's *Negro College Quarterly*. Others issued works of African-American scholars in their bulletins and other publications.

■ Opportunities for Self-Expression

For black Americans the New Deal and post-New Deal years were not merely years of trying to survive and perhaps become a part of the larger community. They were also years in which they sought to improve the quality of their own lives. They had never felt that it was necessary to sacrifice their own personal tastes or occasions for self-expression just to conform to what "others" expected of them. Even as slaves they had written poetry, composed music, sung, and danced, as indeed they did during World War I and succeeding years. The richness of the Harlem Renaissance was both a stimulant and an inspiration for the wealth of talent displayed in later years. Jazz no longer belonged to Harlem—if it ever had—but flourished in New Orleans and Memphis, from which it sprang, as well as in Chicago, Detroit, Los Angeles, and San Francisco, to which it migrated. Fletcher Henderson, the premier stylist of the 1920s, now shared center stage with Jimmie Lunceford, Duke Ellington, Cab Calloway, Count Basie, and other groups of the big-band era. Meanwhile, the virtuosity of such soloists as trumpeter Louis Armstrong, vibraphonist Lionel Hampton, and pianists Teddy Wilson, Earl "Fatha" Hines, and Mary Lou Williams commended them to white musical combinations as well as to black ones.

While black male vocalists on the jazz circuit were a common part of the musical scene, especially when they doubled as instrumentalists, female vocalists became an important added attraction during these years. Mamie Smith, Ma Rainey, Bessie Smith, and Ethel Waters pioneered in the 1920s not only as singers on the stage but as recording artists as well. In succeeding years, Billie "Lady Day" Holiday, Adelaide Hall, Maxine Sullivan, Ella Fitzgerald, and Lena Horne led a growing number of outstanding blues and jazz singers. Through their recordings and appearances on stage and radio, they were bestowed with a much larger audience and thus a larger following than their predecessors.

As significant as almost any other musical development in the black community following the Harlem Renaissance was the emergence of gospel music. In *The Music of Black Americans,* Eileen Southern calls gospel music the sacred counterpart of the city blues, "sung in the same improvisatory tradition with piano, guitar, or instrumental-ensemble accompaniment." The success of gospel music in the 1930s and later was due largely to composer-performer-promoter Thomas A. Dorsey. Unable to get his songs published, he went from church to church and sang them until, as Southern says, eventually they "caught on." His most popular one, "Precious Lord, Take My Hand," was one of more than 400 that Dorsey composed. Subsequently

BESSIE SMITH, BLUES SINGER. A protégé of Gertrude "Ma" Rainey, Smith sang, danced, and played comic sketches. Her most successful career was in her recordings, some of which sold 100,000 within one week. *(Schomburg Center for Research in Black Culture.)*

there were gospel choirs and choruses singing in churches, night clubs, jazz festivals, and concert halls. Soon, gospel-song records were best sellers, thanks to Dorsey and several "queens" of gospel music, including Sister Rosetta Tharpe, Clara Ward, and Mahalia Jackson.

Although this period saw little in the way of a revival of the large, all-black musical revue reminiscent of the smash hits of the early 1920s, blacks continued to play an important part in the field of light entertainment. The major night clubs of New York, Chicago, Los Angeles, and other cities frequently employed black orchestras, singers, and dancers. In 1939 Billy Rose gave many blacks an opportunity to perform in his New York World's Fair production of a popular version of Gilbert and Sullivan's *Mikado*. Later, both Murial Rahn and Muriel Smith rose to fame in the title role of Rose's *Carmen Jones*. Still later, singers like Lena Horne, Diahann Carroll, and Nat "King" Cole became popular on the stage and through their recordings.

In what was widely regarded as "serious" music, William Grant Still was the outstanding composer. His symphonies—*Africa, Afro-American Symphony*, and *Symphony in G Minor: Song of a New Race*—were performed by many of the major orchestras in the United States. He was commissioned to write many works, including the one he created for the New York World's Fair in 1939, and was named by Howard Hanson as one of the four leading composers in this country. Ulysses Kay, who studied at the University of Rochester and Yale, won numerous awards, including the Prix de Rome, for compositions such as his *Concerto for Orchestra* and *Sinfonia in E: A Short Overture*. Meanwhile, R. Nathaniel Dett continued to compose works for the piano and vocal ensembles until his death in 1943. William L. Dawson of Tuskegee Institute, John W. Work of Fisk University, and Warner Lawson of Howard University composed and arranged numerous works, primarily for choruses and choirs. Among the conductors who achieved international reputations were Dean Dixon, conductor of the American Youth Symphony Orchestra, and Rudolph Dunbar, who was guest conductor of several major orchestras in both Europe and the United States.

There was a steady increase of widely acclaimed African-American singers. Paul Robeson and Roland Hayes continued to draw large audiences and generous critical praise during the second period. They shared the spotlight with Edward Matthews, Aubrey Pankey, Kenneth Spencer, and William Warfield. In 1935 Marian Anderson, acclaimed in Europe by Sibelius and Toscanini as one of the great singers of the world, returned to the United States in a veritable blaze of glory and was regarded by many as the greatest living contralto. Dorothy Maynor and Carol Brice won the praise of Serge Koussevitsky as well as thousands of music lovers. Ann Brown and Todd Duncan added to their laurels with their interpretations of the title roles in George Gershwin's opera *Porgy and Bess*. Even before major opera companies of the United States were using African Americans in their casts, Camilla Williams sang the title role of *Madame Butterfly* with a group of New York artists in 1946. At the same time Ellabelle Davis was invited to sing *Aïda* with the Mexican Grand Opera Company.

Only here and there did a color line appear on the American concert stage. There were some incidents, such as the refusal of the Daughters of the American Revolution (DAR) to permit Marian Anderson to use Constitution Hall in Washington in 1939, after which Eleanor Roosevelt resigned from the DAR. A smashing victory over segregation was rendered when Anderson was invited by Harold L. Ickes, secretary of the interior, to sing on the steps of the Lincoln Memorial on Easter Sunday 1939. The victory of African-American singers in later years was symbolized not only by the opening of Constitution Hall to many of them but also by their acceptance in the major opera companies of the United States. By 1956 the Metropolitan Opera Association of New York had signed contracts with several African-American singers, including Marian Anderson, Robert McFerrin, and Mattiwilda Dobbs, who had already sung with several major opera companies in Europe. Meanwhile, singers like Leontyne Price and Lawrence Winters were singing opera on television and with the New York City Opera company.

This was merely the beginning of the operatic triumphs of African-American singers. In the 1960s Gloria Davey, Thurman Bailey, and Grace Bumbry became regular members of European companies. At the Metropolitan in New York, the number of African Americans on the roster climbed steadily. In 1961 Leontyne Price sang the title role on opening night and received this signal honor again in 1966, when the new home of the Metropolitan Opera Association was opened. Meanwhile, George Shirley became one of the most durable and admired tenors with the New York company.

In the Depression and post-Depression years, white writers and artists evinced an interest in black themes and materials similar to what they had shown in the earlier period. Paul Green and a number of his colleagues at the University of North Carolina continued to employ black materials and themes in their works. Carl Van Vechten maintained the lively interest that he had shown from the beginning, and the group was widened to include such sponsors as Fannie Hurst, Stephen Vincent Benét, and H. A. Overstreet. New white writers such as Lillian Smith, Hodding Carter, Frances Gaither, Henrietta Buckmaster, and Howard Fast won recognition for their works with black themes, and some of them consciously sought to argue the case for the black American in their prose and poetry. If depressions and war years serve to inhibit certain cultural and social activities, it cannot be said that they either dampened the interest in blacks or stifled creative expression on their part. The 1930s and 1940s were years of rich harvest for blacks in almost all fields of creative activity.

Among the poets of this period was Melvin B. Tolson, then a professor of English at Wiley College. He published poems in newspapers and magazines during the 1930s and won numerous prizes and awards. Although his volume of poems, *Rendezvous with America,* was not issued until 1944, one of the principal poems, "Dark Symphony," had been published previously in the *Atlantic Monthly*. While at the University of Michigan, Robert Hayden won the Jule and Avery Hopwood Prize for his poems, and

MARIAN ANDERSON AT THE LINCOLN MEMORIAL. When the Daughters of the American Revolution refused to permit Marian Anderson to sing in Constitution Hall, the secretary of the interior invited her to give a recital on the steps of the Lincoln Memorial. More than 75,000 people gathered on Easter Sunday 1939 to hear her. (*UPI/Bettmann.*)

in 1940 his first volume, *Heart-Shape in the Dust,* was published. In 1966 his poetry won first prize at the World Festival of Negro Art at Dakar, Senegal. Owen Dodson, one of the youngest of the well-known poets and playwrights, became seriously interested in writing while a student at Bates College. After writing traditional and experimental verse for several years, he collected his works in a volume, *Powerful Long Ladder,* in 1946. Two young women also won recognition in the field of poetry, Margaret Walker and Gwendolyn Brooks. While on the Chicago Federal Writers' Project, Margaret Walker wrote "For My People," which later won first prize in the Yale University competition for younger poets. Stephen Vincent Benét praised Walker's work generously when it was published in 1942. Her novel *Jubilee,* winner of a Houghton Mifflin Literary Fellowship, was published in 1966. Gwendolyn Brooks's volume *Street in Bronzeville* appeared in 1945. Five years later her *Annie Allen* won the Pulitzer Prize, and more than a decade after that she

LEONTYNE PRICE SANG THE LEADING ROLE in Samuel Barber's *Antony and Cleopatra* when the new Metropolitan Opera House at Lincoln Center opened on September 16, 1966. Shown backstage at the close of the performance are Rosalind Elias as Charmian, Justino Diaz as Antony, Franco Zeffirelli, director, Rudolf Bing, manager, Miss Price, Mr. Barber, and Thomas Schippers, conductor. (*Courtesy, Metropolitan Opera Association.*)

was named poet laureate of Illinois. Later, in 1985–1986, she was poet in residence at the Library of Congress, a post that was elevated at the end of her tenure to poet laureate of the United States.

A profusion of prose writers appeared on the scene during and after the Depression. Among them was Arna Bontemps, who said that he had watched the early stages of the Harlem Renaissance from a grandstand seat, but now had become one of the most productive contributors. In 1931 his *God Sends Sunday* appeared. Then came two historical novels, *Black Thunder* (1936) and *Drums at Dusk* (1939). Bontemps also became one of the most successful writers of children's books. Later, he turned to nonfiction materials. With Jack Conroy he wrote *They Seek a City* (1945), an engrossing story of the urbanization of blacks. The revised edition appeared in 1966 under the title *Any Place But Here.* Bontemp's *They Have Tomorrow* (1945) is a series of biographical sketches of promising young African Americans. Two Southern writers brought out novels of African-American life in the deep South: George W. Henderson wrote *Ollie Miss* in 1935, and in 1946 his second novel, *Jule,* appeared. George W. Lee shed considerable light on black life in Memphis with *Beale Street* (1934). Two years later his *River George* appeared. Meanwhile, a promising young writer, Waters Turpin, was using materials of the upper South for his novels. As a native of the eastern shore of Maryland, Turpin dealt with a familiar area, and his works, *These Low Grounds* (1937) and *O Canaan* (1939), have an authoritativeness about them that is lacking in many similar works.

William Attaway pointed to new areas and materials for the African-American writer in his novels. In *Let Me Breathe Thunder* (1939) Attaway showed that an African-American writer could deal successfully with a work made up primarily of white characters. In *Blood on the Forge* (1941) he indicated the wealth of materials to be found in industrial communities where there was a problem of racial competition in the struggle for existence. This theme was exploited to a greater degree by Chester Himes in his novel of race friction in a wartime industrial community, *If He Hollers, Let Him Go* (1945). Himes, who had attracted attention with his short stories in *Opportunity, Esquire,* and *Coronet,* demonstrated vividly the impact of the war upon black migrants to industrial communities and the bitterness that stems from frustration and despair. Ann Petry, winner of a Houghton Mifflin Literary Fellowship, depicted the problems of a young African-American woman attempting to live a respectable life in the undesirable section of a large urban center. *The Street,* published in 1946, had wide circulation and received considerable praise.

In the 1940s the best known of the younger African-American writers was Richard Wright. It became clear that he was the master of the short story when his *Uncle Tom's Children* appeared in 1938. *Native Son,* which came out in 1940, immediately placed Wright in the front ranks of contemporary American writers. The stark, tragic realism with which he described the frustrations of a young black living in the blighted slums of a great American city may be compared favorably with the best similar works in American literary history. The work was widely circulated by the Book-of-the-Month Club as one of its selections and enjoyed considerable success in general bookstores. In 1941 Wright brought out *Twelve Million Black Voices,* a folk history of African Americans. In 1945 *Black Boy,* a record of Wright's childhood and youth in Mississippi, was a Book-of-the-Month Club selection. Although there was disagreement over the accuracy of the work as an autobiography, there was no dissent about its power as a story of life among poor, underprivileged, Southern blacks. *The Outsider,* which appeared in 1953, did not receive the favorable critical acclaim that Wright's earlier works enjoyed, but by that time he was firmly established as one of the major writers in the country.

Ralph Ellison has been compared by some critics with Richard Wright for his talents as a writer and for his insight into important social problems. *The Invisible Man* received the National Book Award in 1952, and in 1955 Ellison received the Prix de Rome and went to the American Academy in Rome to complete work on a second novel. His volume of essays, *Shadow and Act,* was published in 1964. The most widely read writer was Frank Yerby. In 1944 he v ı the O. Henry Memorial Award with his short story

"Health Card." In 1946 *The Foxes of Harrow* remained on the best-seller list for many months and was reported to have approached the million-copy mark. In succeeding years he published numerous novels; all of them reached the best-seller list and some were filmed in Hollywood.

In the post-World War II years several other African-American writers won wide critical acclaim. John Oliver Killens showed great talent in his novel of Southern life, *Youngblood* (1945), and in the film scripts he wrote for Harry Belafonte. His *And Then They Heard the Thunder* was regarded by many as the most important novel about blacks during World War II; *Blackman's Burden* (1965) contains lively essays on the question of race. James Baldwin, who showed much early promise as an essayist and novelist, followed Richard Wright into a Paris exile. Unlike Wright, however, he returned to the United States. The promise of *Go Tell It on the Mountain* (1953) and *Notes of a Native Son* (1955) is fulfilled in *Nobody Knows My Name* (1960) and *Another Country* (1962). Baldwin's *The Fire Next Time* (1963) is one of the most important pieces of writing to come out of the Black Revolution. Amiri Baraka (LeRoi Jones), an angrier and more solemn writer, used his ample talents in a volume of poetry, *Preface to a Twenty Volume Suicide Note* (1961), a nonfiction work, *Blues: Negro Music in White America* (1963), and his highly controversial and thoroughly engaging *System of Dante's Hell* (1965).

In dramatic arts African-American writers contented themselves, for the most part, with writing one-act plays for the little theater. Most of the writing was done by teachers of dramatic art at black colleges. Randolph Edmonds of Florida Agricultural and Mechanical University published several volumes of plays about African-American life, including *Six Plays for a Negro Theater* (1934) and *Land of Cotton and Other Plays* (1942). At Howard University James W. Butcher, Jr., wrote *The Seer* and several other plays. Owen Dodson, also of Howard University, wrote *The Divine Comedy* and *The Garden of Time* while a student at Yale University. These plays were produced at Yale and at several other Eastern institutions. Thomas D. Pawley, Jr., of Lincoln University in Missouri, published a number of plays in 1938, including *Judgement Day, Smokey,* and *Son of Liberty.*

While many black colleges stimulated an interest in the dramatic arts through the work of campus little theaters, there was scant opportunity for young African Americans to pursue acting as a career because of the limitations placed upon blacks by the demands of the theatergoing public. African Americans in roles other than those portraying them as servants were likely to hamper the success of a play, especially on cross-country runs, and few authors and producers were willing to run the risk. Some substantial progress was made with Paul Robeson as Othello, a role he had previously played in London; Hilda Simms in *Anna Lucasta;* Gordon Heath in *Deep Are the Roots;* and Canada Lee in *On Whitman Avenue.* The last two plays dealt with two of America's most pressing social problems: the return of African-American soldiers to Southern communities and the housing of blacks in Northern cities. With the advances gained by these productions African Americans could look forward to a more secure place in the American theater. American blacks in the field of drama made a significant step forward with Lorraine Hansberry's *A Raisin in the Sun* in 1959. This moving story about the housing problems of an African-American family won the New York Critics Circle Award. Lorraine Hansberry's second play, *The Sign in Sidney Brustein's Window,* was produced shortly before her death in 1964. Although James Baldwin's novels and essays won for him his greatest acclaim, he did enjoy moderate success with his plays, the outstanding one of which was *Blues for Mister Charlie,* produced in 1964.

In motion pictures the problem of using African-American actors was even more serious than it was in the theater because of the tremendous influence of Southern box offices on motion picture production. In 1929 the first major all-black picture, *Hallelujah,* was produced by King Vidor. Although it was well received, it did not open the doors for the general participation of African Americans as actors in Hollywood. In 1934 Fannie Hurst's *Imitation of Life,* with Louise Beavers and Fredi Washington as well as several outstanding white actors and actresses, emphasized the difficulties confronting African Americans of light complexion. This, however, was not the typical role played by blacks in Hollywood. Blacks such as Etta Moten, Bill Robinson, Hazel Scott, and Lena Horne succeeded in securing contracts from major producers that made it possible for them to play respectable roles as entertainers. Until World War II the greater portion of blacks who secured parts in movie productions played servants, laborers, or criminals. As a servant in *Gone with the Wind,* Hattie McDaniel won the Academy Award for best supporting actress in 1939. Unlike the legitimate stage, Hollywood showed little inclination to undertake the integration of African Americans into productions on the basis of equality. Except in the area of purveying news, black film companies experienced little success in the field of motion picture production.

■ The World of African Americans

The forces that operated on the African-American population for three centuries and more were of such nature as to create a distinctly separate black world within the American community. It was the system of slavery with its basic assumption of the inherent inferiority of blacks that gave rise to the deliberate separation of the races. During the period of freedom, moreover, that assumption survived the most searching scientific findings, and it gave strength and persistence to the separate African-American world. Not even the social upheaval brought about by the migration of large numbers of blacks from rural areas to urban industrial centers did much to disturb the existence that African Americans led apart from the rest of the community. Indeed, the policy of forcing them into ghettoes in larger cities had the effect of creating new forces for perpetuation of the black world. In a nation dedicated to the idea of the essential equality of humanity and in which there was a general commitment to a policy of the integration of races and cultures, the existence of a separate African-American community constituted one of the remarkable social anomalies of the twentieth century. Needless to say, this situation created innumerable problems of a political, social, and economic nature that confounded both blacks and whites who sought solutions to them.

With the migration of large numbers of African Americans to the cities during and after World War I, it became difficult even for black families with traditions of stability to remain immune to the unfavorable conditions that tended to destroy normal, healthy human relationships. Poor housing, unemployment, inadequate recreational facilities, and similar conditions contributed to delinquency among children and crime and separation among parents. The occupational differentiation that followed in the wake of industrialization and urbanization drew class lines more distinctly among African Americans. While few could be regarded as upper class, a substantial middle class emerged composed of people in the professions and business. The great mass of African-American industrial workers formed the broad base on which the African-American social structure was built. The contact that these various segments of the black population had with white Americans served to bring about a considerable amount of similarity between the social structure, interests, and tastes of the two groups. Seldom, however, did the contact reach the point where racial identity and interests disappeared. The world of African Americans continued to exist apart from the larger community.

As far as new religious institutions in the postwar years were concerned, none attracted more outside attention or more dramatically pointed up the theme of African-American alienation than the Nation of Islam, commonly called the Black Muslims. The religious group undertook, modestly enough, to offer encouragement and some security to unemployed, disinherited blacks who had sought in vain for some sign of faith in them on the part of the larger community. Accepting the general tenets of the religion of Islam, the Black Muslims, under the leadership of Elijah Poole, who renamed himself Elijah Muhammad, renounced their faith in the ultimate solution of the race problem in the United States, rejected all names that might imply a connection with white America, and sought complete separation from the white community. The ablest and most eloquent spokesperson was Malcolm X, who was read out of the Black Muslims when he described the assassination of President Kennedy as "chickens coming home to roost." Malcolm X was himself assassinated early in 1965 at a New York mass meeting of his newly formed group that competed with the Black Muslims.

The Nation of Islam, bitter in its denunciation of American racism, was a voice of disgust and despair. With its widely circulated paper, *Muhammad Speaks,* its numerous temples, and its farms, bakeries, supermarkets, and restaurants, it was as much a political and social movement as it was a religious organization. After the death of Elijah Muhammad in 1975, his son

Wallace became chief minister. One could immediately see evidence of a change in policy. The name was changed to the World Community of Islam in the West, and membership was opened to people of all races. Wallace Muhammad became active in non-Muslim affairs, and even visited the White House with other African-American leaders. By 1978 he had redefined his own role, giving up his title as chief minister and engaging in missionary work and other religious as well as secular activities.

Perhaps the most powerful institution in the black world was the church. Barred as they were from many areas of social and political life, African Americans turned more and more to the church for self-expression, recognition, and leadership. Nothing in their world was so completely their own as their church. Early in the century church membership grew as it had in the post-Reconstruction period. As African Americans migrated to the cities, old denominations increased in membership and new denominations sprang up. It was an exhilarating experience for blacks to participate in the ownership and control of their own institutions. It stimulated their pride and preserved the self-respect of many who had been humiliated in their efforts to adjust to American life.

The lack of opportunities for African Americans to participate fully in the affairs of other institutions caused many to concentrate their energies and attention on the church. The consequent scramble for leadership and control led to schisms, withdrawals, and reorganization. In 1917 the National Baptist Convention split into two groups, with the older organization keeping almost twice as many members as the new one. In 1944 the National Baptist Convention, Inc., had more than 4 million members, while the National Baptist Convention of America had more than 2 million members. Meanwhile, most older denominations continued to grow, giving little evidence of being hurt by the schisms that gave birth to new groups. By midcentury thirty-four all-black denominations claimed a membership of more than 5 million, more than 35,000 churches, and property valued at nearly $200 million. The Roman Catholic church made substantial gains among African Americans in some parts of the country, while the Episcopal church and other "integrated" denominations seemed to hold their own. On the whole, however, it may be said that despite trends to desegregate some institutions the black church remained what one observer called "the place of refuge for the black community."

As the African-American community came more and more to take on the attributes of an entirely separate world, the black press performed an increasingly important function. Whereas Douglass's *North Star* fought the institution of slavery and Fortune's *New York Age* fought the relegation of African Americans to second-class citizenry, black newspapers of the twentieth century took up the cudgel in behalf of the underprivileged. They became the medium through which the yearnings of the race were expressed, the platform from which African-American leaders could speak, the coordinator of mass action which African Americans felt compelled to take, and a major instrument by which many African Americans were educated with respect to public affairs. During World War I the black newspaper came into its own. It encouraged African Americans to move to industrial centers in search of work, it urged support of the war, and it also led in the fight for complete integration of blacks into American life. Older newspapers, such as the Baltimore *Afro-American* and the *Chicago Defender*, enjoyed unprecedented growth, while newer ones like the *Pittsburgh Courier* and the *Norfolk Journal and Guide*, made rapid strides both in circulation and influence. Editors, notably John Murphy of the *Afro*, Robert S. Abbott of the *Defender*, Robert L. Vann of the *Courier*, and P. B. Young of the *Journal and Guide*, seemed to have had the capacity to combine an effective editorial policy with a shrewd business sense to make their newspapers important institutions in the African-American world. By 1920 several of them had reached a weekly circulation of more than 100,000, while twenty years later several reported circulations above 200,000.

In the decades following World War I the number of black newspapers increased steadily. Every African-American community apparently felt the need for its own newspaper to perform the services that few white newspapers could or would undertake to perform. Here and there a white paper devoted part of a page to black news, while most of them reported a generous share of news of crimes committed by African Americans. None of the Southern white papers, however, had an editorial policy or an interpretation of the news that satisfied the black ghetto. Therefore, most communities where there was an appreciable African-American population saw fit to support black newspapers: Houston had its *Informer*; Los Angeles, its *Eagle* and *Sentinel*; Kansas City, its *Call*; and Oklahoma City, its *Black Dispatch*. The larger papers began to publish several editions to serve various areas of the country, while some, such as the *Afro-American* and the *Houston Informer*, established chains of newspapers. Several news-gathering agencies were established, the most important of which was Claude Barnett's Associated Negro Press. The editors organized the Negro Newspaper Publishers' Association (later changed to the National Newspaper Publishers' Association), and together they sought to establish uniform policies and views with regard to the important issues affecting African Americans.

By 1979 there were more than 350 black newspapers, magazines, and bulletins that were issued on a regular weekly, monthly, or quarterly basis. Only two newspapers, the *Atlanta World* and the *Chicago Defender*, were published daily. In later years the most significant growth was in the field of the monthly or quarterly magazine, where a number of publications vied for control of the field. Among them were *Ebony, Jet, Essence, Visions, Reconstruction, Tuesday*, a Sunday supplement in numerous white daily papers, and *Monitor*, a supplement in many black weeklies. Each African-American fraternity and sorority had an official journal, while numerous large business institutions issued weekly or monthly periodicals for their employees and patrons. The African-American world thus produced a journalistic business that represented an investment of more than $35 million and provided employment for more than 10,000.

While it cannot be said that the rise of African Americans in the professions was altogether an achievement of the post-Civil War period, it was largely the growth of the free, separate black community that provided the greatest stimulation for such a development. The African-American world needed not only teachers and clergy but also physicians, dentists, pharmacists, nurses, attorneys, social workers, recreation leaders, morticians, and others to perform a variety of personal services. The great growth in the African-American professional class followed World War I, and the numbers in each group continued to increase. As the standards for qualification were raised by state or municipal licensing boards, black professionals increased their training at white or black educational institutions. The members of practically every group organized associations for their protection and mutual assistance. In so doing, they conformed to the American practice whereby people with similar interests translated them into a formal organization. They were also responding to the fact that all too frequently they were barred from membership in white professional groups. Even after white groups began to admit blacks to membership, the latter maintained their own professional organizations. Through these associations African-American professionals were able to wield influence not only in the African-American world but in the larger communities as well.

African Americans experienced great difficulty in developing satisfactory programs for wholesome recreation. The YMCA and the YWCA, usually segregated until the 1950s, were able to flourish only in cities of considerable size, and community centers that received public support were likely to be as inadequately equipped and staffed as the separate school. Fraternities and sororities, which seldom had physical facilities to provide for recreation, still served as a nucleus from which both civic and recreational activities emanated. The membership of these organizations, however, was confined to college-trained men and women. Fraternal organizations, such as the Masons and Odd Fellows, increased in number of chapters and in membership, and many established clubhouses and centers where members and friends could enjoy the fellowship that comes from association. The most important of the newer fraternal organizations of a semisocial nature was the Improved Benevolent and Protective Order of Elks of the World.

The Boy Scout and the Girl Scout movements did not seek to involve African-American youth until the late 1920s. After that time black membership grew rapidly. Still, the majority of African-American boys and girls were without any organized out-of-school recreational activity, and only a small number of black associations, fraternities, and clubs had programs for younger people. Motion pictures in the black community, frequently operated by white business people, became one of the most important sources of recreation for African Americans, both young and old. In later years, many cities employed black recreational leaders who undertook to set up programs for young people that were designed to reduce the social maladjustments of the African-American population.

The growth and persistence of the African-American world did not result in the resignation of blacks to life in this relatively small orbit. There were numerous manifestations of efforts to rise above the proscriptions thrown around the African-American community. Black editors, for the most part, fought against the existence of an isolated black world, as did numerous other groups and individuals. The National Negro Congress, which was organized in 1936, represented a most vigorous effort of African Americans to present a solid front against the confinements to which their color apparently condemned them. It consisted of more than 500 black organizations and represented a large cross section of African-American life. Its protests against various forms of discrimination and segregation were vehement, but after 1940 it disintegrated rapidly as many members withdrew because they believed the congress was becoming a Communist front.

The Southern Negro Youth Congress, formed in 1937, was composed of various types of youth organizations. Local councils were established, and efforts were made to help young African Americans out of their many difficulties. Its program had only limited success, however. Numerous local protests and fights against restrictive covenants, separate schools, segregation in public carriers, and other policies that blacks considered un-American showed clearly that they were consistently determined to eradicate all practices that implied their racial inferiority. Evidence of the relentless drive against segregation, for example, was their successful legal action in 1946 against a Virginia bus company that segregated interstate black passengers. The Supreme Court held that such segregation was unconstitutional since it placed an undue burden on interstate commerce.

The protests of African Americans against their status did not imply that they took no pride in their race and its possibilities. Pride grew almost as rapidly as institutions in the African-American community. In inaugurating Negro Health Week, Booker T. Washington hoped to inspire blacks to guard their health and to develop habits of cleanliness that would help them become a stronger and more effective racial group. Carter G. Woodson conceived Negro History Week as a period in which the contributions of African Americans to the development of civilization would be sufficiently emphasized to impress blacks as well as whites. In 1914 the NAACP instituted an annual award—the Spingarn Medal—to be given to the African American who "reached the highest achievement in his field of activity." Beginning in 1926, the William E. Harmon Foundation undertook to select for awards those African Americans who had contributed most notably to the fields in which they were working. Both the Spingarn and Harmon medalists came from a variety of fields, but the racial nature of the achievement was always emphasized, thus stimulating pride in race.

African Americans paid considerable respect to their leaders and heroes, even the controversial ones. They pointed with pride to the fact that Matt

Henson was with Admiral Peary when he reached the North Pole in 1909, that in the twentieth century seven heavyweight champions and a host of other greats in professional sports were black, and that in few walks of life did blacks fail to make notable achievements. It was the kind of pride that naturally and pardonably stemmed from a racial group as peculiarly situated as they were. Their world was a small one, the opportunities were relatively few, and what achievements there were, of course, loomed up all the greater.

■ One World or Two?

In the three centuries that blacks had been a part of the evolving American civilization two important processes vitally affecting them were in operation. They were compelled to live in a world apart from the dominant group in the community and, therefore, developed institutions of their own in order to preserve their identity and individuality. At the same time, however, they participated to some limited extent in the affairs of the larger community. That experience helped to shape their own institutions and also promoted their integration, to a degree, into the pattern of life of the community. It seems unnecessary to add, of course, that their presence in America vitally affected the course of its development, for the most cursory glance at what has already been said will reveal that fact. These two processes went on simultaneously and imposed on blacks a most difficult task: that of trying to live in two worlds at the same time. Meanwhile, there was a considerable attempt to move from one world into the other. These efforts were motivated by the desire to make the problem of existence easier by reducing the many duplications of effort involved in living in two worlds and to move closer to realization of the American concept of equality, which they took as seriously as any group in American life.

In the period following the Civil War white America was compelled to consider the problem of the extent to which African Americans would be permitted to move into the mainstream of American life. There was no general agreement on the way in which the problem should be solved, and the heritage of the slave period merely served to inhibit any movement toward integration. It was not a problem that blacks could themselves solve, for it involved acceptance. African Americans continuously sought opportunities to participate more fully in the affairs of American life, but their overtures were more frequently spurned than not. They were forced back into their own world, and as they erected more institutions and ways of life uniquely their own, the prospect of full equality became more remote.

The effect of this whole experience upon African Americans cannot be fully measured or even appreciated. Many students of race relations and intergroup relations had much to say about the matter. Opponents of integration concentrated their attention on the black community, and when they found crime, delinquency, disease, and illiteracy, they insisted that these shortcomings were positive proof of the inability of African Americans to become equal participants in the affairs of a civilized community. Friends of the idea of integration held that such shortcomings were manifestations of frustration and were in themselves suggestive of the abnormality, as well as the difficulty, of living in a world that had the stigma of inferiority and instability placed upon it.

As African Americans made attempts to live in one world or in two worlds of race, their efforts were the object of serious study by many in the behavioral sciences, who employed new psychological and sociological techniques of studying race and community. They looked at the influence of the nation's democratic tradition on groups of diverse racial origins, and they examined the influence of economic problems on the matter of race. Many blacks began to object to being studied as a problem, frequently accusing the investigators of being more interested in new techniques and new approaches than in the human condition itself. While the Black Revolution of the 1960s and 1970s would require a full-scale reexamination of the place of African Americans in American life, it would also demand more involvement by blacks themselves and more action to relieve the conditions that the investigations revealed.

Many studies of African Americans' place in American social and economic life came out of the research of federal departments, such as the Office of Education, the Department of the Interior, and the Department of Commerce. Educational institutions, such as the Institute for Research in Social Science of the University of North Carolina and the Department of the Social Sciences of Fisk University, undertook to present graphic and scientific pictures of the status of blacks in American society. The works of Howard Odum, Charles S. Johnson, Rupert Vance, Gordon Blackwell, Guy B. Johnson, and others provided hitherto unavailable information concerning blacks and their relation to the worlds in which they lived. In a series of significant volumes the American Council on Education published the findings of the American Youth Commission, which had studied the effect of the proscriptive influences of American society on personality development of African-American youth. The studies of these investigators—among whom were Allison Davis, E. Franklin Frazier, Charles S. Johnson, John Dollard, W. Lloyd Warner, Ira DeA. Reid, and Robert L. Sutherland—revealed that the vast majority of black youth did not get an opportunity to share in the American dream of equal opportunities. They pointed out that the environment of black youth often forced them to react in a manner that many regard as shiftless, irresponsible, and aggressive. The opportunities for young African Americans to live normal lives were so few as to challenge any serious students interested in seeing even an approximation of the American dream.

The most ambitious study of the place of blacks in American life was undertaken by Gunnar Myrdal of the University of Stockholm and a large staff of sociologists, historians, economists, political scientists, psychologists, anthropologists, and other specialists for the Carnegie Corporation of New York. Several major works were published: *Myth of the Negro Past*, by Melville J. Herskovits; *Patterns of Negro Segregation*, by Charles S. Johnson; *The Negro's Share*, by Richard Sterner and others; *Characteristics of the American Negro*, by Otto Klineberg; and *An American Dilemma*, by Gunnar Myrdal. In addition, more than a score of exhaustive studies of various aspects of African-American life were made but not published. The inescapable conclusions running through all the studies were that the treatment of African Americans was America's greatest scandal and that the almost universal rejection of them was America's outstanding denial of its own profession of faith in the equality of humanity.

While some studies did make recommendations for improvement of the status of blacks in American life, the researchers were primarily concerned with revealing facts and did not concentrate on outlining programs of action. But African-American organizations continued to fight for a larger share of every aspect of American life for blacks. To these may be added a growing number of white and interracial organizations which evolved programs for the greater integration of African Americans in American life. In 1944 a group of white and black Southerners met and organized the Southern Regional Council, which was in fact a revitalized and expanded Commission of Interracial Cooperation. It declared itself to be "a Council to attain, through research and action, the ideals and practices of equal opportunity for all peoples in the South." A preliminary statement in August 1943 contained the assertion that "the Negro in the United States and in every region is entitled to and should have every guarantee of equal opportunity that every other citizen of the United States has within the framework of the American democratic system of government." The council participated actively in an attempt to secure political and economic equality for the African Americans of the South.

An organization that sought to secure a larger following of the masses, and whose program was more action-oriented, was the Southern Conference for Human Welfare. Organized in 1938, the conference tried to promulgate a program of aggressive action to raise the general level of underprivileged groups in the South. Through its state committees and local chapters it endeavored to create a wide interest in political affairs and in some instances went so far as to throw its support behind some candidates for public office while opposing others. Its stand against lynching, discrimination, the poll tax, and similar matters was unequivocal, and it usually allied itself with liberal labor forces. It was frequently accused of left-wing leanings and was listed as a subversive group by the House Committee on Un-American Activities.

People in the Midwest found it necessary, in 1944, to seek more satisfactory adjustments for minority groups in community life. Accordingly, they established the American Council on Race Relations with headquarters in Chicago. As a consultant organization the council was instrumental in advising communities in the resolution of minority group difficulties, especially industrial communities, and in establishing programs for inter-group education where necessary. With ample funds and a staff of highly trained white and black specialists, the council moved from the experimental stage to a position where it was recognized as an important agency in the area of race.

In the 1950s and 1960s efforts to educate the school and community in matters of race were greatly expanded. Outstanding psychologists, such as Kenneth Clark, showed how prejudice among children merely reflected the attitudes of their parents. School officials began to introduce courses de-signed to explain racial and cultural differences and at the same time to stimulate greater achievement by African-American children. Several cities, with the encouragement of the United States Office of Education, adopted Operation Headstart, which was designed to enrich the training of preschool children. This, in addition to the Higher Horizon program in New York City and the program of compensatory education in San Francisco, led many educators to believe that they had found models that demonstrated a greater understanding of the problem of minorities. Some programs, such as SEEK at the City University of New York and Access to Excellence in the public schools of Chicago, were highly controversial and invited much public opposition. SEEK's critics, largely white, feared the admission of unqualified students to the City University. The Chicago program drew the ire of many blacks who were convinced that it was merely a ruse to avoid desegregation. To offset the unfavorable image, or indeed the neglect of blacks in many texts, African Americans began to demand textbooks that gave a more adequate treatment of African Americans in the history of the United States.

While it was not possible to measure the results of the numerous efforts to bridge the gap between the two worlds in which most African Americans lived, there was rather general agreement by the end of the 1960s that at least some of the approaches being tried helped to check the increase in racial antipathy. If the agencies, councils, and bureaus did not succeed in accom-plishing their aims in trying to get America's melting pot to boil, they did dramatize the importance of the problem. They called attention to the fact that the great test of America's democratic tradition was the acceptance of blacks into the mainstream of American life.

CHAPTER 21

Fighting for the Four Freedoms

■ Arsenal of Democracy

The international anarchy that characterized the period before the outbreak of World War I reasserted itself shortly after the "War to End Wars" was over. To be sure, there were gestures in the direction of a lasting peace. The machinery of the League of Nations sought feebly to check aggression and to settle international disputes amicably, but the powerful nations too frequently used the organization as a cloak behind which they imposed their will on weaker members. The seizure of Manchuria by Japan in 1931, and the failure of various international organizations to do anything about it, demonstrated the ineffectiveness of such agencies in the face of determined cupidity. As early as 1922, Mussolini had come to power in Italy, and by 1935 he was seeking to resurrect the Roman Empire by overrunning Ethiopia. These developments gave encouragement to Adolf Hitler, who was waiting for a chance to use his newly won authority in Germany to extend his control over neighboring nations.

African Americans watched events in other parts of the world with growing concern. When Italy invaded Ethiopia, they protested with all the means at their command. Almost overnight even the most provincial among black Americans became international-minded. Ethiopia was a black nation, and its destruction would symbolize the final victory of whites over blacks.

In many communities funds were raised for the defense of the African kingdom, while in larger cities elaborate organizations were set up. In New York the International Council of Friends of Ethiopia was organized, with Willis N. Huggins as executive secretary. In 1935 Huggins pleaded for Ethiopia before the League of Nations. Other organizations, such as the United Aid to Ethiopia (later the Ethiopian World Federation), raised funds for the beleaguered African country. The Pittsburgh *Courier* sent its historian-news analyst, J. A. Rogers, to cover the war. Upon his return he issued a booklet, "The Real Facts About Ethiopia," and lectured to many black and white groups.

African Americans were among the earliest and most energetic Americans to condemn the fascism that was rising in Europe. They quickly learned to hate Nazism and its Aryan doctrines. Some had read Hitler's *Mein Kampf* and had resented its unfavorable comments about blacks. It had been claimed, moreover, that in 1936 Hitler had refused to treat the African-American Olympic stars Jesse Owens and Ralph Metcalfe with civility in Berlin. When Max Schmeling knocked out the black idol, Joe Louis, in 1936, African Americans had little to say for Hitlerism. Not until Louis gained complete revenge in 1938 could the average black speak of Nazis without a feeling of personal antagonism. By that time, however, public opinion in America was generally censuring Hitler's tactics in overthrowing Austria and dismembering Czechoslovakia, and African Americans joined in the loud condemnation.

When Europe was plunged into war as a result of Hitler's invasion of Poland in September 1939, the position of the United States as a neutral nation became more and more untenable. Within two months Congress, at the stern insistence of the president, passed an act permitting arms to be purchased on a cash-and-carry basis. When Germany unleashed its furious attack in the west in the spring of 1940, conquering Denmark, Norway, the Netherlands, Luxembourg, and Belgium, the people of the United States became alarmed. The fall of France in June 1940 added to the panic. It looked as though Britain would also fall before the Nazi *Blitzkrieg*. As Americans asked themselves what disposition Germany would make of the New World colonies of the conquered nations, they realized that the war had come frightfully close to them. It was time to prepare, and the following year witnessed a feverish effort to do so.

The low state of America's army by 1940 stemmed not so much from the fact that people were pursuing a policy of disarmament in a search for peace as it did from an almost natural disinclination to support a large standing peacetime army. As the number of officers and soldiers steadily decreased after World War I, the number of African-American soldiers in the army of the United States diminished to one of relative inconsequence. By 1940 there were less than 5,000 African Americans in an army composed of 230,000 enlisted men and officers. Only four black units, the Twenty-fourth and Twenty-fifth Infantries and the Ninth and Tenth Cavalries, were up to full strength. As early as 1939, however, several other black units were activated, including three quartermaster regiments, two antiaircraft battalions, one field artillery unit, a chemical warfare company, and several corps of engineers. At the beginning of the emergency there were less than a dozen African-American officers in the regular army. The difficulties involved in maintaining an active status in the Reserve Officers Corps had caused many African Americans who were eligible for commissions to allow their eligibility to lapse.

As the United States began to put itself on a war footing, African Americans wondered what consideration would be given them, both in the building up of a large fighting force and in the manufacture of the materials of modern warfare. When the Selective Service Act was passed in 1940, it was amended by a clause forbidding discrimination in the drafting and training of men. For a time, however, some draft boards accepted only white men for training, on the grounds that there was a lack of housing facilities for blacks at the camps. At the first signs of discrimination African Americans began to protest loudly. In September 1940 a group of black leaders, including A. Philip Randolph and Walter White, submitted a seven-point program to President Roosevelt outlining minimum essentials in giving African Americans just consideration in the defense program. They urged that all available reserve officers be used to train recruits; that black recruits be given the same training as whites; that existing units of the army accept officers and enlisted men on the basis of ability and not race; that specialized personnel, such as physicians, dentists, and nurses, be integrated; that responsible African Americans be appointed to draft boards; that discrimination be abolished in the navy and air force; and that competent African Americans be appointed as civilian assistants to the secretaries of war and the navy.

The policy of the War Department became clearer in the fall of 1940 when a statement was issued that African Americans would be received into the army on the general basis of the proportion of the African-American population of the country. They were to be organized into separate units, however, and existing black units that were officered by whites would receive no African-American officers other than medical officers and chaplains. African Americans were furious and made known their indignation. They admitted that Hitlerism was to be despised, but they insisted that discrimination against blacks was to be fought with desperate and equal vigor. Significant appointments and promotions of African Americans did little to quiet the voice of protest. On October 25, 1940, Col. B. O. Davis became the first black to be promoted to the rank of brigadier general, but election day was too close to convince all African Americans that the promotion was made without political considerations. William H. Hastie was appointed civilian aide to the secretary of war, and Col. Campbell Johnson became an executive assistant to the director of Selective Service. Senior ROTC units were added at West Virginia State College, Hampton Institute,

North Carolina Agricultural and Technical College, Prairie View State College, and Tuskegee Institute. Although these steps pleased African Americans, they were insufficient to convince them that Washington had made a significant change in policy. Too many clear signs indicated that the United States was committed to maintaining a white army and a black army, and ironically these forces had to be used together somehow to carry on the fight against the powerful threat of fascism and racism in the world.

As industrial plants began to convert for the purpose of producing weapons of war, African Americans found great difficulty in securing employment. Approximately 5 million whites were still unemployed—a significant contrast with the situation immediately before World War I—and employers were generally inclined to absorb them first. Since the vast majority of blacks were unskilled, the explanation for failure to employ them was usually that skilled workers were needed. The first benefits that African Americans derived from the boom in defense industries were in securing jobs that had been deserted by whites who were attracted by the higher wages paid by defense plants. The federal government made several gestures to discourage discrimination. The United States Office of Education declared that in the expenditure of funds in the defense training program there should be no discrimination on account of race, creed, or color. In August 1940, the National Defense Advisory Committee issued a statement against the refusal to hire African Americans at defense plants. In September the president spoke out against discrimination in a message to Congress. The Office of Production Management established a black employment and training branch in its labor division to facilitate the hiring of African Americans in defense industries. None of these actions brought satisfactory results, and blacks made it clear that they wished more than gestures from their government.

As African Americans saw wages skyrocket at plants holding large defense contracts and no change in the rigid antiblack policy in industry, they developed a program for drastic action. In January 1941, A. Philip Randolph, president of the Brotherhood of Sleeping Car Porters, advanced the idea of 50,000 to 100,000 blacks marching on Washington and demanding that their government do something to ensure the employment of blacks in defense industries. Almost immediately, African Americans showed enthusiasm for the idea, and as plans were laid for the march, high government officials became alarmed. Around Washington the question was frequently asked, "What will they think in Berlin?" Blacks became accustomed to replying, "Oh, perhaps no more than they already think of America's racial policy." By June, African Americans all over the United States—certainly many thousands if not 100,000—were making preparations to go to Washington to march to the Capitol on July 1. Seeking redress for grievances was an old American custom, and in this form it was reminiscent of the march on Washington of Coxey's army of unemployed men in 1894 and of the Bonus Expeditionary Force in 1932.

During the last three weeks of June 1941, much was done to prevent the march on Washington from taking place. Mayor Fiorello LaGuardia of New York, Eleanor Roosevelt, Aubrey Williams of the National Youth Administration, Walter White of the NAACP, and Randolph discussed the matter in New York. Mrs. Roosevelt and Mayor LaGuardia, among others, asserted that the march would do no good and would perhaps cause reprisals against blacks. Randolph, however, was adamant. The president sent for Randolph and conferred at length with him, along with Secretary of War Stimson, Secretary of the Navy Knox, and others. Nothing could dissuade Randolph. As the time for the march drew closer, government officials became more desperate. After several conferences, the president said that if Randolph would call off the march, he would issue an order "with teeth in it," prohibiting discrimination in employment in defense industries and in the government. On June 25, 1941, the president issued his famous Executive Order 8802, in which he said that "there shall be no discrimination in the employment of workers in defense industries or Government because of race, creed, color, or national origin. . . . And it is the duty of employers and of labor organizations . . . to provide for the full and equitable participation of all workers in defense industries, without discrimination because of race, creed, color, or national origin. . . ."

In pursuance of the executive order a clause prohibiting discrimination was placed in all defense contracts, and a Fair Employment Practices Committee (FEPC) was set up to receive and investigate complaints of discrimination in violation of the order. The committee, which was composed of representatives of the public, management, and labor, held hearings in industrial centers such as Los Angeles, Chicago, and New York. Many evidences of discrimination were, of course, uncovered. Although the committee had no power to institute punishment and was disinclined to recommend the cancelation of war contracts because of the emergency, its existence had a salutary effect on the employment status of African Americans. Employers and trade unions did not like to appear at hearings as defendants, and occasionally they were willing to change their policies to avoid being called up. The unfavorable publicity involved in an appearance before the committee, moreover, caused some employers to revise their employment policy. Finally, the embarrassment that some employers suffered as a result of their proved misrepresentation of employment practices moved them to change their practices in an effort to restore their good name.

The reaction to the executive order and the committee was mixed. African Americans hailed the order as the most significant document affecting them since the Emancipation Proclamation. They were, of course, disappointed when widespread discrimination continued in defiance of the committee. White employers and Southern whites generally were opposed to it. Mark Ethridge, a Louisville newspaperman and an original member of the committee, said that the order was not a social document and it had no concern with racial segregation. He added, significantly, "All the armies of the world, both of the United Nations and the Axis, could not force upon the South the abandonment of racial segregation." A white Alabama lawyer was so furious that he organized a League to Maintain White Supremacy, while the governor of that state declared that he would refuse to sign a contract that would force him to abandon a policy of segregation that he regarded as essential to racial peace.

Thus did the United States struggle in the early days of the European war when it was called upon by the enemies of the Axis powers to be the arsenal of democracy. It was expected to provide an increasing amount of the goods of war through sale, lend-lease, gift, relief, and the like. It experienced a major difficulty in attempting to serve as the arsenal of democracy and at the same time hold fast to its pattern of a free economy in which labor had the right to strike and management had the right to hire only people of a certain color. The task of giving spiritual as well as material succor to nations under the Axis heel and maintaining simultaneously discriminatory policies based on race, creed, and national origin required remarkable ambidexterity. The president had outlined quite clearly the international aspirations of the world to achieve "freedom of speech, freedom to worship, freedom from want, and freedom from fear." But the inability of the United States to enunciate a strong position on democracy that stemmed from honest practices doubtless had the effect of weakening its position as the arsenal of democracy.

■ Blacks in the Service

Under the Selective Service Act of 1940 more than 3 million African Americans registered for service in the armed forces. Largely because of educational deficiencies, alleged social diseases, and the discriminatory attitudes of draft boards, however, the rate of rejection of blacks was 18.2 percent as compared with 8.5 percent for whites. In the first year of the operation of the act only 2,069 African Americans were drafted into the armed services. In the following year, more than 100,000 entered the service, while in 1942 approximately 370,000 joined. In September 1944, when the army was at its peak, there were 701,678 blacks in that branch of the service alone. Approximately 165,000 served in the navy, 5,000 in the Coast Guard, and 17,000 in the Marine Corps. A rough estimate of the total number of blacks in the armed services during World War II places the figure in the neighborhood of 1 million men and women, which approximates the ratio that African Americans bore to the general population.

The participation of African Americans in the administration of the Selective Service doubtless reduced discrimination in accepting blacks into the armed forces. In various parts of the United States, blacks served in almost every capacity under Selective Service. On the national level, in addition to the executive assistant to the director, an African American served on the president's Advisory Committee on Selective Service. On the lower levels blacks served as local board members, as members of the registrants' advisory board, as examining physicians, as appeal board members, and in various other capacities. The impression was rather general among African Americans that the Selective Service in World War II was administered more impartially than in World War I.

Although there was much discrimination in the armed forces, blacks had a greater opportunity to serve their country than in any previous war. They were in the infantry, coast and field artillery, cavalry, tank battalions, transportation units, signal corps, engineer corps, medical corps, and many other branches in most of which they had previously served. When the Women's Army Corps (WAC) was organized, blacks were admitted, and before the end of the war more than 4,000 African-American women had enlisted. Late in 1940 the War Department announced that African Americans would be trained as aviation pilots at Tuskegee, Alabama. While some African Americans violently objected to the segregation of blacks in the air force, others viewed the announcement as a step forward since no provisions had hitherto been made. As pilots began their training at Tuskegee, ground crews were prepared at Chanute Field, Illinois. Late in 1941 the Ninety-ninth Pursuit Squadron was ready for organization into a fighting unit, and other groups of black fighter pilots were undergoing training. Approximately 600 African-American pilots had received their wings before the end of the war.

In June 1940 there were only 4,000 African Americans in the navy, a majority of whom served as messmen. They had no opportunity either to learn the many trades provided in the naval training program or to become combat seamen. After the beginning of the war African Americans protested the discrimination in the navy, and for several months navy officials made it clear that they had no intention of revising their policy regarding blacks. In April 1942, however, the secretary of the navy announced that the navy would accept the enlistment of blacks for general service and as noncommissioned officers. A separate unit, Camp Robert Smalls, was established for them at the Great Lakes Naval Training Station. Promising recruits were sent from there to Hampton for further training. Others were sent to sea or to naval ammunition depots. When the Navy decided in 1943 to allow African Americans to enter its training program for officers, sixteen men were selected on the assumption that no more than twelve would qualify. At the end of the program, however, all sixteen passed. Twelve were commissioned ensigns and one a warrant officer. The others "were returned to the enlisted ranks without further explanation." Later, African-American women gained admission to the Women Accepted for Volunteer Emergency Service (WAVES). At the same time it was announced that African Americans would be received into the Marine Corps, thereby smashing an exclusion policy that was as old as the corps itself. African-American leathernecks began their training late in the summer of 1942 at the marine base at Camp Lejeune, North Carolina. Within a short period the Fifty-first Composite Defense Battalion was in the process of organization.

The question of African-American officers was a delicate one because of the experience of blacks as well as military officials during the previous war. African Americans were determined to secure equal and integrated training as officers, and the fight to accomplish this was high on the agenda of black leaders. In October 1940 the War Department stated, "When officer candidate schools are established opportunity will be given for Negroes to qualify for reserve commissions." It was decided, moreover, that black and white soldiers should be admitted to the same officer candidate schools and classes. The following summer, classes began at officer candidate schools. The problem that developed was that of getting commanding officers at the various camps to recommend African Americans for advanced training. In the first six months, less than thirty blacks were admitted to the schools. Only after the secretary of war issued a stern order that African Americans be sent to the candidate schools on the basis of no discrimination did blacks get into the schools in considerable numbers. By the middle of 1942 black officers were graduating at the rate of approximately 200 per month. They received commissions from the adjutant general's school in the armored forces, air corps administration, cavalry, coast artillery, infantry, chemical warfare, quartermaster service, and other branches. In each instance they studied and graduated with whites. Only in the air corps were commissions given at a segregated school. Even the navy commissioned African Americans as officers in 1944. Before the end of the war more than fifty blacks were ensigns, lieutenants, medical and dental officers, nurses, WAVES officers, and chaplains. In the marines and Coast Guard there was also a small number of African-American officers.

Approximately a half-million African Americans saw service overseas during World War II. On September 30, 1944, there were 411,368 in foreign theaters, while on February 28, 1945, the number had reached 497,566. In the European theater, almost half of the transportation corps was composed of blacks. They served in port battalions, in truck companies, and in other similar units. Port battalions composed of blacks came ashore shortly after an invasion and unloaded supplies for the use of assault troops. During the summer of 1944 and the remainder of the war black amphibian truck companies made a significant contribution to the successful drive across France. After D-Day more than 50,000 African-American engineers erected camps, tents, and buildings; cleared debris; rebuilt cities; and performed other important services. They constituted about one-fifth of the American engineers in the European theater. Approximately 11 percent of the ordnance men in Europe were African Americans. The chief of ordnance reported that not only did they "pass the ammunition" but on numerous occasions they also fought the Germans, participating in patrols and taking prisoners. One of the most troubling results of the service of African-American soldiers in the European theater was the execution after military courts-martial of almost four times as many black soldiers as whites, despite the fact that African Americans constituted less than 10 percent of the troops there. This has caused criminologist Robert Lilly to conclude that "blacks were . . .

BLACK NURSES GO TO THE WARFRONT. Landing in Scotland from the United States, these nurses would soon serve on several European fighting fronts. *(Courtesy U.S. Signal Corps.)*

punished in all instances . . . more for their behavior, proportionate to their presence, than the white soldiers were."

Twenty-two black combat units were active in ground operations in the European theater. There were nine field artillery battalions, one antiaircraft battalion, two tank battalions, two tank destroyer battalions, and eight engineer combat battalions. The 761st Tank Battalion was one of the outstanding fighting units. It fought in the Battle of the Bulge and saw service in six European countries. Although four major generals and the undersecretary of war commended the battalion for its gallant service, the unit was repeatedly denied the prestigious Presidential Distinguished Unit Citation until 1978 when President Jimmy Carter presented it. The 614th Tank Destroyer Battalion served in several important actions, and one of its officers, Capt. Charles L. Thomas, received the Distinguished Service Cross for heroism in the action before Climbach, France. Black units of field artillery were in France within ten days after the invasion. The 333rd fought through Brittany and northern France and against vicious German attacks in the fall of 1944. Several other units provided artillery backing for other divisions.

In January 1945 it was announced that African-American troops would

BLACK COAST GUARDSMEN.
Aboard the U.S.S. *Big Horn*, north-
west of the Azores, these men en-
gage in target practice. (*U.S. Coast
Guard photo no. 26-G-4284, National
Archives.*)

be integrated with white troops in a unit to fight on German soil. The
integration was of platoons rather than of individual men. Volunteers soon
doubled the quota of 2,500. After a short period of training they were in
action on the east side of the Rhine, with various divisions of the First Army.
African Americans everywhere were elated at the news of the experiment
and were delighted to learn that the racially mixed units were a success. On
April 30, 1945, the War Department said that the volunteer black infantrymen
had "established themselves as fighting men no less courageous or aggressive
than their white comrades." Their performance was short, for the war was
soon over, but not before they won the plaudits of many high-ranking
officers. One said to them, "I have never seen any soldiers who have
performed better in combat than you." When the units were broken up at
the end of the European conflict, African Americans protested, but the War
Department seemed to be finished with experimenting.

In the Mediterranean theater the principal black combat unit was the
Ninety-second Division, which had been reactivated at Fort McClellan,
Alabama, in 1942. In 1943 it was moved to Fort Huachuca, Arizona, where
it went into intensive training. In June 1944 it was sent to Africa and later
to Italy, where it served with the Fifth Army. It was composed of four
regiments of infantry and four battalions of field artillery, as well as other
service units. Its first major offensive action was in crossing the Arno River
in September 1944. Its drive was successful until December, when it was
driven out of several towns that it had taken earlier. Within a few days,
however, all of the lost ground had been recaptured. The following February
the Ninety-second suffered serious reverses, for which it was severely
criticized. After a visit to the division, William Hastie's successor as civilian

THE S.S. "HARRIET TUBMAN." This vessel was named for the "Moses of her people," who was active in the Underground Railroad and served as a Union spy during the Civil War. Completed in 1943 at the New England Shipbuilding Corporation, it was one of fourteen Liberty ships named for outstanding African Americans. *(U.S. Maritime Administration.)*

aide to the secretary of war, Truman K. Gibson, Jr., was reported to have said that the Ninety-second had not made a good showing. Many critics of African-American combat troops immediately took up the report and, by quoting it out of context, used it to bolster their arguments that blacks could not fight. African Americans severely criticized Gibson for his statements. Later it became clear that Gibson had been misquoted. He had only said that whatever poor showing there was of the Ninety-second was doubtless due to the low educational equipment of a large part of the rank and file of the division. He pointed out that 17 percent belonged in class five, the lowest literacy class admitted to the army. The more than 12,000 decorations and citations that the division received indicated that its performance was a creditable one under unusually unfavorable circumstances.

The two major black combat air units overseas were the 99th Pursuit Squadron and the 332nd Fighter Group. The 99th went overseas in April 1943, and in February of the following year the 332nd went to the Mediterranean theater. Both groups participated in various types of fighting over Europe. They escorted bombers and went on strafing and other missions. The 332nd was instrumental in sinking an enemy destroyer off the Istrian peninsula, and it protected the 15th Air Force bombers in important attacks on the oil fields of Rumania. Under the command of Col. Benjamin O. Davis, Jr., the fighter group won the admiration of African Americans everywhere and the generous praise of high officials in the air force. More than eighty pilots won the Distinguished Flying Cross, having destroyed 111 planes in the air and 150 on the ground. The 477th Bombardment Group, which was activated late in the war, did not see action.

From the time that engineers landed in New Guinea to prepare landing strips, African Americans took an increasingly active part in the war in the Pacific and the Orient. Approximately 10,000 black troops worked on construction of the Ledo Road, and it was necessary for many of them to fight the enemy as well as build the road. There were also the usual service troops, including engineers, port companies, quartermasters, amphibians, and chemical warfare units. Among the combat units that saw service against the Japanese was the Twenty-fourth Infantry, which helped take the New Georgia Islands in May 1942. There were several other outfits, including two battalions of coast artillery and one antiaircraft barrage balloon battalion. The main black combat unit was the Ninety-third Division, which saw its first action at Bougainville in the Solomons. From there it proceeded against the Japanese on the Treasury Islands, on the Dutch East Indian island of Morotai, and in the Philippines. While the Ninety-third Division did not perform the kind of spectacular deeds that captured the imagination of citizens on the home front, its fighting was steady and consistent under adverse tropical conditions, and it was never severely criticized for failures in any way.

The opportunities that African Americans had to serve in the navy were in distinct contrast to those they had had in World War I. Thousands of blacks were trained to perform numerous technical tasks and were given ratings accordingly. On March 20, 1944, the destroyer escort *Mason* was commissioned, and African Americans of various grades were assigned to duty on it. Later, blacks manned a patrol chaser and hunted enemy submarines in the Atlantic. By the fall of 1944 the navy was able to announce that 500 black seamen were on duty on twenty-five large auxiliary vessels operating primarily in the Pacific. Among the African Americans with ratings were storekeepers, yeomen, radiomen, shipfitters, carpenter's mates, gunner's mates, quartermasters, and coxswains. Meanwhile, approximately 12,500 black Seabees served in the Pacific, constructing advanced naval bases and doing other jobs. The work they performed, frequently under severe enemy attack, was praised by high navy officials. African-American marines were stationed at several strategic Pacific outposts to defend areas taken from the enemy. Their conduct caused the commander of the corps to say, "Negro Marines are no longer on trial. They are Marines, period." The more than 900 African Americans in the Coast Guard did rescue work in the Atlantic, in the Pacific, and in Alaskan waters. They were among the first to go ashore at Okinawa early in 1945 and on occasion performed invaluable services on shore duty both at home and abroad.

Approximately 24,000 African Americans served in the merchant marine, and some of them had enlisted before the navy relaxed its restrictions on the enlistment of blacks. There seemed to be a minimum of segregation and discrimination, and African Americans were given opportunities to serve in responsible capacities. They worked as able and ordinary seamen, engineers, radio operators, and the like. Four black captains commanded Liberty ships, the crews of which were made up of various races. Eighteen ships were named for African Americans—fourteen for noted African Americans and four for African-American merchant seamen who had lost their lives while in active service with the merchant marine. One of them, the *Booker T. Washington,* was commanded by an African American, Capt. Hugh Mulzac. During the course of the war two of the ships, S.S. *Frederick Douglass* and S.S. *Robert L. Vann,* were sunk. The black press and African-American leaders did not fail to use the merchant marine as an outstanding example of an enterprise in which blacks and whites could work together successfully.

The problem of maintaining high morale among African Americans in the service was most difficult. To be sure, the War and Navy Departments made some concessions, but the black press and African-American leaders were always demanding more. Black soldiers, taking their cue from the more articulate African Americans, demanded equality of treatment whenever it was possible to do so without breaking military discipline. Even among the considerable number of black soldiers and sailors who had but a small amount of formal training, there was much dissatisfaction with the discriminatory policies of the army and navy and disgust with the way in which they were treated by many white civilians. In Durham, North Carolina, a white bus driver was found not guilty of murder after he left his bus in July 1944 and killed a black soldier after an argument. In several communities in the South, African-American soldiers were refused food in places where German prisoners of war were eating and enjoying American hospitality. In a Kentucky railroad station three African-American WACs were beaten by civilian policemen when the women did not move promptly enough from the white waiting room when asked to do so. In South Carolina a white policeman gouged out a black soldier's eyes in an altercation.

On military posts the situation was scarcely better. Several commanding officers forbade the reading of black newspapers, and there were instances in which black newspapers were taken from newsboys or soldiers and burned. At many camps transportation for African-American soldiers was most unsatisfactory. They were frequently forced to wait until buses had been loaded with white soldiers before they were permitted to board them. At post exchanges they were segregated and given inferior merchandise. Theaters and other entertainment facilities were frequently set apart, and

LT. GARVIN

BLACK WOMEN SERVE. Lt. Stella G. Garvin of the Women's Army Corps interviews a job applicant at the rapidly expanding Jersey City Quartermaster Repair Sub-Depot. *(U.S. Signal Corps Photo.)*

accommodations for blacks were below the standard of those provided for white soldiers. The War Department took cognizance of the discrimination against African-American soldiers in its order of July 8, 1944, which forbade racial segregation in recreational and transportation facilities. A veritable storm of protest arose in the South as the order was made known. The Montgomery *Advertiser* said, "Army orders, even armies, even bayonets, cannot force impossible and unnatural social race relations upon us." The order was regarded as merely a "directive" by some commanding officers, and it was not strictly enforced; others sought to wipe out discrimination as the order required. Many black soldiers, seeking equal treatment in pursuance of the order, were rebuffed and denied service at post exchanges and theaters.

The attempts of African Americans to resist segregation and discrimination led, of course, to innumerable clashes both on and off military posts. Few camps could boast at the end of the war that there had been no racial clashes. There were serious riots at Fort Bragg, Camp Robinson, Camp Davis, Camp Lee, and Fort Dix. At Freeman Field, Indiana, more than 100 black officers were arrested for attempting to enter an officers' club maintained for whites. They were later exonerated, but irreparable damage had been done to the morale of the 477th Bombardment Group. At Mabry Field, Florida, and at Port Chicago, California, black servicemen were charged with mutiny when they refused to perform work that they felt was assigned to them because of their color. There were more experiences that served to depress the morale of African-American soldiers than ones that raised their morale. The emotional conflicts and frustrations they experienced as they

BLACK PILOTS. Taking time out between missions in Italy in 1944, these five pilots of the all-black Mustang Group of the Fifteenth Air Force were among the first African Americans to be admitted to the pilot training program in the air force. *(Office of War Information photo no. 208-NP-6XXX-1, National Archives.)*

sought to reconcile the doctrine of the Four Freedoms with their own plight discouraged many of them. Neither the antidiscrimination orders of the War Department nor the concessions made in the commissioning of African-American officers in the navy could compensate for the hurt that blacks felt when rebuffed while wearing the uniform of their country. At the end of the war realists would admit that the morale of African-American soldiers could be substantially raised only by granting to them the Four Freedoms for which they had been fighting.

There were, of course, many critics of black soldiers who insisted that they were incapable of participating efficiently in modern warfare. To be sure, it was strange indeed that no African Americans had been awarded the Congressional Medal of Honor since the Spanish-American War, but blacks could well argue that there had been a change in the policy of those responsible for the awards rather than any change in the heroism and gallantry of the black soldier. In the Civil War sixteen soldiers and five sailors won the coveted medal, while in the Spanish-American War seven black servicemen had received it. Fifteen African Americans on other occasions had served their country in such a manner as to merit the award. In World

War I not even Henry Johnson was awarded the Medal of Honor, and blacks began to ask if the nation was reserving its highest award for white soldiers. African-American soldiers concluded that they would have to content themselves with less significant recognitions, and of those there were plenty. The secretary of war, the chief of staff, and the high military officials in the various theaters of war praised the heroism and service of the black soldier. Through their own newspapers African Americans followed the exploits of their soldiers, and they were satisfied with their performance.

Many units received the Presidential Distinguished Unit Citation for their gallantry. Individual men received recognitions that ranged from good conduct medals to the Distinguished Service Cross, which five African Americans received. For the late Private George Watson the citation read, "Extraordinary heroism—on March 8, 1943, when he lost his life in Portlock Harbor, New Guinea, after assisting several men to safety on a raft from their sinking boat, which had been attacked by Japanese bombers. Overcome by exhaustion, he was pulled under and drowned by the suction of the craft." Steward's Mate 2/c Eli Benjamin, Mess Attendant Leonard Harmon, Messman Doris Miller, and Cook William Pinckney received the Navy Cross for their outstanding heroism. In the now famous incident at Pearl Harbor, Doris Miller, "Without previous experience . . . manned a machine gun in the face of serious fire during the Japanese attack on Pearl Harbor, December 7, 1941, on the Battleship *Arizona,* shooting down four enemy planes." Eighty-two black pilots received the Distinguished Flying Cross. Other African Americans received the Croix de Guerre and the Partisan Medal from Yugoslavia for Heroism, and one received the Order of the Soviet Union. With some justification the black members of the armed services could feel that they had made their contribution to the preservation of at least the ideal, if not the reality, of the Four Freedoms.

■ The Home Fires

The global nature of the war and its demands on the resources of the belligerents implied from the beginning that its successful prosecution involved the utilization of every factor that could possibly contribute strength. For the United States the waging of total warfare presented innumerable difficult problems. It could not be achieved without erecting some controls that served to reduce the freedom of the individual, a move which was strenuously resisted by a considerable portion of the population. Nor could total warfare be achieved without the country's making substantial concessions to its minority groups so that they could make their contribution to the defeat of the Axis powers. This also found considerable opposition among groups determined to carry on the fight abroad without upsetting the existing pattern of race relations at home. Many admitted, however, that for the sake of consistency with the ideology of the United

Nations (U.N.), as well as for the purpose of increasing efficiency, the United States would have to deal more justly with all its people. On numerous occasions African Americans at various levels of social and economic life pointed to the tremendous waste of human effort in their struggle for the right to work and fight for victory. It was indeed embarrassing to Americans, and more than once they asked themselves, "What will Berlin say?"

Thanks to the training programs of the NYA and the WPA, thousands of African Americans were ready for employment in industry when the defense program began. The number was increased substantially by the training programs of the United States Office of Education, the Vocational Training for War Production Workers, and the Engineering, Science, and Management War Training (ESMWT) program. By December 1942 more than 58,000 African Americans were enrolled in preemployment courses. In the summer of 1943 sixty-five black colleges were participating in the ESMWT program, and more than 50,000 students were enrolled. African Americans were thus prepared for work in aircraft industries, shipbuilding, welding, automotive mechanics, electricity and radio, and numerous other defense activities. The nondiscriminatory provisions of the federal training programs ensured the preparation of African Americans for defense work, but the difficulty of securing employment was one that plagued blacks and the federal government all during the war.

Before establishment of the FEPC the black employment and training branch of the labor division of the Office of Production Management had a limited amount of success in negotiating with employers and persuading them to use African Americans on war construction projects and in defense plants. Within a year after creation of the FEPC it was evident that it had experienced some success both directly and indirectly in increasing the number of blacks in government service and in war industries. After its transfer to the War Manpower Commission its techniques were improved and the results were more gratifying. Considerable antagonism to the FEPC developed, however, because of its practice of citing industries for violation of the president's executive order even after those industries had initiated programs for the integration of minorities. The FEPC was also instrumental in putting pressure on the United States Employment Service to give preference, in job referrals, to employers who did not discriminate against minority groups. These various forms of government pressure resulted in much greater utilization of the total work force of the country.

Despite serious criticisms leveled at the FEPC and other agencies of the government that tried to eliminate discriminatory policies, their activities showed clearly that the federal government could do much to modify racial employment practices. By the end of the war few major industries were without at least some African Americans in their plants. At the beginning of the emergency almost no blacks were employed in aircraft industries, but at the end of the war thousands worked in them. The shipyards increased their black workers, both in quantity and quality. More than 100,000 found

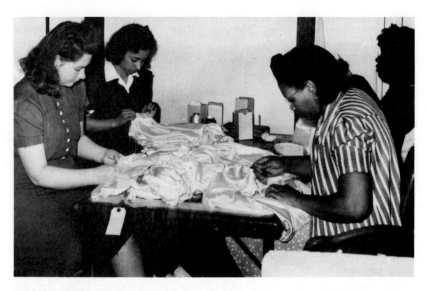

WOMEN PARACHUTE MAKERS. In one Eastern navy yard in 1942 black and white women worked together making parachutes for the armed forces. *(Photo by Office of War Information.)*

employment in the iron and steel industries. Although the problem of upgrading remained unsolved during the war, there were indications that industries were beginning to yield. Perhaps the increased participation of African Americans in labor organizations had something to do with this. During and after the war blacks played an increasingly important role at the conventions of organizations like the United Automobile Workers, the United Steel Workers, the National Maritime Union, and the United Rubber Workers, and on the national councils of the CIO. Many Americans became convinced that the public, through its government, should guarantee employment on a basis of nondiscrimination. As a result there was considerable discussion of a permanent FEPC in the federal government, and the National Committee for a Permanent FEPC did much to rally public sentiment behind such a proposition. In the campaign of 1944 both major parties committed themselves to the proposal, but no headway was made in securing the necessary legislation. Meanwhile, several states, among them New York and Massachusetts, set up such agencies.

As a matter of course, African Americans gave generous support to the war effort on the home front. They purchased bonds, and many corporations reported that black employees signed up for the payroll savings plan, whereby regular amounts were deducted from wages for the purchase of bonds. In every bond campaign African Americans held rallies in schools, churches, and community centers to sell war bonds. With the help of blacks on the staff of the Treasury Department, especially William Pickens and Nell

WORKER IN NORFOLK NAVY YARD. This worker is in the plate-bender's shop, where steel plates are bent to fit the sidings of warcraft under construction. This operation requires a high degree of skill. *(OEM defense photo by Palmer.)*

Hunter, the campaigns among African Americans were almost always successful.

When the Office of Civilian Defense was established, African Americans became active in the preparations to defend the country against possible enemy attack. On the national level Crystal Bird Fauset served as race relations adviser, while on the local level blacks served as block managers, messengers, and auxiliary firefighters and police officers. In air-raid drills they were especially cooperative. Since blacks lived in ghettoes in most American communities, violations by them could be easily detected, and they were determined that there would be none. In Southern communities blacks facetiously speculated on what accommodations would be made for them in shelters in case of an air raid, but fortunately the South was never called upon to provide such facilities. It was perhaps the fear of what would happen in such a case that prompted a paranoid Southern senator to charge that Senegalese soldiers were criminally assaulting large numbers of German women in the subway shelters of Stuttgart, although the German city had no subways at all.

In the program to conserve foods and other essential commodities and to control prices, African Americans also played their part. When the Office of

Price Administration (OPA) was established, blacks were employed as attorneys, price analysts, and economists. They worked in regional and state offices as information specialists and in the local offices of some communities as clerks as well as members of ration boards. There seemed to be more general satisfaction among African Americans with the way in which the OPA was administered than with any other wartime agency, perhaps because of the rather general policy of the agency to employ workers for jobs regardless of race. It was not difficult, moreover, for blacks to cooperate with programs of conservation because of their traditionally impoverished condition. When a white representative from the War Foods Administration was lecturing to a black audience on ways of saving fats, a housewife asserted that many African Americans, through the years, had been forced to use fats over and over again and were, therefore, already quite familiar with the techniques.

In the agencies established for the purpose of building morale, African Americans participated in larger numbers than during World War I. They served the Red Cross as Gray Ladies, as nurses' aides, and as drivers in the motor corps. In fighting areas they worked in camps, clubs, and hospitals. During the war approximately 200 professional workers served as club directors and in other capacities in four theaters of war. To be sure, segregation and discrimination existed, and the workers themselves, as well as the soldiers, protested against such practices. The United Service Organization (USO), organized in February 1941, undertook to channel the activities of the YMCA, YWCA, National Catholic Community Service, Salvation Army, Jewish Welfare Board, and Travelers Aid Society into one great effort for sustaining the morale of the fighting men and women. During the course of the war more than 300 USO clubs were staffed by African-American personnel, while approximately a dozen were staffed by blacks and whites. There were, moreover, approximately 30 Travelers Aid Case Service Units with interracial staffs and 25 Travelers Aid Lounges staffed by African Americans. In Southern states these services were dispensed on a segregated basis, but in most Northern communities both black and white service personnel enjoyed the same facilities. Several black USO shows were organized and sent overseas to entertain those in the war zones.

In contrast to their state of mind at the outbreak of World War I, African Americans had no illusions about the benefits they would derive from World War II. Had there been any doubts, they would have been dispelled during the period of the emergency before the beginning of hostilities, when blacks had such great difficulties in securing opportunities to work in defense industries. At the outbreak of the war African-American civilians made it clear that they were suspicious of the white man's good intentions, and one went so far as to say, "This is very likely to be the last war that the white man will be able to lead humanity to wage for plausible platitudes." Upon occasions of mistreatment, black soldiers were heard to grumble that they would prefer to die for some rights in the United States than to die overseas to secure those rights for peoples in foreign lands.

Experiences on the home front during the war drove the morale of African Americans to a new low. The migration of large numbers of blacks to the North and the West in search of employment raised anew the difficult question of how blacks and whites could live together peacefully in communities where the patterns of race relations were at best confused. Within the five-year period between 1940 and 1945 the African-American population of Los Angeles County, for example, increased from 75,000 to 150,000. Added to that community's problems involving Mexican Americans and Japanese Americans were the newly arrived blacks, and interracial clashes seemed inevitable. In the industrial communities of San Francisco, Oakland, Portland, and Seattle there was similar growth, with correspondingly increased problems in the field of race relations. Among the Midwestern cities that witnessed an influx of blacks and whites, Detroit showed the greatest strains in the problem of achieving adjustment. Approximately 50,000 African Americans had come into the city, along with 450,000 other people, in the three years preceding 1943. The lack of housing, the presence of race baiters and demagogues, the problem of organizing newly arrived workers, and the impotence of the government created an ideal atmosphere in which a riot could flourish.

On June 20, 1943, the most serious race riot of the war period broke out in Detroit. The months of tension reached a climax after a fistfight occurred between a black man and a white man. The altercation rapidly spread to involve several hundred people of both races. Wild rumors, as usual, swept through the town. Within a few hours blacks and whites were fighting throughout most of Detroit. When the governor hesitated to declare martial law and call out troops, whites began to roam the streets, burning blacks' cars and beating large numbers of black people. Nothing effective was done to bring order out of the chaos until President Roosevelt proclaimed a state of emergency and sent 6,000 soldiers to patrol the city. At the end of more than thirty hours of rioting 25 African Americans and 9 whites had been killed, and property valued at several hundred thousand dollars had been destroyed.

Other Northern cities as well as large metropolitan areas in the West feared that they would have the same experience as Detroit, and numerous efforts were made to prevent interracial clashes. New York City and Los Angeles did not escape completely, but many communities were able to avert riots by making intelligent and careful approaches to solution of the problems that created riots. African Americans, however, continued to demand better treatment and a larger share of the benefits that came from the huge expenditures in the war effort. They were willing to do their part and to make necessary sacrifices to ensure victory, but they never failed to remind the people of the United States that they resented all forms of mistreatment. African Americans even criticized Joe Louis when he fought Buddie Baer in January 1942 and gave his entire purse for navy relief. This gesture outraged many African Americans because at the time the navy did not permit blacks to enter the service in other than menial capacities. The Pittsburgh *Courier* waged a vigorous "Double-V" campaign, victory at home as well as abroad. Everywhere blacks registered their protest against the practice of the Red Cross of separating black and white blood in blood banks established for the relief of wounded service personnel. They were quick to point out that there would perhaps have been no blood banks without the work of a black physician, Charles Drew. They also censured the USO when that organization banned the circulation of Ruth Benedict's *Races of Mankind* throughout its clubs.

The government took official cognizance of the importance of African-American morale by appointing Ted Poston, a veteran black newspaperman, as racial adviser in the Office of War Information (OWI). Through Poston's office news of how blacks were faring in the armed services and on the home front was sent to newspapers that were read by African Americans. The OWI also employed black artists, photographers, and others to assist in telling the story of what African Americans were doing to help win the war. Early in 1943 the OWI distributed 2 million copies of a large pamphlet entitled "Negroes and the War," which contained numerous pictures of black service personnel, war workers, scholars, scientists, and artists. It was of course calculated to raise the morale of African Americans, but there are serious doubts that it succeeded. Lester Granger of the National Urban League asserted that the publication was a "monumental mistake and a disservice to the government and the Negro. I say this . . . because it is like kicking a man who is down and congratulating him because he is not yet dead."

The War Department sought to raise the morale of African Americans not only by maintaining a black officer in its press section but also by accrediting black newspapermen as war correspondents. During the war about twenty African Americans covered various theaters of war for the press, but far from raising the morale of blacks, some of the reports had the opposite effect. The reports of correspondents like Ollie Stewart of the *Afro-American* and Lem Graves of the *Journal and Guide* made it clear that all was not well with African-American servicemen overseas, while Walter White's book, *A Rising Wind,* based on his visits to the war fronts, contained revelations that depressed blacks at home even more. Both the War and Navy Departments made possible the visits of leading African Americans to the war fronts in order to raise the morale of service personnel and to inform civilians at home of the activities of those at the front. Among those who went to the theaters of operation were Bishop J. A. Gregg of the AME church, Lester Granger of the National Urban League, and Matthew Bullock of the Massachusetts Parole Board.

The experience of living in two worlds had prepared blacks to wage two fights simultaneously. They felt compelled to carry on the fight for better treatment at home so as to give real meaning to the ideal of the Four Freedoms. While the double preoccupation must have caused both efforts

Walter White's Call for Victory at Home and Abroad—1944

The Negro people, like all other Americans, recognize the war as the chief issue confronting our country. We demand of any political party desiring the support of Negroes a vigorous prosecution of the war. We are opposed to any negotiated peace as advocated by the Hitler-like forces within our country. Victory must crush Hitlerism both at home as well as abroad.

In evaluating the merits of parties and candidates we must include all issues— those touching the life of Negroes as a group as well as those affecting the entire country. The party or candidate who refuses to help control prices, or fails to support the extension of social security, or refuses to support a progressive public program for full post war employment, or opposes an enlarged and unsegregated program of government-financed housing, or seeks to destroy organized labor, is as much the enemy of the Negro as is he who would prevent the Negro from voting.

Walter White and others, "A Declaration by Negro Voters," *The Crisis*, LI (January 1944), pp. 16–17.

to suffer, there is merit in the argument that both efforts were necessary. Eleanor Roosevelt had said early in the war, "The nation cannot expect colored people to feel that the United States is worth defending if the Negro continues to be treated as he is now." African Americans were determined to do all within their power to improve their own status. For them the task of keeping the home fires burning involved the elimination of discrimination and maltreatment. For them that task was as important as that of protecting the Four Freedoms abroad. If their morale continued to sink, it was because the people of the United States failed to agree with one black psychologist who observed that the morale of African Americans would not be appreciably raised "as long as concessions are made within a rigid framework of segregation." At the end of the war most blacks realized that the struggle to save America's own ideals from destruction had just begun. If America was to assume a more important role in world affairs, many African Americans became determined to see to it that race hatred was not one of the items on America's export list. Perhaps, moreover, in the broader sphere and through contact with the hundreds of millions of darker peoples the world over, America could face its own problem and solve it more effectively. At the end of the war, discerning African Americans, therefore, began to look to world organizations to help in the solution of their problems at home. It was a desperate, almost forlorn, hope, but in the face of growing reaction at home, it was one worth pursuing.

▪ The United Nations and Human Welfare

The interest of African Americans in world affairs lagged very little after Italy invaded Ethiopia in 1935. In the following year black Americans manifested considerable interest in the Spanish Civil War, and some went to Spain to fight with the Loyalist forces. The black press loudly condemned Generalissimo Franco and even warned that if he went unchallenged, his regime would constitute a threat to peace and freedom throughout the world. World War II greatly stimulated the interest of African Americans in world affairs, as it did for most Americans. A noticeable concern with colonial problems was displayed by the black press, as several newspapers engaged Japanese, Hindu, and Chinese columnists. Long before the end of the war African Americans sought to influence the course of postwar adjustment by calling attention to the importance of establishing a peace based on justice without regard to race. In 1943 Merze Tate, for example, grimly warned that "the peace that follows World War II may prove only an interlude—a breathing spell before the race and class war—unless Great Britain and the United States act to implement their professed aims. In the coming global order there must be freedom for all or freedom for none." Most African Americans seemed to feel that this was a reasonable assessment. More and more they looked toward San Francisco to see if their desires had any possibility of realization.

When the conference for the establishment of the United Nations opened in San Francisco late in April 1945, Americans were deeply mourning the recent death of President Franklin D. Roosevelt. African Americans were especially dejected. Some had deserted him in the election of 1944, but the great majority still regarded him as their best president since Lincoln. Many heaped extravagant praise on him. Some black writers "revealed" that Roosevelt had wanted to do much more for African Americans than he was able to do, that he was instrumental in securing commissions for blacks in the navy, and that he deplored conditions among colonials the world over. Now that he was gone, African Americans seemed to feel that their problems could not be solved without help from the outside. More and more they thought in terms of bringing world opinion to bear on their plight, in the hope that a healthier atmosphere would be generated. The meeting at San Francisco, coming so close upon the death of the president, was, to many blacks, "the last best hope of earth." Such a point of view could be born only of the most abject disillusionment and the most desperate plight.

They did not exaggerate the importance of the San Francisco conference. The peoples of the world looked to the meeting for formulas to eliminate war and its causes and to guarantee freedom and security. They interpreted the importance of the meeting in terms of their own difficulties. Big powers wanted machinery that would end German and Japanese aggression. Colonial peoples wanted guarantees against encroachments upon their rights by the imperial powers. Minority groups wanted guarantees that they, too, would have the opportunity to enjoy the Four Freedoms. African Americans, one of the world's most important minority groups, wanted relief from the discrimination, segregation, and oppression that the world's "arsenal of democracy" had imposed upon them.

Among American observers who were accredited by the State Department to attend the organizational meeting at San Francisco were several African Americans, including Mary McLeod Bethune of the National Council of Negro Women, Mordecai W. Johnson of Howard University, and W. E. B. Du Bois and Walter White of the NAACP. Ralph Bunche, acting chief of the division of dependent territories of the Department of State, went as a member of the official staff. Most black newspapers with national circulations sent reporters to cover the conference. Many African Americans went to San Francisco for no reason except to see if the nations of the world were capable of establishing an organization that could give relief to the many peoples who were seeking it. Most observant African Americans maintained a lively interest in the official delegates from the darker countries, especially those from India, Liberia, Ethiopia, and Haiti. There was the feeling that when these delegates spoke, they represented underprivileged peoples everywhere. Conversely, delegates from certain imperial powers, especially those from Holland, Belgium, and South Africa, were viewed with utter disgust by African Americans, who made their feelings known in their speeches and writings.

African Americans as well as other Americans had considerable difficulty in following the deliberations at San Francisco. Few understood the intricacies of international politics, and too frequently reporters and observers regarded the meetings as any other large gathering of peoples of different tongues and cultures. Many had little background to understand the numerous problems involved in establishing an organization that transcended national boundaries and at the same time sought to reconcile the desires of scores of different peoples. African Americans kept their eyes on developments that suggested that consideration was being given to underprivileged peoples. "Small Nations Demand Race Plank" and "British Evasive on Colonial Question" were typical headlines in the black press. When it became known that the black people of South Africa were protesting the treatment they received at the hands of their government, the black press of the United States emphasized that fact and pointed out that Jan Smuts had devoted his whole life to obtaining "Nazi-like domination" over his subjects. When General Smuts pleaded for an article on human rights in the United Nations charter, African Americans remembered that he had once said that every white man in South Africa except those that are "mad, quite mad" believes in the suppression of black people.

No previous international document had given such great attention to the rights of human beings as the United Nations charter. Small nations, minority groups, and colonials were pleased with the preamble to the charter which, instead of speaking of "high contracting parties," began simply, "We, the peoples of the United Nations." They begrudgingly gave General Smuts credit for wording it and wondered exactly what he meant by it. The preamble further reaffirmed "faith in fundamental human rights, in the dignity and worth of the human person, in the equal rights of men and women and of nations large and small." African Americans were especially pleased with the chapter that asserted that the United Nations would promote "Universal respect for, and observance of, human rights and fundamental freedoms for all without distinction to race, language, or religion."

Of the agencies provided for by the charter, African Americans took the liveliest interest in the Economic and Social Council and the Trusteeship Council. Under the Economic and Social Council there was established the Educational, Scientific and Cultural Organization (UNESCO), whose responsibility was to develop a worldwide program of fundamental education. It was to be concerned with those tensions that led to misunderstanding and distrust. At the first meeting of UNESCO in Paris, late in 1946, an American black, Charles S. Johnson, was in attendance as a member of the United States National Commission. There seemed to be much hope that this agency would do a great deal to promote the program that was originally conceived for it. Blacks in America hoped, too, that UNESCO would develop a program of fundamental education for Americans as well as for Europeans. Later, the creation of a Commission on Human Rights and the appointment of Eleanor Roosevelt to that body encouraged African Americans even more.

The Trusteeship Council was to safeguard the interests and welfare of non-self-governing peoples in territories held either under League of Nations mandates or detached from enemy countries after World War II. The Mandates Commission had failed to safeguard satisfactorily the welfare of dependent territories, and the mandatories too frequently administered the territories in their own interests. Membership in the Trusteeship Council was to be divided equally between countries administering trust territories and countries that had no such responsibility. Even before the formal establishment of the council, African Americans complained that it was unsatisfactory. George Padmore, writing in London, asserted that it was nothing more than a continuation of the mandates system, "modified and refurbished to accommodate the conflicting ideologies of the great powers." He admitted, however, that the provision that the council could receive petitions from people in trust territories was a "small advance." African Americans were heartened, moreover, when Ralph Bunche of the State Department's division of dependent territories joined the United Nations to work with the Trusteeship Council. They hoped that this black American specialist would somehow be able to advance substantially the welfare and interests of peoples who would be unable to promote their own interests.

African Americans admitted that it would be naive to imagine that the United Nations would be able to end racial discrimination in the United States immediately, but it seemed not too much to hope that blacks in

America would benefit by the general tendency to give greater consideration to underprivileged peoples the world over. At a meeting of the United Nations General Assembly in the autumn of 1946, that body recognized India's charges of racial discrimination practiced against East Indian nationals and their descendants in South Africa. The two-thirds majority by which the resolution was passed requiring South Africa to report at the next meeting the steps that it had taken to rectify the situation was a signal victory for domestic minorities. The delight that blacks in the United States took in the defeat of General Smuts was dampened somewhat by the fact that the United States, along with Great Britain, voted against the resolution. The assembly also approved a resolution asking that the extermination of minorities and racial and ethnic groups, such as the Nazis had practiced, be declared an international crime. This seemed to be further recogntion of the rights of minorities. The editor of the *Crisis* could correctly observe that the U.N. discussions on race were "far ahead of Versailles when President Wilson and the British would not even permit race to be discussed formally even in a committee meeting."

Encouraged by the rather liberal charter and the early actions of U.N. agencies, the National Negro Congress, late in 1946, filed a petition with the Economic and Social Council. On behalf of the black people of America, the congress sought the aid of the United Nations in the struggle to eliminate political, economic, and social discrimination in the United States. Opponents of such petitions argued that the treatment of African Americans in the United States was purely a domestic matter. They reminded American blacks that the charter of the United Nations prevented it from intervening in local and domestic problems. African Americans countered with the argument that one of the main purposes of the U.N. was to achieve international cooperation in solving problems of an economic, social, cultural, or humanitarian character. Writing on the subject, Charles H. Houston admitted that the U.N. did not have jurisdiction to investigate every lynching in Georgia or denial of the ballot in Mississippi, but "where the discrimination and denial of human rights reach a national level or where the national government either cannot or will not afford protection and redress for local aggression against colored peoples, the national policy of the United States itself becomes involved." He further pointed out that at the national policy level the U.N. can take jurisdiction. "A national policy of the United States which permits disfranchisement in the South is just as much an international issue as elections in Poland or the denial of democratic rights in Franco Spain," Houston concluded.

Houston's point was illustrated graphically by a series of events that occurred in the United States in the early months of 1947. In February the State Department inaugurated a series of broadcasts to Communist Russia to keep the people of that country informed of events in democratic America. One of the events that the Voice of America felt compelled to report on its first broadcast was the brutal lynching of a young South Carolina black who was being held in connection with the murder of a taxicab driver. In May an all-white jury exonerated twenty-eight men who had confessed that they participated in the lynching. Repercussions from the verdict could be heard in London, Paris, and Moscow. African Americans began to wonder if the outcome of the trial was a signal for a reign of terror. Within a few days a group of white North Carolinians tried to lynch a black accused of attempted assault, and only his agility in getting away prevented a repetition of the South Carolina atrocity. Again, foreign capitals manifested great interest in the form of "justice" peculiar to America. Again, African Americans wondered if America was prepared to lead the world toward a saner approach to human relations.

Some African Americans had the opportunity to serve the cause for peace and freedom by working in the United Nations. Ralph Bunche was not only the director of the Trusteeship Council but was also the winner of the Nobel Peace Prize in 1950 for his work as United Nations mediator in the Palestine dispute. Later he served as deputy secretary-general until his death in 1971. For several years William H. Dean was an economist with the Trusteeship Council, and E. Franklin Frazier was chairman of the Department of Applied Social Sciences in UNESCO for two years. Meanwhile, African Americans served regularly on the United States National Commission for UNESCO. The United States delegation to the General Assembly of the United Nations usually included a black delegate or an alternate, among them Edith Sampson, Archibald Cary, Charles H. Mahoney, Marian Anderson, and Jewell Lafontant. In 1972 an African-American congressman, Charles Diggs, resigned from the United States delegation to protest the policies of the United States in Africa.

The presence of African delegations at the United Nations headquarters in New York aroused a new interest in the international organization on the part of black Americans. It was heartening to see almost thirty new African states take their places in the family of nations, and it was particularly thrilling to see Alex Quaison-Sackey of Ghana preside over the General Assembly in 1963–1964 and Angie Brooks of Liberia serve in that capacity in 1970–1971. African Americans regarded these events as concrete evidence that black people could reach the summit in world affairs, and they hoped that white Americans would take notice. They believed, moreover, that as Africans proceeded to enjoy civil rights in the United States, except among the crudest, most bigoted Americans, they too would be the beneficiaries. Even more important for African Americans was the new stance of the United States government that sought to improve its racial policies in order to win support from the African states in the continuing rivalry with the Communist bloc.

CHAPTER 22

African Americans in the Cold War Era

■ Progress

Among the numerous adjustments the American people had to make at the end of World War II was adaptation to a new position of African Americans in the United States. This new status arose not merely because a substantial portion of the gains made during the war were retained but also because of intensification of the drive, in several quarters, to achieve equality for blacks. The war had created a climate in which substantial gains could be made, but the very nature of the emergency imposed certain restraints that could no longer be justified after 1945. Black organizations, notably the NAACP, began to press more vigorously for full equality. They were effectively assisted by numerous groups, many of them new, in various parts of the country, including political organizations and civic, labor, and religious groups. The courts, chiefly but not exclusively the federal ones, increasingly took cognizance of racial questions and rather frequently ruled in favor of equality. The executive branch of the federal government, moreover, sensitive to both domestic and foreign pressures, exerted considerable influence in eradicating the gap between creed and practice in American democracy. The interaction of these forces created a better place for African Americans as the nation moved into the second half of the twentieth century.

In several significant ways President Harry S. Truman contributed to the creation of a climate in which the status of African Americans could be improved. In 1946 he appointed a committee of distinguished black and white Americans to inquire into the condition of civil rights and to make recommendations for their improvement. The report, "To Secure These Rights," strongly denounced the denial of civil rights to some Americans, and it called for a positive program to strengthen civil rights including "the elimination of segregation, based on race, color, creed, or national origin, from American life." In the same year the president appointed another interracial committee to look into the problem of higher education. In its report the committee recommended not only the elimination of inequalities in educational opportunities but the abandonment of all forms of discrimination in higher education.

The president's efforts in the armed services did more than lend moral support to the cause for equality. The integration that had been inaugurated in the closing years of World War II was greatly accelerated in the postwar years. In 1948 the president appointed a committee to study the problem, and its report, "Freedom to Serve," was a blueprint of the steps by which integration was to be achieved. Acting on the recommendations of the committee, the army adopted a new policy in 1949 opening all jobs to qualified personnel without regard to race or color and abolishing the racial quota. The navy and air force adopted similar policies; with very few incidents to mar the transition, the armed services of the United States moved steadily toward integration, and this progress was significant.

In Korea in 1950 a battlefield test of integration was in the making. When North Korean forces began pressing the United Nations forces, especially the Ninth United States Infantry Regiment, the commanding officer began to use men from his all-black Third Battalion. They were immediately acceptable to the whites "because at a time like that, misery loves company." After Gen. Matthew Ridgway assumed command of all forces in the Far East, he asked permission from the Defense Department to integrate all African Americans throughout his command. Between May and August 1951 the extent of integration in Korea jumped from 9 percent to 30 percent of troops in the field. A special army report declared that the integration of blacks had resulted in an overall gain for the army. At long last, black Americans had become a vital and integral part of the military pool of the nation.

In public statements President Truman also lent the prestige of his office to improvement of the status of African Americans. In 1948 he issued an executive order requiring fair employment in the federal service and declared that "the principles on which our Government is based require a policy of fair employment throughout the Federal establishment without discrimination because of race, color, religion, or national origin. . . ." Despite the fact that enough Southerners were outraged with certain portions of Truman's Fair Deal policy to form the Dixiecrat party and oppose his election in 1948, the president remained firm. Four years later, after announcing his retirement from office, he said at the Howard University commencement that there should be a civil rights program backed "by the full force and power of the Federal Government" to end discrimination against minorities. He declared that the more the nation practiced the belief in equality, "the stronger, more vigorous, and happier" it would become.

The armed services were not alone in reflecting the assault on discrimination and segregation. In public housing, efforts were made to move away from segregation and toward integration. In 1950, for example, there were 177 local housing projects open to families of all races and creeds; in addition, nine states and eight cities forbade discrimination or segregation in public housing. In 1955 the administrator of the Federal Housing and Home Finance Agency called on the nation's lending agencies to lend money to members of minority groups for the purchase and construction of homes. Meanwhile, as the full implications were felt of the 1948 Supreme Court decision outlawing the enforcement of restrictive covenants, the opportunities for African Americans to secure satisfactory housing began to increase. The resultant subtle and not so subtle opposition of whites to anything resembling a black "invasion" of their neighborhoods could be seen in every section of the United States.

There were also some increases in employment opportunities for African Americans notably in the aircraft, electronics, automotive, and chemical industries. Signs of change were witnessed, moreover, in retailing establishments when firms began to hire blacks as clerks, bookkeepers, and buyers. Upgrading of African-American workers and recognition of seniority rights made it possible for some blacks to move into positions of responsibility that had hitherto been closed to them.

An important factor in the increased opportunities of black workers was the role of the unions, especially the CIO. When the much-heralded drive of the CIO to unionize Southern workers failed, African Americans in that region were left without a vigorous protagonist. Elsewhere, however, there was a general tendency for unions to increase their black membership and to elevate African Americans to positions of leadership. When the American Federation of Labor merged with the CIO in 1955, two African Americans, A. Philip Randolph and Willard Townsend, were elected vice presidents of the new organization. As black workers came to be accepted as union members and as participants in the formulation of union policy, there was some hope that the second half of the twentieth century would witness elimination of much of the racial discrimination in employment.

One of the most important influences in improving the position of blacks in American life at midcentury was the role of religious institutions and organizations. Groups like the American Friends Service Committee and the American Missionary Association gave specific attention to the problem of race tensions in communities, set up programs to improve intergroup relations, and published reports and studies involving race. The social action divisions of the major denominations became involved in racial matters, while the National Council of Churches employed staff members who gave

AFRICAN AMERICANS VOTE IN GEORGIA. For the first time in the twentieth century blacks in Marietta and other Georgia communities cast their votes in the 1946 Democratic primary. *(UPI/Bettmann.)*

full time to social problems of this nature. The Anti-Defamation League of B'nai B'rith and numerous Roman Catholic priests and bishops issued statements and adopted policies that supported the elimination of segregation and discrimination. Here and there churches began to integrate. The Church of All People in San Francisco had black and white ministers, while white and black Baptists in a small Arkansas community merged their churches, to the amazement of most observers. By contrast, the interracial, interdenominational congregation of the Reverend Jim Jones in San Francisco had a most bizarre and tragic end. Led by Jones into exile in Guyana, virtually the entire group died by murder and suicide in November 1978 following the murder of California Congressman Leo J. Ryan, whose visit greatly disturbed Jones and his assistants.

Nowhere was the change in the status of African Americans more dramatic than in the nation's capital. As early as 1947 the larger hotels in Washington began to accept black guests, and by 1956 most of them were doing so. Motion picture houses and theaters followed suit. The desegregation of the facilities of the Department of the Interior and the City Recreation Board made it possible for African Americans to use all the public parks, playgrounds, and swimming pools within the District of Columbia. In 1953 all restaurants in Washington were opened when the Supreme Court upheld the validity of an 1872 statute requiring such establishments to serve "all well-behaved" persons. One of the school desegregation cases arose in the

District of Columbia, and when the decision was handed down, President Eisenhower expressed the hope that the nation's capital would be a model for the rest of the country. Plans to desegregate went forward immediately, with the result that numerous whites fled to the suburbs in Virginia and Maryland.

By midcentury the courts and the Interstate Commerce Commission were protecting the rights of African Americans to travel without the restrictions imposed by state segregation laws. In 1950 the Supreme Court ruled that the segregation of blacks on dining cars of interstate railways was an undue burden on interstate commerce. Although an increasing number of African Americans were traveling on commercial airlines that had never been segregated, those who continued to travel by rail experienced little or no difficulty in securing first-class accommodations and in traveling across state lines without being segregated. In 1955 the Interstate Commerce Commission decreed that all racial segregation on interstate trains and buses must end by January 10, 1956. The decree also applied to waiting rooms in railway and bus terminals. As the Southern states reluctantly began to comply with the decree, some of them held to the principle of segregation by setting up separate waiting rooms for intrastate black passengers.

The steady migration of African Americans to the North and West and their concentration in important industrial communities gave them a new powerful voice in political affairs. In cities like Chicago, Detroit, and Cleveland they frequently held the balance of power in close elections, and in certain pivotal states the votes of African Americans came to be regarded as crucial in national elections. One of the institutions helping to promote this change was the Highlander Folk School founded by Myles Horton and Don West, both white Southerners, at Monteagle, Tennessee, in 1932 to promote social change through democracy, justice, and the eradication of racism. Septima Clark and Esau Jenkins, African Americans from South Carolina, played crucial roles in establishing Highlander's "citizenship schools," where black adults learned to read and register to vote. Over time, the citizenship schools produced "tens of thousands" of registered African-American voters, "profoundly altering the Southern political landscape," as Horton indicated. Meanwhile, an increasing number of blacks in the South were registering and voting. In 1947 a federal district judge, J. Waties Waring, declared that African Americans could not be excluded from the Democratic primary in South Carolina. The following year 35,000 blacks voted in the Democratic primary in that state. By 1948 the number of registered black voters in Georgia had already exceeded 150,000, and this number was even higher by the time of the next presidential election. In 1952 it was estimated that 63 percent of the eligible black electorate in Durham, North Carolina, voted regularly.

While the efforts of Southern black leaders to raise the number of African-American voters to 2 million in the election of 1952 perhaps fell short of the mark, the influence of the black voter could clearly be seen in some areas. The African-American vote was doubtless an important factor in holding Louisiana and South Carolina in the Democratic column. A survey of the vote in predominantly black districts revealed a majority for the Democratic presidential candidate, Adlai Stevenson, ranging from 56 percent in two Jersey City wards to 99 percent in one ward in Darlington, South Carolina. In 1952, as twenty years earlier, African-American voters did not follow the national trend. While some black newspapers attributed the widespread opposition of African Americans to Eisenhower's candidacy to his stand favoring army segregation as late as 1948, others said that African Americans were more concerned with retaining the gains made under the New Deal and Fair Deal programs of Roosevelt and Truman.

At state and local levels the rising influence of the African-American electorate was clearly perceptible. In 1954 Illinois sent black Democrat William Dawson to the House of Representatives of the United States Congress for his seventh consecutive term, while Adam Clayton Powell was returned from New York for his sixth term. When Charles C. Diggs, Jr., of Detroit was elected to the House on the Democratic side in the same year, it marked the first time in the twentieth century that as many as three African Americans were in Congress. Detroit sent a second black to Congress in 1964, by which time six African Americans were in the lower house. By 1956 there were about forty blacks in state legislatures, all in the North and West. The number of African Americans elected to city councils, judgeships, and boards of education increased each year. Significant among such victories were the election of Rufus E. Clement, the president of Atlanta University, to the Atlanta School Board in 1953, and in the same year the election of Hulan Jack to the presidency of the borough of Manhattan of New York City.

Appointments of African Americans to high posts in the national government were indicative of a new position of influence and respect. In 1949 William H. Hastie, with many years of distinguished public service behind him, became a judge on the Third United States Circuit Court of Appeals. Thurgood Marshall went to the circuit court in 1961 but resigned in 1965 to become solicitor general of the United States. In 1953 J. Ernest Wilkins became assistant secretary of labor, E. Frederick Morrow became an administrative assistant in the executive offices of the president, and Scovel Richardson was appointed chairman of the United States Parole Board. In the offices of several senators and members of the House of Representatives there were African-American secretaries and assistants, and others served as register of the Treasury, governor of the Virgin Islands, assistant to the director of Selective Service, and assistant to the secretary of Health, Education and Welfare.

■ Reaction

The improvement in the status of African Americans was neither uniform nor without vigorous opposition in some quarters. On the job, white workers frequently threatened to quit if blacks were employed or upgraded. While the threats were not always successful, they served to retard the advancement of blacks, as in the case of the proposed integration of the fire department in Washington, D.C. There was, likewise, resistance to any change in the voting habits of African Americans. When Judge Waring ordered that the South Carolina Democratic primary be opened to African Americans in 1947, there was a bitter denunciation of the decision. The Waring family was ostracized by whites in Charleston, and hoodlums threatened them with bodily harm. In 1956, when a Louisiana registrar disqualified whites as well as blacks who did not satisfactorily demonstrate their understanding of the Constitution, she was summarily dismissed—obviously because she failed to discriminate against blacks.

African Americans who sought to improve their own status were frequently singled out for attack. In 1956 the blacks of Montgomery, Alabama, boycotted city bus lines to avoid the alleged abuse of black passengers by white drivers, to obtain a more satisfactory seating regulation, and to secure the employment of black drivers on buses serving predominantly black sections. Almost immediately about ninety African Americans were indicted under a 1921 antiunion law forbidding conspiracy to obstruct the operation of a business. The leader, the Reverend Martin Luther King, Jr., was the first to be tried. He was found guilty. He immediately served notice of appeal, while the bus company frantically sought to settle the problem lest it go into bankruptcy. But the effective weapon of the boycott gained in popularity as the blacks of Tallahassee, Florida, followed the Montgomery plan in June 1956 and cut the local bus company's business by almost 75 percent.

There was moreover an intensification of resistance that corresponded roughly to improvement in the status of African Americans. As blacks pressed to desegregate schools, whites organized for a last-ditch stand. Among the new antiblack groups was the National Association for the Advancement of White People, with national headquarters in Washington, D.C. The organization became discredited in 1954, however, as a result of the numerous legal entanglements in which its executive director became involved. More widespread and more effective were the White Citizens' Councils, which a leading white Mississippi editor called the "Uptown Ku Klux Klans." Frankly admitting their determination to resist enforcement of the school desegregation decision, the councils called on their members to use economic reprisals against blacks who were active in the fight to desegregate the schools and against whites who favored compliance with the law. In some communities, in retaliation, African Americans began to boycott businesses operated by members of the councils. Thus, by 1956 something akin to economic warfare was being waged in the South, with many business firms caught in the middle for being regarded as either "soft" on the NAACP or favorable to the program of the councils.

In other ways Southern leaders fought the school desegregation decisions.

They considered numerous plans to avoid compliance, including turning over the public schools to private organizations, punishing as criminals anyone who attended or taught mixed classes, and encouraging "voluntary segregation." In the area of political theory they resurrected the doctrine of interposition set forth by South Carolina's chancellor, William Harper, in 1832. Early in 1956 the governors of South Carolina, Georgia, Mississippi, and Virginia called on the Southern states to declare that the federal government had no power to prohibit segregation and to "protest in appropriate language, against the encroachment of the central government upon the sovereignty of the several states and their people." Among the states that passed resolutions of interposition were Georgia, Mississippi, and Virginia, while several others considered such action.

Southern members of Congress also came forth with a vigorous denunciation of the desegregation decision. In March 1956 more than ninety Southerners, led by Sen. Walter George, presented in Congress their "declaration of Constitutional Principles," commonly known as the "Southern Manifesto." The document condemned the decision as a usurpation of the powers of the states and encouraged the use of "every lawful means" to resist its implementation. Of the three North Carolina members of Congress who refused to sign the manifesto, two were defeated in the Democratic primary the following May.

Since the NAACP had led in the fight for desegregation, it was natural that it should become the special object of attack in the resistance to change. It was widely denounced in the South as subversive, and in 1956 several states, by means of legal devices, virtually stopped its operations. In Louisiana an injunction was granted that restrained the NAACP from holding meetings until it had filed with the secretary of state a complete list of its membership. In Alabama a local judge granted an injunction against any further activities by the NAACP. In South Carolina the general assembly called for its classification as a subversive organization. Meanwhile, a member of Congress from Arkansas entered into the *Congressional Record* about forty pages of "evidence" in an attempt to show that the officers and leading members of the NAACP were un-American.

Southern resistance to any change in the status of African Americans often degenerated into violence; the machinery for maintaining law and order apparently was unable or unwilling to operate. While the bombing of black homes was not confined to the South, there were other forms of violence to be found almost exclusively in the South. Encouraged by many of their leaders to defy and disobey the law and inspired by citizens' councils and similar groups to take matters into their own hands, many white Southerners assumed responsibility for maintaining segregation at all costs. In some parts of the South the amount of violence rose to the proportions of a reign of terror. In Mississippi, for example, several African-American leaders who had urged their people to vote were murdered, one of them on the courthouse lawn in Brookhaven in the summer of 1955. A few months

INADEQUACY OF BLACK SCHOOLS. In this one-room school in Person County, North Carolina, all the facilities are in view, including the "library," "running water," and "central heating." Seven classes were taught in the room. *(Photo by Alex Rivera.)*

later the president of the NAACP in Belzoni was shot when he ignored an order to remove his name from the voting register. Near Greenwood a fourteen-year-old black boy from Chicago was murdered for allegedly whistling at a white storekeeper's wife. In few of these incidents was any white person even accused of having committed a crime, and in none of them was there a conviction.

By early 1956, as Southern whites despaired of retaining segregation, they became increasingly immoderate in their actions. When the state of Alabama was ordered to admit Autherine Lucy, a black applicant, to the University of Alabama, the students and townspeople of Tuscaloosa resorted to violence to prevent her from remaining at the university. Even with heavy police escort and in the company of the dean of women, her car was pelted with stones and some people even jumped on top of the car. When she was suspended because of the rioting, she accused university officials of conspiring to keep her out of the university. As a result she was expelled by the board of regents. A few weeks later, in Birmingham, Nat "King" Cole, an

African-American singer, was attacked by a group of whites while he was performing on the stage of the city auditorium before an all-white audience.

Responsible citizens in the North and South began to express concern over mounting race tensions. Some called for moderation, without too carefully defining it. Others called for federal action, but neither the president nor Congress seemed inclined to enter the picture. All agreed, however, that the problem of African Americans' status continued to be disturbing at home and embarrassing abroad.

■ Urbanization and Its Consequences

One of the most dramatic facts of life for black Americans in the postwar years was their continuing urbanization and the profound impact this process had on them both as individuals and as a community. Of the 15 million blacks in the United States in 1950 about 52 percent were living in metropolitan areas. Thirty years later, there would be approximately 26 million blacks, 81 percent of whom were living in metropolitan areas. Meanwhile, the statistics for whites living in metropolitan areas for the same years would show a more modest, but nevertheless substantial, increase from 56 to 73 percent. Looked at another way, the black central-city population increased from 6.1 million in 1950 to 15.3 million in 1980. During these years there was a steady flow of whites from the central city to the suburbs, with a slight trend back to the city just becoming noticeable in the 1980s. In 1968 only two major cities in the United States, Washington and Charleston, had more blacks than whites. By 1980 no fewer than fifteen major cities, including Atlanta, Detroit, New Orleans, Baltimore, and Richmond, had a majority of blacks in their populations.

Just as blacks arrived in the central city, whites not only departed but took with them the employment opportunities that blacks sought. Consequently, with industrial parks opening in the suburbs and beyond, far out of the reach of blacks who sought employment and often in communities where they were not welcome as residents, blacks remained in the central city, often subsisting on part-time work, unemployment benefits while they lasted, or welfare in one form or another. Factories and shops that had once graced the central city and given it life as well as hope were shut down, began to deteriorate, and frequently were razed to make way for a new highway leading to the suburban industrial parks, shopping malls, and carefully zoned residential areas. The factories that remained, if any, were updated into high-tech industries requiring special skills and fewer personnel, thus creating structural unemployment that would doubtless remain a critical problem for blacks and for many other Americans for the remainder of the century.

The black ghetto that had become a fixture in urban America earlier in the twentieth century gained a measure of permanence during the black

TABLE 7

The Growth and Distribution of the African-American Population in Selected Cities, 1940 and 1990

CITY	1940[a] (IN THOUSANDS)	1990 (IN THOUSANDS)
Birmingham	109	158
Boston	25	126
Chicago	282	1,197
Detroit	151	759
Los Angeles	98	505
Miami	37	87
New Orleans	150	308
New York	477	1,784
Oakland	14	159
Philadelphia	253	639
San Francisco	32	86
Seattle	14	47
Washington D.C.	189	448

[a]*1940 figures include all nonwhites.*

Source: U. S. Department of Commerce. Statistical Abstract of the United States, 1946, 1981, 1986. Bureau of the Census. Washington, D. C., 1946, 1981, 1986.

migration of the war and postwar years. While Supreme Court decisions barred both the exclusion of blacks from certain sections or blocks in the city and covenants that restricted residential occupancy to certain preferred groups, usually white, race-based housing patterns tended to remain the same. If African Americans attempted to move into neighborhoods where they were not wanted, they often met stern resistance, hostility, and even violence. In 1951 a black couple was all but driven from a home they had purchased in Cicero, Illinois. The angry mob broke windows, mutilated the exterior, and shouted vile epithets at the couple. In succeeding decades, into the 1980s, there were repetitions of the Cicero incident. In Birmingham, Chicago, and Detroit, homes of blacks were attacked by whites who resented their presence. In New York City the policy of excluding blacks from the Stuyvesant Town housing project aroused a controversy that stimulated the drive for legislation against discrimination in housing. Indeed, as Reynolds Farley has pointed out, there persisted a high level of racial segregation in housing, "with no more than modest changes in recent decades." Even after the 1968 passage of the Fair Housing Act which barred racial discrimination in the sale, rental, or financing of most housing units, there were no substantial decreases in housing segregation during the ensuing years.

James Baldwin Reflects on the Ghetto—1960

They work in the white man's world all day and come home in the evening to this fetid block. They struggle to instill in their children some private sense of honor or dignity which will help the child to survive. This means, of course, that they must struggle, stolidly, incessantly, to keep this sense alive in themselves, in spite of the insults, the indifference, and the cruelty they are certain to encounter in their working day. They patiently browbeat the landlord into fixing the heat, the plaster, the plumbing; this demands prodigious patience, nor is patience usually enough. . . . Such frustration, so long endured, is driving many strong, admirable men and women whose only crime is color to the very gates of paranoia. . . .

The people who have managed to get off this block have only got as far as a more respectable ghetto. This respectable ghetto does not even have the advantages of the disreputable one—friends, neighbors, a familiar church, and friendly tradesmen. . . . Every Sunday, people who have left the block take the lonely ride back, dragging their increasingly discontented children with them. They spend the day talking, not always with words, about the trouble they've seen and the trouble—one must watch their eyes as they watch their children—they are only too likely to see. For children do not like ghettos. It takes them nearly no time to discover exactly why they are there.

James Baldwin, *Nobody Knows My Name* (New York, 1960), pp. 59–63.

Seldom did whites, Northern or Southern, yield to blacks who sought housing among them. The violence that arose from such efforts in the 1970s and 1980s was a painful reminder that the nation had far to go before racially integrated neighborhoods would be a reality.

The northward migration of African Americans that began during the war continued in ensuing decades, complicating not only the problem of housing but that of employment as well. Discrimination in employment persisted, despite gains that had been made during the war. In 1947 the president's Committee on Civil Rights recommended the enactment of fair employment legislation at both the federal and state levels. When no such legislation was forthcoming, Presidents Truman and Eisenhower established committees to see that there was no discrimination in companies that were filling government contracts. Meanwhile, some states had already begun to set up fair employment committees, and as early as 1956 sixteen states and thirty-six cities had such committees working toward the elimination of discrimination in employment.

For many black newcomers to the city, employment failed to materialize. Without decent places to live and with unemployment or underemployment as their fate, they were vulnerable to most of the forces that operated to debase and degrade them. Men were less likely to secure employment than women, thus replicating the Southern rural experience where the perception of black masculinity was constantly challenged at home and in the workplace. Unemployment and idleness brought on frustration, not infrequently culminating in abuse of family at home and criminal acts away from home, such as petty thievery, public drunkenness, and street brawls. The long-revered extended family, where aunts and grandmothers assumed the role of homemakers and keepers of family traditions while husbands and wives were at work, seemed, in the absence of a stable family organization, both redundant and out of place.

These were among the major factors that have led to the dramatic deterioration of the African-American family in recent years. Even in the face of such obstacles as the slave system, legal segregation, discrimination, poverty, and racially hostile policies of government and society, the fabric of the African-American family had managed to hold together until about three decades ago. Indeed, until the 1960s, a remarkable 75 percent of black families included both husband and wife. The sharp rise in black female-headed households since 1970 was the most significant indication of the deterioration of the black family. In 1983 about 48 percent of black families with related children under 18 were headed by women, 50 percent of all black children under 18 lived in female-headed households, and the vast majority of these women suffered from an oppressive poverty that made it impossible for them to care adequately for their children.

More stable than the African-American family perhaps, but also deeply affected by urbanization, was the black church. As African Americans went to the city in ever-increasing numbers, they took with them their habits of church affiliation, churchgoing, and a general loyalty to religious institutions. The older, established denominations cautiously welcomed the newcomers and at times assisted them in their adjustment. There were, in addition, new religious groups and cults that began to compete with the older groups. Some were mere variations of the older groups, emphasizing greater fundamentalism and emotionalism in an attempt to save the newcomers from the sinister attractions of the city. Others were independent, with no denominational affiliation, appealing primarily to the new materialism with which many of the newcomers were obsessed. All of them sought to fill the void in the lives of the new arrivals by providing social as well as religious communion for their members. No one realized more than church leaders how easy it was for newcomers to fall into the habit of remaining at home on Sunday or becoming involved with a variety of secular activities to the exclusion of churchgoing. Despite the vigorous efforts of many ministers and pastors, they lost many of their members to the other attractions that the city offered.

Churches themselves became involved in numerous secular activities in their efforts to provide better services for their members. Since the 1920s many of them had begun day-care services for working parents, Boy and Girl Scout troops, couples clubs for young married people, and a variety of other social services. With the increase in the number of senior citizens and with a growing consciousness of their special needs, many churches also established clubs for them and developed special programs for their benefit. Assistance with Social Security matters, sightseeing excursions, and recreational activities were merely a few of the programs arranged for older members. For the restive black youth, dissatisfied with the slow pace of improvement in the status of African Americans, churches set up groups that attempted to channel the energies of these young people into activities more creative and more "constructive" than the activities of the radical groups that sought to attract them away from the church or those who sought to lure them into immoral and illegal habits and activities. Meanwhile, an increasing number of African-American clergy became politically active and in numerous instances ran for public office themselves.

The increase in the African-American urban population significantly affected certain types of black businesses that performed special services in the black community. One was newspaper publishing, the character of which changed even as it grew. The pioneer newspapers, such as the New York *Amsterdam News*, the Pittsburgh *Courier*, the Chicago *Defender*, the Norfolk *Journal and Guide*, and the Baltimore *Afro-American*, were no longer papers with a national circulation and a readership from coast to coast. They continued, nevertheless, to serve the community in which they were published and its surrounding areas with perhaps an intensity of focus that had been somewhat lacking in earlier years. Some of their functions as national newspapers had been preempted by local predominantly white newspapers that gave increasing attention to events in the African-American community including weddings, funerals, and church news. Some functions were taken up by *Jet*, the Johnson Publishing Company's mass-circulation pocket-size weekly magazine that contained all the news and more than the national weekly newspapers had once carried. Finally, many of the local black weeklies grew in size and influence (thanks to advertising revenue primarily from white businesses) and provided local news and information much better than any national paper had ever done. The Winston-Salem *Chronicle*, the Tulsa *Oklahoma Eagle*, and the New Orleans *Louisiana Weekly* are examples of new or reinvigorated weekly newspapers that effectively served their local customers. Specialty magazines that appeared and have met with success ranging from moderate to spectacular include the durable *Black Enterprise; Dollars and Sense*, a rapidly growing Chicago-based business magazine; *Essence*, devoted to the interests of black women; and *Visions*, a new magazine of African-American culture. Johnson Publishing Company's *Ebony*, with a monthly circulation well beyond 1 million, continued to be the most successful publishing venture in the history of black journalism.

Black-owned or -operated financial institutions grew steadily in the postwar years. The few savings and loan associations operated by African

Americans at the beginning of the century had increased to thirty-seven by 1980, with assets approaching 1 billion dollars. Banks likewise multiplied. Most major cities in the North and East had at least one black-owned bank, while some, like Chicago, had as many as three. Where branch banking was permitted, as in North Carolina, the Mechanics and Farmers Bank maintained five branches in Durham and nearby communities. In later years, the presence of blacks on the staffs of predominantly white banks, where they filled positions from teller to vice president and board member, opened up employment and financial opportunities to African Americans that had not hitherto existed. For years, insurance companies serving African Americans had been strong, thanks to the tradition of self-supporting benefit societies dating from the years following the Civil War. In the postwar years black insurance companies ranked among the most stable financial institutions in the black community. This was in marked contrast to the years of the Depression when several of the presumably stronger ones went into insolvency. This did not cause African Americans to lose faith in the insurance business, and by 1985 there were some fifty black-owned insurance companies, of which the North Carolina Mutual Life Insurance Company, the Atlanta Life Insurance Company, and the Golden State Life Insurance Company were the largest.

In general, large-scale manufacturing seemed to be beyond the resources available to African Americans. In areas where competition was keen and large outlays of capital were required, African Americans as a rule simply were unable to make a serious effort. There were a few exceptions, however, the most notable of which was in the manufacture of beauty aids and hair grooming products. Here, tradition and experience gave blacks an advantage. In the postwar years several companies undertook the manufacture of such items, of which the Johnson Products Company of Chicago was the most successful. With Afro-Sheen as its leading item, the company came to dominate the field of cosmetics and hair grooming products for African Americans. It was such a lucrative field that it soon attracted other manufacturers, both black and white. Soon the Johnson Publishing Company came out with a whole line of beauty aids called Fashion Fair, advertised as "another fine product from *Ebony*," which garnered a portion of the market. White companies, notably Revlon, entered the field apparently to make the point that beauty that was merely skin deep could be improved by anyone, without regard to race, color, or national origin.

African Americans also entered the white business world in increasing numbers. Realizing, apparently, that the 100 leading black businesses listed annually by *Black Enterprise* were not even in the same league with the *Fortune* 500 as far as financial strength and power were concerned, they went into the white world of banking, mercantile establishments, manufacturing, high-tech industries, transportation, fast food, and a variety of service agencies. Some moved up to managerial positions and even served as vice presidents. Although most remained below the policy-making level, in sheer numbers they augmented significantly the group known as the black middle class. Some of the more skilled and gifted of the black executives in the white corporate world began to feel that there were clearly defined limits beyond which they could not go, regardless of their abilities. Reluctantly reaching the conclusion that the business world was not color blind, they began to leave their companies to establish businesses of their own or to open consulting firms that served whites as well as blacks.

■ Writers and Artists in Later Years

African-American writers of the prewar and war years continued to produce, even as new writers vied for center stage. Ralph Ellison, who became Albert Schweitzer Professor Emeritus at New York University in 1979, continued to write critical essays and short stories, bringing out *Going to the Territory* in 1986. James Baldwin, compromising his expatriation sufficiently to spend months at a time in the United States, maintained his popularity and influence, especially with the 1986 publication of *Evidence of Things Not Seen.* Leon Forrest's *There Is a Tree More Ancient Than Eden* was described by one critic as a highly experimental work, while his *The Bloodworth Orphans* was praised for its dramatic realism. Both were remarkable for their controlled force and power, so central to their messages. Toni Morrison, an editor at Random House, became recognized as a major author with three highly successful novels, *The Bluest Eye, Sula,* and *Song of Solomon,* which was a Book-of-the-Month Club selection in 1977.

One of the most successful and fascinating works of this period was *Roots,* by Alex Haley, which became the basis for a television miniseries; for an entire week in 1977 millions of viewers saw *Roots,* and in 1978, *Roots, the Next Generation.* This dramatic story of an African-American family—from the capture of an African in the eighteenth century to the time of Haley himself—together with the subsequent heightened interest by Americans of all races in family history and genealogy, produced what some have called "the *Roots* phenomenon."

The number and variety of African-American writers increased markedly in the 1970s and 1980s. Among the novelists was Albert Murray, whose *Trainwhistle Guitar* is a poignant, realistic story of growing up in Alabama, which he followed with two more successful works, *The Hero and the Blues* and *Stomping the Blues.* A similar appreciation for the connection between art and life characterizes much of the work of Maya Angelou, especially her autobiographical writings such as *I Know Why the Caged Bird Sings* and *The Heart of a Woman.* The master of the short story, James A. McPherson, was trained in law at Harvard before he turned to a writing career. *Hue and Cry* won him critical acclaim in 1969, while *Elbow Room* won the Pulitzer Prize for fiction in 1978, followed by his receiving a coveted MacArthur Fellowship. One of the writers whose work shows a deep understanding of time

NOBEL LAUREATE TONI MORRISON. At the National Writers Convention in New York City, Morrison, author of a Pulitzer Prize novel and other works, chats with Chicago author and interviewer Studs Terkel. *(AP/Wide World Photos.)*

and place and uses it to advantage in writing about the Deep South was Ernest J. Gaines, who was born in Louisiana and remained there long enough to absorb its special ways before moving to California. His best-known work, *The Autobiography of Miss Jane Pittman,* viewed by millions on television, reveals a familiarity with Southern habits and mores and demonstrates both sensitivity and compassion.

Among the poets, Robert Hayden proved to be one of the most durable writers. As poetry consultant at the Library of Congress (preceding Gwendolyn Brooks by a decade), he did some of his most interesting and effective work. In *American Journal,* named after his University of Michigan Phi Beta Kappa poem of 1976, Hayden paid tribute to his predecessors, Phillis Wheatley and Paul Laurence Dunbar. But his sense of the present is reflected in "Elegies for Paradise Valley," a Detroit subcommunity, and "Astronauts." There were younger poets too—Nikki Giovanni, Sam Allen, Audre Lorde, Lucile Clifton, Michael Harper—who were as observant of life's cruelties as they were of its pleasures. Another, Rita Dove, not only won the Pulitzer Prize for her volume of poetry, *Thomas and Beulah,* but in 1993 became the youngest United States poet laureate.

While the number of African-American playwrights remained relatively small, there was ample talent among them, just as in the other areas of literary expression. The versatile and gifted Amiri Baraka (Le Roi Jones) added to his influence and prestige when he founded the Black Arts Repertory Theater School in Harlem in 1964. There he presented his own plays, as well as those of his colleagues and students, and gave promising young playwrights the opportunity to read their plays. Playwright Douglas Turner Ward founded the Negro Ensemble Company, whose rendition of his *Day of Absence,* a satire in which he explores what happens when for one day all blacks who work for white people take the day off, was seen by a nationwide television audience. Lonnie Elder's *Sounder* was also seen on nationwide television, while his *Ceremonies in Dark Old Men* won many kudos, including the Los Angeles Drama Critics Award. Meanwhile, Charles Gordone's *No Place to Be Somebody* won the Pulitzer Prize for drama in 1970.

Three trends in African-American writing were discernible in the postwar years, although not all black writers could be identified with one or any of them. One was the Black Arts Movement in which its leaders, including Amiri Baraka (Le Roi Jones), insisted that black art was the "esthetic and spiritual sister of the Black Power concept." These writers, most of whom were young and shared similar revolutionary visions, sought to create a "separate symbolism, mythology, critique, and iconology." Aside from Jones and Laurence Neal (one of the theoreticians of the movement), several members of the movement are outstanding poets, among them Don Lee, Sonia Sanchez, and Nikki Giovanni.

Another trend was a response to the Black Arts Movement by its critics who sought to develop what they called a Black Aesthetic. Principal among them were George Kent and Addison Gayle who believed that the black writer, while not ignoring social themes, should be concerned primarily with constructing a set of critical opinions, rules, and criteria by which black writing should be judged. A group of these critics presented their views in a 1971 volume, edited by Gayle, titled simply, *The Black Aesthetic.* In *Blackness and the Adventure of Western Culture,* Kent emphasized the importance of folk and cultural tradition, "loosely defined, on which the writer can enforce as much signification as definitions can be made to bear." For Kent and his colleagues, those traditions should in turn reflect theories and values which at times may or may not be the same as those one finds in Western culture.

Finally, there was the trend that can best be described as the domination of the broad field of literary expression by African-American women writers. Since Phillis Wheatley's time there have been black women writers—including some outstanding ones during the Harlem Renaissance—but never in the number, power, and influence that they reached by the mid-1960s. This trend was in part a result of the determination of women of all races to gain more independence, as well as respect, from men, coupled with the growing awareness by African-American men and women that they had an important role to play in this society: in politics, the world of business, and everything else, including writing. Moreover, black women writers assumed a special role in voicing the long-suppressed feelings of women about the insensitivity, neglect, and abuse they had suffered at the hands of their menfolk. Although not always a major theme in their writing, in many instances it was there for all to see. Although Carlene Hatcher Polite's *The Flagellants* appeared in 1967 depicting the disintegration of a black couple's relationship, it was a Broadway play, *For Colored Girls Who Have Considered Suicide/When the Rainbow Is Enuf* by Ntozake Shange, that served notice that the tension between black women writers and black men was building.

The basic theme was carried forward in 1979 by Michelle Wallace in *Black Macho and the Myth of the Superwoman.* While Wallace criticized African-American males for being interested primarily in securing their own rights, she conceded that black women were angry with black men as a way of "blaming someone else for their underdevelopment." There were others: Gayle Jones's *Corregidora* and Toni Cade Bambara's *The Seabirds Are Still Alive.* The most widely read and most influential black woman writer, however, was Alice Walker, whose *The Third Life of Grange Copeland* was a portent of what was to come. In *The Color Purple,* for which she received the Pulitzer Prize in 1982 and which was subsequently made into a highly successful film, Walker spoke her piece about African-American men. The unspeakable sexual abuse of Celie, the heroine, by her stepfather, and the many years of beating by a husband, set the stage for a far-ranging indictment of the African-American male. The ensuing bitter reaction by the outraged and shaken black male population neither softened the blow nor caused Walker and her fellow sufferers to retreat. It was a bold warning that African-American women would no longer pander to the demands of a polite society that wished them to remain silent. Even so, some women began to feel that they had perhaps become a bit excessive. Shange's *Betsey Brown,* Gloria Naylor's *Linden Hills,* and even Walker's *Meridian* were not nearly as preoccupied with the brutality of the black male as some of their earlier writings had been.

Even as the gender gap began to manifest itself, African Americans—women and men—were beginning to take stock of their own writings, and their critical evaluations were generally free of carping or grudge. With the perspective provided by his commitment to the Black Aesthetic, George Kent dealt with African-American authors from Claude McKay to Ralph Ellison in *Blackness and the Adventure of Western Culture.* Much more traditional, but reflecting the wisdom that years of study and teaching had provided, Arthur P. Davis covered essentially the same ground in *From the Dark Tower: Afro-American Writers, 1900 to 1960.* Displaying a versatility and range which few writers or critics could boast, Houston Baker produced two volumes, *The Journey Back: Issues in Black Literature and Criticism* and *Blues, Ideology, and Afro-American Literature: A Vernacular Theory.* Several literary critics joined in the effort to view the entire field and produced, under the editorship of Henry L. Gates, *Black Literature and Literary Theory.*

Meanwhile, women writers began to look at themselves, with the result that two important works undertook the evaluation of their work: *Black Women Writers at Work,* edited by Claudia Tate, and *Black Women Writers,*

1950–1980, edited by Mari Evans. Blyden Jackson was not only senior editor of *The History of Southern Literature* (to which Trudier Harris contributed a comprehensive essay on recent writings) but also brought out *The Waiting Years: Essays on American Negro Literature.* Finally, Michael Harper and Robert Stepto edited *Chant of Saints,* containing some of the best prose, poetry, and literary criticism of the period. As one views these and other productions, one cannot resist the temptation to compare the intellectual and literary vitality of the 1970s and 1980s with that of the 1920s. The comparison would seem to be on the whole favorable.

In the graphic arts, African Americans received much recognition in the postwar years. The painter Hale Woodruff of Atlanta University and New York University won numerous prizes for his works; his murals in the Talladega College Library, portraying the mutiny of the slaves aboard the *Amistad* in 1839, were regarded as artistic history at its best. Charles Alston of New York proved to be one of the most versatile of the African-American artists. His portraits, caricatures, and pieces of sculpture are to be found in several major American museums. Lois Mailou Jones and James Porter of Howard University won recognition for their work in oils, and by midcentury Ernest Crichlow, Romare Bearden, and E. Simms Campbell were among the leading illustrators and caricaturists in the United States. Meanwhile, Charles White became a leading interpreter of African-American life by depicting, in the words of Samella Lewis, "idealized Black heroes and the struggling Black masses." Elizabeth Catlett, already a leading printmaker and sculptor in the early postwar years, became one of the pioneer expatriots of this period by moving to Mexico where she continued to turn out works of distinction. Part of her series on black heroes, *Malcolm Speaks for Us,* is a prize-winning linocut that won acclaim from major art critics when it appeared in 1969.

Like James Porter before him, David Driskell was both an artist and a scholar in the field. From Fisk University, and later at the University of Maryland, Driskell was a commanding voice in the promotion of African-American art. There were others, including Herman Bailey and Raymond Saunders, whose works reflect their contact with African techniques and materials, and Lucile Roberts and Paul Keene whose works show the influence not only of Africa and the United States but other parts of the world as well. The premier painter of the period, however, was Jacob Lawrence who has been described as an artist of "remarkable personal vitality" with a "strong command of pictorial organization." Perhaps more importantly, he represented the first generation of recognized artists nurtured, as Samella Lewis indicated, by the black experience: "his community [Richmond and Chicago] was Black, his early teachers were Black, and his first encouragement came from Blacks." His works on the black diaspora, migration, city life, slums, Toussaint L'Ouverture, and numerous other subjects have been acclaimed in many parts of the world. A retrospective exhibition, shown in many cities in 1986–1987, was a fitting tribute to his high standing in the world of art.

HALE WOODRUFF, "TRIAL OF THE AMISTAD MUTINEERS." A mural in the Savery Library of Talladega College celebrating the centennial of the trial and acquittal of the slave mutiny in 1839. *(Courtesy, Savery Library, Talladega College, Alabama.)*

In sculpture one finds both men and women in the top ranks. Elizabeth Prophet's work in wood and stone was outstanding. Her *Congolaise* and *Head of a Negro* were widely reproduced as examples of the successful use of black subjects in these difficult mediums. Augusta Savage's *Head of Dr. Du Bois* was one of the best-known pieces of black sculpture in America, while her *Lift Every Voice and Sing* was praised by many at the 1939 New York World's Fair as a noble expression of African Americans in music. Selma Burke achieved wide recognition for her work on a statue of Franklin D. Roosevelt for the Recorder of Deeds building in Washington. Richmond Barthé became a celebrated sculptor of the postwar years. His busts of famous actors and actresses, including John Gielgud and Katherine Cornell, displayed his talents in the field. *Shoe Shine Boy* and *The Boxer* were highly praised by art critics. His preeminence was acknowledged in 1946 when he was commissioned to do a bust of Booker T. Washington for the Hall of Fame at New York University and later to do one of George W. Carver, also for the Hall of Fame. Still later, Richard Hunt became one of America's leading direct-metal sculptors, specializing in large pieces cast in bronze and steel for outdoor settings. *Why* at the University of Chicago, *Orpheus* at the Azalee Marshall Activities Center in Temple, Texas, and *Mountain Flight* at the Greenville County Museum in South Carolina, are examples of his work and the recognition it has received.

One rarely saw a black face in a major symphony orchestra as late as

Mary McLeod Bethune's Last Will and Testament

I leave you love. Love builds. It is positive and helpful. It is more beneficial than hate. . . .

I leave you hope. The Negro's growth will be great in the years to come. Yesterday, our ancestors endured the degradation of slavery, yet they retained their dignity. Today, we direct our economic and political strength toward winning a more abundant and secure life. . . .

I leave you the challenge of developing confidence in one another. As long as Negroes are hemmed into racial blocs by prejudice and pressure, it will be necessary for them to band together for economic betterment. . . .

I leave you a thirst for education. Knowledge is the prime need of the hour. More and more, Negroes are taking full advantage of hard-won opportunities for learning, and the educational level of the Negro population is at its highest point in history. . . .

I leave you a respect for the uses of power. We live in a world which respects power above all things. Power, intelligently directed, can lead to more freedom. Unwisely directed, it can be a dreadful, destructive force. . . .

I leave you faith. Faith is the first factor in a life devoted to service. Without faith, nothing is possible. With it, nothing is impossible. . . .

I leave you racial dignity. I want Negroes to maintain their human dignity at all costs. We, as Negroes, must recognize that we are the custodians as well as the heirs of a great civilization. . . .

I leave you a desire to live harmoniously with your fellow men. The problem of color is world-wide. . . .

I leave you finally a responsibility to our young people. . . . Our children must never lose their zeal for building a better world. They must not be discouraged from aspiring to greatness. . . . Nor must they forget that the masses of our people are still underprivileged, ill-housed, impoverished and victimized by discrimination. . . .

The Freedom Gates are half ajar. We must pry them fully open.

Mary McLeod Bethune, "Last Will and Testament," *Ebony*, August, 1955.

1986, and several African-American performers have insisted that it was old-fashioned racism manifesting itself. A violinist resigned as the sole African-American member of the New York Philharmonic, indicating that he was weary of being the "token" black. A few instrumentalists reached the top of their fields, however. One of the most popular and successful among the piano virtuosos was André Watts. Having performed with the Philadelphia Symphony Orchestra at age ten and with the New York Philharmonic under Leonard Bernstein at age sixteen, he was considered by many critics to be one of the "deans" of world pianists as he approached his fortieth birthday in 1986. For the time being, African-American conductors have had to content themselves with serving as associate or guest conductors, except in Europe where Dean Dixon and several others have held regular posts.

Vocalists have fared much better. Although Leontyne Price retired from the Metropolitan Opera to devote herself to the concert stage, Shirley Verrett, Grace Bumbry, and Jessye Norman became the mainstays and, in addition, captivated audiences on both sides of the Atlantic. There were several bright stars at the Met and elsewhere. Kathleen Battle joined the select few as a leading coloratura soprano, Leona Mitchell inherited much of the Price repertoire, Barbara Hendricks added important new roles, including *Der Rosenkavalier*, and Simon Estes, fresh from European triumphs, became a leading bass at the Metropolitan. The Met's production of George Gershwin's *Porgy and Bess* in its 1985–1986 season provided several new opportunities for African-American singers since Gershwin stipulated that only blacks should sing in the opera. Thus, singers such as Gregory Hubbard, Bruce Everett, Gregory Baker, and Vinson Cole secured opportunities not only to perform in that opera but to take on numerous other roles as well.

■ Heard and Seen by Millions

The vibrancy and creativity that had characterized African-American musical expression during the Depression and war years continues down to the present. The growth in the influence of black popular music as an expression of aesthetic, political, and religious values widely held in the African-American community was directly related to the increased earning power of many blacks during the postwar years. Those able to secure jobs with decent or better wages in industry, the service sector, the civil service, or through work in the professions, now had the means to patronize the theaters, night clubs, and cabarets in which their favorite artists performed and, more importantly, to purchase their records. Recordings enhanced and established the reputations of artists by giving them access to larger audiences, and in some cases they provided African-American artists with their most stable source of income, thus encouraging them to continue to refine and develop their skills in the face of many other discouragements.

Jazz, both instrumental and vocal, continued to show great dynamism. Instrumentalists such as Charlie Parker, Dizzy Gillespie, Thelonious Monk, and Max Roach, all of whom had begun their careers as innovative developers of the jazz idiom on the eve of World War II, were joined during the postwar period by equally talented and inventive younger musicians such as Miles Davis, John Coltrane, Cannonball Adderly, and the composer Quincy Jones. In the 1970s, the ascendancy of Wynton Marsalis, who received acclaim for performances on both the jazz and the classical trumpet, provided another expression of the versatility and musical sensitivity of black artists.

FILM DIRECTOR, TRAIL BLAZER. Spike Lee, director of numerous films, including *School Daze, Do the Right Thing, Jungle Fever,* and *Malcolm X,* arriving at the 62nd Academy Awards. *(Reuters/Bettmann.)*

Jazz vocalists played an important role in the popularization of jazz; Sarah Vaughan, Dinah Washington, Al Jarreau, and Lou Rawls were among the most popular.

The creative ferment in African-American music was so diverse and widespread in the postwar decades that categories such as rhythm and blues, soul, balladeer, gospel, and crossover artist were utilized to denote various singing styles. James Brown, Muddy Waters, Aretha Franklin, and groups like the Shirelles, the Four Tops, the Supremes, and the Jackson Five were representative of some of the most successful rhythm and blues and soul singers. Leading gospel singers included Mahalia Jackson, James Cleveland, the Five Blind Boys, and the Staple Singers. Balladeers, many of whom sang music that included a variety of so-called black-and-white styles, included Nat "King" Cole, Billy Eckstein, Dionne Warwick, and George Benson. The outstanding new feature in the career pattern of African-American artists in

BILL COSBY'S "HUXTABLES." The "Cosby Show," through its comic depictions of the adventures of an upper-middle-class family, gave many American television viewers a new perspective on the black experience. Cosby portrayed "Heathcliffe Huxtable, M.D.," on the Emmy award winning show. *(1986, National Broadcasting Company, Inc. All Rights Reserved.)*

the popular-music field during these years was the crossover phenomenon, a term used to describe artists such as Johnny Mathis, Ray Charles, Stevie Wonder, Diana Ross, and Michael Jackson who gained large followings in white as well as black communities, placing them among the highest earners in the entertainment industry. In return, a number contributed financially and artistically to the various movements for African-American equality or to international causes such as the African Famine Relief Fund.

After World War II talented and versatile African Americans had careers that traversed stage and screen. Ossie Davis and his wife Ruby Dee starred

BRYANT GUMBEL AND SOVIET LEADERS. Bryant Gumbel became the co-host on NBC's "Today" Show in 1982. Here, he is interviewing the Soviet chief of general staff Sergei Akhromeyev (center) and the Soviet deputy foreign minister Grigori Kornienko (right). *(AP/Wide World Photos.)*

in the Broadway hit *Purlie Victorious*—also written by Davis—and in the film version of *Gone Are the Days*. Sammy Davis, Jr., played numerous roles in motion pictures, became a television star, and had a long, successful run on Broadway in the title role of *Golden Boy*. Comedians such as Dick Gregory and Godfrey Cambridge introduced biting satire on racial themes in their night club and television performances. Harry Belafonte attracted huge audiences with his unique singing of folk music and his dramatic roles in motion pictures. In films, however, the outstanding star during the 1950s and 1960s was Sidney Poitier, who won the coveted Academy Award for best actor in 1963 for his performance in *Lilies of the Field*.

After 1960, in response to pressures generated by the civil rights movement, many more films with African-American actors were made and the range broadened in depicting the black experience. These films were not only sources of jobs, training, and exposure for underemployed black performers, but in some instances film companies utilized black directors, a major breakthrough. Some of these pictures, however, produced mixed feelings in the African-American community, where they were often called "blaxploitation films," and were sharply criticized by some individuals and organizations for their heavy focus on crime, sex, and violence. By the mid-1970s, the film industry's intense interest in black themes had ebbed, and black actors "virtually disappeared from the screen."

The only variants during the 1980s were the popularity of films starring

The Passion of Muhammad Ali

"THE PASSION OF MUHAMMAD ALI." Muhammad Ali's refusal, on religious grounds, to serve in the United States Armed Forces and his opposition to the Vietnam War resulted in the loss of his title as world heavyweight champion. After lengthy court battles, the title was restored and he was given a military exemption. (*Courtesy of* Esquire.)

comedians Richard Pryor and Eddie Murphy and the box office successes of the film version of Alice Walker's *The Color Purple* (1986) and black filmmaker Spike Lee's low-budget *She's Gotta Have it* (1986). Lee's film, as cinema historian Donald Bogle pointed out, "introduced a new type of black movie comedy" and gave the "black independent [film] movement . . . commercial viability." The series of exciting, controversial, and commercially successful films Lee produced over the next few years, including *Malcolm X* in 1992, identified him as one of the most creative and challenging figures in American cinema. He was representative of a growing group of black male and female filmmakers whose works received increasingly serious attention from Americans of all races.

Moving from isolated appearances as servants and comic figures, most notably in *Beulah*, whose title character (played at various times by actresses

1975 WIMBLEDON CHAM-PION. Arthur Ashe trium-phantly holds aloft the Cup after defeating another Ameri-can, Jimmy Connors. Ashe later served as captain of the United States Davis Cup team. *(UPI/Bettmann Newsphotos.)*

Ethel Waters, Hattie McDaniel, and Louise Beavers) was a black maid with an inexhaustible supply of patience, and *Amos and Andy* (whose lead characters were played by Alvin Childress, Spencer Williams, Jr., and Tim Moore), the show about which the NAACP said "every character is either a clown or a crook," blacks began to be featured in positive roles in major series and on variety shows. A few performers even hosted their own television specials. In 1956 the widely popular singer Nat "King" Cole briefly hosted his own show, which was eventually canceled for lack of a national sponsor. This disappointment was reversed by the "breakthrough" success of *The Flip Wilson Show* which ran from 1970 to 1974; it was the first variety show hosted by an African American to be consistently rated among the top programs on television. In 1966 Bill Cosby received an Emmy Award for his role in the television series *I Spy*. And the comedy series *Julia* (featuring Diahann Carroll) depicted a beautiful, talented nurse living and working in an integrated world. By the early 1970s African Americans were also major characters in a number of situation comedies, some of which, particularly those produced by Norman Lear, enjoyed long, popular runs. Throughout the 1980s and 1990s, in drama and comedy series, television featured more

**WOMEN'S HEPTATHLON CHAM-
PION.** Jackie Joyner-Kersee clears a
hurdle en route to winning the gold
medal at the Olympic games in 1992.
(Reuters/Bettmann.)

blacks portraying characters of individual achievement, upward mobility, and middle-class status. The most outstanding expression of this trend was the phenomenally successful series, *The Cosby Show,* and its "spinoff" series, *A Different World,* that focused on the adventures of a group of students at a historically black college. Black visibility on television also increased in 1980 when black entrepreneur Robert L. Johnson established the Black Entertainment Network (BET) as part of the cable television system.

The coverage of the civil rights movement provided by television, the major newspapers, and national news magazines did a great deal to make a national issue of African-American efforts to achieve equality. This in turn created a push for enhanced minority representation in the white-owned news media that led to employment in this influential area for a small number of African Americans. Initially, black newscasters, columnists, and reporters associated with the major television stations and magazines were expected, and often directed, to focus solely on race-related news, which frequently limited them to coverage of sports, crime, and civil rights. Slowly, beginning in the mid-1960s, there was a slight but perceptible shift in policy as a handful of black columnists and newscasters gained positions that gave them access to a national audience and set no restrictions on the subjects about which they wrote or commented. In 1965 Carl Rowan began to write a syndicated column and to appear regularly on national radio and television as a commentator. Max Robinson became a national anchorman for the *ABC Evening News* in 1974. And in 1983 Bryant Gumbel was selected to co-host NBC's *The Today Show.* Three years later Charlayne Hunter-Gault became a regular correspondent for the *MacNeil/Lehrer Newshour.* And when Cable

U.S.A.'s BASKETBALL DREAM TEAM. With African Americans making up more than half the team, members pose with their Olympic gold medals in Barcelona in 1992. *(AP/Wide World Photos.)*

News Network (CNN) was launched in 1989, Bernard Shaw became its principal anchor in Washington, D.C. In 1993 two major breakthroughs occurred in print journalism: William A. Hilliard, editor of the Portland *Oregonian,* the only statewide daily in Oregon, was elected the first black president of the American Society of Newspaper Editors; later in the year Bob Herbert, who had worked as a reporter and columnist for the New York *Daily News* and, since 1991, as a network television correspondent for NBC News, joined the *New York Times* as a columnist on its "Op-Ed" (opinion and editorial) page.

Another development that greatly expanded black visibility on television in the last two decades of the twentieth century was the growth in the number and popularity of so-called talk shows. On these locally and nationally televised programs, hosts discussed national and international issues and cultural phenomena with selected guests, the studio audience, and sometimes call-in viewers. Blacks were featured frequently as guests, and a small number of these programs were hosted by African Americans. Oprah Winfrey, whose program, *The Oprah Winfrey Show,* was launched in 1985 to serve the Chicago market, quickly emerged as one of the most successful of the talk show hosts and the dominant black in this field. Within a year Winfrey's skills in relating to her guests and television viewers had launched her show into national syndication, where it consistently attracted a large and faithful television audience. Even as she used her skills to push her talk show repeatedly to the top of the ratings charts, Winfrey achieved additional acclaim as a successful actress, producer, and promoter of employment for African Americans.

During World War II and the years immediately thereafter, the barriers against African-American participation in amateur and professional sports began to crumble. The professional leagues in baseball, basketball, and football began to schedule regular competitions between white players and blacks in the Negro leagues, either through all-star games or contests between the best white and black teams in their respective leagues. A major breakthrough occurred in 1947 when Jackie Robinson was signed by the Brooklyn Dodgers as the first African-American player in major league baseball. This was followed by the steady integration of that sport. In 1950 professional basketball and tennis were integrated with the admission of African-American players to teams and competitions. Throughout the 1950s and 1960s this trend continued as the black presence increased and high achievement by individual black players became an accepted reality.

Boxing is a sport in which African Americans had long been major figures—from 1910 to 1915 Jack Johnson was the world heavyweight champion, and from 1937 to 1949 Joe Louis held the same title, for example. One of the most able and controversial fighters was Muhammad Ali, the former Cassius Clay who, while the reigning world heavyweight champion, refused to be drafted into the United States Army on religious grounds. Ali argued that military service was incompatible with his membership in the Nation of Islam (Black Muslims). After being convicted of violating the Selective Service Act, he was barred from the ring and stripped of his crown. In 1971, his conviction was reversed by the United States Supreme Court. Seven years later Ali regained the championship title. Always a popular figure in the African-American community, Ali's struggle made him a symbol of resistance to racism, not only for numerous black Americans but throughout much of the nonwhite world. In the late 1960s, many other African-American athletes, both professional and amateur, began to use the prestige and publicity they received to challenge remaining forms of discrimination in American sport and to protest the inclusion in the Olympic Games and other international competitions of nations that espoused racial discrimination.

■

CHAPTER 23

The Black Revolution

■ The Road to Revolution

Many factors stimulated the resorting to direct and more drastic action to secure the rights of African-Americans. Few if any were more important than the widespread, massive resistance of whites to the extension of those rights. In many Southern communities economic sanctions were invoked against blacks who were active in civil rights. Dismissals from jobs, denials of loans, and foreclosures of mortgages were some of the tactics used to decimate the ranks of "aggressive Negroes." Violence was a cruder and more direct method, and in 1957 and 1958 African Americans were murdered with impunity in South Carolina, Alabama, Georgia, and other Southern states. Such incidents were extremely discouraging to those who had hoped for an early and peaceful extension of civil rights to all.

Equally discouraging was the official opposition in many Southern states and complacency and indifference elsewhere. Taking their cue from the call for massive resistance by the Virginia senator, Harry F. Byrd, all of the eleven states of the old Confederacy enacted interposition, nullification, or protest resolutions against the Supreme Court decision in the school desegregation cases. "Black Monday," a bitter tirade against the decision, written by a Mississippi circuit court judge, Tom P. Brady, helped to stiffen the opposition by arguing that blacks were not capable of becoming equal citizens. In 1957 segregationists cheered the active opposition of Governor Orval Faubus to the desegregation of Central High School in Little Rock, Arkansas. Not until President Eisenhower sent federal troops in response to the governor's defiance of a court order did African-American children gain admission to the school. The weeks and months of intimidation and harassment of the children on the part of white students and their parents suggested how bitter and harsh the resistance could be.

African Americans themselves became increasingly impatient with the intransigence of the opponents of civil rights. They became bolder and more aggressive and began to press for their rights with relentless vigor. Their action in boycotting the Montgomery buses set an example that was followed in other Southern communities. It was in the cities that they most clearly began to manifest their impatience, and blacks were steadily becoming urban dwellers. Between 1940 and 1970 the black population outside the old Confederacy increased from nearly 4 million to more than 11 million, representing almost 50 percent of the total black population. Most of the growth outside the South was in the central cities of the twelve largest metropolitan areas: New York, Los Angeles, Chicago, Philadelphia, Detroit, San Francisco-Oakland, Boston, Pittsburgh, St. Louis, Washington, Cleveland, and Baltimore. By 1970 these twelve areas held 28 percent of all the African Americans in the United States. There were 1,667,000 blacks in New York City, 1,103,000 in Chicago, 654,000 in Philadelphia, 660,000 in Detroit, and 504,000 in Los Angeles. In Southern cities, such as Atlanta, Birmingham, Houston, and Dallas, the African-American population grew steadily. The Northern black was already a city dweller, and the Southern black was rapidly becoming one. In both sections, however, there was a trend toward the suburbs by 1970.

If African Americans moved to the cities to solve their problems, they soon discovered that their problems persisted, even increased. Poor housing and unemployment were twin evils that spawned new frustrations and difficulties. But new contacts and new associations provided opportunities to discover the strength that they possessed. Some African Americans, in such cities as Chicago, Detroit, Washington, and New York, turned to the racial segregation advocated by the Black Muslims. From their modest beginning in the mid-1930s, the Black Muslims had grown under the leadership of Elijah Muhammad into a vocal and vigorous religious sect by 1960. By the early 1970s conservative estimates indicated that the group numbered nearly 100,000, with a much larger number of sympathizers. Easily the best known member of the sect was the world heavyweight boxing champion, Muhammad Ali, formerly Cassius Clay. (See Chapter 22.)

A more likely response to their plight—and one that appealed to a much larger number of urban blacks—was to seek improvement through political action. To most blacks city hall, the state capital, and Washington seemed proper targets for their efforts. They had seen government wield enormous power in new areas during the Depression and the war. They began to feel that government would do more for them if they could harness and use their political strength wisely. In Northern cities more African Americans had begun to vote, while even in the South—after the white primary was outlawed—they became more active politically. Political activity had undoubtedly influenced the enactment of fair employment laws in New York (1945), Michigan, Minnesota, and Pennsylvania (1955), and California and Ohio (1959). Political influence could, perhaps more than any other means, secure favorable action on behalf of African Americans on the state level and even on the national level.

By the second half of the twentieth century there were important indications that the national government might soon act to improve the status of African Americans. From the time of President Truman's civil rights proposals in 1948, Congress had begun to consider civil rights legislation. Indeed, between 1953 and 1957 the House of Representatives passed civil rights bills several times, but none ever came to a vote in the Senate. In 1957 President Eisenhower presented a four-point proposal for civil rights, a very important feature of which was that the attorney general should be empowered to seek injunctive relief in the federal courts for people whose constitutional rights had been violated. Although this feature was stricken from the bill that was introduced following the president's suggestion, Congress did pass a civil rights bill after much bitter debate and much pressure from civil rights advocates. This was one of the earliest pieces of legislation fought for by Clarence Mitchell, Jr., director of the Washington Bureau of the NAACP. From 1950 until his death in 1984 Mitchell was so active and so effective in pressing for legislation favorable to blacks and to disadvantaged people generally that he was frequently referred to as the "101st senator."

The new law, the first civil rights act since 1875, authorized the federal government to bring civil suits in its own name to obtain injunctive relief, in federal courts, where anyone was denied or threatened in his or her right to vote. It elevated the civil rights section of the Department of Justice to the status of a division, with an assistant attorney general over it. It also created the United States Commission on Civil Rights, with authority to investigate allegations of denial of the right to vote, to study and collect information concerning legal developments constituting a denial of equal protection of the laws, and to appraise the laws and policies of the federal government with respect to equal protection. One senator called the new law a "sham," while another called it "a limited and modest step." The real significance of the legislation lay not so much in its provisions as in its recognition of federal responsibility and its reflection of a remarkable and historic reversal of the federal policy of hands off in matters involving civil rights.

Congress was impelled to enact civil rights legislation not merely in response to the president's suggestion or even to the mounting pressure by advocates of civil rights. It was also responding to the rapidly changing international scene in which the status of blacks in the United States was playing an increasingly important part. On March 8, 1957—six months before the new civil rights act was passed—Ghana became the first former African colony to join the United Nations. As Talcott Parsons has aptly observed,

> ## Henry Lee Moon on the Power of the Black Vote—1948
>
> . . . The ballot, while no longer conceived of as a magic key, is recognized as the indispensable weapon in a persistent fight for full citizenship, equal economic opportunity, unrestricted enjoyment of civil rights, freedom of residence, access to equal and unsegregated educational, health, and recreational facilities. In short, a tool to be used in the ultimate demolition of the whole outmoded structure of Jim Crow.
>
> Already recognized as an important and sometimes decisive factor in a dozen northern states and in at least seventy-five nonsouthern congressional districts, the Negro is beginning to exert increasing political influence in the nation, although still not accorded the recognition his voting strength warrants. Meanwhile, he is again emerging as a positive political factor in the South, where for nearly two generations his suffrage rights have for all practical purposes been nullified.
>
> Henry Lee Moon, *Balance of Power: The Negro Vote* (Garden City, 1948), pp. 9–11.

the emergence into independence of the sub-Saharan nations enormously changed the worldwide significance of the American race problem and provided a considerable stimulus to the movement for racial equality in the United States. As Congress began to debate the proposed civil rights bill in the summer of 1957, diplomatic representatives from Ghana had taken up residence at the United Nations and in Washington. This important fact could not be ignored by responsible members of Congress. It seemed that black men from the Old World had arrived just in time to help redress the racial balance in the New.

■ The Beginnings

On February 1, 1960, four students from the black Agricultural and Technical College in Greensboro, North Carolina, entered a variety store, made several purchases, and then sat down at the lunch counter and ordered coffee. They were refused service because they were black, but they continued to sit at the counter until the store closed. This was the beginning of the sit-in movement which spread rapidly through the South and to numerous places in the North. In the spring and summer of 1960 young people, white and black, participated in similar peaceful forms of protest against segregation and discrimination. They sat in white libraries, waded at white beaches, and slept in the lobbies of white hotels. Many were arrested for trespassing,

SIT-INS ENDURE HARASSMENT. In Jackson, Mississippi, whites poured sugar, mustard, and ketchup on the heads of sit-ins seeking to desegregate a lunch counter. *(Fred Blackwell,* Jackson Daily News.*)*

disorderly conduct, and disobeying police officers. When African-American students were criticized for sitting in, they placed full-page advertisements in several newspapers, including the Atlanta *Constitution,* in which they said, "We do not intend to wait placidly for those rights which are already legally and morally ours to be meted out to us one at a time." Soon, many lunch counters across the South began to serve blacks, and other facilities were opened.

By the time the four black students launched the sit-in movement, the stage was already set for the beginning of the most profound, revolutionary changes in the status of black Americans that had occurred since emancipation. The road to revolution had been paved by significant shifts in the black population from rural areas to the cities and from the South to the North and West, by Supreme Court decisions on voting and school desegregation, by the refusal of Rosa Parks to move to the back of the bus, by the Montgomery bus boycott that followed and the emergence of Martin Luther King, by the passage of the Civil Rights Act of 1957, and by the rise of national states in Africa. The revolution would have many facets. The changes in public policy, in the way that African Americans viewed themselves and their place in American life, and in the attitudes and thoughts of the larger community toward them were about as far-reaching as the changes in the status of African Americans themselves. The decision of the young college students to sit in symbolized some of these changes and suggested the nature of others yet to come.

Underlying these impulses for change in the African-American community, and reinforcing them, was the widespread activism of black women of varying backgrounds and occupations, North and South, in rural and urban areas. Innumerable black women emerged as catalysts of the Black Revolution, sometimes through their support of black males but just as often as strategists and inspiring leaders in their own right. Pauli Murray, a lawyer and legal scholar who had been fighting restrictions based on race and gender as far back as the 1930s, brought her ardent concern for both of these causes to the civil rights movement. Ella Baker, who was an NAACP field organizer in the 1940s, served as executive secretary of the Southern Christian Leadership Conference (SCLC) during the 1960s and was the "political and spiritual midwife for the Student Nonviolent Coordinating Committee (SNCC)." Fannie Lou Hamer was a "natural leader" who was active in SCLC and SNCC. Her commitment to civil rights caused her to lose her home and job, and a severe beating while jailed for civil rights activities left her permanently disabled. A founder of the Mississippi Freedom Democratic party, Hamer's demands for an end to the disfranchisement of Southern black voters received national television coverage at the 1964 Democratic National Convention. Gloria Richardson, who led demonstrations in Cambridge, Maryland, to combat poor housing conditions and unfair employment practices; Jo Ann Robinson, a founder of the Montgomery Improvement Association; Daisy Bates, one of the most effective black leaders in Little Rock during the crisis surrounding the integration of Central High School; Angela Davis, who worked with SNCC, the Black Panthers, and the Communist Party; and Ann Moody, a dedicated field worker for the NAACP, SNCC, and Congress of Racial Equality (CORE), along with numerous other little-known and unsung African-American women, were major contributors to the struggle for black equality.

In the months and years that followed, an interesting and at times exciting interplay of action and response developed between government and civil rights advocates. And it was this interplay that did so much to carry the revolution forward. After passage of the act of 1957 the federal government increased its activity in the civil rights field, and so did the opponents of the movement. The Commission on Civil Rights held hearings on black voting in several cities, North and South, and discovered that blacks were being regularly denied the right to vote by certain Southern white registrars. The Department of Justice then instituted suits in Alabama, Georgia, and Louisiana charging that registrars had failed to register qualified African-American voters solely because of race. Although the Supreme Court upheld the right of the Department of Justice to bring such suits, which had been bitterly challenged, it became clear that the act needed strengthening to prevent evasive action by registrars.

In 1960, after much debate and some filibustering in the Senate, Congress passed another civil rights bill. It provided that if a registrar resigned after complaints had been filed, the proceeding could be instituted against the state. The act further required that voting records be preserved for twenty-two months following any primary, special, or general election. The records were to be available to the attorney general in order to determine whether proceedings were warranted. To strike at a malicious practice that had sprung up in recent years, the law singled out for punishment anyone found guilty of defacing churches, synagogues, or other buildings. The Department of Justice then proceeded successfully to enjoin many white citizens of Haywood and Fayette counties, Tennessee, from employing economic repri-sals against blacks who had attempted to vote. By 1962 more than thirty cases had been brought by the attorney general to protect blacks in their efforts to vote in Mississippi, Louisiana, Alabama, Tennessee, and Georgia.

By the summer of 1960 the question of the status of African Americans had become such a burning issue that neither major party, facing the presidential campaign, could fail to recognize its importance. There were already more than 1 million registered black voters in twelve Southern states. In at least six of the eight most populous states in the country, blacks held the balance of power in closely contested elections. In their platforms in 1960 both major parties took strong stands for racial justice and equality. They hoped not to be guilty of what Theodore White observed in *The Making of the President 1960* when he said, "To ignore the Negro vote and Negro insistence on civil rights must be either an act of absolute folly—or one of absolute miscalculation."

Sen. John F. Kennedy easily outmaneuvered his opponent, Vice President Richard M. Nixon, in the quest for the African-American vote in 1960. Long before the nomination, Kennedy's black staff members briefed him well on the problems and aspirations of blacks. During the campaign Kennedy chided the Republicans for not having done more to advance the cause of African Americans. He criticized President Eisenhower for not having put an end to discrimination in federally supported housing and declared that it could be done "with the stroke of a pen." (President Kennedy did not take that step until November 1962, two years after his election.)

Even more astute than his attacks on the Republican administration was Kennedy's action regarding the imprisonment of Martin Luther King. On October 19, 1960 King and about fifty other blacks were arrested for sitting in at the Magnolia Room of Rich's Department Store in Atlanta. The others were released, but King was sentenced to four months of hard labor in Reidsville State Prison, to the dismay and fear of those who knew what Georgia justice might lead to. On the morning of October 26, Kennedy called Mrs. King and expressed his sympathy and concern. His campaign manager and brother, Robert F. Kennedy, telephoned the Georgia judge who had sentenced King and pleaded for his release. On the following day King was released, although it is not clear what effect Robert Kennedy's intervention actually had. The news of the action of the Kennedy brothers swept through the African-American community, assisted by the distribution in black churches and elsewhere of more than a million pamphlets telling of their deed. The point was not lost on the black voters that neither Dwight D. Eisenhower, the president, nor Vice President Nixon, the candidate, took any action at all.

By 1960 blacks were so preoccupied with civil rights that they were scarcely influenced by other considerations in their decisions to support parties and candidates. Southern blacks who could vote overcame their Protestant bias and cast their votes for Kennedy, the Catholic presidential candidate, who appeared to be more prepared to advance the cause of civil rights. Northern blacks, aware of their critically important strength, were determined to use it to compel equality for their less privileged kin. When the votes were counted—in the closest presidential election of the century— African Americans had reason to believe that they were responsible for the election of John F. Kennedy. In Illinois, which Kennedy carried by 9,000 votes, it was estimated that 250,000 blacks voted for him. In Michigan, where he won by a margin of 67,000 votes, about 250,000 blacks supported him. He carried South Carolina by 10,000 votes, including an estimated 40,000 black votes. African Americans now hoped that the New Frontier would also be theirs.

The young president had no ambitious plans for new legislation to elevate the African American in America life. Instead, he looked toward expanded executive action, especially in those areas where federal authority was most complete and undisputed. He hoped, moreover, to use the prestige of his office to exercise the "moral leadership" to which he had referred during the campaign. He encouraged the Department of Justice, headed by his brother Robert, to carry forward its efforts to secure the right to vote through negotiation and litigation. He pressed for increased employment of African Americans in federally connected programs and established the Committee on Equal Employment Opportunity, with Vice President Lyndon B. Johnson as chairman. The committee took steps to eliminate discrimination in employment in government and private enterprise. After President Kennedy issued the order to prevent discrimination in new federally supported housing, he appointed a Committee on Equal Opportunity in Housing headed by former Governor David Lawrence of Pennsylvania.

Kennedy showed little hesitation in appointing blacks to important federal positions. As judges he appointed Thurgood Marshall to the circuit court in New York, Wade McCree to the district court for Eastern Michigan, James Parsons to the district court of Northern Illinois, and Marjorie Lawson, Joseph Waddy, and Spottswood Robinson to the bench in the District of Columbia. Robert Weaver became head of the Housing and Home Finance

Agency; and when the agency was elevated to cabinet rank in 1965, President Johnson appointed Weaver secretary of the new Department of Housing and Urban Development, the first African American to hold a cabinet office. President Kennedy also appointed George L. P. Weaver to be assistant secretary of labor, Carl Rowan to be deputy assistant secretary of state (and later ambassador to Finland), and Clifton R. Wharton and Mercer Cook to be ambassadors to Norway and Niger, respectively. He appointed two blacks, Merle McCurdy and Cecil F. Poole, as United States attorneys, and several others to presidential committees working in the civil rights field and to other boards and commissions, including John B. Duncan to the Board of Commissioners of the District of Columbia.

On the whole, however, the picture of federal employment for African Americans continued to be dark. Between June 1961 and June 1962 federal employment of blacks increased by only 11,000, with most of these new workers getting jobs only at the lower levels, while the total number of federal employees increased by more than 62,000. Discrimination in federal employment persisted. Indeed, in some agencies there were scarcely any black employees at all. Only in the subprofessional categories, paying less than $5,000 per year, did African Americans constitute any substantial proportion, 23 percent, of the federal service.

African Americans and others in the civil rights field were not satisfied by the actions of the Kennedy administration. Soon civil rights advocates were applying new pressures to secure equal rights for blacks. In May 1961 the Congress of Racial Equality, an interracial direct-action group founded in 1942, sent "freedom riders" into the South to test segregation laws and practices in interstate transportation. In Anniston and Birmingham, Alabama, the interracial teams were attacked by angry segregationists. Attorney General Robert Kennedy was obviously a bit annoyed by the aggressiveness of these unorthodox fighters for civil rights and expressed a desire for a cooling-off period. He nevertheless ordered the Federal Bureau of Investigation to look into the matter and made it clear that the freedom riders would be protected. When the riders were set upon by a mob in Montgomery, where the police intervened only belatedly, the attorney general dispatched a force of 600 deputy marshals and other federal officers to the scene, thus narrowly averting further violence.

Other groups, including the new Student Nonviolent Coordinating Committee, the Southern Christian Leadership Conference, and the Nashville Student Movement, became interested and joined in sending more than 1,000 volunteers on freedom rides through the South. Federal marshals escorted them to Jackson, but local officials arrested at least 300, including 15 priests. Reacting to the pressures of the freedom riders and the intervention of the attorney general, the Interstate Commerce Commission ruled on September 22, 1961, that passengers on interstate carriers would be seated without regard to race and that such carriers could not use segregated terminals.

School desegregation had moved at a snail's pace since the Supreme Court issued its decrees in the school desegregation cases in 1955. In the North de facto segregation of schools was deeply entrenched, thanks to rigid patterns of segregation in housing. In such cities as New Rochelle, New York; Englewood, New Jersey; Chester, Pennsylvania; and Chicago, Illinois, however, strong protests in 1960 and 1961 were a portent of what was to come. In the South, resistance to school desegregation had stiffened to the point that by 1958 the slow pace had come to a virtual standstill. In 1961 a total of 775 of the 2,839 biracial school districts in the seventeen Southern and border states underwent some desegregation, an increase of only 1.5 percent in the two preceding years. Most of the increase had been in the border states.

Since Autherine Lucy's expulsion from the University of Alabama in 1956, African Americans had been admitted in small numbers to Southern white colleges and universities, public and private. Although there were some local objections, the University of Georgia and the University of South Carolina admitted blacks without much excitement. The most dramatic and violent effort to bar an African American from public higher education was the attempt by the state of Mississippi in 1962, in defiance of a court order, to prevent the enrollment of James Meredith. When it became clear that the state would not maintain order and ensure Meredith's admittance, despite Governor Ross Barnett's promise to the president, Kennedy sent deputy marshals and later federalized National Guardsmen to secure Meredith's admission and maintain order. Before the rioting had subsided, two people had been killed and many injured. Meredith's enrollment and graduation the following year indicated the futility of attempting to deny higher education to an African American in the face of a federal government determined to secure it for him. George Wallace, governor of Alabama, would learn that lesson in 1963, when he unsuccessfully attempted to block the enrollment of a black student at the University of Alabama by "standing in the schoolhouse door." Another disadvantage from which Wallace suffered was the fact that by 1963 the Black Revolution was approaching full tide.

■ Marching for Freedom

For several years before 1963 the National Association for the Advancement of Colored People used the motto "Free by '63." Other groups adopted the motto and focused more attention on the drive for equality. Many leaders were especially sensitive to the significance of the Emancipation Centennial in pointing up racial inequality in American life. On September 22, 1962, when Governor Nelson Rockefeller of New York spoke in Washington to open an exhibit of the Preliminary Emancipation Proclamation, "the state's most treasured possession," he said, "The very existence of this document

FREEDOM RIDERS VIOLATE LOCAL LAWS. Teams of black and white travelers, sitting together in all-white waiting rooms, were arrested when they refused to leave. *(UPI/Bettmann.)*

stirs our conscience with the knowledge that Lincoln's vision of a nation truly fulfilling its spiritual heritage is not yet achieved."

During the centennial year itself, the United States Commission on Civil Rights presented to the president a report on the history of civil rights, "Freedom to the Free," in which it declared that "a gap between our recorded aspirations and actual practices still remains." On Lincoln's birthday in 1963, President and Mrs. Kennedy received more than 1000 black and white citizens at the White House and presented to each of them a copy of the report. Speaking at Gettysburg that year, Vice President Lyndon B. Johnson said, "Until justice is blind, until education is unaware of race, until opportunity is unconcerned with the color of men's skins, emancipation will be a proclamation but not a fact." President Kennedy took note of the absence of equality when he said, "Surely, in 1963, one hundred years after emancipation, it should not be necessary for any American citizen to demonstrate in the streets for an opportunity to stop at a hotel, or eat at a lunch counter . . . on the same terms as any other American."

Theoretically, the president was right, but blacks had discovered that demonstrations had accomplished what other measures had not. They had gained valuable experience in Montgomery, Greensboro, Albany, Georgia, and elsewhere. They were determined to use that experience during the centennial year in pressing for equality. Consequently, demonstrations broke out in many places during the spring of 1963. The most critical demonstration began in Birmingham on April 3, under the leadership of Martin Luther King and the Southern Christian Leadership Conference. As they marched, the

Martin Luther King, Jr., on Families Demonstrating Together—1967

A hundred times I have been asked why we have allowed little children to march in demonstrations, to freeze and suffer in jails, to be exposed to bullets and dynamite. The questions imply that we have revealed a want of family feeling or a recklessness toward family security. The answer is simple. Our children and our families are maimed a little every day of our lives. If we can end an incessant torture by a single climactic confrontation, the risks are acceptable. Moreover, our family life will be born anew if we fight together. Other families may be fortunate enough to be able to protect their young from danger. Our families, as we have seen, are different. Oppression has again and again divided and splintered them. We are a people torn apart from era to era. It is logical, moral and psychologically constructive for us to resist oppression united as families. Out of this unity, out of the bond of fighting together, forges will come. The inner strength and integrity will make us whole again.

Martin Luther King, Jr., *Where Do We Go from Here: Chaos or Community* (New York, 1967), p. 128.

demonstrators demanded fair employment opportunities, desegregation of public facilities, creation of a committee to plan desegregation, and the dropping of charges against King and the 2,500 others arrested in the course of the demonstrations.

Up to May 3 the demonstration was notable merely because of the large number of participants, including many schoolchildren, and the large number of arrests. On that day the Birmingham police began to use dogs and high-pressure water hoses on the marchers, who defended themselves with rocks and bottles. The action of the police caused consternation and dismay in many parts of the country, where sympathy demonstrations were held. During the week of May 18, the Department of Justice noted forty-three major and minor demonstrations, ten of them in Northern cities. More such demonstrations were held the following month when Medgar Evers, the leader of the Mississippi NAACP, was shot in the back outside his home in Jackson. The border town of Cambridge, Maryland, was the scene of many weeks of peaceful demonstrations in the spring, but rioting erupted in July, and the National Guard was called out. A semblance of peace was restored only when an agreement was reached with Cambridge officials to desegregate schools and public accommodations, to enlarge employment opportunities for African Americans, and to build low-rent housing that would be available to them.

THIS SPECIAL ISSUE OF "EBONY" to commemorate the centennial of the Emancipation Proclamation sold more than a million copies. (*Courtesy* Ebony *Magazine.*)

There were about as many demonstrations in the North and West as in the South. The emphasis was on increased job opportunities and an end to de facto segregation in housing and education. In New York and Philadelphia demonstrators sought to block tax-supported construction where African Americans received little or no employment. They also sought to prevent the construction of schools in all-black neighborhoods. They staged sit-ins in the offices of Mayor Robert Wagner of New York City and Governor Nelson Rockefeller of New York. In Boston, Chicago, New York, and Englewood, New Jersey, they organized sit-ins in schools or staged school strikes to protest racial imbalances. In Los Angeles and San Francisco crowds of more than 20,000 held rallies to protest the slayings of Medgar Evers and of William Moore, a Baltimore postal employee who was shot from ambush while making a one-man freedom march to Mississippi.

Neither the president nor Congress could be indifferent to the large-scale demonstrations and the resistance of white segregationists. In February, before the demonstrations reached their peak, President Kennedy sent a special message to Congress recommending legislation to strengthen voting rights. In June, largely because of events in Birmingham and elsewhere, he submitted a new and broadened civil rights program. A few days earlier he had spoken to the American people by radio and television—on the same day that National Guardsmen had been used to secure the admission of two African Americans to the University of Alabama. The president said, "We

THE MARCH ON WASHINGTON FOR JOBS AND FREEDOM.
On August 28, 1963, more than 200,000 people gathered at the
foot of the Lincoln Memorial and heard speeches from leaders
in the civil rights movement. (*Courtesy* Ebony *Magazine.*)

face . . . a moral crisis as a country and as a people. It cannot be met by
repressive police action. It cannot be left to increased demonstrations in the
streets. It cannot be quieted by token moves or talk. It is a time to act in the
Congress, in your state and local legislative body and, above all, in all of our
daily lives."

The bill containing the president's recommendations occupied much of
the attention of Congress during the summer of 1963. There was bitter
opposition to the public accommodations provision on the ground that it
interfered with property rights. Opponents of the bill also declared that the
proposal to withhold federal funds from programs where discrimination was
practiced was vindictive and, perhaps, unconstitutional. Advocates of the
measure pointed to the unconscionable delay in granting African Americans
equal rights, and they called on Congress to pass the bill as a first step toward
the achievement of racial equality. Attorney General Robert F. Kennedy
testified before congressional committees ten times in support of the proposed legislation.

As Congress and the nation debated the proposed civil rights bill, the
"March on Washington for Jobs and Freedom" occurred. Those who regarded the march as an idle threat were astounded to discover that even in
the planning stages it was receiving broad support from many sectors of

THE PRESIDENT AND THE LEADERS. At the end of the March on Washington, August 28, 1963, President Kennedy met with the leaders of the march. From the left: Whitney Young, National Urban League; Dr. Martin Luther King, Southern Christian Leadership Conference; John Lewis, Student Nonviolent Co-ordinating Committee; Rabbi Joachim Prinz, American Jewish Congress; Dr. Eugene C. Blake, National Council of Churches; A. Philip Randolph, AFL-CIO vice-president; President Kennedy; Walter Reuther, United Auto Workers; Vice President Johnson (rear); and Roy Wilkins, NAACP. *(AP/Wide World Photos.)*

American life. All of the major civil rights groups were joined by many religious, labor, and civic groups in planning and executing the gigantic demonstration. The American Jewish Congress, the National Conference of Catholics for Interracial Justice, the National Council of Churches, and the AFL-CIO Industrial Union Department were among the strong supporters of the march. On August 28, 1963, more than 200,000 blacks and whites from all over the United States staged the largest demonstration in the history of the nation's capital. The orderly procession moved from the Washington Monument to the Lincoln Memorial, where A. Philip Randolph, Martin Luther King, Roy Wilkins, Walter Reuther, and others addressed the throng. This was the occasion on which King delivered his celebrated "I Have a Dream" speech. Two noted civil rights leaders were absent. James Farmer, in a Louisiana jail for his activities in a demonstration, sent a message. After seventy years of crusading for civil rights, W. E. B. Du Bois had joined the Communist party, renounced his United States citizenship, and moved to Ghana in 1961. In his ninety-sixth year, he died in Accra on the eve of the march.

Congressional opponents of civil rights legislation had insisted that they would not be intimidated by the marchers. Some members of Congress were "out of town" or "previously engaged" when the marchers who were their constituents called on them to enlist their support. Some other members of Congress, however, supported the march and cordially received the demonstrators. President Kennedy, who had refused to criticize the march, received the leaders and pledged his continued support of the drive for equality. As Congress continued to debate the bill and as the threat of a filibuster held out the promise of killing it, many civil rights supporters became discouraged and pessimistic.

The September bombing of a black church in Birmingham in which four children were killed was as discouraging as the delay in enacting the civil rights bill. The election in November of numerous Southerners who ran for public office on strong prosegregation platforms was also discouraging. Nothing, however, filled blacks with such despair as the murder of the young president in Dallas on November 22, 1963. President Kennedy had said that enactment of the pending civil rights bill was imperative, regardless of how long it took. The year of 1963 was drawing to a close, and African Americans were not yet free. They had not even been guaranteed the right to sit down at a lunch counter and have a cup of coffee. But they had gained a few victories. The Supreme Court, in *Edwards v. South Carolina,* had upheld their right to demonstrate and, in *Johnson v. Virginia,* had reversed the contempt conviction of a black man who refused to obey a judge who ordered him to sit in the section of the courtroom reserved for blacks. More people openly supported racial equality than ever before in the history of the country. But at the same time the opposition was at least as openly hostile as ever.

■ The Illusion of Equality

Lyndon B. Johnson, who became the thirty-sixth president of the United States on November 22, 1963, was quick to make known his strong support of Kennedy's civil rights program. Five days after he took office he told Congress that he desired "the earliest possible passage of the civil rights bill." In the weeks and months that followed, the acrimonious debate in Congress continued, with the usual parliamentary maneuvers and delays. The only bright spot on the horizon as the new year opened was the ratification in January 1964 of the Twenty-fourth Amendment to the Constitution, which outlawed the requirement of the poll tax, long a means of disfranchising blacks in federal elections. In the following month, however, the pressure of the president and of civil rights groups began to take effect, and the House of Representatives passed the civil rights bill by a substantial majority, 290 to 130. In June the Senate, for the first time, voted cloture to break a civil rights filibuster, thus assuring final passage of the bill. The vote in the upper house was 73 to 27, with Senate Republican leader, Everett M. Dirksen of Illinois, voting for the bill, and the front-running Republican candidate for the presidency, Barry Goldwater of Arizona, voting against it.

The Civil Rights Act of 1964 was the most far-reaching and comprehensive law in support of racial equality ever enacted by Congress. It gave the attorney general additional power to protect citizens against discrimination and segregation in voting, education, and the use of public facilities. It forbade discrimination in most places of public accommodation and established a federal Community Relations Service to help individuals and communities solve civil rights problems. It established a federal Equal Employment Opportunity Commission (EEOC) and extended the life of the Commission on Civil Rights to January 1968. One of the most controversial provisions required the elimination of discrimination in federally assisted programs, authorizing termination of programs or withdrawal of federal funds upon failure to comply. Finally, the United States Office of Education was authorized to provide technical and financial aid to assist communities in the desegregation of schools. While some African Americans criticized the act for not going far enough, others were delighted that a semblance of equality might now be attainable.

Although there was a notable decline in discrimination in some fields, the period following the passage of the Civil Rights Act of 1964 was marked by strong resistance to its enforcement and indeed considerable violence in some places. There was what some called a "white backlash" created by blacks who pushed "too hard" for equality. In the North it manifested itself in the actions of whites who discovered their prejudices for the first time or who resented direct-action protests to eliminate discrimination in their own communities. It accounts, at least in part, for the strong showing that the segregationist governor of Alabama, George Wallace, made in the 1964 presidential primaries in Wisconsin, Indiana, and Maryland. The backlash in the South was merely the normal determination with which some segregationists went about the task of preserving the old order. Some public places transformed themselves into private clubs—as they had done after the passage of the Civil Rights Act of 1875. The proprietor of an Atlanta restaurant specializing in fried chicken vowed that he would go out of business before he would desegregate it, and he finally did. Before the end of the year it was the segregationists' turn to be discouraged, when the United States Supreme Court on December 14 upheld the constitutionality of the public accommodations section of the Civil Rights Act.

Neither congressional legislation nor executive action could stem the violence that was a feature of the so-called long, hot summer of 1964. In mid-July the violence that broke out in the Yorkville section of New York City was touched off by the killing of a black teenage youth by an off-duty policeman. Protest demonstrations against police brutality spread to Harlem, Bedford-Stuyvesant, and other parts of the city, often accompanied by rioting and looting. There were similar disturbances in Rochester, New York; Paterson, Elizabeth, and Jersey City, New Jersey; Philadelphia, Pennsylvania; and Chicago, Illinois. It was reported by one observer that roving gangs of "unemployed youths were conspicuously involved in most of the disorders."

Following the decision in the school desegregation cases, the Ku Klux Klan had surrendered to the citizens councils its position as leading defender of white supremacy. During the debates over the Civil Rights Act of 1964, however, the Klan reclaimed its position of leadership. In Mississippi, Alabama, Louisiana, and Georgia, its members paraded in protest against racial equality. In Georgia, Klansmen picketed a hotel that had desegregated, carrying posters stating, "Don't trade here! Owners of this business surrendered to the race mixers." Much more serious was the violence, attributed to the Klan and similar groups, that broke out in the South during the summer as SNCC and SCLC stepped up their voter registration drives. In July an African-American educator, returning to his home in Washington from reserve officer training, was killed in Georgia by a shotgun blast from a passing automobile. Two men, identified as Klansmen, were tried for the crime but were acquitted. In July three young civil rights workers—one black Mississippian and two white New Yorkers—disappeared after having been arrested in Mississippi on speeding charges. Weeks later their bullet-riddled bodies were discovered buried in an earthen dam. During the search for the civil rights workers the bodies of two blacks were found floating in the Mississippi River. Several whites were arrested in connection with both crimes, but there were no convictions. Between June and October about twenty-four black churches in Mississippi were totally or partially destroyed by bombings and fire.

Although both major parties continued to recognize the importance of the African-American vote in national elections, the odds greatly favored the Democrats capturing it in 1964. African Americans were generally pleased with the civil rights record of Lyndon B. Johnson as vice president and president. His choice for second place on the ticket, Sen. Hubert Humphrey of Minnesota, who had a strong pro-civil rights record, was additional reassurance that the executive was committed to continued support of the African-American cause. If the Democrats failed to seat the delegates from the Mississippi Freedom Democratic party, who argued that the regular Mississippi Democrats were "lily white," they did mollify blacks by outlawing segregated delegations at future conventions. On the other hand the Republicans nominated for president Barry Goldwater, who had voted in the Senate against the Civil Rights Act of 1964, and for vice president the little-known Rep. William E. Miller of New York. Most African Americans regarded Goldwater's persistent references during the campaign to "crime in the streets" as a thinly veiled condemnation of civil rights demonstrations. The overwhelming victory for the Johnson-Humphrey ticket was one to which the vast majority of African-American voters contributed.

Despite existing civil rights legislation, hundreds of thousands of blacks in the South continued to have difficulty in voting or were barred altogether. During the summer and fall of 1964 the Council of Federated Organizations, composed of the major civil rights groups, the National Council of Churches, and others, faced strong opposition in their drive to increase voter registration among blacks. Even after the election, they continued to face bitter opposition. Southern whites, especially in areas where the black population was large, seemed more opposed to voter registration drives than to demonstrations to desegregate public accommodations. In Selma, Dallas County, Alabama, the opposition, led by the county sheriff, was particularly fierce. In February 1965 a black civil rights worker was killed, and a few weeks later a young white minister from Boston was killed. These acts of violence, together with the sheriff's use of tear gas, whips, and clubs against the demonstrators, attracted worldwide attention.

Still further attention was attracted by the demonstrators' decision to march from Selma to Montgomery. When Alabama public officials sought to prevent the march, the United States District Court judge in Montgomery ordered state officials to permit the march, and President Johnson called the Alabama National Guard into federal service to protect the demonstrators. On the final day of the march the 300 demonstrators were joined by about 50,000 black and white supporters from all over the country. Martin Luther King, who a few months earlier had received the Nobel Peace Prize for his civil rights leadership, told the crowd in Montgomery that "no tide of racism can stop us." Nobel Prize winner Ralph Bunche, another speaker, apologized for having to speak from the steps of a state capitol over which waved the flag of the Confederacy. That night, as if to reaffirm the motto "The Deep South says 'Never,'" snipers shot and killed a white woman from Detroit as she transported passengers from Montgomery back to Selma. In December her assailants, who had been exonerated on a charge of murder, were convicted, under an 1870 federal statute, for violating her civil rights.

As the Selma-Montgomery march got under way, the president recognized the clear need for additional legislation to protect the rights of voters. In an address to Congress and the nation he said that the real hero in the struggle for equality was the African American. "His actions and protests— his courage to risk safety and even life—have awakened the conscience of the nation. His demonstrations have been designed to call attention to injustice, to provoke change and stir reform. He has called upon us to make good the promise of America. And who among us can say we would have made the same progress were it not for his persistent bravery, and his faith in American democracy. . . . We intend to fight this battle where it should be fought—in the courts, in the Congress, and in the hearts of men. And we shall overcome." African Americans everywhere were gratified that the president of the United States should end his stirring address with words from the theme song of the civil rights movement.

A few days later the president sent to Congress his proposals for a right-to-vote law. Congress passed the law with unusual swiftness. It authorized the attorney general to send federal examiners to register black voters when he concluded that local registrars were not doing their job. It suspended all literacy tests and other devices in states and counties that used them and where less than 50 percent of the adults had voted in 1964. The

IN MONTGOMERY, ALABAMA, IN MARCH 1965, approximately fifty thousand people joined those who had marched from Selma and then proceeded to the capitol grounds to air their grievances. *(Courtesy* Ebony *Magazine.)*

states affected were Alabama, Georgia, Louisiana, Mississippi, South Carolina, Virginia, twenty-six counties in North Carolina, Alaska, and scattered counties in Arizona, Idaho, and Hawaii. There was opposition to the measure, and some blacks accused Attorney General Nicholas Katzenbach of not sending federal examiners quickly enough. Nevertheless, by the end of the year nearly a quarter of a million new African-American voters had been registered, one-third by federal examiners and two-thirds by local officials. In that year African Americans won seats in the Georgia legislature and in city councils of several Southern cities.

Even before larger numbers of African Americans began to register to vote under the protection of the new legislation, it became clear that they needed much more than the franchise if they were to enjoy equality. After World War II blacks moved from rural areas to cities at an enormous rate, but the move failed to solve many of their problems. Between 1940 and 1960 the black population of New York City increased two and one-half times, but fully 85 percent of the newcomers were crowded into the already overcrowded black ghettoes. The situation was similar in other cities. As whites departed from the inner city to more attractive sections of the city or to the suburbs, African Americans found housing not on their own terms but on those arranged by owners, mortgage companies, and other beneficiaries. All too often they paid premium prices for housing that was already outmoded and becoming dilapidated.

Discrimination in housing was not only private practice but public policy. Between 1935 and 1950, 11 million homes were built. Wherever there was federal assistance, the racial policy was laid down in the manual of the Federal Housing Administration that declared, "If a neighborhood is to retain stability it is necessary that properties shall be continued to be occupied by the same social and racial classes." One housing authority has claimed that this policy did more to entrench housing bias in American neighborhoods than any court could undo by a ruling. Despite the fact that by 1962 about seventeen states and fifty-six cities had passed laws or resolutions against housing discrimination, the bias persisted. Banks, insurance companies, real estate boards, and brokers greatly benefited from segregated housing for which they received a maximum profit from a minimum of expenditure.

African Americans were greatly embittered to discover that they were being exploited by landlords and real estate brokers who took their rents but refused to comply with the minimum housing and health standards established by the city and state. As they paid high rents for rat-infested slums, they discovered that in such neighborhoods their children received inferior education, found few job opportunities, and had few, if any, public facilities. What was even worse, they discovered that cities were unwilling to enforce their own antibias housing codes. This led blacks in New York City in 1963 to launch rent strikes against slumlords and in Chicago in 1966 to join in Martin Luther King's all-out war against discrimination in housing. In California, the supporters of equal opportunity in housing suffered a setback in 1964 when the voters adopted, by an overwhelming vote, a cleverly framed constitutional amendment ostensibly guaranteeing a property owner the right to dispose of his property to any person he chose. Backed by the California Real Estate Association and the National Association of Real Estate Boards, the amendment was in fact a bulwark against open occupancy in housing. It was so construed in 1966 by the California supreme court, which declared the amendment unconstitutional. But African Americans in any American city continued to experience untold difficulty in finding decent housing.

Urban blacks suffered even more, if possible, from a lack of equal opportunity in employment. President Johnson attempted to set a pattern of fair employment by continuing to appoint African Americans to high government posts. As ambassadors he appointed Mercer Cook to Senegal, Hugh Smythe to Syria, Franklin Williams to Ghana, Elliott Skinner to Upper Volta, and Patricia Harris to Luxembourg. He promoted Wade McCree from the United States District Court to the Circuit Court, and appointed Circuit Judge Thurgood Marshall to be solicitor general and later justice of the

Supreme Court, Hobart Taylor to the board of the Export-Import Bank, Andrew Brimmer to the Federal Reserve Board, and Walter Washington as mayor of the nation's capital. Early in 1965, moreover, he set up the Council on Equal Opportunity, composed of cabinet officers and heads of agencies with overall civil rights responsibilities, and appointed Vice President Humphrey as chairman. The council was to have a staff and could require reports from agencies and departments. This arrangement was terminated in September 1965, and the vice president was relieved of his civil rights assignments. The attorney general became head of the administration's civil rights program, and the emphasis shifted from economic opportunity to the problems of compliance under the Civil Rights Act of 1964. There remained some of the momentum created during the Kennedy years in seeking to persuade private industry to increase employment opportunities for blacks. This, however, was not sufficient to change the picture significantly.

It was widely assumed that the vigorous thrust for equality had begun to close the economic gap between blacks and whites. The assumption, which was entirely erroneous, was caused in part by the opening of a few widely publicized opportunities that can best be described as "massive tokenism." In many cities African Americans became vice presidents of banks and major industrial and commercial institutions. Many secured positions as clerks and white-collar workers in department stores and other businesses. Some joined the boards of major automobile manufacturers, airlines, public utilities, and other businesses and industries. But the economic disparities between blacks and whites not only failed to decrease but actually increased, especially among blue-collar workers and lower-income groups.

Between 1949 and 1964 the relative participation of African Americans in the total economic life of the nation declined significantly. During that period the unemployment rate of blacks was at least double that of whites. Even in 1963, a prosperous year, the unemployment rate for blacks was 114 percent higher than it was for whites. Where blacks were employed, more than 80 percent worked at the bottom of the economic ladder, as compared with 40 percent of employed whites. In later years it was no better. In 1964 the unemployment rate among blacks was 9.6 percent as against 4.6 among whites; in 1971 it was 9.9 percent among blacks and 5.4 among whites. In 1969 the median income of blacks with eight years of schooling was $4,472, while it was $7,018 for whites with the same amount of schooling. In 1970 the Census Bureau, defining poverty as a median income of less than $3,968 for a family of four, reported that one in every three blacks as compared with one in every ten whites was in that category. And the chances for African Americans to move up were greatly restricted not only by general race bias but also by the meager opportunities for apprenticeship training and by discrimination in many labor unions.

In 1962 the Council of Economic Advisors estimated the overall cost of racial discrimination at about $17.3 billion, or 3.2 percent of the gross national product. This cost resulted primarily from failure to utilize fully the existing experience and skills of the total population and failure to fully develop potential experience and skills. The effect of this discrimination against black Americans could be seen in their inability to secure adequate housing even when it was available, to provide a wholesome environment in which to rear and educate their children, and to participate more fully in the economic and social life of the country. There was also the shattering sense of frustration and alienation which could not be measured in monetary terms—at least not until it exploded into violence such as that which occurred in Los Angeles in August 1965.

The immediate cause of the explosion in the Watts area of Los Angeles was the arrest of a young African American who was charged with reckless driving. When a policeman drew a gun, an angry crowd assembled and began to fight the police. On the following day, after an unsuccessful attempt to quiet the tensions, the rioting was resumed, accompanied by looting and burning. At the height of the holocaust blacks were heard to exclaim, "Burn, whitey, burn" and "Get whitey." It was indeed an explosion of tension, bitterness, and hatred. By the time that the police, assisted by the California National Guard, restored peace, the toll had reached 34 dead, 1,032 injured, and 3,952 arrested. Property damage was estimated at $40 million.

The underlying cause of the Watts riot was the demoralization of the black population of Los Angeles. Despite the fact that 20 percent of the houses in Watts were dilapidated, one-sixth of Los Angeles's half-million blacks were crowded into the area in conditions four times as congested as those prevailing in the rest of the city. Because of discrimination and bias, few blacks were able to secure housing elsewhere, even when they could afford it. The employment picture was no better. More than 30 percent of the potential African-American wage earners were unemployed at the time of the riot. Thousands of skilled and unskilled African Americans had no hope of employment. Even in the shops in the Watts area many seeking employment had been turned away by white owners, who preferred white employees who like the owners did not live in Watts. Many blacks resorted to plying a variety of illegal trades. Others, taking counsel with the Black Muslims, whose influence there was growing, concluded that their plight was caused by the injustices of the white man. Thus, they were psychologically prepared to loot and burn. Watts was indicative of the tragedy of the illusion of equality.

At still another level there was the sense of hopelessness. The Student Nonviolent Coordinating Committee had been, for several years, the heaviest contributor of shock troops to the civil rights battle. Its members had braved insults and risked their lives in order to increase voter registration among Southern blacks. They had lived among them, taught them, and built up their self-esteem. Gradually, disillusionment and pessimism overtook some of the members. They felt that some of the black leaders were not pressing hard enough and might be willing to settle for less than full equality. They lost confidence in most public officials and saw a collusion between federal

RESURRECTION CITY, U.S.A.
Resurrection City in Washington, D.C., home of the Poor People's Campaign, is seen from the air May 20, 1968. The Reverend Ralph Abernathy, Martin Luther King's successor as head of the Southern Christian Leadership Conference, told the campaigners that the time was near when they would "raise hell in the daytime" to drive home their demands. *(UPI/Bettmann Newsphotos.)*

officials and state and local leaders, to the detriment of blacks. Laws were weak, they felt, and when they were strong, officials would not enforce them. Members of SNCC, therefore, began to express their own sense of futility in working along traditional lines in fighting for equality. In 1966 the new chairman, Stokely Carmichael, insisted that blacks must think in terms of "black power" and use it to combat the "white power" that had held them down. It was not clear how much white support SNCC was rejecting. It was clear, however, that it preferred black leadership for black goals. By the 1970s it was not unusual for some black groups to reject offers of white support.

The process of school desegregation also showed how illusory freedom could be. Because of opposition to decisions in the school desegregation cases and the techniques used to delay desegregation altogether, African Americans soon discovered that desegregation both in the South and the North would be a very slow process. As late as 1964 less than 2 percent of African-American students in the eleven states of the former Confederacy were in desegregated schools. That year, however, the intransigence of the officials of Prince Edward County, Virginia, was broken when the Supreme

Court ruled that the county was required to maintain a public school. For the first time since 1959 black children were able to attend public school.

Under the Civil Rights Act of 1964 the executive branch of the government gained the means of doing what the Court had been unable to do. Since the act barred discrimination in federally aided projects and programs, school districts receiving federal funds were required to desegregate or to present acceptable plans for desegregating their schools. The Elementary and Secondary Education Act of 1965, with an appropriation of $1.3 billion, was an added incentive to compliance. By September 1965 all but 124 of the school districts in the Southern and border states had presented acceptable plans for compliance, including freedom-of-choice plans, which required black pupils to take the initiative in seeking admission to all-white schools. In the eleven Southern states of the former Confederacy, however, only 6 percent of the black children were attending desegregated schools during the 1965–1966 school year. Southern states were rapidly learning how to satisfy the federal requirement and receive federal funds and at the same time preserve the old order.

In the spring of 1967 the school desegregation process received an unanticipated boost from the United States Circuit Court, Fifth District. In its decision in *United States v. Jefferson County,* a case arising from school systems in Alabama and Louisiana, the court declared that "the only school desegregation plan that meets constitutional standards is one that works." Shortly thereafter about forty desegregation suits were instituted, and the Department of Health, Education and Welfare stepped up its pressure on school districts. By the beginning of the 1968 school year about 20.3 percent of the black schoolchildren in the former Confederate states were in "fully integrated schools." Two years later more than 90 percent of the school systems in the South were classified as desegregated; and school systems in the South—and even in the North—responded to the pressures applied by the courts and the public.

The application of the compliance provision of the Civil Rights Act to de facto segregation in Northern schools presented difficulties. New aid grants to Boston were delayed in 1965 because of complaints that African-American students were treated unfairly. The funds were released during the investigation. In the same year the Office of Education held up more than $30 million in aid to Chicago schools because of complaints that African Americans were kept out of trade schools and that school district lines were gerrymandered. The school board of Chicago agreed to study the situation, and after strong intervention by the mayor and some Illinois members of Congress, the funds were freed. There were complaints in other cities—San Francisco and New York City, for example—but the funds were not held up. Even with its new powerful weapon the Office of Education had not yet learned to use it in moving effectively toward equalizing educational opportunities.

In subsequent years opposition to the desegregation of public schools continued on many fronts. In the South, a considerable amount of "resegregation" occurred as white and black students were racially separated by classes or as black students were excluded from extracurricular activities. Meanwhile, black school officials and teachers either lost their positions or were assigned to inferior ones in situations where whites with no greater training or experience secured the superior positions. In the North, even where school officials enacted programs to achieve racial balance, the opposition was fierce; and in most places neighborhood schools, which most frequently meant racially homogeneous schools, were defended with as much ardor as Southern whites had defended racially segregated schools.

Because of housing patterns in most cities, North and South, few communities could desegregate their schools or achieve racial balance without bodily moving students from one part of the city to another. As early as the mid-1960s some schools began to experiment with that approach. In 1968 Berkeley, California, became the first city to achieve full racial desegregation by crosstown busing. Soon other cities, feeling the pressure of the Department of Health, Education and Welfare, began to follow the Berkeley example.

Despite local resistance, the dual school system was being dismantled, in form at least. Then, in 1971, President Nixon warned federal officials to stop pressing for desegregation of Southern schools through "forced busing" or find other jobs. He also expressed the view that efforts to force integration in the suburbs were "counterproductive, and not in the interest of better race relations." Finally, he threatened to seek legislation or even a constitutional amendment to prevent the courts from promoting racial integration through busing of students. Some school boards, with elaborate plans to achieve racial balance through busing, felt betrayed. Others, committed to the principle of the neighborhood school and to segregation, were overjoyed. The courts would have the last word on the subject, but the position of the United States Supreme Court remained unclear in 1973 when by a four-four decision it permitted a circuit court decision to stand that barred the busing of Virginia schoolchildren across city-suburban lines.

It seemed clear by 1978 that anything resembling racial balance in big-city public schools was virtually out of the question. As the federal government, at times through the states, pressed public schools to achieve a better racial mix, many white parents fled to the suburbs or placed their children in private schools. This often left black children in the majority, with an insufficient number of whites to create racial balance. And both the courts and political leaders frowned on the development of metropolitan (city and suburban) school districts similar to metropolitan districts that were so successful in such areas as transportation, water and sewage, and parks. School desegregation suffered a further setback in 1978 when the Supreme Court ruled in the Bakke case that the factor of race alone could not be used to guarantee the admission of a certain number of blacks to a public medical college in California.

■ Revolution at High Tide

The 1960s was a time of revolution among blacks in the United States. The decade began with high hopes. There was still the belief that the school desegregation decision would somehow bring about a truly democratic educational system in the United States. The sit-in movement, the freedom riders, the marches and demonstrations, and the voter registration drives, supported by untold numbers of whites as well as blacks, suggested that an entirely new and thoroughly effective approach to race relations was in the making. Slowly, then more rapidly, the optimism gave way to pessimism and even cynicism. It was not merely the opposition to equality on the part of white citizens councils or Northern white mothers who railed against school desegregation or white construction workers who bitterly opposed the employment of black workers and apprentices, but the feeling, bolstered by bitter experience, that justice and equality were not to be extended to blacks under any circumstances. This created the gloomy atmosphere out of which the Black Revolution emerged.

There was, first of all, the violence. In 1963 it was the assassination of John F. Kennedy, whom many blacks had come to regard as their friend. Then, there was the murder of Malcolm X in 1965 and the feeling, shared by many blacks, that the prosecution of his assailants was less than vigorous. In the mid-1960s there was, moreover, the murder of numerous civil rights workers as well as innocent children, and for these crimes no one was convicted or even seriously prosecuted. Finally, on April 4, 1968, Martin Luther King, Jr., was shot down in a motel in Memphis, where he had gone to give support to striking garbage workers. To many African Americans this violent act symbolized the rejection by white America of their vigorous but peaceful pursuit of equality. In more than 100 cities several days of rioting and burning and looting ensued, a grave response by many blacks to the wanton murder of their young leader. The subsequent capture of James Earl Ray and his immediate trial, without any testimony after his plea of guilty, further embittered large numbers of blacks who suspected that such speedy "justice" was merely a cover-up for a possible conspiracy. The exhaustive inquiry into the matter by a Select Congressional Committee did not lead to a satisfactory conclusion on the conspiracy question.

Even before his death Martin Luther King had been criticized by militant, action-oriented blacks who insisted that whites would not respond to black demands on the basis of Christian charity, good will, or even peaceful demonstrations. Some also felt that whites would never concede complete equality to African Americans. In 1967 the Black Power Conference in Newark, New Jersey, called for "partitioning of the United States into two separate independent nations, one to be a homeland for white and the other to be a homeland for black Americans." Meanwhile, a group of young California militants led by Huey P. Newton and Bobby Seale organized the Black Panther Party for Self-Defense, and Eldridge Cleaver, its most articulate

TABLE 8
Population of African Americans and Non-African Americans, by States, in 1920 and 1950

STATE	1920 African Americans / Non-African Americans (IN THOUSANDS)		1950 African Americans / Non-African Americans (IN THOUSANDS)	
Alabama	901	1,447	980	2,082
Alaska	(a)	55	–	129
Arizona	8	326	26	724
Arkansas	472	1,280	427	1,483
California	39	3,388	462	10,124
Colorado	11	929	20	1,305
Connecticut	21	1,360	53	1,954
Delaware	30	193	44	274
Dist. of Columbia	110	328	281	521
Florida	329	639	603	2,168
Georgia	1,206	1,690	1,063	2,382
Hawaii	(a)	256	3	497
Idaho	1	431	1	588
Illinois	182	6,303	646	8,066
Indiana	81	2,849	174	3,760
Iowa	19	2,385	20	2,601
Kansas	58	1,711	73	1,832
Kentucky	236	2,181	202	2,743
Louisiana	700	1,099	882	1,802
Maine	1	767	1	913
Maryland	244	1,206	386	1,957
Massachusetts	45	3,807	73	4,618
Michigan	60	3,608	442	5,930
Minnesota	9	2,378	14	2,968
Mississippi	935	856	986	1,193
Missouri	178	3,226	297	3,658
Montana	2	547	1	590
Nebraska	13	1,283	19	1,307
Nevada	(a)	77	4	156
New Hampshire	1	442	1	532
New Jersey	117	3,039	319	4,516
New Mexico	6	354	8	673
New York	198	10,187	918	13,912

TABLE 8
Population of African Americans and Non-African Americans, by States,
in 1920 and 1950 (*Continued*)

	1920 African Americans / Non-African Americans (IN THOUSANDS)		1950 African Americans / Non-African Americans (IN THOUSANDS)	
STATE				
North Carolina	763	1,796	1,047	3,015
North Dakota	(a)	647	(a)	620
Ohio	186	5,573	513	7,434
Oklahoma	149	1,879	146	2,087
Oregon	2	781	12	1,509
Pennsylvania	285	8,435	638	9,860
Rhode Island	10	594	14	778
South Carolina	865	819	822	1,295
South Dakota	1	636	1	652
Tennessee	452	1,886	531	2,761
Texas	742	3,921	977	6,734
Utah	1	448	3	686
Vermont	1	351	(a)	378
Virginia	690	1,619	734	2,585
Washington	7	1,350	31	2,348
West Virginia	86	1,378	115	1,891
Wisconsin	5	2,627	28	3,407
Wyoming	1	193	3	288

(a) Represents less than 500.

– Represents zero statistically.

Source: U.S. Bureau of the Census, *Historical Statistics of the United States, Colonial Times to 1970, Bicentennial Edition,* [Part 2]. Washington, D.C., 1975, pp. 24–37.

spokesman, declared that the choice before the country was "total liberty for black people or total destruction for America."

The Black Panthers became nationally prominent when Huey P. Newton, who had led a group of gun-carrying demonstrators into the California state legislature, was convicted on a charge of manslaughter in the death of an Oakland policeman. Soon chapters of the party sprang up in major cities across the nation. They called for full employment, decent housing, black control of the black community, and an end to every form of repression and brutality. It was not long before they were involved in numerous encounters with the police. Several were sent to prison, charged with murder, attempted

A MUSLIM LEADER TAKES TO THE ROAD. In 1964 Malcolm X traveled widely in Muslim countries. Here, he visits a mosque in Egypt. *(John Launois/Blackstar.)*

murder, and lesser crimes. The Federal Bureau of Investigation declared the Black Panthers to be dangerous and subversive. They became the target of what appeared to be a concerted effort to eliminate them as an effective radical organization. By 1980 the Black Panthers were scarcely a shadow of what they had been. Huey Newton was more a writer than an activist, while Bobby Seale and several other leaders were involved in rather orthodox political activity. Meanwhile, Eldridge Cleaver, who returned from exile to stand trial on some old charges, had become a born-again Christian evangelist, drawing considerable sympathy from his former adversaries.

If the Black Panthers questioned the good intentions of white America,

DR. MARTIN LUTHER KING IN MEMPHIS. Martin Luther King stands
on the balcony of the Memphis Motel at approximately the spot where he
was assassinated. This picture was made on April 3, 1968, the day before
the shooting, shortly after King arrived in Memphis, Tennessee. Standing
next to King, is Jesse Jackson, to whom King was talking the instant he
was shot. At right is Ralph Abernathy. *(AP/Wide World Photos.)*

the national Black Economic Development Conference conceived an acid test
of such intentions. Meeting in Detroit in April 1969, and led by James Forman
of the Student Nonviolent Coordinating Committee, the conference issued a
"Black Manifesto" calling upon the "White Christian Churches and the
Jewish Synagogues in the United States and all other Racist Institutions" to
pay $500 million in reparations and to surrender 60 percent of their assets
to the conference to be used for the economic, social, and cultural rehabilitation of the black community. While some churches appropriated additional
funds for the poor and underprivileged and for the purpose of promoting
racial justice, none of them yielded to the demands of the conference. If the
manifesto did nothing else it affirmed the 1968 findings of the National
Advisory Commission on Civil Disorders that "our nation is moving toward
two societies, one black, one white—separate and unequal."

Numerous other groups of African Americans made moves or uttered
statements that reflected their disillusionment and despair. An increasing

Kenneth Clark on the "Present Dilemma"—1968

The masses of Negroes are now starkly aware that the recent civil rights victories benefited primarily a very small percentage of middle class Negroes while their predicament remained the same or worsened. Added to Ralph Bunche and our traditional civil rights leaders, we now have Thurgood Marshall, Robert Weaver, Walter Washington as the appointed Mayor of Washington, D.C., a few vice-presidents in private industry, a few more Negroes in New England prep schools and Ivy League colleges, and more white colleges and universities are looking for one or two "qualified Negroes" for their faculties. These and other tokens of "racial progress" are not only rejected by the masses of Negroes but seem to have resulted in their increased and more openly expressed hostility toward middle class Negroes. . . .

The present dilemma of the Negro is focused for the trained Negro intellectual. He must dare to say that the enemy was never to be understood in terms of color . . . but in the more difficult and abstract terms of human irrationality, ignorance, superstition, rigidity, and arbitrary cruelty. These are the common enemies which underlie all forms of tyranny—racism, authoritarianism, McCarthyism. . . .

If Negroes and whites who can understand this can make it clear, we can help to save America. We will use the power of disciplined intelligence combined with respect for moral values and humanity to save Negroes from the destructive possibilities of white and black dilemmas and thereby contribute to the survival of America. . . . For America cannot survive if Negroes do not. . . . And Negroes and no other group of human beings are likely to survive if America does not.

Kenneth Clark, "The Present Dilemma of the Negro," *Journal of Negro History*, LIII (January 1968), pp. 1–11.

number regarded themselves as victims of a neocolonialism that was as real to them as it had been to the African victims of British or French or Portuguese rule. Others insisted that they believed that they were scheduled for genocide in the new designs of whites to achieve worldwide racial homogeneity. Still others saw their only hope in somehow joining with their darker brothers, wherever they were, or with the developing nations, wherever they were, in creating a Third World force as a countervailing power to the aggressive, imperialistic designs of the white world.

Some African Americans began to focus their attention on Africa and began to think and speak of it as their home. Some adopted African dress and wore their hair "natural." Some, apparently indifferent to the persistence of slavery in portions of the Arab world, followed the lead of Malcolm X and adopted African or Arabic names to show that they had severed all connections with white Americans. Some, apparently indifferent to the fact

VIOLENCE ERUPTS AFTER MARTIN LUTHER KING'S ASSASSINATION. A group of blacks watches firemen fight a blaze in Pittsburgh's Homewood-Brushton section during an outbreak of looting and vandalism that started after Dr. King's assassination on April 4, 1968. Hundreds of National Guardsmen had to be sent into the area to quell the outbreak. *(AP/Wide World Photos.)*

that during slavery "black" was at least as pejorative as "Negro," rejected the term "Negro," arguing that it was a relic of slavery, and expressed a strong preference for "black" or "Afro-American" as racial designations. They demanded control of all institutions in the black community, including the schools, and they insisted on the introduction of courses in black history, black literature, and other subjects in the area of black studies. In the late 1960s and early 1970s numerous school boards as well as colleges and universities introduced courses in black studies that they hoped would meet the demands of the black community even if the value of these courses to the total curriculum remained open to question. As far as African Americans were concerned, the black pride that a reorganized curriculum could stimulate would compensate for the disillusionment and despair that years of frustration and embitterment had produced.

The Black Revolution of the 1960s and 1970s, along with the rise of the women's movement in America, stimulated the emergence of an African-American women's movement committed to challenging the barriers of racism and sexism that burdened minority women within their racial communities and in the larger society. Significant numbers of black women who were civil rights activists supported or identified with this new emphasis on the liberation of African-American women. The concerns and issues of the black women's movement found powerful expression in the political arena and in the writings of its adherents, many of whom were among the most creative literary and intellectual figures in the African-American community. When the National Black Feminist Organization (NBFO) was founded in 1973, Eleanor Holmes Norton, a member of the New York City Human Rights Commission and a founder of the group, charged that most Americans expected "black women to suppress their aspirations in deference to black males." These sentiments were echoed by Margaret Sloan, another founder, who declared that the new organization would make it clear to "the black liberation movement that there can't be liberation for half a race." In response to critics of the African-American women's movement, Shirley Chisholm, a distinguished and articulate congresswoman who received little support from African-American men in her unsuccessful campaign for the Democratic presidential nomination in 1972, declared that "in many respects it was more difficult to be a woman than a black."

The Black Revolution was, however, more than the disillusionment of those who believed that the dominant forces in American life were neocolonialism and genocide and who responded by advocating cultural nationalism and separatism. It was also the enormous increase in the political power of blacks that reversed the sense of powerlessness and hopelessness of the earlier years. The intense voter registration drives of thousands of black and white civil rights workers, the enactment and enforcement of the Voting Rights Act of 1965, and the growing awareness of African Americans of the power of the ballot created something of a black political revolution in the 1960s and 1970s. In 1966 there were 97 black members of state legislatures and 6 members of the Congress of the United States, but there was no black mayor in any American city. By 1973 more than 200 blacks sat in thirty-seven state legislatures, and 16 were in the Congress of the United States. These included one senator, and the only Republican, Edward Brooke of Massachusetts, and four women, Shirley Chisholm of New York, Barbara Jordan of Texas, Yvonne Burke of California, and Cardiss Collins of Illinois. In 1976 Jordan was a keynote speaker at the Democratic National Convention. By 1979 she and Burke had retired and had been replaced by black men, while Brooke, the lone black in the Senate, had lost to a white Democrat. The Black Congressional Caucus remained strong and aggressive, however, with 17 members in the House of Representatives. During the decade ending in 1973 blacks had served as mayors of Cleveland, Los Angeles, Gary, and Newark, as well as several scores of small Southern towns such as Tuskegee, Alabama, Fayette, Mississippi, and Madison, Arkansas. By 1979 there were also black mayors in major cities in the South, such as Atlanta and New Orleans, and also in Los Angeles and Detroit. By 1979 more than 600 were serving as members of city councils, and over 1,000 had been elected judges, aldermen, constables, marshals, school board members, and to a variety of other public offices at the state and local levels.

In races for statewide offices the record was rather uneven. Not only did Brooke lose his Senate seat in 1978, but Lieutenant Governor Mervyn Dymally of California lost his bid for reelection and Yvonne Burke was an unsuccessful candidate for attorney general of California. On the other hand, Wisconsin elected a black woman as secretary of state, and Illinois sent a black man to the comptroller's office. In North Carolina in 1978 an African American was elected to the state court of appeals, while blacks in the positions of secretary of state in Michigan, treasurer in Connecticut, and superintendent of public instruction in California were all reelected that year.

There were still other manifestations of the new political power of African Americans. Their votes were often decisive in crucial elections. It will be remembered that in several states, such as Illinois and South Carolina, they gave the decisive votes to John F. Kennedy in 1960. In the following year their votes, together with those of Puerto Ricans, were responsible for the reelection of Robert Wagner as mayor of New York and the election of Richard Hughes as governor of New Jersey. This growing power prompted African-American leaders in the late 1960s and early 1970s to demand a greater voice in party affairs. Thus, when it became clear that 20 percent of the Democratic vote in 1968 came from blacks (85 percent of black voters had cast their ballots for presidential candidate Hubert Humphrey that year), they argued that the Democrats should give them greater recognition. Pressures applied by Mayor Richard Hatcher of Gary and others doubtless had the effect of significantly increasing the number of black delegates to the 1972 Democratic National Convention and the selection of Yvonne Braithwaite Burke as cochairperson of the convention.

There were those who feared that the regular political parties would not take blacks seriously, while others were not certain that they could achieve their goals through the established political organizations. These were among the considerations that led to the calling of the first National Black Political Convention, which met in Gary, Indiana, in March 1972. Led by Representative Charles C. Diggs of Michigan, Mayor Richard Hatcher of Gary, and the poet Amiri Baraka (LeRoi Jones), the convention attracted more than 2,700 delegates and 4,000 alternates and observers. For several days the sessions heard various views on what the group should do about such matters as the major political parties, black representation and participation in economic and political matters, school busing, and United States foreign policy in southern Africa, Portugal, and Israel.

When it was not possible to reach definitive positions in the closing hours of the convention, the delegates authorized a committee of leaders to draw up a position paper setting forth a consensus of its views. In May the leaders released a document called the "National Black Political Agenda," which revealed deep divisions regarding major policy issues. Hatcher and Diggs expressed opposition to provisions opposing school busing and United States support of Israel. In this they were joined by the Congressional Black Caucus. Meanwhile, Hatcher criticized Roy Wilkins for withdrawing NAACP support for the agenda. Covering a wide range of problems, the agenda

SHIRLEY CHISHOLM CAMPAIGNS. This picture shows Rep. Shirley A. Chisholm campaigning hand-to-hand in March 1972 in the Roxbury section of Boston during her articulate but unsuccessful campaign for the Democratic presidential nomination in 1972. *(AP/Wide World Photos.)*

contained a poor people's platform, model pledges for black and nonblack candidates seeking convention support, the outline of a voter registration bill, and a bill for community self-determination. It ended on a note of optimism, saying, "All things are possible."

Even as African-American leaders disagreed over the course of action they should take, they fully appreciated the growing awareness in the black community of its political role in American life. The ambivalence regarding racial integration, the sense of alienation, the doubts about the relevance of white values to the problems of the black ghetto, and the strong support for community self-determination merely underscored the vigor of the response of the black community to white resistance to equality. Reverend Jesse Jackson, the head of People United to Save Humanity (PUSH), accelerated the pressure of his organization to secure equal opportunity in the larger community and to control every aspect of life in the black community. The projects under Jackson's leadership included the 1979 campaign, "PUSH for Excellence." As Amiri Baraka reached a position of great influence in Newark, he urged a more independent and unequivocal stand by African Americans in their drive for equality. Even as Gwendolyn Brooks served as poet laureate of Illinois, she became more deeply committed to far-reaching changes in the status of blacks.

The dissatisfaction with conditions was so deep in the black community that few developments, however significant, seemed satisfactory or even noteworthy. Many blacks had become so embittered that they were inclined to interpret individual advancement in the public and private sectors as nothing more than cunning designs of whites to buy off, and thus to silence, their most talented and influential leaders. In 1971 a Gallup poll reported that 25 percent of employed blacks were dissatisfied with their jobs, while only 9 percent of whites were dissatisfied. Meanwhile, the dissatisfaction with the quality of community life was 44 percent for blacks and 18 percent for whites. Small wonder that there was considerable apprehension among African Americans as they faced the future.

■ Balance Sheet of the Revolution

By the mid-1970s many factors contributed to a heightened sense of power on the part of African Americans. They held elective offices to which they could not possibly have thought of aspiring only two decades earlier. At every level of government they held appointive offices, although they continued to insist that they were denied their full share of such positions. The Legal Defense Fund (LDF), the NAACP, the United States Commission on Civil Rights, and the Civil Rights Division of the Department of Justice were quick to take action against the violation of voting rights of blacks. The influence of the Congressional Black Caucus was increasing not only in its effect on legislation but also in its monitoring of law enforcement by the executive departments and the president. To many blacks, the political power they enjoyed was real, and in due course the rewards would be considerable.

But the power as well as the rewards could have been greater. In 1976 only 58.5 percent of all eligible black voters were registered and only 48.7 percent actually voted. The Voting Rights Act of 1965, which theoretically opened the door of political power to all blacks, had not been successful in getting out the black vote. And groups such as the Voter Education Project did not have sufficient funds to mount a successful campaign to get blacks to register and vote. Even more discouraging was the fact that among younger blacks, between eighteen and twenty-four, apathy was so great that in 1976 only 38 percent were registered and only 26 percent voted.

The power of the African-American vote was quite evident in the presidential election of 1976. More than 90 percent of all black voters supported Jimmy Carter, the nominee of the Democratic party. Except for Virginia, the Carter ticket swept the entire South, although white Southerners favored Gerald Ford, the Republican nominee, by about 55 percent to 45 percent. Because the whites of the South rejected Carter, the first president born in the Old South since Woodrow Wilson, blacks, Northern and Southern, laid a firm claim on the credit for his election. He appointed Patricia Harris to the Cabinet as secretary of housing and urban development and Andrew Young ambassador to the United Nations. He tapped Wade McCree to be solicitor general and appointed blacks as undersecretaries and assistant secretaries in executive departments. In his earliest ambassadorial

SECRETARY OF HOUSING AND URBAN DEVELOPMENT, PATRICIA HARRIS, with President Jimmy Carter and New York Mayor Abraham Beame, as they inspect a depressed area of the South Bronx in 1977. *(Courtesy Department of Housing and Urban Development.)*

appointments, he sent at least nine blacks to represent the United States abroad. They were ambassadors to Spain, Rumania, and East Germany as well as to African and Caribbean nations. He also appointed former Ambassador John Reinhardt to be head of the newly organized International Communications Agency.

Blacks insisted that they were entitled to more than Carter was giving them. There was no influential African American on the White House staff until Louis Martin went there as special assistant to the president in September 1978. Many felt that he did not give adequate support to Patricia Harris in her effort to liberalize the rules regarding government subsidy of housing for the poor. Others were distressed about what seemed to be his greater concern for balancing the budget and fighting inflation than for relief and assistance to the disadvantaged. But they had to admit that Carter's door was open to them, and in 1978 and 1979 a veritable stream of delegations representing various black constituencies urged the president to give more attention to the black and the poor.

Even though the president listened attentively and expressed sympathy, the problem of the economic disadvantages of black Americans did not go away. It was true that in 1976 about 30 percent of all black families earned $15,000 or more, while only 2 percent had been at that level in 1966. But in 1976 about 31 percent of all blacks lived below the poverty line, compared to 42 percent in 1966. Over this ten-year period the unemployment rate for blacks was consistently higher than for whites. When the jobless rate was 6.3 percent for whites in 1977, it was 13.2 for blacks. For white teenagers it was about 15 percent, while for black youths it ranged from 40 to 55 percent. Indeed, so many black families within the decade of the 1970s were unemployed and on welfare that it was quite likely that the nation would spawn an entire generation of blacks who had simply never worked to support themselves. The implications of such a possibility were almost too frightening to contemplate.

In 1978 and 1979 many Americans, black and white, were debating the argument advanced by University of Chicago sociologist William J. Wilson in *The Declining Significance of Race.* Wilson contended that "trained and educated blacks, especially the younger ones who have recently entered the labor market, are experiencing unprecedented job opportunities that are at least comparable to those of whites with equivalent qualifications." Those who differed with Wilson seemed not to heed his other argument, namely, that in past years discrimination and oppression had created "a huge black underclass, and the technological and economic revolutions threaten to solidify its position in society." What he feared was a widening economic gap in the black community "with the black poor falling further and further behind the more privileged blacks." Such an eventuality could create tensions and even strife within the black community.

But in the last quarter of the twentieth century, there could be little doubt that an African-American middle class was growing in both size and influence. To the minister, lawyer, teacher, and physician could now be added the civil servant in the upper ranks, the retail clerk in a variety of mercantile establishments, the banker, the corporate manager, the media producer, the publisher of books and periodicals, the account executive, and the elected official. Although many of them served the black community primarily or exclusively, an increasing number had "made it" in the white world. The magazine *Black Enterprise* took pride each year in recognizing the top 100 businesses owned and/or controlled by African Americans, but it did not neglect those who were moving up in the white corporate world. There were bankers such as Lucius Gregg of Chicago's First National and financial consultants such as former Federal Reserve Board Governor Andrew Brimmer, whose firm enjoyed enormous influence among some of the country's most powerful businesses.

As early as the late eighteenth century there had been a few blacks

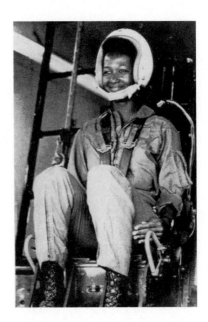

FIRST FEMALE AFRICAN-AMERICAN ASTRO-NAUT. Mae Jemison, M.D., flew her first mission in June, 1991, that was dedicated to a series of life sciences and material processing experiments. *(AP/Wide World Photos.)*

possessing great wealth. From the end of World War II to the end of the 1970s the number of affluent blacks increased markedly. Millionaires could be found in traditional pursuits such as insurance, banking, manufacturing, publishing, and retail enterprises. But they could also be found in the world of entertainment and sports. By 1980 it was not unusual for black athletes, especially basketball, football, and baseball players, to sign multiple-year contracts running into the millions, and even a few boxers aspired to make a fraction of the millions that Muhammad Ali earned as heavyweight boxing champion.

There were nonfinancial rewards that African-Americans reaped in the wake of their changing status. One of the most visible was the participation of black astronauts and scientists in the well-publicized and highly visible programs of the National Aeronautics and Space Administration (NASA). This elite group included Air Force Lt. Col. Guion S. Bluford, Jr., who in 1983 became the first African-American astronaut, and Mae E. Jemison, a physician and chemical engineer, whose 1991 space flight made her the first female African-American astronaut. Television, radio, and other forms of mass communication provided new opportunities for many blacks to affect the way that they were perceived by others. Entertainers such as Bill Cosby, Sammy Davis, Jr., and Nancy Wilson commanded huge followings, while television commercials sought to include blacks, in recognition of the very important market among them as well as to promote a feeling of good will through interracial advertising. Thus, in at least some instances, the Black Revolution had ushered blacks into realms of American life that could not have been foretold two decades earlier.

CHAPTER 24

New Forms of Activism

■ The Reagan Years

If the Black Revolution did not come to a halt during the Carter years, it at least shifted gears. While African Americans were pleased that Carter had appointed more blacks to important positions in the government than had any previous president, they were not happy about other developments. Unemployment continued to rise, putting thousands of black workers out of jobs, and there was general dissatisfaction with Carter's lack of success in handling certain domestic problems such as energy, welfare, and taxes. Even so, the more they heard about Republican nominee Ronald Reagan, the more they felt that they had no alternative to Carter. They viewed Reagan as being too far to the right to suit anyone except the ideological purists in the Republican party. They were mistaken, however, for his position on social issues, especially his criticism of "welfare queens" and big government, greatly appealed to white blue-collar workers who were generally opposed to affirmative action and the equal economic opportunity programs of the federal government. On November 4, 1980, Ronald Reagan won 489 electoral votes to Carter's 49, capturing every Southern state except Carter's home state, Georgia. But Carter did about as well among African Americans as he had done in 1976 by taking approximately 90 percent of the black vote again. Blacks could not help wondering if Carter's liberal racial policies had turned the white South against him.

African Americans did not have to wait long to see how the Reagan policies would affect them. Before the new president took office, the director of his transition team, Edwin Meese, said that more than one black would be appointed to posts in the new cabinet. He added that Reagan was "committed to putting blacks in nontraditional roles." He observed, in addition, that the new president's staff would have no black appointees for what could be regarded as "black" posts. But there was, after all, only one black cabinet member named by President Reagan, and that was Samuel R. Pierce, Jr., the new secretary of housing and urban development. (Since its creation, this post had been something of a traditionally black one, having first been held by Robert C. Weaver and later by Patricia R. Harris and being the only cabinet post in which more than one African American had served.) There was one top-ranking African American on the White House staff, Melvin Bradley, named senior adviser of policy development and later special assistant to the president. At the end of five months, no blacks had been appointed to any of the approximately 100 subcabinet positions.

There were posts in the federal establishment to which it was expected that the new administration would appoint African Americans. One was chairman of the Equal Employment Opportunity Commission, a position that had been held by five other blacks, the most recent of whom was Eleanor Holmes Norton who left the EEOC to accept a professorship at Georgetown Law Center. In June 1981, President Reagan appointed to that position William Bell of Michigan, who from the outset was opposed by civil rights groups and by blacks who claimed that, having only had experience in supervising four people in his consulting firm, he had no demonstrated ability to administer an agency with 3,300 employees. Perhaps not since 1885 when blacks protested the nomination of George Washington Williams to be United States minister to Haiti had blacks so aggressively opposed the appointment of one of their own to a high government post. Under pressure from blacks and civil rights groups, the president felt compelled to withdraw the nomination.

The furor over the Bell affair had not subsided before another one rose as the result of another Reagan appointment. Early on the president had made clear his intention to appoint people to public office who shared his views regarding the role of government and its various agencies. Since its establishment in 1957, the United States Commission on Civil Rights had enjoyed remarkable independence from presidential interference, even when it was critical of presidential policies. It had been bipartisan, an example of which was the appointment of a prominent white Republican, Jill Ruckelshaus, to the commission by Democratic President Jimmy Carter. In November 1981, Reagan notified the chairman, Arthur S. Flemming, that he would replace him, and he nominated Clarence Pendleton, a conservative black Republican who had been executive director of the San Diego Urban League. This was the first time in its twenty-four-year history that a president had removed the chair of the Commission on Civil Rights. Then, in February

1982, the president announced that he would nominate the Reverend B. Sam Hart of Philadelphia to this commission, presumably to replace Ruckelshaus. Hart, a black and a Republican, was described at the time as a right-wing evangelical known to be opposed to virtually every item on the civil rights agenda. Vigorous protests over the appropriateness of Hart's credentials grew to the point where he withdrew his name before ever being formally nominated. Then the president sent up three more names to replace commissioners Mary Frances Berry, Blandina Cárdenas Ramirez, and Murray Saltzman, all known to be critical of the administration's opposition to affirmative action as a remedy for discrimination in employment and education.

The president's nominees, Robert Destro, a law professor, John Bunzel of the Hoover Institute, and Morris Abram, former president of Brandeis University, were known to have views similar to the president's on matters such as affirmative action and busing. This was the first time that a president had attempted to refashion the Commission on Civil Rights in a way that its views and policies would reflect his own. Some members of the Senate Judiciary Committee asked that the names be withdrawn because efforts to replace incumbent Commission members clearly "tainted the independence and integrity" of the commission. Many civil rights leaders urged that if the names were not withdrawn, the nominees should all be opposed. Meanwhile, the House voted to extend the life of the commission beyond its expiration date of September 30, 1982, with an amendment prohibiting removal of commissioners except for neglect of duty or malfeasance in office. As the Senate wrangled over pending nominations, a compromise plan was worked out to permit the six incumbents to remain and to empower the president to appoint two additional nominees.

Facing certain defeat in the passage of the compromise and in a new effort to control the commission, President Reagan fired commissioners Berry, Ramirez, and Saltzman, thus sabotaging the carefully worked out compromise and leaving the Commission on Civil Rights in danger of extinction. The feverish behind-the-scenes maneuvering resulted in renewal of the compromise in which the House and the Senate would share with the president the appointment of members of the commission. The incumbent members would remain, and the president could appoint two new members, presumably Abram and Bunzel. The president would also be able to retain Clarence Pendleton as chairman. But the House Republican leader, Robert Michel who, under the compromise, was expected to appoint Ruckelshaus, appointed Destro instead. The vice president was expected to appoint Mary Louise Smith, who had been confirmed at the same time as Pendleton, but he declined to do so, saying that she had refused to pledge support for the president's designation of Pendleton as chairman. Civil rights advocates and many members of Congress called this a "double cross." For the next several years, the United States Commission on Civil Rights, which for twenty-five years had been a strong voice for justice and equality under the law, became a debating society. It dispensed with hearings and exhaustive studies, limiting itself to pronouncements from the chairman and the executive director, with the members whom the president had tried unsuccessfully to dismiss issuing only minority statements.

Almost no blacks were moving to the top in the foreign service, whether they were career officers or those appointed from the outside by the president. In 1979 members of minority groups accounted for 8.3 percent of foreign service officers on duty in this country and abroad. In 1983 about 6.3 percent of foreign service officers were black. For the first time in more than a decade there were no blacks serving as assistant secretary of state, and only four at the next level, deputy assistant secretary of state. Of the 127 current ambassadorial positions, only 7 were held by blacks in 1983, down from 14 during the Carter years, with but one serving in Europe in 1986 while the others were assigned to posts in the Third World. George Crockett of Michigan, a member of the House Foreign Affairs Committee, lamented the fact that there were 5 black ambassadors "wandering the corridors of the State Department. . . . While other career officers have been given assignments comparable to their grade level . . . the blacks have been passed over," he said.

It became increasingly clear that the things African Americans had taken for granted during the previous two decades were no longer so. There had been, as we have seen, support and respect for the United States Commission on Civil Rights regardless of the politics of the president. Now it was on the road to being reduced to a mere administration mouthpiece. Through a program of weakening the Legal Enforcement Assistance Administration the president not only curtailed the enforcement of laws against housing discrimination but also took from poor people the one opportunity they had to obtain assistance for legal redress of their grievances against landlords, shopkeepers, loan sharks, and the like. He also insisted that the enforcement of civil rights should be left to the states.

Meanwhile, the new administration interested itself in reducing the role of government in dealing with matters arising under the provisions of such legislation as the Civil Rights Act of 1964 and the Voting Rights Act of 1965—indeed, the president was slow to support the renewal of the Voting Rights Act in 1982, and when he finally did so it was with apparent reluctance. Under the leadership of white Reagan appointee William Bradford Reynolds, who replaced Drew Days, the black Carter appointee, the Civil Rights Division of the Department of Justice became the principal opponent of blacks seeking relief through the courts in matters pertaining to affirmative action. In December 1985, Julius Chambers, director-counsel for the NAACP Legal Defense Fund, reflected on this shift in the role of government. "LDF used to be able to count on the federal government as an active partner in civil rights enforcement," he said. "Today—indeed, since 1981—the Department is more often than not fighting us every step of the way in voting rights, school desegregation, equal employment opportunity, and affirmative action. I felt the weight of the burden of this change. Battling the federal government is both disheartening and expensive."

Chambers was referring specifically to his experiences during the 1985 term of the United States Supreme Court. In *Thornburg v. Gingles,* he had presented a challenge to the redistricting plan adopted by North Carolina in 1982 for elections to the state legislature. He argued that the plan was illegal under the Voting Rights Act as amended in 1982 which prohibited voting practices that afforded minorities "less opportunity than other members of the electorate to participate in the political process and elect representatives of their choice." His argument had been upheld in the lower court, and the state appealed. The Justice Department, despite having previously conceded that aspects of the plan were discriminatory, reversed itself and supported the state's claim. Nevertheless, a bipartisan group of United States senators and representatives supported the claim of the LDF. The Court rejected the arguments of the state of North Carolina and the United States Department of Justice and upheld the LDF's contention regarding proof of violation of the act and the type of statistical evidence necessary to establish a violation. During the same term, the Supreme Court upheld affirmative action plans that included goals and timetables, thus rejecting the government's argument that the Civil Rights Act of 1964 restricted relief to identified victims of discrimination. The Court held in *Local 98, International Association of Fire- fighters v. Cleveland* that affirmative action plans were appropriate if carefully drawn and limited so as to address identified problems and discriminatory patterns or practices.

In January 1982, the Reagan administration reversed an eleven-year-old policy that denied tax-exempt status to private educational and certain other nonprofit institutions that practiced racial discrimination. Apparently, the two institutions for which the benefit was intended were Bob Jones University in South Carolina, which admitted African-American students but forbade interracial dating and racial intermarriage, and Goldsboro Christian School in North Carolina, which barred the admission of blacks. When the inevitable uproar came, the administration insisted that administrative agencies, such as the Internal Revenue Service, should not exercise powers that the Constitution assigns to Congress. Congress, by specific legislation, had already sanctioned procedures requiring private schools, as a condition of obtaining tax exemption, to publish and advertise that they did not practice racial discrimination. Thus, Congress insisted that it did not need to act in the matter. The *New York Times* declared, "The Reagan Administration is picking the pocket of every American taxpayer to subsidize racism in education," while the *Washington Post* called the policy "outrageous." The matter soon quieted down, and the schools did not get the tax-exempt status they hoped for.

Ronald Reagan had said during his campaign—and he repeated it after his election—that government handouts made people "government depend- ent, rather than independent," and he wanted to put a stop to that. Once in

THE PRESIDENT SIGNS THE KING HOLIDAY BILL. Ronald Reagan signs a bill establishing a national holiday in honor of slain civil rights leader Martin Luther King, Jr., as his widow, Coretta Scott King, looks on. Among those invited to the ceremony were Vice President George Bush and Congresswoman Katie Hall, who introduced the bill in Congress. *(UPI/Bettmann Newsphotos.)*

office he pushed through Congress a number of programs in keeping with these views. His first budget, as well as subsequent ones, reduced the number of people eligible to participate in federal social programs such as food stamps, Medicaid, student loans, unemployment compensation, child nutrition assistance, and Aid to Families with Dependent Children. Even his tax program reflected his view that low-income groups should not become more dependent on the government. The 31.7 million taxpayers making $15,000 or less were to receive 8 percent of the tax reduction, while the 12.5 million earning $50,000 or more per year were to get 35 percent of the reduction. Meanwhile, the contribution of corporations to federal revenues was reduced from 13 cents to 8 cents for each tax dollar. Since most blacks were in the low-income group, they not only suffered from reductions in federal programs but also from receiving less tax relief than did the higher-income groups. It was difficult not to conclude that President Reagan did not regard people at the lower end of the income levels to be of urgent interest to him and his advisers.

For almost fifteen years the friends and admirers of Martin Luther King, Jr., had worked for a national holiday commemorating his birthday. Many opponents pointed to scores of presidents and hundreds of great Americans

TABLE 9
Unemployment Rate by Race (White and Black) between 1965 and 1990

	1965	1970	1975	1980	1985	1990
White	4.3%	3.9%	8.5%	6.0%	6.6%	3.8%
Black	8.5%	6.7%	14.7%	13.4%	15.6%	8.6%

Source: U. S. Department of Commerce. Statistical Abstract of the United States, 1992. Bureau of the Census. Washington, D.C., 1992.

whose birthdays had not been commemorated with a national holiday. Each year, nevertheless, members of the Congressional Black Caucus and other members of Congress pushed for the passage of such a bill, but to no avail. On January 15, 1981, five days before Ronald Reagan took the oath of office as president, more than 100,000 marchers converged on Washington to rally for a King holiday. The president, preoccupied with other matters, indifferent to the mounting pressures, or downright opposed to the proposition, did nothing. Finally, his silence was interpreted as opposition. When asked about the matter, he usually parried the question or deflected it in some way.

When Senator Jesse Helms raised questions about King's alleged Communist associations, the White House defended Helms's sincerity. When the president was asked about King's alleged Communist ties, he said, "We'll find out in 35 years," alluding to the period after which the raw files of the FBI could be reviewed. He later apologized to the King family for the remark. But the pressure continued to mount, especially when Strom Thurmond, a former Dixiecrat, came out in support of the proposed holiday. When, finally, the bill passed both houses of Congress, the president transformed his final approval into a gala occasion by signing the bill in the White House rose garden on November 2, 1983, in the presence of the King family, leaders of both houses of Congress, and other dignitaries. He said on that occasion: "But traces of bigotry still mar America. So each year on Martin Luther King Day, let us not only recall Dr. King, but rededicate ourselves to the commandments he believed in and sought to live every day."

Even as the president's popularity soared in the white community, African Americans were never reconciled to Ronald Reagan. To be sure, a steady but small trickle went into the Republican party to join the "hard core" of party faithfuls who had remained in the face of mounting criticism of many blacks. In a survey made in 1984 by a Gallup Poll and the Joint Center for Political Studies, 83 percent of the blacks interviewed felt that "Reagan's policies have been harmful to blacks," and a massive 94 percent disapproved of the president's handling of "the situation of poor people." The study concluded that the most dramatic economic recovery of the postwar period "has left many blacks feeling like spectators rather than as participants." With unemployment among blacks rising at an alarming rate, they had reason to be apprehensive about the future. In 1982 the black unemployment rate was 18.9 percent, more than twice the white rate of 8.4 percent. Even by 1985, when times were better, the unemployment rate among blacks was 16.3 percent when the unemployment rate among whites had dropped to 6.2 percent. Meanwhile, the unemployment rate for young blacks, ages 16 to 19, soared to more than 50 percent for the first time in history. When one looked at earnings, the picture was similarly bleak. Black workers in the early 1980s earned less than white workers in every meaningful classification, whether by age, education, sex, or occupation. Small wonder that, in *The Myth of Black Progress*, Alphonso Pinkney concluded that even if the number of middle-class blacks had increased in recent years, "there has been a startling growth in the black underclass."

■ A New Economic and Political Thrust

For a man so young, Jesse Jackson had followed several careers before 1984, when he was forty-three years old. He had begun his civil rights activities while still a student at North Carolina Agricultural and Technical State University. Going on to Chicago Theological Seminary, he left before graduation to join Martin Luther King, Jr., and the Southern Christian Leadership Conference in their crusade for civil rights all over the South. Soon Jackson was placed in charge of Operation Breadbasket, the economic arm of SCLC, and he was with King in Memphis when he was assassinated in April 1968. After he broke with SCLC in 1971, he founded Operation PUSH (People United to Save Humanity which was later modestly changed to People United to Serve Humanity), which quickly grew to comprise about seventy chapters totaling more than 80,000 members. With headquarters in Chicago and annual meetings in cities where there were thriving PUSH chapters, Jackson and PUSH began to press the business and financial community for economic parity for African Americans.

Jackson became the self-appointed black ambassador to the white business community, gently threatening to boycott selected firms if they did not move toward parity for blacks. In August 1981, the Coca-Cola Company was the first to sign an agreement to increase its benefits to the black community. It agreed to spend $14 million with minority vendors, and within a year it had exceeded its goal by more than 22 percent. It also sold thirty-two fountain-syrup distributorships and set a goal to increase the management staff from 5 percent black to 12.5 percent. Similar agreements were reached with Kentucky Fried Chicken, the Southland Corporation, Anheuser-Busch, Seven-Up, and Burger King. When the CBS-TV affiliate in Chicago replaced a black anchorman with a white one who had returned after a stint in New York, Jackson organized a boycott of the station that was eminently successful; the Chicago station even named a black manager in 1986. This convinced

AN AFRICAN AMERICAN BECOMES VIRGINIA'S GOVERNOR. Governor L. Douglas Wilder was sworn in by retired Supreme Court Justice Lewis Powell, thus becoming the first African American elected chief executive of a state. *(UPI/Bettmann.)*

Jackson and many others that by careful planning and targeting, blacks could secure a larger share of job opportunities and economic power than they had ever had.

Jackson began to apply the same creative imagination and insight to the political sphere. He told African Americans that they had enormous political power if they would but use it. Speaking at the twentieth anniversary of the March on Washington, he indicated how black Americans could have changed the outcome of the election in 1980. "Reagan won Alabama by 17,500 votes, but there were 272,000 unregistered blacks. He won Arkansas by 5,000 votes, with 85,000 unregistered blacks. He won Kentucky by 17,800 votes, with 62,000 unregistered blacks. . . . So the numbers show that Reagan won through a perverse coalition of the rich and the unregistered. But this is a new day. Hands that picked cotton in 1884 will pick the President in 1984." He electrified the crowd, and he repeated that message wherever he went. It was not so easy, however.

It was clear from the summer of 1983 that he would make a run for the Democratic nomination for president—especially after hearing the shouts of "Run, Jesse, run" welling up from the crowds. But he needed money—lots of it—and he needed support from the black establishment, which he did not get. Benjamin Hooks, executive director of the NAACP, said, "If an

BIG CITY MAYORS. Tom Bradley of Los Angeles, Colman Young of Detroit, W. Wilson Goode of Philadelphia, Harold Washington of Chicago, Sharon Pratt Kelly of Washington, Maynard Jackson of Atlanta, and David Dinkins of New York City were among the scores of African Americans serving as Mayors of their cities in 1980s and 1990s. *(Bradley; AP/Wide World Photos; Young, UPI/Bettmann; Goode, UPI/Bettmann; Washington, AP/Wide World Photos; Dixon, AP/Wide World Photos; Jackson, UPI/Bettmann; Dinkins, AP/Wide World Photos.)*

overwhelming number of black voters are voting for a black, then we've lost our voice in selecting the white candidate who will be the Democratic choice." John Jacob, president of the National Urban League, added that "A black presidential candidate would be a retreat to symbolism and would shatter black expectations."

Jackson was not daunted. He had seen how the rising tide of black voters had done much to make Harold Washington mayor of Chicago in 1983 and how blacks were coming into power in increasing numbers at the local level, for example, as mayors of Charlotte, North Carolina, Birmingham, Alabama, and New Orleans, Louisiana. That power could be mobilized at higher levels to elect more black members to Congress, to make a run for the presidency, or at least to influence the choice that the Democratic convention would make. Others agreed with him. Barry Commoner, who in 1980 had campaigned as an environmentalist candidate, came out for Jackson, as did feminist organizer, Gloria Steinem, former Attorney General Ramsey Clark, Congressman John Conyers, California Assemblywoman Maxine Waters, and Mayor Richard Hatcher of Gary, Indiana.

When Jackson announced his candidacy in October 1983, he made it clear that one of his main goals was to induce the disfranchised to register and vote, "thus vesting them with a kind of power they had not had before." His "Rainbow Coalition" symbolized for many the unity that could be forged when people of all races, creeds, and colors joined together for a common purpose: to place men and women in public service whose primary purpose was to serve the best interests of their constituents. He placed his emphasis on registration, and at his campaign appearances he arranged to have registrars present to make certain that people in the audience who had not registered could do so. He would begin the chant that his listeners would repeat: "There is a freedom train a comin', But you got to register to ride, So get on board and get on with it." Then the audience would shout, "Run, Jesse, run! Run, Jesse, run!" There can be no doubt that the Jackson candidacy was a great stimulus to black registration and voting.

The American public had never seen and heard a black person make a serious bid for nationwide public office. James W. Ford had run for vice president on the Communist ticket in the 1930s, but neither the ticket nor Ford was taken seriously. Here was Jackson in 1984, however, stumping the nation, running in Democratic primaries, debating the other candidates—Cranston, Hart, Hollings, and Mondale—and acquitting himself well as an attractive, personable, intelligent, articulate, well-informed American citizen. That, in itself, was an important experience for Americans, black and white alike.

Jackson had serious problems, however. In 1979 he had traveled to the Middle East and met with President Hafez al-Hassad of Syria and, to the horror of many pro-Israeli Americans, with the head of the Palestine Liberation Organization (PLO), Yasir Arafat. Jackson defended the meeting, declaring that any long-term peace settlement in the Middle East had to take the Palestinians into consideration. His critics said that such an argument was no defense at all, since the PLO did not recognize the existence of Israel. Later, in an off-the-record interview with a reporter from the *Washington Post*, Jackson referred to New York City as "Hymie Town," which many considered to be a slur against Jews. Jackson insisted that no slur was intended, but many Jews continued to feel that he had insulted them.

In a remarkable feat of courage and daring, Jackson went to Syria at the end of December 1983, to plead with President Hassad for the release of a young black, Lt. Robert Goodman, a navigator-bombardier. Goodman's reconnaissance plane had been shot down over Syria, killing the pilot, and Goodman taken prisoner. After hearing Jackson's plea, President Hassad turned Goodman over to Jackson to the great joy of many Americans, including President Reagan, who welcomed Jackson and Goodman in a White House ceremony. But not all were pleased. Some Americans said that Jackson was not only grand-standing but was also interfering in the conduct of his country's foreign affairs. Others were severely critical of Jackson for

CANDIDATE JESSE JACKSON. Jackson and his family immediately following his address at the Democratic National Convention in 1988. (*Sygma.*)

including in his delegation Louis Farrakhan, who had called Judaism "a gutter religion." Jackson was called upon to reject Farrakhan's support, but he would only go so far as to differ with Farrakhan on specific items and issues.

By the time of the Democratic National Convention in San Francisco in July 1984, Jackson had garnered approximately 300 delegates, but since Walter Mondale, the front runner, had 200 black delegates, Jackson's bargaining power was limited. He made a well-crafted speech to the convention in which he again apologized for any statements he had made that were regarded as offensive. There did not seem to be much forgiveness in response. Walter Mondale and Geraldine Ferraro came away with the nominations for president and vice president, and Jackson became an unenthusiastic supporter of the Democratic ticket which went down to ignominious defeat in November.

Black voters, however, had voted in larger numbers than ever before. An estimated 3.05 million blacks voted in the Democratic primaries, representing 18 percent of the 16.94 million Democratic primary voters. The surge of black registration and voting was due largely to Jackson's candidacy. In the November elections, about 10 million blacks voted, 89 percent of whom supported Mondale. If there was little enthusiasm for Mondale, blacks continued to feel that they had no alternative. They could derive considerable satisfaction, nevertheless, from the increase in their political power between

CLARENCE THOMAS BECOMES SUPREME COURT JUSTICE. President Bush and his wife, Barbara, look on as Supreme Court Justice Byron White administers the oath and Virginia Thomas, the wife of the new justice, holds the Bible. *(AP/Wide World Photos.)*

1970, when there were 1,469 black elected officials, and 1985, when there were 6,056. For black officeholders in general, Jackson's candidacy had a salutary effect. Some even believed that it had something to do with the election in 1985 of Virginia's first black lieutenant governor, Douglas Wilder, who was elected governor four years later. The defeat of the Democrats in 1984 ensured four more years of the Reagan administration and its policies. With increasing concern and pessimism, black leaders continued to pursue the well-being of their racial community in the face of a White House they considered uninterested and unfriendly. As the nation moved toward the 1988 presidential election, the bulk of the African-American community focused attention on the nominating process of the Democratic party in the hope that it would select a candidate effective enough to wrest the Oval Office from the Republicans.

■ The Bush Quadrennium

Surely one of the most significant factors for African Americans in the 1988 electoral year was the second candidacy of Jesse Jackson in the Democratic presidential primaries. As he crisscrossed the United States debating with the other contenders for the nomination, among them Michael Dukakis, Gary

Hart, Richard Gephardt, Albert Gore, Jr., and Bruce Babbitt, many Americans saw for the first time an African American who could speak as knowledge-ably about structural unemployment as about civil rights and who could comment on United Nations policies as well as discuss problems in the ghetto. He impressed many voters, regardless of race, and many more voted for him in 1988 than in 1984.

In the primaries Jesse Jackson received 6.6 million votes, or 24 percent of the approximately 23 million votes cast, while the front-runner, Michael Dukakis, received 9.7 million votes, or 43 percent. Jackson's showing in the primaries was by far the most serious bid that an African American had ever made for the presidency. He won seven primaries, compared to two in 1984. With 92 percent of the black vote and 17 percent of the white vote, which translated into 1,200 votes in the 1988 convention compared to 400 in 1984, Jackson made a very impressive showing. Having failed to secure the nomination, after he and his family had electrified the Atlanta convention with their appearance and speeches, Jackson concentrated on voter registra-tion among African Americans and other minorities.

Vice President George Bush was a formidable candidate, made more so by incumbency and by his long service in public life. He had been a member of the lower house of the United States Congress, director of the Central Intelligence Agency, director of the United States Liaison Office in China, and United States ambassador to the United Nations. He had long been interested in the United Negro College Fund, but those who knew of his vigorous opposition to the Civil Rights Act of 1964 questioned his commit-ment to racial equality.

During the campaign Bush cultivated upper-class suburban voters and conservatives by accusing Dukakis of being soft on crime. The example that became a central feature of Republican strategy was the televised accusation that Dukakis granted parole to a black felon, Willie Horton, who then committed another felony. In *Chain Reaction: The Impact of Race Rights and Taxes on American Politics,* Thomas and Mary Edsall claimed that this and similar tactics "conjured up the criminal defendants' and prisoners' rights movements, black crime, permissive liberal elites, a revenue-hungry state, eroding traditional values, tattered patriotism, and declining American prestige." While this was sufficient to sweep another Republican into the White House, it occurred without substantial African-American support.

Approximately 90 percent of African-American voters cast their ballots for Michael Dukakis for president and Lloyd Bentsen for vice president. When asked at his first news conference as president-elect why he had not campaigned for votes in the black community, Bush replied candidly that he had to work for votes in the suburbs and among more likely supporters in the middle- and upper-income elements in the cities. He hastened to add that he would be president of all the people, regardless of race, religion, or ethnic origin.

Despite the fact that President George Bush assumed office in January

1989 with eight years of a sense of national well-being behind him and with optimism for the future exuding in some places, many Americans were apprehensive. The economy did not appear to be healthy, and the maldistribution of property, as described by Kevin Phillips in *The Politics of Rich and Poor*, was disturbing. In 1980 there were 574,000 millionaires in the United States. Eight years later, there were 1.3 million Americans who were millionaires. In 1981 there was a mere handful of billionaires, but by 1988 there were at least fifty-two. Put another way, the average per capita income of the top 1 percent of Americans increased from $270,000 in 1977 to $404,500 in 1988. Meanwhile, the average per capita income of the lower 10 percent fell from $4,113 in 1977 to $3,504 in 1988. With the vast majority of blacks among the lower 40 percent in income, they were especially hard hit by redistribution of the national income.

The erratic movement of the American economy, with a brief recession in the early months of 1980, finally settled into a real recession during the Bush years. One feature of these years was the steady, relentless climb in the number of unemployed. Another was the failed savings and loan associations that were bailed out by the federal government at a cost of billions of dollars. Still another was the dramatic increase in the trade deficit that indicated American goods were not attracting foreign purchasers, except perhaps of the American dollar itself. Another was the increase in plant closings, business failures, and home foreclosures that made millions of Americans feel the sharp pinch of the recession. These economic setbacks hung like a pall over most of the Bush quadrennium.

President Bush appointed only a few African Americans to highly visible and influential positions. Gen. Colin Powell, who had been the president's national security adviser during the waning years of the Reagan administration, was a member of the Bush transition team and soon became chairman of the Joint Chiefs of Staff, easily the most important military post ever occupied by an African American. Louis W. Sullivan, president of Morehouse Medical School, became secretary of the Department of Health and Human Services and presided over a department whose budget was exceeded only by that of the Department of Defense. He attracted considerable attention by speaking out against manufacturers of tobacco products who made special efforts to lure African Americans into buying their products.

The president initiated no special programs to help African Americans or other disadvantaged Americans to improve their status in American life. Indeed, in vetoing significant pieces of legislation, he indicated his view of problems affecting African Americans and other minorities better than any executive initiatives he might have taken during his term as president. In June 1989, his first veto was of a bill to raise the minimum wage to $4.55 from $3.35, where it had been since 1977. Congress was finally able to forge a compromise increase to $4.25. In 1990 he vetoed the Civil Rights Act, claiming that it was a "quotas bill," despite the fact that some Republican leaders, such as Sen. John C. Danforth of Missouri, insisted that it was not.

Congress was unable to override the veto. After the elections that year, and after a groundswell of public opinion favoring the bill made it no longer politically desirable to oppose it, Bush signed the bill, insisting that it was no longer a quotas bill. In fact it was substantially the same legislation that he had vetoed the previous year.

Bush also vetoed the so-called motor voter bill that would have permitted people to register to vote when they applied for a driver's license or sought to renew one. The president said that the bill easily lent itself to fraud and placed an undue burden on the states, and the veto was sustained. He also vetoed a bill to extend unemployment benefits for a longer period, an action that was especially hard on those who had lost their jobs during the prolonged recession. Likewise, he vetoed the family leave bill that would have called for unpaid maternity leave or leave in cases of adoption, illness, or other emergencies. While such actions by the president were reactions to legislative initiatives, they clearly indicated his own views regarding contemporary social problems.

If President Bush was unusually successful in stemming the tide of what some called progressive social legislation, the Supreme Court performed its share of the task in a series of important but stunning decisions that it handed down. Under the leadership of William H. Rehnquist, who had been promoted to chief justice in 1986, supported by such Reagan appointees as Anthony Scalia and Anthony Kennedy, as well as others, the Court went far in reversing the gains that had been made under civil rights legislation in the previous decade. In 1988, the stage was set for these sweeping reversals when the Court in *City of Richmond v. J. A. Crosson Company* ruled that the city's set-aside program under which a certain portion of public contracts were awarded to minority contractors was unconstitutional. It violated the rights of competing white contractors, the Court claimed. That was the prelude to "the year of judicial activism," as some observers described it.

In June 1989, in *Patterson v. McLean Credit Union,* the Court reversed its 1976 ruling in holding that the Civil Rights Act of 1866 protected an employee in making a contract but did not extend protection to the employee once the contract was made. During the same month the Court, in *Wards Cove Packing Company v. Atonio,* held that an employer accused of discrimination against minority employees in the interest of promoting a business no longer had to prove his or her case. Instead, the aggrieved employee had to prove that no legitimate business interest was involved. In yet another decision handed down the same month, the Court, in *Martin v. Wilks,* permitted white firefighters in Birmingham to sue the city at any time for making race-conscious promotions to eradicate egregious past discrimination when no blacks were employed in the city fire department.

With President Bush's successful veto of legislation affecting them and with the Supreme Court providing no protection, African Americans felt thwarted if not altogether powerless. Perhaps the decisions of the Supreme Court were the most disheartening since, from the 1950s, African Americans could reasonably expect the Court to give them a fair and often favorable hearing. That is why they faced the retirement of Justice Thurgood Marshall with apprehension and dismay. While in the latter years he was compelled to dissent more often than to concur, his was a voice with which even the majority had to reckon. Some African Americans were quite surprised when President Bush nominated Clarence Thomas, a black conservative, to succeed Marshall. Not all of them could agree with the president when he declared that Thomas was "the best qualified" person for that high office and that race played no role in the nomination, a characterization described by Erwin Griswold, the 87-year-old former dean of Harvard Law School, as "fantasy."

Clarence Thomas, a graduate of Yale Law School, was appointed by President Reagan as assistant secretary for civil rights in the Department of Education and, in 1982, as chairman of the Equal Employment Opportunity Commission, where he served until March 1990. Then President Bush nominated him for the United States Court of Appeals for the District of Columbia. He was subsequently confirmed by a voice vote in the Senate. His tenure at EEOC was at best controversial, but his job never seemed in jeopardy despite regular complaints that EEOC was getting farther and farther behind in processing grievances. His nomination to the high court did provoke widespread discussion regarding his fitness for the office. Some African Americans were pleased that the president had seen fit to appoint another member of their race, although staunchly conservative, to succeed Thurgood Marshall. When he picked up support from Senators Strom Thurmond of South Carolina, Sam Nunn of Georgia, and Orrin Hatch of Utah, some observers concluded that many whites in and out of Congress would think it unseemly to oppose the nomination of an African American to the Supreme Court.

Seldom in a fight over a Supreme Court nomination had lines been so quickly and sharply drawn. Among the organizations favoring the nomination of Thomas were the National Black Nurses Association, the Congress of Racial Equality, Americans for a Balanced Budget, Family Research Council, Women for Judge Thomas, Knights of Columbus, Catholic Golden Age, Conservative Caucus, United Conservatives, National Jewish Coalition, United States Chamber of Commerce, and Young Americans for Freedom. Among those opposed to Thomas were the AFL-CIO, American Federation of Teachers, National Bar Association, National Council of Jewish Women, Gray Panthers, National Organization for Women, People for the American Way, National Lawyers Guild, United States Student Association, and the NAACP Legal Defense and Educational Fund. By September 1991, when the Senate Judiciary Committee began hearings on the nomination, about seventy-six organized groups had expressed support for Thomas, while fifty-four groups opposed him.

While the National Urban League decided to remain neutral on the Thomas nomination, the Congressional Black Caucus, with the exception of its lone Republican member, Gary Franks of Connecticut, came out firmly against Thomas. After postponing a decision at its national meeting in order to provide more time to study the Thomas record, the NAACP came out against Thomas. Meanwhile, individuals on both sides had their say. One said that Thomas had both "the intellect and the intellectual honesty for the job." Another called him "a counterfeit hero." One said that she was as proud of his achievements and promise as she would be of those of her own son. Another, referring to the nominee as "Uncle Justice Thomas," asserted that "no white man with his credentials could be appointed to the Supreme Court."

As the hearings on the Thomas nomination moved toward a conclusion, Anita Hill, a professor of law at the University of Oklahoma, accused Thomas of sexual harassment during her employment in the Department of Education and at EEOC. Her testimony, carried nationwide on television, drew millions into a discussion of the nomination and obscured the important issues of training, experience, and other qualifications. When the dust settled and the controversy receded, Clarence Thomas was confirmed as the second African American to serve as a justice on the Supreme Court.

■ Stirrings

The growing widespread use and abuse of drugs in all segments of American society, along with the attendant violence produced by proliferating drug markets and dealers in urban communities, were major factors in the passage by Congress of the Anti-Drug Abuse Act of 1988. This move, hailed by many African-American leaders who saw it as a tardy but timely response to the problems of their beleaguered communities, resulted in the appointment of a "drug czar" or director to oversee and coordinate the actions of more than thirty federal agencies involved in fighting drugs. The responsibility of naming an official to oversee the "war against drugs" fell to newly elected President George Bush. His choice was William J. Bennett, who had served as secretary of education under outgoing President Reagan. Although the law directed that the post be cabinet level, Bush decided against this, prompting critics to charge that "the new anti-drug post had been downgraded by the administration."

During the year and seven months that Bennett was drug czar, he expended considerable energy in efforts to find new approaches to solving the drug problem, but most of these had little immediate effect. His most visible activity was to use his post as a "bully pulpit" to launch attacks against liberal intellectuals, academics, and journalists for what he termed their "morally scandalous positions" advocating either tolerance of drug use or legalization. When he left the post, Bennett claimed that America was gaining ground in its war against drugs. His critics argued, more persuasively, that he and the Bush administration had failed to produce an effective strategy to confront the problem and that drug trafficking and the violence associated with it had soared to even higher levels. Bennett's successors in the post of drug czar, none of whom had his ability to capture public attention, seemed to make even less impact on these worsening problems.

Since George Bush had promised to be the "education president," African Americans wondered how his policies might affect them. Access to education was of special importance to them, and they watched with interest any policy moves that would make education more or less accessible. In December 1990, Michael L. Williams, an African American who was assistant secretary for civil rights in the Department of Education, issued a directive placing restrictions on "race-specific" scholarships with the explanation that such scholarships were discriminatory. The directive immediately produced a barrage of angry criticism from educational institutions and civil rights organizations, among others, who charged that the Bush administration was attempting to subvert good faith attempts to provide access to higher education for disadvantaged minorities and to falsely categorize these efforts as a form of "reverse discrimination." The outcry from all political quarters was so intense that the policy announced by Williams was quickly discarded by the Department of Education.

The 1980s brought a new and fearful challenge to African Americans in the form of acquired autoimmune deficiency syndrome (AIDS), an epidemic that began to affect the black community as early as 1981. Initially, most Americans identified AIDS as a gay or homosexual disease until the death toll began to include people outside the gay community, including children. Gradually, segments of the African-American community responded to the threat of the disease in ways that complemented the efforts of national governmental, health, civic, and religious organizations to stem the soaring rate of infection with human immunodeficiency virus (HIV), the cause of AIDS and AIDS-related deaths. Such efforts most often took the form of preventive education, the creation of institutions to house those living with the disease, and providing emotional and spiritual support, as well as practical services such as medical care, counseling, legal assistance, food deliveries, and hospice care. One of the products of these new forms of activism was the establishment in 1986 of the National Black Gay and Lesbian Conference, an organization committed to addressing and devising solutions to the prejudice and problems faced by African-American gays and lesbians both as a racial and a sexual minority. When gays and lesbians of all races and from all regions of the United States traveled to Washington, D.C., in 1993 for one of the largest rights marches in American history, the NAACP, the nation's oldest civil rights organization, endorsed the march and was an official participant.

Two widely publicized events heightened consciousness of the dangers posed by AIDS. Earvin "Magic" Johnson, a popular and uniquely talented basketball star, revealed in 1991 that he was infected with HIV. Later, Arthur Ashe, one of the most gifted professional tennis players of his generation and a distinguished civic figure, made public the information that he had contracted AIDS as a result of surgery. Less than a year later Ashe was dead. Following their public statements, both Johnson and Ashe devoted considerable time to AIDS education and efforts to raise financial support for AIDS research and better medical treatment and services for victims of AIDS.

Almost immediately after assuming the presidency, George Bush was confronted by a report of the bipartisan National Commission on AIDS (NCA) urging him to take a stronger leadership role than his predecessor Ronald Reagan had in raising the consciousness of the nation about the increasingly rapid spread of AIDS, in pushing Congress for larger expenditures for medical research, public education, and treatment centers, and in developing greater appreciation among all Americans concerning the urgent need for an immediate overhaul of the American health care system. Throughout the Bush quadrennium, the commission essentially repeated the same message, though each time with increased volume and sharpness. As early as the second year of Bush's presidency, the commission charged that the country's indifference to the impact of AIDS was compounded by the president's failure to provide national leadership.

Bush's initial response was to call for an end to discrimination against those infected with AIDS and to praise his administration's efforts to combat the disease. Later, Vice President J. Danforth Quayle, often a spokesman for the administration on domestic issues, asserted that the best response of the American people to the AIDS threat was to cultivate higher moral standards, especially through the practice of sexual abstinence.

For many Americans, one of the president's most dramatic gestures of concern was his appointment of "Magic" Johnson to the National Commission on AIDS. Bush's critics, however, used even this action to question the genuineness of the president's commitment. Derek Hodel, executive director of the People with AIDS Health Group, challenged "Magic" Johnson to give legitimacy to his appointment to the NCA by confronting President Bush on his failure to stem the AIDS epidemic. Johnson's service on the commission was also complicated by a report in March 1992 from the National Minority AIDS Council accusing federal agencies of providing inadequate financial support to prevent the spread of AIDS among Americans of African, Hispanic, Asian, and Native American ancestry. This charge would be repeated and amplified by numerous organizations and individuals in these minority communities, where the percentage of AIDS victims was growing more rapidly than in the society as a whole.

In September 1992 "Magic" Johnson created serious embarrassment for the Bush administration by his abrupt resignation from the National Commission on AIDS. Johnson justified his departure by sharply criticizing the President for fighting the disease with "lip service and photo opportunities." By the time Bush left the White House, there was general consensus among his friends and enemies that his administration had accomplished little in the way of an effective response to the AIDS crisis.

The last two decades of the twentieth century saw heightened economic deprivation and social problems in poor black communities: chronic unemployment, rampant violence, drug addiction, HIV infection and AIDS, soaring homicide rates for young black males, high levels of illegitimate births to young black females, and public school systems overwhelmed by all these problems. Not surprisingly, many residents of those communities felt deeply alienated from and hostile to middle- and upper-class Americans. An expression of this was the emergence, as early as 1974, of what has been described as "a kind of in-your-face culture" that reflected a profound sense of alienation. Rap music, its colorful, profane performers, and the "hip-hop" culture it spawned was one of the most visible and controversial expressions of this alienation. While music critics and others debated the merits of rap music as a form of African-American musical and cultural expression, some rap pieces caused numerous listeners to denounce rap and rap artists as sexist, homophobic, anti-Semitic, racist, antiauthoritarian, and sexually explicit. Some sought a ban on performances and sales of albums of certain rap artists. Whatever view listeners had of rap, to those who understood America's racial politics, this musical form was, as one writer observed in the *New York Times,* an unmistakable reflection of the "poverty, violence, lack of education, frustration, and rage of the ghetto."

During the 1980s a body of ideas labeled Afrocentrism came to be an important part of public discourse in various segments of the African-American community. Some of these ideas could be traced back to a small group of black writers and intellectuals in the nineteenth century who, at various times, stressed the uniqueness and greatness of ancient African cultures. Some attributed the achievements of ancient Greek societies to ties of culture and blood with Africa or argued that the historical Jesus, the founder of Christianity, was wholly or in part African. The New Negro movement which found such powerful expression in the cultural and political activities of the Harlem Renaissance in the 1920s reinforced some of these ideas and added to them. And the Black Power movement, a product of the racial challenges and tensions faced by the African-American community during the 1960s, generated intellectual and cultural expressions adding to the appeal of Afrocentric thought.

During the last two decades of the twentieth century, some exponents of Afrocentrism attracted widespread attention with vigorous arguments that Africa and African cultures were the original sources of world civilization, that peoples of African descent have a unique "humanistic, spiritualistic value system" unmatched by any other racial group, that European cultural and economic systems are inherently exploitative, and that blacks' high melanin content makes them "inherently more creative." Opponents of the more extreme tenets of Afrocentrism charged that its advocates lacked scholarly proof of their claims or based them on distortions of historical research and that many of the arguments of Afrocentrists were implicitly racist, in particular often viciously anti-Semitic. The debate remained unresolved as the scholarly community continued to appropriate new research concerning the origins of cultures, societies, and races.

DESTRUCTION DURING LOS ANGELES RIOT. Following the acquittal of four white police officers for allegedly beating a black man, Rodney King, protesters burned and looted portions of South Central Los Angeles. Here, residents view a burned-out building along Vermont Avenue in early May, 1992. *(Reuters/Bettmann.)*

All the social ills and deep resentment in the most beleaguered sections of black America seemed to reach a flash point in March 1991 when Rodney King, an African American, was arrested after a high-speed chase by white Los Angeles policemen. King was severely beaten, after allegedly resisting and threatening the officers, and released without being charged. Perhaps that would have been the end of it, except that the encounter was videotaped by an observer and subsequently shown on television throughout the world. The outcry was loud and the demand was insistent that the unpopular chief of police, Daryl Gates, be dismissed and the offending policemen brought to trial for using excessive force. Many Americans, including a significant portion of the African-American community, viewed the trial of the four white policemen (as many as fifteen had been present at the beating) as a major test of the system's ability to deliver justice on behalf of a victim of racism and police brutality.

The difficulty in securing an "impartial jury" in Los Angeles for the trial led to the choice of Simi Valley, a largely white and Hispanic community. The protracted trial ended in April 1992 with the acquittal of the officers by a jury of eleven whites and one Hispanic. The verdict of not guilty was shocking to most citizens who had seen the beating on television, and it plunged Los Angeles into several days of rioting, looting, and burning. Four days later, the count was 38 deaths, 4,000 arrests, 3,700 burned-out buildings, and damage estimated at more than $500 million. Visiting the riot area, both President Bush and presidential candidate Bill Clinton expressed dismay and called for action to address the problems of the inner cities. The following year, the four policemen were tried in a federal court for violating the civil rights of Rodney King. This time two were found guilty and two were acquitted. There was peace in Los Angeles, but not happiness in the African-American community.

■ African Americans and the World

In the years that followed the end of World War II, African Americans more and more viewed their fate as inextricably connected with the fate of darker peoples throughout the world. Regardless of what attitude the United Nations took toward the domestic problems of the United States, some African Americans sensed, more strongly than many others, the implications of the interdependence of the world brought about by the revolutionary developments in transportation and communication and by the use of atomic energy. It was no sudden, newly awakened realization on the part of blacks. Diplomacy, disarmament, colonial problems, and international relations had for years occupied the attention of a growing number of African-American scholars, including W. E. B. Du Bois, Ralph Bunche, Rayford Logan, and Merze Tate. The black press, as well as a considerable number of black organizations, became interested in the international aspects of the struggle for freedom. They sought to define the roles that they as well as their country should play in achievement of the great dream of peace and equality.

African Americans assumed a strong moral position as they became more articulate in the area of peace and freedom for the world. They praised America's goal of a world community of peaceful nations. They were quick to point out, however, that in order to achieve such a goal, discrimination, race hatred, and segregation must be replaced by equality for all citizens at home. They chided the Truman administration for embarrassing the United States in appointing as secretary of state James F. Byrnes of South Carolina, where blacks were excluded from white primaries, at a time when it became necessary to protest against the "undemocratic character" of elections in Bulgaria. Later, many would question their country's involvement in the war in Vietnam to achieve there what had not been achieved at home. They also reminded their government that the peoples of India, Indonesia, Burma, and elsewhere were following in the footsteps of the United States in their struggle for independence. It would be most unfortunate if the country that had early set the example for the right of peoples to be independent should

TABLE 10
Number of Blacks in Selected Categories of Elected Officials, 1970–1990

	MEMBERS OF CONGRESS	STATE SENATORS	STATE REPRE-SENTATI VES	COUNTY OFFICIALS	MAYO RS	CITY COUNCIL MEMBERS	SCHOOL BOARD MEMBERS	TOTAL BLACK ELECTED OFFICIALS	PERCENTAGE OF CHANGE
1970	10	31	137	92	48	552	362	1,469	—
1975	18	53	223	305	135	1,237	894	3,503	138.5
1980	17	70	247	451	182	1,809	1,149	4,912	40.2
1985	20	90	302	611	286	2,189	1,368	6,056	23.3
1990	26	108	340	810	314	2,972	1,561	6,131	1.2

Source: Black Elected officials, 1991. *Joint Center for Political Studies.*

now seek to thwart the effort of African Americans to participate fully in the political process.

When the Fifth Pan-African Congress met at Manchester, England, in October 1945, it was concerned not so much with problems peculiar to Africa as with taking steps toward implementing the efforts of darker peoples everywhere to secure a greater share of democracy for themselves. African Americans in attendance hoped that the congress would inspire a greater measure of cooperation between Africans and their descendants in the United States. Even if the sons and daughters of Africa in the United States were not enthusiastic about working within the framework of such an organization, they were willing to take up the cudgel in behalf of darker peoples everywhere.

African Americans were particularly interested in the movement for self-government in West Africa, and they applauded the independence movements in Nigeria and the Gold Coast. As they became world-minded, thousands of them traveled to Europe, Asia, and Africa. Expatriate Richard Wright left his Paris home, visited numerous countries in Africa, and wrote a moving account of the continent's progress and problems in *Black Power*. Era Bell Thompson, the international editor of *Ebony* magazine, recorded her impressions in *Africa, Land of My Fathers*. African-American observers, newspaper editors, and one member of Congress attended the Conference on Asian-African Problems at Bandung, Indonesia, in the spring of 1955 and reported the proceedings to their constituents in the United States. Meanwhile, black physicians, engineers, teachers, and other highly trained personnel went to Ethiopia, Liberia, and other countries to contribute what they could to the growth and development of those countries.

When Africans south of the Sahara began to win their independence, they

ANDREW YOUNG, UNITED STATES AMBASSADOR TO THE UNITED NATIONS,
speaking before the Security Council, proposes an interim Security Council
Force for southern Lebanon, March 18, 1978. In 1982 he was elected mayor of
Atlanta, Georgia. *(Courtesy United States Mission to the United Nations. United
Nations/Photo by Sam Lwin.)*

could hardly have been more delighted than African Americans, who were
present in large numbers for the ceremonies marking the independence of
Ghana, Nigeria, Tanganyika, Kenya, Zanzibar, Sierra Leone, and Uganda.
They agonized over the tribulations and the conflicts in Rhodesia and
rejoiced when Zimbabwe came into existence. It was clear that they wished
to be identified with the peoples of Africa who were moving to an important
position on the world stage. They were not unaware of the effect that the
emerging black nations might have upon their own status. The studied insult
in a Maryland coffee shop of a black finance minister from an African nation
or the presence of a black man on the United Nations Security Council was
enough to elicit support from the highest United States officials for the equal
treatment of all peoples, including African Americans. Nor could those in
high government positions lose sight of the fact that the entire world was
interested in the fight over the admission of an African American to the
University of Mississippi, in the bombing of black churches by white
hoodlums, and in the denial of equal employment and housing opportunities
to black Americans.

PEACE CORPS VOLUNTEER
Theresa Hicks serves as a nurse in
a hospital in Rio de Janeiro. (AC-
TION *photo by Paul Conklin.*)

The widening horizons of African Americans, the increasing world interest in the American race problem, and the leadership of the United States in world affairs were factors that commended the greater participation of blacks in the foreign relations work of the United States government. One of the duties of Assistant Secretaries of Labor J. Ernest Wilkins and George L. P. Weaver was to represent the United States at international labor meetings. In 1965 James M. Nabrit became deputy chief of the United States mission to the United Nations. The culmination came with Andrew Young's appointment in 1977 as United States ambassador to the United Nations and his strong advocacy of majority rule in Rhodesia, South Africa, and elsewhere.

The war in Vietnam underscored African Americans' increased involvement in world affairs. At home many of them raised questions about the presence of American troops in Southeast Asia. Some joined with other Americans who insisted that the United States could not and should not undertake the task of policing the world. Others insisted that the escalation of the war and the bombing of North Vietnam went beyond the commitment of the United States and indeed rendered impossible any meaningful peace talks. Some opposed the war because it used up resources that could better

THE WAR IN VIETNAM. The African Americans in this photograph were among the 22,000 blacks in Vietnam in 1966. *(Courtesy Department of Defense.)*

RAFER JOHNSON CARRIES OLYMPIC TORCH. 1960 Olympic Decathlon champion Rafer Johnson carries the torch to light the Olympic flame opening the 1984 summer Olympics in Los Angeles. *(UPI/Bettmann Newsphotos.)*

TABLE 11
Black Population Growth and Percentage of U.S., 1790–1990

YEAR	TOTAL POPULATION	BLACK POPULATION	PERCENTAGE
1790	3,929,214	757,181	19.3
1800	5,308,483	1,002,037	18.9
1810	7,239,881	1,377,808	19.0
1820	9,638,453	1,771,656	18.4
1830	12,866,020	2,328,642	18.1
1840	17,169,453	2,873,648	16.1
1850	23,191,876	3,638,808	15.7
1860	31,443,790	4,441,830	14.1
1870	39,818,449	4,880,009	12.7
1880	50,155,783	6,580,793	13.0
1890	62,947,714	7,488,676	11.0
1900	75,994,775	8,833,994	11.6
1910	93,402,151	9,827,763	10.7
1920	105,710,620	10,463,131	9.9
1930	122,775,046	11,891,143	9.7
1940	131,669,275	12,865,518	9.8
1950	150,697,361	15,042,286	10.0
1960	179,323,175	18,871,831	10.5
1970	203,302,031	22,580,289	11.1
1980	226,504,825	26,488,218	11.7
1990	248,710,000	29,986,000	13.2

Source: U.S. Department of Commerce. *Statistical Abstract of the United States, 1992.* Bureau of the Census. Washington, D.C., 1992.

be utilized in fighting for equal economic and civil rights at home or because it was a war against other darker peoples.

Civil rights groups were divided over the Vietnamese question. The older organizations tended to be less critical of United States policy and to view their role as that of continuing to fight for their stated objectives. The newer ones, such as the Congress of Racial Equality and the Student Nonviolent Coordinating Committee, viewed the war as closely related to the civil rights question. Some of the leaders declared that they would not fight in the war even if drafted. Julian Bond, the director of publicity for SNCC, was denied his seat in the Georgia legislature because he had praised young men who burned their draft cards. He was not seated until the United States Supreme Court decided that he could not be denied his seat because of the opinions he held. It was Martin Luther King's opposition to the war in Vietnam that

UNITED SUPPORT OF ARTISTS FOR AFRICA. Many of America's best known enter-tainers volunteered their talent to help produce an album and video cassette whose sales benefitted African famine victims. The artists participating in this project in-cluded Harry Belafonte, Ray Charles, Michael Jackson, Bette Midler, Lionel Ritchie, Di-ana Ross, Paul Simon, Bruce Springsteen, Tina Turner, and Stevie Wonder. *(AP/Wide World Photos.)*

CONGRESSIONAL BLACK CAUCUS PROTESTS APARTHEID. During the Congres-sional Black Caucus Weekend in 1985 its members led a march against apartheid in South Africa. In 1986 they helped override the president's veto of sanctions against South Africa. *(William Gray, House Budget Committee.)*

TABLE 12
Growth and Distribution of the African-American Population, by States, in 1940 and 1990

STATE	1940[a] (IN THOUSANDS)	1990 (IN THOUSANDS)
Alabama	983	1,021
Alaska	(b)	22
Arizona	15	111
Arkansas	483	374
California	124	2,209
Colorado	12	133
Connecticut	33	274
Delaware	36	112
District of Columbia	187	400
Florida	514	1,760
Georgia	1,085	1,747
Hawaii	(b)	27
Idaho	1	3
Illinois	387	1,694
Indiana	122	432
Iowa	17	48
Kansas	65	143
Kentucky	214	263
Louisiana	849	1,299
Maine	1	5
Maryland	302	1,190
Massachusetts	55	300
Michigan	208	1,292
Minnesota	10	95
Mississippi	1,075	915
Missouri	244	548
Montana	1	2
Nebraska	14	57
Nevada	1	79
New Hampshire	(b)	7
New Jersey	227	1,037
New Mexico	5	30
New York	571	2,859
North Carolina	981	1,456
North Dakota	(b)	4

TABLE 12
Growth and Distribution of the African-American Population, by States,
in 1940 and 1990 (*Continued*)

STATE	1940[a] (IN THOUSANDS)	1990 (IN THOUSANDS)
Ohio	339	1,155
Oklahoma	169	234
Oregon	3	46
Pennsylvania	470	1,090
Rhode Island	11	39
South Carolina	814	1,040
South Dakota	(b)	3
Tennessee	509	778
Texas	924	2,022
Utah	1	12
Vermont	(b)	2
Virginia	661	1,163
Washington	7	150
West Virginia	118	56
Wisconsin	12	245
Wyoming	1	4

[a]*1940 figures include all nonwhites.*
[b]*Less than 500.*

Source: U.S. Department of Commerce. Historical Statistics of the United States: Colonial Times to 1970, Part 1. *Bureau of the Census. Washington, D.C., 1975. U.S. Department of Commerce.* Statistical Abstract of the United States, 1992. *Bureau of the Census. Washington, D.C., 1992.*

was the most embarrassing to the administration. At Riverside Church in New York, he told an overflow audience that "The Great Society has been shot down on the battlefields of Vietnam. . . . It would be very inconsistent for me to teach and preach nonviolence in this situation and then applaud violence when thousands and thousands of people . . . are being maimed and mutilated and many killed in this war, so that I still feel and live by the principle, 'Thou shalt not kill.'" More than in any other war in the nation's history, African Americans were signing peace petitions, participating in peace demonstrations and rallies, and criticizing the administration of the armed services and their country's role in the war.

In contrast to the critical view of the war that many blacks held was their participation in the war itself. In the 1960s proportionately more blacks (30 percent) than whites (18 percent) from the group that qualified for military

THE LATE DR. RALPH BUNCHE, undersecretary for special political affairs of the United Nations, who received the Nobel Prize for Peace in 1950, confers with the United Nations Secretary-General, U Thant. (*Courtesy United Nations.*)

AFRICAN AMERICANS SERVE ABROAD. Dr. Roscoe L. McKinney, Howard University anatomy professor, makes suggestions to a tutor in anatomy at the Osmania University Medical College in Hyderabad, India. (*Courtesy A.I.D.*)

FIRST AFRICAN AMERICAN AND YOUNGEST CHAIRMAN OF THE JOINT CHIEFS OF STAFF. In 1989 President Bush listens to General Colin Powell, former National Security Adviser, as he responds to the President's announcement that he had been appointed chairman of the Joint Chiefs of Staff. Reappointed in 1991, Powell retired in September, 1993. *(AP/Wide World Photos.)*

service were drafted. While enlistment rates of blacks and whites were about equal, first-term reenlistments of blacks were more than double those of whites. At the end of December 1965, there were more than 20,000 African Americans in Vietnam, including 16,531 in the army, 500 in the navy, 3,580 in the marines, and 908 in the air force. In 1967 African Americans constituted 11 percent of the total United States enlisted personnel in Vietnam, but black soldiers comprised 14.5 percent of all army units, and in army combat units the proportion was, according to the Department of Defense, "appreciably higher" than that. In 1972 blacks in Vietnam comprised 17 percent of all combat forces, but only 10 percent of all service personnel. During the first eleven months of 1966, black soldiers constituted 22.4 percent of all army troops killed in action. Plagued by discrimination while in the armed services and the inability to secure satisfactory employment after discharge, black veterans of the war in Southeast Asia became a part of the group that was most apprehensive about the future.

African Americans also took the initiative in pressing their government and the American people to oppose injustice in another part of the world. On Thanksgiving eve in 1984, Randall Robinson, executive director of Trans-

Africa, Mary Frances Berry of the United States Commission on Civil Rights, Eleanor Holmes Norton of Georgetown Law Center, and Walter Fauntroy, District of Columbia delegate to the House of Representatives, began a sit-in in the South African Embassy in Washington to protest apartheid in general and the detention of black South African labor leaders in particular. This was the beginning of a sit-in campaign at the embassy that lasted for more than a year and that led to the arrests of hundreds of people who protested the racial policies of the Republic of South Africa. This surely had much to do with encouraging the black majority in South Africa to fight more vigorously for their rights and to arouse world opinion and indignation against apartheid. By 1986 Congress had responded with the passage of bills favoring economic sanctions against South Africa, although President Reagan continued to oppose sanctions, even after Congress overrode his veto, insisting that not only would such moves hurt black South Africans but also that he knew responsible blacks there also opposed sanctions. While the final solution to the problem seemed not to be immediately at hand, African Americans waited impatiently and anxiously to see what the government and what American businesses in South Africa would do.

The pressures on South Africa to promote greater democracy began to have an effect once F. W. de Klerk became president in 1989. Early in 1990 de Klerk lifted the thirty-year ban on the African National Congress (ANC) that had been fighting to end minority rule. The announcement was followed within days with the release, after twenty-eight years in prison, of Nelson Mandela, titular head of the ANC and a universal symbol of the black liberation movement in South Africa.

In June 1990, Mandela visited eight American cities as part of a twelve-day tour of the United States. Arriving in New York, he was greeted with a tumultuous welcome from crowds that included thousands of blacks as well as numerous Americans of all backgrounds. In an address to a joint meeting of the two houses of the United States Congress, Mandela invoked the names of American heroes who had been sources of inspiration to him. The only discordant note came during Mandela's visit to South Florida, where his refusal to disavow Fidel Castro earned him the emnity of many in the powerful Cuban-American community. Five of the region's Cuban-American mayors, including the mayor of Miami, signed a statement criticizing the South African leader for not denouncing human rights violations in Cuba and refused to provide an official welcome for him. Many African Americans in Florida expressed outrage and anger, and some promised to use their votes to eject these mayors from office.

Several events in the post-Carter years signaled the continuing interest of African Americans in events in other parts of the world. One was Panama, where strongman Gen. Manuel Antonio Noriega, sometime paid operative for the Central Intelligence Agency, thwarted local and outside efforts to establish democratic rule in Panama. As early as March 1988, Jesse Jackson made a "moral appeal" to Noriega to step down, for which Jackson was criticized by administration officials and others for opening up a new line

THE CONGRESSIONAL BLACK CAUCUS. These members of the 103rd Congress were the largest number of African Americans ever to sit in that body. *(Copyright Congressional Black Caucus.)*

of communication with the Panamanian leader. When elections were held in 1989, former president Jimmy Carter and his international monitoring delegation observed numerous irregularities, including fraud.

At various times in the early months of the Bush administration there were calls for Noriega, who had ignored the election of the previous year, to step down, with strong suggestions that the Panamanian people overthrow him. In December 1989, Gen. Colin Powell, recently appointed chairman of the Joint Chiefs of Staff, began to reverse the long-standing opposition by senior military officers to the use of United States military forces to oust Noriega. Meanwhile, about 10,000 United States troops were deployed in what was called "Operation Just Cause." Soon they were in hot pursuit of Noriega. Under the circumstances, his capture was a foregone conclusion. He was brought to Miami where he was tried, found guilty of involvement in drug traffic to the United States, and sentenced to forty years in prison. Just as one African American, writing in the *Washington Post*, expressed doubts that the United States would have undertaken the "Rambo-style invasion" of a white country, others wondered if the arrest and conviction of Noriega had had any appreciable effect on the drug traffic between the United States and Panama.

Although the United States tended to support Iraq in its decade-long war with Iran, the move of President Saddam Hussein against oil-rich Kuwait drew immediate and strong reaction from the United States. President Bush condemned the invasion on August 3, 1990, the day after it occurred, and called on world leaders to take collective action against Iraq. He also vowed to defend Saudi Arabia and its oil resources. Soon United States troops were on their way to protect the line that President Bush said he had "drawn in the sand." Gen. Colin Powell, the African-American chairman of the Joint Chiefs of Staff, seemed to be less fearful of using force than any senior American officer since the Vietnam War. He reminded his officers that the use of armed force was a political matter, and it was clear that he had presented a strong case to the president for sending troops to Saudi Arabia. Meanwhile, two former chairmen of the Joint Chiefs of Staff urged the president to defer military action and give sanctions, imposed by the United Nations, time to work.

Early in January 1991, by which time the national debate over using force in the Middle East had reached its peak, Congress, by a vote of 52 to 47 in the Senate and 250 to 183 in the House, voted to give the president authority to use military force against Iraq and to end its occupation of Kuwait. Deep divisions remained in the country, however, and antiwar protesters held rallies and peace vigils in many cities. Soon, nevertheless, 500,000 United States troops were in the Middle East.

Since blacks, who made up 13.2 percent of the population, accounted for 25 percent of the United States troops in the Persian Gulf, some African Americans feared that their community would pay disproportionately for a war that many of them did not even support. A reliable poll reported that blacks were split about evenly on the question of military action, while whites were in favor of it by a ratio of 4 to 1. In Congress, every black Democrat voted against the measure authorizing the use of force in "Operation Desert Storm," as the action was called. African Americans, nevertheless, expressed pride in the leadership of Gen. Colin Powell. They also recognized that their disproportionate presence in the armed forces, where many blacks were volunteers, was rooted in the lack of job opportunities in the civilian sector. By the time the military operation was over in late February 1991, and African Americans began to witness a reduction in the military force, they realized that job opportunities in civilian life, if anything, had decreased, thanks to the persistent recession that dogged the Bush quadrennium.

It seemed that the problem of establishing and maintaining normal relations with the New World's black nation, Haiti, was never-ending. (See Chapters 6, 15, and 17.) For more than half a century, the United States had withheld recognition from the island state of Haiti, the only self-governing country in the New World. During periods of instability, however, such as those of the early twentieth century, the United States did not hesitate to occupy and impose its will on the country and its people. The United States was barely critical of the Duvaliers, father and son, whose corrupt rule lasted from 1957 to 1986. It was not until February 1991 that the first democratically elected president of Haiti, Jean-Bertrand Aristide, took office, only to be ousted by a military junta in October of that year and deported to France. The Bush administration immediately suspended economic aid to Haiti and refused to recognize the military regime. Subsequently, however, the administration retreated from its strong support of Aristide, claiming that his human rights record was not as clean as previously thought.

When large numbers of Haitians began to leave their country and seek a haven in the United States, this country's Coast Guard began to intercept them in international waters and escort them back to Haiti or to the United States naval base at Guantanamo Bay in Cuba. Haitians continued to leave their country in large numbers, and many of them drowned because of unseaworthy vessels. The United States then defended its action on humanitarian grounds. There were those who rejected such claims, arguing that Cuban refugees were treated differently either because the Cuban government refused to repatriate them or because the Cubans made a good case in their quest for political asylum. In any case, the United States regularly gave Cubans permanent residence status after one year in residence in the United States. Even the courts seemed opposed to asylum for the Haitians. In 1991 the United States Court of Appeals ruled that the United States could send home thousands of Haitians intercepted at sea, and in 1993 the Supreme Court upheld that policy.

■ "On the Pulse of Morning"

African Americans were clearly interested in the outcome of the presidential election in 1992, as well as in congressional and local elections. With Jesse Jackson on the sidelines, they seemed to see in the Democratic candidate, Governor Bill Clinton of Arkansas, and his running mate, Sen. Al Gore, Jr., of Tennessee, an interest in their problems that had not been evident during the Reagan and Bush years. Ronald Brown, who had managed Jackson's campaign in 1988, had become chairman of the Democratic National Committee, and from that very important position that no African American had previously occupied, he was a powerful force in attracting African Americans to the Clinton-Gore ticket.

According to the Joint Center for Political and Economic Studies, black voter turnout in November 1992 was approximately 8 percent of the total voter turnout, with 83 percent of black voters supporting the victorious Clinton-Gore ticket. Of course, local and state races featuring black candidates contributed to the high black voter turnout. In Illinois, Carol Mosely Braun defeated United States Sen. Alan Dixon in the Democratic primary and went on to win the Senate seat in November, thus becoming the only African American in the twentieth century, besides Republican Edward Brooke of Massachusetts, to go to the upper house and the first African-American woman to sit in the United States Senate.

CAROL MOSELY BRAUN GREETS COLLEAGUES. Elected to the U.S. Senate in 1992, Braun was the fourth African American and the first African-American female to be elected to the upper house of the U.S. Congress. *(AP/Wide World Photos.)*

Thanks to congressional redistricting and the appearance of several attractive and politically adroit candidates, sixteen African Americans— eleven men and five women—gained new seats in the House of Representatives. This ran the total number of African Americans in the lower house to thirty-nine, a record high for all time. Eight of the new members of the House represented five states that had not sent any African Americans to Congress in the twentieth century. Among them were Earl Hilliard of Alabama, Corrine Brown, Alcee Hastings, and Carnie Meek of Florida, Eva Clayton and Melvin Watt of North Carolina, Jim Clyburn of South Carolina, and Bobby Scott of Virginia. Eddie Bernice Johnson of Texas was the first African American ever to sit in Congress from that state.

With forty African Americans in the 103rd Congress, they were in a position to exert considerable influence in decision making. Several of them already had had legislative experience. Twenty-nine year old Cleo Fields of Louisiana had been chairman of the committee in his state legislature that passed on all major appointments. Carnie Meek of Florida had been chair of a major appropriations committee in the Florida senate. One keen observer described the group as having "political savvy."

More than once during the campaign and again after his election, Clinton said that the personnel of his administration "would look like America." Many waited to see just what he meant. The president-elect began by

ONE OF CLINTON'S FIRST APPOINT-
MENTS, WHO SERVED ALMOST A
YEAR AS DEPUTY SECRETARY OF
STATE. Former President of Michigan
State University, the State University of
New York, and the Teachers Insurance
Annuity Association, Clifton Wharton's
father was the first African American to
attain full ambassadorial status. Here
he testifies before the Senate Commit-
tee on Foreign Relations. (AP/World
Wide Photos.)

appointing as chairman of his transition team Vernon Jordan, a prominent
Washington attorney and former president of the National Urban League.
At President Clinton's inauguration, Maya Angelou read her poem, "On the
Pulse of Morning," written for the occasion. For his cabinet, he selected the
following African Americans: Ronald Brown, chairman of the Democratic
National Committee, secretary of commerce; Mike Espy, United States
representative from Mississippi, secretary of agriculture; Hazel O'Leary,
executive vice president of the Northern States Power Company of Minnesota, secretary of energy; and Jesse Brown, executive director of Disabled
American Veterans, secretary of veterans affairs. No previous president had
had more than one African American in his cabinet. Other African Americans
whom Clinton named in the early days of his administration were Joycelyn
Elders, surgeon general of the United States; Clifton Wharton, deputy
secretary of state; Walter D. Broadnax, deputy secretary of health and human
services; Terrence Duvernay, deputy secretary of housing and urban development; and Drew Days, solicitor general of the United States. In other
departments, African Americans became undersecretaries and assistant
secretaries. Thus, as far as African Americans were concerned, the new
president had made a significant beginning toward making his administration look like America.

Looking back on almost four centuries of residence in the Western world,
African Americans could correctly visualize themselves, from the beginning,
as an integral part of the struggle for freedom. At times they were passive
symbols of the struggle that was carried on by others. Frequently, however,
they were active participants in the valiant warfare to destroy bigotry,

Excerpts from Marian Wright Edelman's Litany for Children

We pray for children . . .
   who stare at photographers from behind barbed wire,
   who can't bound down the street in a new pair of sneakers,
   who never "counted potatoes,"
   who are born in places we wouldn't be caught dead,
   who never go to the circus,
   who live in an X-rated world.
And we pray for those . . .
   who never get dessert,
   who have no safety blanket to drag behind them,
   who watch their parents watch them die,
   who can't find any bread to steal,
   who don't have any rooms to clean up,
   whose pictures aren't on anybody's dresser,
   whose monsters are real.
We pray for children . . .
   whose nightmares come in the daytime,
   who will eat anything,
   who have never seen a dentist,
   who aren't spoiled by anybody,
   who go to bed hungry and cry themselves to sleep,
   who live and move, but have no being.

Marian Wright Edelman, *The Measure of Our Success: A Letter to My Children and Yours.* (Boston, Beacon Press, 1992), pp. 86–97.

repression, and subjugation. Studying carefully their role in the growth and development of the United States, they could see that they were more than very important contributors to the economic, political, and social development of their country. They had also been important factors in the ageless struggle between freedom and slavery. They had been the nation's constant reminders of the imperfection of its social order and the immorality of its human relationships. They had witnessed a nation dedicated to liberty move toward the brink of destruction in the struggle to settle the question of freedom. They had seen that same nation compromise its position in the family of nations because of its inability to face squarely the problem of freedom for all at home.

This was a rich experience that African Americans had undergone. As they moved together with other peoples into another era in the final years

THE 1993 INAUGURAL. President Clinton greets poet Maya Angelou following her reading her poem "On the Pulse of Morning" at his inauguration. (*Copyright Lisa Quinones/Black Star.*)

of the twentieth century they gave evidences of greater maturity. They had become an integral part of Western culture and civilization, and their fate was inextricably connected with it. The rejections that they had suffered doubtless wounded them considerably, but such treatment also gave them a perspective and an objectivity that others had greater difficulty in achieving. They could, therefore, point out more clearly than some others the weaknesses that seemed to be inherent in Western civilization. They could counsel their country, if it cared to listen, concerning its own position in an atomic world. They could tell it, as the National Urban League did at the close of World War II, "The United States must hold to the elemental principles of cooperation in a family of diversified nations, none of which can escape the obligations of world responsibility. Back of all that is planned or achieved is the fact that henceforth it is ONE WORLD OR NONE." If America's role was to lead the world toward peace and international understanding, African Americans had a special function to perform in carrying forward the struggle for freedom at home, for the sake of America's role, and abroad, for the sake of the survival of the world.

Bibliographical
Notes

We shall make no attempt here to list all of the primary and secondary works that we consulted in writing this book. Instead, we shall cite a selected number of the more important works, primarily those in English that are generally available, with a view to guiding the interested reader to further study. Those available in paperback editions are marked with an asterisk. It is well to mention that in this computer age most libraries can provide bibliographies through an on-line catalog. On-line catalogs also allow researchers to create specialized bibliographies for their research needs. For many years the best general bibliographical aid in the study of African Americans was Monroe R. Work's *A Bibliography of the Negro in Africa and America* (New York, 1928). Although out of date, it continues to have value, but it should be supplemented by other aids. The most exhaustive and excellent bibliographical aid is James M. McPherson and others, *Blacks in America: Bibliographical Essays** (Garden City, N.Y., 1971), now unfortunately out of print. There are several other bibliographies of value. Among them are Dorothy B. Porter, *The Negro in the United States: A Selected Bibliography* (Washington, D.C., 1970); and Elizabeth W. Miller, *The Negro in America, A Bibliography** (Cambridge, Mass., 1966, revised edition, 1970). The lists of materials in the major African-American collections should also be consulted. Among them are those at Fisk University and Hampton University, the Moorland-Spingarn Research Center at Howard University, the Slaughter Collection at Atlanta University, the James Weldon Johnson Collection at Yale University, the Schomburg Center for Research in Black Culture at the New York Public Library, and the Vivian Harsh Collection at the Chicago Public Library. Of special interest and importance is Debra Newman Ham, ed., *The African American Mosaic: A Library of Congress Resource Guide for the Study of Black History and Culture* (Washington, D.C., 1993).

It is widely known that a large and curious assortment of general histories of

African Americans has appeared in the past century. While some have only historiographical value, others are important sources of information. Among the former are James W. C. Pennington, *Text Book of the Origin and History of the Colored People* (Hartford, Conn., 1841); William T. Alexander, *History of the Colored Race in America* (Kansas City, 1887); Harold M. Tarver, *The Negro in the History of the United States from the Beginning of the English Settlements in 1607, to the Present Time* (Austin, Tex., 1905); and E. A. Johnson, *School History of the Negro Race* (Raleigh, N.C., 1893). Of much greater value is George W. Williams, *History of the Negro Race in America*, two volumes (New York, 1882, reprinted 1968), which was the first such work to attract the attention of serious students. Two works of a similar nature, but less exhaustive, are Booker T. Washington, *The Story of the Negro: The Rise of the Race from Slavery*, two volumes (New York, 1909) and Willis D. Weatherford, *The Negro from Africa to America* (New York, 1924). Other efforts in the general field include Benjamin Brawley, *A Short History of the American Negro* (New York, 1913); Merle R. Eppse, *The Negro, Too, in American History* (Chicago, 1939); and Edwin R. Embree, *Brown Americans: The Story of a Tenth of the Nation** (New York, 1945).

The pioneer modern work was written in 1922 by Carter G. Woodson. The tenth edition was prepared by Charles H. Wesley under the title *The Negro in Our History* (Washington, D.C., 1962). For certain aspects of the history of African Americans, the work of W. E. B. Du Bois, *Black Folk, Then and Now: An Essay in the History and Sociology of the Negro Race** (New York, 1939), is invaluable. In the last four decades the number of general histories of African Americans has greatly increased. Among them are Roi Ottley, *Black Odyssey* (New York, 1948); Rayford W. Logan, *The Negro in the United States** (New York, 1957); Lerone Bennett, *Before the Mayflower,** revised edition (Chicago, 1987); J. Saunders Redding, *They Came in Chains* (New York, 1952, revised edition, 1973) and *Lonesome Road* (New York, 1958); W. Z. Foster, *The Negro People in American History** (New York, 1970); Benjamin Quarles, *The Negro in the Making of America** (New York, 1964); Eli Ginzberg and Alfred S. Eichner, *The Troublesome Presence: American Democracy and the Negro* (Glencoe, Ill., 1964); August Meier and Elliott Rudwick, *From Plantation to Ghetto: An Interpretive History of American Negroes,** third edition (New York, 1976); C. Eric Lincoln, *The Negro Pilgrimage in America** (New York, 1969); Nathan Huggins, *Black Odyssey: The Afro-American Ordeal in Slavery** (New York, 1977); Philip S. Foner, *History of Black Americans,* three volumes (Westport, Conn., 1975), which brings the story up until the end of the Civil War; Vincent Harding, *There Is a River: The Black Struggle for Freedom in America** (New York, 1981); and Mary Frances Berry and John Blassingame, *Long Memory: The Black Experience in America** (New York, 1982). One should not miss an especially unique and thoroughly fascinating work by John Langston Gwaltney, *Drylongso: A Self-Portrait of Black America** (New York, 1981).

Three works of a special nature that cover most of the period are Vincent P. Franklin, *Black Self-Determination: A Cultural History of the Faith of the Fathers* (Westport, Conn., 1984); Jacqueline Jones, *Labor of Love, Labor of Sorrow: Black Women, Work, and the Family from Slavery to the Present* (New York, 1985); and Darlene Clark Hine, *Black Women in United States History* (New York, 1993).

A different approach to the history of black Americans is undertaken in Earl E. Thorpe, *The Mind of the Negro: An Intellectual History of Afro-Americans* (Baton Rouge, La., 1961). The interest of foreign writers in the subject can be seen in J. W. Schulte Nordholdt, *The People That Walk in Darkness* (London, 1960); Frank K. Schoell, *Histoire de la race noire aux Etats-Unis du XVIIe siècle à nos jours* (Paris, 1959); and Jean Daridan,

De Lincoln à Johnson: noirs et blancs (Paris, 1965). There is much historical material in Gunnar Myrdal, *An American Dilemma: The Negro Problem and Modern Democracy** (New York, 1944 and 1964); E. Franklin Frazier, *The Negro in the United States,* revised edition (New York, 1957); Margaret J. Butcher, *The Negro in American Culture** (New York, 1956, revised edition, 1972); and Mabel M. Smythe, ed., *The Black American Reference Book* (Englewood Cliffs, N.J., 1976).

Volumes documenting the general history of African Americans have not been numerous. Outstanding are Herbert Aptheker, *A Documentary History of the Negro People in the United States,** three volumes (New York, 1951, 1973, 1974); Leslie Fishel and Benjamin Quarles, *The Black American: A Documentary History** (Glenview, Ill., 1976); and William Loren Katz, *Eyewitness, The Negro in American History** (New York, 1967, revised edition, 1974). See also Richard Wade, *The Negro in American Life, Selected Readings** (New York, 1970); Milton Meltzer, *In Their Own Words: A History of the American Negro, 1619–1865,** three volumes (New York, 1967); and Milton Sernett, *Afro-American Religious History: A Documentary Witness* (Durham, N.C., 1985). Richard Bardolph, *The Negro Vanguard* (New York, 1959) contains a wealth of material on individual African Americans. A monumental achievement dealing with individual African Americans is Rayford W. Logan and Michael R. Winston, eds., *Dictionary of American Negro Biography* (New York, 1982). See also, Edgar A. Toppin, *A Biographical History of Blacks in America Since 1528* (New York, 1971). Among pictorial representations are the following: Langston Hughes and Milton Meltzer, *A Pictorial History of the Negro in America* (New York, 1968); Russell L. Adams, *Great Negroes, Past and Present** (Chicago, 1969); Year's *Picture History of the American Negro* (New York, 1965); Lucille A. Chambers, *America's Tenth Man* (New York, 1957); *Ebony Pictorial History of Black America,* three volumes (Chicago, 1971); and John Hope Franklin and the editors of Time-Life Books, *An Illustrated History of Black Americans* (New York, 1970).

With the increased interest in the history of African Americans, a considerable number of anthologies, curriculum guides, and teachers' aids have appeared. Among the better anthologies are August Meier and Elliott Rudwick, eds., *The Making of Black America,** two volumes (New York, 1969); Nathan Huggins and others, eds., *Key Issues in the Afro-American Experience,** two volumes (New York, 1971); Eric Foner, ed., *America's Black Past, A Reader in Afro-American History** (New York, 1970); Melvin Drimmer, ed., *Black History, A Reappraisal** (Garden City, N.Y., 1968); and Talcott Parsons and Kenneth B. Clark, eds., *The Negro American** (Boston, 1966). The following are valuable as curriculum aids and teachers' guides: Philip T. Drotning, *A Guide to Negro History in America** (Garden City, N.Y., 1970); William Loren Katz, *Teachers' Guide to American Negro History** (Chicago, 1971); San Francisco Unified School District, *The Negro in American Life and History** (San Francisco, 1967); and Robert L. Harris, *Teaching Afro-American History** (Washington, D.C., 1985).

There have been many books and articles dealing with the treatment of African Americans in American history. Among them are Earl E. Thorpe, *Negro Historians in the United States* (Baton Rouge, La., 1958), and *Black Historians: A Critique* (New York, 1971); John Hope Franklin, "The New Negro History," *Journal of Negro History,* XLII (April 1957), "The Future of Negro American History," *University of Chicago Magazine,* LXII (January–February 1970), and "Mirror for Americans: A Century of Reconstruction History," *American Historical Review,* LXXXV (February, 1980); and Ernest Kaiser, "Trends in American Negro Historiography," *Journal of Negro Education,* XXXI (Fall 1962). John Hope Franklin, *George Washington Williams: A Biography* (Chicago, 1985), is a full-length study of the first serious historian of African Americans. Recent works on the state of the art are Eugene D. Genovese, *In Red and Black: Marxian Explorations in Southern and Afro-American History* (New York, 1968); Darlene Clark Hine, *The State of Afro-American History* (Baton Rouge, La., 1986); and August Meier and Elliott Rudwick, *Black History and the Historical Profession, 1915–1980* (Urbana, Ill., 1986). See also John Hope Franklin, *Race and History: Selected Essays, 1938–1988** (Baton Rouge, La., 1989).

More and more African Americans have become the subject of serious study, and numerous monographs have appeared that shed considerable light on their condition. While these works are specialized in subject matter, their scope in time or approach is sufficiently broad to warrant their consideration among the studies that are generally useful in works of this nature. The problems of adjustment and integration are extensively discussed in Myrdal, *An American Dilemma*; Melville J. Herskovits, *The American Negro: A Study in Racial Crossing** (New York, 1928); John G. Van Deusen, *Black Man in White America* (Washington, D.C., 1944); E. Franklin Frazier, *The Negro in the United States*; Maurice R. Davie, *Negroes in American Society* (New York, 1949); and Oscar Handlin, *Race and Nationality in American Life** (Boston, 1948). A wide-ranging effort to update the Myrdal study was made by the National Research Council, through the Committee on the Status of Black Americans, in a volume edited by Gerald David Jaynes and Robin M. Williams, Jr., *A Common Destiny: Blacks and American Society* (Washington, D.C., 1989). The pioneer study of the history and sociology of the black family is E. Franklin Frazier, *The Negro Family in the United States* (Chicago, 1939). A new and revisionist approach is Herbert Gutman, *The Black Family in Slavery and Freedom, 1750–1825** (New York, 1976). Sociobiological problems are treated in Samuel J. Holmes, *The Negro's Struggle for Survival: A Study in Human Ecology* (Berkeley, Calif., 1937) and Julian H. Lewis, *The Biology of the Negro* (Chicago, 1942).

The political and legal aspects of African-Americans' history and status have been treated in several books, among which are Paul Lewinson, *Race, Class and Party: A History of Negro Suffrage and White Politics in the South** (London, 1932); and Charles S. Mangum, *The Legal Status of the Negro* (Chapel Hill, N.C., 1940). More recent and more sophisticated are Pauli Murray, *States' Laws on Race and Color* (Cincinnati, 1950); V. O. Key, *Southern Politics in State and Nation** (New York, 1949); and Jack Greenberg, *Race Relations and American Law* (New York, 1959). Three works by Paul Finkelman should be consulted: *An Imperfect Union: Slavery, Federalism, and Comity* (Chapel Hill, N.C., 1981); *Slavery in the Courtroom* (Washington, D.C., 1985); and *The Law of Freedom and Bondage: A Casebook** (New York, 1986). A valuable study is A. Leon Higginbotham, Jr., *In the Matter of Color: Race and the American Legal Process* (New York, 1978). See also Howard Brotz, ed., *Negro Social and Political Thought, 1850–1920** (New York, 1966); Richard Bardolph, ed., *The Civil Rights Record: Black Americans and the Law, 1849–1970** (New York, 1970); Albert Blaustein and Robert Zangrando, eds., *Civil Rights and the American Negro: A Documentary History** (New York, 1968); and Herbert Storing, ed., *What Country Have I? Political Writings by Black Americans** (New York, 1970).

In the field of the economic history of African Americans, Charles H. Wesley, *Negro Labor in the United States, 1850–1925* (New York, 1927, reprinted 1967) is much more comprehensive than the title suggests, while *The Negro Wage Earner* (Washington, D.C., 1930) by Lorenzo J. Greene and Carter G. Woodson confines itself primarily to the history of black labor. A penetrating study of the history of African Americans and organized labor is the work by Sterling D. Spero and Abram L. Harris, *The Black*

Worker: The Negro and the Labor Movement* (New York, 1931); but for a very special aspect of the problem, see Herbert Hill, *Black Labor and the American Legal System** (Washington, D.C., 1977). Another phase of economic life is treated in Abram L. Harris, *The Negro as Capitalist: A Study of Banking and Business among American Negroes* (Philadelphia, 1936).

Among the better general studies on the social and intellectual history of African Americans are the following. For education, Horace M. Bond, *The Education of the Negro in the American Social Order* (New York, 1934, revised edition, 1965); Dwight O. W. Holmes, *The Evolution of the Negro College* (New York, 1934); and Henry Allen Bullock, *A History of Negro Education in the South from 1619 to the Present* (Cambridge, Mass., 1967). In the area of the fine arts, two works by Alain Locke, *Negro Art: Past and Present** (Washington, D.C., 1936) and *The Negro and His Music** (Washington, D.C., 1936) should be consulted, as well as James Porter, *Modern Negro Art* (New York, 1943) and Samella Lewis, *Art: African American* (New York, 1978). These works should be supplemented by use of the periodical *The International Review of African American Art* (formerly *Black Art*) edited by Samella Lewis. Significant recent works in the history of music are LeRoi Jones, *Blues People: Negro Music in White America** (New York, 1963); Eileen Southern, *The Music of Black Americans, A History** (New York, 1971); John Lovell, *Black Song: The Forge and the Flame* (New York, 1972); and Mildred Roach, *Black American Music: Past and Present* (Boston, 1973). The best studies in religion are Carter G. Woodson, *History of the Negro Church* (Washington, D.C., 1921); Benjamin E. Mays and Joseph W. Nicholson, *The Negro's Church* (New York, 1933); E. Franklin Frazier, *The Negro Church in America** (New York, 1963); Joseph R. Washington, *Black Religion** (Boston, 1964); C. Eric Lincoln and Lawrence H. Mamiya, *The Black Church In The African American Experience** (Durham, N.C., 1990); and Cyprian Davis, *The History of Black Catholics in the United States* (New York, 1990). The literary history of the Negro may be traced in Benjamin Brawley, *The Negro in Literature and Art in the United States*, third edition (New York, 1971); Vernon Loggins, *The Negro Author: His Development in America* (New York, 1931); Sterling Brown, *The Negro in American Fiction** (Washington, D.C., 1937); J. Saunders Redding, *To Make a Poet Black* (Chapel Hill, N.C., 1939); Hugh Gloster, *Negro Voices in American Fiction* (Chapel Hill, N.C., 1948); and Robert Bone, *The Negro Novel in America** (New Haven, Conn., 1958, revised edition, 1965). See also Seymour Gross and John E. Hardy, eds., *Images of the Negro in American Literature** (Chicago, 1966); Loften Mitchell, *Black Drama: The Story of the American Negro in the Theatre** (New York, 1967); and Edith J. R. Isaacs, *The Negro in the American Theater* (New York, 1947). Satisfactory collections of Negro writings are Otelia Cromwell and others, *Readings from Negro Authors* (New York, 1931); Sterling Brown and others, *The Negro Caravan* (New York, 1941); Ruth Miller, ed., *Black American Literature: 1760 to the Present** (Encino, Calif., 1971); Charles T. Davis and Daniel Walden, eds., *On Being Black; Writings by Afro-Americans from Frederick Douglass to the Present** (New York, 1970); and Robert Hayden and others, eds., *Afro-American Literature: A Thematic Reader** (New York, 1971). For representative recent writing, do not overlook Herbert Hill, *Soon One Morning: New Writing by American Negroes* (New York, 1963); Francis Kearns, ed., *The Black Experience: An Anthology of American Literature for the 1970s** (New York, 1971); Michael S. Harper and Robert B. Stepto, eds., *Chant of Saints: A Gathering of Afro-American Literature, Art, and Scholarship** (Urbana, Ill., 1979); Blyden Jackson, *A History of Afro-American Literature, Volume I: The Long Beginning, 1746–1895* (Baton Rouge, 1989). The pioneer study on African-American newspapers was done by Irvine Garland Penn in *The*

Afro-American Press and Its Editors (Springfield, 1891, reprinted 1975). Less encyclopedic but more critical is Frederick G. Detweiler, *The Negro Press in the United States* (Chicago, 1922). More recent treatments are Maxwell Brooks, *The Negro Press Re-examined* (Boston, 1959); and Jack Lyle, ed., *The Black American and the Press* (Los Angeles, 1968).

1. Land of Their Ancestors

Maurice Delafosse has made many important contributions to the history of African civilization. Among those that have been translated from the French is *The Negroes of Africa: History and Culture* (Washington, D.C., 1931), which contains a mine of information on the early African states. Carter G. Woodson, *Africa Background Outlined* (Washington, D.C., 1936) is excellent for its bibliographical and other study aids, while his *African Heroes and Heroines* (Washington, D.C., 1939) contains informal human interest accounts of many of the leaders in West Africa. Among the many works that Basil Davidson has written to illuminate the history of West Africa, *The Lost Cities of Africa** (Boston, 1959, revised edition, 1970) is especially valuable. Generally helpful works are Philip Curtin and others, *African History** (Boston, 1978); J. D. Fage, *A History of Africa** (New York, 1978); J. F. A. Ajayi and Michael Crowder, *History of West Africa* (London, 1976); and J. D. Fage and Roland Oliver, *Cambridge History of Africa* (Cambridge, 1975–1984). Du Bois' *Black Folk, Then and Now* has excellent chapters on the early African states. A classical and reliable description of the political and social scene may be found in the writings of a contemporary, Joannes Leo Africanus, *The History and Description of Africa* (London, 1896). A popular but generally reliable account of the early history of the Western Sudan is Flora Louisa Lugard, *A Tropical Dependency* (London, 1905).

In *Black Athena: The Afroasiatic Roots of Classical Civilization*, Volume 2: *The Archaeological and Documentary Evidence* (New Brunswick, N.J., 1991), Martin Bernal offers a complex and controversial argument that the culture and thought of ancient Greece were similar to and in many ways derived from the cultures of the darker peoples of the eastern and southern Mediterranean. For critical and qualifying responses to Bernal, see Molly M. Levine, "The Use and Abuse of *Black Athena*"; Robert L. Pounder, "*Black Athena 2:* History Without Rules"; and Janet J. Ewald, "Slavery in Africa and the Slave Trades in Africa" in "Review Articles," *American Historical Review*, LXXXXVII (April 1992).

2. The African Way of Life

Perhaps the best general accounts of the culture and civilization of West Africa in addition to those previously mentioned are to be found in Delafosse, *The Negroes of Africa;* Du Bois, *Black Folk, Then and Now;* Basil Davidson, *The African Past** (Boston, 1964); E. W. Bovill, *Golden Trade of the Moors** (New York, 1958, reprinted 1970); John K. Thornton, *The Kingdom of Kongo* (Madison, Wisc., 1983); Alia A. Mazrui, ed., *The Warrior Tradition in Modern Africa* (Leiden, 1977); and Woodson, *The African Background Outlined.* The works of Melville J. Herskovits in the field have long been regarded as highly significant. Among them are *Dahomey; An Ancient West African Kingdom,* two volumes (New York, 1938, reprinted 1967), a modern anthropological study that sheds considerable light on the earlier period, and "The Art of the Congo," *Opportunity,* V (May 1927). A provocative work by the same author is *Myth of the Negro Past** (New York, 1941, reprinted 1958), in which Herskovits contends that the blacks of West Africa had developed a complex civilization and that much of it survived in the New World. In this connection one should also read his "On the Provenience of the New World Negroes," *Social Forces,* XII (December 1933). George W. Ellis, *Negro Culture in West Africa* (New York, 1914, reprinted 1971) is valuable largely for its discussion of how an African group developed its own alphabet and written language. An important work dealing with various aspects of African culture, including the complex problem of language, is Robin Hallett, *Africa to 1875* (Ann Arbor, Mich., 1970). See also Basil Davidson, *The African Genius** (Boston, 1969) and John A. Davis, ed., *Africa from the Point of View of American Negro Scholars** (Paris, 1958). Three brief studies that emphasize the importance of the culture of Africans are Franz Boas, *Old African Civilizations* (Atlanta, 1906); James Weldon Johnson, *Native African Races and Culture* (Charlottesville, Va., 1927); and Roland F. Oliver, *Africa in the Iron Age* (Cambridge, 1975).

Special aspects of African culture are treated in *Harvard African Studies,* No. 1 (Cambridge, Mass., 1917) and No. 11 (Cambridge, Mass., 1918), edited by Oric Bates. These studies are especially satisfactory for their treatment of early African art and of implements. A. O. Stafford, "The Tarik E. Soudan," *Journal of Negro History,* II (April 1917) is a valuable study of an early African literary work. In addition to several works already mentioned, two special studies of African art will prove helpful. They are James J. Sweeney, *African Negro Art* (New York, 1935) and Frank Willett, *African Art* (London, 1971).

3. The Slave Trade and the New World

Of the works dealing with the history of the slave trade, there is nothing to compare with the monumental four-volume work of Elizabeth Donnan, *Documents Illustrative of the History of the Slave Trade to America* (Washington, D.C., 1930–1935). The introductions to each volume provide a most satisfactory running account of the traffic, and the notes on the documents themselves illuminate the period considerably. A good general account of the trade is presented in Daniel R. Mannix, *Black Cargoes: A History of the Atlantic Slave Trade, 1518–1865** (New York, 1962). See also Basil Davidson, *Black Mother: The Years of the African Slave Trade** (London, 1961). An exhaustive examination of the slave trade in terms of numbers involved, sources of supply, and distribution in the New World is Philip D. Curtin, *The Atlantic Slave Trade: A Census** (Madison, Wisc., 1969). A vigorous challenge to what he calls Curtin's underestimation is in J. E. Inikori, "Measuring the African Slave Trade: A Rejoinder," *Journal of African History,* XVII (No. 4, 1976). Another valuable work is Peter Duignan and Clarence Clendenen, *The United States and the African Slave Trade, 1619–1862* (Westport, Conn., 1963). The significance of the trade in the growth of capitalistic enterprise is discussed in Wilson E. Williams, *Africa and the Rise of Capitalism** (Washington, D.C., 1938) and Eric Williams, *Capitalism and Slavery** (Chapel Hill, N.C., 1944). Two pioneer works that give some attention to the slave trade are W. E. B. Du Bois, *Suppression of the African Slave Trade to the United States, 1638–1870** (Cambridge, Mass., 1896, reprinted 1969) and U. B. Phillips, *American Negro Slavery** (New York, 1918). Herbert S. Klein, *The Middle Passage: Comparative Studies in the Atlantic Slave Trade* (Princeton, N.J., 1978), is most valuable for perspective and balance. Specific phases of the trade are discussed in several papers published in the *Journal of Negro History:* Jerome Dowd, "The African Slave Trade," II (January 1917); George F. Zook, "The Company of Royal Adventurers Trading in Africa," IV (April 1919); Luther P. Jackson, "Elizabethan Seamen and the African Slave Trade," IX (January 1924); and Eric Williams, "The Golden Age of the Slave System in Britain," XXV (January 1940).

For a discussion of Africans in the New World before Columbus, see Leo Wiener, *Africa and the Discovery of America,* three volumes (Philadelphia, 1922); Harold G. Lawrence, "African Explorers of the New World," *The Crisis,* CLIX (June–July 1962); and Ivan Van Sertima, *They Came Before Columbus* (New York, 1976). The participation of blacks in the exploration of the New World first received attention at the hands of Richard R. Wright in an article published in *The American Anthropologist* in 1902. It is reprinted under the title, "Negro Companions of the Spanish Explorers," *Phylon,* II (Fourth Quarter 1941), to which Rayford W. Logan has appended some valuable notes. Other papers on the subject include J. F. Rippy, "The Negro and Spanish Pioneers in the New World," *Journal of Negro History,* VI (April 1921); James B. Browning, "Negro Companions of the Spanish Pioneers in the New World," *Howard University Studies in History* (Washington, D.C., 1930); and Rayford W. Logan, "Estevanico, Negro Discoverer of the Southwest," *Phylon,* I (Fourth Quarter 1940).

The horrors of the middle passage are described in several of the preceding works, notably in the *Documents* edited by Donnan and in the work by Phillips. See also Du Bois, *Black Folk, Then and Now;* Weatherford, *The Negro from Africa to America;* and Mannix, *Black Cargoes.* H. A. Wyndham, *The Atlantic and Slavery* (London, 1935), deals in a scholarly manner with this and many other aspects of the slave trade. The effect of the slave trade on the future of Africa is treated by a number of scholars in J. E. Inikori, ed., *Forced Migration: The Impact of the Export Slave Trade on African Societies* (New York, 1982).

One of the most important works in the economic history of the Caribbean is Lowell J. Ragatz, *The Fall of the Planter Class in the British Caribbean* (New York, 1928), in which ample attention is given to the institution of slavery. The rivalry of the European countries is treated by Arthur P. Newton, *The European Nations in the West Indies, 1493–1688* (London, 1933). For the treatment of slavery on an important British island, see W. J. Gardner, *A History of Jamaica* (London, 1909). Herbert S. Klein, *Slavery in the Americas* (Chicago, 1967) compares slavery in Cuba with slavery in Virginia. A fresh approach is in David Barry Gaspar, *Bondmen and Rebels: A Study of Master-Slave Relations in Antigua* (Baltimore, 1985). There are several important essays on the West Indies in Laura Foner and Eugene Genovese, eds., *Slavery in the New World: A Reader in Comparative History* (Englewood Cliffs, N.J., 1969).

Among general works on Latin America that give some attention to various aspects of life among Africans in the New World are Charles E. Chapman, *Colonial Hispanic America: A History* (New York, 1933) and Bernard Moses, *South America on the Eve of Emancipation* (New York, 1908). Considerable statistical data as well as provocative interpretations are provided in Frank Tannenbaum, *Slave and Citizen** (New York, 1947). Especially important are Herbert S. Klein, *Slavery in the Americas* (Chicago, 1967); David B. Davis, *The Problem of Slavery in Western Culture* (Ithaca,

N.Y., 1966); and Franklin W. Knight, *The African Dimension in Latin American Societies* (Madison, Wisc., 1970).

The literature on Brazil is abundant. Among the more important pioneer works of scholarship are the following: Gilberto Freyre, *The Masters and the Slaves: A Study in the Development of Brazilian Civilization** (New York, 1946); Donald Pierson, *Negroes in Brazil, A Study of Race Contact at Bahia* (Chicago, 1942); Florestan Fernandes, *The Negro in Brazilian Society* (New York, 1969); Robert B. Toplin, *The Abolition of Slavery in Brazil* (New York, 1972); and Carl N. Degler, *Neither Black Nor White: Slavery and Race Relations in Brazil and the United States** (New York, 1971). C. R. Boxer, *The Golden Age of Brazil, 1695–1750: Growing Pains of a Colonial Society* (Berkeley, Calif., 1969) contains many valuable insights and interpretations.

4. Colonial Slavery

A good way to begin a study of Africans in the English colonies is with David B. Davis, *The Problem of Slavery in Western Culture* (Ithaca, N.Y., 1966) and Winthrop Jordan, *White over Black; American Attitudes toward the Negro, 1550–1812** (Chapel Hill, N.C., 1968). See also Gary B. Nash and Richard Weiss, eds., *The Great Fear: Race in the Mind of America** (New York, 1970). A clear exposition of this period is in Donald R. Wright, *African Americans in the Colonial Era: From African Origins Through the American Revolution* (Arlington Heights, Ill., 1990). The view that the first blacks in Virginia were servants rather than slaves is set forth by John H. Russell in *The Free Negro in Virginia, 1619–1865** (Baltimore, 1913). Details concerning the early years of slavery in Virginia are provided in James C. Ballagh, *A History of Slavery in Virginia* (Baltimore, 1902), while *The Negro in Virginia* (New York, 1940) by the Writers' Program of the Work Projects Administration furnishes valuable additional information. See also Thad W. Tate, Jr., *The Negro in Eighteenth-Century Williamsburg** (Williamsburg, Va., 1965); Gerald W. Mullin, *Flight and Rebellion: Slave Resistance in Eighteenth-Century Virginia** (New York, 1972); and T. H. Breen and Stephen Innes, *"Myne Owne Ground": Race and Freedom on Virginia's Eastern Shore, 1640–1676** (New York, 1980). Jeffrey R. Brackett, *The Negro in Maryland: A Study of the Institution of Slavery* (Baltimore, 1889) gives the essential information concerning slavery in that colony. The problem for North Carolina has been treated by John Spencer Bassett in *Slavery and Servitude in the Colony of North Carolina* (Baltimore, 1896), but Guion G. Johnson, *Antebellum North Carolina* (Chapel Hill, N.C., 1937) deals most satisfactorily with the colonial as well as the later period. Frank J. Klingberg, *An Appraisal of the Negro in Colonial South Carolina* (Washington, D.C., 1941, reprinted 1975) is a pioneer modern treatment, but one must also study carefully Peter Wood's *Black Majority: Negroes in Colonial South Carolina from 1670 through the Stono Rebellion** (New York, 1974) and Daniel F. Littlefield, *Rice and Slaves: Ethnicity and the Slave Trade in Colonial South Carolina* (Baton Rouge, La., 1981). A special problem is treated in Thomas J. Davis, *A Rumor of Revolt: The Great Negro Plot in Colonial New York* (New York, 1985). Beginnings in Georgia are covered in Ralph B. Flanders, *Plantation Slavery in Georgia* (Chapel Hill, N.C., 1933). A more modern and up-to-date version is Betty Wood, *Slavery in Colonial Georgia, 1730–1775* (Athens, Ga., 1984). Marcus W. Jernegan, *Laboring and Dependent Classes in Colonial America, 1607–1783* (Chicago, 1931) illuminates many aspects of the problem.

The social and economic life of Negroes in early New York is treated in Samuel McKee, *Labor in Colonial New York, 1664–1776* (New York, 1935) and Edwin V. Morgan, *Slavery in New York* (Washington, D.C., 1891). William R. Riddell, "The Slave in Early New York," *Journal of Negro History,* XIII (January 1928) is a valuable addition to the literature. Another useful study is Edgar J. McManus, *A History of Negro Slavery in New York* (Syracuse, N.Y. 1966). Henry S. Cooley, *A Study of Slavery in New Jersey* (Baltimore, 1896, reprinted 1973); Marion T. Wright, *Education of Negroes in New Jersey* (New York, 1941) and "New Jersey Laws and the Negro," *Journal of Negro History,* XXVIII (April 1943) by the same author all shed considerable light on blacks in that colony. Standard works on Pennsylvania are Edward R. Turner, *The Negro in Pennsylvania* (Washington, D.C., 1911, reprinted 1969) and Jean R. Soderlund, *Quakers and Slavery: A Divided Spirit* (New York, 1985). For an excellent survey of some works on the early history of African Americans see Peter Wood, "'I Did the Best I Could for My Day': The Study of Early Black History during the Second Reconstruction, 1960 to 1976," *William and Mary Quarterly,* Third Series, XXXV (April 1978).

The most important single volume dealing with slavery in the New England colonies is Lorenzo J. Greene, *The Negro in Colonial New England** (New York, 1942). Valuable studies on individual states are George H. Moore's anti-Puritan *Notes on Slavery in Massachusetts* (New York, 1866); William Johnston, *Slavery in Rhode Island, 1755–1776* (Providence, 1894); Edward Channing, *The Narragansett Planters* (Baltimore, 1886, reprinted 1973); and Bernard C. Steiner, *History of Slavery in Connecticut* (Baltimore, 1893). An interesting sidelight on New England social history is provided in Lorenzo J. Greene, "The New England Negro as Seen in Advertisements for Runaway Slaves," *Journal of Negro History,* XXIX (April 1944). Two general works are valuable: Edmund Morgan, *American Slavery, American Freedom* (New York, 1975) and Jack P. Greene and J. R. Pole, *Colonial British America: Essays in the New History of the Early Modern Era* (New York, 1984).

Two studies that put forth the provocative argument that Christianity in the British North American colonies played a crucial role in the construction of racist thought and practice in the future United States are H. Shelton Smith, *In His Image, But . . . : Racism in Southern Religion, 1780–1910* (Durham, N.C., 1972) and Forrest G. Wood, *The Arrogance of Faith: Christianity and Race in America from the Colonial Era to the Twentieth Century* (New York, 1990).

5. That All May Be Free

The outstanding work covering the period of the American Revolution is Benjamin Quarles, *The Negro in the American Revolution** (Chapel Hill, N.C., 1961). The paradoxes of slavery and the revolutionary philosophy are discussed in George Livermore, *An Historical Research Respecting the Opinions of the Founders of the Republic on Negroes as Slaves, as Citizens, and as Soldiers* (Boston, 1862); George H. Moore, *Historical Notes on the Employment of Negroes in the American Army of the Revolution* (New York, 1862); Walter H. Mazyck, *George Washington and the Negro* (Washington, D.C., 1932); Duncan J. MacLeod, *Slavery, Race and the American Revolution** (Cambridge, 1975); and Ira Berlin and Ronald Hoffman, *Slavery and Freedom in the Age of the American Revolution* (Charlottesville, Va., 1983). In Sylvia Frey's study, *Water From the Rock: Black Resistance In a Revolutionary Age* (Princeton, N.J., 1991), white southerners' fight for independence is secondary to their struggle to retain control of their slave property and to preserve order. Two works that argue that the failure to rid the former British colonies of slavery lay as much with white northerners as with white southerners are Gary B. Nash, *Freedom and Revolution* (Madison, Wisc., 1991) and Gary B. Nash and Jean R. Soderlund, *Freedom by Degrees: Emancipation in Pennsylvania and Its Aftermath* (New York, 1991). A useful study of emancipation in northern cities is Shane White, *Somewhat More Independent: The End of Slavery in New York City, 1770–1810* (Athens, Ga., 1991). Among the studies of African Americans as fighters in the War for Independence, the following are outstanding: William C. Nell, *The Colored Patriots of the American Revolution* (Boston, 1855) and Luther P. Jackson, "Virginia Negro Soldiers and Seamen in the American Revolution," *Journal of Negro History*, XXVII (July 1942). In George W. Williams, *A History of the Negro Troops in the War of the Rebellion* (New York, 1887) and Joseph T. Wilson, *The Black Phalanx* (Hartford, Conn., 1888) there are chapters on black soldiers in the War for Independence. A unique work with numerous authentic illustrations is Sidney Kaplan, *The Black Presence in the Era of the American Revolution, 1770–1800** (Boston, 1973).

The antislavery movement in the Revolutionary period is treated in Quarles, *The Negro in the American Revolution*, as well as in Mary S. Locke, *Antislavery in America* (Boston, 1901). More recent scholarship on the subject is in Arthur Zilversmit, *The First Emancipation: The Abolition of Slavery in the North** (Chicago, 1967) and David Brion Davis, *The Problem of Slavery in the Age of Revolution* (Ithaca, N.Y., 1975). See also William Cohen, "Thomas Jefferson and the Problem of Slavery," *Journal of American History*, LVI (December 1968) and Paul Finkelman, "Jefferson and Slavery" 'Treason against the Hopes of the World'," in Peter S. Onuf, *Jeffersonian Legacies* (Charlottesville, Va., 1993). Important for its interpretation is John Franklin Jameson, *The American Revolution Considered as a Social Movement* (Princeton, N.J., 1926). Charles A. Beard, *An Economic Interpretation of the Constitution of the United States* (New York, 1913) is an excellent interpretation of the problem of slavery at the Constitutional Convention. See also Staughton Lynd, *Class Conflict, Slavery, and the United States Constitution** (Indianapolis, Ind., 1967). One of the best brief accounts of the convention is Max Farrand, *The Framing of the Constitution* (New Haven, Conn., 1913), but there is no substitute for the monumental *Records of the Federal Convention of 1787*, three volumes (New Haven, Conn., 1911), edited by Max Farrand. It contains much discussion on the status of blacks at the time that has not been extensively used in other works.

6. Blacks in the New Republic

The best source of information concerning the numbers and distribution of the black population is the publication by the United States Bureau of the Census, *Negro Population, 1790–1915* (Washington, D.C., 1918), while significant changes of an economic and social nature are dealt with in Charles A. Beard, *Economic Origins of Jeffersonian Democracy* (New York, 1915) and in Ira Berlin, "Time, Space, and the Evolution of Afro-American Society on British Mainland North America," *American Historical Review*, 85, 1 (February, 1980). An excellent general treatment is Donald R. Wright, *African Americans in the Early Republic, 1789–1831* (Arlington Heights, Ill., 1993). One should not overlook Robert McColley, *Slavery and Jeffersonian Virginia,**

second edition (Urbana, Ill., 1974). The impact of the Industrial Revolution on slavery is treated in Lewis C. Gray, *History of Agriculture in the Southern United States to 1860* (Washington, D.C., 1933). The uprising in the Caribbean is vividly described in C. L. R. James, *The Black Jacobins: Toussaint Louverture and the San Domingo Revolution* (New York, 1938). *The Suppression of the African Slave Trade* by W. E. B. Du Bois is an early but still authoritative account of the movement to close the slave trade.

Brief discussions of the works of early black writers are given in Benjamin Brawley, *Early Negro American Writers* (Chapel Hill, N.C., 1935); Brown and others, *The Negro Caravan;* and Dorothy B. Porter, ed., *Early Negro Writings, 1760–1837* (Boston, 1971). The following are satisfactory treatments of individual Negroes: Edward D. Seeber, "Phillis Wheatley," *Journal of Negro History,* XXIV (July 1939); Henry Baker, "Benjamin Banneker, Negro Mathematician and Astronomer," *Journal of Negro History,* III (April 1918); P. L. Phillips, "The Negro, Benjamin Banneker: Astronomer and Mathematician," *Records of the Columbia Historical Society,* XX (Washington, D.C., 1917); H. N. Sherwood, "Paul Cuffe," *Journal of Negro History,* VIII (April 1923); and W. H. Morse, "Lemuel Haynes," *Journal of Negro History,* IV (January 1919). Essays of Phillis Wheatley and George Moses Horton are in M. A. Richmond, *Bid the Vassal Soar* (Washington, D.C., 1974). One treatment of Cuffe is Sheldon H. Harris, *Paul Cuffe, Black America and the African Return** (New York, 1972). The most recent, however, is Lamont D. Thomas, *Rise to Be a People, A Biography of Paul Cuffe* (Champaign, Ill., 1986). For discussions of education, see Carter G. Woodson, *Education of the Negro Prior to 1861* (New York, 1915) and Charles C. Andrews, *History of the New York African Free Schools* (New York, 1830). The best accounts of the origins of black religious constitutions are Woodson, *History of the Negro Church;* Charles H. Wesley, *Richard Allen, Apostle of Freedom* (Washington, D.C., 1935); and Mechal Sobel, *Traveling On: The Slave Journal to an Afro-Baptist Faith* (Westport, Conn., 1979). For information on African-American Masonry, see George W. Crawford, *Prince Hall and His Followers* (New York, 1914) and William Upton, *Negro Masonry* (Cambridge, 1902, reprinted 1975). A useful study of blacks in an urban setting is Gary B. Nash, *Forging Freedom: The Formation of Philadelphia's Black Community, 1720–1840* (New York, 1988).

7. Blacks and Manifest Destiny

Frontier influences are treated in a series of highly significant essays in Frederick J. Turner, *The Frontier in American History* (New York, 1920). William Loren Katz, *The Black West** (New York, 1971) is a documentary and pictorial history of African Americans in the westward movement. Two other works on the subject are Kenneth W. Porter, *The Negro on the American Frontier* (New York, 1971) and W. Sherman Savage, *Blacks in the West* (Westport, Conn., 1976). The movement of African Americans into frontier areas has also been discussed in several essays in the *Journal of Negro History,* among which are the following: Eugene P. Southall, "Negroes in Florida Prior to the Civil War," XIX (January 1934); Harry E. Davis, "John Malvin, A Western Reserve Pioneer," XXIII (October 1938); Alrutheus A. Taylor, "The Movement of Negroes from the East to the Gulf States from 1830 to 1850," VIII (October 1923); and Carter G. Woodson, "Freedom and Slavery in Appalachian America," I (April 1916). The War of 1812 is treated in Laura E. Wilkes, *Missing Pages* *in American History* (Washington, D.C., 1919); George W. Williams, *A History of Negro Troops in the War of the Rebellion* (New York, 1888); Roland McConnell, *Negro Troops in Antebellum Louisiana* (Baton Rouge, La., 1968); and Wilson, *The Black Phalanx*. William C. Nell, *Services of Colored Americans in the Wars of 1776 and 1812* (Boston, 1851) should also be read.

The growth of the cotton kingdom is treated in William E. Dodd, *The Cotton Kingdom* (New Haven, Conn., 1919); Gray, *History of Agriculture in the Southern United States;* Frederick J. Turner, *Rise of the New West* (New York, 1906); and Ulrich B. Phillips, *American Negro Slavery** (New York, 1918). For a critical discussion of the highly questionable conclusions reached by Phillips, see Richard Hofstadter, "U. B. Phillips and the Plantation Legend," *Journal of Negro History,* XXIX (April 1944). The influence of the doctrine of Manifest Destiny on the emergence of the cotton kingdom is handled in Albert K. Weinberg, *Manifest Destiny, A Study of National Expansionism in American History** (Baltimore, 1935). Most of the works on slavery deal with the domestic slave trade, but the best account is in Frederick Bancroft, *Slave Trading in the Old South** (Baltimore, 1931). W. H. Stephenson, *Isaac Franklin, Slave Trader and Planter of the Old South* (University, La., 1938) is an important supplement. See also William T. Laprade, "The Domestic Slave Trade in the District of Columbia," *Journal of Negro History,* XI (January 1926). For discussions of the persistence of the African Trade, see Du Bois, *Suppression of the African Slave Trade;* Charles H. Wesley, "Manifests of Slave Shipments along the Waterways, 1808–1864," *Journal of Negro History,* XXVII (April 1942); and Eric Williams, "The British West Indian Slave Trade after Its Abolition in 1807," *Journal of Negro History,* XXVII (April 1942).

8. That Peculiar Institution

Most of the works on slavery in the United States should be read with critical care because of their tendency to emphasize the large plantation at the expense of the smaller unit, on which most of the slaves were to be found. A convenient and reliable reference is Randall M. Miller and John David Smith, eds., *Dictionary of Afro-American Slavery* (New York, 1968). A monumental work on the subject is the several volumes by David Brion Davis beginning with *The Problem of Slavery in Western Culture* (Ithaca, N.Y., 1960). For a detached view of how United States historians deal with slavery, see the work by British historian Peter J. Parish, *Slavery: History and Historians* (New York, 1989). Ulrich B. Phillips, *Life and Labor in the Old South** (Boston, 1929), like his *American Negro Slavery,* tends to apologize for the institution.

Kenneth M. Stampp, *The Peculiar Institution** (New York, 1956) is a more exhaustive study of slavery that takes sharp issue with Phillips on many points. Eugene D. Genovese, *The Political Economy of Slavery** (New York, 1965) discusses slavery as a part of a total way of life in the South. See also his *The World the Slaveholders Made** (New York, 1971). His *Roll, Jordan, Roll: The World the Slaves Made** (New York, 1974) is an extensive examination of slave life and the relationship of masters to it. The most recent and one of the best general treatments of slavery is Peter Kolchin, *American Slavery, 1619–1877* (New York, 1993). In *Slavery and Freedom: An Interpretation of the Old South* (New York, 1990), James Oakes argues that the Civil War was a conflict rooted in the fundamentals of capitalistic society, a salient feature of the slave system. Discussions of the development of culture and institutions from the slave perspective are found in John Blassingame, *The Slave Community, Plantation Life in the Antebellum South** (New York, 1974); Leslie Howard Owens, *This Species of Property: Slave Life and Culture in the Old South** (New York, 1976); Thomas L. Webber, *Deep Like the Rivers: Education in the Slave Quarter Community, 1831–1865** (New York, 1978); and Charles Joyner, *Down by the Riverside: A South Carolina Slave Community* (Urbana, Ill., 1984). See also Blassingame's *Slave Testimony: Two Centuries of Letters, Speeches, Interviews, and Autobiographies** (Baton Rouge, La., 1977). Stanley Elkins, *Slavery: A Problem in American Institutional and Intellectual Life,** third edition (Chicago, 1976), is concerned primarily with the effect of slavery on personality. For a critical discussion of the Elkins thesis, see Ann J. Lane, ed., *The Debate over Slavery: Stanley Elkins and His Critics** (Urbana, Ill., 1971). Richard C. Wade, *Slavery in the Cities: The South 1820–1860** (New York, 1964) argues that slavery in urban areas was different in virtually every way from slavery in rural areas. A counterargument is advanced in Claudia D. Goldin, *Urban Slavery in the American South, 1820–1860: A Quantitative History* (Chicago, 1976). For a discussion of the problem of determining the profitability of slavery, see Alfred H. Conrad and John R. Meyer, *The Economics of Slavery and Other Econometric Studies* (Chicago, 1964) and Robert W. Fogel and Stanley L. Engerman, eds., *The Reinterpretation of American Economic History* (New York, 1971). See also Thomas P. Govan, "Was Plantation Slavery Profitable," *Journal of Southern History,* VII (November 1942) and Harold D. Woodman, "The Profitability of Slavery: A Historical Perennial," *Journal of Southern History,* XXIX (August 1963). An excellent recent addition to this discussion is Michael Tadman, *Speculators and Slaves: Masters, Traders, and Slaves in the Old South* (Madison, Wisc., 1989). In *Time on the Cross,* two volumes (New York, 1974), Robert Fogel and Stanley Engerman make greater claims for the mitigating factors in slavery than they are able to prove. Among the several critical analyses of their position see Paul David and others, *Reckoning with Slavery: A Critical Study in the Quantitative History of American Negro Slavery* (New York, 1976) and Herbert Gutman, *Slavery and the Numbers Game: A Critique of Time on the Cross* (Urbana, Ill., 1975). Other problems of management are discussed in John S. Bassett, *The Southern Plantation Overseer as Revealed in His Letters* (Northampton, Mass., 1925, reprinted 1968) and in William L. Van Deburg, *The Slave Drivers: Black Agricultural Labor Supervisors in the Ante-Bellum South** (Westport, Conn., 1979). Janet Duitsman Cornelius, *"When I Can Read My Title Clear": Literacy, Slavery, and Religion in the Antebellum South* (Columbia, S.C., 1991) is an important contribution to this subject.

The following are among the more satisfactory discussions of slavery in specific states: Guion Johnson, *Ante-Bellum North Carolina;* Charles S. Sydnor, *Slavery in Mississippi* (New York, 1933); Roger W. Shugg, *Origins of Class Struggle in Louisiana** (University, La., 1939); Chase C. Mooney, *Slavery in Tennessee** (Bloomington, Ind., 1957); J. Winston Coleman, *Slavery Times in Kentucky* (Chapel Hill, N.C., 1940); Harrison A. Trexler, *Slavery in Missouri, 1804–1865* (Baltimore, 1914); James B. Sellers, *Slavery in Alabama* (University, Ala., 1950); Julian Floyd Smith, *Slavery and Plantation Growth in Antebellum Florida, 1821–1860* (Gainesville, Fla., 1973); and Orville W. Taylor, *Negro Slavery in Arkansas* (Durham, N.C., 1958). One of the very best treatments of slavery in one state that goes beyond the borders of the state is Ann Patton Malone, *Sweet Chariot, Slave Family and Household Structure in Nineteenth Century Louisiana* (Chapel Hill, N.C., 1992). The best travel account, more authoritative than many secondary works, is Frederick L. Olmsted, *The Cotton Kingdom: A Traveller's Observations on Cotton and Slavery in the American Slave States,* two volumes (New York, 1861). A special aspect of slavery in treated in Robert S. Starobin, *Industrial Slavery in the Old South** (New York, 1970).

The laws affecting slaves are summarized in John C. Hurd, *Law of Freedom and Bondage in the United States,* two volumes (Boston, 1858), while interpretations of the law may be found in Helen T. Catterall, ed., *Judicial Cases Concerning American Slavery and the Negro,* five volumes (Washington, D.C., 1926). Howell M. Henry, *The Police Control of the Slave in South Carolina* (Emory, Va., 1914) and Wilbert E. Moore, "Slave Law and the Social Structure," *Journal of Negro History,* XXVI (April 1941) discuss the problem of enforcing the Black Codes. Numerous slaves have told of their own experiences, often with the assistance of others. *The Narrative of Frederick Douglass** (Boston, 1845) is the best known; another is *Father Henson's Story of His Own Life* (Boston, 1858). A remarkable document is Harriet A. Jacobs, *Incidents in the Life of a Slave Girl Written by Herself,* edited by Jean F. Yellin (Cambridge, Mass., 1987). The reminiscences of several slaves are recorded in the following works: B. A. Botkin, ed., *Lay My Burden Down: A Folk History of Slavery** (Chicago, 1945); George P. Rawick, *The American Slave: A Composite Autobiography,* nineteen volumes (Westport, Conn., 1971); Arna Bontemps, ed., *Great Slave Narratives** (Boston, 1969); Gilbert Osofsky, ed., *Puttin' on Ole Massa** (New York, 1969); and Charles H. Nichols, *Many Thousand Gone** (Bloomington, Ind., 1969). Evaluations of the importance of the narrative are in Marion W. Starling, *The Slave Narrative: Its Place in American History* (Boston, 1981); John Sekora and Darwin T. Turner, eds., *The Art of Slave Narrative: Original Essays in Criticism and Theory* (Macomb, Ill. 1983); and Charles T. Davis and Henry L. Gates, *The Slave's Narrative* (New York, 1985).

The problems of the slave family are discussed in Frazier, *The Negro Family in the United States,* and Gutman, *The Black Family in Slavery and Freedom.* See also Deborah Gray White, *Ar'nt I a Woman? Female Slaves in the Plantation South* (New York, 1985). See Elizabeth Fox Genovese, *Within the Plantation Household: Black and White Women of the Old South* (Chapel Hill, N.C., 1989) that argues that a special relationship existed between female members of the ownership class and those who were slaves. Melton McLaurin, *Celia, A Slave* (Athens, Ga., 1992) examines a female slave's resistance to sexual exploitation. A special aspect of social relationships is considered in E. Ophelia Settle, "Slave Attitudes during the Slave Regime: Household Servants versus Field Hands," *Publications of the American Sociological Society,* XXVIII (1934). The relationships of slaves with others is discussed in several works, including the following: James H. Johnston, *Race Relations in Virginia and Miscegenation in the South, 1776–1860* (Amherst, Mass., 1970); Carter G. Woodson, "Beginnings of the Miscegenation of the Whites and Blacks," *Journal of Negro History,* III (October 1918); Avery O. Craven, "Poor Whites and Negroes in the Antebellum South," *Journal of Negro History,* XV (January 1930); and Kenneth W. Porter, "Relations between Negroes and Indians within the Present Limits of the United States," *Journal of Negro History,* XVII (July 1932). In addition to Woodson, *History of the Negro Church,* Henry J. Cadbury, "Negro Membership in the Society of Friends," *Journal of Negro History,* XXI (April 1936) and Luther P. Jackson, "Religious Development of the Negro in Virginia from 1760 to 1860," *Journal of Negro History,* XVI (April 1931) may be read with profit. Albert Raboteau, *Slave Religion: The Invisible Institution in the Antebellum South* (New York, 1978), with its careful discussion of African survivals, brings a fresh perspective to this discussion, while Jon Butler, *Awash in a Sea of Faith: Christianizing the American People* (Cambridge, Mass., 1990) focuses on the ways in which Christianity eliminated African religious practices. For a discussion of the origins of spirituals and work songs, see Miles M. Fisher, *Negro Slave Songs in the United States** (Ithaca, N.Y., 1953). An interesting form of slave recreation is handled in Ira DeA. Reid, "The John Canoe Festival," *Phylon,* III (Fourth Quarter 1942). For a stimulating discussion of the influence of Africa on slave culture, see Sterling Stuckey, *Slave Culture: Nationalist Theory and the Foundations of Black America** (New York, 1987). See also Barbara H. Fields, *Slavery and Freedom on the Middle Ground: Maryland during the Nineteenth Century* (New Haven, Conn., 1985).

The best account of resistance to slavery is Herbert Aptheker, *American Negro Slave Revolts** (New York, 1943). His "Maroons within the Present Limits of the United States," *Journal of Negro History*, XXIV (April 1939) is also valuable. Other studies are Joseph C. Carroll, *Slave Insurrections in the United States, 1800–1860* (Boston, 1938); Nicholas Halasz, *Rattling Chains: Slave Unrest and Revolt in the Antebellum South* (New York, 1966); Raymond and Alice Bauer, "Day to Day Resistance to Slavery," *Journal of Negro History*, XXVII (October 1942); Lorenzo J. Greene, "Mutiny on the Slave Ships," *Phylon*, V (Fourth Quarter 1944); Vincent Harding, "Religion and Resistance among Ante-Bellum Negroes, 1800–1860," in August Meier and Elliott Rudwick, eds., *The Making of Black America*, Volume I* (New York, 1969); and Gerald W. Mullin, *Flight and Rebellion: Slave Resistance in Eighteenth Century Virginia* (New York, 1972). An engrossing account of one slave uprising is contained in John Lofton, *Insurrection in South Carolina: The Turbulent World of Denmark Vesey* (Yellow Springs, Ohio, 1964), but see also Richard Wade, "The Vesey Plot: A Reconsideration," *Journal of Southern History*, XXX (May 1964). William Styron's novel, *The Confessions of Nat Turner** (New York, 1966), was bitterly assailed by many, and the principal attacks may be found in John Henrik Clarke, ed., *William Styron's Nat Turner: Ten Black Writers Respond** (Boston, 1968). See also John B. Duff and Peter M. Mitchell, eds., *The Nat Turner Rebellion: The Historical Event and the Modern Controversy** (New York, 1971). Surprisingly little has been written on runaway slaves beyond several volumes of advertisements for fugitives. But see Freddie L. Parker, *Running for Freedom: Slave Runaways in North Carolina, 1775–1840* (New York, 1993) and Michael P. Johnson, "Runaway Slaves and the Slave Community in South Carolina, 1799–1830," *William and Mary Quarterly*, Third Series, XXXVIII (July 1981).

9. Quasi-Free Blacks

The first full-length general treatment of free blacks is Ira Berlin, *Slaves without Masters: The Free Negro in the Antebellum South** (New York, 1975). A detailed study of free blacks in one locale is offered in Michael P. Johnson and James L. Roark's two books, *No Chariot Let Down: Charleston's Free People of Color on the Eve of the Civil War* (Chapel Hill, N.C., 1984) and *Black Masters: A Free Family of Color in the Old South* (New York, 1984). See also Larry Koger, *Black Slaveowners: Free Black Slave Masters in South Carolina* (Jefferson, N.C., 1985) and Loren Schweninger, *Black Property Owners in the South, 1790–1915* (Urbana, Ill., 1990). An excellent summary statement concerning the group is found in Carter G. Woodson, *Free Negro Heads of Families in the United States in 1830* (Washington, D.C., 1925). The problem in the North is treated in Leon Litwack, *North of Slavery, The Negro in the Free States, 1790–1860** (Chicago, 1961); Emma L. Thornbrough, *The Negro in Indiana, A Study of a Minority* (Indianapolis, Ind., 1957); James Oliver Horton and Lois Horton, *Black Bostonians: Family Life and Community Struggle in the Ante-Bellum North** (New York, 1979); James Oliver Horton, *Free People of Color: Inside the African American Community* (Washington, D.C., 1993); Leonard P. Curry, *The Free Black in Urban America, 1800–1850* (Chicago, 1981); and

Robert Cottrol, *The Afro-Yankees: Providence's Black Community in the Ante-Bellum Era* (New York, 1982). Information on Southern free black women is presented in Suzanne Lebsock, *The Free Women of Petersburg: Status and Culture in a Southern Town* (New York, 1984) and Ellen N. Lawson and Marlene D. Merrill, *The Three Sarahs: Documents on Antebellum Black-College Women* (Lewiston, N.Y., 1984). Several monographs deal with the subject in different states. They are James M. Wright, *The Free Negro in Maryland, 1634–1860* (New York, 1921); John Russell, *The Free Negro in Virginia, 1619–1865** (Baltimore, 1913); Luther P. Jackson, *Free Negro Labor and Property Holding in Virginia, 1830–1860** (New York, 1942); H. E. Sterkx, *The Free Negro in Antebellum Louisiana* (Rutherford, N.J., 1972); Edward F. Sweat, *Economics Status of Free Blacks in Antebellum Georgia* (Atlanta, 1974); and John Hope Franklin, *The Free Negro in North Carolina, 1790–1860** (Chapel Hill, N.C., 1943). For a discussion of free blacks in the nation's capital, see Letitia Woods Brown, *Free Negroes in the District of Columbia, 1790–1846* (New York, 1972) and James Borchert, *Alley Life in Washington, D.C.: Family, Community, Religion and Folklife in the City, 1850–1870* (Urbana, Ill., 1980). A rare personal testimony is found in W. R. Hogan and E. A. Davis, eds., *William Johnson's Natchez: The Ante-Bellum Diary of a Free Negro* (Baton Rouge, La., 1951). Briefer works deal with free blacks in other localities: E. Horace Fitchett, "The Origin and Growth of the Free Negro Population of Charleston, South Carolina," *Journal of Negro History,* XXVI (October 1941); Ralph B. Flanders, "The Free Negro in Ante-Bellum Georgia," *North Carolina Historical Review,* IX (July 1932); W. McDowell Rogers, "Free Negro Legislation in Georgia," *Georgia Historical Quarterly,* XVI (March 1932); David Y. Thomas, "The Free Negro in Florida before 1865," *South Atlantic Quarterly,* X (October 1911); J. Merton England, "The Free Negro in Ante-Bellum Tennessee," *Journal of Southern History,* IX (February 1943); William L. Imes, "The Legal Status of Free Negroes and Slaves in Tennessee," *Journal of Negro History,* IV (July 1919); Charles S. Sydnor, "The Free Negro in Mississippi before the Civil War," *American Historical Review,* XXXII (July 1927); Alice D. Nelson, "People of Color in Louisiana," *Journal of Negro History,* I (October 1916) and II (January 1917); and Harold Schoen, "The Free Negro in the Republic of Texas," *Southwestern Historical Quarterly,* XL (April 1926) and succeeding issues. A special phase of the free black's legal status is treated in Roger W. Shugg, "Negro Voting in the Ante-Bellum South," *Journal of Negro History,* XXI (October 1936). For the fortunes and misfortunes of an individual free black, see John Hope Franklin, "James Boon, Free Negro Artisan," *Journal of Negro History,* XXX (April 1945) and Juliet E. K. Walker, *Free Frank: A Black Pioneer on the Ante-Bellum Frontier* (Lexington, Ky., 1984).

The ownership of slaves by free blacks is discussed in John H. Russell, "Colored Freemen as Slave Owners in Virginia," *Journal of Negro History,* I (July 1916); C. D. Wilson, "Negroes Who Owned Slaves," *Popular Science Monthly,* LXXXI (November 1912); Michael P. Johnson and James L. Roark, *Black Masters: A Free Family of Color in the Old South* (New York, 1984); and Loren Schweninger, "John Carruthers Stanly and the Anomaly of Black Slaveholding," *North Carolina Historical Review* LXVII (April 1990). Statistics are provided in Carter G. Woodson, *Free Negro Owners of Slaves in the United States in 1830* (Washington, D.C., 1925).

Some of the peculiar social problems of free blacks are treated in E. Franklin Frazier, *The Free Negro Family* (Nashville, 1932), while economic matters are handled in Martin R. Delany, *The Condition, Elevation, Emigration, and Destiny of the Colored People of the United States* (Philadelphia, 1852) and Wesley, *Negro Labor in the United States.* Other works that deal with the problems that Northern free blacks faced are

Edward R. Turner, *The Negro in Pennsylvania* (Washington, D.C., 1911) and Carter G. Woodson, "The Negroes of Cincinnati Prior to the Civil War," *Journal of Negro History,* I (January 1916). White Southerners viewed the plight of Northern free blacks in John Hope Franklin, *A Southern Odyssey: Travelers in the Antebellum North** (Baton Rouge, La., 1976). Early African-American organizations are considered in John W. Cromwell, *The Early Negro Convention Movement* (Washington, D.C., 1904) and Bella Gross, "The First National Negro Convention," *Journal of Negro History,* XXXI (October 1946). For an important phase of cultural history, see Dorothy B. Porter, "The Organized Educational Activities of Negro Literary Societies, 1828–1846," *Journal of Negro Education,* V (October 1936).

The pioneer work on the major colonization organizations is Early L. Fox, *The American Colonization Society, 1817–1840* (Baltimore, 1919). It has been superseded by Philip J. Staudenraus, *The African Colonization Movement, 1816–1865* (New York, 1961) and by the essays of Frederick Bancroft in Jacob E. Cooke, *Frederick Bancroft, Historian* (Norman, Okla., 1957). H. N. Sherwood, "The Formation of the American Colonization Society," *Journal of Negro History,* II (July 1917) should also be read. Additional works on various phases of the subject are Charles A. Earp, "The Role of Education in the Maryland Colonization Movement," *Journal of Negro History,* XXVI (July 1941); Miles M. Fisher, "Lott Cary, the Colonizing Missionary," *Journal of Negro History,* VII (October 1922); H. N. Sherwood, "Early Negro Deportation Projects," *Mississippi Valley Historical Review,* II (March 1916); N. Andrew Cleven, "Some Plans for Colonizing Liberated Negro Slaves in Hispanic America," *Journal of Negro History,* XI (January 1926); Louis R. Mehlinger, "The Attitude of the Free Negro toward Colonization," *Journal of Negro History,* I (July 1916); and Floyd John Miller, *The Search for a Black Nationality: Black Colonization and Emigration, 1787–1863* (Urbana, Ill., 1975).

10. Slavery and Intersectional Strife

The beginnings of abolition are discussed in Alice D. Adams, *The Neglected Period of Anti-Slavery in America, 1808–1831* (Boston, 1908). For the relationship between abolitionism and the other reform movements, see Alice F. Tyler, *Freedom's Ferment: Phases of American Social History to 1860** (Minneapolis, Minn., 1944). One of the best discussions of the abolition movement is Gilbert H. Barnes, *The Antislavery Impulse, 1830–1844** (New York, 1933). Several works of excellent quality that deal with abolitionism are Louis Filler, *The Crusade against Slavery, 1830–1860** (New York, 1960); Dwight L. Dumond, *Anti-Slavery: The Crusade for Freedom in America** (Ann Arbor, Mich., 1961); Martin L. Duberman, ed., *The Antislavery Vanguard** (Princeton, N.J., 1965); and Hugh Hawkins, ed., *The Abolitionists: Immediatism and the Question of Means** (Boston, 1964). An important reexamination of the movement is in Aileen Kraditor, *Means and Ends in American Abolitionism: Garrison and His Critics on Strategy and Tactics, 1834–1850** (New York, 1969). Biographies of abolitionists that should be consulted include Irving Bartlett, *Wendell Phillips, Brahmin Radical* (Boston, 1961) and John L. Thomas, *The Liberator: William Lloyd Garrison* (Boston, 1963). One excellent work on this subject is Herbert Aptheker's "Militant Abolitionism," *Journal of Negro History,* XXVI (October 1941). The international aspects of abolitionism are treated in Frank J. Klingberg, *The Anti-Slavery Movement in England* (New Haven, 1926). The growth and dissemination of ideas in the abolition movement may be studied in

Lorenzo D. Turner, *Anti-Slavery Sentiment in American Literature* (Washington, D.C., 1929) and W. Sherman Savage, *The Controversy over the Distribution of Abolition Literature* (Washington, D.C., 1938). The *Dictionary of American Biography* and W. J. Simmons, *Men of Mark* (Louisville, Ky., 1887, reprinted 1970) include sketches of the lives of the leading abolitionists.

The major work on black participation in the antislavery movement is Benjamin Quarles's excellent *Black Abolitionists** (New York, 1969). Other noteworthy studies are Herbert Aptheker, *The Negro in the Abolitionist Movement* (New York, 1941); Charles H. Wesley, "The Negroes of New York in the Emancipation Movement," *Journal of Negro History*, XXIV (January 1939); John Bracey and others, eds., *Blacks in the Abolitionist Movement* (Belmont, Calif., 1971); R. J. M. Blackett, *Building an Anti-Slavery Wall: Black Americans in the Atlantic Abolitionist Movement** (Baton Rouge, La., 1983); and Merton L. Dillon, *Slavery Attacked: Southern Slaves and Their Allies, 1619–1865* (Baton Rouge, La., 1990). *Witness for Freedom: African American Voices on Race, Slavery, and Emancipation*, three volumes (Chapel Hill, N.C., 1985–1991), edited by C. Peter Ripley, Roy E. Finkbine, Michael F. Hembree, and Donald Yacovone, is an invaluable source of information on African-American abolitionist thought and activity. The outstanding piece of abolitionist writing by a black person is David Walker's *Appeal in Four Articles* (Boston, 1830), two paperback editions of which appeared in 1965. The narratives mentioned in the text of Chapter 8 provide valuable information concerning blacks in the abolition movement, as does Carter G. Woodson, *The Mind of the Negro as Reflected in Letters during the Crisis, 1800–1860** (Washington, D.C., 1926). There are numerous biographies and sketches of individual blacks. *The Life and Times of Frederick Douglass* (Hartford, Conn., 1881) is a classic of American autobiography. The work by Shirley Graham, *There Was Once a Slave* (New York, 1947) is one of the best biographies. The definitive biography of Douglass is Benjamin Quarles, *Frederick Douglass** (Washington, D.C., 1948). One should also consult Philip S. Foner, *Frederick Douglass* (New York, 1964) and, of course, Foner's *The Life and Writings of Frederick Douglass**, four volumes (New York, 1950–1955). Publications offering additional insights on Douglass include Waldo E. Martin, Jr., *The Mind of Frederick Douglass* (Chapel Hill, N.C., 1984) and the comprehensive new edition of Douglass's *Papers* edited by John Blassingame and others, of which two volumes have been published (New Haven, Conn., 1979, 1982); David W. Blight, *Frederick Douglass' Civil War: Keeping Faith in Jubilee* (Baton Rouge, La., 1989); William S. McFeely, *Frederick Douglass* (New York, 1991); and Shirley J. Yee, *Black Women Abolitionists: A Study in Activism, 1828–1860* (Knoxville, Tenn., 1992). See also Earl Conrad, *Harriet Tubman** (Washington, D.C., 1943); Arthur H. Fauset, *Sojourner Truth, God's Faithful Pilgrim* (Chapel Hill, N.C., 1938); Dorothy B. Porter, "David M. Ruggles, An Apostle of Human Rights," *Journal of Negro History*, XXVIII (January 1943); Monroe N. Work, "The Life of Charles B. Ray," *Journal of Negro History*, IV (October 1919); William E. Farrison, *William Wells Brown: Author and Reformer* (Chicago, 1969); and William Cheek and Aimee Lee Cheek, *John Mercer Langston and the Fight for Black Freedom* (Urbana, Ill., 1989). The conflict between the leading white and black abolitionists is discussed in Benjamin Quarles, "The Breach between Douglass and Garrison," *Journal of Negro History*, XXIII (April 1938).

The works of Wilbur H. Siebert have made him the outstanding authority on the Underground Railroad. His major work is *The Underground Railroad from Slavery to Freedom* (New York, 1898). Others include "The Underground Railroad in Massachusetts," *Proceedings of the American Antiquarian Society*, New Series, XLV (Worcester,

Mass., 1935) and "Light on the Underground Railroad," *American Historical Review,* I (April 1896). An invaluable collection of documents and accounts of incidents by a participant is William Still's *The Underground Railroad* (Philadelphia, 1872). See also Horatio T. Strother, *The Underground Railroad in Connecticut** (Middletown, Conn., 1962) and Henrietta Buckmaster, *Let My People Go** (New York, 1941), a popular account of the railroad. Two articles by E. D. Preston in the *Journal of Negro History* shed considerable light on two aspects of the Underground Railroad: "Genesis of the Underground Railroad," XVIII (April 1933) and "The Underground Railroad in Northwest Ohio," XVII (October 1932). A critical view of the railroad is given in Larry Gara, *The Liberty Line: The Legend of the Underground Railroad** (Lexington, Ky., 1961). The Southern fight against the Underground Railroad is discussed in Stanley W. Campbell, *The Slave Catchers: Enforcement of the Fugitive Slave Law, 1850–1860** (Chapel Hill, N.C., 1970). The definitive work on the Canadian phase is Robin Winks, *Blacks in Canada* (New Haven, 1971), but one should not overlook William H. and Jane Pease, *Black Utopia: Negro Communal Experiments in America** (Madison, Wisc., 1963).

The fate of the antislavery movement in the South is discussed in John S. Bassett, *Anti-Slavery Leaders in North Carolina* (Baltimore, 1931); Ruth Scarborough, *The Opposition to Slavery in Georgia Prior to 1860* (Nashville, 1933); and Kenneth M. Stampp, "The Fate of the Southern Antislavery Movement," *Journal of Negro History,* XXVIII (January 1943). The growth of proslavery sentiment in the South is carefully traced and analyzed in William S. Jenkins, *Pro-Slavery Thought in the Old South* (Chapel Hill, N.C., 1935). An excellent collection of proslavery essays is edited and introduced by Drew Gilpin Faust, *The Ideology of Slavery: Proslavery Thought in the Antebellum South, 1830–1860** (Baton Rouge, La., 1981). See also William R. Stanton, *The Leopard's Spots: Scientific Attitudes toward Race in America, 1815–1859** (Chicago, 1960) and William B. Hesseltine, "Some New Aspects of the Proslavery Argument," *Journal of Negro History,* XXI (January 1936). The disappearance of liberalism is treated in Clement Eaton, *Freedom of Thought in the Old South* (Durham, N.C., 1940), while the psychological effect of proslavery thought is discussed in Jesse Carpenter, *The South as a Conscious Minority, 1789–1861* (New York, 1930). Two works by Dwight L. Dumond discuss the breakdown of intersectional relations: *The Secession Movement* (New York, 1931) and *Antislavery Origins of the Civil War in the United States** (London, 1939). In this connection see also Arthur C. Cole, *The Irrepressible Conflict* (New York, 1938) and John Hope Franklin, *The Militant South 1800–1861** (Cambridge, Mass., 1956) and *Southern Odyssey.*

11. Civil War

For general works on blacks in the Civil War, see the able study by the pioneer black historian, George W. Williams, *A History of the Negro Troops in the War of the Rebellion* (New York, 1888). Another study that may also be consulted with profit is Joseph T. Wilson, *The Black Phalanx: A History of the Negro Soldiers of the United States in the Wars of 1775–1812, 1861–1865* (Hartford, Conn., 1888). Of less importance, but of some value, is William W. Brown, *The Negro in the American Rebellion* (New York, 1888). Easily the outstanding modern treatment is Benjamin Quarles, *The Negro in the Civil War** (Boston, 1953). See also his *Lincoln and the Negro* (New York, 1962) and William O. Douglas, *Mr. Lincoln and the Negroes: The Long Road to Equality* (New York, 1963).

Herbert Aptheker, *The Negro in the Civil War* (New York, 1938) is a brief but valuable work. Bell Irvin Wiley, *Southern Negroes, 1861–1865** (New York, 1953) ably deals with numerous aspects of the Union and the Confederate policies. Emerson D. Fite, *Social and Industrial Conditions in the North during the Civil War* (New York, 1910) discusses the effect of draft laws on blacks. The problem of emancipation is covered in John Hope Franklin, *The Emancipation Proclamation** (New York, 1963). See also Hans L. Trefousse, *Lincoln's Decision for Emancipation* (Philadelphia, 1975) and Charles H. Wesley and Patricia Romero, *Negro Americans in the Civil War: From Slavery to Citizenship* (Washington, D.C., 1969). Works dealing with problems of transition from slavery to freedom during the war are Clarence L. Mohr, *On the Threshold of Freedom: Masters and Slaves in Civil War Georgia* (Athens, Ga., 1985); C. Peter Ripley, *Slaves and Freedmen in Civil War Louisiana* (Baton Rouge, La., 1975); Roger L. Ransom and Richard Sutch, *One Kind of Freedom: The Economic Consequences of Emancipation* (Cambridge, 1977); Louis Gerteis, *From Contraband to Freeman: Federal Policy toward Southern Blacks, 1861–1865* (Westport, Conn., 1973); and LaWanda Cox, *Lincoln and Black Freedom: A Study in Presidential Leadership* (Columbia, 1981) and Samuel L. Horst, *Education for Manhood: The Education of Blacks in Virginia during the Civil War* (Lanham, 1987). See also Herman Belz, *Emancipation and Equal Rights: Politics and Constitutionalism in the Civil War Era* (New York, 1978) and Eric Foner, *Nothing But Freedom* (Baton Rouge, La., 1983). Among the many works on the service of black soldiers, Thomas W. Higginson, *Army Life in a Black Regiment* (Boston, 1870) is outstanding. Also of great merit is Dudley T. Cornish, *The Sable Arm: Negro Troops in the Union Army, 1861–1865** (New York, 1956). The most recent discussion of the subject is in Ira Berlin, Joseph P. Reidy, and Leslie S. Rowland, *The Black Military Experience* (Cambridge, Mass., 1982). Herbert Aptheker, "Negro Casualties in the Civil War," *Journal of Negro History*, XXXII (January 1947) is an invaluable study on the subject. The black's own experience is conveyed in James McPherson, *The Negro's Civil War: How American Negroes Felt and Acted during the War for the Union** (New York, 1965). See also McPherson's *The Struggle for Equality: Abolitionists and the Negro in the Civil War and Reconstruction** (Princeton, N.J., 1964) and Joseph T. Glatthar, *Forged in Battle: The Civil War Alliance of Black Soldiers and White Officers* (New York, 1990).

Several works deal primarily with the condition of blacks under the Confederacy. Robert F. Durden, *The Gray and the Black: The Confederate Debate on Emancipation* (Baton Rouge, La., 1972) and Charles B. Dew, *Ironmaker to the Confederacy: Joseph R. Anderson and the Tredegar Iron Works* (New Haven, Conn., 1966) are important. See also Brainerd Dyer, "The Treatment of Colored Union Troops by the Confederates, 1861–1865," *Journal of Negro History*, XX (July 1935); Charles H. Wesley, "The Employment of Negroes as Soldiers in the Confederate Army," *Journal of Negro History*, IV (July 1919); and Harvey Wish, "Slave Disloyalty under the Confederacy," *Journal of Negro History*, XXIII (October 1938). The role of blacks on the home front and with the Confederate military forces is well treated in James H. Brewer, *The Confederate Negro: Virginia's Craftsmen and Military Laborers, 1861–1865* (Durham, N.C., 1969).

12. The Effort to Attain Peace

For many years a great portion of the literature on Reconstruction, while written in the framework of "scientific" history, contained such strong presuppositions regarding the inherent unfitness of blacks for citizenship and the justification for the Ku Klux Klan to restore "order" in the South that its value was severely limited by its bias. That was especially true of the works written under the supervision of William Archibald Dunning at Columbia University early in the twentieth century. Among the better-known works of this "school" of writing are Walter L. Fleming, *Civil War and Reconstruction in Alabama* (New York, 1905) and Joseph G. DeRoulhac Hamilton, *Reconstruction in North Carolina* (New York, 1914). The problems involved in the writing of Reconstruction history have been ably discussed by several historians: Howard K. Beale, "On Rewriting Reconstruction History," *American Historical Review*, XLV (July 1940); Francis B. Simkins, "New Viewpoints of Southern Reconstruction," *Journal of Southern History*, V (February 1939); A. A. Taylor, "Historians of the Reconstruction," *Journal of Negro History*, XXIII (January 1938); and Bernard Weisberger, "The Dark and Bloody Ground of Reconstruction Historiography," *Journal of Southern History*, XXV (November 1959). See also W. E. B. Du Bois, "Reconstruction and Its Benefits," *American Historical Review*, XV (July 1910). A broader approach to the problems of Reconstruction was made by Francis B. Simkins and R. H. Woody in *South Carolina during Reconstruction* (Chapel Hill, N.C., 1932), while an attempt to redress the balance was made by W. E. B. Du Bois, in *Black Reconstruction** (New York, 1935), which seeks to apply Marxist doctrine to the problem of Reconstruction. See also James Allen, *Reconstruction: The Battle for Democracy** (New York, 1937).

Two works by Horace M. Bond suggest a revision of the history of Reconstruction in terms of the influence exercised by powerful business interests: "Social and Economic Forces in Alabama Reconstruction," *Journal of Negro History*, XXIII (July 1938) and *Negro Education in Alabama** (Washington, D.C., 1939). See also A. B. Moore, "Railroad Building in Alabama during the Reconstruction," *Journal of Southern History*, I (November 1935) and James L. Sellers, "The Economic Incidence of the Civil War in the South," *Mississippi Valley Historical Review*, XIV (September 1927). During the period of initial reexamination of Reconstruction several general studies appeared. E. Merton Coulter, *The South during Reconstruction* (Baton Rouge, La., 1947) reaffirmed the position advanced by the Dunning School. Hodding Carter, *The Angry Scar* (New York, 1959) is a popular account. John Hope Franklin, *Reconstruction after the Civil War** (Chicago, 1961) and Kenneth M. Stampp, *The Era of Reconstruction** (New York, 1965) are revisionist in approach and interpretation. See also Robert Cruden, *The Negro in Reconstruction** (Englewood Cliffs, N.J., 1969); Lerone Bennett, *Black Power, U.S.A.: The Human Side of Reconstruction, 1867–1877** (Chicago, 1967); Peter Kolchin, *First Freedom: The Responses of Alabama's Blacks to Emancipation and Reconstruction* (Westport, Conn., 1972); and Forrest G. Wood, *Black Scare: The Racist Response to Emancipation and Reconstruction** (Berkeley, 1968). In recent years there have been numerous general works and monographs that have provided new perspectives as well as new knowledge about the era of Reconstruction. Among them are Leon F. Litwack, *Been In the Storm So Long: The Aftermath of Slavery* (New York, 1979); Claude F. Oubre, *Forty Acres and a Mule: The Freedmen's Bureau and Black Land Ownership* (Baton Rouge, La., 1978); Lawrence Levine, *Black Culture and Black Consciousness* (New York, 1977); Howard Rabinowitz, ed., *Southern Black Leaders of the Reconstruction Era* (1982); Otto Olsen, ed., *Reconstruction and Redemption in the South* (Baton Rouge, La., 1980); J. Morgan Kousser and James M. McPherson, eds., *Region, Race and Reconstruction* (New York, 1982); and George C. Cable, *But There Was No Peace* (Athens, Ga., 1984). A well-received general work is Eric Foner, *Reconstruction: America's Unfinished Revolution, 1863–1877* (New York, 1988). Two stimulating works by Michael Perman have contributed to the understanding of politics in the Reconstruction South: *Reunion without Compromise: The South and Reconstruction, 1865–1868* (Cambridge, Mass., 1973) and *The Road to Redemption: Southern Politics, 1869–1878* (Chapel Hill, N.C., 1984). Two recent works in this area are Earl M. Maltz, *Civil Rights, The Constitution, and Congress, 1863–1869* (Lawrence, 1990) and Eric Anderson & Alfred A. Moss, Jr., eds., *The Facts of Reconstruction: Essays in Honor of John Hope Franklin* (Baton Rouge, 1991). Important documents of the period, with interpretation, are in Ira Berlin, and others, eds., *Freedom: A Documentary History of Emancipation, 1861–1867: Selected from the Holdings of the National Archives* (Cambridge, Mass., 1985).

Several African Americans who lived through the period have attempted to tell their story. Among them are John R. Lynch, *The Facts of Reconstruction** (New York, 1913); John Hope Franklin, ed., *Reminiscences of an Active Life: The Autobiography of John Roy Lynch* (Chicago, 1970); John Wallace, *Carpetbag Rule in Florida* (Jacksonville, Fla., 1888); and Ray Billington, ed., *The Journal of Charlotte Forten* (New York, 1953). Among the better biographical studies are Loren Schweninger, *James T. Rapier and Reconstruction* (Chicago, 1978); Peter D. Klingman, *Josiah Walls: Florida's Black Congressman of Reconstruction* (Gainesville, Fla., 1976); Okon E. Uya, *From Slavery to Public Service, Robert Smalls, 1839–1915** (New York, 1971); and Edward F. Sweat, "Francis L. Cardoza: Profile of Integrity in Reconstruction Politics," *Journal of Negro History,* XLVI (January 1961). The works of Alrutheus A. Taylor should be consulted. They are *The Negro in the Reconstruction of Virginia* (Washington, D.C., 1926); *The Negro in South Carolina during Reconstruction* (Washington, D.C., 1924); and *The Negro in Tennessee, 1865–1880* (Washington, D.C., 1938). Local studies of Reconstruction in the several states have illuminated the greater picture. One of the most significant is Vernon L. Wharton, *The Negro in Mississippi, 1865–1890** (Chapel Hill, N.C., 1947). Another is Thomas Holt, *Black over White: Negro Political Leadership in South Carolina during Reconstruction* (Urbana, Ill., 1977). Others are Joel Williamson, *After Slavery, The Negro in South Carolina during Reconstruction** (Chapel Hill, N.C., 1965); Joe M. Richardson, *The Negro in the Reconstruction of Florida, 1865–1877* (Tallahassee, Fla., 1966); Alan Conway, *The Reconstruction of Georgia* (Minneapolis, 1966); Joe Gray Taylor, *Louisiana Reconstructed, 1863–1877* (Baton Rouge, La., 1975); Carl H. Moneyhon, *Republicanism in Reconstruction Texas* (Austin, 1980); John Blassingame, *Black New Orleans, 1860–1880* (Chicago, 1973); Roberta Alexander, *North Carolina Faces the Freedmen: Race Relations during Presidential Reconstruction, 1865–1867* (Durham, N.C., 1985); and Barbara J. Fields, *Slavery and Freedom on the Middle Ground: Maryland during the Nineteenth Century* (New Haven, Conn., 1985).

Among the numerous works dealing with the conflict between the president and Congress and the triumph of Radical Reconstruction is Howard K. Beale, *The Critical Year, A Study of Andrew Johnson and Reconstruction* (New York, 1930). It has been superseded, to a great extent, by Eric L. McKitrick, *Andrew Johnson and Reconstruction** (Chicago, 1960), La Wanda and John Cox, *Politics, Principle, and Prejudice** (Glencoe, Ill., 1963); Hans L. Trefousse, *Impeachment of a President: Andrew Johnson, the Blacks, and Reconstruction* (Knoxville, Tenn., 1975); and David Warren Brown, *Andrew Johnson and the Negro* (Knoxville, Tenn., 1989). See also David Donald, *The Politics of Reconstruction** (Baton Rouge, La., 1965). Other important works are Horace E. Flack, *The Adoption of the Fourteenth Amendment* (Baltimore, 1908); Benjamin B. Kendrick, *The Journal of the Joint Committee of Fifteen on Reconstruction* (New York, 1914); Jacobus Ten Broek, *The Anti-Slavery Origins of the Fourteenth Amendment* (Berkeley, Calif.,

1951); and William Gillette, *The Right to Vote: Politics and the Passage of the Fifteenth Amendment** (Baltimore, 1965). The pioneer study of the Freedmen's Bureau was Paul S. Peirce, *The Freedmen's Bureau, A Chapter in the History of Reconstruction* (Iowa City, Iowa, 1904). A more recent work is George R. Bentley, *A History of the Freedmen's Bureau* (Philadelphia, 1955). Excellent state studies are Martin Abbott, *The Freedmen's Bureau in South Carolina, 1865–1872* (Chapel Hill, N.C., 1967) and Howard A. White, *The Freedmen's Bureau in Louisiana* (Baton Rouge, La., 1970). Educational activities are covered in Bullock, *A History of Negro Education in the South** (Cambridge, Mass., 1967); Holmes, *The Evolution of the Negro College;* Luther P. Jackson, "The Educational Efforts of the Freedmen's Bureau and Freedmen's Aid Societies in South Carolina, 1862–1872," *Journal of Negro History,* VIII (January 1923); Henry L. Swint, *The Northern Teacher in the South, 1862–1870* (Nashville, Tenn., 1941); Willie Lee Rose, *Rehearsal for Reconstruction: The Port Royal Experiment** (Indianapolis, Ind., 1964); Robert C. Morris, *Reading, 'Riting and Reconstruction: The Education of Freedmen in the South, 1861–1870* (Chicago, 1981); and Ronald E. Butchart, *Northern Schools, Southern Blacks, and Reconstruction: Freedmen's Education, 1862–1875* (Westport, Conn., 1980). In addition to the works already cited, Carl R. Osthaus, *Freedmen, Philanthropy and Fraud: A History of the Freedmen's Savings Bank* (Urbana, Ill., 1976) and Wesley, *Negro Labor in the United States* shed considerable light on certain economic aspects of Reconstruction.

Political currents are discussed in Luther P. Jackson, *Negro Office-Holders in Virginia** (Norfolk, Va., 1945); Samuel D. Smith, *The Negro in Congress, 1870–1901* (Chapel Hill, N.C., 1940); Peggy Lamson, *Glorious Failure: Black Congressman Robert Brown Elliott and the Reconstruction in South Carolina** (New York, 1973); Alrutheus A. Taylor, "Negro Congressmen a Generation After," *Journal of Negro History,* VII (April 1922); G. David Houston, "A Negro Senator," *Journal of Negro History,* VII (July 1922); William A. Russ, "The Negro and White Disfranchisement during Radical Reconstruction," *Journal of Negro History,* XIX (April 1934); and R. H. Woody, "Jonathan J. Wright, Associate Justice of the Supreme Court of South Carolina, 1870–1877," *Journal of Negro History,* XVIII (April 1933). A convenient source for studying the careers of African Americans in Congress is by a member of Congress in the 1990s, William L. Clay, *Just Permanent Interests: Black Americans in Congress, 1870–1991* (New York, 1992). For other aspects, see Otis A. Singletary, *Negro Militia and Reconstruction* (Austin, Tex., 1957) and McPherson, *The Struggle for Equality.* The major documents may be examined in La Wanda and John N. Cox, eds., *Reconstruction, the Negro and the New South** (New York, 1973).

13. Losing the Peace

Many of the titles listed for the previous chapter provide valuable information on the overthrow of Reconstruction. Michael W. Fitzgerald's *The Union League Movement in the Deep South: Politics and Agricultural Change during Reconstruction* (Baton Rouge, La., 1989) is an excellent resource. A fresh and stimulating discussion of the forces behind the overthrow and the way in which the compromise of 1877 was reached is contained in C. Vann Woodward, *Reunion and Reaction: The Compromise of 1877 and the End of Reconstruction** (Boston, 1951). For a general view of the plight of African Americans, see Rayford W. Logan, *The Negro in American Life and Thought: The Nadir,*

1877–1901* (New York, 1954). Southern blacks are discussed in C. Vann Woodward, *Origins of the New South, 1877–1913** (Baton Rouge, La., 1951). Two books covering Republican policy are Vincent P. DeSantis, *Republicans Face the Southern Question* (Baltimore, 1959) and Stanley P. Hirshon, *Farewell to the Bloody Shirt** (Bloomington, Ind., 1962). Reconstruction and post-Reconstruction violence is treated in many of the preceding titles. For Klan activities see John C. Lester, *The Ku Klux Klan: Its Origin, Growth, and Disbandment* (New York, 1905); Stanley F. Horn, *Invisible Empire: The Story of the Ku Klux Klan, 1866–1871* (Boston, 1939); Allen W. Trelease, *White Terror: The Ku Klux Klan Conspiracy and Southern Reconstruction* (New York, 1971); and David M. Chalmers, *Hooded Americanism: The First Century of the Ku Klux Klan** (New York, 1965). See also Francis B. Simkins, *The Tillman Movement in South Carolina* (Durham, N.C., 1926) and Alfred B. Williams, *Hampton and His Red Shirts* (Charleston, S.C., 1935).

The deterioration of the status of African Americans has been discussed by many authors. For general treatments of the political situation, see Key, *Southern Politics*; Lewinson, *Race, Class, and Party**; William A. Mabry, *Studies in the Disfranchisement of the Negro in the South* (Durham, N.C., 1933); Michael L. Lanza, *Agrarianism and Reconstruction Politics: The Southern Homestead Act* (Baton Rouge, La., 1990); and Loren Schweninger, *Black Property Owners in the South* (Urbana, Ill., 1990). At the state level consult Wharton, *The Negro in Mississippi**, Albert D. Kirwan, *Revolt of the Rednecks: Mississippi Politics, 1876–1925** (Lexington, Ky., 1951, reprinted 1964); Helen G. Edmonds, *The Negro and Fusion Politics in North Carolina* (Chapel Hill, N.C., 1951); Eric Anderson, *Race and Politics in North Carolina, 1872–1901* (Baton Rouge, La., 1981); H. Leon Prather, *We Have Taken a City: The Wilmington Massacre and Coup of 1898* (Rutherford, N.J., 1984); Frenise A. Logan, *The Negro in North Carolina, 1876–1894* (Chapel Hill, N.C., 1964); George Tindall, *South Carolina Negroes, 1877–1900** (Columbia, S.C., 1952); and Robert E. Martin, *Negro Disenfranchisement in Virginia** (Washington, D.C., 1938). Economic deterioration can be followed in Daniel A. Novak, *The Wheel of Servitude: Black Forced Labor after Slavery* (Lexington, Ky., 1978); Dwight B. Billings, *Planters and the Making of a "New South": Class Politics and Development in North Carolina* (Chapel Hill, N.C., 1980); Peter J. Rachleff, *Black Labor in the South: Richmond, Virginia, 1865–1890* (Philadelphia, 1984); Charles L. Flynn, *White Land, Black Labor: Caste and Class in Late 19th Century Georgia* (Baton Rouge, La., 1983); Stephen J. DeCanio, *Agriculture in the Post-Bellum South: The Economics of Production and Supply* (Cambridge, Mass., 1974); and John William Graves, *Race Relations in an Urban-Rural Context, Arkansas, 1865–1905* (Fayetteville, Ark., 1990). Various aspects of the problem are explored in William Cohen, *At Freedom's Edge: Black Mobility and the Southern White Quest for Racial Control, 1861–1915* (Baton Rouge, La., 1991).

The effect of the decline of the blacks' position on African Americans themselves is ably discussed in August Meier, *Negro Thought in America, 1880–1915** (Ann Arbor, Mich., 1963). Many aspects of life among blacks are explored in Arnold Taylor, *Travail and Triumph: Black Life and Culture in the South Since the Civil War* (Westport, Conn., 1976). For a discussion of the role of women, see Paula Giddings, *"When and Where I Enter . . .": The Impact of Black Women on Race and Sex in America* (New York, 1984). For an articulate African American's reaction, see T. Thomas Fortune, *Black and White: Land, Labor, and Politics in the South* (New York, 1884) and Emma Lou Thornbrough, *T. Thomas Fortune, Militant Journalist* (Chicago, 1972). The views of a Southern white man sympathetic to African Americans are expressed in George Cable, *The Negro Question,** edited by Arlin Turner (New York, 1958).

C. Vann Woodward has discussed the beginnings of segregation in several of his books. See especially the revised edition of *The Strange Career of Jim Crow,** third edition (New York, 1974). An important work is Howard Rabinowitz's *Race Relations in the Urban South, 1865–1890* (New York, 1978). For other aspects of the start of segregation, see Joseph H. Cartwright, *The Triumph of Jim Crow: Tennessee Race Relations in the 1880s* (Knoxville, Tenn., 1976); Charles E. Wynes, *Race Relations in Virginia, 1870–1902* (Charlottesville, Va., 1961); and John Hope Franklin, "Jim Crow Goes to School: The Genesis of Legal Segregation in Southern Schools," *South Atlantic Quarterly,* LVIII (Spring 1959). Phillip Durham and Everett L. Jones, *Negro Cowboys** (New York, 1965) describes a little-known phase of African-American life.

14. Philanthropy and Self-Help

The effect of philanthropy on the development of American education in general receives able treatment in Jesse B. Sears, *Philanthropy in the History of American Higher Education* (Washington, D.C., 1922), while philanthropic activities among African Americans are discussed in Ullin W. Leavell, *Philanthropy in Negro Education* (Nashville, Tenn., 1930) and Alfred A. Moss, "Northern Philanthropy," *Encyclopedia of Southern Culture* (Chapel Hill, N.C., 1989). For the growth of education among African Americans during the period, see Bond, *Education of the Negro in the American Social Order;* Holmes, *Evolution of the Negro College;* and Bullock, *History of Negro Education in the South.* J. L. M. Curry, a leader in the program for developing education among African Americans in the South, discusses the problem in *A Brief Sketch of George Peabody and A History of the Peabody Education Fund through Thirty Years* (Cambridge, Mass., 1898) and *Difficulties, Complications and Limitations Connected with the Education of the Negro* (Baltimore, 1895). A work that goes beyond these titles and discusses the role of philanthropy in the discrimination against blacks in education is Louis R. Harlan, *Separate and Unequal** (Chapel Hill, N.C., 1958). Studies that provide useful information on developments in black education during this period are Vincent P. Franklin and James D. Anderson, eds., *New Perspectives on Black Educational History* (Boston, 1978); Vincent P. Franklin, *The Education of Black Philadelphia: The Social and Educational History of a Minority Community, 1900–1950* (Philadelphia, 1979); James D. Anderson, *The Education of Blacks in the South, 1860–1935* (Chapel Hill, N.C., 1988); Robert A. Margo, *Race and Schooling in the South, 1880–1950: An Economic History* (Chicago, 1990); and Edmund L. Drago, *Initiative, Paternalism, and Race Relations: Charleston's Avery Normal Institute* (Athens, Ga., 1990).

The views of Booker T. Washington have been discussed by numerous friends and enemies. His views, as expressed by himself, may be found in the following works: *The Negro in the South: His Economic Progress in Relation to his Moral and Religious Development,* with W. E. B. Du Bois (Philadelphia, 1907); E. David Washington, ed., *Selected Speeches of Booker T. Washington* (Garden City, N.Y., 1932); and *Up from Slavery; An Autobiography** (Garden City, N.Y., 1900). See also Emmett J. Scott and Lyman B. Stowe, *Booker T. Washington, Builder of a Civilization* (Garden City, N.Y., 1916). W. E. B. Du Bois, the most relentless critic of Washington, has aired his views in many books and articles. Among them are *The Souls of Black Folk, Essays and Sketches** (Chicago, 1903) and *Dusk to Dawn, An Essay toward the Autobiography of a Race Concept* (New York, 1940). For other discussions of Washington's program, see Merle Curti,

The Social Ideas of American Education* (New York, 1935); Charles S. Johnson, "The Social Philosophy of Booker T. Washington," *Opportunity,* VI (April 1928); and W. Edward Farrison, "Booker T. Washington: A Study in Educational Leadership," *South Atlantic Quarterly,* XLI (July 1942). Later studies of Washington include Basil J. Mathews, *Booker T. Washington* (Cambridge, Mass., 1948); Samuel R. Spencer, Jr., *Booker T. Washington and the Negro's Place in American Life** (Boston, 1955); and Meier, *Negro Thought in America.* An indispensable source on Washington is the two-volume study by Louis R. Harlan, *Booker T. Washington, The Making of a Black Leader, 1856–1901** (New York, 1972) and *Booker T. Washington: The Wizard of Tuskegee, 1901–1915* (New York, 1983). Harlan is also the editor of *The Booker T. Washington Papers* (Urbana, Ill., 1972–1985). For studies on Du Bois, see Francis L. Broderick, *W. E. B. Du Bois: Negro Leader in Time of Crisis* (Stanford, Calif., 1959); Elliott M. Rudwick, *W. E. B. Du Bois: A Study in Minority Group Leadership** (Philadelphia, 1961); Arnold Rampersad, *The Art and Imagination of W. E. B. Du Bois* (Cambridge, Mass., 1976); David Lewis, *W. E. B. Du Bois, Biography of a Race, 1868–1919* (New York, 1993); and Herbert Aptheker, ed., *The Correspondence of W. E. B. Du Bois* (Amherst, Mass., 1973–1978).

The problems of African-American labor and other aspects of economic life are treated in Spero and Harris, *The Black Worker* and Wesley, *Negro Labor in the United States.* Recent works that expand on earlier studies are Dennis C. Dickerson, *Out of the Crucible: Black Steelworkers in Western Pennsylvania, 1875–1980* (Albany, N.Y., 1986); Joe William Trotter, *Coal, Class, and Color: Blacks in Southern West Virginia, 1915–1932* (Urbana, Ill., 1990); and Eric Arnesen, *Waterfront Workers of New Orleans: Race, Class, and Politics, 1863–1923* (New York, 1991). The status of black business enterprises at the turn of the century is discussed in W. E. B. Du Bois, *The Negro in Business* (Atlanta, Ga., 1899) and Booker T. Washington, *The Negro in Business* (Boston, 1907). Banking enterprises among African Americans have been carefully analyzed and criticized in Harris, *The Negro as Capitalist,* while another phase of economic life is treated in William J. Trent, *Development of Negro Life Insurance Enterprises* (Philadelphia, 1932); Walter B. Weare, *Black Business in the New South: A Social History of the North Carolina Mutual Life Insurance Company* (Urbana, Ill., 1975); and Alexa Benson Henderson, *Atlanta Life Insurance Company: Guardian of Black Economic Dignity* (Tuscaloosa, Ala., 1990).

The Atlanta University Studies, edited by W. E. B. Du Bois, are an important source concerning the social and cultural development of African Americans during the period. See, for example, *The College-Bred Negro* (Atlanta, Ga., 1900); *The Negro Common School* (Atlanta, Ga., 1901); and *Some Efforts of American Negroes for Their Own Social Betterment* (Atlanta, Ga., 1898). An effort by black intellectuals to provide racial leadership is discussed in Alfred Moss, *The American Negro Academy: Voice of the Talented Tenth** (Baton Rouge, La., 1981). Additional insight on the complexity of the lives of members of the African-American elite is provided in Willard B. Gatewood, *Aristocrats of Color: The Black Elite, 1880–1920* (Bloomington, Ind., 1990); Wilson Jeremiah Moses, *Alexander Crummell: A Study of Civilization and Discontent* (New York, 1989); and Dickson D. Bruce, Jr., *Archibald Grimke: Portrait of a Black Independent* (Baton Rouge, La., 1993). For religious developments, see Woodson, *History of the Negro Church;* David M. Reimers, *White Protestantism and the Negro* (New York, 1965); and Stephen J. Ochs, *Desegregating the Altar: The Josephites and the Struggle for Black Priests* [in the Roman Catholic Church], *1871–1960* (Baton Rouge, La., 1990). Three useful studies that focus on the activities of African-American women are Cynthia Neverdon-Morton, *Afro-American Women of the South and the Advancement of the Race,*

1895–1925 (Knoxville, Tenn., 1989); Adele Logan Alexander, *Ambiguous Lives: Free Women of Color in Rural Georgia, 1789–1879* (Fayetteville, Ark., 1992); and Evelyn Brooks Higginbotham, *Righteous Discontent: The Women's Movement in the Black Baptist Church, 1880–1920* (Cambridge, Mass., 1993). An able analysis of the growth of social institutions is in Guy B. Johnson, "Some Factors in the Development of Negro Social Institutions in the United States," *American Journal of Sociology,* XXX (November 1934). Literary activities of African Americans are carefully traced in Loggins, *The Negro Author,* while journalistic activities receive attention in Penn, *The Afro-American Press and Its Editors;* Detweiler, *The Negro Press in the United States;* and Henry Lewis Suggs, *P.B. Young, Newspaperman: Race, Politics, and Journalism in the New South, 1910–1962* (New York, 1988). For a definitive treatment of the leading writer of the period see Frances R. Keller, *An American Crusade: The Life of Charles Waddell Chesnutt* (Provo, Utah, 1977). For sketches of prominent contemporary African Americans, see William J. Simmons, *Men of Mark: Eminent, Progressive, and Rising* (Cleveland, 1887). For discussion of general problems and frustrations, see Logan, *The Negro in American Life and Thought;* Edwin S. Redkey, *Black Exodus: Black Nationalists and Back-to-Africa Movements 1890–1910** (New Haven, Conn., 1969); and Nell Painter, *Exodusters: Black Migration to Kansas after Reconstruction* (New York, 1977).

15. The Color Line

Although there is no exhaustive account of African Americans' part in the Spanish-American War, Willard Gatewood's collection of letters written by black soldiers, *Smoked Yankees and the Struggle for Empire* (Urbana, Ill., 1971) offers an excellent introduction to the subject. The following titles are among the better ones available: Edward L. N. Glass, *The History of the Tenth Cavalry, 1866–1901* (Tucson, Ariz., 1921); James M. Guthrie, *Campfires of the Afro-American* (Philadelphia, 1899); Edward A. Johnson, *History of Negro Soldiers in the Spanish American War and Other Items of Interest* (Raleigh, N.C., 1899); Miles V. Lynk, *The Black Troopers, or the Daring Heroism of the Negro Soldiers in the Spanish American War* (Jackson, 1899, reprinted 1972); and *A New Negro for a New Century* (Chicago, 1900). For a full treatment of the Brownsville riot, see Ann J. Lane, *The Brownsville Affair: National Crisis and Black Reaction* (Port Washington, N.Y., 1971).

The emergence of an American imperial policy is discussed in Howard C. Hill, *Roosevelt and the Caribbean* (Chicago, 1927) and Theodore Roosevelt, Jr., *Colonial Policies of the United States* (Garden City, N.Y., 1937). The American administration (of Puerto Rico) is treated in Pedro Capo-Rodriguez, "Some Historical and Political Aspects of the Government of Puerto Rico," *Hispanic American Historical Review,* II (November 1919) and Bolivar Pagan, *Puerto Rico: The Next State* (Washington, D.C., 1942). Luther H. Evans ably handles the acquisition and administration of the Virgin Islands in *The Virgin Islands: From Naval Base to New Deal* (Ann Arbor, Mich., 1945). The relations of the United States and Haiti receive attention in George W. Brown, "Haiti and the United States," *Journal of Negro History,* VIII (April 1923) and Rayford W. Logan, *Diplomatic Relations of the United States with Haiti 1776–1891* (Chapel Hill, N.C., 1941). See also James A. Padgett, "Diplomats to Haiti and Their Diplomacy," *Journal of Negro History,* XXV (July 1940); "The Ministers to Liberia and Their

Diplomacy," *Journal of Negro History*, XXII (January 1937), by the same author, traces the influence of American diplomats on Liberia's history. For a different approach see George P. Marks, comp., *The Black Press Views American Imperialism, 1898–1900* (New York, 1971) and Willard B. Gatewood, *Black Americans and the White Man's Burden, 1898–1903* (Urbana, Ill., 1975).

The main problems arising during the Roosevelt administration are discussed in H. F. Pringle, *Theodore Roosevelt** (New York, 1931). For a criticism of Roosevelt's policy with regard to African Americans, see Alfred H. Stone, *Studies in the American Race Problem* (New York, 1908). The impact of the city upon the condition of blacks is treated in Thomas J. Woofter, *Negro Problems in Cities* (Garden City, N.Y., 1928). For information concerning the problems of blacks in New York, see George E. Haynes, *The Negro at Work in New York City* (New York, 1912); James W. Johnson, *Black Manhattan** (New York, 1930); and Claude McKay, *Harlem: Negro Metropolis** (New York, 1940). Full-length studies that should be consulted are Gilbert Osofsky, *Harlem: The Making of a Ghetto** (New York, 1966); Seth M. Scheiner, *Negro Mecca** (New York, 1965); Allan Spear, *Black Chicago, The Making of a Negro Ghetto, 1890–1920** (Chicago, 1967); Kenneth Kusmer, *A Ghetto Takes Shape: Black Cleveland, 1870–1930* (Urbana, Ill., 1976); and David M. Katzman, *Before the Ghetto: Black Detroit in the Nineteenth Century* (Urbana, Ill., 1973). Various aspects of the problems of African-American life in urban centers are discussed in Woodson, *A Century of Negro Migration*; Caroline B. Chapin, "Settlement Work among Colored People," *Annals of the American Academy of Political and Social Science*, XXI (March 1903); and R. E. Clark, "Negro Home Life and Standards of Living," *Annals of the American Academy of Political and Social Science*, XLIX (September 1913).

Violence in both the South and the North receives special attention in Ray S. Baker, *Following the Color Line** (New York, 1908). For a discussion of the growth of prejudice in a Northern state, see Frank U. Quillen, *The Color Line in Ohio* (Ann Arbor, Mich., 1913). Much more recent is David A. Gerber, *Black Ohio and the Color Line, 1860–1915* (Urbana, Ill., 1976). For an account of black experiences in a border city see George C. Wright, *Life Behind a Veil: Blacks in Louisville, Kentucky, 1865–1930* (Baton Rouge, La., 1985). Antiblack views are canvassed in I. A. Newby, *Jim Crow's Defense: Anti-Negro Thought in America, 1900–1930** (Baton Rouge, La., 1965). The status of lynching is the concern of Arthur Raper in *The Tragedy of Lynching* (Chapel Hill, N.C., 1933). See also Ida Wells Barnett, "Our Country's Lynching Record," *Survey*, XXIV (January 1913) and E. B. Reuter, *The American Race Problem** (New York, 1927). Two recent works that deepen understanding of the causes and consequences of racial violence are George C. Wright, *Racial Violence in Kentucky, 1865–1940: Lynchings, Mob Rule, and 'Legal Lynchings'* (Baton Rouge, La., 1990) and Roberta Senechal, *The Sociogenesis of a Race Riot: Springfield, Illinois, in 1908* (Urbana, Ill., 1990). W. E. B. Du Bois traces the growth of organized protest against violence to Negroes in *Dusk to Dawn*. The story of the emergence of the major protest organization is told in several works: Mary W. Ovington, *How the National Association for the Advancement of Colored People Began* (New York, 1914); Robert L. Jack, *History of the National Association for the Advancement of Colored People* (Boston, 1943); Langston Hughes, *Fight for Freedom: The Story of the NAACP* (New York, 1962); and Robert L. Zangrando, *The NAACP's Crusade against Lynching, 1909–1950* (Philadelphia, 1980). An excellent account of one of the major figures is Barbara Joyce Ross, *J. E. Spingarn and the Rise of the NAACP, 1911–1939* (New York, 1972). The most detailed study is by Charles F. Kellogg,

NAACP (Baltimore, 1967). *The National Urban League, 1910–1940* (New York, 1974) by Nancy Weiss is an excellent treatment of a pioneer service organization. Stephen R. Fox, *Guardian of Boston: William Monroe Trotter** (New York, 1971) treats one of the ablest blacks of the period. See also J. E. Moorland, "The Young Men's Christian Association among Negroes," *Journal of Negro History*, IX (January 1924). Dilemmas that African Americans faced are discussed in Kelly Miller, *Race Adjustment** (New York, 1909); Alfreda M. Duster, ed., *Crusade for Justice: The Autobiography of Ida B. Wells** (Chicago, 1970); and Emma Lou Thornbrough, *T. Thomas Fortune: Militant Journalist* (Chicago, 1972). For a discussion of politics, see Key, *Southern Politics* and Brotz, *Negro Social and Political Thought.*

16. In Pursuit of Democracy

The first general account of African Americans in World War I was Emmett J. Scott's *The American Negro in the World War* (Washington, D.C., 1919). A more recent one is Arthur E. Barbeau and Florette Henri, *Unknown Soldiers: Black American Troops in World War I* (Philadelphia, 1974). The difficult problems that blacks faced both at home and abroad are treated in Arthur W. Little, *From Harlem to the Rhine, The Story of New York's Colored Volunteers* (New York, 1936) and Charles H. Williams, *Sidelights on Negro Soldiers* (Boston, 1923, reprinted 1970). Chester D. Heywood's *Negro Combat Troops in the World War: The Story of the 371st Infantry* (Worcester, Mass., 1928) is diminished in importance by the condescending attitude of the author. The difficulties of the ranking African-American officer are related in Abraham Chew, *A Biography of Colonel Charles Young* (Washington, D.C., 1923). The efforts to raise the morale of black soldiers are described in Addie W. Hunton and Katherine M. Johnson, *Two Colored Women with the American Expeditionary Forces* (New York, 1920). See also Robert R. Moton, *Finding a Way Out* (Garden City, N.Y., 1921).

The phenomenon of African-American migration during the war is treated in a variety of ways in numerous works. Among the better analyses are the following: Louise V. Kennedy, *The Negro Peasant Turns Cityward* (New York, 1930); Emmet J. Scott, *Negro Migration during the War* (New York, 1920); Ray S. Baker, "The Negro Goes North," *World's Work*, XXXIV (July 1917); and Henderson Donald, "The Negro Migration, 1916–1918," *Journal of Negro History*, VI (October 1921). Four works with valuable discussions of African-American patterns of migration in the United States during the twentieth century are Jacqueline Jones, *Labor of Love, Labor of Sorrow: Black Women, Work, and the Family from Slavery to the Present* (New York, 1985); James R. Grossman, *Land of Hope: Chicago, Black Southerners, and the Great Migration* (Chicago, 1989); Carole Marks, *Farewell—We're Good and Gone: The Great Black Migration* (Bloomington, Ind., 1989); and Joe William Trotter, *The Great Migration in Historical Perspective* (Bloomington, Ind., 1991). For articles dealing with the problems of adjustment, see John H. Bracey and others, *The Rise of the Ghetto** (Belmont, Calif., 1971). The impact of migration on Washington, D.C., is discussed in Constance M. Green, *The Secret City: A History of Race Relations in the Nation's Capital** (Princeton, N.J., 1967). For discussions of the problems of black labor, see Spero and Harris, *The Black Worker;* Wesley, *Negro Labor in the United States;* and three works by George E. Haynes: "The Effect of War Conditions on Negro Labor," *Proceedings of the Academy of Political Science*, VIII (February 1919); *The Negro at Work during the World War and* *during Reconstruction* (Washington, D.C., 1921); and *The Trend of the Races* (New York, 1922). Examples of wartime violence are extensively treated in Elliott M. Rudwick, *Race Riot at East St. Louis, July 2, 1917** (Carbondale, Ill., 1964) and Robert V. Haynes, *A Night of Violence: The Houston Riot of 1917* (Baton Rouge, La., 1976).

The way in which America's attitude toward blacks influenced the treaties is discussed by Rayford W. Logan in *The Senate and the Versailles Mandate System* (Washington, D.C., 1945). See also George L. Beer, *African Questions at the Paris Peace Conference* (New York, 1923). Such periodicals as *Crisis, Afro-American,* and the Pittsburgh *Courier* are important sources of information on the conditions among African Americans during World War I.

17. Democracy Escapes

The violent reaction against African Americans in the postwar period is described in Walter White, *Rope and Faggot, A Biography of Judge Lynch* (New York, 1929); Frank Tannenbaum, *Darker Phases of the South* (New York, 1924); and Moorfield Storey, *Problems of Today* (Boston, 1920). The rise of the new Ku Klux Klan is traced and analyzed in John M. Mecklin, *The Ku Klux Klan: A Study of the American Mind* (New York, 1924); Walter White, "Reviving the Ku Klux Klan," *Forum,* LXV (April 1921); and Chalmers, *Hooded Americanism.* The best report of a race riot during the period of reaction is the study made by the Chicago Commission on Race Relations, *The Negro in Chicago: A Study of Race Relations and a Race Riot* (Chicago, 1922). An excellent study of that riot is William M. Tuttle's *Race Riot: Chicago in the Red Summer of 1919** (New York, 1970). Several of the postwar riots are discussed as a background to recent developments in Arthur I. Waskow, *From Race Riot to Sit-In: 1919 and the 1960s* (New York, 1966). For the reaction of blacks, see the collection of articles from newspapers in Robert T. Kerlin, *The Voice of the Negro, 1919* (New York, 1920). See also Mary Frances Berry, *Black Resistance, White Law: A History of Constitutional Racism in America* (New York, 1971).

Efforts to find solutions to the problems during the period are discussed in Paul Baker, *Negro-White Adjustments* (New York, 1934); Herbert A. Miller, *Races, Nations and Classes* (Philadelphia, 1924); and Thomas J. Woofter, *The Basis of Racial Adjustment* (Boston, 1925). Programs that African Americans developed to improve their status are vividly described by James Weldon Johnson in *Along This Way** (New York, 1933). See also Abram L. Harris, "The Negro Problem as Viewed by Negro Leaders," *Current History,* XVIII (June 1923) and Horace M. Bond, "Negro Leadership Since Washington," *South Atlantic Quarterly,* XXIV (April 1925). The efforts to secure relief in the courts are described in Bernard Nelson, *The Negro and the Fourteenth Amendment Since 1920* (Washington, D.C., 1946); Mangum, *The Legal Status of the Negro;* and Darlene Clark Hine, *Black Victory: The Rise and Fall of the White Primary in Texas* (Millwood, N.Y., 1979). For information on the Garvey movement, see Amy Jacques-Garvey, *Philosophy and Opinions of Marcus Garvey** (New York, 1923); McKay, *Harlem: Negro Metropolis;* Roi Ottley, *New World A-Coming* (New York, 1943); E. David Cronon, *Black Moses: The Story of Marcus Garvey and the Universal Negro Improvement Association,** second edition (Madison, 1969); and Robert A. Hill, ed., *The Marcus Garvey and Universal Negro Improvement Association Papers,* seven volumes (Berkeley, Calif., 1984–1991), an invaluable resource. See also Theodore Draper, *The Rediscovery of Black*

*Nationalism** (New York, 1970). Father Divine's movement is described in Robert Weisbrot, *Father Divine and the Struggle for Racial Equality* (Urbana, Ill., 1983) and Jill Watts, *Harlem U.S.A.: The Father Divine Story* (Berkeley, Calif., 1992).

18. The Harlem Renaissance and the Politics of African-American Culture

Many of the important works that shed light on the new African-American literary movement were mentioned in the text. In Spero and Harris, *The Black Worker*, important socioeconomic aspects of the movement are discussed. The forces that gave rise to the Renaissance are taken up in Rollin L. Hartt, "The New Negro," *Independent*, CV (January 15, 1921), while the difficulties involved in the new movement are the concern of James Weldon Johnson in "The Dilemma of the Negro Author," *American Mercury*, XV (December 1928). A careful and successful treatment of the period is Nathan I. Huggins's *Harlem Renaissance** (New York, 1971). A quite different but excellent work is David L. Lewis, *When Harlem Was in Vogue* (New York, 1981). For a very critical assessment of the period, see Harold Cruse, *The Crisis of the Negro Intellectual** (New York, 1967). The movement is traced carefully and ably by Langston Hughes in *The Big Sea** (New York, 1940) and by James Weldon Johnson in two of his works, *Black Manhattan* and *Along This Way*. An authoritative biography of Johnson is by Eugene Levy, *James Weldon Johnson: Black Leader, Black Voice** (Chicago, 1973). For an account by participants see Arna Bontemps, ed., *The Harlem Renaissance Remembered* (New York, 1972). See also Blanche Ferguson, *Countee Cullen and the Harlem Renaissance** (New York, 1966); Claude McKay, *A Long Way from Home** (New York, 1937); James Richard Giles, *Claude McKay* (Boston, 1976); Wayne F. Cooper, *Claude McKay, Rebel Sojourner in the Harlem Renaissance* (Baton Rouge, La., 1986); and Robert E. Hemenway, *Zora Neale Hurston: A Literary Biography* (Urbana, Ill., 1978). For the impact of the movement on a philosopher and a scientist, see Russell J. Linneman, ed., *Alain Locke: Reflections on a Modern Renaissance Man* (Baton Rouge, La., 1983) and Kenneth R. Manning, *Black Apollo of Science: The Life of Ernest Everett Just** (New York, 1983). See also, Linda O. McMurry, *George Washington Carver: Scientist and Symbol* (Baton Rouge, La., 1981). Outstanding is Arnold Rampersad, *The Life of Langston Hughes*, Volume 1: *1902–1941—I, Too, Sing, America* and Volume 2: *1941–1967—I Dream a World* (New York, 1986, 1988). Every aspect of the movement is analyzed and interpreted in Alain Locke, *The New Negro: An Interpretation** (New York, 1925). Among the many critical studies of the literary aspects of the movement, the following are outstanding: Brown, *The Negro in American Fiction*; Elizabeth L. Green, *The Negro in Contemporary American Literature* (Chapel Hill, N.C., 1928); J. Saunders Redding, *To Make a Poet Black* (Chapel Hill, N.C., 1939); and Frederick W. Bond, *The Negro and the Drama* (Washington, D.C., 1940); the works mentioned in the first section of "Bibliographical Notes" can also be consulted. See also Benjamin Brawley, "The Negro Literary Renaissance," *Southern Workman*, LVI (April 1927). Anthologies that furnish satisfactory selections of African-American writers are Brown and others, *The Negro Caravan*; Calverton, *Anthology of American Negro Literature*; James Weldon Johnson, *The Book of American Negro Poetry*,* revised edition (New York, 1969); Arna Bontemps, *American Negro Poetry*, revised edition (New York,

1974); James Weldon Johnson, *The Book of American Negro Spirituals* (New York, 1925); James Weldon Johnson, *The Second Book of Negro Spirituals* (New York, 1926); Miller, *Black American Literature;* and Southern, *The Music of Black Americans.* For an able discussion of art during the period, see Porter, *Modern Negro Art;* Marcia M. Mathews, *Henry Ossawa Tanner: American Artist* (Chicago, 1969); and Samella Lewis, *Art: African American* (New York, 1978).

19. The New Deal

The impact of the Depression on African Americans has claimed the attention of several authors. See, for example, T. Arnold Hill, *The Negro and Economic Reconstruction* (Washington, D.C., 1937); Myrdal, *An American Dilemma;* Richard Sterner, *The Negro's Share* (New York, 1943); and Raymond Wolters, *Negroes and the Great Depression: The Problem of Economic Recovery** (Westport, Conn., 1970). The political regeneration of African Americans is an engrossing story that is told, for one locality, by Harold F. Gosnell, *Negro Politicians: The Rise of Negro Politics in Chicago** (Chicago, 1935). See also James Q. Wilson, *Negro Politics: The Search for Leadership** (Glencoe, Ill., 1960); Margaret Price, *The Negro Voter in the South* (Atlanta, Ga., 1957); Ralph Bunche, "The Negro in the Political Life of the United States," *Journal of Negro Education,* X (July 1941); Kenneth W. Goings, *'The NAACP Comes of Age': The Defeat of Judge John J. Parker* (Bloomington, Ind., 1990); and Paula F. Pfeffer, *A. Philip Randolph, Pioneer of the Civil Rights Movement* (Baton Rouge, La., 1990). The desertion of the Republican party by blacks is treated in Nancy Weiss, *Farewell to the Party of Lincoln: Black Politics in the Age of F.D.R.* (Princeton, N.J., 1983). The role of the Communist party is the focus of several works: Mark Naison, *Communists in Harlem during the Depression* (Urbana, Ill., 1983); Wilson Record, *The Negro and the Communist Party* (Chapel Hill, N.C., 1951); Nell I. Painter, *The Narrative of Hosea Hudson: His Life as a Negro Communist in the South* (Cambridge, Mass., 1979); and Charles H. Martin, *The Angelo Herndon Case and Southern Justice* (Baton Rouge, La., 1976). The political implications of one of the best-known incidents of the period are examined in Dan Carter, *Scottsboro: A Tragedy of the American South** (Baton Rouge, La., 1969).

The black press, especially *Afro-American,* Norfolk *Journal and Guide,* the Chicago *Defender,* Pittsburgh *Courier, Crisis,* and *Opportunity,* are important sources of information concerning political activities among African Americans. Analyses of the political activities of African Americans are made in "The Fortune Quarterly Survey: XIII," *Fortune,* XVIII (July 1938); James E. Allen, "The Negro and the 1940 Presidential Election," unpublished master's thesis (Howard University, 1943); and Harold F. Gosnell, "The Negro Vote in Northern Cities," *National Municipal Review,* XXX (May 1941). For an able description of the rise of the New Deal, see Louis M. Hacker, *A Short History of the New Deal* (New York, 1934). The activities of the African-American "advisers" in the federal government are discussed in Laurence J. W. Hayes, *The Negro Federal Governmental Worker* (Washington, D.C., 1941); Ottley, *New World A-Coming;* and William J. Davis, "The Role of the Adviser on Negro Affairs and the Racial Specialist in National Administration, 1933–1940," unpublished master's thesis (Howard University, 1940).

The relationship of African Americans to the many new government agencies formed in the New Deal era is treated in John P. Davis, "Blue Eagles and Black

Workers," *New Republic,* LXXXI (November 14, 1934); Marian T. Wright, "Negro Youth and the Federal Emergency Programs, CCC and NYA," *Journal of Negro Education,* IX (July 1940); John H. Kirby, *Black Americans in the Roosevelt Era: Liberalism and Race* (Knoxville, Tenn., 1980); Harvard Sitkoff, *A New Deal for Blacks: The Emergence of Civil Rights as a National Issue: The Depression Decade* (New York, 1978); and Nancy L. Grant, *TVA and Black Americans: Planning for the Status Quo* (Philadelphia, 1990). See also Charles S. Johnson, *The Economic Status of Negroes* (Nashville, Tenn., 1933) and Bernard Sternsher, ed., *The Negro in Depression and War: Prelude to Revolution, 1930–1945** (Chicago, 1969). There have been several excellent studies of African-American labor. Among them are Horace Cayton and George S. Mitchell, *Black Workers and the New Unions* (Chapel Hill, N.C., 1939); Charles L. Franklin, *The Negro Labor Unionist of New York* (New York, 1936); Herbert R. Northrup, *Organized Labor and the Negro* (New York, 1944); Robert C. Weaver, *Negro Labor, A National Problem* (New York, 1946); August Meier and Elliott Rudwick, *Black Detroit and the Rise of the UAW* (New York, 1979); and Donald H. Grubbs, *Cry from the Cotton: The Southern Tenant Farmers Union and the New Deal* (Chapel Hill, N.C., 1971). See also Milton Cantor, ed., *Black Labor in America* (Westport, Conn., 1970). The story of the growth of a powerful African-American labor union is ably told by B. R. Brazeal in *The Brotherhood of Sleeping Car Porters* (New York, 1946) and William H. Harris, *Keeping the Faith: A. Philip Randolph, Milton P. Webster, and the Brotherhood of Sleeping Car Porters, 1925–1937* (Urbana, Ill., 1977).

20. The American Dilemma

Walter A. Jackson, *Gunnar Myrdal and America's Conscience: Social Engineering and Racial Liberalism, 1938–1987* (Chapel Hill, N.C., 1990) and David R. Goldfield, *Black, White, and Southern: Race Relations and Southern Culture, 1940 to the Present* (Baton Rouge, La., 1990) contain valuable intellectual histories of American race relations in the mid-twentieth century, while satisfactory general statements concerning trends in the education of African Americans may be found in Bond, *Education of the Negro in the American Social Order* and Holmes, *Evolution of the Negro College.* The psychological and social factors involved in separate education are treated in Buell G. Gallagher, *American Caste and the Negro College* (New York, 1938) and Doxey A. Wilkerson, *Special Problems in Negro Education* (Washington, D.C., 1939). For discussions of the influence of education on the process of integration, see Charles S. Johnson, ed., *Education and the Cultural Process* (Westport, Conn., 1943) and Paula S. Fass, *Outside in: Minorities and the Transformation of American Education* (New York, 1989). The yearbook issue of the *Journal of Negro Education* deals with some aspects of the problem of African-American education each year. Especially important are the issues for July 1933, "A Survey of Negro Higher Education," and for July 1940, "A Critical Survey of the Negro Adolescent and His Education." The inequalities of African-American education receive special attention in Rayford W. Logan, "Educational Segregation in the North," *Journal of Negro Education,* II (January 1933); Henry J. McGuinn, "The Courts and Equality of Educational Opportunity," *Journal of Negro Education,* VIII (April 1939); and Leon A. Ransom, "Legal Status of Negro Education under Separate School Systems," *Journal of Negro Education,* VIII (July 1939). For discussions of the growing interest in provisions for graduate training, see Rufus E.

Clement, "Legal Provisions for Graduate and Professional Instruction for Negroes in States Operating Separate School Systems," *Journal of Negro Education,* VIII (April 1939); Oliver C. Cox, "Provisions for Graduate Work among Negroes and the Prospects of a New System," *Journal of Negro Education,* IX (January 1940); and Fred McCuiston, *Graduate Instruction for Negroes in the United States* (Nashville, Tenn., 1939).

Material on education and especially on school desegregation has been exceedingly voluminous. Virtually all yearbook (summer) editions, as well as other issues, of the *Journal of Negro Education* contain material on the subject. *Southern School News* began publication shortly after the 1954 Supreme Court decision on desegregating the schools and has valuable information on events and trends. *Integrated Education* also should be consulted. Herbert Hill and Jack Greenberg, *Citizen's Guide to Desegregation** (Boston, 1955) and Harry Ashmore, *The Negro and the Schools,** revised edition (Chapel Hill, N.C., 1970) provide excellent overall treatments of school desegregation. Specific experiences and examples of school desegregation are presented in Robin Williams and Margaret W. Ryan, eds., *Schools in Transition: Community Experiences in Desegregation* (Chapel Hill, N.C., 1954); Numan Bartley, *The Rise of Massive Resistance: Race and Politics in the South in the 1950s* (Baton Rouge, La., 1969); Robert C. Smith, *They Closed Their Schools* (Chapel Hill, N.C., 1965); James H. Tipton, *Community in Crisis* (New York, 1953); Wilson and Jane Record, *Little Rock, U.S.A.: Materials for Analysis** (San Francisco, 1960); and James W. Silver, *Mississippi: The Closed Society** (New York, 1964). The drama of fighting segregation in the courts is captured in Richard Kluger, *Simple Justice: The History of Brown v. Board of Education and Black America's Struggle for Equality** (New York, 1976). Jennifer L. Hochschild, in *Thirty Years after Brown* (Washington, D.C., 1985), surveys the process of desegregation since the Supreme Court decision, while Raymond Wolters's *The Burden of Brown: Thirty Years of School Desegregation* (Knoxville, Tenn., 1984) regards the effort as essentially a failure.

Concerning the problems and achievements of African Americans in various fields, see Harry W. Greene, *Holders of Doctorates among American Negroes* (Boston, 1946); Charles S. Johnson, *The Negro College Graduate* (Chapel Hill, N.C., 1938); Carter G. Woodson, *The Negro Professional Man and the Community* (Washington, D.C., 1934); G. Franklin Edwards, *The Negro Professional Class* (Glencoe, Ill., 1959); Dietrich C. Reitzes, *Negroes and Medicine* (Cambridge, Mass., 1958); and Daniel C. Thompson, *The Negro Leadership Class** (Englewood Cliffs, N.J., 1963). Eliza Atkins Gleason has discussed the African-American library as an educative force in *The Southern Negro and the Public Library* (Chicago, 1941). Books dealing with music and art discussed in Chapter 18 should be consulted for this period, especially Southern, *The Music of Black Americans,* and Lewis, *Art: African American.* A recent study that provides valuable information is Michael W. Harris, *The Rise of Gospel Blues: The Music of Thomas Andrew Dorsey in the Urban Church* (New York, 1992). An important but seldom noticed aspect of the two worlds of race is explored in Donn Rogosin, *Invisible Men: Life in Baseball's Negro Leagues* (New York, 1985).

The African-American world is exhaustively described in Myrdal, *An American Dilemma.* Shorter, but able descriptions of the African-American community are contained in Van Deusen, *Black Man in White America;* Davie, *Negroes in America;* and Frazier, *The Negro in the United States.* Two useful community studies are Joe William Trotter, *Black Milwaukee: The Making of an Industrial Proletariat* (Urbana, Ill., 1985) and Earl Lewis, *In Their Own Interests: Race, Class, and Power in Twentieth-Century Norfolk,*

Virginia (Berkeley, Calif., 1991). For a searching, critical analysis of the black middle class, see E. Franklin Frazier, *Black Bourgeoisie** (Glencoe, Ill., 1957). Important sources of information are Florence Murray, *The Negro Handbook* (New York, 1946); Smythe, *The Black American Reference Book*; Talcott Parsons and Kenneth Clark, *The Negro American** (Boston, 1966); Karl and Alma Taeuber, *Negroes in Cities** (Chicago, 1965); Stanley Lieberson, *Ethnic Patterns in American Cities* (New York, 1963); and Hollis R. Lynch, ed., *The Black Urban Condition* (New York, 1973). Special aspects of the African-American world are discussed in Detweiler, *The Negro Press in the United States*; Mays and Nicholson, *The Negro's Church*; and the yearbook issue of the *Journal of Negro Education,* VIII (July 1939), "The Position of the Negro in the American Social Order." Privation and opportunities are discussed in Michael Harrington, *The Other America: Poverty in the United States** (New York, 1962) and Eli Ginzberg, *The Negro Potential** (New York, 1962). One should also consult Gerda Lerner, ed., *Black Women in White America** (New York, 1972) and George Frederickson, *The Black Image in the White Mind** (New York, 1971).

Lives of individual African Americans are presented in Bardolph, *The Negro Vanguard*; Logan and Winston, *Dictionary of American Negro Biography*; Ridgeley Torrence, *The Story of John Hope* (New York, 1948); Mary Church Terrell, *A Colored Woman in a White World* (Washington, D.C., 1940); Helen Buckler, *Dr. Dan: Pioneer in American Surgery* (Boston, 1954); Roi Ottley, *The Lonely Warrior: The Life and Times of Robert S. Abbott* (Chicago, 1955); Rackham Holt, *George Washington Carver* (Garden City, N.Y., 1943); Edwin R. Embree, *Thirteen against the Odds* (New York, 1945); *The Autobiography of Malcolm X** (New York, 1965); Anthony M. Platt, *E. Franklin Frazier Reconsidered* (New Brunswick, N.J., 1991); and Martha Graham Goodson, *Chronicles of Faith: The Autobiography of Frederick D. Patterson* (Tuscaloosa, Ala., 1991). Three valuable works that illuminate the lives and experiences of African-American women are Sara Lawrence Lightfoot, *Balm in Gilead: Journey of a Healer* (Reading, Mass., 1988); Idella Parker with Mary Keating, *Marjorie Rawlings' "Perfect Maid"* (Gainesville, Fla., 1992); and Carole Ione, *Pride of Family: Four Generations of American Women of Color* (New York, 1992). The problem of the relationship between blacks' Americanization and African background is discussed in Harold R. Isaacs, *The New World of Negro Americans** (New York, 1963).

The American Youth Commission studies shed considerable light on the problem of adjustment that African Americans in America faced in this period. The principal titles are J. H. Atwood and others, *Thus Be Their Destiny** (Washington, D.C., 1941); Allison Davis and John Dollard, *Children of Bondage** (Washington, D.C., 1940); E. Franklin Frazier, *Negro Youth at the Crossways** (Washington, D.C., 1940); Charles S. Johnson, *Growing Up in the Black Belt** (Washington, D.C., 1941); Ira DeA. Reid, *In a Minor Key** (Washington, D.C., 1940); Robert L. Sutherland, *Color, Class, and Personality** (Washington, D.C., 1942); and W. Lloyd Warner and others, *Color and Human Nature** (Washington, D.C., 1941). Programs for the improvement of the status of African Americans are discussed in Rayford W. Logan, ed., *What the Negro Wants* (Chapel Hill, N.C., 1944); the entire issue of *Survey Graphic,* XXXI (November 1942), "Color, Unfinished Business of Democracy"; and Ralph J. Bunche, "The Programs of Organizations Devoted to the Improvement of the Status of the American Negro," *Journal of Negro Education,* VIII (July 1939). See also *Crisis, Opportunity, Southern Patriot,* and *New South,* the last two journals being the official publications of the Southern Conference for Human Welfare and the Southern Regional Council, respectively. Linda Reed provides a full account of the work of the Southern Conference for

Human Welfare in *Simple Decency and Common Sense: The Southern Conference Movement, 1938–1963* (Bloomington, Ind., 1991). Broader programs for the improvement of intergroup relations are discussed in Theodore Brameld, *Minority Problems in the Public Schools* (New York, 1946); Rachel David Du Bois, *Build Together Americans* (New York, 1945); Hortense Powdermaker, *Probing Our Prejudices* (New York, 1944); Kenneth B. Clark, *Prejudice and Your Child** (Boston, 1955); and George E. Simpson and J. Milton Yinger, *Racial and Cultural Minorities*, revised edition (New York, 1972).

21. Fighting for the Four Freedoms

William R. Scott, *The Sons of Sheba's Race: African Americans and the Italo-Ethiopian War, 1935–1941* (Bloomington, Ind., 1992) illustrates the connections American blacks made between their battles in the United States and the Ethiopian conflict. Releases of the press sections of the War and Navy Departments and of the Office of War Information provide considerable information on the activities of African Americans both on the home front and on the battlefields during World War II. Many excellent pictures of African Americans in the war are provided in John D. Silvera, *The Negro in World War II* (New York, 1947, reprinted 1969). A good summary of the military operations is included in Roger W. Shugg and H. A. De Weerd, *World War II* (Washington, D.C., 1946). The definitive work on African Americans in the army is the volume in the Special Studies Series of the United States Army in World War II: Ulysses Lee, *The Employment of Negro Troops* (Washington, D.C., 1966). The basic history of racial military policy is set forth in Morris J. MacGregor, Jr., *Integration of the Armed Forces, 1940–1965* (Washington, D.C., 1981). See also Richard M. Dalfiume, *Fighting on Two Fronts: Desegregation of the U.S. Armed Forces, 1939–1953* (Columbia, Mo., 1969); Dennis D. Nelson, *The Integration of the Negro into the United States Navy* (New York, 1951); Alan Gropman, *The Air Force Integrates, 1945–1964* (Washington, D.C., 1978); Robert J. Jakeman, *The Divided Skies: Establishing Segregated Flight Training at Tuskegee, Alabama, 1934–1942* (Tuscaloosa, Ala., 1992); Ralph W. Donnelly, *Blacks in the Marine Corps* (Washington, D.C., 1975); and Lee Nichols, *Breakthrough on the Color Front* (New York, 1954). Walter White's *A Rising Wind* (New York, 1945) is an excellent account of the activities of African Americans on the fighting front. An overall perspective is provided in Jack D. Foner, *Blacks and the Military in American History: A New Perspective* (New York, 1974); and Mary Penick Motley, *The Invisible Soldiers: The Experience of the Black Soldier in World War II* (Detroit, 1975).

The black press is indispensable in getting a complete picture of African Americans during the war. See also L. D. Reddick, "The Negro in the Navy in World War II," *Journal of Negro History*, XXXII (April 1947). The problem of integrating blacks in the war efforts is the principal concern of Earl Brown, "American Negroes and the War," *Harper's Magazine*, CLXXXIV (April 1942); Earl Brown and George R. Leighton, *The Negro and the War* (New York, 1942); and "The Negro's War," *Fortune*, XXV (June 1942). Several journals have devoted entire issues to the problem of the impact of the war on African Americans. Among them are *Survey Graphic*, "Color, Unfinished Business of Democracy," XXX (November 1942); *Annals of the American Academy of Political and Social Science*, "Minority Peoples in a Nation at War," CCXXIII (September 1942); *Journal of Negro Education*, "The American Negro in World War I and World War II," XII (Summer 1943); and two issues of the *Journal of Educational*

Sociology with L. D. Reddick as special editor, "The Negro in the North during Wartime," XVIII (January 1944) and "Race Relations on the Pacific Coast," XIX (November 1945). Dominic J. Capeci, Jr., and Martha Wilkerson, *Layered Violence: The Detroit Rioters of 1943* (Jackson, 1991), offers a fresh perspective on the race riot in that city. The apprehension of Southern whites concerning African Americans and the war is expressed by John Temple Graves in "The Southern Negro and the War Crisis," *Virginia Quarterly Review,* XVIII (Autumn 1942).

The part that African Americans played in producing the goods of war has received special attention in the Council for Democracy's *The Negro and Defense* (New York, 1941); Weaver, *Negro Labor;* and Northrup, *Organized Labor and the Negro.* African-American morale was the concern of many writers, but the following were particularly concerned about this subject: Horace M. Bond, "Should the Negro Care Who Wins the War?" *Annals of the American Academy of Political and Social Science,* CCXXIII (September 1942); James A. Bayton, "The Psychology of Racial Morale," *Journal of Negro Education,* XI (April 1942); Guion G. Johnson, "The Impact of the War upon the Negro," *Journal of Negro Education,* X (July 1941); and J. Saunders Redding, "A Negro Looks at This War," *American Mercury,* LV (November 1942).

22. African Americans in the Cold War Era

For a discussion of some of the major problems confronting African Americans during the postwar years, see Rayford W. Logan, *The Negro and the Post-War World: A Primer* (Washington, D.C., 1945). The several publications of the Truman administration that deal with postwar problems are mentioned in the text. The development of legal machinery with respect to fair employment is discussed in Malcolm Ross, *All Manner of Men* (New York, 1948); Louis Ruchames, *Race, Jobs, and Politics* (New York, 1953); and Louis Kesselman, *The Social Politics of FEPC* (Chapel Hill, N.C., 1948). For trends in housing, see Morton Deutsch, *Interracial Housing* (Minneapolis, Minn., 1951) and Robert C. Weaver, *The Negro Ghetto** (New York, 1948). Race and radical politics are discussed in Wilson Record, *The Negro and the Communist Party** (Chapel Hill, N.C., 1951), and Martin Bauml Duberman, *Paul Robeson* (New York, 1988), while other political matters are covered in Henry L. Moon, *Balance of Power: The Negro Vote* (New York, 1948). Two valuable studies of the leading African-American politician during these years are Charles V. Hamilton, *Adam Clayton Powell, Jr.: The Political Biography of an American Dilemma* (New York, 1991) and Wil Haygood, *King of the Cats: The Life and Times of Adam Clayton Powell, Jr.* (New York, 1992). The successful fight to make their vote effective in the Democratic party is described in Darlene Clark Hine, *Black Victory, The Rise and Fall of the White Primary in Texas* (Millwood, N.Y., 1979). See also Steven Lawson, *Black Ballots: Voting Rights in the South, 1944–1969* (New York, 1976). Leadership in the fight to secure equality for blacks in voting, education, and civil rights has been portrayed in Genna Rae McNeil, *Groundwork: Charles Hamilton Houston and the Struggle for Civil Rights* (Philadelphia, 1983); Gilbert Ware, *William Hastie: Grace under Pressure* (New York, 1984); Benjamin Rivlin, *Ralph Bunche: The Man and His Times* (New York, 1990); and Brian Urquhart, *Ralph Bunche: An American Life* (New York, 1993). Various problems of the postwar years are treated in Paul Burstein, *Discrimination, Jobs, and Politics: The Struggle for Equal Employment Opportunity in the United States Since the New Deal* (Chicago, 1985). For a view of problems related to foreign policy, see Gerald Horne, *Black and Red: W. E. B. Du Bois and the Afro-American Response to the Cold War, 1944–1963* (Albany, N.Y., 1986). For treatment of a racial incident that helped set the agenda for the African-American civil rights movement of the 1950s and 1960s, see Stephen J. Whitfield, *A Death in the Delta: The Story of Emmet Till* (Baltimore, 1991).

The civil rights record of the Truman administration is examined in Donald R. McCoy and Richard T. Ruetten, *Quest and Response: Minority Rights and the Truman Administration* (Lawrence, Kans., 1973) and William C. Berman, *The Politics of Civil Rights in the Truman Administration* (Columbus, Ohio, 1970). For a critical assessment, see Barton J. Bernstein's essay in a book edited by him, *Politics and Policies of the Truman Administration** (Chicago, 1970).

In Howard Zinn, *The Southern Mystique** (New York, 1964) there is a stimulating analysis of the forces in the South that are opposed to change. Carl Rowan, *Go South to Sorrow* (New York, 1957) discusses the South's resistance to social change in a climate that calls for economic change. There are several valuable treatments of Southern reaction to the move to desegregate the schools, including Hodding Carter, *The South Strikes Back* (New York, 1959) and John B. Martin, *The Deep South Says "Never"* (New York, 1957). The Southern position is summarized in William D. Workman, *The Case for the South* (New York, 1960).

Demographic changes in the African-American population are discussed in William P. O'Hare, *Blacks on the Move: A Decade of Demographic Change* (Washington, D.C., 1982). See also Daniel M. Johnson and Rex R. Campbell, *Black Migration in America: A Social Demographic History* (Durham, N.C., 1981). Allan B. Ballard, *One More Day's Journey: The Story of a Family and a People* (New York, 1984); Nicholas Lemann, *The Promised Land: The Great Black Migration and How It Changed America* (New York, 1991); and James R. Grossman, *Land of Hope: Chicago, Black Southerners, and the Great Migration* (Chicago, 1989) deal with the impact of migration on African-American families. For an examination of the extent of progress among blacks, see Reynolds Farley, *Blacks and Whites: Narrowing the Gap?* (Cambridge, Mass., 1984). The problems of the black church are canvassed in James H. Cone, *For My People: Black Theology and the Black Church: Where Have We Been and Where Are We Going?* (Maryknoll, N.Y., 1984); C. Eric Lincoln, *Race, Religion, and the Continuing American Dilemma* (New York, 1984); and Rubye F. Johnston, *The Religion of Negro Protestants: Changing Religious Attitudes and Practices* (New York, 1956).

The files of *Black Enterprise* and *Dollars and Sense* provide intimate details and important generalizations about black businesses in the postwar years. Many important sources about African-American writers are provided in the text. Developments in the literary, artistic, and musical fields can be followed in the sources provided in Chapter 18. See also Dexter Fisher and Robert B. Stepto, *Afro-American Literature: The Reconstruction of Instruction* (New York, 1979); Elsa Honig Fine, *The Afro-American Artist: A Search for Identity* (New York, 1982); and Frank Kotsky, *Black Nationalism and the Revolution in Music* (New York, 1970). A perceptive critical analysis of recent writing is Nathan A. Scott, Jr.'s "Black Literature," in Daniel Hoffman, ed., *Harvard Guide to Contemporary American Writing* (Cambridge, Mass., 1979).

Southern's *The Music of Black Americans* contains considerable information on the evolution of black popular music in the decades after World War II. Two standard histories of jazz are Marshall Stearns, *The Story of Jazz** (New York, 1962) and Winthrop Sergeant, *Jazz: A History* (New York, 1964). Three other studies that contain valuable information on other forms of black music are Harold Courlander, *Negro

Folk Music U.S.A. (New York, 1963); Paul Oliver, *The Story of the Blues* (Philadelphia, 1969); and Mahalia Jackson, *Movin' On Up: The Mahalia Jackson Story** (New York, 1966).

The expanded African-American presence in popular culture has only recently begun to receive the attention of historians. Three significant works on the cinema are M. Donald Bogle, *Toms, Coons, Mulattoes, Mammies, and Bucks: An Interpretive History in American Films* (New York, 1973); Thomas Cripps, *Slow Fade to Black: The Negro in American Film, 1900–1942* (New York, 1977); and *Making Movies Black: The Hollywood Message Movie from World War II to the Civil Rights Era* (New York, 1993). Two insightful works on television are F. Fred McDonald, *Blacks and White T.V.: Afro-Americans in Television Since 1946* (Chicago, 1983) and Melvin Patrick Ely, *The Adventures of Amos 'n' Andy: A Social History of an American Phenomenon* (New York, 1991). The late Arthur P. Ashe, Jr., wrote the first general history of African Americans in sports in *A Hard Road to Glory: A History of the African-American Athlete, 1919–1945,* three volumes (New York, 1988). A number of other significant works have also appeared, among them Randy Roberts, *Papa Jack: Jack Johnson and the Era of White Hopes* (New York, 1983); Al-Tony Gilmore, *Bad Nigger: The National Impact of Jack Johnson* (Port Washington, N.Y., 1975); Jules Tygiel, *Baseball's Great Experiment: Jackie Robinson and His Legacy* (New York, 1984); and Janet Bruce, *The Kansas City Monarchs: Champions of Black Baseball* (Lawrence, Kans., 1985). See, also, Donald Spivey, ed., *Sport in America: New Historical Perspectives* (Westport, Conn., 1985).

23. The Black Revolution

The beginnings of the Black Revolution are discussed in Martin Luther King, Jr., *Stride toward Freedom: The Montgomery Story** (New York, 1962); Robert F. Burk, *The Eisenhower Administration and Black Civil Rights* (Knoxville, Tenn., 1984); and Louis Lomax, *The Negro Revolt** (New York, 1962). For a treatment of the Black Muslims as a factor in the growing black revolt, see C. Eric Lincoln, *The Black Muslims in America** (Boston, 1973) and Essien U. Essien-Udom, *Black Nationalism: A Search for Identity in America** (Chicago, 1962). The work of the United States Commission on Civil Rights is set forth in its own publications, including its annual reports, the reports of its state advisory committees, and its hearings.

There are considerable materials on the militant drive for equality. Among the works that give perspective and background are Loren Miller, *The Petitioners: The Story of the Supreme Court of the United States and the Negro* (New York, 1966); Milton Konvitz, *A Century of Civil Rights** (New York, 1961); United States Commission on Civil Rights, *Freedom to the Free** (Washington, D.C., 1963); and Rhoda L. Blumberg, *Civil Rights: The 1960s Freedom Struggle** (New York, 1984). Also valuable are two recent biographies: Nancy J. Weiss, *Whitney M. Young, Jr., and the Struggle for Civil Rights* (Princeton, N.J., 1989) and Denton L. Watson, *Lion in the Lobby: Clarence Mitchell, Jr.'s Struggle for the Passage of Civil Rights Laws* (New York, 1990).

The problems which the militant movement addressed are the main interest of several works. See especially, John P. Roche, *The Quest for the Dream: The Development of Civil Rights and Human Relations in Modern America* (New York, 1963); Charles Silberman, *Crisis in Black and White** (New York, 1964); William J. Brink and Louis Harris, *The Negro Revolution in America** (New York, 1964); August Meier and Elliott

Rudwick, *CORE: A Study of the Civil Rights Movement** (New York, 1973); and Robert Brisbane, *Black Activism: Black Revolution in the U.S., 1954–1970** (Valley Forge, Pa., 1984). The student group most influential in the movement is treated in Howard Zinn, *SNCC: The New Abolitionists** (Boston, 1964) and Clayborne Carson, *In Struggle: SNCC and the Black Awakening of the 1960s* (Cambridge, Mass., 1981). See also William H. Chafe, *Civilities and Civil Rights: Greensboro North Carolina and the Black Struggle for Freedom** (New York, 1980). For a discussion of the movement by some of the leaders, see Kenneth B. Clark, ed., *The Negro Protest** (Boston, 1963).

Militant positions are set forth in Stokely Carmichael and Charles Hamilton, *Black Power: The Politics of Liberation in America** (New York, 1967); Eldridge Cleaver, *Soul on Ice** (New York, 1968); Bobby Seale, *Seize the Time** (New York, 1970); and the *Autobiography of Malcolm X*. See also LeRoi Jones and Billy Abernathy, *In Our Terribleness* (Indianapolis, Ind., 1971). More recent writings on the Black Panther Party and its leaders include Kathleen Rout, *Eldridge Cleaver* (Boston, 1991); Elaine Brown, *A Taste of Power: A Black Woman's Story* (New York, 1993); and David Hilliard and Lewis Cole, *This Side of Glory: The Autobiography of David Hilliard and the Story of the Black Panther Party* (Boston, 1993). The most noteworthy of the recent publications on Malcolm X include Clayborne Carson, *Malcolm X and the F.B.I.* (New York, 1991); David Gallen, *Malcolm X as They Knew Him* (New York, 1992); and Bruce Perry, *Malcolm: The Life of a Man Who Changed America* (New York, 1991). Discussions and analyses of black militancy can be followed in John H. Bracey and others, eds., *Black Nationalism in America** (Indianapolis, Ind., 1970); Theodore Draper, *The Rediscovery of Black Nationalism** (New York, 1970); August Meier and Elliott Rudwick, eds., *Black Protest in the Sixties** (Chicago, 1970); and Lerone Bennett, *Confrontation: Black and White** (Chicago, 1965). Violence in the Black Revolution is discussed in *Report of the National Advisory Commission on Civil Disorders*, Kerner Commission (New York, 1968); Richard Hofstadter and Michael Wallace, eds., *American Violence: A Documentary History** (New York, 1970); Robert H. Connery, ed., *Urban Riots: Violence and Social Change* (New York, 1968); Arthur Waskow, *From Race Riot to Sit-In;* and James W. Button, *Black Violence: Political Impact of the 1960s Riots* (Princeton, N.J., 1978).

For a unique, highly imaginative appraisal of the civil rights movement that also has merit for its literary quality, see Derrick Bell, *And We Are Not Saved: The Elusive Quest for Racial Justice* (New York, 1987). Even more pessimistic is Bell's *Faces at the Bottom of the Well: The Permanence of Racism* (New York, 1992). Civil Rights leaders themselves have begun to tell their own story. See, for example, James Farmer, *Lay Bare the Heart: An Autobiography of the Civil Rights Movement* (Ann Arbor, Mich., 1985) and *Standing Fast: The Autobiography of Roy Wilkins* (New York, 1982).

The experiences of participants in marches, demonstrations, and other forms of protest are covered in the following works: Martin Luther King, Jr., *Why We Can't Wait** (New York, 1964); James Forman, *The Making of Black Revolutionaries* (New York, 1972); Len Holt, *The Summer That Didn't End* (New York, 1965); Merrill Proudfoot, *Diary of a Sit-In** (Chapel Hill, N.C., 1962); James Peck, *Freedom Ride* (New York, 1962); Nicholas Von Hoffman, *Mississippi Notebook* (New York, 1964); John Ehle, *The Free Men* (New York, 1965); James W. Silver, *Mississippi: The Closed Society;* and J. L. Chesnut, Jr., and Julia Cass, *Black in Selma: The Uncommon Life of J. L. Chesnut, Jr.* (New York, 1990). Lorraine Hansberry, *The Movement: Documentary of a Struggle for Equality** (New York, 1964) and Doris E. Saunders, *The Day They Marched** (Chicago, 1963) contain excellent photographs of events in the movement. President Kennedy's role is assessed in Harry Golden's *Mr. Kennedy and the Negroes** (Cleveland, 1964) and in Doris Saunders, ed., *The Kennedy Years and the Negro: A Photographic Record** (Chicago, 1964). The best biography of Martin Luther King is by David Lewis, *King, A Critical Biography** (New York, 1970). A more recent one is Stephen B. Oates, *Let the Trumpet Sound: The Life of Martin Luther King, Jr.* (New York, 1982). In 1986, *American Visions, Ebony,* and the *Union Seminary Quarterly Review* devoted entire issues to various aspects of King's life and work. An excellent collection of King's writings is James M. Washington, ed., *A Testament of Hope: The Essential Writings of Martin Luther King, Jr.* (San Francisco, 1986). Recent noteworthy works on King include Taylor Branch, *Parting the Waters: America in the King Years, 1954–1963* (New York, 1988); James H. Cone, *Martin & Malcolm & America: A Dream or a Nightmare* (New York, 1991); and Vincent Harding, *Hope and History: Why We Must Share the Story of the Movement* (New York, 1990). An especially valuable source on King is the publication project on his papers, one volume of which has already been issued: Clayborne Carson, Ralph E. Luker, and Penny A. Russell, eds., *The Papers of Martin Luther King, Jr.,* Volume 1: *Called to Serve, January 1929–June 1951* (Berkeley, Calif., 1992).

Various aspects of the Black Revolution have been treated by a number of authors who can be read with profit. Virginia Durr, an Alabama white woman, tells of the involvement of herself and her family in the civil rights struggle in *Outside the Magic Circle* (University, Ala., 1985). Tony Freyer, *The Little Rock Crisis: A Constitutional Interpretation* (Westport, Conn., 1984) deals with a critical juncture in the Black Revolution. See also E. Culpepper Clark, *The Schoolhouse Door: Segregation's Last Stand at the University of Alabama* (New York, 1993). Others are Aldon D. Morris, *The Origins of the Civil Rights Movement: Black Communities Organizing for Change* (New York, 1984); Robert J. Norrell, *Reaping the Whirlwind: The Civil Rights Movement in Tuskegee* (New York, 1985); and David J. Garrow, *Protest at Selma: Martin Luther King, Jr. and the Voting Rights Act of 1965* (New Haven, Conn., 1978). For an insightful study of civil rights activity in the North, see Ronald P. Formisano, *Boston against Busing: Race, Class, and Ethnicity in the 1960s and 1970s* (Chapel Hill, N.C., 1991). The growing number of writings that describe the involvement and perspective of women in the civil rights movement include Daisy Bates, *The Long Shadow of Little Rock: A Memoir* (Fayetteville, Ark., 1987); Sheyann Webb and Rachel West Nelson, *Selma, Lord, Selma: Girlhood Memories of the Civil Rights Days* (Tuscaloosa, Ala., 1980); Septima Clark, *Ready from Within: Septima Clark and the Civil Rights Movement* (Navarro, 1986); Catherine Clinton, "Ella Baker (1903–1986)," *Portraits of American Women* (New York, 1991); and Vickie L. Crawford, Jacqueline Anne Rouse, and Barbara Woods, *Women in the Civil Rights Movement, 1941–1965* (New York, 1990). Children and young adults have told of their role in the civil rights movement in Ellen Levine, *Freedom's Children: Young Civil Rights Activists Tell Their Own Stories* (New York, 1993). A seasoned head of the Southern Poverty Law Center has recounted his experiences in Morris Dees, *A Season for Justice: The Life and Times of a Civil Rights Lawyer* (New York, 1991).

Important social and economic problems related to the Black Revolution are discussed in Parsons and Clark, *The Negro American* and Daniel P. Moynihan, *The Negro Family: The Case for National Action* (Washington, D.C., 1965), as well as in President Lyndon B. Johnson's commencement address at Howard University in June 1965. There are illuminating discussions of discrimination in industry and the relationship between black employment and the national economy in the following: Dale L. Hiestand, *Economic Growth and Employment Opportunities for Minorities* (New York, 1964); Paul Bullock, *Merit Employment* (Los Angeles, 1960); and Vivian W. Henderson, *The Economic Status of Negroes: In the Nation and in the South** (Atlanta, Ga., 1963). The search for new industrial opportunities for African Americans is discussed in Eli Ginzerg, ed., *The Negro Challenge to the Business Community* (New York, 1964). For other aspects of the problem of equal economic opportunity, see Whitney M. Young, *To Be Equal** (New York, 1964) and Nat Hentoff, *The New Equality* (New York, 1964). Kenneth B. Clark, *Dark Ghetto: Dilemmas of Social Power** (New York, 1965) discusses poverty in the inner city and ways of solving the problem. Also important are Arthur M. Ross and Herbert Hill, *Employment, Race, and Poverty** (New York, 1967); Dawn Day Wachtel, *The Negro and Discrimination in Employment** (Ann Arbor, Mich., 1965); and Charles C. Killingsworth, *Jobs and Income for Negroes** (Ann Arbor, Mich., 1968). For a different perspective see Thomas Sowell, *The Economics and Politics of Race: An International Perspective* (New York, 1983). Two works by Theodore Cross suggest strategies that blacks could pursue in two important areas. They are *Black Capitalism: Strategy for Business in the Ghetto* (New York, 1969) and *The Black Power Imperative: Racial Inequality and the Politics of Nonviolence* (New York, 1984).

There have already been numerous assessments of the significance and consequences of the Black Revolution. Frank Hercules, *American Society and the Black Revolution* (New York, 1972) regards the positive results as minimal. In *Protest, Politics, and Prosperity: Black Americans and White Institutions, 1940–75* (New York, 1978), Dorothy K. Newman and her associates do not paint a very favorable picture of the results. Less pessimistic is William J. Wilson, *The Declining Significance of Race: Blacks and Changing American Institutions* (Chicago, 1978). See also John Hope Franklin, *Racial Equality in America* (Chicago, 1976); Steven F. Lawson, *Running for Freedom: Civil Rights and Black Politics in America Since 1941* (Philadelphia, 1991); Hugh Davis Graham, *The Civil Rights Era: Origins and Developments of National Policy, 1960–1972* (New York, 1990); and Donald G. Nieman, *Promises to Keep: African Americans and the Constitutional Order* (New York, 1991). Current assessments may be found in special reports as well as the annual reports of such organizations as the NAACP, the National Urban League, and the Joint Center for Political and Economic Studies.

24. New Forms of Activism

In moving so close to the period of the 1990s one has to rely increasingly on television, radio, and the print media for information. Already, however, a number of monographs, biographies, and special studies have appeared that provide fairly reliable information as well as some tentative interpretations. *Focus,* the monthly newsletter of the Joint Center for Political and Economic Studies, contains current information regarding housing, employment, demographic changes, and voting patterns among African Americans. Some books, moreover, have appeared that assist one in understanding developments during the Reagan years. Among them are Robert Dallek, *Ronald Reagan: The Politics of Symbolism* (Cambridge, Mass., 1984); Richard Reeves, *The Reagan Detour* (New York, 1985); Laurence I. Barrett, *Gambling with History: Ronald Reagan in the White House* (Garden City, N.Y., 1983); Lloyd Demause, *Reagan's America* (New York, 1984); Ronnie Dugger, *On Reagan: The Man and His Presidency* (New York, 1983); and Haynes Johnson, *Sleepwalking through History: America in the Reagan Years* (New York, 1991).

Understandably, there is no satisfactory biography of Jesse Jackson as indeed there is none of Ronald Reagan or George Bush. Several years ago, Barbara Reynolds published a study of Jackson called *Jackson, the Man, the Movement and the Myth* (Chicago, 1975). Recently, it was issued as *Jesse Jackson, America's David* (Washington,

1985). In Adolph Reed, Jr.'s *The Jesse Jackson Phenomenon: The Crisis in Afro-American Politics* (New Haven, Conn., 1986), the author argues that the Jackson candidacy was untimely and smacked of opportunism more than a serious bid for office. But see Charles P. Henry's *Jesse Jackson: The Search for Common Ground* (Oakland, Calif., 1991). Jackson's efforts on behalf of black businesses and black labor are described in detail in *Black Enterprise* and *Dollars and Sense*. Several works issued by the Joint Center for Political and Economic Studies deal not only with Jackson's candidacy but the black electorate in general. They are Thomas E. Cavanagh, *The Impact of the Black Electorate* (Washington, D.C., 1984); Thomas E. Cavanagh and Lorn S. Foster, *Jesse Jackson's Campaign, the Primaries and Caucuses* (Washington, D.C., 1984); and Thomas E. Cavanagh, *Inside Black America: The Message of the Black Vote in the 1984 Elections* (Washington, D.C., 1985).

Political and economic problems of African Americans in the Reagan and Bush years receive attention in several significant works, including Kevin Phillips, *The Politics of Rich and Poor: Wealth and the American Electorate in the Reagan Aftermath* (New York, 1990); Andrew Hacker, *Two Nations: Black and White, Separate, Hostile, Unequal* (New York, 1992); Thomas Byrne Edsall with Mary D. Edsall, *Chain Reaction: The Impact of Race, Rights, and Taxes on American Politics* (New York, 1991); Katherine Tate, *From Protest to Politics: The New Black Voters in American Elections* (Cambridge, Mass., 1993); John Hope Franklin, *The Color Line: Legacy for the Twenty-first Century* (Columbia, 1993); and Carol M. Swain, *Black Faces, Black Interests: The Representation of African Americans in Congress* (Cambridge, Mass., 1993).

Works dealing with social and intellectual matters in recent years include Andrew Billingsley, *Climbing Jacob's Ladder: The Enduring Legacy of African-American Families* (New York, 1993); Jannette L. Dates and William Barlow, eds., *Split Image: African Americans in the Mass Media* (Washington, D.C., 1990); Toni Morrison, ed., *Race-ing Justice En-Gendering Power: Essays on Anita Hill, Clarence Thomas and the Construction of Social Reality* (New York, 1992); and Cornel West, *Race Matters* (Boston, 1993).

Ralph Bunche, *A World View of Race** (Washington, D.C., 1936) calls attention to the relationship between imperialism, colonialism, and the problem of race. See also Merze Tate, "The War Aims of World War I and World War II and Their Relation to the Darker Peoples of the World," *Journal of Negro Education*, XII (Summer 1943). W. E. B. Du Bois discusses the connection between colonies and world peace in two works: *Color and Democracy* (New York, 1945) and *The World and Africa* (New York, 1947). For discussions of the interest of African Americans in Africa see Harold Isaacs, *The New World of Negro Americans** (New York, 1963) and *Emergent Americans: A Report on Crossroads Africa** (New York, 1961); John A. Davis, ed., *Africa As Seen by American Negroes** (Paris, 1958); and articles in *Freedomways* and the *Journal of African History*. Publications by TransAfrica and the African-American Institute may also be read with profit.

For a delineation of the attitudes of black Americans toward the war in Vietnam, see Wallace Terry, *Bloods: An Oral History of the Vietnam War by Black Veterans** (New York, 1984). Martin Luther King, Jr., set forth his views on the Vietnam War on numerous occasions. Some of his statements on the subject are in Washington's *A Testament of Hope*. A comment on King's views of the war is made by Vincent Harding in "The Land Beyond: Reflections on Martin Luther King, Jr.'s 'Beyond Vietnam' Speech," in *Sojourners* (Washington, D.C., 1986). The role of the highest-ranking African-American military officer is examined in Howard Means, *Colin Powell: Soldier/Statesman—Statesman/Soldier* (New York, 1992).

Appendixes

The Emancipation Proclamation

By the President of the United States of America. A Proclamation.

Whereas on the 22d day of September, A. D. 1862, a proclamation was issued by the President of the United States, containing, among other things, the following, to wit:

> That on the 1st day of January, A. D. 1863, all persons held as slaves within any State or designated part of a State the people whereof shall then be in rebellion against the United States shall be then, thenceforward, and forever free; and the executive government of the United States, including the military and naval authority thereof, will recognize and maintain the freedom of such persons and will do no act or acts to repress such persons, or any of them, in any efforts they may make for their actual freedom.
>
> That the Executive will on the 1st day of January aforesaid, by proclamation, designate the States and parts of States, if any, in which the people thereof, respectively, shall then be in rebellion against the United States; and the fact that any State or the people thereof shall on that day be in good faith represented in the Congress of the United States by members chosen thereto at elections wherein a majority of the qualified voters of such States shall have participated shall, in the absence of strong countervailing testimony, be deemed conclusive evidence that such State and the people thereof are not then in rebellion against the United States.

Now, therefore, I, Abraham Lincoln, President of the United States, by virtue of the power in me vested as Commander in Chief of the Army and Navy of the United States in time of actual armed rebellion against the authority and Government of the United States, and as a fit and necessary war measure for suppressing said rebellion, do, on this 1st day of January, A. D. 1863, and in accordance with my purpose so to do, publicly proclaimed for the full period of one hundred days from the days first above mentioned, order and designate as the States and parts of States wherein the

617

people thereof, respectively, are this day in rebellion against the United States the following, to wit:

Arkansas, Texas, Louisiana (except the parishes of St. Bernard, Plaquemines, Jefferson, St. John, St. Charles, St. James, Ascension, Assumption, Terrebonne, Lafourche, St. Mary, St. Martin, and Orleans, including the city of New Orleans), Mississippi, Alabama, Florida, Georgia, South Carolina, North Carolina, and Virginia (except the forty-eight counties designated as West Virginia, and also the counties of Berkeley, Accomac, Northampton, Elizabeth City, York, Princess Anne, and Norfolk, including the cities of Norfolk and Portsmouth), and which excepted parts are for the present left precisely as if this proclamation were not issued.

And by virtue of the power and for the purpose aforesaid, I do order and declare that all persons held as slaves within said designated States and parts of States are and henceforward shall be free, and that the executive government of the United States, including the military and naval authorities thereof, will recognize and maintain the freedom of said persons.

And I hereby enjoin upon the people so declared to be free to abstain from all violence, unless in necessary self-defense; and I recommend to them that in all cases when allowed they labor faithfully for reasonable wages.

And I further declare and make known that such persons of suitable condition will be received into the armed service of the United States to garrison forts, positions, stations, and other places and to man vessels of all sorts in said service.

And upon this act, sincerely believed to be an act of justice, warranted by the Constitution upon military necessity, I invoke the considerate judgment and mankind and the gracious favor of Almighty God.

In witness whereof I have hereunto set my hand and caused the seal of the United States to be affixed.

Done at the city of Washington, this 1st day of January, A. D. 1863, and of the Independence of the United States of America the eighty-seventh.

ABRAHAM LINCOLN.

By the President:
WILLIAM H. SEWARD, *Secretary of State.*

Fair Employment Executive Order[*]

Executive Order

Reaffirming Policy of Full Participation in the Defense Program by All Persons, Regardless of Race, Creed, Color, or National Origin, and Directing Certain Action in Furtherance of Said Policy

WHEREAS it is the policy of the United States to encourage full participation in the national defense program by all citizens of the United States, regardless of race, creed, color, or national origin, in the firm belief that the democratic way of life within the

---

[*]Presidential Executive Order No. 8802.

Nation can be defended successfully only with the help and support of all groups within its borders; and

WHEREAS there is evidence that available and needed workers have been barred from employment in industries engaged in defense production solely because of considerations of race, creed, color, or national origin, to the detriment of workers' morale and of national unity:

NOW, THEREFORE, by virtue of the authority vested in me by the Constitution and the statutes, and as a requisite to the successful conduct of our national defense production effort, I do hereby reaffirm the policy of the United States that there shall be no discrimination in the employment of workers in defense industries or government because of race, creed, color, or national origin, and I do hereby declare that it is the duty of employers and of labor organizations, in furtherance of said policy and of this order, to provide for the full and equitable participation of all workers in defense industries, without discrimination because of race, creed, color, or national origin;

And it is hereby ordered as follows:

1. All departments and agencies of the Government of the United States concerned with vocational and training programs for defense production shall take special measures appropriate to assure that such programs are administered without discrimination because of race, creed, color, or national origin;

2. All contracting agencies of the Government of the United States shall include in all defense contracts hereafter negotiated by them a provision obligating the contractor not to discriminate against any worker because of race, creed, color, or national origin;

3. There is established in the Office of Production Management, a Committee on Fair Employment Practice, which shall consist of a chairman and four other members to be appointed by the President. The Chairman and members of the Committee shall serve as such without compensation but shall be entitled to actual and necessary transportation, subsistence and other expenses incidental to performance of their duties. The Committee shall receive and investigate complaints of discrimination in violation of the provisions of this order and shall take appropriate steps to redress grievances which it finds to be valid. The Committee shall also recommend to the several departments and agencies of the Government of the United States and to the President all measures which may be deemed by it necessary or proper to effectuate the provisions of this order.

FRANKLIN D. ROOSEVELT
THE WHITE HOUSE
June 25, 1941

Government's Responsibility: Securing the Rights*

The National Government of the United States must take the lead in safeguarding the civil rights of all Americans. We believe that this is one of the most important

*From *To Secure These Rights,* the Report of the President's Committee on Civil Rights, 1947.

observations that can be made about the civil rights problem in our country today. We agree with words used by the President, in an address at the Lincoln Memorial in Washington in June, 1947:

> We must make the Federal Government a friendly, vigilant defender of the rights and equalities of all Americans. . . . Our National Government must show the way.

It is essential that our rights be preserved against the tyrannical actions of public officers. Our forefathers saw the need for such protection when they gave us the Bill of Rights as a safeguard against arbitrary government. But this is not enough today. We need more than protection of our rights against government; we need protection of our rights against private persons or groups, seeking to undermine them. In the words of the President:

> We cannot be content with a civil liberties program which emphasizes only the need of protection against the possibility of tyranny by the Government. . . . We must keep moving forward, with new concepts of civil rights to safeguard our heritage. The extension of civil rights today means not protection of the people against the Government, but protection of the people by the Government.

There are several reasons why we believe the federal government must play a leading role in our efforts as a nation to improve our civil rights record.

First, many of the most serious wrongs against individual rights are committed by private persons or by local public officers. In the most flagrant of all such wrongs—lynching—private individuals, aided upon occasion by state or local officials, are the ones who take the law into their own hands and deprive the victim of his life. The very fact that these outrages continue to occur, coupled with the fact that the states have been unable to eliminate them, points clearly to a strong need for federal safeguards.

Second, it is a sound policy to use the idealism and prestige of our whole people to check the wayward tendencies of a part of them. It is true that the conscience of a nation is colored by the moral sense of its local communities. Still, the American people have traditionally shown high national regard for civil rights, even though the record in many a community has been far from good. We should not fail to make use of this in combating civil rights violations. The local community must be encouraged to set its own house in order. But the need for leadership is pressing. That leadership is available in the national government and it should be used. We cannot afford to delay action until the most backward community has learned to prize civil liberty and has taken adequate steps to safeguard the rights of every one of its citizens.

Third, our civil rights record has growing international implications. These cannot safely be disregarded by the government at the national level which is responsible for our relations with the world, and left entirely to government at the local level for proper recognition and action. Many of man's problems, we have been learning, are capable of ultimate solution only through international cooperation and action. The subject of human rights, itself, has been made a major concern of the United Nations. It would indeed be ironical if in our own country the argument should prevail that safeguarding the rights of the individual is the exclusive, or even the primary concern of local government.

A lynching in a rural American community is not a challenge to that community's conscience alone. The repercussions of such a crime are heard not only in the locality, or indeed only in our own nation. They echo from one end of the globe to the other, and the world looks to the American national government for both an explanation of how such a shocking event can occur in a civilized country and remedial action to prevent is recurrence.

Similarly, interference with the right of a qualified citizen to vote locally cannot today remain a local problem. An American diplomat cannot forcefully argue for free elections in foreign lands without meeting the challenge that in many sections of America qualified voters do not have free access to the polls. Can it be doubted that this is a right which the national government must make secure?

Fourth, the steadily growing tendency of the American people to look to the national government for the protection of their civil rights is highly significant. This popular demand does not by itself prove the case for national government action. But the persistent and deep-felt desire of the American citizen for federal action safeguarding his civil rights is neither a request for spoils by a selfish pressure group, nor is it a shortsighted and opportunistic attempt by a temporary majority to urge the government into a dubious or unwise course of action. It is a demand rooted in the folkways of the people, sound in instinct and reason, and impossible to ignore. The American people are loyal to the institutions of local self-government, and distrust highly centralized power. But we have never hesitated to entrust power and responsibility to the national government when need for such a course of action has been demonstrated and the people themselves are convinced of that need.

Finally, the national government should assume leadership in our American civil rights program because there is much in the field of civil rights that it is squarely responsible for in its own direct dealings with millions of persons. It is the largest single employer of labor in the country. More than two million persons are on its payroll. The freedom of opinion and expression enjoyed by these people is in many ways dependent upon the attitudes and practices of the government. By not restricting this freedom beyond a point necessary to insure the efficiency and loyalty of its workers, the government, itself, can make a very large contribution to the effort to achieve true freedom of thought in America. By scrupulously following fair employment practices, it not only sets a model for other employers to follow, but also directly protects the rights of more than two million workers to fair employment.

Brown v. Board of Education*

Mr. Chief Justice Warren delivered the opinion of the Court.

These cases come to us from the States of Kansas, South Carolina, Virginia, and Delaware. They are premised on different facts and different local conditions, but a common legal question justifies their consideration together in this consolidated opinion.

In each of the cases, minors of the Negro race, through their legal representatives, seek the aid of the courts in obtaining admission to the public schools of their

---

*The Supreme Court's school desegregation decision, delivered May 17, 1954.

community on a nonsegregated basis. In each instance, they had been denied admission to schools attended by white children under laws requiring or permitting segregation according to race. This segregation was alleged to deprive the plaintiffs of the equal protection of the laws under the Fourteenth Amendment. In each of the cases other than the Delaware case, a three-judge federal district court denied relief to the plaintiffs on the so-called "separate but equal" doctrine announced by this Court in *Plessy* v. *Ferguson*, 163 U. S. 537. Under that doctrine, equality of treatment is accorded when the races are provided substantially equal facilities, even though these facilities be separate. In the Delaware case, the Supreme Court of Delaware adhered to that doctrine, but ordered that the plaintiffs be admitted to the white schools because of their superiority to the Negro schools.

The plaintiffs contend that segregated public schools are not "equal" and cannot be made "equal," and that hence they are deprived of the equal protection of the laws. Because of the obvious importance of the question presented, the Court took jurisdiction. Argument was heard in the 1952 Term, and reargument was heard this Term on certain questions propounded by the Court. . . .

In approaching this problem, we cannot turn the clock back to 1868 when the Amendment was adopted, or even to 1896 when *Plessy* v. *Ferguson* was written. We must consider public education in the light of its full development and its present place in American life throughout the Nation. Only in this way can it be determined if segregation in public schools deprives these plaintiffs of the equal protection of the laws.

Today, education is perhaps the most important function of state and local governments. Compulsory school attendance laws and the great expenditures for education both demonstrate our recognition of the importance of education to our democratic society. It is required in the performance of our most basic public responsibilities, even service in the armed forces. It is the very foundation of good citizenship. Today it is a principal instrument in awakening the child to cultural values, in preparing him for later professional training, and in helping him to adjust normally to his environment. In these days, it is doubtful that any child may reasonably be expected to succeed in life if he is denied the opportunity of an education. Such an opportunity, where the state has undertaken to provide it, is a right which must be made available to all on equal terms.

We come then to the question presented: Does segregation of children in public schools solely on the basis of race, even though the physical facilities and other "tangible" factors may be equal, deprive the children of the minority group of equal educational opportunities? We believe that it does. . . .

We conclude that in the field of public education the doctrine of "separate but equal" has no place. Separate educational facilities are inherently unequal. Therefore, we hold that the plaintiffs and others similarly situated for whom the actions have been brought are, by reason of the segregation complained of, deprived of the equal protection of the laws guaranteed by the Fourteenth Amendment. This disposition makes unnecessary any discussion whether such segregation also violates the Due Process Clause of the Fourteenth Amendment.

Because these are class actions, because of the wide applicability of this decision, and because of the great variety of local conditions, the formulation of decrees in these cases presents problems of considerable complexity. On reargument, the consideration of appropriate relief was necessarily subordinated to the primary question—the constitutionality of segregation in public education. We have now announced that such segregation is a denial of the equal protection of the laws.

John F. Kennedy: Special Message to the Congress on Civil Rights*

To the Congress of the United States:

"Our Constitution is color blind," wrote Mr. Justice Harlan before the turn of the century, "and neither knows nor tolerates classes among citizens." But the practices of the country do not always conform to the principles of the Constitution. And this Message is intended to examine how far we have come in achieving first-class citizenship for all citizens regardless of color, how far we have yet to go, and what further tasks remain to be carried out—by the Executive and Legislative Branches of the Federal Government, as well as by state and local governments and private citizens and organizations.

One hundred years ago the Emancipation Proclamation was signed by a President who believed in the equal worth and opportunity of every human being. That Proclamation was only a first step—a step which its author unhappily did not live to follow up, a step which some of its critics dismissed as an action which "frees the slave but ignores the Negro." Through these long one hundred years, while slavery has vanished, progress for the Negro has been too often blocked and delayed. Equality before the law has not always meant equal treatment and opportunity. And the harmful, wasteful and wrongful results of racial discrimination and segregation still appear in virtually every aspect of national life, in virtually every part of the Nation.

The Negro baby born in America today—regardless of the section or state in which he is born—has about one-half as much chance of completing high school as a white baby born in the same place on the same day—one-third as much chance of completing college—one-third as much chance of becoming a professional man—twice as much chance of becoming unemployed—about one-seventh as much chance of earning $10,000 per year—a life expectancy which is seven years less—and the prospects of earning only half as much.

No American who believes in the basic truth that "all men are created equal, that they are endowed by their Creator with certain unalienable Rights," can fully excuse, explain or defend the picture these statistics portray. Race discrimination hampers our economic growth by preventing the maximum development and utilization of our manpower. It hampers our world leadership by contradicting at home the message we preach abroad. It mars the atmosphere of a united and classless society in which this Nation rose to greatness. It increases the costs of public welfare, crime, delinquency and disorder. Above all, it is wrong.

Therefore, let it be clear, in our own hearts and minds, that it is not merely because of the Cold War, and not merely because of the economic waste of discrimination, that we are committed to achieving true equality of opportunity. The basic reason is because it is right.

The cruel disease of discrimination knows no sectional or state boundaries. The continuing attack on this problem must be equally broad. It must be both private and public—it must be conducted at national, state and local levels—and it must include both legislative and executive action.

In the last two years, more progress has been made in securing the civil rights of all Americans than in any comparable period in our history. Progress has been

---

*Delivered February 28, 1963.

made—through executive action, litigation, persuasion and private initiative—in achieving and protecting equality of opportunity in education, voting, transportation, employment, housing, government, and the enjoyment of public accommodations.

But pride in our progress must not give way to relaxation of our effort. Nor does progress in the Executive Branch enable the Legislative Branch to escape its own obligations. . . .

The Civil Rights Act of 1964*

AN ACT

To enforce the constitutional right to vote, to confer jurisdiction upon the district courts of the United States to provide injunctive relief against discrimination in public accommodations, to authorize the Attorney General to institute suits to protect constitutional rights in public facilities and public education, to extend the Commission on Civil Rights, to prevent discrimination in federally assisted programs, to establish a Commission on Equal Employment Opportunity, and for other purposes. . . .

TITLE I—VOTING RIGHTS

. . . .

(2) No person acting under color of law shall—

(A) in determining whether any individual is qualified under State law or laws to vote in any Federal election, apply any standard, practice, or procedure different from the standards, practices, or procedures applied under such law or laws to other individuals within the same county, parish, or similar political subdivision who have been found by State officials to be qualified to vote;

(B) deny the right of any individual to vote in any Federal election because of an error or omission on any record or paper relating to any application, registration, or other act requisite to voting, . . . or

(C) employ any literacy test as a qualification for voting in any Federal election unless (i) such test is administered to each individual and is conducted wholly in writing, and (ii) a certified copy of the test and of the answers given by the individual is furnished to him within twenty-five days of the submission of his request made within the period of time during which records and papers are required to be retained and preserved pursuant to title III of the Civil Rights Act of 1960. . . .

TITLE II—INJUNCTIVE RELIEF AGAINST DISCRIMINATION IN PLACES OF PUBLIC ACCOMMODATION

SEC. 201. (a) All persons shall be entitled to the full and equal enjoyment of the goods, services, facilities, privileges, advantages, and accommodations of any place of public

---

*These are the major provisions of the Act, Public Law 88–352, the full text of which may be consulted in *U.S. Statutes At Large*, Vol. 78, pp. 241–268.

accommodation, as defined in this section, without discrimination or segregation on the ground of race, color, religion, or national origin.

(b) Each of the following establishments which serves the public is a place of public accommodation within the meaning of this title if its operations affect commerce, or if discrimination or segregation by it is supported by State action:

(1) any inn, hotel, motel, or other establishment which provides lodging to transient guests, other than an establishment located within a building which contains not more than five rooms for rent or hire and which is actually occupied by the proprietor of such establishment as his residence;

(2) any restaurant, cafeteria, lunchroom, lunch counter, soda fountain, or other facility principally engaged in selling food for consumption on the premises, including, . . . any such facility located on the premises of any retail establishment; or any gasoline station;

(3) any motion picture house, theater, concert hall, sports arena, stadium or other place of exhibition or entertainment; and

(4) any establishment (A) (i) which is physically located within the premises of any establishment otherwise covered by this subsection, or (ii) within the premises of which is physically located any such covered establishment, and (B) which holds itself out as serving patrons of such covered establishment. . . .

TITLE III—DESEGREGATION OF PUBLIC FACILITIES

SEC. 301. (a) Whenever the Attorney General receives a complaint in writing signed by an individual to the effect that he is being deprived of or threatened with the loss of his right to the equal protection of the laws, on account of his race, color, religion, or national origin, by being denied equal utilization of any public facility which is owned, operated, or managed by or on behalf of any State or subdivision thereof, other than a public school or public college as defined in section 401 of title IV hereof, and the Attorney General believes the complaint is meritorious and certifies that the signer or signers of such complaint are unable, . . . to initiate and maintain appropriate legal proceedings for relief and that the institution of an action will materially further the orderly progress of desegregation in public facilities, the Attorney General is authorized to institute . . . a civil action in any appropriate district court of the United States against such parties and for such relief as may be appropriate, and such court shall have and shall exercise jurisdiction of proceedings instituted pursuant to this section. . . .

(b) The Attorney General may deem a person or persons unable to initiate and maintain appropriate legal proceedings within the meaning of subsection (a) of this section when such person or persons are unable, either directly or through other interested persons or organizations, to bear the expense of the litigation or to obtain effective legal representation; or whenever he is satisfied that the institution of such litigation would jeopardize the personal safety, employment, or economic standing of such person or persons, their families, or their property. . . .

SEC. 303. Nothing in this title shall affect adversely the right of any person to sue for or obtain relief in any court against discrimination in any facility covered by this title. . . .

TITLE IV—DESEGREGATION OF PUBLIC EDUCATION

DEFINITIONS

SEC. 401. As used in this title—

(a) "Commissioner" means the Commissioner of Education.*

(b) "Desegregation" means the assignment of students to public schools and within such schools without regard to their race, color, religion, or national origin, but "desegregation" shall not mean the assignment of students to public schools in order to overcome racial imbalance.

(c) "Public school" means any elementary or secondary educational institution, and "public college" means any institution of higher education or any technical or vocational school above the secondary school level, . . .

(d) "School board" means any agency or agencies which administer a system of one or more public schools. . . .

TECHNICAL ASSISTANCE

SEC. 403. The Commissioner is authorized, upon the application of any school board, State, municipality, school district, or other governmental unit legally responsible for operating a public school or schools, to render technical assistance to such applicant in the preparation, adoption, and implementation of plans for the desegregation of public schools. . . .

TRAINING INSTITUTES

SEC. 404. The Commissioner is authorized to arrange, through grants or contracts, with institutions of higher education for the operation of short-term or regular session institutes for special training designed to improve the ability of teachers, supervisors, counselors, and other elementary or secondary school personnel to deal effectively with special educational problems occasioned by desegregation. . . .

GRANTS

SEC. 405. (a) The Commissioner is authorized, upon application of a school board, to make grants to such board to pay, in whole or in part, the cost of—

(1) giving to teachers and other school personnel inservice training in dealing with problems incident to desegregation, and

(2) employing specialists to advise in problems incident to desegregation.

(b) In determining whether to make a grant, and in fixing the amount thereof and the terms and conditions on which it will be made, the Commissioner shall take into consideration the amount available for grants under this section and the other applications which are pending before him; the financial condition of the applicant and the other resources available to it; the nature, extent, and gravity of its problems incident to desegregation; and such other factors as he finds relevant. . . .

---

*In 1980, the office of Commissioner of Education was transformed into a cabinet level Department of Education.

SEC. 407. (a) Whenever the Attorney General receives a complaint in writing—

(1) signed by a parent or group of parents to the effect that his or their minor children, as members of a class of persons similarly situated, are being deprived by a school board of the equal protection of the laws, or

(2) signed by an individual, or his parent, to the effect that he has been denied admission to or not permitted to continue in attendance at a public college by reason of race, color, religion, or national origin,

and the Attorney General believes the complaint is meritorious and certifies that the signer or signers of such complaint are unable, in his judgment, to initiate and maintain appropriate legal proceedings for relief and that the institution of an action will materially further the orderly achievement of desegregation in public education, the Attorney General is authorized, after giving notice of such complaint to the appropriate school board or college authority and after certifying that he is satisfied that such board or authority has had a reasonable time to adjust the conditions alleged in such complaint, to institute for or in the name of the United States a civil action in any appropriate district court of the United States against such parties and for such relief as may be appropriate, . . .

(b) The Attorney General may deem a person or persons unable to initiate and maintain appropriate legal proceedings within the meaning of subsection (a) of this section when such person or persons are unable, either directly or through other interested persons or organizations, to bear the expense of the litigation or to obtain effective legal representation; or whenever he is satisfied that the institution of such litigation would jeopardize the personal safety, employment, or economic standing of such person or persons, their families, or their property. . . .

TITLE V—COMMISSION ON CIVIL RIGHTS

. . .

DUTIES OF THE COMMISSION

SEC. 104. (a) The Commission shall—

(1) investigate allegations in writing under oath or affirmation that certain citizens of the United States are being deprived of their right to vote and have that vote counted by reason of their color, race, religion, or national origin; which writing, under oath or affirmation, shall set forth the facts upon which such belief or beliefs are based;

(2) study and collect information concerning legal developments constituting a denial of equal protection of the laws under the Constitution because of race, color, religion or national origin or in the administration of justice;

(3) appraise the laws and policies of the Federal Government with respect to denials of equal protection of the laws under the Constitution because of race, color, religion or national origin or in the administration of justice;

(4) serve as a national clearinghouse for information in respect to denials of equal protection of the laws because of race, color, religion or national origin, including but not limited to the fields of voting, education, housing, employment, the use of public facilities, and transportation, or in the administration of justice;

(5) investigate allegations, made in writing and under oath or affirmation, that

citizens of the United States are unlawfully being accorded or denied the right to vote, or to have their votes properly counted, in any election of presidential electors, Members of the United States Senate, or of the House of Representatives, as a result of any patterns or practice of fraud or discrimination in the conduct of such election; . . . .

(b) The Commission shall submit interim reports to the President and to the Congress at such times as the Commission, the Congress or the President shall deem desirable, and shall submit to the President and to the Congress a final report of its activities, findings, and recommendations not later than January 31, 1968. . . .

(f) The Commission, or on the authorization of the Commission any subcommittee of two or more members, at least one of whom shall be of each major political party, may, . . . hold such hearings and act at such times and places as the Commission or such authorized subcommittee may deem advisable. Subpenas for the attendance and testimony of witnesses or the production of written or other matter may be issued in accordance with the rules of the Commission as contained in section 102 (j) and (k) of this Act, over the signature of the Chairman of the Commission or of such subcommittee, and may be served by any person designated by such Chairman. The holding of hearings by the Commission, or the appointment of a subcommittee to hold hearings pursuant to this subparagraph, must be approved by a majority of the Commission, or by a majority of the members present at a meeting at which at least a quorum of four members is present.

(g) In case of contumacy or refusal to obey a subpena, any district court of the United States or the United States court of any territory or possession, or the District Court of the United States for the District of Columbia, within the jurisdiction of which the inquiry is carried on or within the jurisdiction of which said person guilty of contumacy or refusal to obey is found or resides or is domiciled or transacts business, or has appointed an agent for receipt of service of process, upon application by the Attorney General of the United States shall have jurisdiction to issue to such person an order requiring such person to appear before the Commission or a subcommittee thereof, there to produce pertinent, relevant and nonprivileged evidence if so ordered, or there to give testimony touching the matter under investigation; and any failure to obey such order of the court may be punished by said court as a contempt thereof.

SEC. 507. Section 105 of the Civil Rights Act of 1957 . . . , as amended by section 401 of the Civil Rights Act of 1960, . . . is further amended by adding a new subsection at the end to read as follows:

(i) The Commission shall have the power to make such rules and regulations as are necessary to carry out the purposes of this Act.

TITLE VI—NONDISCRIMINATION IN FEDERALLY ASSISTED PROGRAMS

SEC. 601. No person in the United States shall, on the ground of race, color, or national origin, be excluded from participation in, be denied the benefits of, or be subjected to discrimination under any program or activity receiving Federal financial assistance.

SEC. 602. Each Federal department and agency which is empowered to extend Federal financial assistance to any program or activity, by way of grant, loan, or contract other than a contract of insurance or guaranty, is authorized and directed to effectuate the provisions of section 601 with respect to such program or activity by issuing rules, regulations, or orders of general applicability which shall be consistent with achievement of the objectives of the statute authorizing the financial assistance in connection with which the action is taken. No such rule, regulation, or order shall become effective unless and until approved by the President. Compliance with any requirement adopted pursuant to this section may be effected (1) by the termination of or refusal to grant or to continue assistance under such program or activity to any recipient as to whom there has been an express finding on the record, after opportunity for hearing, of a failure to comply with such requirement, but such termination or refusal shall be limited to the particular political entity, or part thereof, or other recipient as to whom such a finding has been made and, shall be limited in its effect to the particular program, or part thereof, in which such noncompliance has been so found, or (2) by any other means authorized by law: *Provided, however,* That no such action shall be taken until the department or agency concerned has advised the appropriate person or persons of the failure to comply with the requirement and has determined that compliance cannot be secured by voluntary means. In the case of any action terminating, or refusing to grant or continue, assistance because of failure to comply with a requirement imposed pursuant to this section, the head of the Federal department or agency shall file with the committees of the House and Senate having legislative jurisdiction over the program or activity involved a full written report of the circumstances and the grounds for such action. No such action shall become effective until thirty days have elapsed after the filing of such report.

SEC. 603. Any department or agency action taken pursuant to section 602 shall be subject to such judicial review as may otherwise be provided by law for similar action taken by such department or agency on other grounds. In the case of action, not otherwise subject to judicial review, terminating or refusing to grant or to continue financial assistance upon a finding of failure to comply with any requirement imposed pursuant to section 602, any person aggrieved (including any State or political subdivision thereof and any agency of either) may obtain judicial review of such action in accordance with section 10 of the Administrative Procedure Act, and such action shall not be deemed committed to unreviewable agency discretion within the meaning of that section. . . .

TITLE VII—EQUAL EMPLOYMENT OPPORTUNITY

. . .

DISCRIMINATION BECAUSE OF RACE, COLOR, RELIGION, SEX, OR NATIONAL ORIGIN

SEC. 703. (a) It shall be an unlawful employment practice for an employer—

(1) to fail or refuse to hire or to discharge any individual, or otherwise to discriminate against any individual with respect to his compensation, terms, conditions, or privileges of employment, because of such individual's race, color, religion, sex, or national origin; or

(2) to limit, segregate, or classify his employees in any way which would deprive or tend to deprive any individual of employment opportunities or otherwise adversely affect his status as an employee, because of such individual's race, color, religion, sex, or national origin.

(b) It shall be an unlawful employment practice for an employment agency to fail or refuse to refer for employment, or otherwise to discriminate against, any individual because of his race, color, religion, sex, or national origin, or to classify or refer for employment any individual on the basis of his race, color, religion, sex, or national origin.

(c) It shall be an unlawful employment practice for a labor organization—

(1) to exclude or to expel from its membership, or otherwise to discriminate against, any individual because of his race, color, religion, sex, or national origin;

(2) to limit, segregate, or classify its membership, or to classify or fail or refuse to refer for employment any individual, in any way which would deprive or tend to deprive any individual of employment opportunities, or would limit such employment opportunities or otherwise adversely affect his status as an employee or as an applicant for employment, because of such individual's race, color, religion, sex, or national origin; or

(3) to cause or attempt to cause an employer to discriminate against an individual in violation of this section. . . .

EQUAL EMPLOYMENT OPPORTUNITY COMMISSION

SEC. 705. (a) There is hereby created a Commission to be known as the Equal Employment Opportunity Commission, which shall be composed of five members, not more than three of whom shall be members of the same political party, who shall be appointed by the President by and with the advice and consent of the Senate. One of the original members shall be appointed for a term of one year, one for a term of two years, one for a term of three years, one for a term of four years, and one for a term of five years, beginning from the date of enactment of this title, but their successors shall be appointed for terms of five years each, except that any individual chosen to fill a vacancy shall be appointed only for the unexpired term of the member whom he shall succeed. The President shall designate one member to serve as Chairman of the Commission, and one member to serve as Vice Chairman. The Chairman shall be responsible on behalf of the Commission for the administrative operations of the Commission, and shall appoint, in accordance with the civil service laws, such officers, agents, attorneys, and employees as it deems necessary to assist it in the performance of its functions and to fix their compensation in accordance with the Classification Act of 1949, as amended. The Vice Chairman shall act as Chairman in the absence or disability of the Chairman or in the event of a vacancy in that office. . . .

(d) The Commission shall at the close of each fiscal year report to the Congress and to the President concerning the action it has taken; the names, salaries, and duties of all individuals in its employ and the moneys it has disbursed; and shall make such further reports on the cause of and means of eliminating discrimination and such recommendations for further legislation as may appear desirable. . . .

(g) The Commission shall have power—

(1) to cooperate with and, with their consent, utilize regional, State, local, and other agencies, both public and private, and individuals;

(2) to pay to witnesses whose depositions are taken or who are summoned before the Commission or any of its agents the same witness and mileage fees as are paid to witnesses in the courts of the United States;

(3) to furnish to persons subject to this title such technical assistance as they may request to further their compliance with this title or an order issued thereunder;

(4) upon the request of (i) any employer, whose employees or some of them, or (ii) any labor organization, whose members or some of them, refuse or threaten to

refuse to cooperate in effectuating the provisions of this title, to assist in such effectuation by conciliation or such other remedial action as is provided by this title;

(5) to make such technical studies as are appropriate to effectuate the purposes and policies of this title and to make the results of such studies available to the public;

(6) to refer matters to the Attorney General with recommendations for intervention in a civil action brought by an aggrieved party under section 706, or for the institution of a civil action by the Attorney General under section 707, and to advise, consult, and assist the Attorney General on such matters. . . .

TITLE VIII—REGISTRATION AND VOTING STATISTICS

SEC. 801. The Secretary of Commerce shall promptly conduct a survey to compile registration and voting statistics in such geographic areas as may be recommended by the Commission on Civil Rights. Such a survey and compilation shall, to the extent recommended by the Commission on Civil Rights, only include a count of persons of voting age by race, color, and national origin, and determination of the extent to which such persons are registered to vote, and have voted in any statewide primary or general election in which the Members of the United States House of Representatives are nominated or elected, since January 1, 1960. Such information shall also be collected and compiled in connection with the Nineteenth Decennial Census, and at such other times as the Congress may prescribe. . . . *Provided, however,* That no person shall be compelled to disclose his race, color, national origin, or questioned about his political party affiliation, how he voted, or the reasons therefore, nor shall any penalty be imposed for his failure or refusal to make such disclosure. . . .

TITLE IX—INTERVENTION AND PROCEDURE AFTER REMOVAL IN CIVIL RIGHTS CASES

SEC. 901. Title 28 of the United States Code, section 1447(d), is amended to read as follows:

An order remanding a case to the State court from which it was removed is not reviewable on appeal or otherwise, except that an order remanding a case to the State court from which it was removed pursuant to section 1443 of this title shall be reviewable by appeal or otherwise.

SEC. 902. Whenever an action has been commenced in any court of the United States seeking relief from the denial of equal protection of the laws under the fourteenth amendment to the Constitution on account of race, color, religion, or national origin, the Attorney General for or in the name of the United States may intervene in such action upon timely application if the Attorney General certifies that the case is of general public importance. In such action the United States shall be entitled to the same relief as if it had instituted the action.

TITLE X—ESTABLISHMENT OF COMMUNITY RELATIONS SERVICE

SEC. 1001. (a) There is hereby established in and as a part of the Department of Commerce a Community Relations Service (hereinafter referred to as the "Service"), which shall be headed by a Director who shall be appointed by the President with the advice and consent of the Senate for a term of four years. . . .

SEC. 1002. It shall be the function of the Service to provide assistance to communities and persons therein in resolving disputes, disagreements, or difficulties relating to discriminatory practices based on race, color, or national origin which impair the rights of persons in such communities under the Constitution or laws of the United States or which affect or may affect interstate commerce. The Service may offer its services in cases of such disputes, disagreements, or difficulties whenever, in its judgment, peaceful relations among the citizens of the community involved are threatened thereby, and it may offer its services either upon its own motion or upon the request of an appropriate State or local official or other interested person. . . .

The Voting Rights Act of 1965*

AN ACT

To enforce the fifteenth amendment to the Constitution
of the United States and for other purposes

. . .

SEC. 2. No voting qualification or prerequisite to voting, or standard, practice, or procedure shall be imposed or applied by any State or political subdivision to deny or abridge the right of any citizen of the United States to vote on account of race or color.

SEC. 3. (a) Whenever the Attorney General institutes a proceeding under any statute to enforce the guarantees of the fifteenth amendment in any State or political subdivision the court shall authorize the appointment of Federal examiners by the United States Civil Service Commission in accordance with section 6 to serve for such period of time and for such political subdivisions as the court shall determine is appropriate to enforce the guarantees of the fifteenth amendment. . . .

SEC. 4. (a) To assure that the right of citizens of the United States to vote is not denied or abridged on account of race or color, no citizen shall be denied the right to vote in any Federal, State, or local election because of his failure to comply with any test or device in any State with respect to which the determinations have been made in any political subdivision with respect to which such determinations have been made as a separate unit. . . .

If the Attorney General determines that he has no reason to believe that any such test or device has been used during the five years preceding the filing of the action for the purpose or with the effect of denying or abridging the right to vote on account of race or color, he shall consent to the entry of such judgment. . . .

The provisions . . . shall apply in any State or in any political subdivision of a state which (1) the Attorney General determines maintained on November 1, 1964, any test or device, and with respect to which (2) the Director of the Census determines

---

These are the major provisions of the Act, Public Law 89–110, the full text of which may be consulted in *U.S. Statutes At Large, 1965* Vol. 79 (Washington, 1966), pp. 437–446.

that less than 50 per centum of the persons of voting age residing therein were registered on November 1, 1964, or that less than 50 per centum of such persons voted in the presidential election of November 1964.

The phrase "test or device" shall mean any requirement that a person as a prerequisite for voting or registration for voting (1) demonstrate the ability to read, write, understand, or interpret any matter, (2) demonstrate any educational achievement or his knowledge of any particular subject, (3) possess good moral character, or (4) prove his qualifications by the voucher of registered voters or members of any other class. . . .

For purposes of this section no State or political subdivision shall be determined to have engaged in the use of tests or devices for the purpose or with the effect of denying or abridging the right to vote on account of race or color if (1) incidents of such use have been few in number and have been promptly and effectively corrected by State or local action, (2) the continuing effect of such incidents has been eliminated, and (3) there is no reasonable probability of their recurrence in the future. . . .

Congress hereby declares that to secure the rights under the fourteenth amendment of persons educated in American flag schools in which the predominant classroom language was other than English, it is necessary to prohibit the States from conditioning the right to vote of such persons on ability to read, write, understand, or interpret any matter in the English language. . . .

SEC. 5. Whenever a State or political subdivision with respect to which the prohibitions set forth in section 4 (a) are in effect shall enact or seek to administer any voting qualification or prerequisite to voting, or standard, practice, or procedure with respect to voting different from that in force or effect on November 1, 1964, such State or subdivision may institute an action in the United States District Court for the District of Columbia for a declaratory judgment that such qualification . . . does not have the purpose and will not have the effect of denying or abridging the right to vote on account of race or color, and unless and until the court enters such judgment no person shall be denied the right to vote for failure to comply with such qualification. . . .

SEC. 6. Whenever . . . the Attorney General certifies . . . that he has received complaints in writing from twenty or more residents of such political subdivision alleging that they have been denied the right to vote under color of law on account of race or color, and that he believes such complaints to be meritorious . . . the Civil Service Commission shall appoint as many examiners . . . as it may deem appropriate to prepare and maintain lists of persons eligible to vote in Federal, State, and local elections. . . .

SEC. 7. . . . The examiners . . . shall . . . examine applicants concerning their qualifications for voting. . . . Any person whom the examiner finds . . . to have the qualifications prescribed by State law not inconsistent with the Constitution and laws of the United States shall promptly be placed on a list of eligible voters. . . . The examiner shall certify and transmit such list . . . at least once a month, to the offices of the appropriate election officials, with copies to the Attorney General and the attorney general of the State and any such lists and supplements transmitted during the month shall be available for public inspection on the last business day of the month and in any event not later than the forty-fifth day prior to any election. The appropriate State or local election officials shall place such names on the official voting list. Any person whose name appears on the examiner's list shall be entitled and allowed to vote in the election district of his residence. . . .

SEC. 8. Whenever an examiner is serving under this Act . . . the Civil Service Commission may assign, at the request of the Attorney General, one or more persons . . . to enter and attend at any place for holding an election . . . for the purpose of observing whether persons who are entitled to vote are being permitted to vote and . . . to enter and attend at any place for tabulating the votes cast . . . for the purpose of observing whether votes cast by persons entitled to vote are being properly tabulated. . . .

SEC. 9. . . . Any challenge to a listing on an eligibility list . . . shall be heard and determined by a hearing officer appointed for and responsible to the Civil Service Commission. . . . Such challenge shall be entertained only if filed . . . within ten days after the listing of the challenged person is made available for public inspection. . . .

SEC. 10. . . . The Congress finds that the requirement of the payment of a poll tax as a precondition to voting (i) precludes persons of limited means from voting or imposes unreasonable financial hardship upon such persons as a precondition to their exercise of the franchise, (ii) does not bear a reasonable relationship to any legitimate State interest in the conduct of elections, and (iii) in some areas has the purpose or effect of denying persons the right to vote because of race or color. Upon the basis of these findings, Congress declares that the constitutional right of citizens to vote is denied or abridged in some areas by the requirement of the payment of a poll tax as a precondition to voting. . . .

SEC. 11. . . . No person acting under color of law shall fail or refuse to permit any person to vote who is entitled to vote under any provisions of this Act or is otherwise qualified to vote, or willfully fail or refuse to tabulate, count, and report such person's vote. . . .

Whoever knowingly or willfully gives false information . . . for the purpose of establishing his eligibility to register or vote . . . shall be fined no more than $10,000 or imprisoned not more than five years, or both. . . .

Whoever . . . knowingly and willfully falsifies or conceals a material fact . . . shall be fined not more than $10,000 or imprisoned not more than five years, or both. . . .